South African Human Resource Management | Theory and Practice

South African
Human Resource Management   Theory and Practice

Authors:

BEN SWANEPOEL (*Editor*)

Barney Erasmus
Marius van Wyk
Heinz Schenk

Co-authors
David Beaty
Lize Booysen
Lukas Ehlers
Dries Schreuder

Contributors:

Paolo Ciucci
Karin Liebenberg
Du Toit Visser
Johannes Visser
Retha Wiesner

Juta

First published 1998

© Juta & Co, Ltd
PO Box 14373, Kenwyn 7790

This book is copyright under the Berne Convention. In terms of the Copyright Act 98 of 1978, no part of this book may be reproduced or transmitted in any form or by any means (including photocopying, recording, or by any information storage and retrieval system) without permission in writing from the publisher.

ISBN 0 7021 3330 2

Typographic design, typesetting and illustrations by Zebra Publications, Cape Town

Cover design by Comet Design, Cape Town

Printed and bound in South Africa by Creda Communications, Eliot Avenue, Eppindust II, Cape Town

The authors

Authors

- **Ben Swanepoel**, the editor, is associate professor of human resource and labour relations management at Unisa's Graduate School of Business Leadership. He is the editor of the *South African Journal of Labour Relations*; chairs the management committee of the Industrial Relations Association of South Africa (IRasa); is a part-time commissioner of the Commission for Conciliation, Mediation and Arbitration (CCMA); and is an IMSSA panelist. He acts as an advisor and consultant in labour relations and human resource management.
- **Barney Erasmus** is professor of human resource management in the Department of Business Management at Unisa. He is a registered generalist practitioner with the South African Board of Personnel Practice, and a full member of the Institute of Personnel Management (IPM). He specialises in training management and acts as a consultant in industrial relations, human resource development and general human resource management.
- **Marius van Wyk** is associate professor of Industrial Relations, Labour Law and Business Ethics at the Graduate School of Business Leadership of Unisa. He is a panelist of Independent Mediation Services of South Africa (IMSSA), an ad hoc member of the Industrial Court, an advocate of the High Court and a registered psychometrist. He acts as a consultant in labour law, dispute resolution, facilitation and employment equity issues.
- **Heinz Schenk** is the Executive Director: Human Resource Management at Technikon Southern Africa, and a registered industrial psychologist. He is registered as a personnel practitioner (generalist) with the South African Board of Personnel Practice (SABPP) and is a mentor of the SABPP. He also serves on the professional education and development board of the IPM.

Co-authors and contributors

- **David Beaty** is professor of organisational behaviour at Unisa's Graduate School of Business Leadership
- **Lize Booysen** is a senior lecturer in organisational behaviour at Unisa's Graduate School of Business Leadership.
- **Lukas Ehlers** is a consultant in human resource and industrial relations management.
- **Karin Liebenberg** is Manager: Economic Research and Development at the Industrial Development Corporation of South Africa.

- **Dries Schreuder** is associate professor and head of the Department of Industrial Psychology at Unisa.
- **Du Toit Visser** is an independent consultant and part-time lecturer at Unisa's Graduate School of Business Leadership.
- **Johannes Visser** used to be a senior lecturer in human resource management in the Department of Business Management, Unisa.
- **Retha Wiesner** lectures in human resource management at the University of Southern Queensland in Australia.

Preface

Few of you who read this textbook will disagree that the last few years have brought fundamental challenges to the South African business environment. The complete transformation of South African society, coupled with the fact that one can nowadays almost refer to "borderless economies", means that South African organisations are faced with external environmental forces requiring change and transformation within the organisation in order to be able to survive and grow. It is well known that the way in which we manage the people within our organisations — the employees, the human resources — holds the key to managing these forces of change and transformation in today's highly competitive environment.

The foundation of this book is the belief that successful human resource management is a prerequisite for overall organisational success, and that HRM is therefore a top management responsibility requiring a general management and strategic approach. In addition, because a strategic approach implies a good "fit" between internal and external environments, the heart of this text revolves around unique South African HRM challenges. Challenges related to aspects such as: balancing economic growth and wealth redistribution; dealing with changing worker expectations; adapting leadership and motivational theories to the South African situation; strategically implementing affirmative action; coping with fast-changing labour legislation; enhancing labour productivity; dealing with unions; working towards cultures of union–management cooperation; and welcoming unions as partners in our endeavours to better develop, empower, utilise and reward our employees.

In other words, this textbook recognises that human resource management should not be hived off into some separate personnel "ghetto". All managers should explore and adapt HRM strategies and practices that add value in a South African environment, an environment quite distinct from that in countries such as the USA, Japan or Sweden. In order to assist South African managers to do this, the text is divided into seven parts, covering twenty four chapters:

- Part 1, **Orientation and General Overview**, contains five chapters, and has the overall aim of introducing HRM as a field of study from a general international and South African perspective. It specifically covers the broad South African HRM environment, and because affirmative action impacts on all other HRM functions, and, because of its prominence in the South African context, it is comprehensively dealt with in a separate chapter.
- Part 2, **Strategising, Structuring and Planning**, consists of three chapters covering the longer-term preparatory decisions that every top management team in South Africa has to consider. It deals with strategic HRM decisions related to the overall approaches we have to follow in respect of managing human

resources and labour relations, regarding structural dimensions such as work and organisation design and in respect of planning how to balance the supply and demand of our workforces.

- Part 3, **Establishing Employment Relationships**, consists of two chapters dealing with the strategies, processes and practices involved in staffing our organisations with the right quality and quantity of people.

- Part 4, **Utilising and Developing Employees**, is made up of six chapters. The spectrum of topics covered include motivation and leadership, performance and career management, and two comprehensive chapters covering essential material relating to the huge challenge of training and developing human resources in South Africa.

- Part 5, **Compensating and Caring for Employees**, covers strategies, practices and processes to reward, retain and maintain employees. The three chapters deal with remuneration, incentives and benefits and employee well-being respectively.

- Part 6, **Managing Labour and Employee Relations**, consists of two chapters dealing comprehensively with South Africa's labour relations challenges and the dynamics related to establishing climates of trust, cooperation, disciplined behaviour and optimal conflict levels in our organisations. Special attention is devoted to the LRA 66 of 1995 and union–management interaction through processes such as negotiation, consultation and cooperation. The individual dimension of employment relations is also addressed, and aspects such as communication, discipline and grievance handling are well covered.

- Part 7, **Special Topics in Human Resource Management**, rounds off this textbook with three chapters, each dealing with a particular topic warranting special treatment. One such topic is organisational transformation and change. Aspects related to human resource management are covered in another chapter, and the last chapter focuses on the all-important but specialised topic of how to terminate the services of employees.

By covering such a broad spectrum of topics, integrating all of it into a whole and blending it with a unique South African flavour, it is believed that this comprehensive textbook on the theory practice of South African Human Resource Management, will enhance the appreciation and understanding of this all important management challenge facing all South African organisations. Meeting this challenge is necessary to become more competitive, to create value, and to fairly distribute the fruits accruing from the value creation processes. Without this we will fail to bring about the stability, peace and general quality of life so eagerly sought by the ordinary citizens of this country: the challenge is ours, let's not let it slip by.

"Wealth is the means and people the ends. All our material riches will avail us little if we do not use them to expand the opportunities of people." (John F Kennedy.)

BEN J SWANEPOEL
(*Editor*)

Contents

part one
Orientation and General Overview

part two

Strategising, Structuring and Planning

6. Strategic Decisions Regarding HRM
Part 1: Formulating HRM Strategies

7. Strategic Decisions regarding HRM
Part 2: Structural Dimensions and Considerations

Contents

part three

Establishing employment relationships

part four

Utilising and Developing employees

part five
Compensating and caring for employees

Contents

part six

Managing Labour and Employee Relations

part seven

Special Topics in Human Resource Management

part one

Orientation and General Overview

chapter 1 Human Resource Management: Orientation and General Introduction

STUDY OBJECTIVES

After studying this chapter you should be able to:

- briefly explain the management context of this book;
- give a brief overview of the evolution of human resource management from an international-historical perspective;
- analyse the semantic debate underlying the evolution from personnel to human resource management;
- explain the systems-functional perspective of the human resource management process;
- illustrate and describe what is meant by human resource management as an interventionary process;
- list and briefly discuss the scope of human resource management functions and activities;
- analyse and discuss the debate surrounding the people responsible for performing human resource management functions;
- explain how a typical human resource department fits into organisational structures;
- give a general overview of work opportunities in the human resource field.

1.1 INTRODUCTION

Work occupies a central part in life. Most people, at some stage, have to engage in some form of work activity to earn a living. Most do so within the context of some or other organisation in which they are employed. Such people can be classified as the "personnel" of an organisation. It is well known today that the quality of the people in organisations can make a major difference in the competitiveness of organisations. It is therefore beneficial to study human resource management, even though not everyone will become human resource professionals. The issues related to work and the management of people at work form an interesting, dynamic and challenging field of study. The overall aim of this book is to introduce those interested in management, to state-of-the-art theory and practice of human

resource management in South Africa. This book is therefore about the management of people in relation to their work and the organisations where they work.

1.2 MANAGEMENT: THE CONTEXT OF THIS BOOK

This book is written from a management perspective.

 As a well-established, applied and normative science at most academic institutions in South Africa, and as an important and omnipresent phenomenon in
modern society, *management* can, in broad terms, be regarded as that field
which concerns itself with all the factors, methods, principles and processes
involved in the successful functioning of organisations (Cronje, Hugo, Neuland & Van Reenen 1994: 18–20)

 In this context, *organisations* can be regarded as all those consciously coordinated social entities in modern society, with relatively identifiable boundaries, that function on a relatively continuous basis to achieve specific goals
(Robbins 1987: 3–4).

Organisations are created by people in order to help fulfil their vast range of needs.
Some organisations are business enterprises which ascribe to a profit motive (for
example Pep Stores and Pick 'n Pay), some are government organisations or parastatal institutions (such as local authorities, ESKOM and the SABC) and some are
non-profit-seeking organisations (such as churches, trade unions and welfare institutions). All of these organisations consist of people who interact consciously in an
endeavour to achieve certain goals and to serve a particular need in society — in
order to be successful.

Successful, in this context, means doing the right things the right way. The
"right things" refer to the specific goods (products and/or services) which a particular organisation serves to provide. The provision of such goods or services constitutes the basic *raison d' être* of any such social entity. Any organisation is thus set
up specifically to cater for certain needs in society, to provide need-satisfying products and/or services (goods). Organisations can only be successful if they deliver
the right goods — in other words, the goods that people want. Furthermore, however, all organisations also have to do things the right way. This means that, in
providing these "right goods", organisations must also function in such a way that
all the stakeholders (not only the owners) — in particular the customers, consumers or end users of these goods — are satisfied with the products or services
provided. The nature and quality of the goods must be right, and they must be
provided at the right price, at the right time and at the right place. If they are happy
and they use the products/services, the organisation's chances of surviving are
better.

Students of management therefore study all the activities and decisions of
managers which aim to ensure the success of their organisations and the gradual
improvement of the quality of life of all their stakeholders (such as the customers,

the owners, the employees and the community at large). In this sense the organisation is goal driven and managers are responsible for ensuring goal achievement.

Management as a field of study is complex and vast. It is concerned with the utilisation and mobilisation of all of the organisation's resources so that it can survive and success be achieved in the changing environment within which any organisation exists and operates. These resources can be tangible or intangible and include natural resources such as water and land, financial resources such as cash and debtors, technological resources such as machinery, equipment and computer technology, information and knowledge-based resources, energy-related resources and human resources. All of these resources have to be utilised, combined and transformed into need-satisfying goods. It is the responsibility of management to manage all of these resources, including human resources.

The focus of this book is on how the human resources of an organisation can be managed in order to help ensure that need-satisfying goods are delivered in such a way that all stakeholders are optimally satisfied.

In section 1.4 this management perspective is taken a step further when organisations and human resource management are discussed from a systems and process perspective. At this stage it is important to clarify important concepts which are used throughout the book.

1.3 HUMAN RESOURCE MANAGEMENT IN AN INTERNATIONAL-HISTORICAL CONTEXT

Few areas of research, teaching or writing have evoked as much semantic debate as that which abounds in the literature concerning the field of human resource management. Terms or concepts used to describe this field include *labour management, employment management, personnel management, personnel administration, manpower management, industrial relations, human resources management, human resource management* and *employment relations* (Beach 1980; Cuming 1989; Pieper 1990; Brewster & Tyson 1991; Storey 1992). It seems that this semantic confusion stems partly from international and historical differences which have developed in theories relating to this field of knowledge and practice. It is therefore necessary to focus briefly on this concept in a historical and international context.

1.3.1 Managing human resources: A brief evolutionary overview

As the twenty-first century approaches and one looks back in time, it seems that not only life in general but working life in particular is today significantly different from what it used to be; it can, however, be concluded with reasonable certainty that it will be even more significantly different another fifty years from now.

Before the Industrial Revolution most people were engaged in home crafts or in agriculture. There was virtually no such thing as modern-day employment or employment relationships. With the coming of the Industrial Revolution, however, daily life and the world of work changed dramatically as technological developments led to the establishment of factories where people went to work.

Working life came to be removed from the family or household context. Specific employer-employee relationships were established, which had to be managed by those in charge of and responsible for these factories or organisations. The real origins of personnel management practice can hence actually be traced back to all those efforts by employers who over the years tried to devise ways to maintain and utilise their workers better. For example, Robert Owen (1771–1858), a Scottish textile manufacturer, spent company profits on efforts to improve the living and working conditions of his labour force at New Lanark, Scotland. These efforts included the provision of villages for workers near their places of work, schooling facilities, as well as decent health and sanitation facilities in his cotton mill factories (Beach 1980; Cuming 1989). On the other hand, in the United States of America the earliest strike ever to be documented was organised by Philadelphia printers who claimed minimum weekly wages as long ago as in 1786. In addition, as early as 1794 Albert Gallatin had already established the first profit-sharing scheme in the United States, at his glass works in Pennsylvania (Cherrington 1983: 15).

During the period 1820–1850 many factories were established —to an extent that at some stage then only about 50 % of American workers were engaged in agriculture (Cherrington 1983; Beach 1980).

During the period 1880–1920 three important changes came about: a massive growth in factory-type work; serious efforts to improve the general welfare of factory workers; and scientific management to improve production levels. Due to the growth in larger factories, an American, Frederick W Taylor (the so-called father of scientific management), began to conduct research. He propagated the use of "scientific techniques" to elicit higher output, higher profits (and higher wages) through a differential piece rate wage incentive system. He believed in using scientific methods to study working conditions and jobs in order to identify the "best working methods" (tools, equipment, machinery and process) and to recruit and appoint the "right" people for the "right" jobs. Scientific management protagonists, such as Taylor, the Gilbreths and Henry Grant, also advocated clearly defined jobs with concomitant organisational structures.

During the early 1900s the welfare phase gained momentum in the United Kingdom as well as in America. Typical personnel departments were established and filled by welfare workers who provided welfare facilities and programmes (related to aspects such as health and recreation) in order to enhance the general wellbeing of the workers within the factories — the so-called paternalism paradigm of personnel management. By this time other functions performed by these so-called employment departments included all the basic administrative activities of record keeping and, based on the principles of scientific management, the specialised functions involved in recruitment and selection. In 1912 the managers of these departments formed the first "employment managers" association in the

United States of America (Beach 1980: 15). In 1913 a separate Department of Labour was created in the United States of America and the Welfare Workers Association was formed in the United Kingdom, an association which eventually evolved into the Institute of Personnel Management in 1946 (Cherrington 1983; Cuming 1989).

By 1915 the first official training programme for these "employment managers" was launched in the USA (Beach 1980: 15). By this time industrial psychological research had also paved the way for the use of sophisticated selection tests, such as the first large-scale group intelligence tests, the Army Alpha and Beta tests, which were used for the first time in 1917 in the USA (Cherrington 1983: 15). Hugo Munsterberg's famous book, *Psychology and Industrial Efficiency*, was published in 1913 — a work regarded by many as the authoritative source in the field of applying psychological knowledge to the management of work and human resources. These developments made important contributions to existing knowledge on aspects such as training techniques, the relationship between working conditions and work performance, work motivation and morale, as well as on performance evaluation.

During the period 1924 to 1933, Elton Mayo and some of his colleagues at Harvard University also conducted a series of research studies at the Hawthorne Works of the Western Electric Company in Chicago, USA. Their work related to the role of aspects such as lighting, rest pauses and group norms on work performance levels, and laid the foundation for the so-called human relations movement which highlighted the social drives of man within the context of work. This movement emphasised that approaches which were too impersonal and task orientated, rational and scientific, were of little value in the field of people management and that the "softer" or social aspects of people management needed more attention. This movement, which marked the beginning of the era of applying behavioural sciences in the work place, put forward the view that employees could not be seen merely as "factors of production" just like materials, money and natural resources. Personnel management as a distinct field of theory and practice thus came to be appreciated and recognised more and more. At this stage the concepts *personnel management* and *personnel administration* were widely used, although, according to Staehle, the concept *human resource management* was coined only in the 1950s (Staehle, in Pieper 1990).

Personnel management was largely regarded at this stage as a reactive function which had to serve or support other functions within the context of pre-existing organisational structures and established goals and objectives. The other functions (like production and marketing) would keep the personnel department informed of its needs regarding employees, and the latter then had to see to it that, through the use of specialised knowledge, these needs were satisfied by means of recruitment, selection, training, compensation and administrative work.

During the 1950s and 1960s various behavioural scientists were influential in the evolution of the human relations school of thought. Humanistic psychologists such as Abraham Maslow (1954), Chris Argyris (1957), Douglas McGregor (1960) and Frederick Herzberg (1966) were prominent figures in this regard.

In 1965 Miles published an article in the *Harvard Business Review* in which he explicitly made the distinction between *human relations* and *human resources*. Whereas in the former the emphasis was said to be on the *human* aspect, on the "softer" issues of supportive, friendly people management styles where employees' feelings and needs were emphasised, the latter was said to emphasise the potential value of the *resource* aspect in terms of which each employee's potential talents, qualities and abilities would contribute. In a broader sense Becker's work *Human Capital* (1964) in many respects laid the foundation for the idea of *human resource management*. Frederick Herzberg's *Work and the Nature of Man* (1966) also made major contributions to developments in the field of people management. He emphasised the necessity of incorporating certain "motivational" principles (such as challenging work and responsibility), as well as "hygiene principles" (such as good pay and good interpersonal relations between superiors and subordinates), in the design of work and processes and systems to manage the people who execute the work. Rensis Likert's work (1967) emphasised the quantification of all these aspects through the development of the first human resource accounting systems. This again emphasised the "harder", economic or "business value" aspects of the idea of *human resource management*. Employees were viewed as highly valued assets rather than as cost factors of production.

By the late 1970s all these developments contributed to the more official rechristening of traditional, reactive "personnel administration or management" as "human resource management" in the USA. Developments such as new safety and equal opportunity laws and souring economic circumstances in the USA gave further impetus to many innovative human resource management practices (many of which came from line and top management itself, rather than from the so-called personnel experts), in order to reduce costs and increase flexibility in increasingly volatile and competitive environments (Strauss, in Towers 1992: 27–29).

1.3.2 From personnel management to human resource management: recent developments and contemporary viewpoints

Whereas most experts would agree that *human resource management* is the concept that has replaced concepts such as *personnel administration* or *personnel management*, there is considerable debate in the western world regarding what exactly *human resource management* (HRM) entails. Various authors (Brewster & Tyson 1991; Pieper 1990) ascribe these variations in the interpretation of the concept *human resource management* to international differences. This section therefore provides a brief overview of some of these different conceptions.

1.3.2.1 *Something old, something new: generalistic conceptions of human resource management*

Although the concept *human resource management* (HRM) has largely come to replace the concept *personnel management* internationally, there is little consensus regarding the degree to which this development constitutes something qualitatively new in people management. To some, *human resource management* is a rather loosely used concept — a more modern or trendy name for what has traditionally been termed *personnel management*. Many second and third editions of textbooks in this field have been retitled without much change to their content. The majority of authoritative American writers follow a similar approach in their textbooks where the terms are used interchangeably (Klatt, Murdick & Schuster 1985; Leap & Crino 1993; Byars & Rue 1994: 6).

In many of the titles of these works reference is made to "something in addition": for example, the titles *Personnel and Human Resource Management* or *Human Resource and Personnel Management* (Byars & Rue 1984; Schuler 1987). This rechristening seems partly to be symbolic of the actual nature/content of this field of theory and practice which has undergone substantial qualitative changes. Traditionally personnel administration or management was viewed as a second-class function where "washed-up" or substandard line managers would land up, with a reactive role to play. At most these personnel functionaries fulfilled administrative tasks related to recruitment, selection, compensation and some welfare service orientated functions. Personnel management was viewed as a separate, distinct area for administrators and perhaps behavioural scientists who could help with some of the sociopsychological support functions such as selection, appraisal and counselling. In addition, with the growth of the trade union movement, personnel managers were also seen to be responsible for labour or industrial relations matters, dealing with issues related to trade unions, grievances, discipline and dismissals.

The modern American view is that human resource management (HRM) is a more business orientated and integrated general management function with a qualitatively different role to fulfil. To a large extent it can be said that Beer, Spector, Lawrence, Mills and Walton's (1985) Harvard Business School text, *Human Resource Management: A General Manager's Perspective*, took the lead in this regard. Klatt et al (1985: 5), for example, also state that *human resource management* 'covers all activities by both line managers and the "personnel department" that deal with them. The term personnel/human resource (P/HR) management comprises the managerial activities involved in planning for recruiting, staffing, training, developing, rewarding, utilising and maintaining human resources', and further that 'human resource management is an integral function of line management and, therefore, an important training step for high general management positions' (Klatt et al 1985: 8). This generalist conception is upheld in many authoritative American textbooks.

It seems that this broad conception of the concept *human resource management* is of a generalist nature: most or all of the typical old aspects are retained, some aspects are considered to be somewhat different and some totally new ideas regarding people management are incorporated.

There are, however, other narrower or more absolutist interpretations and approaches to the concept *human resource management*.

1.3.2.2 *More specific views of the concept human resource management*

To some analysts and commentators, in particular those from the United Kingdom, *human resource management* represents a very specific way or style of managing people at work. Two of the United Kingdom's most authoritative researchers and writers on the topic, Guest and Storey (Guest 1987, 1989; Storey 1989, 1992), view human resource management as a new and very distinct approach to people management. This "human resource management approach" has specific characteristics, based on the belief that:

- it is essentially the quality of organisations' human resources which makes the difference between those which are more and those which are less successful and that all employees as resources therefore have to be developed and valued;

- due to the strategic importance of human resource management decisions, all such decisions have to be taken in direct relation to and as an integral part of the corporate and/or business planning decisions of the organisation;

- human resource management decisions have long-term business related implications and therefore have to be the concern of the line managers, who are the key figures in and "owners of" human resource management;

- a specific model of personnel management, superior to all others, has certain distinct "key levers" fostering development, flexibility, commitment, involvement, customer orientation and hence competitive advantage for the enterprise;

- human resource management is essentially unitaristic and thus individualistic as opposed to collectivistic. It is thus a non-trade unionist approach.

- Table 1.1 is adapted from Storey's work (1992: 35) (inspired by Guest (1987)) and represents a summary of so-called differences between the more traditional personnel and industrial relations management approach as opposed to the human resource management approach — as conceived in an absolutist sense.

Having introduced you to some of the different international viewpoints regarding the concept of human resource management, the next step is to spell out the systems-functional perspective of HRM, a perspective which underlies the approach taken in this book.

Table 1.1
Some points of difference between 'Personnel & IR' and 'HRM'*

Aspect	Personnel and IR	HRM
Employment contract	Clear delineation of formalised contracts	Try going 'beyond formal contracts'
Rule orientation	Importance of rules/ stressed	Much less rule-based
Management actions driven by	Procedures	'Business-needs'
Management's role iro labour	To monitor	To nurture
Frame of reference	Pluralist	Unitarist
Key relations focus	Internal: Labour-management	External: Customer
Initiatives/Interventions	Piecemeal	Integrated
Corporate strategy	Not important	Very important
Line Management's role	Transactional	Transformational leadership
Key role players	Specialists	Line managers
Communication	Indirect	Direct
Degree of standardisation	High	Low
Selection	Separate, marginal task	Integrated, key task
Pay thrust	Fixed ito job evaluation	Performance based
Conditions of service	Separately negotiated	Harmonisation
Collectivism/Individualism	Collective agreements	Towards individual agreements
Job levels and categories	Many	Few
Work design	Mechanistic	Motivational
Human resource development	Controlled access to courses	Learning organisations
Foci of attention for interventions	Personnel and IR procedures	Wide ranging cultural, structural and HR strategies

*Source: Adapted from Storey 1992: 3

1.4   A SYSTEMS-FUNCTIONAL PERSPECTIVE OF THE HUMAN RESOURCE MANAGEMENT PROCESS

Human resource management is viewed by the authors as an intrinsic part of an organisation and its management. As mentioned earlier, it is management's task to combine, deploy and utilise all resources and/or inputs available to the organisation in a way which will ensure long-term organisational success in a changing environment — to the benefit of all its stakeholders.

From a systems perspective, a visual presentation of the basic task and process of management can be set out as shown in figure 1.1. All the organisation's resources and/or inputs have to be planned for, organised, activated and directed (by means of the function of leading) and controlled on a continuous basis. Various functional areas have to be managed in the organisation in this way.

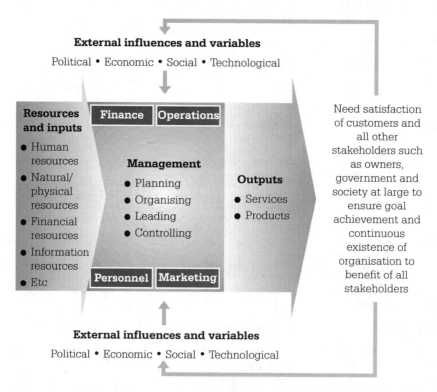

Figure 1.1

Management of the organisation: A process perspective

According to the traditional functional approach to management, there are various *functions* in the organisation. These include the technical/operational or production function (concerned with the actual production of goods), the financial function, the marketing function, the public relations function and the personnel or human resource function. These functional areas can all be viewed as subsystems of the organisation as a system. Each functional area or subsystem has to be planned for, organised, directed/led and controlled in an integrated and coherent way.

This systems-functional perspective of management is theoretical by nature. It is a simplified version, for conceptual, research and teaching purposes, of what happens in "the real world" (in practice). In practice all these functional areas or subsystems, management processes, decisions and activities, as well as all the environmental factors, are interrelated and in dynamic interaction, making for a very complex phenomenon.

The human resource management process as such can be viewed as the planning and organising for, and the directing/leading and control of, the organisation's human resource subsystem. Figure 1.2 is a more detailed visual presentation

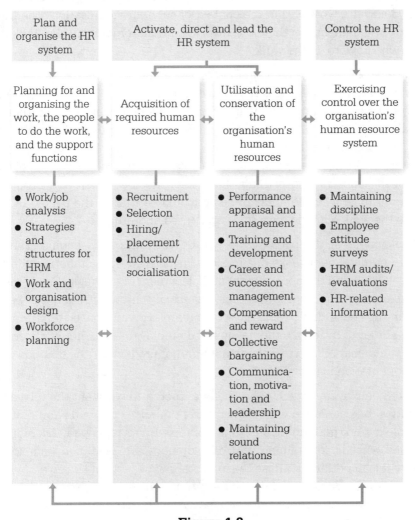

Figure 1.2

Human resource management: a general process approach

of this basic human resource management process. Please note again that this visual presentation and categorisation is theoretical and for conceptual purposes only. In practice things are much more complex.

The basic process can be summarised in the following way: Any organisation, in order to provide the necessary goods, needs to have some sort of work done. During the planning and organising process of human resource management, the nature of the work to be done is analysed. *Work or job analysis is therefore one of the most basic human resource management tasks or functions.* Jobs are designed (or redesigned) in that certain tasks are grouped together into various "positions" which stand in specific relation to each other.

In this way work is structured and organisational structures are designed. The definition of an organisation (see section 1.1) as a consciously coordinated social entity, emphasises the need to coordinate formally the interaction between the people doing the work within the context of such an organisation. The design or redesign of organisations therefore revolves around organising the work and the people who have to do the work.

However, this is only the beginning of human resource management. Management must also plan which positions have to be filled when, by what type and what quality of persons. Workforce planning must thus be undertaken. Furthermore, it must also be decided how the people, once employed, will be dealt with or managed. The necessary HRM strategies or plans must thus be formulated, and the necessary structures or mechanisms to facilitate the execution of these plans must be devised. Once all these things have been decided upon and arranged, the human resource subsystem has to be activated — that is, the people required to execute the work actually have to be appointed and utilised.

Employment of the people who will do the work thus begins. The human resource management tasks or functions involved at this stage include recruitment, selection and the appointment and placement of the newly hired employees. This means that the human resource system of the organisation has been activated, in the sense that people have been employed and have started to do their work. In order to introduce the newly hired employee to his/her work, colleagues and the organisation and in order to get him/her productive, the function of induction or orientation is embarked upon.

As the employee settles in, he/she is expected to carry out the relevant tasks and duties in accordance with the work performance standards and criteria. The employee's work performance is thus appraised and managed. Accordingly the employee's needs for training and development are identified and addressed. Because it is important to utilise the full potential of each and every employee, it is necessary to plan for his/her future career within the organisation, based on potential, preferences and current competencies, as well as the organisation's projected future work-related needs. In the process it is necessary to manage and direct the employee; this calls for communication, motivation and leadership.

It is necessary to ensure that the employee is compensated adequately and that the health, safety and general wellbeing of the employee are maintained. Traditionally many of these areas did not receive the necessary attention from employers, resulting in dissatisfied workers and leading to the formation of trade unions to act as their representatives in the workplace. Collective bargaining has therefore become an important dimension of managing employment relationships, especially in South Africa. Negotiating and interacting with trade unions and worker representatives has thus become another management function related to the organisation's human resource subsystem.

The process of control is important throughout. The employee's work performance, behaviour at work, and satisfaction levels have to be monitored and kept in line with the requirements of the organisation. Control can, for example, be exercised by means of employee attitude surveys and disciplinary processes. Furthermore it is necessary continuously to ensure that all the human resource management functions are executed according to plan or in line with HRM strategy. To this end extensive use is made of human resource related information and certain functions are performed to evaluate the contribution made by the organisation's human resource subsystem to the overall success of the organisation. This completes the cycle of managing the HR subsystem of the organisation. It is, however, an ongoing, interventionary cycle.

1.5 HUMAN RESOURCE MANAGEMENT AS AN INTERVENTIONARY PROCESS

In its most basic form, when any person is employed by an organisation, an employment relationship of exchange comes into being. There is an exchange of energy, knowledge, skills, attitudes and abilities (EKSAs) to do certain work in return for some form of compensation or reward. The employing organisation's management establishes what work needs to be done — the tasks, duties and responsibilities (TDRs). An employment relationship is thus created when the EKSAs of the employee are utilised to perform the TDRs related to certain work that needs to be done. In return, the employee gets some sort of compensation or reward, monetary and otherwise.

In essence, then, we view the scope of human resource management as having to do with managing all aspects related to and flowing from the employment relationships between the organisation as employing entity (the employer) and those persons employed to do the work (employees). All these aspects have to be managed in such a way that organisational success is enhanced and all stakeholders (for example employees, customers, owners or shareholders and the public at large) are optimally satisfied.

All aspects relating to the interaction between these employees — that is, the human resources — and the organisation where they work must thus be managed. Figure 1.3 is a visual presentation of this idea.

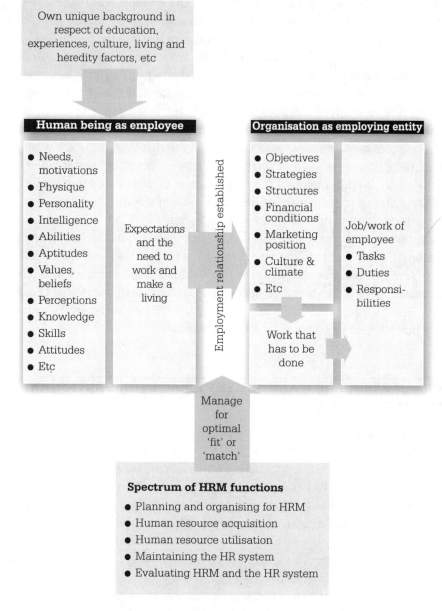

Figure 1.3

Human resource management as an interventionary process to establish,
enhance and maintain "fit for purpose" employment relationships

From this perspective human resource management is an intervening process
aimed at continuously establishing an optimal fit or match between people and
their employing organisations. To achieve this, makes human resource management a very dynamic, complex and demanding area of management because each
employee is a complex human being and each organisation is a complex social

entity. Human resource management is not merely concerned with ensuring employee compliance with the organisation's rules, regulations, procedures and policies, but (even more so) with establishing employee commitment and cooperation and with creating all the necessary circumstances conducive to the optimal utilisation of each and every dimension of the person in employment. An important concept within this context is that of the *psychological contract*.

Apart from the formal employment relationship embodied in the *employment contract*, each employee can be said to enter into a more informal and tacit employment agreement — the so-called *psychological contract*. These contracts basically embody the sense of reciprocal commitment that employees feel exists between themselves and the organisation which employs them. Employees enter the organisation with certain tacit expectations regarding the employment relationship. Employees generally expect to receive something in addition to the formal contractually agreed upon salary, benefits and other conditions of employment; these expectations relate to aspects such as the way they will be treated, the nature of their work, the quality of their working life, and so forth. Employees' returns to the organisation, in terms of aspects such as work behaviour, performance, commitment, cooperation, loyalty, productivity, and so forth, may largely be the result of how they experience or perceive the fulfilment of their psychological contracts with the organisation. These contracts are not static and change over time. Employees who, at any time, perceive this informal dimension of the employment relationship negatively, or the basic employment exchange as inequitable, may not be willing to give their best and may eventually even decide to terminate the employment relationship. In this way low quality HRM as an intervening process can cause the organisation to lose potentially high value human resources. On the other hand, a situation may arise where the staff of an organisation become a major cost factor or liability rather than an asset to the organisation.

Human resource management is thus aimed at constantly enabling employees and their employing organisations to be in agreement, as far as possible, about the nature of their working relationships and their reciprocal expectations, and at ensuring that these agreements are fulfilled as far as possible. The authors' "philosophy of HRM" is based on the belief that employee commitment to an organisation's success, is largely dependant on the employees' perception of the extent to which their own needs and personal objectives will be met through their continuous commitment to the success of the organisation. Only HRM practice which is underscored by this basic belief of the reciprocal dependence between employee and employing organisation (for organisational success on the one hand and individual success and happiness on the other) can hope to achieve an optimal fit or match between employees and organisations, by means of a wide spectrum of typical HRM activities and functions.

1.6 THE SCOPE OF HUMAN RESOURCE MANAGEMENT FUNCTIONS AND ACTIVITIES

From previous sections (and especially figure 1.3) one can already form a fair impression of the type of functions/activities involved in human resource management (HRM) as the intervening process in matching organisations and employees. Although it is an almost impossible task to list all the typical HRM functions/activities, an attempt is made in exhibit A to provide a brief overview of the major functions/activities involved in HRM. This section can thus, in a sense, also serve as a preview of the topics covered in the remaining chapters of this textbook.

Exhibit A

The scope of HRM

1. Planning and organising for work, people and human resource management (HRM)
   - Strategic planning for HRM
     - formulating strategy
     - structuring the work and the organisation through work analysis, job design/redesign, and designing appropriate organisational structures to facilitate optimal flow of work
   - Workforce planning through the preparation of job descriptions and specifications and matching projected supply and demand of labour
2. Staffing the organisation with the necessary employees
   - Recruiting job candidates
   - Selecting the most suitable persons
   - Appointing employees (including new appointments, transfers, promotions, etc)
   - Socialising newly appointed employees (induction or orientation)
3. Utilising and maintaining human resources
   - Appraising and managing the work performance of employees
   - Leading/directing all employees in the performance of their tasks and duties (including the application of motivation and leadership principles)
   - Training and developing all levels of employees
   - Maintaining employee wellbeing (including safety and health, sport and recreation, canteen facilities and accommodation, welfare services and transportation)
   - Compensating and rewarding employees (including remuneration structures, job evaluations, fringe benefit and incentive schemes)
   - Ensuring compliance with labour-related legislation
   - Negotiating with employee representatives and engaging in other collective bargaining processes (including dispute settlement and strike handling)
   - Maintaining discipline and dealing with employees' grievances
   - Ensuring that employees agree with proposed changes and are prepared to help the organisation constantly to change in order to cope with an ever-changing external environment
   - Maintaining and using all employee and human resource management related information and statistics, including maintaining HR information systems, undertaking all sorts of HR related research and evaluating or measuring the quality and nature of the HRM system of the organisation.

The question which now arises regarding the execution of all these types of HRM activities and functions is: Who is responsible?

1.7 WHO PERFORMS HUMAN RESOURCE MANAGEMENT FUNCTIONS?

This is a complex question that cannot be given one definitive answer. As mentioned earlier, most (if not all) managers, at some time or another, are involved in the execution of human resource management functions. Consider, for example, the role of the manager of any section in an organisation (that is, as a supervisor of personnel under his/her authority) in terms of the following:

- When a subordinate resigns and has to be replaced, the manager is normally one of first to know about the vacancy and will consider the replacement of this person by means of internal promotions/transfer or external recruitment.
- The manager is also usually closely involved in making appropriate selection decisions regarding a new appointment.
- The manager is usually responsible for ensuring that the job description is a true reflection of the TDRs attached to the vacant position and that the minimum entry requirements (job specification) are in line with the TDRs, so that a capable person is appointed.
- The manager introduces the new employee to his/her colleagues, working environment and job.
- The manager, as time goes by, not only appraises the progress and performance of the employee (and all other employees) but also provides the necessary on-the-job training (or arranges for other off-the-job training) to ensure that the employee/s can perform as required.
- The manager also usually recommends the relevant pay increases (apart from the general increases for all workers negotiated with trade unions) when merit pay is involved. In addition, the manager is also usually involved as member of job evaluation committees when critical comparisons of relative job worth are made.
- The manager also discusses the subordinate's career prospects, future transfers or promotion prospects, to set objectives in this regard, in collaboration with the subordinate, and thus is responsible for the career planning and management of his/her personnel.
- The manager is responsible for dealing with employee problems and grievances, for maintaining discipline (and even for instituting disciplinary hearings and taking disciplinary action if necessary) and for negotiating with representatives of subordinates in the workplace (mostly shop stewards).
- The responsibility for safety and health in the workplace also lies with the manager who has to ensure that general conditions in the workplace are conducive to the employee's safety and general wellbeing.

From the foregoing it should be quite clear that human resource management functions are not necessarily executed by a human resource specialist or department. The distinction drawn by some between human resource management and the management of human resources, thus seems to be quite vague and possibly confusing. Few contemporary authoritative international textbooks on human resource management draw such a distinction — and the reasons for this should be quite clear from the above. The view taken in this book is that human resource management is, in the final analysis, a function of all managers. Human resource management strategies, practices and decisions have to be integrated and synchronised with, and be supportive of, the organisation's business objectives and strategies. To this end there has to be a partnership between line managers and HR specialists.

Apart from the role played by all managers (who, by definition, manage people), there is thus also very often, especially in medium to large organisations, the need for separate human resource departments or sections. Working in these departments are the so-called human resource specialists or practitioners. The head of such a department is called, for example, the HR manager or Chief Executive: Human Resources. The question therefore arises: Who plays what role in HRM?

This question can also only be answered within the context of a contingency approach. This concerns, in essence, the degree of specialisation and/or devolution involved — in other words, the degree to which HRM will be left to the specialists or the extent to which all managers will themselves perform HRM functions. Precisely how the human resource management functions are divided between the human resource department's specialists and the organisation's other managers varies from situation to situation and is contingent upon a vast number of circumstantial factors. These factors include organisational history, size, structure and location, the values, philosophies and management styles of top management, the nature of the workforce, the type of industry, as well as external factors such as economic conditions, legislative requirements, industrial relations and trade union developments, and other broader social factors which have an influence on the country's human resources and thus on labour market demographics.

The issue of specialisation (versus devolution) in HRM thus lies at the heart of this question. In some organisations, such as in a small-sized engineering firm, there might be a lot of devolution with almost no room for HRM specialisation in the sense that there simply is no human resource department/section or specialists. General managers will, in such an extreme case of devolution, perform all the HRM functions from HR planning, job and organisation design, through to the hiring, training, disciplining and firing of employees.

Many organisations (especially smaller ones) do not need, cannot afford, or simply do not want a form of specialisation in HRM where most of the HRM functions are executed by a separate department staffed with specialists. However, in many organisations, especially as they grow and increase in terms of size and complexity, the general line managers cannot or may not want to perform all the HRM functions on their own any longer, and the need will thus arise for separate human resource departments. These are normally staffed by various HR specialists/functionaries/practitioners. From a functional management perspective, then, just as organisations have marketing departments responsible for the marketing function (or subsystem) and public relations departments responsible for the public relations function (or subsystem), they can also have human resource departments responsible for the human resource function. There is, however, a subtle but fundamental difference.

The human resource subsystem overarches and dominates the other subsystems in the sense that it is **people** who design, activate, implement and control all the other subsystems of the organisation. Thus, although not all managers are, for example, directly involved in operations/production, marketing or public relations, all managers are, by definition, involved in human resource management because they are responsible for the employees under their authority. The human resource subsystem is thus superimposed over all other subsystems or functions.

The distinction between *line* and *staff authority*, however, adds another dimension to the question of roles and responsibilities.

Line authority refers to the authority which runs from top to bottom in a hierarchical organisational structure and where superiors have the right to give and enforce instructions; *staff authority*, on the other hand, really refers to the right to give advice and to render services which may or may not be accepted. Unfortunately, in line with 'Taylorism' and the specialisation phenomenon, organisations used and adapted these concepts to create a distinction between what is traditionally termed *line management* and *staff management*. In this way the concept *line management* came to be used to refer to those organisational functions directly responsible for the business objectives of the organisation. Typically in line with Taylorism, this way of thinking was traditionally taken within the context of the factory, or the manufacturing industry, where the line managers were those who were held directly responsible for the production of the goods (the "lifeblood" of the organisation). Line managers were thus traditionally those in charge of activities in production departments. Staff management, then, within this context, was viewed as being responsible for rendering advisory and other support services, based on the specialised knowledge possessed by the personnel employed in these so-called staff departments. It therefore seems that, partly due to this extension of the line/staff concept (and perhaps wrongly), confusion tends to exist regarding whether human resource management is a staff or line function of management.

Traditionally *personnel management* or the *personnel function* was viewed as being a typical example of a staff management function as opposed to a line management function. However, with the adoption of the concept *human resource management*, this issue took on a new dimension. As the human resource subsystem is increasingly viewed as the dominant subsystem in the organisation's strive towards excellence, and since this aspect is superimposed over all other management subsystems or functions, HRM is increasingly viewed as a general function of management. The question is therefore redirected at the role to be played by the HR department vis-à-vis the other general managers.

Due to circumstantial changes (such as a worldwide shift from a pure production orientation to one of total quality or customer satisfaction/service or marketing), and the vagueness of the distinction between line and staff authority/

management, the idea of making a rigorous distinction between line and staff functions and/or managers has been losing a lot of ground lately — especially within the HRM context. Torrington and Hall (1991: 21), for example, say that this "distinction is getting more and more blurred as all managers become progressively more general in the range of their responsibilities".

The exact nature of the role to be played by the HR department vis-à-vis other managers with regard to human resource management within a particular organisation remains an area of debate and an aspect about which each organisation's top management will have to decide. It is actually an area for strategic decision making, and is dealt with in greater detail in chapter 7. In general it can be said, however, that, to a greater or lesser extent, HR departments (where they exist) will normally fulfil roles and functions which have one or more of the characteristics in the box below:

Typical characteristics of the role of the department

- Catalystic (devising/drafting/initiating strategies, policies and systems)
- Advisory/consultative
- Coordinative and controlling
- Counselling/facilitating/mediating
- Supportive

Irrespective of the exact nature of the role of HR departments, the emphasis will be on their ability to 'add value'. As Beatty and Schneier (1997:29) say: "HR must now be judged on whether it enhances the firm's competitive advantage by adding **real**, measurable economic value ... Whatever HR does must not only add value to its internal clients, but also (more importantly) add economic value to the organization's external customers and investors."

In line therefore with the latest trend to make human resource management a general management responsibility, HR specialists and departments are expected to be active players and partners in the challenge of making organisations more competitive and successful. As Lobel (1997:135) puts it: "... HR managers recognize that, like line managers, they are accountable for business results".

1.8 MAKING A SPECIALISED CAREER IN THE HR FIELD

Although it was clearly illustrated earlier that all managers, by definition, in fact perform HRM functions, specific jobs and careers specialising in the HR field can be identified. Especially over the last ten to fifteen years, the HR field as a career option has become very prominent and rewarding (both in monetary terms and otherwise), as well as challenging. The view taken in this book is that HR specialists/departments work in partnership with general/line management in so far as it concerns HRM.

However, in this section the focus is on HR specialists and the perspective is that of the individual (not the organisation or management) who might be interested in following a career of HR specialisation.

1.8.1 Types of HR jobs and careers

Career opportunities for HR professionals vary within and across organisations. In general the number and types of HR jobs offered by an organisation will largely depend on both the size of the organisation and on its management philosophy with regard to HRM (particularly with regard to the role of the HR specialist or department). Larger organisations usually offer more opportunities for specialisation in the field of HR practice, as research has indicated over the years that ratios tend to exist between the numbers of HR staff employed and the total number of employees in any organisation. In some instances the specialist-to-employee ratio (excluding clerical staff) might be 0,5:100 (one HR specialist for every 200 employees), whereas in other cases it might be 1,2:100 (six HR specialists for every 500 employees). Regarding the specific ratio, much will depend on the specialisation/devolution policy of the particular organisation. A top management decision to move away from HR specialisation towards "giving HRM back to line" might therefore mean a lowering of the HR specialist-to-employee ratio. Be that as it may, in similar types of organisations (in terms of industry and business), the larger ones will normally employ more HR specialists and the HR career opportunities will thus be greater. In such cases the degree of specialisation vis-à-vis a more generalist role within the particular HR job will also usually depend upon the size of the organisation and its HRM philosophy. In a large, multiestablishment organisation with an HRM policy of specialisation rather than devolution, the contents of the various HR positions would also of necessity be of a much more specialised nature than would be the case in a smaller, single plant organisation with a policy of high devolution. In the latter case it might be required of all of the few HR specialists sometimes to give advice to line on a vast number of HR issues, ranging from selection techniques, remuneration/benefits and workforce planning and information systems, through to questions of dispute settlement with trade unions and the training of managers and technical personnel. In some organisations the HR departments are themselves highly specialised with the roles of some HR specialists restricted to one particular area such as supervisory training or psychometric testing. In general terms a distinction can thus be drawn between generalist types of HR jobs or careers on the one hand and specialist types of HR jobs or careers on the other.

1.8.1.1 Specialising in HR

In most cases anyone who is interested in a career in the HR field, and who has no work experience, will have to start in a typical entry-level position in the HR field of practice. In such cases the different areas of specialisation are vast, ranging from *employment* or *staffing* (where a person may specialise in one or more areas such as recruitment or selection interviewing, job analysis, workforce planning, or administrating psychometric tests on candidates), to *labour relations* (negotiating with unions, reviewing disciplinary appeal cases or preparing dispute settlement cases), *compensation administration* (performing job evaluations, conducting wage/salary surveys or administering employee benefit schemes) or *training and development* (running induction/orientation programmes, conducting training needs analyses, presenting general supervisory training or being involved in management and organisation development interventions). Note that, in order to enter these areas of specialisation, some form of formal education and/or training is normally required in order to ensure that those who enter this field of practice have the minimum knowledge base. Qualifications in the social and business sciences are normally required. The individual can then as a rule choose to remain engaged in a specific HR specialist area, or he/she might decide to gain experience in various specialist areas in order to later move on to more generalist positions.

An individual may, for example, decide on a career in the field of human resource development. He/she may then start off as an assistant training officer, later became a skills training instructor, and carry on to gain experience in the fields of training and development, until such time as he/she can be appointed to the position of "Senior Manager: Human Resource Development" in a large multinational organisation employing over 10 000 people. Similarly, a person may decide to specialise in labour relations until such time as he/she can become the "General Manager: Labour Relations" of a large organisation like Telkom, or a specialist industrial relations consultant (or training/development or remuneration consultant for that matter) who will deal with specialised cases in the particular field on a daily basis on behalf of his/her clients. An HR specialist type of job or career therefore often involves a specialised consultative type of work.

1.8.1.2 Generalist HR practitioners

In the case of a more generalist career in the human resource field, the individual may decide not to remain in any one subfunctional area of HR specialisation for too long. In relatively smaller organisations with smaller HR departments, the HR specialists execute various HR-related functions because there are not as many HR specialists.

As a rule, HR generalists prefer to gain broader based knowledge and experience by working in various HR functional areas, rather than to gain highly specialised, in-depth knowledge and experience in one specific area (such as labour relations or personnel selection). Such an individual will also have to start in one or other specialist area, but will see this simply as a stepping stone to get into the HR field.

Apart from young graduates in the social and/or business sciences, sometimes line functionaries who become interested in the HR field make career shifts into the HR generalist field. The senior HR practitioner at a particular establishment or plant of an organisation, who assumes responsibility for all the HR department's functions at that organisational level (including, for example, recruitment, selection, induction, training, remuneration and labour relations), is a typical example of an HR generalist. If such a plant is relatively small (say 30–100 employees), the HR manager or personnel officer at the plant may be all on his/her own, having to deal with most of these aspects on a daily basis. If such an HR generalist needs any highly specialised advice in the HR field, he/she will usually approach the relevant HR specialists at corporate/head office level (if they are available) or make use of specialist consultants. In the case of a larger organisational setup, it may be that the HR manager (the HR generalist) of a plant with, say, approximately 1 000–1 500 employees, may have his/her own specialists reporting to him/her. As head of an HR department which has to deal with all or most of the various areas in HRM, the top level HR practitioner will thus usually also be more of a generalist.

1.9 STUDYING HRM: AN OUTLINE OF THIS BOOK

One of the most important first steps to take in order to become more knowledgeable and competent in the field of HRM is, however, to study this broad and interesting field in a systematic way. This book has been devised to help those interested in this topic to do just that. In the next chapter we introduce you to human resource management from a South African perspective. Chapters 3 and 4 form the cornerstone of your studies in this field by explaining some of the dynamics that underlie and impact on this area of management, first at a micro- and then at a macrolevel (in other words, external to the organisation). Chapter 5 deals with affirmative action and equal employment opportunities — an aspect that has a profound influence on almost every human resource management function. The three chapters that follow cover the decisions, processes and practices related to planning and organising the human resource systems of organisations. Chapters 9 and 10 deal with the employment of personnel. Chapters 11 to 16 have to do with how we can go about utilising and developing the people employed to do the work. Chapters 17 to 19 focus on meeting the needs of the workforce through remuneration, reward and general employee care practices like health and safety management. Because labour relations — and especially trade unions — play such an important role in the management of employment relationships in South African organisations, these topics are dealt with quite comprehensively in chapters 20 and 21. The last part of this book deals with certain special topics. Chapter 22 revolves around the management of organisational transformation and change, while chapter 23 covers various aspects related to human resource management information. The last chapter deals with the termination of employment relationships.

SELF-EVALUATION QUESTIONS

1. Briefly explain what "management" is all about.
2. Provide an overview of historical developments in the management of human resources up to the late 1970s.
3. Differentiate between broad and generalistic perspectives of HRM as concept and, narrower/or absolutist viewpoints.
4. Describe what HRM entails from a systems-functional perspective.
5. 'Human resource management can basically be viewed as an interventionary process focused on establishing and maintaining "good fit" employment relationships within an organisational context.' Discuss.
6. Outline the scope of typical HRM functions and activity areas.
7. 'The traditional view that HRM is a staff function is outdated.'
    Critically comment on the above statement and explain who performs HRM functions in organisations.
8. Suppose that you have just been approached by a high school pupil with the following request/question: "I've heard that I ought to consider a career in the field of HR; what can you tell me about such a career?"
    How would you respond to this question?

BIBLIOGRAPHY

Beach, DS. 1980. *Personnel: The Management of People at Work*, 4 ed. New York: MacMillan

Beatty, RW & Schneier, CE. 1997. New HR roles to impact organizational performance: from "partners" to "players". *Human Resource Management*, vol 38, no 1, 29–37

Beer, M, Spector, B, Lawrence, P, Mills, D & Walton, R. 1985. *Human Resource Management: A General Manager's Perspective*. New York: Free Press

Brewster, C & Tyson, S. 1991. *International Comparisons in Human Resource Management*. London: Pitman

Byars, LL & Rue, LW. 1984. *Human Resource and Personnel Management*. Homewood, Illinois: Irwin

Byars, LL & Rue, LW. 1994. *Human Resource Management*, 4 ed. Boston, Massachusetts: Irwin

Cherrington, DJ. 1983. *Personnel Management: The Management of Human Resources*. Dubuque, Iowa: WMC Brown

Cronje, GJ de J, Hugo, WMJ, Neuland, EW & Van Reenen, MJ. 1994. *Introduction to Business Management*, 3 ed. Halfway House: Southern

Cuming, MW. 1989. *The Theory and Practice of Personnel Management*, 6 ed. Oxford: Heinemann

Guest, D. 1987. Human resource management and industrial relations. *Journal of Management Studies*, 24(5)

Guest, D. 1989. Personnel and HRM: Can you tell the difference? *Personnel Management*, 21, January, 48–51

Klatt, LA, Murdick, RG & Schuster, FE. 1985. *Human Resource Management*. Columbus, Ohio: Charles E Merill/A Bell & Howell

Leap, TL & Crino, MD. 1993. *Personnel/Human Resource Management*, 2 ed. New York: MacMillan

Lobel, SA. 1997. In praise of the "soft" stuff; a vision for human resource leadership. *Human Resource Management*, vol 38, no 1, 135–39

Pieper, R. 1990. *Human Resource Management: An International Comparison*. Berlin: Walter de Gouyter

Robbins, SP. 1987. *Organisation Theory: Structure, Design and Applications*, 2 ed. Englewood Cliffs, New Jersey: Prentice-Hall

Schuler, RS. 1987. *Personnel and Human Resource Management*, 3 ed. St Paul: West

Smit, PS & Cronje, GJ de J. 1992. *Principles of Management: A Contemporary South African Perspective*. Cape Town: Juta

Staehle, WH. 1990. Human resource management and corporate stategy. In Pieper, R. *Human Resource Management: An International Comparison*. Berlin: Walter de Gouyter

Storey, J (ed). 1989. *New Perspective on Human Resource Management*. London: Routledge

Storey, J. 1992. *Developments in the Management of Human Resources*. Oxford: Blackwell

Strauss, G. 1992. Human resource management in the USA. In Towers, S (ed) *The Handbook of Human Resource Management*, 27–29. Oxford: Blackwell

Torrington, D & Hall, L. 1991. *Personnel Management: A New Approach*. London: Prentice-Hall

STUDY OBJECTIVES

After studying this chapter, you should be able to:

- describe developments in human resource management (HRM) in South Africa over a seven-phase period;
- explain at least nine characteristics of a South African perspective of human resource management;
- briefly discuss how one can pursue a career in the HR field in South Africa;
- identify the role of the South African Board for Personnel Practice (SABPP) in human resource management in South Africa by explaining its philosophy, strategy, objectives and functions;
- explain the process of registration with the South African Board for Personnel Practice (SABPP);
- discuss the SABPP's code of professional conduct;
- give an overview of the South African Board for Personnel Practice (SABPP's) generic competency model for HR practitioners in South Africa;
- explain how one can remain a valued HR practitioner in South Africa.

2.1 INTRODUCTION

In chapter 1 you were introduced to human resource management (HRM) from a general, international perspective. However, this book deals with human resource management in South Africa and it is therefore necessary to shed some more light on HRM from a South African perspective. Although by now you should already have a fair idea of the authors' approach to HRM in this book, this chapter is intended to highlight some additional important issues which are peculiar to HRM theory and practice in South Africa.

2.2 SOME HISTORICAL PERSPECTIVES ON HRM DEVELOPMENTS IN SOUTH AFRICA

Any textbook on South African human resource management would be incomplete without some reflections on how this field of knowledge and practice has evolved over time within this country. However, this topic raises all sorts of difficulties. Not only will any attempt to analyse, document and outline historical events inevitably be flawed with the value-laden frame of reference through which the historian selectively interprets past developments, but, when it comes to the history of personnel management in South Africa, a lack of systematically documented information compounds the problem. Some two decades ago Verster (1979) had the following to say in this regard: "The history and development of personnel management in South Africa is a subject on which apparently very little research has been done and few publications have seen the light." Within the context of these difficulties, the section which follows can be viewed as an attempt to fill the current gap in the literature.

2.2.1 The world of work in preindustrial South Africa

Due to the fact that South Africa was chiefly an agrarian society prior to the discovery of diamonds in 1867 and gold in 1872, most of the country's inhabitants were engaged in household and agrarian activities. The SAN people, probably the first inhabitants of South Africa, were, for example, highly competent and prolific hunters. The Khoikhoi, who lived at the Cape when the first Europeans came ashore in 1488, were nomadic herdsmen and also proficient hunters. These indigenous peoples bartered their cattle in exchange for the copper, beads, iron and tobacco offered by the early European visitors. Later some of the Khoikhoi became the servants and slaves of the Dutch settlers.

As more and more immigrants settled at the Cape after Jan van Riebeeck arrived in 1652 to set up a refreshment post, trade between these groups increased. The Khoikhoi provided fresh vegetables and fruit. More people were required to help build the growing settlement (colony). Many of the passing crewmen stayed on and the first Cape community thus came to include skilful people like millers, bakers and blacksmiths.

Because the settlers needed more and more help, and the Khoikhoi people were reluctant to work for them, Van Riebeeck, who was well acquainted with the slave trade in the East, arranged for the first shipment of slaves from Angola in 1658. Gradually more slaves were "imported" from places like West Africa, the East, Madagascar and Mozambique. The slaves had to work hard maintaining gardens and buildings, chopping trees and working on farms for six days a week — all without pay. Their working conditions were poor and they were often punished — for example by taking away their tobacco rations if they did not perform or behave as required. In this way the Cape Colony joined in the East African slave trade. Finnemore and Van der Merwe (1992: 17) state that "by the end of the 18th century slavery had become an integral part of the Cape Colony. The nomadic Boer farmers carried these ideas into the interior, where manual labour was expected to be done by blacks who rendered their services to the farmer in return for squatting rights."

The basic relationship was thus mainly one of slavery — of master and servant. Slaves, as the property of the owners who bought them at auctions, had to obey their masters and work hard without really obtaining anything in return. In these early days there was no other form of "personnel management" (if we can call it that at all). Slavery was eventually officially abolished in 1834 (Nel & Van Rooyen 1993: 54,) and the first real formal regulation of some form of individual employment relationship came into being with the Masters and Servants Act of 1841. Later the Masters and Servants Act 15 of 1856 repealed the Act of 1841 and increased the strict legalistic and paternalistic nature of "people management" in South Africa. Servants were subjected to a host of rules and Acts dealing with aspects such as failure to commence work on an agreed date, intoxication, disobedience to the master, unauthorised absence from work, substandard work performance, negligence, the use of abusive language — all of which were viewed in terms of this Act (15 of 1856), as offences punishable by imprisonment with or without hard labour for a period of not more than one month (Nel & Van Rooyen 1993:54). The personnel, or rather servants, were thus managed in a very strict, almost subhuman manner. They were motivated in a negative way (with threats of punishment) and did not enjoy any real form of security or any guarantees of the protection of their wellbeing.

2.2.2 People and work in the period following the South African Industrial Revolution

With the discovery of diamonds and gold and the accompanying advent of the South African industrial revolution in the late 1860s and 1870s, life and the world of work in this country changed dramatically.

The need arose for mining and engineering-related skills to mine the diamonds and gold. Other industries, such as building, engineering and the railways, developed around the mining industry. In order to satisfy the need for skilled people in these areas, European immigrants (mostly from the United Kingdom due to historical ties through the British settlers) were recruited. These skilled people were paid high wages because of the increasing demand for their services and know-how. In the meantime local inhabitants were utilised to perform some of the less skilled tasks in these industries. There was thus an increased movement away from traditional, mainly agrarian and household activities as people entered into formal employment relationships with the growing number of industrial types of organisations.

While the need for cheap labour to support the skilled workers increased, the latter kept their labour scarce by, for example, establishing trade unions (the first one was the Amalgamated Society of Carpenters and Joiners of Great Britain, established during December of 1881), limiting membership exclusively to the British skilled worker (excluding blacks as well as Afrikaans-speaking whites) and preventing the entry of others into these jobs, and by resisting job fragmentation.

The ideas of scientific management (Taylorism) were also "imported" in the sense that, as mechanisation increased, mining employers turned their attention to breaking down the many skilled jobs into smaller, simpler units — in order to be able to employ cheaper, unskilled or semiskilled labour to perform these tasks. This was resisted by the unions. Strict control was thus very much the watchword of people management during these times. Not only was labour mobility and entry into certain job categories strictly controlled, but mine owners also tried to control the supply of cheap labour by, for example, extending unskilled workers' employment contracts (Finnemore & Van der Merwe 1992:18). Rules and regulations on the mines were extensive. A regulation which required miners who came off duty to be searched and stripped led to the first official strike in South Africa, which took place on the Kimberley diamond fields in 1884.

In 1886 the Witwatersrand Chamber of Mines was formed and, after brainstorming the labour problems faced by mine owners, it was decided, inter alia, to attempt to lower the wages of black workers (which had by now started to rise due to shortages of cheap labour). In 1897 white miners went on strike when attempts were also made to lower their wages in line with the wages of black mine workers. The late 1800s and early 1900s were thus characterised by the legalistic management of people, strict control and a lack of flexibility, with little room for individualism in employment relations. There was also an underlying lack of concern for the worker's needs, which resulted in increased conflict in the field of people management in South Africa. This is clearly demonstrated by the relatively high number of strikes which occurred during these years (for example, seven strikes between 1904 and 1908) (Nel & Van Rooyen 1993: 57). Workers were required to work very hard and for very long hours. In 1907, for example, white miners went on strike due to dissatisfaction with their heavy workloads (according to them, they had to supervise too great a number of drill bits). The widespread strike of 1913 (involving some 20 000 strikers) was initially the result of dissatisfaction with the decision of the management of Kleinfontein Gold Mine to compel underground mechanics to work longer hours on Saturdays (from 7:00 to 15:30 and not to 12:30) (Cunningham, Slabbert & De Villiers 1990: 2.5).

The result of this widespread dissatisfaction was that the majority of workers joined trade unions; while management practices relating to the individual were still sadly deficient, collective aspects were becoming increasingly important during this period of personnel management in South Africa. Nel and Van Rooyen (1993: 59), for example, report that "during the period of 1915 to 1917, there was a fourfold increase in worker representation through trade unions". By 1921/22 white-led trade union membership figures had grown to approximately 118 000 and, between 1918 and 1922, organised collective industrial action (strikes) involved, on the average, 42 000 black workers striking for 16,8 days each (Cunningham et al 1990: 2.4–2.6; Coetzee 1976: 6, 12). Trade unions thus played a prominent role in sensitising management in South Africa to the needs of workers. Most of the dissatisfaction on the mines can also be traced back to the strong racial undertones characterising people management practices at this time.

As secondary industries (mainly manufacturing) grew along with the expanding mining industry, and in line with "scientific management" thinking, mass production increased and the need arose for predominantly semiskilled workers in industries such as furniture, clothing and shoe manufacturing. Many white females and black males were prepared to do this type of work for lower wages than those paid to skilled labourers. Whereas whites in the mining industry were largely to be found in supervisory positions, there was a greater mix of race groups on the shop floors of these manufacturing organisations (Finnemore & Van der Merwe 1992: 22). The spectrum of people who had to be managed throughout industrialised South Africa was thus basically multiracial, multicultural (due to the presence, for example, of former slaves and indentured labourers of Asiatic and Chinese origin and not limited only to the male sex). Although there were efforts during the late 1920s and in 1930 to establish a culture of non-racialism in South African industrial relations (for example the multiracial conference of 1930 which resulted in the establishment of the South African Trades and Labour Council which called unsuccessfully for the inclusion of blacks under the Industrial Concil- iation Act) (Finnemore & Van der Merwe 1992: 22), race continued to play a domi- nant role in all people management issues in South Africa. Various labour-related Acts made sure of this. For example, in terms of the Industrial Conciliation Act 11 of 1924, later repealed by Act 36 of 1937, blacks were excluded from the definition of "employee".

Partly due to the high cost of industrial action and the rise in collectivism (trade unionism) in South Africa, awareness of the necessity for greater sensitivity towards the needs, welfare and rights of employees gradually increased during the first three to four decades of the twentieth century. The Industrial Conciliation Act 36 of 1937 and the new Wage Act 44 of 1937 can, for example, be viewed partly as attempts by government to provide, amongst others, for the welfare and rights of certain groups of workers and to remove the need to belong to trade unions (Nel & Van Rooyen 1993: 62). Although union membership figures generally kept on growing (black workers, for example, organised and went on to form the Council for Non-European Trade Unions in 1941, claiming 158 000 individual members and 119 union members in 1945), managers gradually began to realise that people are not the same as other production factors and cannot simply be treated and con- trolled like extensions of the machine. In South Africa, as in other parts of the world, it became clear that people as employees needed some form of special treat- ment.

2.2.3 Isobel White and the real advent of personnel management in South Africa[1]

South Africa was indeed fortunate that Isobel H B White, the wife of a professor who was appointed to the chair of classics at Rhodes University College, Grahams- town, in 1938 accompanied her husband to South Africa. Isobel White can truly be regarded as the mother of South African personnel management. It is, for instance, her pioneering work which eventually led to the establishment of the Institute of Personnel Management of South Africa.

Towards the end of 1940, Mrs White gave her first six lectures on industrial psychology at Rhodes University College, at that time a residential college of the University of South Africa.

As an industrial psychologist, holding a Diploma in Social Studies as well as an MA degree from St Andrew's University, she began to conduct research in the personnel field during the 1940s, published extensively and addressed various meetings in order to propagate and publicise the need for personnel managers and welfare officers in larger factories in South Africa.

In September 1941 she was requested to conduct pilot research at seven footwear factories in the Port Elizabeth area, with the aim of investigating possible personnel-related problems. A report with a series of recommendations for future work subsequently followed. In October 1941 she addressed a special joint meeting in Port Elizabeth of the South African Institute of the Boot and Shoe Industry, and the Port Elizabeth (Shoe Trade and Training Industry) Managers and Foremen's Association, on "Human Problems of Management".

In this paper she emphasised, for example, the need for a new attitude towards labour, including the training and follow-up of new employees, and the necessity of fostering a spirit of cooperation between management and non-management employees. She also emphasised the need for paternalistic practices related to the maintenance of employee health, proper nutrition and the importance of "good working conditions for workers".[2]

In the meantime she also published two articles in the *South African Industry & Trade Journal*, under the heading "Selecting employees for maximum efficiency". Mrs White was subsequently requested to carry on with her personnel research work as an Assistant Research Officer with the Leather Industries Research Institute, Rhodes University College, as from January 1942.

Before taking up this full-time position, South Africa's "mother of personnel management" insisted that the Footwear and Leather Workers Trade Union should approve of this type of research work. She thus emphasised individualism in personnel management — but not at the cost of collectivism. Indeed, as early as 1941/42 she advocated the collaboration of unions with management on personnel-related matters. This did in fact take place, and the trade union eventually responded positively by making monthly contributions and receiving in return all relevant reports, bulletins and recommendations arising from her personnel related work.[3]

In recognition of her pioneering work in South Africa, Isobel White was elected to the Fellowship of the Institute of Personnel Management of Great Britain (then called the Institute of Labour Management) in 1943.

In collaboration with Professor E H Wild, she also worked on aptitude tests and recruitment methods. In addition, because of Isobel's intense interest in the general welfare of workers, she established a Factory Welfare Board in Port Elizabeth in 1944, to work towards the improvement of the general environment of factory workers. This Board consisted of representatives of footwear manufacturers, the Red Cross, factory inspectors and Child Welfare.

Also, her research work emphasised welfare aspects and related these to analyses of factors such as employee absenteeism and labour turnover. Various articles in this regard subsequently appeared in *'The Manufacturer'*, *'The Engineer'* and *'Industry and Trade'*, and the awareness of need for welfare supervisors and personnel managers was thus spread.

Having attempted to sensitise managers to the need for these specialists, Mrs White felt that the time was right to work more formally towards the establishment of an official personnel management training course at tertiary level. In this regard she realised that South Africa had its own unique situation and that a course in personnel management in South Africa had to have its own character. In 1944/45 she wrote on this subject as depicted in exhibit A (White 1944/45: 144).

Exhibit A

Early comments on the industrial population in SA

"There are many more problems involved in planning a course of personnel management training in this country than there are in Great Britain due to the character of the industrial population and the attitude to work of the people as a whole. During the agricultural depression of 1932 there was a decided drift of the poorer and less successful European farmers and their families to the towns, and these began to drift into industry. They are the "poor white" type and have come into both skilled and semi-skilled jobs in industry. On the whole they are Afrikaans speaking and there is no long tradition of industrial background, so that the pride in craftsmanship has to be built up. Many foremen are still overseas men.

Alongside the white industrial workers, but segregated from them, there are the coloured girls who are often employed on similar types of work machining in the footwear and clothing industries, biscuit packing, sweet wrapping, etc. Coloured girls are employed a great deal in factories in the Cape, but not nearly so much in factories in the Eastern Province and on the Reef owing to the population distribution. In Natal many Indian boys and men are employed in industry, where in Great Britain we would use girls and women. African native men are used for packing, factory sweeping, etc. This all adds to the problem of the personnel officer as he cannot, by law, mix these different races in the factory. Messrooms, cloakrooms and lavatories all have to be quadrupled, different exits and clocking arrangements have to be provided. The personnel officer must be familiar also with the racial background of the various groups and with their taboos, as well as be fluent in Afrikaans."

The need to introduce an obligatory scheme of **welfare supervision** was also advocated by Isobel White. In 1945 she advanced her reasons for this in the following way (White 1945: 313).

"1. The Factories' Act will remain a dead letter unless someone is appointed to see that the spirit of the Act is carried out, e.g., supervision of cloakrooms, washing accommodation, rest rooms, etc.
2. First Aid.

3. Extra supervision is necessary because of the influx of women and young people. Married women also raise a special problem, unless there is someone outside of the production side to whom these employees can take their personal problems. Employees who are worried are not efficient, and production will always be hampered.

4. Utilisation of manpower. The welfare supervisor can ensure that each one is doing the job for which he is mentally and physically capable. This induces contentment.

5. Canteens. Much more attention must be paid to the nutrition of our industrial workers. The importance of a sound midday meal in preventing fatigue and ill-health cannot be overrated.

6. Working conditions. Supervision of lighting, seating, ventilation, etc.

7. Resolving problems, mental and physical, in so far as they affect the relations between the individual and the organisation by personal influence and by calling in all the resources which the organisation provides."

In January 1944 White instituted a special postgraduate "Diploma in Personnel Welfare and Management" at Rhodes University College. Recognition for this diploma was obtained from the Institute of Labour Management (Great Britain). Any prospective candidate had to have at least a BA, BA (Social Sciences), BSc or BCom degree. It was a twelve-month course and candidates had to be selected. The curriculum of this first diploma in the personnel field in South Africa was documented by White (1945: 317–318) as per exhibit B on page 37.

At the end of 1944 the first two graduates qualified for this diploma and went into industry.

As more and more personnel managers and "welfare supervisors" went to work in factories throughout South Africa, it was realised that these specialists felt a bit isolated. South Africa's mother of personnel management thus felt it necessary to establish some forum for interaction amongst these specialists. A local branch of the Institute of Personnel Management (UK) was thus formed in Port Elizabeth in 1945. Other separate branches were subsequently formed: the Johannesburg branch in December 1945; the Cape Town branch in September 1946; the Durban branch in June 1947.

In the light of the foregoing it is clear that in the beginning personnel management in South Africa had very much a welfare-oriented and paternalistic character. See, for example, the typical duties of a personnel manager as spelled out by Isobel White (1945: 314–316) in exhibit C on page 38.

It was also sometime during 1945/46 that the South African mining industry's first personnel department was set up, also presumably very much along the lines of welfarism and personnel administration.

By 1955, however, there were signs of a gradual shift from *welfarism* to *human relations*.

Extracts from Isobel White's address delivered to a one-day conference of the Port Elizabeth branch of the SA Institute of Personnel Management, on Tuesday, 9 August 1955 (the first conference of this kind in South Africa), serve to illustrate this shift in thinking (White 1955: 1–2). (See exhibit D on page 39.)

Exhibit B

Curriculum: First Diploma course in Personnel Welfare and Management*

The Diploma will be awarded to candidates who have passed the following courses either for their degrees or subsequently in the Diploma course. (A full course extends over four terms, half course over two terms.)

A. University degree courses
1. Economics and Economics His. I: full bachelor's degree course.
2. Economics II.
3. Psychology I.
4. Psychology II.

B. Courses covered by university degree courses
5. Social problems: full course: (covered by parts of Sociol. I and II).
6. Social Law: full course: (covered by parts of Soc. Work I and II).
7. Industrial Organisation: half course: (covered by half of B.Com. course Indus. Organisation and Management I).
8. Elementary statistics: half course: (covered by half of B.Com. course Elementary Theory of Statistics and Finance).

C. Special courses for the diploma
9. Personnel Management, Factory Planning, etc., full course.
10. Industrial Law — half course.
11. Native and Coloured in industry — half course.
12. Aptitude testing — half course.
13. Industrial Physiology and Hygiene — half course.

D. Practical work
(a) General Social Work with special reference to Industry.
(b) Training in factories-vacation work–eight weeks to be spent in two different industries.
(c) Candidates must pass an examination written and oral, to prove their competence in the use of both official languages. It will be conducted by the Heads of the Language Departments and of the Social Science Department.

*Source: White, IHB. 1945. Personnel management in industry. In *Personnel Research in South Africa,* 317–318. Grahamstown: Personnel Research Section, Leather Industries Research Institute.

From exhibit D it can be seen that as early as 1955 personnel management in South Africa had started to focus on a much broader range of issues. In the same address, for example, White refers to the importance of training all supervisors of people in "the understanding of human beings and on leadership". Other aspects which featured strongly include wage incentives, merit-rating schemes, selection and training of supervisors, motivation of people, attending to morale problems and grievance handling. The human relations movement was thus also propogated in South Africa at that stage. White (1955: 4–6), for example, also stated that

> "The worker is a human being who is also a member of a team . . . It is now clear that the most important single factor in determining output is the emotional attitude of the worker towards his work and his workmates . . . The main problem is how to apply the carrot and stick theory when jobs are open to choice . . . The modern manager, therefore, is not so

Exhibit C

Duties of a personnel manager in the 1940s*

Employment side

1. Maintenance of contacts with schools, Juvenile Affairs Board, etc., in order to obtain co-operation between schools and industry. This is very important in view of the ignorance which exists in schools about factory work.
2. All applicants for work should be interviewed in a room set aside for this purpose and the application details recorded by the welfare officer. This establishes good personal relationships from the beginning, and any necessary advice can be given about health, problems of the care of children in the case of married women workers, etc.
3. Selection of employees in co-operation with foremen. If aptitude tests have been developed these should be administered by the welfare supervisor and records kept.
4. Checking up of training of learners and their progress. In this way a more comprehensive study can be made of the problems of selection. Also, by means of a periodic review, particularly when statutory advances become payable, a more efficient check can be kept on the training of employees.
5. Talks should be given to new employees on factory rules and an opportunity taken to emphasise the firm's policy towards employees and such items as discipline, time-keeping, notification of absence, any sports facilities, and so on. In this talk also, an opportunity should be taken of telling, and if possible, showing the various processes which go to making the firm's product. In this way, the employee discovers how each little bit is related and the importance of the small section which he is doing becomes clear. It should be emphasised how slackness on his part affects the work of the other employees.
6. Record cards should, of course, be kept for each employee, both on the employment side and on the health side. If he should leave, the exact details are then available for any future re-application.
7. A knowledge of the principles of fatigue and their application to rest pauses, accidents, methods of work, is most essential. All this helps to reduce wasteful labour turnover.
8. Any schemes for Health, Unemployment and Pensions should be under the supervision of this department. Talks are to emphasise the firm's policy towards employees and such items as discipline, time-keeping, notification of absence, any sports facilities, and so on. In this talk also, an opportunity should be taken of telling, and if possible, showing the various processes which go to making the firm's product. In this way, the employee discovers how each little bit is related and the importance of the small section which he is doing becomes clear. It should be emphasised how slackness on his part affects the work of the other employees.
9. Interest in works' committees is gradually increasing, and this should be stimulated so that there is more co-operation between workers and management.
10. The welfare supervisor must keep abreast of current practice in labour management so that she can inform her firm on the latest findings.
11. Responsibility for seeing that the provisions of the Factory Act are carried out.
12. A knowledge of suitable lodging and billeting accommodation is most valuable.

Health side

1. Supervision of all first aid. This should be concentrated in one room and under individual control. This avoids wounds being dressed in unsuitable surroundings by works people. The risk of sepsis is diminished and so absences are reduced. Redressing can also be controlled.
2. Supervision of ventilation, lighting, seating and working conditions in general from point of view of health.
3. Supervision of any employee who seems undernourished and the giving of extra milk, cod liver oil, etc. Advising on better food where necessary.
4. Arrangements of scheme for regular medical examination when approved.
5. Maintenance of sickness and accident records so that the firm has full data in considering policy re-effects of ventilation, departmental accident rates, sickness rates, etc.
6. Supervision of cleanliness of factory and cloakrooms.
7. Visiting of sick workers. This establishes a valuable personal contact between the firm and the workers. Advice can be given on convalescence, and financial help when necessary. From this knowledge, care can be exercised as to the type of work to which an employee returns.
8. When necessary a canteen should be established. In any case the personnel manager should be able to advise the employees on nutrition and help the Red Cross Society in its national health campaign by disseminating their literature on health.
9. Supervision of Workmen's Compensation cases.

*Source: Taken from White, IHB. Personnel management in industry. In *Personnel Research in South Africa*. Grahamstown: Personnel Research Section, Leather Industries Research Institute.

Exhibit D

Isobel White's address to IPM in 1955

"In the past the emphasis has been placed on the Welfare aspects, on the housing of the worker, on establishing standards of good cloakrooms and their equipment, washing facilities and good general working conditions. Attention was given to the provision of adequate lighting, protective clothing, rest pauses, and canteen facilities. The personnel manager in earlier days was very much concerned with recreation, social clubs, arranging holiday camps and other activities concerned with the mainte-nance of health. Students in training were taught the importance of these welfare aspects, were encouraged to undertake research in them. They were taught how to educate and convince employers on the need for expenditure on these activities in order to get a more efficient and contented staff. Now it is true that many of these 'welfare activities' are admirable in themselves, but they dealt exclusively with the individual worker in relation to his environment, not with the individual in relation to the group whether co-workers, supervisors or management. Much of the work included in this category has now been covered in our factory legislation and we take these standards for granted . . . Nothing will illustrate the great change in emphasis of which I have spoken more than the successive changes of name which have occurred since the foundation of the Institute in 1909 from Institute of Welfare Workers to Institute of Labour Management and finally to its present title. Today we have moved away from the conception of the factory as a kind of hygienic cowshed where the cows, if given every physical condition that is conducive to content will produce an ever-increasing volume of milk, to one where we realise that we are employing human beings who react in different ways not only to each other but to those who are leading them. The Personnel Manager has, therefore, become much more concerned not so much with the battle for staff comfort . . . but with the human relations side of this job. The function of the Personnel Manager thus becomes:

- Recruitment
- Employment
- Incentives
- Morale"

concerned with machines and materials but with handling people. The need for social skills is a further reason for the interest shown in problems of motivation and morale today . . . One of our crying needs is to find leaders and it is one of the concerns of the Personnel Manager to select leaders and, having found them, to develop them.")

In the meantime the National Party came to power in 1948 and the rigid policy of racial apartheid which was subsequently institutionalised had direct implications for South African workplaces and workers.

Various Acts were enacted during this period to ensure an "apartheid system of people management" in South African organisations, a system which represented an embodiment of current thinking, namely that, as expressed in the senate by Dr H F Verwoerd in 1954 (Cunningham et al 1990: 2.11):

" . . . Natives will be taught from childhood to realise that equality with Europeans is not for them . . . What is the use of teaching a Bantu child mathematics when it cannot use it in practice? . . . That is absurd . . . Education must train people in accordance with their opportunities in life . . . the opportunities are . . . manual labour".

Separate labour-related legislation was thus enacted for blacks in South Africa. The Black Labour (Settlement of Disputes) Act 48 of 1953 was, for example, an outflow of the Botha Commission's (appointed in 1948) recommendations, and later had to complement the Industrial Conciliation Act 28 of 1956 (which repealed Act 36 of 1937). In terms of the former Act, black workers who had problems or disputes with their white employer-managers had to deal with them via a committee system. Clearly, then, already in the fifties there were signs of a very particular South African approach to human resource management, the emphasis being on racial discrimination and a partnership between personnel specialists and line managers.

Interest in the personnel field grew quite rapidly in South Africa during the 1940s and 1950s. The Johannesburg branch of the Institute of Personnel Management, for example, grew so rapidly that it was registered as the South African Institute of Personnel Management in 1959.

2.2.4 The period following Republic status

Personnel management as a field of study, research and practice in South Africa had already become relatively well established at the time when South Africa attained Republic status. On 20 October 1964, all provincial units of the Institute of Personnel Management joined forces to form a single national body, retaining the name South African Institute of Personnel Management.

Estimates from early research (Langenhoven & Verster 1969) indicate that by 1964 South African organisations probably had a ratio of personnel staff to total number of employees of 0,97:100. Although the black to white ratio of total staff complements was in the region of 1,67:1, the ratio of black to white personnel staff was only approximately 0,93:1. Furthermore, in 1964 only approximately 6,24 % of all those performing personnel work exclusively were graduates. Only 2,95 % held degrees with Psychology as a major subject and only 0,34 % with Industrial Psychology as a major subject.

A period of steady growth in the personnel field followed, altering the picture of personnel management in South Africa somewhat by the end of the sixties. The ratio of personnel staff to total number of employees increased to approximately 1:100. According to Langenhoven and Verster (1969: 2–5), the ratio of black to white employees increased to approximately 1,71:1 by 1969, whereas the ratio of black to white personnel staff decreased to approximately 0,79:1. Although relatively more blacks were thus employed by South African organisations, relatively fewer blacks were employed to do personnel work.

By 1969 there were also signs of a qualitative shift in personnel people in so far as it concerned their qualifications. Approximately 8,8 % of staff performing personnel work were graduates. Of these, 3,36 % had majored in Psychology and 1,31 % held degrees with Industrial Psychology as a major subject.

Research indicated that, by 1969, personnel management in South Africa had the following characteristics (Langenhoven & Verster 1969; Marx 1969).

- The majority of organisations did not have a separate personnel department.
- Personnel departments were relatively small and consisted mainly of personnel without formal postmatric qualifications.
- Use was made of personnel specialists particularly in areas such as employment, salary and wage administration and training and development.
- The most general subsections into which personnel departments were organised included (in order of priority): general personnel administration; employment (including recruitment and selection); training and development; welfare, sport, pension and related personnel services; salary and wage administration; and medical scheme and medical services.
- The emphasis in personnel work fell on administrative/clerical, routine work and also, to some extent, on paternalistic, welfare-related activities.
- Most of those in the personnel field who did in fact have formal qualifications were graduates in the social sciences (and these did not number many).

As can be seen, the emphasis was on individualism rather than on collectivism and there had been a gradual movement towards the human relations approach, especially as far as white employees were concerned. Racialism was a dominant force and was rigorously controlled in the South African workplace.

Two other trends did, however, start to emerge:

1. a dawning realisation of the need for more of a "human resources approach"; and
2. a gut feel that collectivism (trade unions) would become more prominent.

In this regard Marx (1969: 59) warned that collectivism was going to need more attention; with regard to the role of the personnel function he pointed out that the "chief function is the provision of personnel, but it should also be responsible for maintaining a high morale and personnel development and utilisation in the interests of higher productivity . . . " (1969: 53). Marx (1969: 58–60) stated further that, although the human relations school of thought had helped a great deal, more emphasis had to be put on actually getting people to contribute towards the success of the organisation, which of necessity meant a shift to better qualified and more highly trained employees.

2.2.5 The decade that shaped the things to come

By the end of the sixties, with the majority of workers being black, it was clear that the face of work, people and personnel management had to change. African workers especially had been suppressed and too strictly controlled for far too long, particularly by means of legal restrictions in keeping with the preceding two decades of apartheid rule. As Friedman (1987: 33) states:

"None of the African union movements before the 1970s endured because none could turn worker support into a permanent source of power . . . By the 1970s new pressures were building which forced those in power to concede that they could no longer simply resist unionism: by then a new generation of unions was beginning to grow."

The decade 1969–1979 thus brought with it all the signs of what was to follow later during the eighties, particularly with regard to the collectivism of black employees. Durban dock workers went on strike in 1969, African workers launched isolated efforts to organise themselves from early 1970, huge numbers of contract workers went on strike on the diamond mines of Namibia (then still South West Africa and controlled by Pretoria), and in 1972 the approximately 9 000 blacks who had embarked on strike action cost management 74 000 shifts (including the Putco strike in June 1972 which stranded 120 000 commuters) (Friedman 1987: 44–45).

However, the real rebirth of African collectivism only hit employers early in 1973, with the outbreak of the biggest wave of strikes in the country since the Second World War. Friedman (1987: 40) states that "between 1965 and 1971, less than 23 000 African workers had struck. In the first three months of 1973, 61 000 stopped work. By the end of the year, the figure had grown to 90 000 and employers had lost 229 000 shifts."

The Natal strikes highlighted the fact that the system of black worker represen-tation — and, in fact, the total approach to the management of black workers in South African organisations — was deficient and that too little proper interaction was taking place between management and black workers (Nel & Van Rooyen 1993: 68). This strike wave also emphasised the need to review labour legislation; the Black Labour Relations Regulation Amendment Act 70 of 1973 followed as a result. Committees (liaison committees in particular) were being established more and more to communicate with black workers. These committees were, however, also used largely as a measure of paternalistic personnel management. In most cases the committees were set up by employers who decided how they were to operate (Friedman 1987: 56).

However, in addition to the collectivism aspect, more and more people had begun to realise the importance of the role of the black worker. A number of exam-ples can serve to illustrate this. In 1973, for example, training centres were set up and tax benefits offered for the training of African workers (Friedman 1987: 52). In July 1973 the Institute of Personnel Management (Southern Africa) (having changed its name from the South African Institute of Personnel Management on 2 February the same year) published the first edition of *People & Profits* and, in this very first edition, an article appeared about black advancement efforts by the Anglo American Corporation (*People & Profits* 1973: 9–12). In the same edition and following from the 1973 strikes, a checklist for action in case of strikes was pub-lished, as well as an article on the representation of black workers. In the November 1973 edition of this journal, the need to train blacks for higher level jobs, and to channel their potential into the field of technology, was emphasised by two different experts (Natrass 1973: 5; Jacobsz 1973: 22). In the December 1973 edition,

Baqwa pleaded for the improvement of welfare facilities for black employees (1973: 12–16). In the very next edition the need to educate African workers in order to help them to participate meaningfully in committees was emphasised, as was the importance of utilising the black personnel officer as "the linkman" (Douwes Dekker 1974: 5–7; Dickenson 1974: 8–19).

Of all these developments, Cunningham et al (1990: 2.16) have the following to say:

> "There was a shift in the political economy of South Africa. Blacks became aware of their economic power . . . There was a restructuring of the power balance within the employment relationship . . . A non-racial (although predominantly black) trade-union movement established itself as a permanent feature . . . In 1975 there were twenty-five exclusively black trade unions, representing 66 000 workers."

Although black trade union figures dropped during the mid-seventies, the foundations had been laid for the era of African collectivism which was to dominate the personnel field in South Africa during the eighties.

By 1975 Professor Langenhoven of the University of the Orange Free State had completed a thorough analysis of definitions of personnel management, and had come up with his own definition, which can in a sense be viewed as the South African perspective of the concept at that time (Langenhoven 1975: 7):

> "Personnel management is one of the responsibilities of management and the full-time function of personnel specialists in regard to the human resources of the organisation to develop, apply and manage a complete network of interdependent processes and systems with a view to achieving the organisation's and its people's objectives, with due consideration to the concepts, principles and techniques of the behavioural sciences and the practical requirements of the situation."

As can be seen, this definition underplayed the collective dimension of trade unions — despite the fact that organised labour and aspects like worker representation and industrial action were becoming more and more prominent.

After the 1976 strikes on the Witwatersrand, it again became apparent that labour legislation in South Africa, as far as it concerned the collective bargaining rights of black workers, was totally inadequate and needed to be completely updated. Eventually Professor Nic Wiehahn of the University of South Africa was appointed as adviser to the then Minister of Labour, Fanie Botha; in May 1977 he was appointed chairman of a commission of inquiry into South African labour legislation — an investigation which was to lead to a break with statutory racialism in the workplace and which therefore altered South Africa's system of industrial relations quite significantly.

Following on the publication of the White Paper on Part 1 of the Wiehahn Commission's report in 1979, the remainder of the report, and the subsequent changes in South Africa's labour legislation, irreversible changes took place in the context of work and personnel management in South Africa.

Another important development which took place in the late seventies was the drive to professionalise personnel work in South Africa. By mid-1978 the initiative had already been taken and the professionalisation of personnel management practice in South Africa was well under way. Mr Gary Whyte, the 1977 President of the Institute of Personnel Management (Southern Africa), presented a paper on this topic at the IPM's Twenty-first Convention in September 1977. Professor Langenhoven published an article in this regard in the June 1978 edition of *People & Profits*, and after this the debate gained momentum (Langenhoven 1978: 14–15; Whyte 1978: 9–10).

The concept of *human resources* had by this time also come to be used more and more often. In 1978 Lombard (after returning from the USA) published an article in the *South African Journal of Labour Relations* entitled "Human resources management: A new approach for South Africa" (Lombard 1978: 12–24). The IPM's journal, *People & Profits*, furthermore started to feature regular articles on industrial relations related issues by 1978/1979, reflecting the then growing importance of the collective dimension of personnel management in South Africa.

The year 1979 saw the publication of some very interesting research results stemming from a survey on developments in personnel management in South Africa conducted by the University of the Orange Free State (Verster 1979). The findings revealed that, by 1979, personnel management in South Africa had acquired the following characteristics.

- Many organisations had independent personnel departments.
- In most cases the top personnel official was called a personnel manager, often a group personnel manager or personnel director.
- As a rule, this top level personnel official reported to the general manager or to a member of the board.
- People performing personnel work exclusively held more clerical positions than managerial or professional positions — especially in the case of black personnel staff.
- The ratio of people performing personnel work to total staff establishment was in the region of 1,26:100.
- Approximately 21 % of those performing personnel work had postmatriculation qualifications.
- Approximately 3,4 % of the personnel staff had degrees with Industrial Psychology as a major subject.
- Another approximately 3,6 % had postgraduate qualifications in a behavioural science.
- Changes in emphasis in personnel management practice from 1976 to 1979 resulted in the emergence of the following top three priority areas: (1) the upgrading of black workers; (2) employee training; and (3) industrial relations.
- More money, time and manpower were spent on administrative personnel work than on professional aspects of personnel management.
- Personnel research work was neglected and viewed as the black sheep of personnel work.

2.2.6 Some HRM developments in a post "labour-apartheid" decade

The South African government's acceptance in principle of the Wiehahn Commission's recommendation that racialism no longer be a consideration in the South African labour dispensation, gave rise to a new era of personnel management in South Africa — an era where black employees were no longer to be excluded from the statutory labour machinery of the country.

Although collectivism — in particular black trade unionism — had by 1980 already become a permanent feature in South Africa, the Wiehahn developments gave further impetus to this aspect of human resource management — an aspect which was to occupy centre stage throughout the eighties and into the nineties.

The realisation of the increasing importance of trade unions led organisations in South Africa to pay increasing attention to the human resource aspects of management. In 1980, in one of the first articles in the IPM's journal with a title referring to "human resources management" (rather than personnel management), Diessnack (1980: 5) specifically stated that "a new union will increase payroll costs by 20 % with no increase in production". The "hard" aspects of human resource management, the impact of people management practices on the bottom line of organisations, thus also came to the fore by the time collectivism gained more official prominence.

Trade union membership figures increased throughout the eighties, and along with these huge organising efforts came the signs of increasing adversarialism in the relationships between (especially black) employees and their trade unions on the one side and employers (and managers, mostly white, as their representatives in the workplace) on the other side. The unions displayed a great deal of militancy and industrial action became a frequent challenge in the area of human resource management in South Africa.

Whereas for the ten-year period 1970–1979 the number of reported strikes stood at 179, the corresponding number for the five-year period 1983–1987 was 3 135. Statistics also reveal that South Africa lost more persondays owing to strike action over the period 1985–1990 than during the entire preceding seventy-five years. It is thus not surprising that a large number of articles published during the eighties dealt with industrial relations and conflict-related topics.

However, the individual dimension of personnel management in South Africa also matured to some extent during the eighties — in particular as far as certain traditional functional areas of personnel management were concerned. Attention was being paid to a whole range of aspects. During the first five years of the eighties, aspects which were emphasised in journal articles included manpower planning, selection, training and development, organisation development, job evaluation and remuneration, career planning, performance appraisal, manpower information systems, and especially black advancement and labour productivity (apart from the large number of industrial relations related articles and books which were published).

In October 1983 the professionalisation of the personnel field in South Africa became a reality with the inauguration of the first South African Board for Personnel Practice (SABPP). In June 1983 it was reported (*IPM Manpower Journal* 1983: 4–5) that "In the first two weeks of registration, over 300 applications were received! . . . The Registrar for the Board, Mr Wilhelm Crous said that he was 'overwhelmed' by the response . . . the Board was now 'truly launched', and will play a 'meaningful role' in South Africa's fields of personnel, training and industrial relations."

Over the next three years an intensive public relations campaign was launched in order to inform organisations of the aims, role and importance of the SABPP.

In the meantime, on 30 November 1985, COSATU (Congress of South African Trade Unions), the giant trade union federation, was born, with an initial membership of thirty-three trade unions. In 1987 strike action in South Africa reached a peak, with 1 148 recorded strikes and 5 825 231 persondays lost. During the eighties, much of the industrial unrest was motivated by political factors due to the fact that the majority of South Africa's people were disenfranchised, the trade unions being their only legitimate public forum. Human resource management in South Africa thus became politicised to a great extent during the eighties and trade unions were very instrumental in the political transformation of the country.

In the meantime, in 1985, another dimension was added to the concept of personnel management in South Africa with Pansegrouw's definition of "strategic HRM" (Pansegrouw: 1985). In 1987 Hill (1987: 6–9) also proposed the adoption of a "strategic approach to human resources management" by South African organisations.

Furthermore, research findings published in 1985 (Hall 1985: 6) showed that the responsibility for decision making with regard to people-related issues had been transferred to the personnel and/or industrial relations departments of South African organisations. According to Horwitz (1988: 6–7), however, this was contrary to a typical international shift from "functionally oriented personnel management" to a more line driven, general management conception of HRM. In the same article, where Horwitz speculated about the differences between "functional, specialist and professional personnel management" on the one hand and "a generalist, organizational conception of HRM" on the other, it was proposed that the differences should be viewed as orientational rather than as substantive, and that the two approaches linked to the terms should not be regarded as being mutually exclusive.

In the meantime also, in 1987, the first local comprehensive academic textbook on the personnel field was published. In this publication the authors held that, due to the rapid developments in industrial relations in South Africa over the preceding decade, employers had been compelled to "resort to the employment of industrial relations specialists to cope with the new demands . . .", and that ". . . the task of the industrial relations manager may come to be as important as that of the human resource manager" (Gerber, Nel & Van Dyk 1987: 315–316). Industrial relations thus became a distinct and extremely important area of people management during the eighties and aspects such as collective bargaining (negotiating recognition and other agreements with trade unions), dispute handling, strike management and fair discipline and labour practices took centre stage in the management of most South African enterprises (see, for example, Horwitz 1988).

Towards the latter part of 1988 other important aspects which began to feature prominently in the literature on personnel management included worker participation, violence and AIDS. At the end of the eighties the following comments were made by Van Wyk (1989: 13–14) regarding the changing role of HR practitioners in South Africa with the nineties approaching:

> "The HR practitioner's role is shifting away from the traditional view of personnel management to one of strategic planning for manpower utilization in **partnership** with the relevant line function. His role is to **support** the managerial population in its quest for obtaining and growing a successful work team . . . the practitioner must develop a business orientation and ensure that it is reflected in the HR interventions in which he is involved . . . The HR practitioner should also reflect a philosophy . . . where he actively seeks out new business . . . A proactive approach . . . also in providing the required consulting service to implement the relevant programmes . . . All in all, the HR practitioner will play a key role in guiding organizations into and through the nineties. Their vision and appropriate framework of strategy changes will be driving forces in their organizations with regard to the adaptations we are all going to have to make."

2.2.7 Human resource management during a period of transformation politics

By the end of the eighties the South African economy was in recession due to, inter alia, political instability, disinvestment and sanctions imposed by overseas countries, and rising labour unit costs (lower labour productivity and higher wages). Poor economic growth had resulted in large-scale unemployment and job creation had become one of the major challenges. While 44 800 new job opportunities had been created during the sixties, the corresponding figure for the eighties was 28 000 (Finnemore & Van der Merwe 1992: 37). Against the background of the gloomy economic situation, the socioeconomic backlogs suffered by the majority of black South Africans became increasingly more apparent. South Africa was in the midst of political and socioeconomic turmoil — a situation felt by virtually every employer and employee.

On 2 February 1990, South Africa's newly elected State President, F W de Klerk, announced the government's intention of trying to resolve South Africa's sociopolitical problems through negotiations with all stakeholders — thus effectively turning around the world of each and every South African. A number of organisations (such as the African National Congress (ANC), the South African Communist Party (SACP), and the Pan Africanist Congress (PAC)) were to be unbanned and restrictions imposed on various other organisations (including COSATU) during the latter part of the eighties were to be lifted. The stage was set for major transformations in the country and the idea of a "new South Africa" and a "postapartheid era" echoed throughout the land. This situation, however, also brought along with it certain dynamics and challenges which spilled over into the world of work and people management.

Some people had extremely high expectations of the future, while others experienced uncertainty and fear. Workplaces in South Africa had by now become involved in a broader community role. Employees had to be educated and sensitised with regard to the changes in the country.

Employers became increasingly aware that not only did they have a welfare role to fulfil in respect of their employees, but that they also had to exhibit a broader social responsibility. Wilhelm Crous, the then Executive Director of IPM (SA), stated, for example, in March 1990 that as political problems were solved, other areas of pressing concern, like unemployment, housing, education, training and health, had to be addressed (Crous 1990: 3). Consequently, during the early 1990s many of the personnel-related publications dealt with these types of issues.

In 1990 the SABPP made available a Board Paper which spelled out a *Generic Competency Model for Human Resource Practitioners*, as developed by the Human Resources Group of Eskom — the national electricity utility. This broad framework identified the knowledge, skills, experiential and behavioural base required to perform competently at the various levels in the HR profession in South Africa. By this time the role of HR practitioners in South Africa had broadened and many managers were turning to them to act as change agents and to help with demands and problems which had no clear-cut, ready-made answers.

Some areas, such as conflict, intimidation and violence (spilling over from the community), became a pressing concern for employers in the early 1990s. Tension and conflict in communities resulted, inter alia, from the newly found freedom experienced by opposing black political forces, and this contributed to disruptions in workplaces. In October 1991 Visser, Douwes Dekker, Majola and Brenner (1991: 22) stated: "As South Africa moves into the transition phase, communities on all sides are drawn into cycles of violence and instability . . . Employers and unions are increasingly drawn into this violence . . . management and union leadership are struggling to come to grips with the violence as they are called upon to intervene and contribute to the hostilities." These were "people problems" and hence the human resource specialists were drawn right into the broader dynamics of a society in transformation.

Gradually the nature of industrial relations also began to show signs of a need for change. Unions and management seemed to become aware that there were areas of common ground. The parties involved had to follow the dictates of the socioeconomic reality and began to realise that outright hostility and severe adversarialism could lead to their mutual demise, especially at a time when economic conditions and business confidence had reached dangerously low levels. Business not only had to become more competitive (especially internationally) so that jobs could be preserved, but also had to grow so that new job opportunities could be created. All of this called for the development and better utilisation of all of the country's human resources, as well as participation and better cooperation by all the stakeholders in the South African industrial relations community. A culture of greater cooperation was necessary and aspects such as "social contracts" at national level and joint decision making at the organisational level were increasingly emphasised in the publications of the day. South Africa's HRM practitioners had been instrumental in all of this, especially the industrial relations specialists who had experienced more than a decade of transition and negotiations in the labour field.

From early 1992, representatives of business and labour engaged in bilateral negotiations with the aim of setting up a national, tripartite economic forum which would include representatives of the government. Eventually the National Economic Forum was formally launched on 29 October 1992. In this regard, Bokkie Botha (then chairman of the South African Consultative Committee on Labour Affairs) pointed out that "human resource practitioners have played an important role" (Botha 1992: 7).

The findings of a survey conducted amongst a number of prominent South African organisations, and covering more than 1,2 million employees, were released in a report published by SPA Consultants in 1992. In this report certain human resource priorities in the medium to short term were identified. These priority areas included aspects such as education/training; affirmative action, discrimination and white resistance; industrial relations (with particular reference to shop-floor relationships and bargaining levels); business literacy; social responsibility and violence (SPA Consultants 1992: 6–24). The most important areas were identified as affirmative action, education and training, and the lack of the necessary strategic orientation by employers to ensure the integration of these aspects with the business aspects of the organisations.

In line with this, research conducted by Grobler led him to conclude, towards the middle of 1993, that "the time has come for South African companies to take stock of their position and to face the challenge of the future and adopt the recommended strategic approach to HRM. This is the obvious course if they wish to remain successful and viable in the long-term" (Grobler 1993: 17).

2.2.8 A research report in the mid-1990s[4]

In 1994 the South African Board for Personnel Practice (SABPP) requested the Human Sciences Research Council (HSRC) to launch an investigation to determine the supply and demand of personnel practitioners in South Africa. The specific objectives of the investigation were the following:

- The development of a **conceptual framework** that can serve as the basis for the investigation. This framework included:
  - the definition of the *work domain* of the personnel practitioner;
  - the selection of *occupational categories* that represent the work domain of personnel practitioners; and

O the identification of the *main fields of study* in which practitioners are trained.

● The estimation of the **demand** for personnel practitioners based on previous trends.

● The identification of **factors** that could influence the **demand** for personnel practitioners.

● The estimation of the **supply** of personnel practitioners based on qualification trends.

● The identification of **factors** which could influence the **supply** of personnel practitioners.

● The identification of the **competencies** that personnel practitioners should possess.

Some of the more important findings that flowed out of this research are outlined below.

According to the report, managers have begun to realise anew that the quality and wellbeing of the workforces of organisations are key influences on their productivity; this has led to a greater awareness of the importance of the personnel function and, consequently, to an improvement in its status. The role of HR functionaries was, however, changing from the provision of primarily support services to involvement in the core business of organisations. Human resource practitioners in South Africa were increasingly expected to participate in the general strategic management of enterprises.

Another trend identified was the devolution of HRM, a shift of the day-to-day human resource management from human resource departments to line managers. Personnel practitioners were thus becoming increasingly responsible for training line managers in human resource management issues and for acting as consultants to line.

Organisations were also apparently tending to reduce their in-house human resource functions — making more use of independent consultants.

Another important finding was that, in line with national, political and social changes, organisations were becoming more democratised, making greater use of worker participation and shifting from authoritarian to participative management styles. Human resources experts thus had to devise organisational strategies in line with these broader trends in the sociopolitical arena.

The importance and high priority of affirmative action has also been identified and all the organisations that took part in the investigation were at that stage involved to some extent in affirmative action. Human resource practitioners were viewed the major driving force behind affirmative action programmes, and also as responsible for managing the process of changing worker groups into multicultural teams.

Linked to the affirmative action programmes and other sociopolitical changes taking place in South Africa was an increasingly strong focus on human resource development.

Human resource development was becoming competency-based and modular and the trend was towards matching it with a "national qualifications framework". There was also an increased emphasis on the development of basic skills, such as literacy and numeracy, and also on accelerated management development. Apparently the challenge now became to devise innovative ways of identifying employees' potential, of recognising prior learning and experience and of accelerating employee development. Multiskilling was also reported to becoming increasingly important.

It was also found that many South African organisations were in the process of large-scale transformation and have been compelled to adapt to a rapidly changing environment, including aspects such as the accommodation of more diverse worker groups, the streamlining of their operations and consequently also often the retrenchment of staff.

An important finding was that most organisations either already actively did, or planned to, implement aspects of the Reconstruction and Development Programme (RDP). These efforts included participation in the upliftment of local communities through, inter alia, the provision of housing, water and health facilities and educational opportunities through job creation and subcontracting.

It was found further that another major trend affecting the work of personnel practitioners lies in the realm of the revolutionary developments in the field of information technology. As systems would become progressively computerised and sophisticated, these systems were expected to relieve HR practitioners of many traditional administrative tasks. The report said that "integrated information management" will become more important as information becomes more accessible and significant to organisations.

2.3 A CONTEMPORARY SOUTH AFRICAN PERSPECTIVE OF THE HRM CONCEPT

In section 1.3 you learned about the international variations in the semantic debate regarding the concept of HRM. You now know that there are different opinions and viewpoints regarding the meaning of the concept "human resource management". Some adopt a generalistic perspective, while others (the "absolutists") view the concept of HRM as denoting a very specific style or way of managing people at work. Although the absolutist approach as presented in section 1.3.2 is not adopted in this book, the authors also do not prescribe to the approach of "old wine in new bottles".

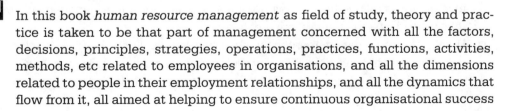

In this book *human resource management* as field of study, theory and practice is taken to be that part of management concerned with all the factors, decisions, principles, strategies, operations, practices, functions, activities, methods, etc related to employees in organisations, and all the dimensions related to people in their employment relationships, and all the dynamics that flow from it, all aimed at helping to ensure continuous organisational success through "good fit" employment relationships — in turbulent and ever-changing environmental conditions.

The perspective taken is thus broad rather than narrow, in that HRM is viewed as referring to all practices and decisions aimed at continuously achieving an optimal match or fit between work, the human resources required to execute the work within an organisational context, and the environment. Some of the more important characteristics of this perspective (which may or may not form part of the approaches or perspectives taken by others), are outlined below:

- Human resources are viewed as an organisation's most important and valued assets. The workforce of any organisation determines what value will be added to all the other resources utilised by an organisation in its striving towards success. The organisation's value system and culture and the quality and commitment levels of its human resources ultimately exert the greatest influence on the organisation's ability to change continuously in line with the demands of its environments.
- All managers are involved in human resource management to a greater or lesser extent and HRM is therefore ultimately the responsibility of top management. Human resource management is a general management function shared by HRM managers, functionaries or specialists on the one hand and all those involved in the management of people within the context of getting the work of an organisation done.
- Human resource management is viewed from a contingency perspective. There is no single, best model of HRM in an absolutist sense and the management of human resources is not only contingent upon organisational strategies (corporate and/or business) but is also influenced by a magnitude of other, ever-changing factors and circumstances, both internal and external to the organisation. Flexible people management, which will vary according to situational factors, is thus supported.
- An open systems and holistic perspective is adopted. The human resource system of any organisation is taken to be one of the many subsystems in the organisation with the organisation also being viewed as an open system existing and functioning in an ever-changing external environment of which it is itself a subsystem.
- A strategic management approach to human resources is generally considered to be essential because of the important role played by this organisational subsystem, and because of the reciprocal relationship existing between the human resource subsystem, all other organisational subsystems and the organisation's market and macro-external environments. Human resource management is thus viewed as a top management concern.
- Human resource management, as viewed from a holistic perspective, is taken to be a comprehensive field of theory and practice including topics which were traditionally studied by personnel management scholars (such as staffing, compensation, training, conditions of the working environment and labour rela-

tions), as well as any contemporary topics covering more proactive, innovative and alternative approaches to the management of the human factor at work.

- Human resource management is not necessarily unitaristic by nature, but is rather concerned with the management of all dimensions of employment relationships, including collectivistic aspects related to trade unionism and collective bargaining, as well as other forms of employment relationships, such as temporary work and contract work.
- Human resource management has both "hard" and "soft" characteristics. The former refers to the rational (quantitative and calculative) and economic/business/financial aspects of people management (such as psychometric evaluation and measurement of work performance, the audit and/or evaluation of HRM — including human asset accounting — as well as the formal, rational functions or activities involved in work force forecasting and planning). The soft aspect stresses that the human dimension (as advocated by human relationists and the work of, for example, Herzberg) be incorporated in the decisions and practices concerning HRM, and emphasises the idea that human resources cannot be dealt with in the same way as other production factors or resources because much more complex and intangible issues (such as feelings, attitudes, perceptions and human needs) are involved.
- Organisational success is not only influenced by the extent to which human resource strategies and practices are closely linked with, and make important contributions to, the organisation's strategic objectives and plans. It is also influenced by the degree to which the various aspects of HRM are synchronised with each other and managed in an integrated, coherent way, with the aim of fostering a culture conducive to organisational success.

2.4 PURSUING A CAREER IN THE HR FIELD IN SOUTH AFRICA

In chapter 1 the types of HR jobs and careers which can be followed in this field of management practice were briefly discussed. The question however arises: How does one embark on a professional career in this field in South Africa?

Although traditionally personnel managers did not require formal qualifications and could become top level managers through experience in administrative personnel departments, over the past two decades or so HRM has become such a complex and demanding field of theory and practice that true professionalism has come to be regarded as a major requirement for HR practitioners.

As mentioned earlier, personnel departments have traditionally been the administrative sections of many an organisation. Consequently, the typical personnel department is involved in data gathering, record keeping and other clerical work. Personnel clerks or officers who have no tertiary qualifications, thus still carry out important supportive work which has to be executed in any organisation (such as record keeping on leave and absenteeism, preparing the payroll inputs, processing medical aid and insurance claims). However, in order to gain access to a professional career in human resource management, one has to acquire additional education, training and development in the field of HRM. External factors such as changes in workforce demographics, changing values in society, economic pressures, globalising competition and corporate reorganisation require the inputs of a new breed of HR practitioners — HR professionals who can add value to organisational success, employee wellbeing and a better society in general. These realities pose peculiar challenges to those interested and involved in the HR field in South Africa — challenges which call for human resource professionalism.

A definite course of action must be determined and followed in order to become a highly valued HR professional. Apart from studying for the recognised qualifications, it is often desirable to gain general business management experience in order to understand the business of an organisation and the type of work in which an organisation's human resources are really involved. This is where integrative HRM thinking begins. However, a crucial aspect is gaining the necessary relevant knowledge base regarding the human factor within the organisational context.

Most tertiary educational institutions in South Africa offer courses in fields relevant to HRM. General social science studies in the fields of psychology or sociology help to provide knowledge of human and behavioural processes in organisational contexts. Similarly, legal studies can provide knowledge of relevant legal requirements which have a bearing on the acquisition, utilisation and separation of the organisation's human resources.

On the other hand, disciplines such as industrial psychology, business economics or business management, as well as public administration, can provide an important foundation in the HRM field. Many tertiary educational institutions in South Africa offer specialised postmatric courses in HRM or personnel management. These include universities, technikons, technical colleges and other business/management educational schools or centres where one can obtain qualifications in this interesting and dynamic field. Furthermore, most of the South African universities' postgraduate business schools offer modules specialising in human resource related topics.

In addition to obtaining the necessary qualifications one must also seek employment in the HR field in order to gain the relevant experience and to apply the theoretical knowledge gained through studies.

Because of the complex and dynamic challenges currently facing the HRM field, more stringent requirements are being applied to those wishing to become true HR professionals. Cuming (1989: 45), for example, says in this regard that "the status of any profession depends in large measure on its requirements and methods for entry into membership and on the existence of a code of professional conduct". This means that, in order to be called an HR professional, one really has to be a professional person, involved in a particular profession.

In this regard a *profession* can be said to be characterised by the existence of a common body of knowledge, a procedure for certifying members of that profession, a set of standards of ethical conduct, and a communication system that can facilitate the exchange of ideas and self-regulation (Cherrington 1983: 26). Thus, to be an HR professional not only requires a professional approach to HR practice but also some form of official professional recognition.

In South Africa one can become an official HR professional through registration with the South African Board for Personnel Practice (SABPP).

2.5 PROFESSIONALISM IN HRM AND THE SOUTH AFRICAN BOARD FOR PERSONNEL PRACTICE (SABPP)[5]

In 1990, the Chairman of the SABPP, Gary Whyte, explained the reason for the decision to set up the SABPP in 1982 (White 1990: 33): "Just like chartered accountants and professional engineers have to be 'registered', and every profession needs to have set standards (related to education and training of new entrants, registration and professional conduct) which are fully credible and are hence set by an impartial body, the need arose for a similar body and registration process in the personnel field." Whyte (1990: 33) then went on to say: "There was a ground swell of opinion and feeling, expressed by the members of the personnel fraternity, that they wanted to pursue the goal of professionalism." Consequently, in 1976 an Ad Hoc Committee on Professional Recognition for Personnel Practitioners was established — paving the way for the eventual establishment of the SABPP on 15 October 1982.

The SABPP's **mission** is to establish, direct and sustain a high level of professionalism and ethical conduct in personnel practice in South Africa.

If a person is registered with the SABPP, this serves as an indication to employers, fellow employees and all other interested parties, that this person meets the very high standards of professional performance and ethical conduct set by the Board; it is also a form of recognition of the individual's professional status and of the contributions which he/she has made to the HR field. Employers often demand registration with the Board as one of the criteria necessary for appointment to HR positions. By setting and protecting these standards of professionalism, the SABPP as an impartial and independent body protects the public, the Board's registered practitioners and their employers. The SABPP monitors the application of (and thus ensures the protection of) professional standards and conduct in the HR field.

2.5.1 The philosophy, strategy and objectives of the SABPP

The **philosophy** of the SABPP is to enable those engaged in the personnel profession to make a significant contribution to:

- the organisation, in terms of its management and utilisation of human resources;
- the individual, in terms of his or her needs and aspirations;

- the community at large, in terms of an enhanced quality of life.

The Board's **strategy** is to direct, influence and promote the development of the personnel profession in South Africa; to set standards of competence for the education, training and conduct of those engaged in the profession; to advise those involved how such competencies can be obtained; and to evaluate achievements in the field of personnel practice.

The **objectives** of the SABPP are to:

- promote the profession of personnel practice in South Africa;
- promote the standard of education and training of persons engaged in personnel practice, and to recognise education and/or training which qualifies persons for registration in terms of the Board's charter;
- promote liaison in the fields of education and training referred to above;
- advise the Minister of Labour or any other party, on any matters falling within the scope of the charter of the Board;
- communicate to the Minister of Labour, or any other party, any relevant information on matters of public or professional importance acquired by the Board in the course of the performance of its functions in terms of its charter; and exercise authority in respect of all matters affecting the standard of professional conduct of persons in personnel practice who are voluntarily registered in terms of the Board's charter.

2.5.2 The functions of the SABPP

The functions of the Board within the HR field in South Africa are to:

- register personnel practitioners, associate personnel practitioners and candidates as generalists, or in prescribed categories of specialist disciplines, within the field of personnel practice;
- in such circumstances as may be prescribed, or where otherwise authorised by the charter, remove any name from a register or, upon payment of the prescribed fee, restore it thereto;
- appoint supervisors, conduct assessments and examinations, and award certificates; and charge such fees in respect of such assessments, examinations or certificates as may be prescribed;
- recognise, on such prescribed conditions as it may deem fit, education and/or training which qualifies a person for registration in terms of the charter;
- upon application of any person, recognise any qualifications held (whether such qualifications have been obtained in the Republic of South Africa or elsewhere) as being equal, either wholly or in part, to any prescribed qualifications;
- establish a code of professional conduct for persons registered in terms of the charter;
- consider any matter which the Board deems pertinent to personnel practice in South Africa;

- perform any other functions which may be prescribed, and generally do all those things which the Board deems necessary or expedient to achieve the objects of its charter.

2.5.3 Registering with the SABPP: Levels, categories, processes and procedures

The SABPP's registration standards and procedures apply to South Africa's personnel fraternity as a whole; various levels and categories of registration are available, each with its own requirements.

Individuals who are interested in registering with the SABPP can apply for registration at various levels, including *Personnel Practitioner*; *Associate Personnel Practitioner*; *Candidate Practitioner* or *Candidate Associate Practitioner*. Furthermore, one can choose to be registered in the category of *Generalist* and/or in any one or more of a number of *Specialist* categories. It is thus possible to register in more than one category; in other words, one can register both as *Generalist* and *Specialist*. The Board's charter provides for registration in specialist categories such as: industrial relations; psychologiae; employee assistance; education and research; personnel services; recruitment and selection; and training and development.

Registered practitioners who meet certain additional criteria set by the Board may, upon invitation from the Board, act as mentors. Such individuals will gain enhanced status and will have the opportunity to make additional contributions to the field by helping new entrants to the profession to qualify for higher levels of registration.

The requirements set for registration at the various levels differ, but usually consist of a combination of relevant experience and qualifications. The following requirements must be met for registration at the different levels.

- **Personnel Practitioner**
  A four-year postmatriculation qualification, accredited by the Board, in the field of personnel practice, plus a two-year candidateship or at least four years' experience in the field; or some other admixture deemed to be of an equivalent standard and acceptable to the Board.
- **Associate Personnel Practitioner**
  A three-year postmatriculation qualification in the field of personnel practice, accredited by the Board, plus at least two years' practical training and experience in the field; or some other admixture deemed to be of an equivalent standard and acceptable to the Board.
- **Candidate Practitioner or Candidate Associate Practitioner**
  Personnel-related employment is a minimum requirement. A person who has completed his or her studies, but who does not have sufficient experience, may register as a candidate at any of the other two levels (whichever is applicable), and a person who is in the process of obtaining qualifications may register for

candidateship at the beginning of the third academic year of study. The candidate may then select a suitable mentor from the Board's list of approved mentors and then gain relevant experience under the guidance of the mentor, who will eventually evaluate the practical experience against the Board's requirements after a specific candidateship period (normally two years). The purpose of such a candidateship period or programme is to structure and focus the development of candidates who aspire to register at a higher level.

In addition to these requirements, the Board provides certain other guidelines regarding the qualifications and relevant experience required in order to qualify for registration. These guidelines are usually provided **quantitatively** by means of **credits** which are calculated according to predetermined values (such as one credit for one year's appropriate experience if one wants to register as a personnel practitioner), as well as **qualitatively** which normally relates to the type of experience required (such as in training and development or industrial relations) and the depth of involvement in the particular HR field. Guidelines are also provided regarding the relevance of different study courses. The Board may furthermore request an applicant to attend a professional interview in a case where there is any doubt as to the applicability of an applicant's experience and/or qualifications.

2.5.3.1 The process and procedure of registering

Any person who is interested in registering can request the Registrar: SABPP to provide him or her with the necessary documentation.

After the relevant documentation has been studied, and if the person thinks that he/she qualifies for registration, the necessary application forms are to be completed and returned to the SABPP, together with a nominal registration fee, certified copies of all relevant certificates, a detailed curriculum vitae (CV), a job description of the person's current post and recommendations from at least two persons (preferably registered with the SABPP). The registration fee is payable with regard to each category of registration applied for and has to be renewed on an annual basis. The processing of such an application normally takes about six weeks and, once it has been finalised, the person is informed and issued with an SABPP certificate stating his or her registration status. The individual may then use the postnominal designation of RPP (Registered Personnel Practitioner) or RAPP (Registered Associate Personnel Practitioner) on CVs, calling cards, and so forth — as long as he/she continues to pay the necessary renewal fees and as long as he/she is not deregistered for any reason.

2.5.4 The SABPP's code of professional conduct

Registration with the SABPP not only offers particular advantages (such as professional recognition and status, recognition of the individual's ability to meet the Board's high professional standards, a postnominal title, and access to research commissioned by the Board and to its publications and newsletters,) but also entails compliance with various requirements — such as adherence to its code of professional conduct at all times. In order to maintain the high standards of the HR profession in South Africa, any person registered with the SABPP shall:

● in executing his or her responsibility to the employer, the client and the profession, have due regard for the public interest;

● conduct him or herself so as to uphold the dignity, standing and reputation of the profession;

● discharge his or her duties to employer, employee or client to the best of his or her ability;

● not undertake work for which he or she is inadequately trained, experienced or qualified;

● not improperly canvass or solicit professional employment;

● not advertise professional services in a self-laudatory manner, or in any other manner derogatory to the dignity of the profession;

● not compete unethically for work;

● not maliciously or recklessly injure, whether directly or indirectly, the reputation, prospects, or business of any other person or organisation;

● not divulge any information which ought not to be divulged, gathered in the course of professional practice, regarding any person or organisation (in a court of law, professional secrecy should be contravened only under protest, after direction from the presiding judicial officer);

● at all times, and in all circumstances, order his or her conduct connected to personnel practice in accordance with the rules prescribed by the Board.

2.5.5 A generic competency model for HR practitioners in South Africa

As indicated in section 2.2.7, the SABPP (1990: 4–5) published a model which can serve as a guideline for the development of HR practitioners in South Africa. This framework serves basically as a guide to the identification, development and evaluation of the competencies (knowledge, skills, experiential and behavioural base) required of those who want to function as professionals at various levels in the HR profession in South Africa. The model is presented in figure 2.1.

2.5.5.1 Work domain and competency requirements: Research reveals some changes

In section 2.2.8 we referred to the research conducted by the HSRC on behalf of the SABPP. The findings of the said research also revealed some changing trends in the work domain and competency requirements of South African personnel practitioners. A few of these trends are summarised below.

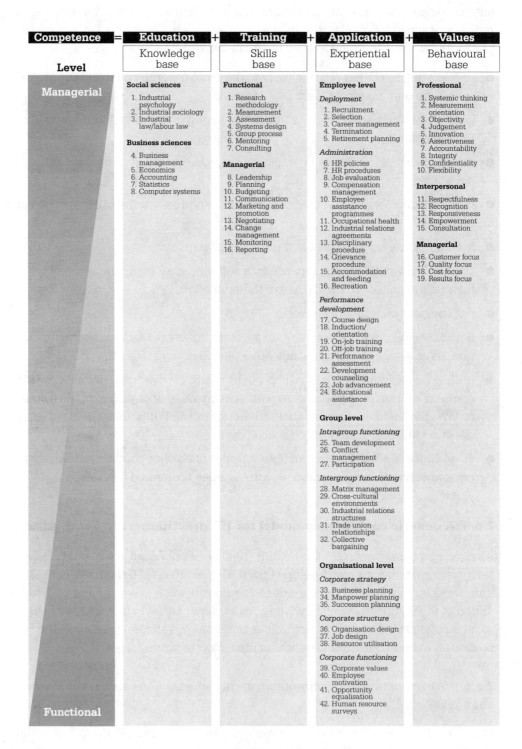

Competence	=	Education	+	Training	+	Application	+	Values
Level		Knowledge base		Skills base		Experiential base		Behavioural base

Managerial

Education — Knowledge base

Social sciences
1. Industrial psychology
2. Industrial sociology
3. Industrial law/labour law

Business sciences
4. Business management
5. Economics
6. Accounting
7. Statistics
8. Computer systems

Training — Skills base

Functional
1. Research methodology
2. Measurement
3. Assessment
4. Systems design
5. Group process
6. Mentoring
7. Consulting

Managerial
8. Leadership
9. Planning
10. Budgeting
11. Communication
12. Marketing and promotion
13. Negotiating
14. Change management
15. Monitoring
16. Reporting

Application — Experiential base

Employee level

Deployment
1. Recruitment
2. Selection
3. Career management
4. Termination
5. Retirement planning

Administration
6. HR policies
7. HR procedures
8. Job evaluation
9. Compensation management
10. Employee assistance programmes
11. Occupational health
12. Industrial relations agreements
13. Disciplinary procedure
14. Grievance procedure
15. Accommodation and feeding
16. Recreation

Performance development
17. Course design
18. Induction/ orientation
19. On-job training
20. Off-job training
21. Performance assessment
22. Development counseling
23. Job advancement
24. Educational assistance

Group level

Intragroup functioning
25. Team development
26. Conflict management
27. Participation

Intergroup functioning
28. Matrix management
29. Cross-cultural environments
30. Industrial relations structures
31. Trade union relationships
32. Collective bargaining

Organisational level

Corporate strategy
33. Business planning
34. Manpower planning
35. Succession planning

Corporate structure
36. Organisation design
37. Job design
38. Resource utilisation

Corporate functioning
39. Corporate values
40. Employee motivation
41. Opportunity equalisation
42. Human resource surveys

Values — Behavioural base

Professional
1. Systemic thinking
2. Measurement orientation
3. Objectivity
4. Judgement
5. Innovation
6. Assertiveness
7. Accountability
8. Integrity
9. Confidentiality
10. Flexibility

Interpersonal
11. Respectfulness
12. Recognition
13. Responsiveness
14. Empowerment
15. Consultation

Managerial
16. Customer focus
17. Quality focus
18. Cost focus
19. Results focus

Functional

Figure 2.1

The generic competency model for HR practitioners

2.5.5.2 Changes in the definition of the work domain and competency requirements of personnel practitioners

The research showed that there has been a shift in focus in HRM; this relates primarily to the increased involvement of personnel practitioners in the strategic management of organisations, in business operational processes and the improvement of productivity levels, in community-related projects and in the implementation of RDP-related projects. It was also found that line managers have become increasingly involved in human resource management.

Work domain

According to the report, the following developments are expected to take place in practice.

- **Administration**, in particular, is subject to the technological revolution. Because personnel administrative systems will become much more sophisticated and computerised, personnel practitioners will become less involved in old-fashioned administrative functions. It will remain their responsibility, however, to manage these systems.
- **Employee welfare and community involvement**

  Because it is expected that organisations will get more involved in social investment projects, personnel practitioners will have to be involved to a much greater extent in such efforts to uplift communities and to provide basic facilities for workers and their dependants (for example recreational facilities, welfare services, housing and educational opportunities) than has traditionally been the case. Employee counselling services are also seen to be of particular importance due to the many retrenchments resulting from restructuring and rationalisation exercises.

  The report states also that the health and safety of workers will remain an important area of responsibility for South African personnel practitioners. It may even become more important as workers become increasingly aware of their right to a safe working environment.

- The **development of human resources** is viewed as one of the most important aspects of personnel practice. The responsibility for job skills training is however, viewed as something to be shared between the HR practitioners and line management. The contributions of the specialists must focus on identifying learning potential and training gaps, ensuring accelerated development of previously disadvantaged groups, facilitating the development of managers' ability to adapt to changing environments and developing more participative management styles. Personnel practitioners will also be required to take the lead in career planning, and development, as well as in the development of systems for the recognition of prior learning.
- With regard to **human resource utilisation**, the study found that line management (in relation to the specialists) is taking much greater responsibility than

used to be the case. Personnel practitioners are, however, required to provide the necessary strategic inputs regarding the improvement of people productivity in the workplace.

- The study found that **industrial relations** will remain an important component of the work domain of personnel practitioners. It is expected that the highly politicised content of negotiations — particularly common during the eighties — will change. Sectors which were previously excluded from labour legislation (such as the public sector and agriculture) will be faced with new challenges in that they will have to deal with less sophisticated labour movements. Specialist practitioners in these sectors will have greater responsibility regarding the training of management to deal constructively with a unionised labour force. It is expected that the interpretation and implementation of labour legislation will remain a pertinent part of the work domain of personnel practitioners.

- Although **organisational development** was traditionally included in the definition of the work domain of personnel practitioners, it was found that the strong emphasis on organisational change, the strategic realignment of organisations and the need for intercultural understanding and tolerance were traditionally not featured prominently enough to reflect current trends. Another aspect that will need particular emphasis is the management and containment of the high levels of uncertainty associated with the host of changes which are taking place in South African organisations.

- The study further showed that **human resource procurement** will in future be approached from a different perspective as affirmative action programmes are implemented. Human resource professionals are increasingly required to champion affirmative action initiatives, to find innovative ways of assessing potential and to facilitate accelerated development.

- Trends in **remuneration** or **compensation management** were also found to be changing in conjunction with other trends in workplaces such as multiskilling, multitasking and the utilisation of matrix structures as people work more in teams. Personnel practitioners will furthermore have to be able to justify compensation structures as all processes have to become more transparent.

- **Systems development** and **research** were also found to be important areas in the work of personnel practitioners. However, few of the respondents interviewed were in fact involved in research or systems development. This seems to be an area in which consultants in the personnel field are making a major contribution.

Competency requirements

For the purposes of the study, the concept **competency** was used to denote the knowledge, skills and orientation or attitudes required by personnel practitioners. It was found that none of the competencies previously identified (see figure 2.1 above) will become redundant. A higher level of skill in certain areas and a different focus will, however, be needed in future. One of the most important requirements is therefore the ability to adapt to a changing environment. Personnel practitioners should thus have a lifelong learning orientation and will have to expand their knowledge base and hone their skills continuously.

According to the report the debate on the need for HR generalists versus specialists was frequently mentioned by respondents. Although there was no consensus with regard to this matter, it still seems as if both generalists and specialists will in future be needed in the personnel profession. The main trends were that generalists with a thorough understanding of all aspects of HR work, as well as advanced managerial skills, were needed in high-level human resource positions. Generalists are also needed to perform the whole array of personnel functions in smaller organisations. Specialist units will still be found in some large organisations. However, many organisations seem to use the services of consultants to perform their specialist functions.

The research also indicated that not all the competencies needed by personnel practitioners necessarily have to be developed through preparatory education. In-service training and development also contribute towards the refinement of skills and the transfer of organisation-specific information. However, almost all the respondents contended that graduates (especially university graduates) need much more practical exposure and opportunities to gain experience during their preparatory education. The report says that the market for personnel practitioners will become increasingly competitive and people without a high level of skills and who cannot immediately function independently will find it difficult to obtain employment.

1. Knowledge

It was found that the increased involvement of personnel practitioners in the core business of organisations requires an in-depth knowledge and understanding of

- the economic environment;
- business economics, including the concept of productivity, value-adding processes and marketing; and
- the business activities of the organisation.

In addition to these, a basic understanding of statistics and a knowledge of current labour legislation are viewed as essential.

The increased demand on personnel practitioners to play a leading role in organisational transformation, the democratisation of the workplace and community involvement and development necessitates a thorough understanding of both individual and group behaviour. On the other hand, involvement in the core business activities of organisations requires the ability to balance business goals with human resource demands (the so-called hard and soft sides of the business).

2. Skills

The study showed that, in future, administrative skills will be required to a lesser degree. However, a wide array of skills are expected to become progressively more important. These skills include the following:

- cognitive skills — the ability to conceptualise, to integrate information, to think strategically and to act proactively;
- problem-solving skills — the ability to reason, identify problems and approach these from a logical and analytical perspective;
- interpersonal skills — the ability to relate with empathy on an interpersonal level in a diverse working environment;
- negotiation and mediation skills;
- facilitation skills — the ability to act as a catalyst for change and to facilitate the process of reconciliation and compromise;
- language skills — the ability to communicate in English (the ability to speak an African language is becoming increasingly important as workers become aware of their right to be served in a language with which they are conversant);
- entrepreneurial skills — the ability to be creative, innovative and to take initiative;
- business skills — the ability to identify business opportunities, to market and to plan and to steer the activities of a business;
- leadership skills.

3. Attitudes

It was found that the nineteen crucial human resource values identified in the generic competency model (see figure 2.1) are still relevant. During the study, respondents indicated, however, that certain modes of behaviour are becoming progressively important. These include assertiveness, accountability and flexibility. In addition to these, emerging value requirements are the following: proactiveness (thinking forward), partnership (being prepared to work with employees at all levels) and enthusiasm (accepting problems as challenges and converting them into opportunities).

2.6 REMAINING A VALUED HR PRACTITIONER: NETWORKING AND READING

Individuals who choose a career in the human resource field specifically and who want to become successful professionals must continuously keep abreast of the latest developments in the relevant fields in order to ensure that they remain knowledgeable, valued, state-of-the-art HR practitioners. They must constantly add to their knowledge of the relevant fields and keep in contact with other professionals. It may not be too difficult to obtain the necessary qualifications, to gain the required experience or even to register with the SABPP, but to remain a highly valued and well-respected HR practitioner means that one must be prepared to go the extra mile. In this regard it is necessary at least to read extensively and to become a member of other associations where interaction with others with similar interests can take place.

The **Institute of Personnel Management (Southern Africa) (IPM)** is the most prominent body or association in the HR field in South Africa. Other relevant associations include **IRasa** (Industrial Relations Association of South Africa), which is affiliated to the **IIRA** (International Industrial Relations Association), the **ITM** (The Institute of Training Management (Southern Africa)) and the **SASTD** (Southern African Society for Training and Development). By joining associations such as these, individuals can come into contact with other professionals who also want to stay on top of their professions. Knowledge and experience can be shared and ideas exchanged and, in this way, not only will the individual enhance his/her own level of professionalism and competence but the community as a whole will also benefit.

Because of the importance of the **IPM** it is necessary to highlight its role in South Africa and to distinguish it from the SABPP.[6]

The IPM (SA) was established in 1946, and although (like the SABPP) it is also concerned with the question of professional competence in the HR field, there is a difference in emphasis. In this regard Whyte (1990: 33) makes the following remarks:

> "The IPM is concerned with promotion and development: which it achieves through activities such as its diploma programmes, its Convention, its Journal, and its seminars. The Board focuses on enablement: which it does through standard setting in areas like registration, education, candidate training, and norms of professional conduct. The Board confines itself to 'Personnel Practice', which is concerned with the unique role of the functional specialist. The remit of the IPM is much wider. It concerns itself with 'Personnel Management' (or 'Human Resource Management', if you prefer), which refers to the generic role of managing people at work."

Accordingly, the goals of the IPM include those listed in exhibit E.

Exhibit E

IPM goals*

- to promote the professional development of members and other interested persons;
- to cooperate and liaise actively with organisations both locally and internationally on relevant human resource issues and to represent human resource and professional personnel management locally and internationally;
- to play a leading role in the field of creating equal employment opportunities;
- to supply specialised, formal and professional training to members and to see that provision is made for professional education;
- to provide and disseminate specified, applicable and current information on developments and trends in the field of personnel management and the Institute;
- to assist the human resource practitioner and personnel profession in playing a strategic role in the areas of social responsibility, quality of working life, unemployment, etc.;
- to provide an appropriate infrastructure that includes a sound organisational structure and a healthy financial resource base to implement and manage the above goals.

*Source: Whyte 1990: 33–34

Apart from the networking which can be undertaken by joining associations such as the IPM or IRasa, and by actively taking part in the activities of these organisations, it is also of extreme importance to read extensively in the relevant field. Reading relevant journals is thus an important part of trying to remain a valued HR practitioner in South Africa. Some of the more prominent international and South African publications are listed in exhibit F.

Exhibit F

Some HRM-related journals

International
- Harvard Business Review
- Human Resource Management
- International Journal of Human Resource Management
- The Journal of Human Resources
- The Journal of Industrial Relations
- Journal of Organizational Behavior
- Human Resource Management Journal
- British Journal of Industrial Relations
- European Industrial Relations Review
- Personnel Journal
- The Personnel Administrator
- Industrial Relations Journal
- Industrial and Labor Relations Review
- Personnel Management

South African
- Contemporary Labour Law
- Employment Law
- Management Today
- People Dynamics (official publication of the IPM)
- South African Journal of Labour Relations
- South African Labour Bulletin

In addition, several publications of the Department of Labour can keep one abreast of general developments in the field of human resources in South Africa.

2.7   CONCLUSION

In this chapter you were introduced to the concept, nature and scope of the field of human resource management from a South African perspective. Specific attention was devoted to historical developments, to the concept of HRM from a South African perspective, to career opportunities in the field and to the profession of human resource management in this country. In this regard the important role of the SABPP was emphasised.

SELF-EVALUATION QUESTIONS

1. Write an essay in which you give a brief overview of the historical developments in South African human resource management.

2. Discuss the role of Isobel White in the historical development of personnel management in South Africa.

3. Write cryptical notes on "The decade that shaped the things to come in South African human resource management".

4. Compile a report on the following topic:
"Human resource management: Recent comparative perspectives and trends from 1990 up to today".

5. Define human resource management from a South African perspective and explain the important characteristics of the South African approach to this concept and field, as spelled out in this chapter.

6. Suppose that you are approached by a friend who would like to pursue a career in the human resource management field in South Africa. What advice would you give him/her regarding the nature of such a career, how to enter the field, what to study and read and which institutions and associations to approach?

7. Provide a detailed discussion on the nature and role of the SABPP.

8. Explain in detail what registration as a professional personnel practitioner in South Africa entails.

ENDNOTES

1. This section is based largely on personal notes of IHB White (kindly supplied to the author by the IPM (SA)), on publications by IHB White, and on a personal interview with IHB White conducted by Ben Swanepoel.

2. *EP Herald,* Friday, 31 October 1941.

3. Personal notes of IHB White, 2–3.

4. This section is based on and adapted from *The Supply and Demand of Personnel Practitioners in South Africa,* published by the Human Sciences Research Council in Pretoria.

5. This section is based on the following sources:

    (a) IPM and SABPP: How do they differ? (IPM in interview with Gary Whyte). 1990. *IPM Journal,* 8 (7), 33–34.

    (b) *People Dynamics,* 11 (8), 1993, 11.

    (c) The *SABPP's Guide to Registration* (June 1992).

6. This outline is based on Whyte, Gary. 1990. IPM and SABPP: How do they differ? (IPM in interview with Gary Whyte). *IPM Journal,* 8 (7), 33–34.

BIBLIOGRAPHY

Bagwa, W. 1973. Welfare facilitaties for black employees. *People & Profits, 1* (6), 12–16.

Botha, B. 1992. Window for opportunity. *People Dynamics,* 10 (12), 7.

Cherrington, DJ. 1983. *Personnel Management: The Management of Human Resources.* Dubuque, Iowa: Brown.

Coetzee, JAG. 1976. *Industrial Relations in South Africa.* Cape Town: Juta.

Crous, W. 1990. 'n Nuwe Suid-Afrika op die horison — Implikasies vir die menslike hulpbronbestuurder. *IPM Journal,* 8 (8), 3.

Cuming, MW. 1989. *The Theory and Practice of Personnel Management.* Oxford: Heinemann.

Cunningham, PW, Slabbert, JA, & De Villiers, AS. 1990. The historic development of industrial relations. In *Managing Industrial Relations in South Africa,* eds JA Slabbert, JJ Prinsloo & W Becker, 2.5. Pretoria: Digma.

Dickenson, J. 1974. The linkman: Selection and training of the black personnel officer. *People & Profits,* 1 (7), 8–19.

Diessnack, CH. 1980. Financial impact of effective human resources management. *People & Profits,* 7 (10), 5.

Douwes Dekker, L. 1974. Workers' education: A prerequisite for effective works committees. *People & Profits,* 1 (7), 5–7.

Finnemore, M & Van der Merwe, R. 1992. *Introduction to Industrial Relations in South Africa.* Johannesburg: Lexicon.

Friedman, S. 1987. *Building Tomorrow Today: African Workers in Trade Unions 1970–1984.* Johannesburg: Raucon Press.

Gerber, PD, Nel, PS & Van Dyk, PS. 1987. *Human Resources Management.* Johannesburg: Southern.

Grobler, PA. 1993. Strategic human resource management models: A review and a proposal for South African companies. *Management Dynamics: Contemporary Research,* 2 (3), 17.

Hall, R. 1985. Some changes in management practice in the Transvaal. *Industrial Relations Journal of South Africa,* 2nd quarter, 6.

Hill, A. 1987. The strategic approach to human resources management. *IPM Journal, 5* (9), 6–9.

Horwitz, FW. 1988. Personnel management or human resource management — Euphemism or new paradigm? *IPM Journal,* 6 (12), 6–7.

IPM Manpower Journal. 1983. News update–South African Board for Personnel Practice. *IPM Manpower Journal,* 2 (2), 4.

Jacobsz, FP. 1973. Herstrukturering van arbeid: 'n Voorvereiste vir ekonomiese groei. *People & Profits,* 1 (5), 22.

Langenhoven, HP & Verster, R. 1969. *Survey of Personnel Management in South Africa.* Bloemfontein: Personnel Research Division, University of the Orange Free State.

Langenhoven, HP. 1975. *The Present State of Black Personnel Management in South Africa*. Bloemfontein: Personnel Research Division, University of the Orange Free State.

Langenhoven, HP. 1978. Industrial psychology and personnel management do not mean the same thing. *People & Profits*, 5 (12), 14–15.

Lombard, BU. 1978. Human resources management: A new approach for South Africa. *SA Journal of Labour Relations*, December, 12–24.

Marx, FW. 1969. *Aspects of Personnel Management*. Pretoria: University of Pretoria.

Natrass, N. 1973. Effective supervision of black employees: Techniques that get results. *People & Profits*, 1 (5), 5.

Nel, PS & Van Rooyen, PH. 1993. *South African Industrial Relations Theory and Practice*. Pretoria: JL van Schaik.

Pansegrouw, G. 1985. Strategic human resource management — An emerging dimension, parts 1 & 2. *IPM Journal*, 4 (5), 22–30; 4 (6), 8–15.

People and Profits. 1973. Anglo sticks its neck out–Dr Alex Boraine plans for black advancement. *People & Pofits*, 1 (1), July, 3–28.

South African Board for Personnel Practice (SABPP). 1990. *Generic Competency Model for Human Resource Practitioners*. Board Paper of the South African Board for Personnel Practice. Johannesburg: Eskom — Human Resources Performance Management.

SPA Consultants. 1992. *Human Resources Survey in 23 Well-Known South African Organisations*, 6–24.

Van Wyk, C. 1989. The human resource practitioner's changing role. *IPM Journal*, 7 (9), 13–14.

Verster, R. 1979. *Personnel Management in South Africa*. Bloemfontein: Personnel Research Division, University of the Orange Free State.

Visser, P, Douwes Dekker, L, Majola, A & Brenner, D. 1991. Community conflict and violence: A human needs perspective. *IPM Journal*, 10 (2), 22.

White, IHB. 1944/45. Personnel management in South Africa. *Labour Management* (Journal of the UK Institute of Personnel Management), 144.

White, IHB. 1945. Personnel management in industry. In *Personnel Research in South Africa*, 313. Grahamstown: Personnel Research Section: Leather Industries Research Institute.

White, IHB. 1955. *The Effect of the Changing Social and Economic Situation on the Training and Experience demanded of the Personnel Manager*. Address delivered at a one-day conference of the Port Elizabeth branch of the SA Institute of Personnel Management on Tuesday 9 August 1955.

Whyte, GS. 1978. The professionalism of personnel management. *People & Profits*, 5 (12), 9–10.

Whyte, Gary. 1990. IPM and SABPP: How do they differ? (IPM in interview with Gary Whyte). *IPM Journal*, 8 (7), 33–34.

chapter 3 The Individual in the Organisation: Dynamics and Variables in Creating the Fit or Match

STUDY OBJECTIVES

After studying this chapter, you should be able to:

- list at least ten variables relating to individuals that can have an impact on human resource management (HRM);
- write an in-depth essay, with practical illustrations, on the interrelation between human resource management; and the attributes and dynamics of individuals;
- list at least seven variables relating to organisation dynamics that can have an impact on human resource management;
- write an in-depth essay, with practical illustrations, on the interrelation between human resource management and the dynamics of organisations as complex social entities;
- explain the meaning of "measurement";
- explain the meaning of "test";
- illustrate, by means of practical examples, how measurements can play a role in matching people and organisations;
- briefly discuss general aspects which are measured;
- explain four types of measurement scales;
- explain the meaning of the concepts *central tendency, variability, skewness* and *correlation* as they relate to describing data;
- explain the outcomes and consequences of matching employees, their work, and the organisation's internal and external environments.

3.1 INTRODUCTION

In section 1.5 it was stressed that human resource management can be viewed as all those intervening processes which are aimed at ensuring a continuous optimal fit or match in the employment relationship that exists between an organisation and the people it employs. In this chapter the focus is on the complex dynamics which underlie this interaction between **human beings** as employees and **organisations** as complex social entities which employ them.

The first section briefly deals with the complexities characteristic of **human beings** while the second part consists of a brief overview of some of the complexities and dynamics peculiar to **organisations** as social entities, made up of people. The chapter concludes with a brief discussion of the role played by **measurement** in achieving an optimal fit between human beings and organisations.

The aim is thus to introduce the complexities and dynamics which are, to a greater or lesser extent, involved in all HRM decisions and practices. The various interrelated factors and variables which form an inherent and natural part of the individual–organisation interface are thus briefly highlighted. Figure 3.1 reflects some of the variables in this regard.

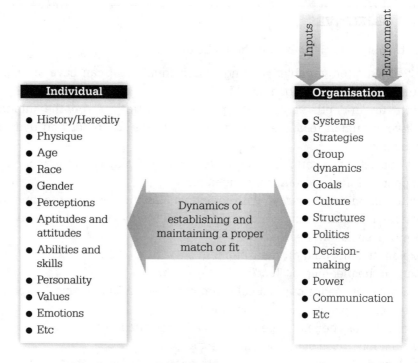

Figure 3.1
The individual–organisation interface

3.2 HUMAN RESOURCE MANAGEMENT AND THE ATTRIBUTES AND DYNAMICS OF INDIVIDUALS

People differ! Just think of your family and friends. Can you make a list of all those aspects in which you differ from them? As you try to do this it will soon become clear that, although you share some characteristics with other people, you are really quite different from them. Some people can be described as friendly, while others are surly or grumpy most of the time. Some are tall, others short, some are skinny, some are fat, some like rock, reggae or jazz music, while others prefer classical music. Some people prefer to work with animals, others with physical objects and still others with people. Whereas some people are well educated, others are illiterate and while some of us prefer to work on our own, others prefer to work in groups. A list of potential differences between individuals, could be extremely long. This section focuses on some of the variables underlying these differences. Reference is made to how such variables can influence HRM. The management of human diversity in the workplace as a vast, interesting and challenging topic is illustrated.

3.2.1 Physique

Some of an individual's most basic attributes manifest in physical terms. Attributes pertaining to, for example, the size of a person's body (height, weight), the strength of the muscles, the basic efficiency of the sensory organs (eyes and ears for example), are all immediately apparent and are largely determined by hereditary factors — although some (or rather most) of these can also be influenced by other factors such as diet, exercise and medical interventions.

What is important is the fact that each employee brings to work all his/ her physical attributes. Certain tasks involving hard labour, for example, require great muscle strength and fitness (for instance the job of a builder or miner). It is obvious that only individuals who are physically strong will be able to perform such tasks. Similarly, excellent eyesight will be a most important physical factor in the case of a fighter pilot. In other jobs perfect colour vision is often a prerequisite. Air hostesses who work for the South African Airways, for example, must have certain physical attributes and, for those interested in a career in modelling, the physique is obviously of utmost importance.

However, another area of human resource management in which the physical attributes of individuals play a role is in the design of equipment, physical work environments and other physical objects which individuals use or with which they come into contact during the course of their work. *Human factors' engineering* or *ergonomics* is the study of the relationship between workers and their environments. Ergonomical factors such as job aids, equipment and the physical working environment must therefore be considered when plant layouts are planned and when facilities at workplaces, such as training rooms, are designed (for example seating, lighting, noise and temperature). All of these aspects are important in the sense that they can have an influence on the individual, physically, in the work situation. An optimal fit between the individual and his/her job, (and thus the organisation) cannot be attained without giving due cognisance to the physical attributes of people.

Another important aspect in this context concerns those individuals who are physically handicapped. Disabled persons have to be accommodated in a very special way by organisations. In some countries employers are legally obliged to create equal employment opportunities by ensuring that a certain proportion of available jobs is reserved for the physically handicapped. In terms of South Africa's Constitution (s 9), unfair discrimination against handicapped people is prohibited.

Although physique is not usually the determining factor in the selection and placement of employees in modern times, the managements of most organisations still insist on their employees undergoing medical examinations (see chapter 10 on selection) which include the investigation of individuals' physical conditions. In the South African National Defence Force and the South African Police Service for example, the physical factor and medical fitness play a prominent role. Physique therefore remains a variable which can influence various decisions and practices. Most of these physical attributes can be measured by means of quite straightforward tests, such as hearing tests, measuring the height of a person or determining his/her fitness level. Other dynamics pertaining to human beings, are less easily measurable (as will be shown later).

3.2.2 Demographic factors

Demographic factors are the general background issues pertaining to individuals which quite often contribute to generalisations, and sometimes even to misconceptions or misperceptions, about what people are like. In this regard aspects such as gender, age, race, culture and nationality (including religion and language), socioeconomic background and status, type and level of education, marriage status, and even family background and history, come into play to influence people and also the way people are perceived. All of these factors or variables contribute to the differences to be observed in the people employed by organisations.

These demographical differences are not important so much in themselves, but rather because of the influence which they have on how people think and behave, on their needs, goals and beliefs, and also on stereotyping or the way in which people are categorised by others.

3.2.2.1 Age

One often hears people saying that in general, older people are resistant to change or conservative. While this may be true in some cases, it may not be true in others. No study has proven a positive correlation between age and resistance to change. Unfortunately, older employees are often labelled as being old fashioned thinkers. Although, in general, the physical abilities of people tend to deteriorate as they get older (for example impairments in hearing and eyesight begin to occur), these factors, under normal circumstances, do not necessarily affect the work performance of people of working age (18 to 65). There are, however, exceptions. In the case of pilots at South African Airways for example, where something like alertness is extremely important, the normal retirement age is 50. Thus age can play a role in certain situations, especially when people approach retirement age or beyond. This is especially true of more physically demanding jobs where muscular fitness and dexterity are essential for optimal work performance. It should also be borne in mind that, as people grow older and become more mature, their career goals and objectives also usually change.

3.2.2.2 Race

Another factor which is extremely relevant in the South African situation is that of race. South Africa's history of apartheid made racial discrimination in the workplace a contentious and ongoing issue in our organisations. For many years the whites in South Africa received preferential employment opportunities at the expense of the black, coloured and Indian communities. One of the major challenges facing the management of South African organisations today is the resolution of this issue in the workplace (see chapter 5).

This issue cannot, of course, simply be addressed by means of legislation, as **perceptual** problems continue to play an important role. Some people believe that the various racial groups differ markedly as far as abilities and intelligence are concerned.

Exhibit A

Management attitude and black advancement in the 80s

A survey conducted amongst 306 South African managers during the latter half of the eighties led Human and Hofmeyr (1987: 5–19) to conclude that employee attitudes, in particular those of South African managers at the time, play a central and determining role in the advancement or otherwise of blacks in South African organisations. As a result of their research, they were able to report that: "This means that although respondents seem to have accepted the principles of equal opportunity, fairness and non-discrimination, they appear to express racialistic attitudes, that is the belief that human abilities are racially determined."

The existence of racially based perceptions in some South African workplaces was again supported by a more recent study undertaken by Kruger and Human who found that " . . . whites generally harbour negative attitudes towards Africans, while expressing positive, although not strong, attitudes towards Indians", (Kruger & Human 1990: 29); and also that "the attitudes of Indians were found to be relatively more positive towards Africans than the attitudes of whites, and the attitudes of Indians towards whites were found to be significantly more positive than the attitudes of whites towards Indians" (Kruger & Human 1990: 39).

Although this study was conducted only in the sugar milling industry in South Africa, and although one should be cautious not to generalise, it still serves to illustrate the continued existence of racial issues in South African workplaces. It must be reiterated that differences in demographic factors (such as race) do not necessarily influence human behaviour in the workplace, but that it is the perceptions, beliefs and attitudes of employees regarding these factors, which play an important role in the management of human resources in South African organisations (see also chapter 5).

3.2.2.3 *Gender*

Gender is another demographic factor that may influence human resource management in organisations, and which can lead to similar problems of discrimination in the workplace. In this regard the results of a study conducted by Human and Allie (1988) led them to state that, although most South African managers believe in fairness, non-discrimination and equal opportunities, many also still had doubts about the ability of women to advance in the field of management. It was also reported that although managers accept affirmative action in relation to blacks, it was not regarded in the same light when it came to women in South African organisations. Many people thus continue to see female–male differences as holding implications for work performance abilities, and this often leads to covert sexual discriminatory management practices. The reality of these perceptions of male–female differences and of their influence on work performance must be taken seriously in HRM in South African organisations, in particular as far as discrimination in job and career opportunities is concerned.

Although the potential influence of only three demographic factors on HRM has been discussed here, other factors such as nationality and culture, hold similar implications for human behaviour in the workplace and hence for HRM.

3.2.3 Perception

Perception refers to those (mainly cognitive and mental) processes which enable us to interpret, give meaning to and understand our internal and external environments. In the previous section reference was made to the fact that people perceive things in certain ways. People tend to "see" things differently; in other words, there are differences in perception, because people recognise, interpret and give different meanings to different stimuli in their environments. Perceptions thus occur every time that certain environmental stimuli activate any of our senses and we try to make sense of, or give meaning to these stimuli by organising and interpreting them (cognitively). Perception is therefore subjective and it involves complex processes such as selective attention, observing objects, symbols or messages, recognising the relevance of stimuli, comprehension, relating these aspects to previous experience, and translating them into specific responses.

In this way the behaviour of people at work is influenced by perceptual issues. Different people respond differently to similar stimuli in the work situation. While one person might perceive an instruction to complete a specific task which falls outside the scope of his/her job description as challenging and fair, another might regard it as unfair. Similarly one manager might perceive English-speaking males as creative, progressive and open-minded workers and Afrikaans-speaking females as conservative and dogmatic, whereas another manager might regard such stereotyping as invalid. The two managers' behaviour and managerial practices will most likely also differ in this regard. This is in line with the so-called *attribution theory*, which holds that people's behaviour is determined by how they perceive the causes and effects of their behaviour. One worker may attribute his/her promotion to hard work and will thus continue to work hard to obtain further promotion. Another worker may see the reason for his/her promotion as a result of the close personal relationship which exists between him/her and a particular influential person in the organisation. In the latter case the employee will most likely work harder at maintaining these kinds of relationships at work than at doing his/her work really well.

The complexity of perception in general and the potential influence of perceptual differences on HRM practices should already be quite clear from the foregoing discussion. Perception is a complex concept, not only because of all the intricacies involved in all cognitive processes but also particularly because of the interrelationships which exist between perception and other individually based variables such as differences in needs, emotions and previous experiences, as well as situational factors. Time as a situational factor can serve as an example. Assume that an important project has to be completed within two weeks and two key members (say engineers) of the five-member project team suddenly withdraw. The project team leader now has to find suitable replacements as soon as possible. The time factor may put so much pressure on this manager that he/she may overlook certain sources of recruitment such as advertisements in weekly, national newspapers (see chapter 9 on recruitment). There may thus very well be signs of so-called selective perception in the sense that some recruitment sources are totally ignored. Similarly, the need to have two engineers on the project team as soon as possible may lead to the perception that "any engineer will now do" because "anything is better than nothing". Had the time constraints been different or had the project team members required less specialised advice, the situation may have been perceived as less urgent and more careful consideration of various potential candidates from various fields would have resulted. Another factor — emotions — can also come into play. The manager may be so negative, angry or upset that he/she may perceive the situation as hopeless and thus decide not to continue with the project at all. Another person, with a different temperament, may well react quite differently.

As can be seen, perception can be influenced by a host of other variables. These perceptual dynamics can play a role in decisions about the recruitment, selection and even performance appraisal and the general management of human resources.

One other aspect relating to perception is that of self-perception: that is, how one sees oneself. We all recognise ourselves as distinct human beings. Every person is conscious of his/her own existence. Some people, however, view themselves in negative terms, while others tend to have more positive perceptions about themselves. How one evaluates one's own worth or value determines one's **self-esteem**. People with a high self-esteem see themselves as valuable, capable and having the potential to contribute and be successful. It follows that individuals who perceive themselves in a negative way will have doubts and be more uncertain about their abilities and potential to contribute and be successful in the work situation. These people with low self-esteem will thus tend to see themselves as less valued and less important members of the organisation, and such individuals will have to be understood and treated differently by management in the workplace. It is thus clear that perceptions and perceptual differences can play an important role in HRM.

3.2.4 Aptitudes, abilities and skills

People often decide to make career moves and to apply for jobs in which they have had no previous experience. Management sometimes decides to employ such people even though they do not yet have the required skills, as long as they show the ability or potential (in terms of mental and physical qualities) to learn or attain those skills. The concepts referred to here, *aptitude* and *ability*, are rather elusive.

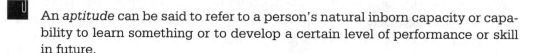

An *aptitude* can be said to refer to a person's natural inborn capacity or capability to learn something or to develop a certain level of performance or skill in future.

Abilities, on the other hand, can be taken to refer to innate or learned general traits that enable people actually to do something.

Experts differ on what *intelligence* really entails, but it is usually taken to include various specific mental abilities such as verbal comprehension, spatial orientation, numerical abilities, span of memory, verbal or word fluency and inductive or deductive reasoning. In this sense it would therefore seem that aptitudes refer to specific abilities.

Intelligence generally refers to each person's mental ability or cognitive capacity to use the intellect, to think, to solve problems, to reason, to learn and to understand.

Most experts, however, also agree that mental abilities or intelligence can be viewed in a **general** sense or in relation to certain **specific** mental aptitudes. Usually when somebody is referred to as intelligent that person is regarded as having a high *intelligence quotient* or IQ. This represents a general measurement of intelligence. Intelligence is therefore not a concrete entity but rather an abstraction used to describe the general mental abilities of a person. A person's IQ is simply a numerical value which indicates the general mental abilities of that person at a specific point in time. Research has shown that, contrary to the earlier belief that a general level of intelligence is inherited or inborn, intelligence can in fact change over time through the influence of various environmental factors encountered, for example, during the learning process. Research has also shown that, when intelligence is tested or measured, both general and specific factors (or groups of factors) and their correlations have to be taken into account. Experience has furthermore shown that high intelligence does not necessarily guarantee commensurate performance in the work situation. Ability to perform is one thing; the *will* to actually perform well is something quite different.

On the other hand, *skills* are those very specific task-related competences that a person already possesses, such as the skill to type, to negotiate, to interview someone or to fix a broken personal computer.

Because the abilities and skills of people differ and, because different jobs require different skills, abilities and/or aptitudes, different people are better suited to different jobs or careers.

Whereas some degree of general mental ability is necessary in all jobs, some jobs require very particular mental abilities or aptitudes. The job of a chartered accountant, for example, requires a greater numerical ability (that is, to make accurate arithmetic computations) than the job of a social worker. On the other hand, the job of a salesperson would normally require greater verbal abilities (to talk, listen, understand and thus communicate with others) than that of a computer programmer. Mechanical and psychomotor abilities would generally be more important for a career in the technical and mechanical field than would be the case with a career in the field of research in the natural or social sciences.

In addition to mental abilities and aptitudes, other human abilities also differ. Psychomotor abilities, for example, include aspects such as finger dexterity, manipulative ability or hand-use coordination. This refers to the ability to manipulate small objects with the fingers, for instance when typing on a word processor or when screwing a nut and bolt into quite a tight space in the engine of a motorcar. Other abilities (such as social abilities) often also relate to certain personality traits (discussed below), such as introversion versus extroversion. All of these human abilities influence human resource management decisions.

Another aspect which must be mentioned, and which also relates to mental abilities, is the individual's ability to **learn**. We all have a general idea of what learning is all about. As you read through the pages of this book you are learning, you are gaining knowledge or influencing your thought patterns. Learning can therefore be viewed as a basic cognitive process which all people engage in from birth.

Learning refers to the process by which relatively enduring changes in thought processes and behaviour or potential behaviour are brought about as a result of indirect or direct experience or practice.

When people are employed in organisations to do specific jobs and to perform particular tasks, they also constantly gain new experience and knowledge and therefore learn. Not all learning, therefore, takes place in a formal way, such as, for example, by studying for a degree or by attending a training course. Some learning takes place informally and indirectly and almost naturally. Such is the case, for example, when we learn how to get along with certain people or how to dress when we go to work or who to trust when we negotiate with a certain interest group.

Nevertheless, all forms of learning can have a bearing on human behaviour in the organisational context and hence on HRM.

Some people have greater learning abilities than others. There are those who tend to cling strongly to what they have already learned in the past and who demonstrate resistance when new things have to be learned. Such people often do not want to learn. There are also those who perhaps want to learn in order to master certain skills, but who lack the necessary aptitude which makes it difficult for them to learn as easily in a particular situation. Some people also tend to learn faster than others. All of these aspects play a role in aspects like making selection decisions, in appraising the performance of subordinates, in training individuals and in planning the careers of individual employees.

From the foregoing it is clear that the dynamics which flow from individual differences, and which can influence HRM decisions in the workplace, are also complicated by the fact that people differ in terms of ability, aptitude and skill.

3.2.5 Personality

From what has already been said it is quite clear that people differ in many respects. The term *personality*, although often used very loosely, is a concept which is difficult to define. Various experts have approached the concept from different theoretical perspectives and one therefore cannot provide a single, definitive definition. The term is thus often misused. You may well have overheard somebody describing someone else as having "absolutely no personality" or as having a "good" or "nice" personality. These are vague generalisations to "sum up" people — often wrongly so. Many view the term *personality* as an aggregate or sum total of almost all the characteristics or traits peculiar to any individual — thus constituting the individual's identity and unique nature.

In terms of this approach personality includes aspects such as emotions, interests, attitudes, values, behaviour and mental characteristics (that is, many of the aspects discussed elsewhere in this chapter).

In this broad sense *personality* can be taken to refer to the way in which the biological, physical, social, psychological and moral traits of an individual are organised into a whole, and also to the relatively stable set of behavioural patterns which flow from the dynamic interaction between the individual and his or her environment in a particular situation.

Various personality traits can therefore be identified, each referring to a relatively stable characteristic responsible for some form of consistency in behaviour. *Temperament* as a trait, for example, refers to the individual's characteristic speed and way of reacting to stimuli and situations, to his or her emotional nature and total disposition, and is usually linked to physical factors such as the individual's nervous system, endocrine and gland system, and other genetic factors.

Human resource specialists tend almost universally to believe that an individual's personality can have a marked influence on his/her work performance and on the extent to which such a person adjusts to his/her job. Assuming that personality do in fact affect job-related behaviour, the argument can be divided into two parts.

First, it is reasonable to assume that in some circumstances personality factors do have an influence on job-related behaviour via a motivational route. One could thus expect individuals with certain personality traits to be more inclined to seek certain types of employment and to be better suited to such jobs than people with other personality traits.

Secondly, it is reasonable to assume that, in some kinds of jobs, personality factors will have a direct bearing on the proficiency with which the individual will be able to perform his/her functions. This is particularly true of jobs that require a great deal of personal contact with other people, such as in public relations work, some management activities, interviewing, and so on.

People are thus often described in terms of various personal qualities or traits such as introversion, extroversion, sociability, dominance and locus of control. It is useful to see the various traits as positions on a continuum. Take locus of control for instance. At the one end of the continuum are people with internal locus of control, who believe that their internal traits determine what happens in a given situation. At the other end of the continuum are people with an external locus of control, who feel that they are at the mercy of chance, fate, other people and outside events. "Internals" not only perceive themselves as having greater control over events in their lives but also seek out situations where they are more likely to be in control — for example by starting their own companies (Sterns & Spector 1987: 227–234). The typical personality tests measure constructs like these.

Although personality has an obvious relation to work-related behaviour (as was pointed out earlier), the use of measures of personality variables is fraught with problems that might preclude these measures from having enough practical value. In view of this, the most defensible use of such tests is under circumstances in which their validity has been clearly demonstrated (see also chapter 10).

3.2.6 Values

In the work situation people's values form a major potential source of performance differences — of variations in quantity and quality of output, absenteeism and other aspects of performance. The values of individuals also influence their perception of other employees, groups, standards and situations. The normative nature of values furthermore determines what is perceived to be ethical or unethical in a particular organisation.

Values can be described as the explicit or implicit conceptions of the desirable held by an individual or a group; they are concerned with what "should be" and are the normative standards by which human beings are influenced when choosing between alternatives.

Whereas values refer to generalised conceptions of what is right or wrong, good or bad, *attitudes* generally refer to one's feelings (positive or negative) about specific objects or situations (Spates 1983: 27–49). Values are thus closely linked to attitudes and together they form an integrated part of the psychic system of the personality of any person. Because values are created as a person develops within a particular culture, they are extremely resistant to change.

Values can clearly make a significant contribution to success and to high levels of performance when the individual's values fit the requirements of his or her job. Yet values can also create problems in the workplace. Because values are difficult to change, problems caused by clashing values are also difficult to solve. Conflicts often arise for instance because people with strong values regarding freedom, fall foul of bureaucratic rules and regulations. Strong religious convictions, which are often supported by moral values, can clash so severely with job demands that the employee experiences difficulty doing his or her work. A congruence of values between individuals and employing organisations can thus substantially benefit both parties. Where such congruence is lacking, the individual can be expected to suffer; if many such individuals are involved, the organisation may suffer as well.

3.2.7 Attitudes

An *attitude* can be defined as the degree of positive or negative feeling a person has towards a particular object, such as a place, thing, situation or other person.

Employees have positive *job attitudes* when they have pleasant internal feelings about their jobs or certain aspects of their jobs (Pinder 1984).

People may have different attitudes regarding groups (eg ethnic groups, political groups, religious groups), social customs (eg fashion, music, art), medical issues (eg abortion, organ transplant), social phenomena (eg marriage, divorce, child abuse), national and international events (eg terrorism, war, civil disobedience), ecological phenomena (eg nature conservation, pollution), work concerns (eg management, labour unions, strikes), and many more.

Primary influences on attitudes include family, peer groups, teachers and representatives of the church. Secondary influences include mass communication media, such as TV, radio and newspapers, experts in a particular field, people with authority and information sources.

Employees' attitudes are important to organisations for at least two reasons. Knowing to which aspects of a job employees respond either favourably or unfavourably can provide a basis for job design decisions. When possible, positive features should be reinforced and negative factors improved or removed. Employees' attitudes are also important for philosophical reasons. Today it is not sufficient simply to provide employees with work: because work forms such a central part of life, employers are expected to provide meaningful and satisfying work, to the extent that it is possible to do so.

Job satisfaction is often thought to be synonymous with job attitudes, but one should be aware that those with different theoretical viewpoints may use the term somewhat differently. Some see job satisfaction as the degree of discrepancy that exists between what a person expects to gain from work and what that person perceives is actually gained. Others measure job satisfaction in terms of the gratification of strong needs in the workplace. Still others see job satisfaction as a purely emotional response to a job situation.

Job satisfaction stems in part from actual workplace conditions and in part from an individual's attitude towards work in general. Since most people want to feel good about their lives, and since work generally takes up half of an individual's waking hours, job satisfaction must be considered as important in its own right and not just as a means to an end. Job satisfaction has a significance independent of its contribution to organisational goals such as productivity.

However, the different reactions which people have to job satisfaction or dissatisfaction can have important implications for work performance. Employees who think that they have been treated badly may even feel justified in stealing from an employer, thereby helping themselves to what they see as a morally justifiable supplement to their wages. Similarly, job dissatisfaction appears to be associated with emotional illness and symptoms of emotional disorder (Wiener, Vardi & Muczyk 1981).

Job satisfaction can therefore have a profound influence on organisational success. It can contribute both to productive output (for example a high quantity and quality of products or services), and to organisational maintenance objectives (for example low absenteeism and labour turnover).

Organisational commitment is another aspect which can be defined from the attitudinal standpoint. Organisational commitment as a work attitude has much in common with job satisfaction, although the two are distinct constructs (Brooke, Russel & Price 1988).

From the attitudinal standpoint *organisational commitment* can be defined as the relative strength of an individual's identification with and involvement in a particular organisation.

Conceptually it can be characterised by at least three factors, namely a strong belief in and acceptance of the organisation's goals and values, a willingness to exert considerable effort on behalf of the organisation and a strong desire to maintain membership of the organisation (Mourday, Porter & Steers 1982).

Inherent in this definition is the idea of organisational loyalty, but commitment goes beyond loyalty to a more active contribution.

Organisational commitment, as an attitude, is more broad than job satisfaction because it applies to the organisation as a whole, not just to the job. It is also more stable, because day-to-day events at work are less likely to influence it.

Once again it is important to note that it takes a good fit between the nature of the individual and the characteristics of the employing organisation to obtain the right level of commitment.

3.2.8 Diverse aspects

The *needs*, *interests* and *emotions* of employees form, like values and attitudes, a major potential source of work performance differences. Employers have therefore much to gain from attending to the needs, interests and emotions of their employees.

Environment and culture develop certain needs in individuals. Most of the physiological needs are congenital, while higher-order needs, such as the need for esteem, acknowledgement, power, acceptance and social interaction, are acquired. The existence of a need can be deduced from an individual's behaviour. For instance, an individual may have an unsatisfied need. As a result he/she develops a drive to satisfy that need. This leads to the release of energy in the form of behavioural patterns directed at a specific goal. When the goal is reached, the behaviour directed at satisfying the need will cease. Other unsatisfied needs will now become more important.

There are a few universal needs which have been identified by most theorists. *Physiological needs* are pre-eminently physiologically based. The manner in which some of these needs are satisfied is socialised in terms of the habits and customs of a particular culture.

The need for *safety* is both physiological and acquired. This need is directly linked to self-preservation and to the survival of the species and is a consequence of any person's physical nature.

Social needs are primarily acquired and develop especially as a result of a person's interaction with other people. Much of a person's everyday behaviour relates to the need for acceptance by and affiliation to a group.

The need for *esteem* relates to the need to be admired by other people, to excel, to achieve in order to promote self-esteem. This need is acquired. Western civilisation in particular tends to shape and teach this need pattern. Praise, rewards and approval are given for achievements.

These needs have practical implications in the work situation. If an employee's needs are satisfied in the work environment, he/she will more likely try to minimise absences from work and will probably do a better job than would have been the case had his/her needs not been met (Steers & Porter 1991).

On the presumption that *interest* in one's work promotes better performance, improved productivity and greater job satisfaction, both employers and employees have much to gain from adopting methods that can help individuals to identify their interests and to design work tailored to those interests. Using such methods (see chapter 14), an individual can determine, for example, whether his/her interests lie in seeking new worlds and exploring new civilisations or in something more along the lines of dermatology.

Interest is thus related to a person's needs, attitudes and values and can be described as a person's tendency to feel attracted to something.

The term "attracted" indicates giving attention to, obtaining knowledge about, moving towards and attempting to obtain that which gives potential value to a person. The development of interest is primarily determined by the experience and knowledge that the individual has gathered over time. This development implies that interest is a continuous process rather than a time-limited characteristic and that it is subject to constant change and transformation.

Although interest is largely determined by environmental influences, it is also closely linked to one's physical characteristics, aptitudes and intellectual abilities, which all have an influence on the development of interests. Employers can use information about their employees' interest patterns to formulate job descriptions and to attract new personnel.

In addition to interests, an individual brings certain *emotions* to the workplace.

Emotion is the complex experiencing of feelings, accompanied by some characteristic physiological states, and finds expression in certain behavioural patterns with a particular function.

All emotions are characterised by feeling and it is this affective experiencing which gives colour to emotions, for example joy, anger, fear, etc. These feelings can be experienced as either pleasant, unpleasant or mixed. For instance, a prerequisite for an emotion like *joy* in the workplace is the satisfaction of needs through the pursuance and achievement of certain goals. The more important the goal, the greater the joy experienced in the achievement of that goal.

In contrast, a prerequisite in the manifestation of *anger* as an emotion is an insurmountable, identifiable obstacle in the way of goal achievement.

In contrast to joy and anger, *fear* is an escapist emotion which serves to protect man against threat. Because of the many potential dangers in society, fear is an emotion which is generally experienced. A change in the environment could lead to fear; new or strange situations may be threatening. For example, workers sometimes don't want to be promoted because of the implied changes in their working environment. Fear is contagious: for example, in a group situation or in the spreading of rumours within an organisation.

One can conclude that when an individual's needs, interests and emotions mesh with the requirements of the organisation and his or her job, chances are greater for success and higher levels of work performance.

3.2.9 Concluding remarks about individual dynamics

As has been explained, the attributes and dynamics of individuals play an extremely important role in organisations. Managers must always bear this in mind when making HRM-related decisions. Also, when conducting surveys care must be taken to develop measurement scales with good psychometric properties (an aspect dealt with later in this chapter and also in chapter 10).

When HRM-related decisions are taken, the inherent dynamics of organisations as social entities (made up of people) should, however, also be taken into account. This is so because individuals as employees are engaged in particular relationships with the organisations that employ them.

3.3 ORGANISATION DYNAMICS AND HUMAN RESOURCE MANAGEMENT

Now that you have been introduced to the complex issue of individual differences and its interrelation with HRM-related decisions and practices, it is necessary to focus on some of the dynamics inherent to the other side of the employment relationship — the organisation as employing entity. Once again the approach will be to illustrate how the characteristics, processes and dynamics peculiar to organisations as social entities interrelate with HRM-related decisions and practices.

3.3.1 Strategies and goals of organisations

As indicated in chapter 1, all organisations exist to fulfil certain needs in society. Organisations are therefore purposeful entities and one of the tasks of management, particularly top management, is to formulate strategic goals and objectives which the total organisation will seek to attain. So, for example, the objective may be an annual average turnover growth rate of 10 % or a 20 % greater share in a particular market. Furthermore, organisations must consider the means to the ends. The *strategies* of the organisation refer to the *ways* in which it hopes to achieve the strategic objectives.

Various types of strategies can be differentiated. *Corporate strategy* decisions revolve around determining which types or areas of business it would be best to get involved in, whereas the management decisions and practices concerned with how to compete and to achieve success in these particular industries or sectors are normally referred to as *business strategy*. *Functional strategy* refers to the strategies relating to the various functional areas such as marketing, public relations, operations and human resources. Decisions relating to any of these strategic issues can have an influence on HRM.

Say, for example, that an organisation wishes to adopt a *divestiture* grand strategy (this type of strategy refers to the sale of an organisation or parts thereof). This may mean that the new owners follow a totally different approach or strategy to human resource management. Similarly, a *turnaround* grand strategy (when profits are declining) may mean cost reduction in various areas, including cutting labour costs, which may lead to retrenchments. Also, top management may decide that, in order to achieve the set growth rate, the organisation should diversify and enter into new markets. This may lead to a need for different types of employees (with different skills, knowledge and abilities), thus spilling over to the areas of workforce planning, recruitment, and so forth. On the other hand, if an organisation fails to do proper financial planning, the resultant financial hardships will almost certainly spill over into the HRM area — for example when pay increases are considered and collective bargaining with trade unions is put under strain.

3.3.2 Organisational structures

Part of management's task is to organise the organisation into a structure of positions (a hierarchy), ranging from the most senior general manager at top management level to the lowest level labourers. Various management decisions in this regard revolve around principles such as specialisation, departmentalisation, centralisation and/or decentralisation of authority, delegation of responsibilities, and so forth. Not only are these types of decisions part of work organisation and job design (see chapter 7) but the outcomes thereof (the resultant structures) can also influence the flow of information and hence communication in the organisation, which in turn can affect other HRM decisions and practices.

You may also have read at sometime or another about the *restructuring* of an organisation. As a rule this refers to rationalising or changing the broad overall structures of organisations, which may also lead to redundant personnel who may have to be retrenched. In an organisation with a great deal of specialisation (employing specialists who perform only a few specified tasks for which they have been specifically trained), some employees may become very bored with the monotonous work. Such job dissatisfaction may lead to low productivity, conflict, lack of discipline and even labour court cases.

Another important aspect revolves around the specialisation/devolution decision regarding HRM in the organisation. In chapter 1 it was shown that management can decide who will be the main role-players with regard to HRM in an organisation (the HR specialists and/or the line managers). These types of decisions will clearly have a fundamental influence on the way in which HRM is conducted in an organisation (more about this in chapter 7).

3.3.3 Group dynamics

Most people spend the greater part of their time at work working within a group context rather than as individuals. In fact, one of management's major organisational functions is to group tasks and people together. The dynamics underlying the formation, development and functioning of groups form a vast and complex field of study. Most management development courses offer a module in group dynamics because of its profound influence on human behaviour in the workplace (and thus on HRM).

Although "*a group*" can be defined in various ways, the perspective taken here is that a group in an organisation refers to a collection of relatively freely and regularly interacting people (thus more than one) who perceive themselves as belonging together in some or other sense because of the common objectives which they collaboratively try to achieve and because their behaviour can influence each other and the extent to which they achieve their common objectives.

Per definition group members are thus interdependent and their interaction is purposeful and structured in a particular way in order to facilitate goal achievement. In this sense a particular department or section thereof, such as the financial services department or the credit control section, can be viewed as a formal group within the organisation. Other groups are formed on an informal basis, such as a group of secretaries who interact regularly to share common problems and to support one another.

Groups are thus formed for different reasons and take on various forms and sizes. Groups also go through various stages of development. All of these variables influence the functioning of groups. Some groups, for example, display signs of high *group cohesiveness* (a sense of closeness and commonness of purpose, norms, values, attitudes and behaviour). In such cases it is often said that a particular group has a good team spirit. In a formal situation group cohesiveness can be good. For example: good team spirit in a particular department or section will result in members who are closely knit, who support one another and who stand in for one another and give their best for the sake of the group. Such closeness may, however, lead to difficulties when a newcomer is employed and has to become part of the group and attain full membership status. Highly cohesive groups may however also result in management problems, especially if the group members do not support the manager. Such situations may lead to lack of discipline and even conflict. Think, for example, of trade unions which sometimes act collectively to resist management decisions and actions.

Within the group context individual group members may be in conflict (intragroup conflict), which may lead to dysfunctional group processes, to the detriment of group goal achievement. Intergroup conflict (between certain groups) can also arise within organisations (for example, when two rival trade unions are trying to recruit members). Within the context of such situations the work performance abilities of individual workers may be influenced negatively. These may spill over into performance appraisal problems and even into labour disputes.

3.3.4 Communication

Communication, within an organisational context, can be described as the process by which people transmit and exchange messages (or information).

Those who send the information want to convey a certain idea and thus encode the idea (translate it into a specific form such as a letter, memorandum or verbal instruction) so that those who receive the message can decode it (interpret the message and form their own idea of what it means). The ideal is that the senders' intended meaning (idea) and the receivers' perceived meaning (idea) should be the same. However, many factors can intervene to have a negative impact on the communication process, thus leading to distorted or poor communication where the receivers' interpretation or perception of the idea or meaning underlying the message differs from that intended by the senders.

Communication is vital to enable employees to do their work and to help people to work harmoniously together towards the achievement of the organisation's goals. For example, the supervisor of a section in which a vacancy has occurred must instruct the personnel department to draw up an advertisement. Recruitment advertisements (a form of communication) may be poorly devised and thus be unsuccessful in attracting enough of the right applicants. The job description is a form of communication — a written message of what is expected of an employee in terms of work performance. During performance appraisals/reviews, superiors and subordinates communicate about work performance levels, requirements, deficiencies, and strengths. The success of training interventions often depends on the extent to which the trainees correctly understand (decode) the new information.

Many obstacles or barriers can harm the quality of communication and, consequently, HRM practices. Apart from semantic problems, other factors such as physical distractions (for example factory noise) and organisation structures which are too bureaucratic can influence communication. Sometimes communication problems can even spill over into disputes in the labour courts — for example when work instructions are not interpreted correctly and employees are disciplined and even dismissed unfairly.

3.3.5 Decision-making processes

Decision making is one of the most fundamental and important management tasks, and refers in essence to the identification and choice of alternatives (usually regarding objectives, priorities and courses of action) in order to solve problems and to achieve organisational objectives.

For example, managers have to decide which business/industry to be in or which business strategies to follow. All work involves some sort of decision making. Some decisions are more complicated and require more information, experience and knowledge, while others are relatively simple and routinised, requiring little information or specialised knowledge.

Decisions are made by people and are therefore exposed to all of the dynamics pertaining to individuals in organisations, such as cognitive abilities, needs, values, attitudes, personality and perception. The risk propensity of individual managers can, for example, influence the extent to which decision-making powers are delegated or decentralised to lower levels. Some managers tend to be very autocratic and non-participative in their decision-making styles and thus do not involve lower-level employees in the decision-making process. This may frustrate those employees who feel the need to take a more active part in decision making (see also chapter 21).

Both superiors and subordinates have to make certain decisions on career planning and training and development opportunities. A manager who decides unilaterally to transfer one of his/her subordinates can expect some sort of resistance with resultant conflict and possible negative attitudes. Furthermore, in some organisations performance appraisals are done in a very haphazard way, allowing individual managers to decide on their own what the performance levels of their subordinates are (see chapter 13).

Many decisions thus have to be made in the process of managing human resources. The way in which this is done often relates directly to the quality of HR management practices.

3.3.6 Power and politics

Power and politics are basic realities present in all organisations.

Power can be described as the ability to control the way things happen. Formal authority, on the other hand, refers to the right to seek or obtain compliance — that is, legitimate power.

In organisations, therefore, the element of power lies in the ability which some people have to exert control over or influence the behaviour or decisions of others.

When people use their power to influence others in order to achieve their own ends (which are often in conflict with the goals of the organisation) we talk of organisational politics.

People who play "power games" in organisations often form political coalitions as informal organisational groups, banding together in order to influence decisions so that they can get their own way. Sometimes these groupings are in conflict within the organisation, leading to counterproductive power struggles.

Empire building takes place when one or more persons decide to gain more power by increasing their influence and role within the organisation. So, for example, the head of an HR department may decide to work deliberately towards gaining greater control over aspects such as budgets and other areas of decision making within the organisation by building up the HR department to an indispensable, vital organisational resource area.

In other areas of HRM, politics and power can also play an important role. People are, for example, often recruited and employed purely because the manager knows that they will support him/her in the organisation. Similarly, managers often evaluate the performance levels of subordinates more positively when they are more willing to be influenced by the superior. People can therefore be manipulated or stepped upon for selfish purposes. The same principles are often also applied in decisions over promotions and pay increases, when powerful individuals promote the interests of those who promote the image, status and role of the superiors themselves.

3.3.7 Organisational culture

As is the case with so many concepts, there is a lack of consensus amongst theorists, researchers and practitioners regarding the precise definition of organisational culture. We propose the following one:

Organisational culture can broadly be defined as the shared understanding which exists amongst organisation members (employees of all levels) regarding "the way things are done" in a particular organisation.

It basically refers to a set or system of shared features such as beliefs, values, assumptions, expectations, norms, sentiments, symbols, rituals, and so forth. For example, if "the customer is always right" is a shared value or norm in a particular retail organisation, and one of the employees at the point of sale is caught quarrelling with a customer, such an employee will not be regarded as "a good corporate citizen", and may even be disciplined.

Newly hired employees quickly begin to learn about an organisation's culture. The role played by the induction process (see also chapter 10) is of extreme importance in this regard, helping employees to understand how things are done and socialising them into the organisation's culture. Likewise, HRM practices and policies relating to aspects such as recruitment (internal versus external), career management, performance management and rewards, can play an important role in creating or facilitating a culture where a sense of belonging, commitment and cohesiveness is shared. During the employment process it is thus important to ensure that those people selected for entry level positions have personal value systems which are compatible with the organisation's culture. In addition, performance appraisal and reward systems must be devised and applied in a way which can foster the culture necessary for the achievement of organisational objectives.

3.4 MEASUREMENT

3.4.1 General

From sections 3.2 and 3.3 in this chapter it should be quite clear that, due to all the variables, the task of establishing an optimal fit between individual employees and organisations can be quite a daunting one. Over the years human behaviour scientists have conducted extensive research into the improvement of this fit through scientific measurements. To this end the issues of *measurement* and *testing* have come to play an important role in the work of HR specialists such as industrial psychologists and psychometrists. The scope of this book does not allow for an in-depth discussion of these topics; in chapter 23 particular aspects relating to measurement or evaluation within the context of human resource management are analysed. At this stage a few introductory remarks regarding *measurement* will suffice.

3.4.2 The meaning of "measurement"

Most fields of human endeavour use measurement in some form and each field has its own set of measuring tools and measuring units. Units of measure with which you may be familiar include a kilometre, a metre, a kilogram, a litre, and so on. Professionals in the fields that employ these units (as well as the various tools used to obtain measurements) are well aware of the potential uses, benefits and limitations of the measuring tools that they use and the measurements that they make. So, too, it is incumbent upon the user or potential user of behavioural measurement devices to have a working knowledge of the nature of measurement and testing.

The concepts *measurement* and *test* are used here in a very broad sense.

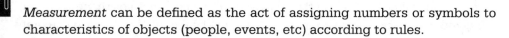

Measurement can be defined as the act of assigning numbers or symbols to characteristics of objects (people, events, etc) according to rules.

A *test* can be viewed as a special form of assessment procedure — a set of tasks or questions intended to elicit particular types of behaviour when presented under standardised conditions and to yield scores that will have desirable psychometric properties such as high reliability and validity.

Tests can be conducted in various ways, including the use of standardised aptitude and achievement instruments, diagnostic and evaluative devices, interest inventories, personality inventories, projective instruments and related denial techniques, and many kinds of personal history forms.

In your role as student (or job applicant) the nature of your relationship to various tests has probably been primarily that of a test taker. But as a researcher, psychologist or human resource manager the primary nature of your relationship with tests could well be that of a user — the person who breathes life and meaning into test scores by applying the knowledge and skill needed to interpret the scores appropriately or by using them for research purposes. Test scores are frequently expressed as numbers, and statistical tools are used to describe, make inferences, and draw conclusions about numbers.

3.4.2.1 *Matching people and organisations: Measurement applications*

The vast differences between individuals and the great variety of available jobs have led to the frequent use of expressions such as "matching people and jobs" and "round pegs in square holes" (when the match is not a good one). "Matching" becomes particularly complicated when the job setting is taken into account.

The fact that many of these matches are far from perfect is reflected in many different ways, such as in the way in which people perform their jobs (that is, in the quality of work performance), in how long people stay in their jobs, how often they are late for work, in how well people like their jobs and in how people adapt to their jobs both physically and psychologically. Let us use the word *behaviour* to describe these (and other) job-related factors. The word "behaviour" can also be used in a broader sense to cover covert, less observable factors, such as people's attitudes towards their jobs and job situations, as well as the physiological or physical effects of work. Most of these things can be measured in some way or another — that is, numerical values can be attached to these factors.

It is often necessary to measure aspects related to employees both for administrative as well as research purposes. Examples of HRM decisions where measurements are made include performance evaluations, selection, transfers, promotions and training. During the whole process of trying to ensure that people fit their positions within the organisation, various measurements can be made to quantify information on which to base decisions.

In selection, for example, choices have to be made: from a number of available candidates, one or more new employees must be chosen. Typically the selection decision is made with a view to assigning an individual to a given job. Such decisions are based on data or on judgements of the various candidates' attributes as related to the requirements of the job (see chapter 10).

Decisions about promotions (that is, the advancement of individuals to higher level jobs) and transfers (that is, shifting people to jobs on similar levels), also require some sort of measurement.

All these HRM functions require matching individuals with their work environments.

In matching individuals to their work, it is necessary to obtain personnel data relevant to the specifications of the jobs. Some of the more commonly used sources of such measurement information are personnel tests and inventories, application forms and other personal data questionnaires, interviews, etc (see chapter 10). These sources of information are used to measure aspects related to work behaviour. Thus measurements of some job-related behaviours often serve both administrative and research purposes.

3.4.3 Aspects which are measured

Most behavioural measurements are aimed at making predictions of relevant behaviour. Such predictions typically require the use (including the measurement) of two types of variables. The first of these variables, that which is being predicted, is usually called the *criterion*, and most typically characterises some type of behaviour (such as job performance, job satisfaction, etc). The other type of variable is the one used in predicting the criterion and is usually called the *predictor* (such as a test or an interview which may measure personal characteristics). The criterion is frequently called the *dependent variable* and the predictor is called the *independent variable* or *controlled variable*.

The latter concepts are used especially when it is possible to control the predictor to a certain extent and when the measure of the criterion (the dependent variable) can be attributed to the effects of the predictor (the independent variable). For example, one might study the effects of organisational culture on employees' attitudes.

3.4.4 Types of measurement scales

Numbers at different levels or scales of measurement convey different kinds of information. It is generally agreed that there are four different levels or *scales of measurement*, namely *nominal scale*, *ordinal scale*, *interval scale* and *ratio scale*.

A *nominal* (or categorical) scale is one that has two or more mutually exclusive classes or categories of the general type of variable in question, such as male and female, rural and urban. Some types of variables that vary in level are occasionally treated as nominal scales. With regard to educational level, for example, individuals might be categorised according to their highest diploma or degree.

An *ordinal* scale is used to characterise the rank order of some variable of individual cases in a sample, such as the rankings of a group of employees according to job performance or the ranking of jobs to pay level.

In an *interval* scale the individual cases have numbers associated with them, and these numbers are significant in that any given numerical difference, anywhere along the scale, theoretically represents an equal difference in the underlying variable. The scale has no absolute zero. Many tests of human attributes and abilities, at least theoretically, are examples of interval scales. With a properly developed test of numerical ability, for example, the difference between a score of 70 and 75 presumably would represent the same difference in numerical ability as would the difference between 80 and 85.

A *ratio scale* is one in which the individual cases have numerical values that, like the interval scale, represent equal differences in the variable being measured. In contrast with the interval scale, however, the ratio scale does have an absolute zero and could probably be best illustrated by variables of physical measurements. One could think, for instance, of measuring the levels of absenteeism in an organisation. Zero will be a meaningful measurement because it is indeed possible to have no absenteeism over a set period of time.

3.4.5 Describing data: Some concepts

Suppose that you are a human resource manager who has just given trainees an examination that consists of 100 multiple-choice items (where one point is awarded for each correct answer). The scores for the 25 students enrolled in your class could theoretically range from 0 (none correct) to 100 (all correct). Assume that it is the day after the examination and you are sitting in your office with the data. One of your tasks is to communicate the test results to your class in such a way that each individual trainee will be able to relate his/her performance in the test to the results obtained by all the other members of the class. How do you accomplish this objective?

You might begin by setting up a *distribution* of the raw scores to help you compare the performance of one student with that of another. In a *frequency* distribution all the possible scores are listed alongside the number of times each score occurred.

In this way, distributions can be described in terms of characteristics such as their *central tendency*, *variability*, *skewness* and *correlation*.

3.4.5.1 Central tendency

Measures of *central tendency* are indices of the central value or location of a frequency distribution. The centre of a distribution can be defined in different ways. Perhaps the most commonly used measure of central tendency is the *arithmetic mean*, referred to in everyday language as the "average". The arithmetic mean, denoted by the symbol $\overline{X}$, is equal to the sum of the observations (or test scores in this case) divided by the number of observations. The *median* is another commonly used measure of central tendency. It is defined as the middle score in a distribution. Suppose that the ICM Corporation has a requirement that all of its clerks be able to do word processing at a rate of 50 words per minute (with total accuracy). Suppose further that the personnel office of this company has a policy of testing job applicants' word-processing speed on seven different days before making any determination as to employment. The word-processing scores in words per minute for applicant Kathy, follow. If you were the personnel officer, would you hire her?

| 52 | 55 | 39 | 56 | 35 | 50 | 54 |

If you were to obtain the arithmetic mean for this distribution of scores, the resulting figure is below 50. Thus, if the company's policy was routinely to take an average of typing-test scores and to reject people whose average score did not meet the minimum of 50 words per minute, Kathy would have to be eliminated from further consideration. However, if you as the personnel officer had some discretion, you might have used the median and not the mean as the preferred measure of central tendency in this situation. You would have then grouped these scores from highest to lowest and located the middle score in the distribution:

35	
39	
50	
52	(the middle score)
54	
55	
56	

If Kathy's résumé looked good in all respects, if the company needed to hire clerks immediately or for any other good reason, a decision to hire Kathy could be justified by the use of the median as the measure of central tendency — in this case, as a measure of Kathy's typing ability. The median may well be the most appropriate measure to use with such a distribution of scores. On the days when Kathy's score was in the 30s, she may not have been feeling well, the typewriter used for the test may not have been operating properly, or other factors could have influenced the score. Technically, while the mean is the preferred measure of central tendency for symmetrical distributions, the median is the preferred measure for skewed distributions.

The most frequently occurring score in a distribution of scores is the *mode*. Despite the fact that the mode is not calculated and is not necessarily a unique point in a distribution (a distribution can have two, three, or even more modes), the mode can be useful in conveying certain types of information. For example, suppose that you wanted an estimate of the number of journal articles published by HR managers in South Africa in the last year. To arrive at this figure, you might total the number of journal articles by each HR manager in South Africa which have been accepted for publication, divide by the number of HR managers, and arrive at the arithmetic mean — an indication of the average number of journal articles published. Whatever that number turns out to be, we can say with certainty that it will be more than the mode: it is well known that most HR managers do not write journal articles; therefore, the mode for publications by HR managers in any given year is zero. The mode in this instance provides useful information in addition to the mean because it tells us that no matter what the figure is for the average number of publications, the fact remains that most HR managers do not publish.

Because the mode is not calculated in the true sense, it is a nominal statistic and cannot legitimately be used in further calculations. The median is a statistic that takes into account the order of scores and is, itself, ordinal in nature. The mean is the most stable and generally the most useful measure of central tendency, and it is an interval statistic.

3.4.5.2 Variability

Variability is an indication of how scores in a distribution are scattered or dispersed. The *variance* is a widely used measure, particularly with respect to a statistical technique called analysis of variance (wherein two or more sets of measurements are analysed for the presence of significant differences between them). To make meaningful interpretations, the test score distribution should be approximately normal, which means that the greatest frequency of scores occurs near the arithmetic mean and correspondingly fewer and fewer scores relative to the mean occur on both sides of it as scores differ from the mean.

The *standard deviation* is one very useful measure of variability since each individual score's distance from the mean of the distribution is employed in its computation.

3.4.5.3 Skewness

Distributions can be characterised in terms of their *skewness*, or the nature and extent to which symmetry is absent. Skewness is another indication of how the measurements in a distribution are distributed. A distribution is said to be skewed positively when relatively few of the scores fall at the positive end of the distribution. Results from an examination that are positively skewed may indicate that the test was too difficult; it would have been better to have included a number of easier questions. A distribution is said to be skewed negatively when relatively few of the scores fall at the negative end of the distribution. Results from an examination that are negatively skewed may indicate that the test was too easy; in such an instance, a number of more difficult questions should have been included.

3.4.5.4 Correlation

An understanding of the concept of *correlation* is fundamental to the study of measurement within the context of human behaviour.

An important aspect of measurement in the field of HRM concerns specialists' attempts to find out how some things (such as traits, abilities or interests) are related to other things (such as behaviour or work performance).

A coefficient of correlation is the number that provides us with an index of the strength of the relationship between two things.

The meaning of a correlation coefficient is interpreted by its sign (positive or negative — indicative of a positive or negative correlation) and by its magnitude (the greater its absolute value, the greater the degree of relatedness). A correlation coefficient can range in value from +1 to –1. If a correlation coefficient is –1, this means that the relationship between the two variables is perfectly negative, without error in the statistical sense. Perfect correlations are difficult to find (just as perfection in almost every field of endeavour is difficult, if not impossible). If a correlation is zero, then no linear relationship exists between the two variables. If two variables simultaneously increase or simultaneously decrease, these two variables could be said to be positively (or directly) correlated. The height and weight of normal, healthy children ranging in age from birth to 10 years of age tends to be positively or directly correlated; as children get older, their height and weight generally increase simultaneously. A positive correlation also exists when two variables simultaneously decrease (for example, the less preparation a student does for an examination, the lower the score in the examination). A negative (or inverse) correlation occurs when one variable increases while the other variable decreases. For example, there tends to be an inverse relationship between the number of miles on your car's odometer (kilometre indicator) and the number of rands a used-car dealer is willing to give you as a trade-in; all other things being equal, as the kilometres increase, the number of rands offered as a trade-in decreases.

The term *correlation* is often confused with *causation*. It must be emphasised that a correlation coefficient is simply an index of the relationship between two variables, not an index of the causal relationship between two variables. If you were told, for example, that from birth to age 5 there is a high positive correlation between hat size and measurable intelligence, would it be appropriate to conclude that hat size causes intelligence? Of course not; this is a time of maturation in all areas, including development in cognitive and motor abilities, as well as growth in physical size. Thus, while intellectual development parallels physical development in these years and while it is true that a relationship clearly exists between physical and mental growth, it is not necessarily a causal relationship.

While correlation does not imply causation, there is an implication of prediction. In other words, if we know that there is a high correlation between X and Y, we should be able to predict — with varying degrees of accuracy, depending on other factors — the value of one of these variables if we know the value of the other.

3.5 OUTCOMES RELATED TO CREATING THE NECESSARY FIT

The purpose of human resource management, from the perspective of a system's approach to management, must at the end of the day always be to add value to the organisation's overall success. The actual value added will thus depend largely on the quality of the match or fit that is established between the employees, their work, the organisation, the environment, etc — through human resource management. Human resource management that is not of an appropriate quality may even lead to a decrease in value. In other words, poor quality HRM may contribute in a negative sense to the downfall, failure or destruction of an organisation.

The idea of measurement in a business sense is to be able to monitor how well an organisation performs. It has traditionally been in the marketing and financial fields that managers have measured the wellness or state of health of organisations. This has always been (and still is) done through the measurement of aspects such as market share, turnover, profit levels, etc. When it comes to the organisation's HR subsystem there are also many measurements that can be taken to evaluate or monitor the quality of the match or fit between the organisation's HR system and the rest of the organisation. As has already been mentioned, we will be taking a more in-depth look at certain measurements in chapter 23. At this stage the various aspects or dimensions that can be looked at (or measured) to monitor the quality of that match or fit will be briefly examined. These basically refer to the different *outcomes* of human resource management — the consequences of the type and quality of the fit or match that is achieved.

The first order outcome relates to the extent of overall employee satisfaction with their employment relationships. If employees are essentially satisfied with the management of their employment relationships, this triggers off a chain reaction that may result in their making fewer mistakes, having fewer accidents, attending work more regularly, being more loyal, committed and positive, filing fewer grievances, misbehaving less, and generally improving their work performance and being more productive. This can result in the provision of better quality products/services by the organisation, which in turn should lead to increased customer satisfaction, an expanding customer base and thus a greater market share, meaning more competitiveness and a generally more successful organisation.

On the other hand, if — because of below-standard HRM practice — there is greater dissatisfaction or unhappiness with the match or fit that is achieved in the employment relationship, the reverse of the above chain reaction may follow as a natural consequence. The final outcome could be a less successful organisation or even perhaps the outright failure of the organisation.

All of these different levels or orders of outcomes can be measured. Employee satisfaction levels can be gauged or monitored by scrutinising symptomatic indicators such as labour turnover, absenteeism rates, grievances, disciplinary cases, accident rates, theft, sabotage incidents, etc. The attitudes and/or opinions of employees with regard to various aspects related to employee satisfaction can even be researched by means of what is commonly known as attitude surveys.

Employees who are generally dissatisfied or unhappy with their employment relationships may show behavioural patterns that signal work withdrawal. Employees may engage in open conflict with superiors/management in order to try to remove the causes of their dissatisfaction. This may include the filing of grievances, declaring disputes or even serious collective action that disrupts the workplace, such as strikes or other forms of industrial action. If these efforts do not help, employees may show other forms of work withdrawal behaviour.

Employee work withdrawal behaviour can take on many different forms. At the level of psychological withdrawal, employees become detached or disinterested in their work and in the organisation. Factors such as diminished loyalty and commitment levels are indicative of psychological level withdrawal. There can, however, also be physical work withdrawal. Going on strike is an example of this. Another example is that of poor timekeeping, being away from the physical work station often. This may include absenteeism and resignations (employee turnover). Absenteeism is one particularly important form of physical work withdrawal — and in many South African organisations absenteeism has become a major problem.

Absenteeism in essence refers to the fact that an employee has failed to be at work as scheduled. This may involve either voluntary or involuntary absenteeism. The important aspect is that it is unscheduled — in other words, it does not concern pre-arranged or scheduled vacation or holiday leave, attending events elsewhere, etc. Involuntary forms of absenteeism include sick leave due to illness. Voluntary absenteeism results when there is no valid excuse for not being at work. Irrespective of whether it is voluntary or involuntary, the employee is physically not there to do the work — and this costs money. It must be remembered that sometimes even poor health — that is, a valid form of absenteeism — may partly be due to HRM-related deficiencies, such as when employees develop work stress related diseases or occupational or mental health problems (see chapter 19). In this sense, then, it is not always that easy to draw absolute distinctions between physical and psychological work withdrawal behaviour. And, as has already been mentioned, employee satisfaction levels that influence withdrawal behaviour patterns can be the consequence of various factors or variables inside or outside the organisation's HRM subsystem. From a management perspective it is therefore important, as a starting point, to 'measure' (monitor) work withdrawal such as absenteeism. This is not enough however. The underlying causes have to be researched.

The causes of employee dissatisfaction may lie primarily within the employee him/herself, or within the immediate physical work environment of the employee. Dissatisfaction may also stem from the social work environment — that is, the interaction between people at work — or it may result from any of the organisa-tional variables discussed earlier in this chapter. The general level of satisfaction will essentially be a consequence of the extent to which the necessary fit or match has been established between the employees, their work, and the organisation's internal and external environments. The basic purpose of HRM must always be to create the most optimal fit or match between an organisation and its employees in order to help ensure the success of the organisation.

3.6   CONCLUSION

In chapter 1 it was shown that HRM can be viewed as an interventionary process aimed at establishing, as far as possible, an optimal fit or match between individ-uals and their employing organisations. In this chapter you were introduced to the complex dynamics which relate both to people as individuals who come to the workplace and to employing organisations as complex social entities. It was shown that many variables can affect either of the two parties to the employment relation-ship and thus can influence the quality of this match or fit. Measurements of var-ious types can be utilised by managers to make better decisions regarding the management of human resources. You were thus also introduced very briefly to the concept of *measurement* and the role that it can play in HRM and in the process of matching people and their employing organisations.

SELF-EVALUATION QUESTIONS

1. "Demographic variables hold no implications for human resource manage-ment."

   Comment critically on the above statement and use illustrations to substantiate your arguments.

2. "People tend to 'see' things differently and this holds implications for human resource management."

   Is this true or false? Why do you think so? Use examples to illustrate that you understand.

3. Differentiate between the role of aptitudes, abilities and skills in matching people, their work and organisations.

4. Explain what you understand by the concept *personality*. Also explain the importance of an understanding of this concept for human resource manage-ment.

5. Differentiate between *values* and *attitudes* and explain the implications thereof for HRM.

6. Think of the possible differences between married and unmarried persons as far as the work environment is concerned. Can you think of any and can you explain, with the aid of examples, what the HRM implications could be?

7. Think of the cultural diversity of the South African population. Do you think that aspects relating to language and/or religious differences can influence HRM in South African organisations? Why/why not? Explain by means of illustrations.

8. Explain how the goals, strategies, structures and decision-making processes in organisations interplay with aspects of human resource management.

9. Describe what you understand by "power, politics and culture in organisations". Do these organisation dynamics hold implications for the way that people in employment situations are managed? Explain.

10. What does "measurement" mean in the context of human resource management? Also differentiate the concept from "test".

11. Write critical notes on how *measurements* can be used to help match people and the organisations that seek to (or indeed do) employ them.

12. Differentiate between four different types of measurement scales.

13. Explain what the following mean in the context of "describing data" in the human resource management field:

    ○ central tendency;
    ○ variability;
    ○ skewness;
    ○ correlation.

BIBLIOGRAPHY

Brooke, PP, Russel, DW & Price, JL. 1988. Discriminant validation of measures of job satisfaction, job involvement and organizational commitment. *Journal of Applied Psychology*, 73, 139–145

Human, L & Allie, F. 1988. Attitudes of white English-speaking male managers to the advancement of women in business. *South African Journal of Labour Relations*, 12(2), 49–50

Human, P & Hofmeyr, K. 1987. Attitudes of South African managers to the advancement of blacks in business. *South African Journal of Labour Relations*, 11(3), 5–19

Kruger, GPN & Human, LN. 1990. The attitudes of skilled and semiskilled white and Indian workers to one another and to the advancement of Africans in the sugar milling industry in South Africa. *South African Journal of Labour Relations*, 14(4), 29

Locke, EA. 1976. The nature and causes of job satisfaction. In *Handbook of Industrial and Organizational Psychology*, ed MD Dunnetti. Chicago: Rand McNally

Miner, JB. 1985. *People Problems: The Executive Answer Book*. Chicago: Rand McNally

Mourday, RT, Porter, LW & Steers, RM. 1982. *Employee-Organization Linkages: The Psychology of Commitment, Absenteeism and Turnover*. New York: Academic Press

Pinder, CC. 1984. *Work Motivation: Theory, Issues and Applications.* Glenview, Illinois: Scott, Foresman

Smit, GJ. 1991. *Psigometrika: Aspekte van Toetsgebruik: Pretoria:* HAUM

Spates, JL. 1983. The sociology of values. *Annual Review of Sociology,* 9, 27–49

Steers, RM & Porter, LW. 1991. *Motivation and Work Behaviour.* New York: McGraw-Hill Book Company

Sterns, PL & Spector, PE. 1987. Relationships of organizational frustration with reported behavioural reactions. The moderating effect of locus of control. *Journal of Occupational Psychology.* 60, 227–234

Wiener, Y, Vardi, Y & Muczyk, I. 1981. Antecedents of employees' mental health — The role of career and work satisfaction. *Journal of Vocational Behaviour,* 19, 50–60

chapter 4 The Macrocontext of Human Resource Management in South Africa

◎ STUDY OBJECTIVES

After studying this chapter, you should be able to:

- briefly explain the variables and changing trends at a global level that may impact on human resource management in South Africa;
- explain the trends and variables in South Africa's broader social, political and economic environment that hold implications for managing people employed by South African organisations;
- describe how the South African economy rates internationally and how this relates to human resource management;
- provide an in-depth discussion of the problems related to inequality in South Africa, and the resultant implications for human resource management;
- give a broad overview of South African labour market dynamics;
- identify the sources of legal rules governing the employment relationship and understand the relationship between them;
- identify the relationship arising from the common-law contract of employment and distinguish it from other types of legal relationships;
- prove basic knowledge of the topics governed by the Labour Relations Act 66 of 1995;
- have a basic understanding of minimum standards legislation and welfare legislation in South Africa.

4.1 INTRODUCTION

In the previous chapter the focus was on the organisation as the unit where human resource management takes place, from the perspective of management. As explained, no organisation exists in isolation and human resource management at the organisational level must thus be contextualised in terms of the external environment in which any organisation operates. Although this macro-external environment constantly changes, it is important to establish some framework of issues that may have an impact on the way one manages people in employment situations. The emphasis in this chapter is therefore on the **wider context**; this means that the immediate contextual factors of the human resource subsystems of organ-

isations — in other words, the internal organisational variables (such as organisations' financial, operations and marketing subsystems) — are not dealt with. In
this chapter the focus is on the broader environment — outside the organisation —
those factors, variables and forces that surround, affect, influence and impact on
the human dimension of management in about all South African organisations.
The perspective of an open system is thus taken further by scanning trends and
variables in the social, economic, political and technological environment. A substantial part of the chapter is therefore devoted to legislative aspects impacting on
human resource management.

The point of departure is, however, that South Africa is part of an even wider
system, namely the international, global system.

4.2   VARIABLES AND CHANGE AT A GLOBAL LEVEL

One can safely say that the world is in the midst of multifaceted and revolutionary
change. From the perspective of world politics and international power relations,
an era has dawned where generally the world over there is a rapidly growing appreciation and acceptance of more democratic systems. The oppressive, authoritarian
and communistic systems that were common for a long period in the world's history have been making way for democracies. A shift has been taking place from a
largely bipolar world order towards a multipolar order.

For many years the United States of America (USA) and the Soviet Union, as the
two world "superpowers" with their distinctive systems of free enterprise and state
socialism respectively, have taken centre stage in debates over world politics and
economics. Instead of this bipolar order we now have a situation where different
power blocs are developing. Not only did the Soviet Union collapse soon after the
fall of the Berlin Wall and the reunification of East and West Germany but a con-
federation of major European countries, the European Economic Community
(EEC), was formed, and a gradual shift of economic power towards the East Asian
bloc has also taken place. It has been estimated, for instance (De Villiers & Slabbert
1996), that over the period 1992 to 2000, 40 % of new purchasing power in the world
will come from East Asia. Furthermore, with the relative declining prominence of
the USA, the conclusion of the North American Free Trade Agreement (NAFTA)
has resulted in the formation of a North American trade bloc consisting of the USA,
Mexico and Canada.

There has thus been a gradual shift away from power dynamics in the military
sense towards economic-driven power relations.

Simultaneously with these trends in international relations and the world
politico-economic order, a revolution has been taking place in the field of technology. This is true especially in the field of information and communication technology. The move from the industrial age into the information age has resulted in
an almost boundaryless world with individuals, businesses, governments, etc
becoming more and more interconnected through computers and on-line systems

like the Internet. Information flow and distance have become crucial variables in transactions between countries and organisations. Revolutionary technological developments have thus created the foundation for more free trade and for faster moving economic transactions and systems across the globe.

A more open and global world order has thus come into existence. Due to these advances in communication technology, the abilities of governments to control information (and thus their sovereignty) have been curtailed quite severely. Because of these and other developments — such as the establishment of economic blocs and more free trade between nations, which has been further facilitated by developments such as the establishment of the World Trade Organisation (WTO) — it is becoming increasingly difficult for governments to retain control over information and money flows, thus impacting negatively on their ability to maintain systems of nation-state sovereignty.

All of this and a host of other complex, multifaceted developments, such as the trend towards the formation of regional and subregional trade blocs, is making for a whole new global village where the internationalisation of markets is commonplace. New markets arise with the concomitant potential to compete across boundaries. Companies are setting up operations in other countries and entering into business alliances outside their home countries. Thus South African organisations now have to compete not only with the providers of products and services from other countries on our local markets but they can also compete with others in markets within other countries. Similarly, our business leaders have to decide whether or not they are interested in setting up operations beyond the boundaries of South Africa. In this competitive world economy the managements of organisations thus have constantly to seek ways of improving their performance in order to survive. So-called total quality and world-class manufacturing systems have thus come to the forefront, all of which place new demands on the management of employment relationships. Within this context of global competition and free trade, countries are tied via their business economic structures, into a game of vigorous competition for foreign investment to stimulate growth. At the same time (or rather as a result of this), labour has become a more fluid production factor in what can almost be termed a global labour market.

Due to factors such as increased competition, the accelerated pace at which economies (and thus organisations) have to operate, the free flow of money, information, products and people, the wave of high-tech developments, as well as the general trend towards more democratic value systems, the world of work and human resource management in South Africa is faced with a multitude of complex challenges and forces.

4.3 SOUTH AFRICA'S SOCIOPOLITICAL ECONOMY: VARIABLES, TRENDS AND CHALLENGES

4.3.1 General

As indicated above, the challenges and complexities facing South Africa cannot be separated from broader international developments. For South Africa to survive in this international war of competition, tremendous efforts will be required from all its citizens, especially the stakeholders of the organisations that deliver the goods. A major challenge in this regard is the need to balance the inherent intricacies and tensions which have resulted from our history of gross unfair discrimination and inequality with the need to stimulate and develop the economy.

The point of departure for any country's economy is, apart from its natural resources, its **people**. The people of any country make the difference between success or failure. Demographic statistics cannot, however, be detached from the circumstances within which the people of the country live and make a living.

South Africa's complex sociopolitical-economic setup is founded today to a large extent on the history of the country. Reference to our history (see chapter 2) shows clearly that the legacies of the apartheid system have permeated all aspects of our lives. The pressures and demands facing South Africa in a global economy — where competitiveness is the watchword — must be seen against the background of the major threat (or challenge) to our country: the problem of **inequality**.

Although South Africa's single major objective may be to stimulate the economy in order to create the means to improve the quality of life of all the country's inhabitants, the real problem that we face is that of the gross socio-economic inequality in our society. Reconciling these two dynamic realities (inequality and growth) embodies one of the greatest challenges facing the country.

Whereas some parties (like organised labour) are fighting to eradicate the socio-economic inequalities through strategies aimed at wealth redistribution, captains of business and industry are adamant that, in order to enrich the traditionally deprived, wealth has first to be created. To them creating wealth means but one thing: business organisations have to become competitive in international terms. This may mean adopting measures to cut costs, to become "lean and mean" which may entail, inter alia, cutting labour costs and improving labour productivity. To the deprived the immediate objective is to get that which was traditionally kept/taken away from them. The essence of the debate thus concerns what comes first: wealth creation or wealth redistribution? This dynamic tension boils over directly into the relations between the parties in the workplace.

4.3.2 Social and demographic dynamics

Because the human resources of a country are so crucially important, we begin by focusing briefly on some important demographic and social factors.

4.3.2.1 The South African population

It is estimated that the South African population has nearly doubled during the period 1970–1994, with a total population of more than 40 million in 1994 — almost the same as that of Spain. More than 75 % of the total South African population are African (black), with approximately 13 % white, 8,5 % coloured and less than 3 % Asian. Our population growth rate is high and some project that our population will have reached between 53 and 60 million by the year 2010. Structural changes in age distribution suggest that the proportion of young blacks in our population is increasing whereas the white population is ageing (see table 4.1).

Table 4.1
South Africa's population: Future projections*

Year	Asians	Blacks	Coloureds	Whites	Total
Population in millions with % of total in brackets					
1995	1,04 (3 %)	31,44 (76 %)	3,48 (8 %)	5,17 (13 %)	41,13
2001	1,12 (2 %)	35,92 (78 %)	3,77 (8 %)	5,32 (12 %)	46,13
2006	1,18 (2 %)	39,70 (79 %)	4,00 (8 %)	5,40 (11 %)	50,28
2016	1,27 (2 %)	47,02 (81 %)	4,38 (8 %)	5,43 (9 %)	58,11
2026	1,32 (2 %)	53,37 (83 %)	4,62 (7 %)	5,34 (8 %)	64,65
Aged under 15 years as % of total population[1]					
1995	28,7	38,0	31,8	21,4	35,2
2006	23,7	35,1	26,3	18,6	32,4
2016	20,6	30,8	22,5	15,8	28,6
2026	17,2	26,4	18,4	14,5	24,7
Aged 15 to 64 years as % of total population[2]					
1995	67,5	58,3	64,8	69,1	60,4
2006	70,0	60,9	69,1	69,8	62,7
2016	69,6	64,4	71,2	68,8	65,4
2026	69,2	67,1	71,5	66,2	67,4
Aged 65 years and older as % of total population[3]					
1995	3,8	3,6	3,4	9,5	4,4
2006	6,3	4,0	4,6	11,6	4,9
2016	9,8	4,7	6,4	15,4	6,0
2026	13,6	6,5	10,1	19,3	7,9

[1] A relatively large number of young people in the population will put pressure on parents' personal income and public funds

[2] Economically active section of the population falls in the category that will gradually become bigger with serious consequences for unemployment.

[3] Note the greater number of whites who will be older than 65 with implications particularly for pensions and sick funds.

*Source: Institute for Future Research, US. In *Finansies en Tegniek* (1996:19).

There is furthermore a discernible trend towards the urbanisation of the South African population (see table 4.2)

Table 4.2
*South African population estimates and projections**

	1995	2000	2011
Metropolitan	16,5 m	18,7 m	23,7 m
Cities and large towns	3,6 m	4,1 m	5,2 m
Small towns	3,3 m	3,7 m	4,5 m
Rural	17,8 m	18,9 m	20,7 m
TOTALS	41,2 m	45,4 m	54,1 m

*Source: Centre for Development and Enterprise (CDE) 1995: 10

According to Cloete (1996), the Institute for Future Research (IFR) at the University of Stellenbosch singles out food production, water resources, education, housing and health services as those areas most threatened by the population explosion (see table 4.1).

As far as food production is concerned, too large a population creates the problem of having to produce more food on existing agricultural land. At present only 10,7 % of the total surface of the country is devoted to agriculture.

With regard to water resources, the IFR points out that there has always been a shortage in South Africa. It is estimated that South Africa will be without sufficient water between 2020 and 2030 — unless drastic steps are taken. Approximately 88 % of all fresh water is used by the agricultural and industrial sectors, which leaves only 12 % for domestic use. Domestic consumption is expected to increase sharply in future.

Together with this, the agricultural sector will have to increase food production 1,5 times between now and 2026 in order to feed an additional 23 million people. This will put further pressure on water resources.

As for education, the IFR estimates that the total schoolgoing population will grow from 11,6 million to 12,6 million in the year 2001 and to 13,4 million in the year 2006. An average annual increase of 164 000 pupils is thus expected, which will mean that about 330 schools with an average of 500 pupils will have to be built annually.

As had already been mentioned, one of South Africa's key problems is the gross socioeconomic inequality that characterises society. A large proportion of our population is very poor. Some estimates indicate that the poorest 40 % of South African households earn less than 6 % of total income, whereas the richest 10 % earn more than 50 % of total income (De Villiers & Slabbert 1996: 47).

With regard to housing, the IFR says that it is almost impossible to meet the demand. The current backlog is already 3 million units, while the population is expected to increase from 41,1 million in 1995 to approximately 46,1 million in 2001.

In respect of health services, it is calculated that up to the year 2006, 710 doctors and 2 969 nurses will have to be trained annually. That does not take retirement, deaths and emigration into account. In respect of AIDS and HIV there is still a great deal of debate regarding facts and figures. Some estimate that the epidemic is growing at a faster rate in South Africa than in most other African countries, and that 7,57 % of the South African population was HIV positive in 1994. Over the next six to ten years up to 10 million more people could be infected (De Villiers & Slabbert 1996: 52; Barker 1995).

Other important characteristics of the South African society include: high rates of crime and violence; high expectations and growing impatience for drastic improvements in quality of life by most; and a fear of losing everything by others. There are still feelings of mistrust and uncertainty and racist attitudes continue to thrive as the country moves through a major transitional phase. Tensions between reconciliation and nation building on the one hand and retribution and dissent on the other have become increasingly apparent (De Villiers & Slabbert 1996).

While the rest of the world thus continues to progress and develop at a dramatic pace, South Africans are spending a great deal of energy, time and resources focusing on the past. As can be seen, the current situation in our country has created a very complex external environment — impacting on the management of human resources within our organisations. Some other external factors relate to economic dynamics.

4.3.3 Some socio-economic dynamics

4.3.3.1 The South African economy in a global context

The performance of the South African economy must be evaluated against the ultimate aim of economic policy, namely to improve the welfare of the population at large. Competitiveness is central to this and is defined by Landau (1992) as follows: "what we should mean by competitiveness, and thus the principal goal of our economic policy, is the ability to sustain in a global economy, an acceptable growth in the real standard of living of the population with an acceptable fair distribution, while efficiently providing employment for substantially all who can and wish to work". The per capita gross domestic product (GDP) is normally used as a measure of standard of living.

Exhibit A

South African standard of living*

In 1970 South Africa was ranked thirty-third in the world in terms of its standard of living according to the WEFA Group. The country's position subsequently deteriorated to forty-fourth in 1980, fifty-seventh in 1990 and sixty-second in 1995.

*Liebenberg 1996: 5

Figure 4.1 compares South Africa's per capita GDP with that of five other countries (USA, United Kingdom (UK), Taiwan, China and Chile), using purchasing power parity (PPP) exchange rates. The graph shows that South Africa's per capita GDP remained almost constant between 1980 and 1995. Of all the countries in the graph only China registered a lower economic standard of living than South Africa in 1980, but managed to catch up with South Africa in 1995.

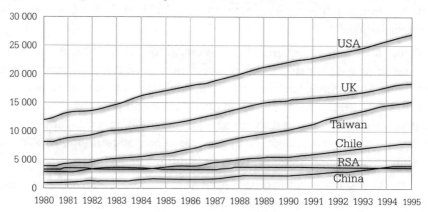

Figure 4.1
Nominal per capita GDP at purchasing power parity, US$

Although the developed countries started off from a much higher level in 1980, they all managed to increase their economic standard of living even further, while South Africa's remained at the same level. The United States is still the country with the highest per capita GDP in the world, followed by Switzerland and Japan.

The growth in per capita GDP or average standard of living has two basic components — the economic growth rate and the population growth rate. Reference has already been made to the latter.

Between 1980 and 1995 the South African economy registered an average annual growth rate of only 1,1 % per annum, whereas the population increased by an average of 2,4 % per annum (see figure 4.2). South Africa's high population growth rate requires an economic growth rate of at least 3,5 % per annum to increase the average economic standard of living by only 1 % per annum. South Africa thus cannot rely only on a higher GDP growth rate in order to obtain a higher standard of living — a lower population growth rate seems to be equally important. A complicating factor in this regard is the high level and growth of immigration (both legal and illegal) from other African countries (particularly in Southern Africa).

Per capita GDP figures serve only as indicators of average living standards and do not reflect the *distribution of income*. The crucial importance of this aspect has been referred to many times already. Let us take a closer look at this issue.

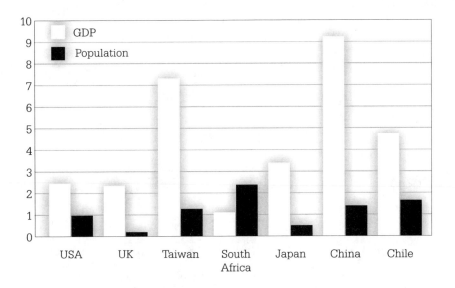

Figure 4.2

GDP and population growth rates 1985–1995

4.3.3.2 Inequalities in income and status in South Africa

As indicated earlier, recent research conducted by the Human Sciences Research Council (HSRC) and the University of Natal indicates that the poorest 40 % of households in South Africa earn less than 6 % of total income, while the richest 10 % earn in excess of half the total income (De Villiers & Slabbert 1996: 47). The average income of the richest 20 % of households is 45 times higher than the average income of the poorest 20 %. In 1993 total personal income amounted to R279 840 million, of which less than 30 % accrued to Africans, despite the fact that they account for more than three-quarters of the population. The per capita income of whites was more than 12 times that of Africans.

The most popular indicator of income inequality is the Gini coefficient, which varies between 0 (perfect equality) and 1 (perfect inequality). South Africa's estimated figure of 0,68 for 1993 was one of the highest recorded in the world. While international comparisons of income distribution are not conducted regularly and are subject to various data problems and other sources of error, the 1993 estimate for the total population remains one of the highest ever recorded (see figure 4.3).

The workers who are employed and who comprise the labour force are typically not part of that group of the population who receive half of the country's income. Instead they have to support the poorest 40 % of households. Policies aimed at employment equity thus gain their urgency from the deep inequalities that rend our society. As mentioned, income distribution in South Africa ranks among the most unequal in the world. An unusually small share of the national income goes to the majority of the population. In that context, black people, and especially black women, are clustered at the bottom, while most whites appear at higher income

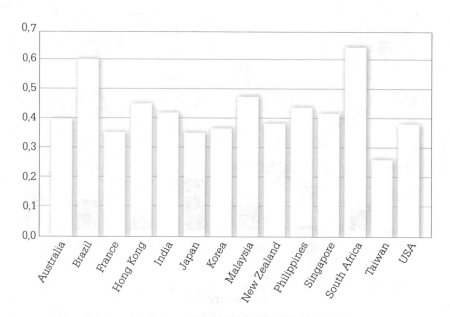

Figure 4.3

International comparison of Gini coefficients for various years

levels. Because of the crucial importance of this socioeconomic problem of inequity in our society, it is necessary to examine it even more closely.

Inequalities in income and status related to race and gender

Differences in income and status in South African society go hand in hand with race and gender. Substantial inequalities exist between blacks and whites and between men and women, even when their occupational status and education are similar.

Statistics highlight the need to define inequalities, not in terms of race or gender, but in terms of how race and gender work together.

Tables A1 to A3 (pp 140–143 of the appendix at the end of this chapter) provide data from the *1994 October Household Survey* on incomes and occupational status by race and gender. The discussion here only identifies the key trends that emerge from these tables.

Table A1 (p 140) outlines differences in access to employment by race and gender. Black people, and especially black women, are much worse off than whites. African women alone make up one in five employees, but one in two unemployed people. In contrast, white men make up one in seven employees, but less than one in a hundred of the unemployed

Table A2 (p 141) indicates incomes for employed and self-employed people by race and gender. Almost one in three African employees earned less than R500 a month, compared to less than one in twenty whites. A third of black people earned under R500 a month, compared to under 5 % of whites. Disparities emerged even within occupational categories. Thus, in top management, only half of black people earned more than R2 000 a month, compared to three-quarters of whites. Among unskilled workers, about 2 % of black people earned over R2 000 a month, compared to over half of white men and a quarter of white women. In respect of disability and inequality, available data do not permit comparisons of the relationship between disability, income and status. Estimates suggest that 5 % to 12 % of the population are moderately to severely disabled. Only one in five disabled people is economically active, and only one in a hundred severely disabled people has a job on the open labour market. The vast majority of the disabled must depend on social pensions and family support, rather than on earned income.

Table A3 (p 143) gives a further indication of the inequities in our society, focusing on representivity in selected occupations in terms of race and gender.

The impact of inequality

Massive inequalities in income and status affect social cohesion, undermine efficiency and economic growth, and have a devastating impact on families and individuals. South Africa cannot sustain the current level of inequalities related to race and gender. Inequalities contribute to high levels of social unrest and crime, which undermine growth and development.

Extreme inequalities also have a direct effect on the economy: they are associated with inefficiencies in the labour market and consequently throughout the economy. In addition, inequalities have prevented the growth of the middle class, which has stunted domestic demand and human resource development.

Apartheid policies led to allocation and technical inefficiency. They marginalised large sections of the labour force, preventing them from engaging in directly productive and sustainable economic activities either as employees or as self-employed individuals. This resulted in an iniquitous waste of resources. Apartheid policies also artificially reduced the labour costs of the majority, and increased the cost of employing a favoured minority. As a result, employers faced higher costs for skilled and supervisory workers, while they had little incentive to improve the productivity of unskilled labour. Since employers could not easily substitute for high-cost, often poor quality protected labour, they endured substantial inefficiency at the microeconomic level.

Consistent inequalities in incomes by race and gender were associated with an unusually skew distribution of income, as table 4.3 illustrates. As a result, poverty and inequality in South Africa are worse than in most Third World countries at a similar level of productivity.

The middle 60 % of South Africans received substantially less than the norm for Third World countries, and far less than in the newly industrialising economies. This compression of the middle class limits the potential for balanced economic growth and social development.

Table 4.3

Income shares in South Africa compared with selected newly industrialising
countries according to the World Bank*

Populations are divided into five groups each, from the poorest 20 %
(group 1) to the wealthiest 20 % (group 5)

	Share (percentage) of income going to:				
	Group 1	Group 2	Group 3	Group 4	Group 5
South Africa	3	6	10	18	63
South Korea	7	12	16	22	42
Thailand	6	9	14	22	50
Singapore	5	10	15	22	49
Malaysia	5	8	12	20	53
Indonesia	9	12	16	21	42

*Source: Republic of South Africa. 1996. *Green Paper: Policy Proposals
for a New Employment and Occupational Equity Statute. Government
Gazette* no 17303, 1 July 1996, p 15. Pretoria: Government Printer

In short, the apartheid legacy distorts resource allocation in the labour market, the way in which capital and labour are combined, the relative costs of inputs, the structure of production and consumption, and the levels of savings and investment in the economy. The costs to society and to individuals remain uncountable. These inequalities have thus imposed heavy burdens on society, the economy, and individuals — and lead to major HRM challenges.

Measures for employment equity are therefore required to help to alleviate inequalities as part of a broader strategy of reconstruction and development in South Africa. Because these inequalities arise, inter alia, from discrimination in the workplace, affirmative action as a measure aimed at bringing about employment equity is a very important factor in the context of human resource management in South Africa. For this reason affirmative action is dealt with separately in the next chapter.

4.3.3.3 The South African labour market: Realities and dynamics

One of the most alarming developments in the South African economy is reflected in figure 4.4. which shows that the gap between the demand and supply of labour in South Africa has increased at an alarming rate since 1976. The labour force or economically active population (EAP) of a country represents the supply of labour in a macro sense. Since the labour force includes the number of people presenting their labour for remuneration on the labour market, whether they are employed or not, the following categories are included:

- workers in the formal sector;
- self-employed persons and employers;
- informal sector workers;
- unemployed persons.

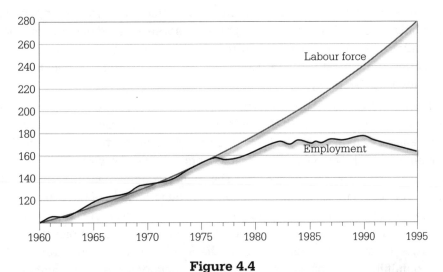

Figure 4.4

Labour force vs formal employment in South Africa, 1960–95

The EAP of South Africa is outlined in table 4.4. Although there appear to be inaccuracies in estimates of the EAP, the total EAP in South Africa for 1994 was in the region of 14,2 million.

Table 4.4

Economically active population (EAP) of South Africa*

Year	Numbers in thousands				
	Total	Asians	Blacks	Coloureds	Whites
1960[1]	5 319	121	3 585	534	1 079
1970[1]	6 989	180	4 643	694	1 381
1980[1]	9 173	254	6 213	924	1 782
1991[1]	12 944	379	8 821	1 358	2 386
1994[2]	14 227	406	9 751	1 458	2 518
1991[3]	13 599	389	9 357	1 409	2 443
1996[3]	15 794	438	11 197	1 574	2 584
2001[3]	18 118	482	13 255	1 711	2 670

	Annual growth rates				
1970–1980[1]	2,89	3,50	2,96	2,90	2,58
1980–1991[1]	3,81	3,71	3,24	3,56	2,6

Sources:
[1]Development Bank of Southern Africa
[2]Barker's own calculations
[3]Calculations by Sadie, 1994 (projections for 1996 and 2001)

*Source: Barker 1995: 31

At least 350 000 persons entered the labour market every year during the 1980s, while only about 50 000 formal job opportunities were created per annum. The consequential high unemployment can thus be attributed to factors such as a high population growth rate, a low economic growth rate and the declining labour intensity of the economy.

The measurement of unemployment presents numerous difficulties in a developing country such as South Africa, but the *October Household Surveys* provide more reliable data as from 1993. According to the 1994 survey, there were 4,7 million unemployed persons, which represents an unemployment rate of 32,6 % (among Africans the rate was 41 %). The high unemployment rate and the large number of people in the informal economy are an indication of the serious dualism that exists in the South African labour market: while one part of the labour force is employed in secure and well-paid jobs, the other part is not employed at all or is employed in low-paying insecure jobs. The South African labour market is therefore not fulfilling the objectives and economic functions of a labour market.

Functions of labour markets

According to Barker (1995), labour markets have the following two economic functions:

- the allocation of human resources among alternative users, that is, among sectors, enterprises, locations and occupations;
- the distribution of income in terms of salaries and wages — both as an incentive and to reward workers.

Labour markets should, therefore, in terms of their functions, contribute to the following objectives:

- *efficiency*, that is, maximum output and maximum income;
- *equity*, that is, equality of opportunity for all in terms of access to jobs, training, treatment at work and payment;
- *growth*, that is, labour market operations should contribute to higher productivity and incomes, as well as to improved employment in the future;
- *social justice*, that is, the extent to which society acts to minimise any negative effects the labour markets may have on workers' welfare, and to redress any harm that has been done.

An active labour market policy

The labour policies of governments in most parts of the world focused until recently on macroeconomic policies, such as the stimulation of economic growth to generate sufficient employment opportunities. The hardship arising from unemployment was then alleviated through unemployment benefits. As a consequence of the disturbing results which were obtained, the concept of active labour market policies has been developed.

The International Labour Organisation (ILO) defines *active labour market policies* as those policies which aim to improve the operation and results of labour markets so as to maximise quality employment and minimise unemployment and underemployment.

While unemployment compensation benefits can help to alleviate the hardship of job loss, active labour market policies aim at preventing unemployment or at remedying it by returning displaced workers to productive jobs.

Since the South African government's policy is rooted in a strong commitment to job creation, fair remuneration and improved working conditions, an active labour market policy will have to play an important role in reversing the negative trends of the past. Figure 4.5 shows that almost all of the formal job opportunities created in South Africa between 1985 and 1995 were in the public sector instead of the private sector. Some 340 000 more people were employed in the government sector, while jobs were lost in the rest of the economy. An important target of the government's macroeconomic strategy ('GEAR') is to create 400 000 or more jobs by the year 2000. It is intended to create these jobs in the private instead of the public sector, while the creation of Small, Medium and Micro enterprises (SMMEs) will also play an important role in providing more employment opportunities. The fact of the matter remains, however, that we have major unemployment and job security problems.

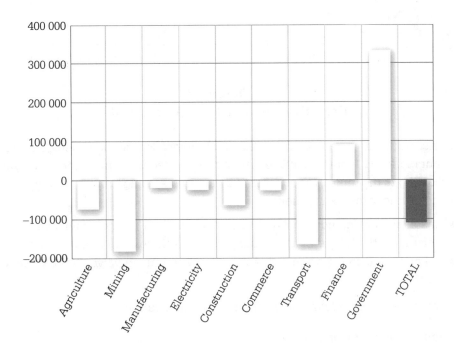

Figure 4.5

Changes in employment in the formal sector, 1985–95

Source: Liebenberg, K. 1996. *South African competitiveness monitor* 1996: Volume 3, *South African Issues* p 3. Pretoria: WEFA Group

Figure 4.6 further shows that the capital intensity of the South African economy has increased sharply over the last two decades. According to the Central Economic Advisory Services (CEAS), the South African economy became more capital intensive at a rate of 3,7 % per annum between 1969 and 1985. This means that, if the capital intensity of the economy increases at the same rate in the future, the GDP will have to grow at an average rate of 5,4 % per annum just to ensure that the new entrants to the labour force are accommodated. If the capital/labour ratio could, however, be kept constant, the economy would need to grow at only 3,7 % per annum. It is therefore in the interests of employment creation to promote more labour-intensive production.

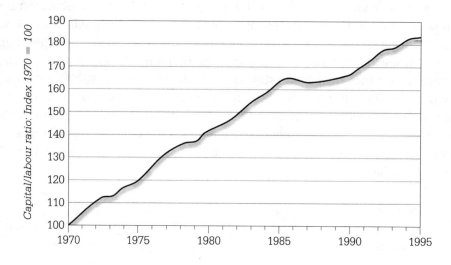

Figure 4.6
Capital intensity in South Africa, 1970–95

According to a report of the Labour Market Commission, deregulating the labour market will not be sufficient to ensure the required growth in employment. According to the report, the success of a labour-absorbing growth strategy rests on the following three requirements:

● macroeconomic, industrial and trade policies must promote employment;
● reforms in the labour market must promote both flexibility and security;
● a national accord for employment and growth must involve all the social partners.

All of these aspects clearly hold serious HRM implications.

Productivity improvement

In the longer term increasing productivity is the principal factor underlying wealth creation for a nation. This leads to higher income and a better quality of life. It must, however, be stressed that productivity is much more than simply an expression of the internal efficiency of organisations. It is invariably a social process with social constraints and incentives. Figure 4.7 shows that multifactor productivity in the private economy remained at almost the same level between 1970 and 1995. This was the net result of a labour productivity increase and a capital productivity decrease. Multifactor productivity increased by 2,6 % in 1995, with labour and capital productivity increasing by 3,1 % and 2,1 % respectively. The increase in productivity since 1992 is noteworthy.

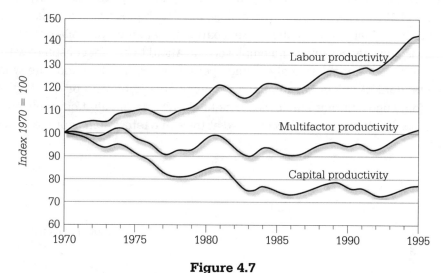

Figure 4.7
Multifactor productivity in the private economy

The capital intensity of the South African economy, as well as the declining capital productivity trend between 1970 and 1992, can to a large extent be attributed to past policies. These policies favoured large, capital-intensive investments and discriminated against labour-intensive downstream activities. The development of SMMEs (small, micro- and medium enterprises) was also restricted and an industrial policy to reverse this trend seems to be of paramount importance to ensure labour-intensive industrial development.

Productivity improvement in South Africa will depend on various factors, of which the following are important examples:

- quality of the labour force;
- management responsibilities;
- sociopolitical circumstances;
- productivity incentive schemes;
- labour market flexibility;
- management-union cooperation.

Nominal and real earnings per employee

The primary means by which labour market policies influence macroeconomic outcomes is through the wage-determination process. When nominal earnings per employee increase more rapidly than labour productivity, the result may be a more rapid rate of inflation. This rise is, however, not synonymous with nor caused solely by rising wage levels. In particular, the degree of competition in product markets is a key factor in determining whether firms are able to pass wage increases along to consumers in the form of higher prices.

Figure 4.8 shows that nominal earnings per employee increased at a much faster rate than labour productivity in the South African private economy between 1970 and 1995. There is, however, a close relationship between real earnings per employee and labour productivity. Real earnings per employee reflect the amount of goods and services which an employee can afford to buy (or consume) with his/her earnings. Changes in real earnings per employee therefore indicate whether the standard of living (consumption per person) is improving or not. Figure 4.8 therefore suggests that employees benefited only marginally from their nominal increases because inflation accelerated at the same rate, wiping out the monetary gains.

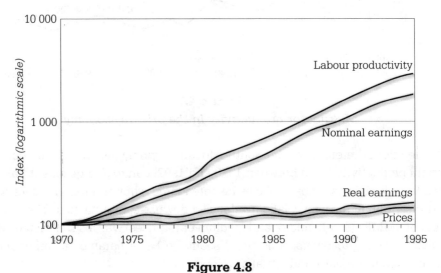

Figure 4.8
Labour productivity and earnings per employee in the private economy

Unit labour cost changes

To determine to what extent changes in labour productivity and wages have moved in tandem, a concept known as *unit labour cost* is used.

Unit labour cost can be defined as the cost of labour to produce one unit of output or the total remuneration cost per unit produced.

An increase in unit labour cost implies that the remuneration of employees is increasing more rapidly than labour productivity, and this would have a negative effect on competitiveness.

Figure 4.9 gives a clear indication of the relationship between wage increases and labour productivity, and how this impacts on unit labour cost. Unit labour costs in South Africa increased much more rapidly than they did for our main trading partners and this had a negative impact on our competitiveness. The depreciation of the rand has, however, helped to lower our unit labour costs relative to the other countries.

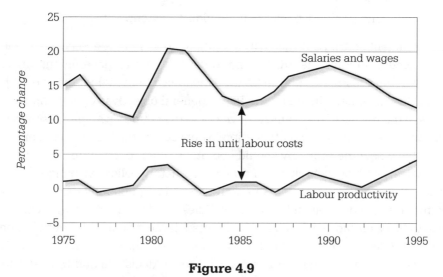

Figure 4.9
Changes in nominal earnings and labour productivity in the private economy

Although the rate of unit labour cost increases have started to decline since 1992, further reductions are desirable to increase competitiveness. Important also, is that unit labour cost increases are not caused by increases in the wage bill of blue-collar workers only, as is often claimed. Such increases are determined by a number of factors, including the level of managerial efficiency and the cost of white-collar salaries and wages. The contribution of blue-collar workers to the total wage bill differs markedly between different sectors of the economy. In mining blue-collar workers' contribution to the total wage bill is 62 % compared to the 30 % in manufacturing. Within manufacturing this contribution ranges between 50 % in footwear and 19 % in printing and publishing. Depressing unskilled wages in some sectors will therefore have a relatively small impact compared to the influence of the other determinants of unit cost, and a strategy to increase productivity and competitiveness will have to take all the relevant factors into account.

4.3.3.4 South Africa's macroeconomic strategy

Earlier we referred to South Africa's macroeconomic strategy for growth, employment and redistribution (GEAR), which was tabled in a document outlining the overall economic policy of the Government of National Unity (GNU). The objectives of this policy are to seek:

- an economy that grows fast and is competitive so that sufficient job opportunities are created for all work seekers;
- the redistribution of income and opportunities in favour of the poor;
- a society in which education and sound health as well as other social services are available to all;
- a secure and productive living and working environment.

The document setting out the GNU's strategy flows from the Reconstruction and Development Programme (RDP) and details how the government envisages rebuilding and restructuring the South African economy. While the overall policy of the GNU is largely driven by the RDP's general objectives of meeting the basic needs of the people of the country, developing the country's human resources, and increasing democracy and participation in our society, the GEAR document details specifically how the economy should operate in order to facilitate such objectives. GEAR deals with aspects such as fiscal and monetary policy, exchange rate policy, trade policy, industrial and small enterprise policy, public investment and asset restructuring, and social and sectional policies. While it is beyond the scope of this book to focus on these policy aspects in detail, it must be noted that the impact of all these policy elements on South African organisations cannot be ignored. GEAR holds definite implications for business economic decisions and thus also for the human resource side of business management. One section of GEAR deals, for instance with "employment, wages and training".

The report states that there are two important factors inherent in the labour market policy. The first of these relates to productivity improvement and it is expressly stated that wage and salary increases should not exceed average productivity growth. This, it is recognised, forms a critical cornerstone of competitiveness over the longer term. The second factor is so-called regulated flexibility of the labour market. This basically means a strategy of regulating the labour market in such a way that it allows, amongst others, for flexible collective bargaining structures, and variable application of employment standards.

The need to develop the more labour-intensive components of the economy with the aid of appropriate industrial policies is also emphasised. It is recognised that South Africa's labour market is very fragmented and that organisations tend to prefer employment relationships that are based on irregular, subcontracted, outsourced or part-time and semiformal contractual terms wherever regulations raise the costs of job creation.

The importance of a greater emphasis on training and education is also highlighted. However, throughout the document it is recognised that all the stakeholders have to be involved in the process of managing the economy. It is stated, for instance, that through the encouragement of the Department of Labour, collective bargaining arrangements will be rationalised to meet the challenges of the new socioeconomic environment. Apart from the discretion of the Minister of Labour to intervene, labour market policies ought to be negotiated between labour, business and government constituencies. In GEAR it is specifically recognised that our country has a strong tradition of collective bargaining in the industrial and broader social environment. It is therefore envisaged that a national social agreement will be drawn up between the government and the other social partners.

4.3.4 The changing political landscape in South Africa

The Government of National Unity (GNU) was formed in 1994 with the African National Congress (ANC), bolstered and supported by the major trade union federation, COSATU (Council of South African Trade Unions), as well as the SACP (South African Communist Party), as the majority party, having received 62,7 % of the votes during the April 1994 elections. The ANC is entitled to 252 seats in the National Assembly and it controls seven out of the nine provinces. The GNU is basically a power-sharing arrangement for a set period, 1994–1999. The GNU resulted from lengthy negotiations which began with the release of Nelson Mandela from prison in February 1990. The arrangement was that, during this period, power would be shared between the ANC, the National Party (NP) and the Inkatha Freedom Party (IFP). The NP received 20,4 % of the votes, which meant that it got 82 seats in the National Assembly and six ministers in Cabinet. Subsequently, the NP has withdrawn from the GNU. The IFP was entitled to 43 seats in the National Assembly as a result of receiving 10,5 % of the national vote. The country is now governed according to the principle that sovereignty no longer resides in Parliament. This essentially means that our political system now accentuates democratic values, constitutionality, human rights, accountability and greater transparency in government and society at large.

The major task of the government is thus to transform South Africa into a true democracy, ensuring equitable treatment and prosperity for all. It has already embarked on this task, a key driving force being its RDP (Reconstruction and Development Programme) and GEAR. Although a lot of progress has been made, and the final Constitution has been adopted, there are still a number of obstacles to overcome in this long road to transformation and reform. Some possible stumbling blocks include the potential effect of legacies of the past which may resurface through institutions like the Truth and Reconciliation Commission, the possibility of tension in the GNU resulting in breakdowns in political cooperation, and, in particular, tensions within the ANC/SACP/COSATU alliance. With regard to the latter it is the sphere of economic policy in particular which will require a great deal of patience, perseverance and hard work.

At the end of the day, the major challenge facing the government in the achievement of its objectives lies in the realm of economic policy. Although the overwhelming emphasis in government policy is on the people of the country, it must always be remembered that it is precisely these people who have to do the work in the organisations which form the engine of economic development. What is essentially required therefore is a balancing act — keeping everyone happy in the context of wealth creation and redistribution.

An important means to this end lies in the amendment of current legislation and in the enactment of new laws. With this in mind, not long after the GNU came into being, the Minister of Labour, Tito Mboweni, announced a five-year plan to overhaul South Africa's labour law dispensation.

The remainder of this chapter is devoted to aspects of South Africa's labour-related legislation, as this feature of the macroexternal environment has a particular and very direct impact on human resource management in our organisations.

4.4   THE LEGISLATIVE FRAMEWORK IMPACTING ON EMPLOYMENT RELATIONSHIPS

Employment relationships in South Africa are governed by many sources of law, the most important being: the common law, the contract of employment, various statutes, collective agreements entered into between employers and trade unions, international labour standards (such as, for example, the various Conventions of the International Labour Organisation (ILO)), workplace practices, customs and traditions, and lastly, the values enshrined in the Bill of Rights contained in our Constitution. The most important labour statutes are: the Labour Relations Act, the Occupational Health and Safety Act (in the mining sector, the Mine Health and Safety Act 29 of 1996 should be consulted for provisions relating to safety and minimum standards), the Compensation for Occupational Injuries and Diseases Act, the Manpower Training Act, the Guidance and Placement Act, the Unemployment Insurance Act, the Basic Conditions of Employment Act, and the Wage Act. The latter two Acts are to be replaced by an Employment Standards Act. Proposed legislation on employment equity is not included in this chapter, but is discussed in chapter 5.

In a book of this nature it is obviously not possible to provide a detailed discussion of the provisions of these Acts, as this would require, in effect, a separate book on labour law. This overview of labour laws is intended simply to make you aware of the existence of these sources of labour law rules and to point out the main objects of the various statutes. The only exception is the discussion of the Labour Relations Act 66 of 1995. As this Act constitutes the most important piece of legislation from an industrial relations perspective, and bearing in mind the importance of trade unions and collective bargaining in South African human resource management practice, a detailed exposition of the most important provisions of this Act is provided in chapter 19. However, readers are cautioned not to rely solely on what is contained in that chapter — it is advisable to consult a specialist textbook on labour law when seeking the answer to any particular labour law problem.

The existence of so many sources of rules governing employment relationships means that we also need rules to determine which source will take precedence in instances where different rules come into conflict! For the purposes of this discussion the hierarchy of sources is depicted in figure 4.10. For example, common-law principles may be amended by the contract of employment, which, in turn, must comply with the Basic Conditions of Employment Act. The provisions of the latter Act may be superseded by the provisions of a wage determination in terms of the Wage Act or by a collective agreement in terms of the Labour Relations Act.

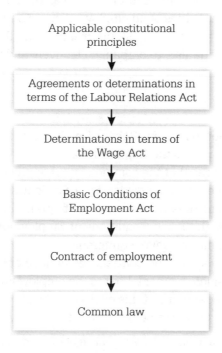

Figure 4.10
Hierarchy of sources of labour law rules

4.4.1 Constitutional law

Chapter 2 of the final Constitution (Chapter 3 of the 1993 Constitution) enshrines certain basic rights as fundamental rights guaranteed by the Constitution. In terms of this Bill of Rights no one (including Parliament) may infringe upon those rights that are regarded as indispensable in a democratic society affirming the democratic values of human dignity, equality and freedom, unless the infringement or limitation of the right in question can be brought under the general limitation clause of the Constitution (section 36). Therefore, any action that is in contravention of the constitutionally guaranteed rights can be challenged on those grounds. Furthermore, any Act of Parliament can be similarly challenged and, indeed, be declared null and void, should it be found to be unconstitutional. The principle is that sovereignty no longer belongs to Parliament — it resides in the Constitution which gives the Constitutional Court the authority to overrule Parliament.

Section 23 of the final Constitution relates specifically to labour relations and makes the following provisions:

- everyone has the right to fair labour practices;
- every worker has the right to form and join a trade union, to participate in the activities of a trade union and to strike;
- every employer has the right to form and join an employers' organisation and to participate in the activities of an employers' organisation;
- every trade union and employers' organisation has the right to determine its own activities, to organise, to bargain collectively and to form and join a federation.

4.4.2 Common law

The common law of South Africa is Roman-Dutch law, that is, the legal system that Jan van Riebeeck brought to the Cape in 1652.

In general one can say that the common law is applicable in all cases except in those instances where it is superseded by a particular statute. For instance, in common law there is no duty on the employer to grant any leave whatsoever; this has been changed by the Basic Conditions of Employment Act 3 of 1983, which prescribes certain minimum leave requirements.

Our common law regards the contract of employment as a contract of letting and hiring; the worker lets his/her labour to the employer (the lessee) who pays the worker a wage. The legal name of this contract is *locatio conductio operarum*. The *locatio conductio operarum* can be defined as follows (Swanepoel 1992: 1):

> "... it is a reciprocal agreement between an employer and an employee in terms of which an employee puts his services at the disposal of the employer usually for an indefinite period, at an agreed remuneration and in such a manner that the employer exercises control over the employee and supervises the rendition of his services".

From the above definition it is apparent that:

1. **there must be an agreement**: this agreement need not be in writing, in fact, it need not even be expressed, as would be the case where the agreement can be inferred from the behaviour of the parties;

2. **it is a reciprocal agreement**: the worker must put his/her services at the employer's disposal and the employer must undertake to pay the former for his/her services, (although payment need not only be in money, as long as the remuneration is calculable);

3. **the element of control is essential:** the single most important distinguishing trait of the employment relationship is the element of control that the employer has over the worker; if this is lacking, then the "worker" is not an employee but an independent contractor. Control implies that not only may the employer tell the worker what must be done but also how it is to be done and that the employer is entitled to closely supervise the manner in which the worker performs his/her task.

In addition, the general common-law requirements for a valid contract to come into existence must be present. These are:

- there must be consensus between the contracting parties regarding the contents of the agreement and the intention to contract;
- both parties must have contractual capacity;
- performance in terms of the contract must be possible at the time of the conclusion of the contract;
- the contract must be lawful in the sense that it must not offend the prevailing good morals of society (it must not be *contra bonos mores*);
- while formalities, such as reducing the contract to writing, are generally not required, in those cases where compliance with formalities is a prerequisite for the validity of a particular contract (such as an apprenticeship contract), those formalities must be complied with.

Both parties to the employment contract have certain rights and duties (generally speaking, the rights of the one party constitute the duties of the other party and vice versa). These rights and duties are summarised in table 4.5 below.

Table 4.5

Common-law duties of employers and employees

Employee's duties	Employer's duties
• to enter and remain in service; • to maintain reasonable efficiency; • to further the employer's business interests; • to be respectful and obedient; • to refrain from misconduct; • not to compete in his/her private capacity with the business of his/her employer.	• to receive the worker into service and to retain him/her; • to pay the worker's wages; • to provide safe working conditions; • not to expect the worker to do work inconsistent with his/her status; • to provide work for the worker.

As mentioned above, the duties of one party constitute the rights of the other. For example, from the duty of the worker to place his/her services at the disposal of the employer is derived the right of the worker to be remunerated for those services. It should be noted that these duties (with their concomitant rights) flow naturally from the employment relationship and need not be contained in any formal contract. Furthermore, many other rights and duties may be included in the contract concluded between the parties (for example hours of work, leave conditions, etc). What is most important is that, in addition to the above rights and duties, our statute law prescribes many other duties, such as the duty to observe prescribed hours of work, to give leave, to give a certificate of service when the relationship is terminated, to keep the prescribed records and not to victimise workers.

The contract of employment can be terminated in a number of ways, namely on expiry of the agreed period, by notice duly given, by mutual agreement, on completion of a specific task, by repudiation, on the death of either party, on the insolvency of the employer and through supervening impossibility of performance.

4.4.3 The Labour Relations Act 66 of 1995

4.4.3.1 Background

In July 1994 the Cabinet approved the appointment of a Ministerial Legal Task Team (MLTT) to draft a new labour relations Bill to address the many deficiencies associated with the Labour Relations Act 28 of 1956. After extensive negotiations between labour, employers and the state (the main social partners constituting NEDLAC), NEDLAC tabled a report on 21 July 1995 in which the adoption of an amended draft Bill was recommended. The Act, after a number of postponements during 1996, finally came into force on 11 November 1996.

According to the MLTT, the Act seeks to balance the demands of international competitiveness and the protection of the fundamental rights of workers, so as to give effect to the stated goals and principles of the Reconstruction and Development Programme of the Government of National Unity. These include the achievement of high productivity, improved efficiency, social justice, the inclusion of all sectors under the new Act and the establishment of collective bargaining at national, industrial and workplace levels. In the view of the MLTT (and of the Minister of Labour), Act 66 of 1995 seeks to avoid the imposition of legal rigidities in the labour market by promoting collective bargaining as the preferred method of regulating labour relations and setting terms and conditions of employment.

We now turn to a very brief overview of the various chapters of the Labour Relations Act 66 of 1995 (the Act). The contents and implications of these chapters are discussed in chapters 19 and 20, which deal with labour relations.

4.4.3.2 Chapters of the Act

Chapter One of the Act covers the purpose, application and interpretation of the Act. In line with the long title of the Act, the overall purpose of the Act is stated as being " . . . to advance economic development, social justice, labour peace and the democratisation of the workplace . . . ". This it intends to achieve by fulfilling the following objectives:

● to give effect to and regulate the fundamental rights conferred by the Constitution;
● to give effect to obligations incurred by the Republic as a member state of the International Labour Organisation;
● to provide a framework within which employees and their trade unions, employers and employers' organisations can:
  ○ collectively bargain to determine wages, terms and conditions of employment and other matters of mutual interest; and

○ formulate industrial policy; and
● to promote:
    ○ orderly collective bargaining;
    ○ collective bargaining at sectoral level;
    ○ employee participation in decision making in the workplace; and
    ○ the effective resolution of labour disputes.

The only categories excluded from the ambit of the Act are members of:

● the National Defence Force;
● the National Intelligence Agency; and
● the South African Secret Service.

The provisions of the Act must be interpreted in the light of its primary objectives, the Constitution and the Republic's obligations in terms of public international law.

Chapter Two deals with freedom of association and with general protections in this regard. *Chapter Three* deals with collective bargaining. It covers aspects such as the organisational rights of trade unions, structures for collective bargaining (such as bargaining and statutory councils), and collective agreements.

Chapter Four of the Act contains lengthy provisions regarding strikes, lockouts and other forms of industrial action and *Chapter Five* deals with workplace forums. The latter are structures that can facilitate indirect worker participation in the form of joint consultation and joint decision making.

Chapter Six contains stipulations regarding trade unions and employers' organisations, such as those relating to their registration and regulation. *Chapter Seven* provides for structures and processes for dispute resolution and *Chapter Eight* deals with unfair dismissal. The Act thus devotes a separate chapter to dismissal law, which is a good indication of the prevalence of disputes surrounding allegedly unfair dismissals. This topic is given exhaustive treatment in the last chapter of this book.

Chapter Nine contains various general provisions. It contains some residual issues as well as definitions.

4.4.3.3 Schedules to the Act

There are eight schedules to the Act, all of which, with the exception of Schedules 4 and 8, are regarded as part of the Act for the purposes of interpretation. As a discussion of the provisions of the schedules falls outside the ambit of this chapter, the schedules are summarised in exhibit B.

4.4.3.4 Schedule 7 to the Act: Residual unfair labour practices

In terms of its jurisdiction relating to unfair labour practices over the past almost two decades, the Industrial Court examined almost all aspects of the conduct of the parties to the employment relationship. It was able to do this because of the extremely open-ended nature of the unfair labour practice definition contained in section 1 of the old Act and because of the fearless and activist disposition of some of the prominent members of the Court. The drafters of the new Act were able to benefit from the fruits of the labour of these members of the Industrial Court in that the new Act is in large part simply a codification of the law as developed by the Industrial Court. (This may be denied by those who do not wish to recognise the good which emanated from that discredited institution despite its limited resources.) In the codification process the drafters classified certain aspects of our unfair labour practice law under specific logical categories. For instance, unfairness in the conduct of the bargaining process is covered in Chapters 2 and 3; unfairness in the context of industrial action is covered in Chapter 4; and unfairness in dismissals is dealt with in Chapter 8. However, there are still a number of unfair labour practices that remain to be dealt with. This is the purpose of Part B of Schedule 7.

Exhibit B

Schedules to the Labour Relations Act

- **Schedule 1.** Provision is made for the establishment of a bargaining council for the public service.
- **Schedule 2.** Detailed guidelines for the establishment and constitution of workplace forums are provided.
- **Schedule 3.** Certain aspects of the Commission for Conciliation, Mediation and Arbitration (CCMA) are dealt with.
- **Schedule 4.** This schedule contains 14 handy flow diagrams to assist users in ascertaining how different disputes should be dealt with.
- **Schedule 5.** This schedule provides for some technical amendments to the Basic Conditions of Employment Act and the Occupational Health and Safety Act.
- **Schedule 6.** Lists all the Acts that have been repealed.
- **Schedule 7.** Contains various transitional arrangements, the most important of which, for our purposes, are those relating to residual unfair labour practices (see below).
- **Schedule 8.** Code of Good Practice: Dismissal (see chapter 24).

For the purposes of this schedule, an unfair labour practice means any unfair act or omission that arises between an employer and an employee and that involves:

- unfair discrimination (see exhibit C);
- unfair conduct on the part of the employer relating to the promotion, demotion or training of an employee or relating to the provision of benefits to an employee;
- unfair suspension of an employee or any other disciplinary action short of dismissal in respect of an employee;
- failure or refusal of an employer to reinstate or re-employ a former employee in terms of an agreement.

Exhibit C

Provisions relating to discrimination

- Job applicants may be regarded as employees
- Direct as well as indirect discrimination are covered
- The open list of arbitrary grounds that may constitute discrimination includes the following: race, gender, ethnic or social origin, colour, sexual orientation, age, disability, religion, conscience, belief, political opinion, culture, language, marital status or family responsibility
- Provision is made for affirmative action measures
- Any discrimination based on an inherent requirement of the particular job does not constitute unfair discrimination

4.4.4 Minimum standards legislation

4.4.4.1 General

Under the present system the Basic Conditions of Employment Act 3 of 1983 and the Wage Act 5 of 1957 set minimum employment standards for the majority of employees in South Africa (these two Acts are to be replaced by a new Basic Conditions of Employment Act — see below and also Appendix B at the end of this chapter). In the previous section we saw that our system of industrial relations is based on the premise that the major actors within the system should regulate their own affairs and, if possible, resolve their disputes, without external interference. However, this scheme of things presupposes that both employer and employee are sufficiently organised to engage with one another in collective bargaining. Does this imply that, where either of the parties is not organised, the common law will prevail? If this was the case, employees would be in a very weak position relative to their employers. It is almost trite to say that, in the absence of a trade union, the ordinary employee as an individual who is dependent upon wages for his/her livelihood is susceptible to exploitation by employers. The object of the Basic Conditions of Employment Act (BCEA) is to lay down minimum conditions of employment to protect employees in the absence of collective agreements regulating such conditions.

One can characterise the BCEA as the default option that comes into play when individual bargaining has to do the job of collective bargaining: it is a safety net in recognition of the much weaker bargaining power of the individual employee. Thus, any actual condition of employment, such as working hours, that is less favourable than the minimum specified in the BCEA, will be regarded as null and void and will be replaced by the corresponding provisions specified in the Act. For example, suppose that, in terms of his common-law contract of employment, an employee is expected to work more than ten hours a week overtime, this stipulation will be of no force and effect because the Act lays down a maximum of ten hours a week overtime. It should be noted, however, that the BCEA **does not** specify minimum wages. The reason for excluding minimum wages from the ambit of the Act is that, while it is possible to specify minima in respect of working hours, leave, notice periods, etc, that could be justified as reasonable irrespective of the area and industry, it is impossible to determine a reasonable minimum wage without investigating the local circumstances within which the employee and employer find themselves (such as the local cost of living and the prevailing local economic climate). Thus the determination of minimum wages is best left to a body such as the Employment Conditions Commission (the successor to the Wage Board — see below) which determines wages (and, incidentally, other minimum conditions of employment) on an ad hoc and local basis, after a thorough investigation.

Seeing that the BCEA is the default option for collective bargaining, it follows that in industries and areas where a collective agreement caters for an issue such as hours of work, these collectively bargained for provisions will prevail over the corresponding provisions of the BCEA. Since the BCEA and the Wage Act are to be replaced by a new Act, these Acts will not be discussed any further here.

4.4.4.2 *Proposed new Basic Conditions of Employment Act*

After protracted negotiations in NEDLAC during 1996–7, and the social partners having failed to reach agreement, the Basic Conditions of Employment Bill of 1997 ("the Bill") was nevertheless tabled in Parliament on 13 October 1997 by the Minister of Labour, who stated that there was "sufficient consensus" on the Bill among the NEDLAC stakeholders for it to be placed before Parliament. The Bill will replace the Basic Conditions of Employment Act of 1983, and the Wage Act 5 of 1957.

According to the Explanatory Memorandum to the Bill, the overall purpose of the Bill is to advance economic development and social justice, and it has two primary objectives:

1. to ensure that working conditions of unorganised and vulnerable workers meet minimum standards that are socially acceptable in relation to the level of development of the country; and
2. to remove rigidities and inefficiencies from the regulation of minimum conditions of employment and to promote flexibility.

The problems the Bill aims to address include:

● inadequate protection of vulnerable workers, such as farm, domestic and part-time workers;
● poverty in employment;
● child labour;
● excessive working hours, particularly in sectors such as security and transport;
● gender discrimination, particularly in relation to maternity leave;
● outdated legislation.

It creates a national set of minimum standards but permits the application of these standards to be varied. There are four mechanisms for variation:

1. collective bargaining

2. sectoral determinations
3. contracts of employment, and
4. variation determinations made by the Minister of Labour.

It is hoped that this approach permits sufficient flexibility for the variation of basic conditions of employment while at the same time creating appropriate safeguards to avoid extremes of exploitation.

The most important provisions of the proposed new legislation are summarised in Appendix B at the end of this chapter (pp 144–148).

4.4.5 Occupational Health and Safety Act

The Occupational Health and Safety Act 85 of 1993 (OHSA) replaced the Machinery and Occupational Safety Act 6 of 1983 and came into operation on 1 January 1994. The objectives of the OHSA are to "provide for the health and safety of persons at work and for the health and safety of persons in connection with the use of plant and machinery; the protection of persons other than persons at work against hazards to health and safety arising out of or in connection with the activities of persons at work; [and] to establish an advisory council for occupational health and safety . . . " (long title of the Act).

The *ambit* of the OHSA is wider than any other labour statute. In addition to covering the private as well as the public sectors, it is also applicable to persons in private households; in fact, this Act covers persons who are exposed to hazards or occupational disease or who are injured through the use of machinery or through exposure to hazardous substances, even though such exposure or injury did not occur in the context of an employment relationship. The major exclusions from the ambit of the Act are the mining industry (only in respect of matters provided for in the Mine Health and Safety Act 29 of 1996), and certain vessels as defined in the Merchant Shipping Act 57 of 1951.

Relevant aspects of the OHSA and the Mine Health and Safety Act are discussed in greater detail in chapter 19.

4.4.6 Compensation for Occupational Injuries and Diseases Act

4.4.6.1 Rationale

The Compensation for Occupational Injuries and Diseases Act 130 of 1993 (COIDA) replaced the Workmen's Compensation Act 30 of 1941, and came into operation on 1 March 1994. The purpose of the Act is to ". . . provide for compensation for disablement caused by occupational injuries or diseases sustained or contracted by employees in the course of their employment, or for death resulting from such injuries or diseases . . ." (long title of the Act). Should an employee die as a result of an accident, injury or disease, the compensation will be paid to his/her dependants. The rationale of the Act is to provide employees (or their dependants in the case of the employee's death) with compensation without their having to prove fault on the part of their employer or any other person (or the absence of fault on the employee's part) and to create a fund from which such compensatory payments can be financed. The logic behind this scheme is that employees are frequently unable to prove fault on the part of their employer (which makes a damages claim impossible), or that the injury/death could be the result of fault on the part of the employee himself/herself (which would likewise be fatal for any civil claim for damages). By removing the fault requirement which is an essential element of a civil claim for damages, employees are guaranteed some compensation, provided that the injury, illness or death arose out of and in the course of their employment (employees who are being transported to or from work by a person appointed by the employer to do so are also regarded as being at work). Furthermore, by instituting a fund, employees are protected from the possibility of their employer being insolvent or otherwise unable to compensate them. The fact that the Act caps the amount of compensation which can be awarded and provides for intercession by the fund on behalf of the employer (an employee is precluded from instituting a claim against his/her employer or any other third party), protects employers from potentially ruinous claims (although the caps on compensation can be seen as a definite disadvantage from the employee's point of view).

4.4.6.2 Ambit

The Act covers almost all employees (including casual and seasonal workers, trainees, and persons employed by an independent contractor). Excluded from the ambit of the Act are: persons performing military service or undergoing military training who are not permanent force members; permanent members of the SANDF and the SAPS while on active duty in defence of the Republic; domestic workers employed in private households; and persons who contract to do work but who engage other persons to perform the work.

4.4.6.3 Duties of employers

The duties of employers include the following.

- Every employer must register with the Compensation Commissioner and supply particulars regarding his/her business and employees.
- Employers must keep records of wages, time worked and payment for overtime and piecework, and retain these records for a period of four years.
- By the end of March of every year, the total salary bill for the preceding financial year must be submitted to the Commissioner in the prescribed form.
- An employer must report any accident within seven days and any occupational disease within fourteen days of its coming to his/her attention.
- Employers must pay an assessed amount (see below) into the Compensation Fund (no contributions may be deducted from employees' wages).

4.4.6.4 Assessment

The Commissioner determines annually the percentage of total salary bill that must be paid by every employer into the Compensation Fund. The Commissioner may decide that different percentages should apply to different employers or to different groups of employers, based, inter alia, on the claims history of an employer or particular group of employers. It is therefore in the interests of employers to introduce measures to decrease the likelihood of accidents and occupational diseases which may result in an unfavourable claims history, as this may in turn cause an increase in the assessed rate for that employer or sector.

4.4.6.5 Benefits

Benefits are payable to three categories of claimants:

- employees who have suffered temporary disability;
- employees who are permanently disabled;
- the dependants of employees who have died as a result of their injuries or occupational disease (occupational diseases are listed in a schedule to the Act).

Claims for compensation must be lodged within twelve months after the accident or illness occurred or after the employee has died. Compensation will not be payable if temporary disablement lasts for three days or less or if an accident is the result of the serious and wilful misconduct of the employee (unless the accident results in the serious disablement of the employee or the employee dies as a consequence thereof). An employee may apply for increased compensation if the accident in which he/she was injured or the occupational disease he/she contracted was caused by the employer's negligence.

4.4.7 Unemployment Insurance Act

4.4.7.1 Rationale

The Unemployment Insurance Act 30 of 1966 came into operation on 1 January 1967. The main purpose of the Act is to provide for the payment of benefits to contributors (to the Unemployment Insurance Fund (UIF)) and to combat unemployment.

4.4.7.2 Ambit

This Act is peculiar in that it does not contain a definition of "employee". Instead it works with the concept of "contributor" (see below) which is central to the scheme envisaged by the Act. Employees who qualify as contributors contribute 1 % of their earnings to the UIF, while their employers contribute an equal amount. When such contributors become unemployed, fall ill for lengthy periods, or give birth to or adopt a child, they may apply for UIF benefits. The dependants of deceased contributors may also apply for benefits. Therefore, the UIF provides financial assistance to contributors or their dependants under the following circumstances:

- during periods of unemployment;
- during periods of illness (it must be a listed illness);
- during pregnancy or on the adoption of a child under two years of age;
- if the contributor dies.

Only persons who are contributors are covered by the Act. The following categories of employees are not regarded as contributors: persons earning more than R69 420 per annum; casual employees; domestic servants; seasonal workers; persons who contribute to the Government Service Pension Fund; persons whose earnings consist solely of a share in takings or who earn commission only; outworkers; the spouse of an employer; officers of Parliament or people who work as permanent staff in Parliament; certain migrant workers; part-time employees employed for less than eight hours or one working day per week; and certain persons in the educational sector.

4.4.7.3 Duties of employers

The Act imposes the following duties on employers.

- Employers must register with the Department of Labour on the prescribed form.
- The employer must supply a list of employees who qualify as contributors.
- The employer must obtain and keep an UIF card for each such contributor.
- On the termination of the employee's employment, the employer must complete the UIF card and give it to the employee.
- The employer must deduct monthly contributions from every employee who is a contributor and must submit these (together with his/her own contributions) to the Unemployment Insurance Commissioner not later than ten days after the end of each month.

4.4.7.4 Benefits

Normally contributors or their dependants are paid benefits at a rate of 45 % of the total weekly or monthly earnings, based on the average earnings at the time they became unemployed, fell ill or died. The contributor receives one week's benefits for every 6 weeks of employment, usually up to a maximum of 26 weeks in any 52-week period. A contributor will not be granted benefits if he/she worked for less than 13 weeks in the 52-week period preceding his/her unemployment, or if he/she refuses to be trained for another job. The contributor will also not receive any benefits for the first week of unemployment (unless his/her last job lasted for less than 9 weeks and he/she was unemployed before that). Benefits will not be paid during the first two weeks of an illness. Should a contributor die, his or her widowed spouse, children under 17 or any other dependant may claim benefits for a maximum period of 26 weeks.

In the case of illness benefits, additional conditions apply: the contributor must be unable to work on account of a listed illness; he/she will be disqualified from claiming benefits if the illness arises from his/her own misconduct, if he/she refuses to undergo medical treatment, or if he/she refuses to carry out the instructions of a medical practitioner.

4.4.8 Manpower Training Act

In South Africa it is almost universally acknowledged that one of our most important national objectives is to develop our human resources. Although it is to be expected that the Manpower Training Act will be extensively overhauled as part of the Department of Labour's five-year programme of labour law reform, the existing Act is still in force and provides an important framework for the establishment of training schemes, training boards and private training centres. For this reason it is important that managers should be acquainted with at least the major provisions of the Act (these are discussed in chapter 15).

4.4.9 Guidance and Placement Act

The Guidance and Placement Act 62 of 1981 came into effect on 29 November 1981 and has as its objective " . . . to provide for the establishment and control of guidance and placement centres and advisory employment boards; [and] for the registration and control of private employment offices . . . " (long title of the Act).

The Act defines a workseeker as " . . . a person over the age of 15 years who, whether or not unemployed or not bona fide engaged in any business, trade, profession or other remunerative activity, is seeking employment, is not required by law to attend school and is not a pupil or student at, or awaiting admission to, a school or other educational institution".

4.4.9.1 Establishment of guidance and placement centres

The Minister may authorise the establishment of a guidance and placement centre in any area for workseekers within that area. The functions of guidance and placement centres include the following: providing guidance to any person regarding choice of vocation by means of the collection and communication of relevant information and the furnishing of advice; maintaining a register of workseekers registered at the centre; placing workseekers in employment; and rendering assistance to employers in connection with the selection of staff.

4.4.9.2 Registration of workseekers

For the purposes of the Act any workseeker may be registered at a particular centre. Any workseeker registered at a centre must notify the centre on obtaining employment. Any employer who engages a workseeker whom the centre has referred to him/her for employment must notify the centre concerned that he/she has engaged the workseeker.

4.4.9.3 Registration and regulation of private employment offices

No person may run a private employment office, or charge or recover any payment or reward for or in connection with procuring employment or procuring a work-seeker through a private employment office, unless that private employment office is registered under the Act.

4.4.10 Employment Equity Legislation

The government has announced its intention of introducing a Bill in Parliament providing for anti-discrimination and affirmative action measures. This Green Paper is discussed in chapter 5.

4.5 CONCLUSION

In this chapter we focused on factors, variables, trends and forces from outside the organisation which have a potential bearing on human resource management. Special emphasis was placed on the relevant legislative aspects. Most of the sources of rules governing the workplace were introduced. It must be emphasised that laws in and of themselves can neither make for sound employment relations nor guarantee a vibrant economy. The role of the law in promoting good quality employment relations and economic growth is limited. The converse is, however, not always true: laws may impact negatively on employment relations and on the economy as a whole. This could happen, for instance, when laws are enacted which disturb the balance of power between capital and labour or which introduce too much rigidity into the employment sphere. The major challenge facing South Africans in the decades to come will be to promote economic growth and social equity (in the workplace and society at large). In this lies the challenge of pre-serving a fine balance between these two somewhat opposing goals. If we fail in either of these tasks, we may well reap social unrest and suffer marginalisation by the international markets. It is therefore the task of management (and trade union leaders) to seize the opportunities created by the structures that the law provides and by all the other external influences and to translate these into constructive employment relations.

SELF-EVALUATION QUESTIONS

1. Write an essay outlining South Africa's competitiveness in international terms. Explain how the characteristics of the human dimension of the country play a role in this regard.
2. "Now that apartheid is gone and the Constitution guarantees equality, South Africa's problem of inequality is something of the past."

Comment critically on the above quotation and explain the implications for human resource management.

3. Explain what is meant by an "active labour market policy". What are the potential implications of such a policy for human resource management in South African organisations?

4. Discuss briefly the implications of constitutional law and common law for human resource management in South Africa.

5. Define and explain the legal concept *locatio conductio operarum*.

6. List the common-law duties of employees and employers.

7. Write brief, explanatory notes on "minimum standards legislation" affecting the management of employees of South African organisations.

8. Briefly outline the rationale and ambit of the Unemployment Insurance Act 30 of 1966. Also explain the implications for human resource management.

 BIBLIOGRAPHY

Barker, FS. 1995. *The South African Labour Market: Critical Issues for Reconstruction*. Johannesburg: Van Schaik

Centre for Development and Enterprise (CDE). 1995. *Post-apartheid Population and Income Trends — A New Analysis*. CDE Research No 1. Johannesburg: CDE

Cloete, G. 1996. Oorbevolking kan HOP verongeluk. *Finansies en Tegniek*, 26 Januarie, 19

De Villiers, AS & Slabbert, JA. 1996. *The South African Organisational Environment*. Johannesburg: RAU

Landau, R. 1992. Technology, capital formation and US competitiveness. In *International Productivity and Competitiveness*, ed BG Hickman. Oxford: Oxford University Press

Liebenberg, K. 1996. *South African Competitiveness Monitor 1996: Volume 1–International Comparisons*. Pretoria: WEFA Group

Republic of South Africa. 1996. *Green Paper: Policy Proposals for a New Employment and Occupational Equity Statute. Government Gazette* no 17303, 1 July 1996: Pretoria: Government Printer

Liebenberg, K. 1996. *South African Competitiveness Monitor 1996: Volume 3–South African Issues*. Pretoria: WEFA Group

Swanepoel, JPA. 1992. *Introduction to Labour Law*, 3 ed. Johannesburg: Lexicon.

APPENDIX A: TABLES SHOWING INCOME AND OCCUPATIONAL STATUS BY RACE AND GENDER

Table A1

Access to employment by race and gender, 1994*

Included under blacks

	Asian women	Asian men	Coloured women	Coloured men	African women	African men	Black women	Black men	White women	White men	TOTAL
Not economically active	2	1	5	3	45	30	52	34	9	5	100
Unemployed	1	1	4	4	48	39	53	44	2	1	100
Total employees	1	3	5	8	18	41	24	52	10	14	100
Employers or workers on own account	0	2	4	2	50	17	55	21	6	18	100

*Source: Calculated from Central Statistical Services (CSS), *October Household Survey 1994*

Table A2
Incomes by race and gender for selected occupations, 1994*
(Figures are percentages)

Included under blacks

		Asian women	Asian men	Coloured women	Coloured men	African women	African men	Black women	Black men	White women	White men
All employees	% employed in group	93	87	87	95	65	93	70	93	90	80
	R0–R499	7	3	20	19	30	30	26	27	4	2
	R500–R999	24	14	28	24	27	26	27	25	2	7
	R1 000–R1 999	49	40	41	37	32	32	35	33	38	2
	R2 000 and more	21	29	11	15	12	12	12	14	43	47
Top management	% employed in group	2	4	1	2	0	1	1	2	4	11
	R0–R499	0	1	0	7	17	7	9	6	0	1
	R500–R999	11	5	5	5	9	15	8	11	9	1
	R1 000–R1 999	66	31	32	47	30	27	36	32	23	11
	R2 000 and more	23	64	63	41	43	50	47	51	67	89
Professionals	% employed in group	7	4	4	3	7	4	7	3	11	8
	R0–R499	5	2	4	1	2	3	2	3	1	1
	R500–R999	7	6	11	6	9	5	9	6	6	4
	R1 000–R1 999	34	16	38	29	49	32	47	30	26	13
	R2 000 and more	55	74	47	63	41	59	42	61	67	82
Clerks	% employed in group	33	14	19	8	8	6	11	7	44	9
	R0–R499	4	2	4	2	11	5	8	4	3	2
	R500–R999	23	17	24	18	29	20	27	19	18	10
	R1 000–R1 999	55	45	58	55	49	55	52	54	45	33
	R2 000 and more	18	36	14	25	12	21	13	23	34	56
Artisans and related occupations	% employed in group	6	13	4	20	3	12	3	13	1	21
	R0–R499	9	1	10	6	33	15	27	12	13	2
	R500–R999	26	2	36	25	34	35	34	32	15	8
	R1 000–R1 999	55	18	50	46	27	39	34	42	16	28
	R2 000 and more	10	80	4	23	6	11	6	15	56	63

Table A2 (cont.)
Incomes by race and gender for selected occupations, 1994*
(Figures are percentages)

		Asian women	Asian men	Coloured women	Coloured men	African women	African men	Black women	Black men	White women	White men
							Included under blacks				
Operators and assemblers	% employed in group	17	15	12	14	4	20	6	19	1	6
	R0–R499	8	5	6	9	23	18	15	16	8	3
	R500–R999	24	18	34	27	33	27	32	26	33	9
	R1 000–R1 999	58	62	59	53	39	43	48	45	41	36
	R2 000 and more	9	15	2	11	5	12	5	12	17	52
Elementary workers	% employed in group	3	4	24	31	22	34	22	32	1	2
	R0–R499	12	12	49	42	57	57	55	55	5	14
	R500–R999	36	38	29	30	31	25	31	26	16	19
	R1 000–R1 999	47	40	21	26	11	16	13	17	23	41
	R2 000 and more	4	10	1	2	1	2	1	2	56	27
Employers and workers on own account	% employed in group	7	13	13	5	35	7	30	7	10	20
	R0–R499	24	3	75	12	69	29	69	25	17	6
	R500–R999	12	5	16	15	21	16	20	15	15	4
	R1 000–R1 999	22	16	7	26	6	24	7	23	16	9
	R2 000 and more	43	76	3	47	4	31	4	37	51	82
Top management on own account	% employed in group	2	6	0	1	2	2	2	2	2	6
	R0–R499	9	0	18	3	25	14	24	11	9	3
	R500–R999	0	2	6	3	18	7	16	6	5	1
	R1 000–R1 999	5	5	51	16	20	23	21	20	9	5
	R2 000 and more	86	93	24	78	37	56	39	63	77	91
Elementary workers on own account	% employed in group	3	2	12	1	30	2	26	2	0	0
	R0–R499	49	13	78	32	74	20	74	21	0	6
	R500–R999	19	9	16	28	20	17	20	18	59	0
	R1 000–R1 999	28	38	5	20	5	24	5	25	0	16
	R2 000 and more	5	40	1	20	1	7	1	11	41	78

*Source: Calculated from Central Statistical Services (CSS), *October Household Survey 1994. (a)* Employment in occupation as a % of employment plus self-employment of group.

Table A3

Index of representivity in selected occupations by race and gender, rounded to nearest 5 points, 1994 (see note at end of table) *

	Asian women	Asian men	Coloured women	Coloured men	African women	African men	Included under blacks			
							Black women	Black men	White women	White men
Total employees	124	152	110	140	57	109	65	115	145	137
Top management	67	213	31	78	9	41	14	53	206	548
Professionals	135	91	72	53	91	59	90	60	262	203
Technicians and associated professionals	114	151	95	62	79	54	83	59	270	224
Clerks	312	171	167	79	50	50	72	59	501	105
Service/retail workers	161	182	154	85	78	99	90	101	129	114
Artisans and related	69	188	41	242	23	111	26	131	16	289
Operators/assemblers	159	185	113	150	31	169	41	168	10	75
Elementary workers	15	27	118	177	75	155	79	152	5	10
Employers and workers on own account	47	116	88	35	160	44	160	44	86	179
Top management on own account	84	314	11	63	48	85	44	91	116	331
Elementary workers on own account	34	33	154	14	261	19	241	19	1	7

Note:

Less than 100 = relative underrepresentation

100 = proportional to participation in labour force

More than 100 = relative overrepresentation

*Source: Calculated from CSS, *October Household Survey 1994*. The index consists of the group's percentage share in each occupation divided by the group's percentage share in the economically active population. These figures understate the poor representation of African women in higher-level positions, since African women were most underrepresented in the economically active population.

APPENDIX B: OVERVIEW OF THE BASIC CONDITIONS OF EMPLOYMENT BILL, 1997

This overview summarises the main provisions of the Bill [with references to the appropriate sections of the Bill].

Chapter 1: Application of the Bill [ss 3–5]

- All employees and employers except members of the National Defence Force, National Intelligence Agency, South African Secret Service and unpaid volunteers working for an organisation with a charitable purpose. [s 3]
- The Bill takes precedence over any agreement, whether entered into before or after the commencement of the Act. [s 5]

Chapter 2: Regulation of working time [ss 6–18]

- This Chapter does not apply to senior managerial employees; employees engaged as sales staff who travel to the premises of customers and who regulate their own hours of work; and employees who work less than 24 hours a month for an employer. [s 6]
- Working time must be regulated with due regard to employees' health and safety and family responsibilities. [s 7]
- The maximum ordinary hours of work for all employees are 45 in a week.. The maximum daily hours of work are 9 for employees who work on 5 days or less a week, and 8 for employees who work 6 days a week. [s 9]
- Schedule 1 sets out procedures for the progressive reduction of maximum working hours to the goal of a 40-hour working week and an eight-hour working day. [schedule 1]
- An employee can, by agreement, work up to 3 hours overtime in a day or 10 hours overtime in a week. Overtime work must be paid at 1,5 times the employee's normal wage, or an employee may agree to receive paid time off. An employee may agree to work up to 12 hours in a day without receiving overtime pay in order to work a compressed work week. [ss 10-11]
- A collective agreement may permit the hours of work to be averaged over a period of up to four months. [s 12]
- An employee must have a meal interval of at least 60 minutes after five hours' continuous work. This may be reduced to 30 minutes by agreement. [s 14]
- An employee must have a daily rest period of at least 12 hours and a weekly rest period of at least 36 consecutive hours each week. The weekly rest period must include Sunday, unless otherwise agreed. [s 15]
- An employee who works on a Sunday must receive double pay. However, if an employee is hired to ordinarily work on a Sunday, he or she must be paid 1,5 times the normal wage for Sunday. An employee may agree to receive paid time off in return for working on a Sunday. [s 16]

- Employees who work at night (between 18:00 and 06:00) are protected and must be compensated by the payment of an allowance or by a reduction of working hours. [s 17]
- Employees must be paid their normal wage for any public holiday that falls on a working day. Work on a public holiday is by agreement and is paid at double rate. [s 18]

Chapter 3: Leave [ss 19–27]

- Employees are entitled to 21 consecutive days' annual leave. An employer must not pay an employee instead of granting annual leave. [ss 20–21]
- An employee is entitled to six weeks' paid sick leave in every 36 months. An employer may require a medical certificate before paying an employee who is frequently absent. [ss 22–24]
- A pregnant employee is entitled to four consecutive months of maternity leave. An employer of a pregnant employee or employee nursing her child is not allowed to permit her to perform work that is hazardous to her or her child. [ss 25–26]
- Full time employees are entitled to three days' paid family responsibility leave annually (if employed for longer than 4 months and works at least 4 days per week for the employer). [s 27]

Chapter 4: Particulars of employment and remuneration [ss 28–35]

- An employer must supply an employee with written particulars of employment when the employee starts employment. These must be revised if the terms of employment change. [s 29]
- Employers must display at the workplace a statement of employees' rights under the Bill in official languages used at the workplace. [s 30]
- Employers must keep a record of the time worked by each employee and their remuneration. [s 31]
- The Bill sets out the manner in which employees must be paid and protects employees from unlawful deductions from their wages. The rules for calculating remuneration and wages are set out. [ss 32–35]

Chapter 5: Termination of employment [ss 36–42]

- Minimum notice periods for terminating employment by employers or employees. This ranges from one week's notice during the first four weeks of employment to one month for employees with more than one year's service. [ss 37–38]
- The termination of employment by an employer on notice in terms of the Bill does not prevent the employee challenging the fairness or lawfulness of the dismissal in terms of the Labour Relations Act or any other law. [s 37(6)]
- An employee who is dismissed for reasons based on the employer's operational requirements is entitled to one week's severance pay for every year of service. [s 41]

- On termination of employment, an employee is entitled to a certificate of service. [s 42]

Chapter 6: Prohibition of employment of children and forced labour [ss 43–48]

- It is an offence to employ a child under 15 years of age or who is under the minimum school leaving age in terms of any law, if this is 15 years or older. [s 43(1)]
- Children under 18 may not be employed to do work inappropriate for their age or that places them at risk. [s 43(2)]
- The use of forced labour is prohibited and is an offence. [s 48]

Chapter 7: Variation of basic conditions of employment [ss 49–50]

- A collective agreement concluded by a bargaining council may replace or exclude any basic condition of employment except certain core rights. The core rights that cannot be varied are the following:
  - the duty to arrange working time with due regard to the health, safety and family responsibility of employees;
  - two weeks of annual leave;
  - maternity leave;
  - sick leave, except to the extent permitted by the Act;
  - to inform employees (who work for a period of longer than one hour after 23:00 and before 06:00 at least five times per month or 50 times per year) of the health and safety hazards associated with night work, enable them to undergo medical examinations at appropriate intervals and to transfer them to suitable day work if the employee suffers from a health condition associated with the performance of night work;
  - the prohibition of child and forced labour. [s 49]
- Other collective agreements and individual agreements may only replace or exclude basic conditions of employment to the extent permitted by the Bill.
- The Minister of Labour may make a determination to vary or exclude a basic condition of employment. This can also be done on application by an employer or employer organisation. [s 50]
- The Minister of Labour and the Minister of Public Service and Administration must make a determination applying to the public sector. [s 50(4)]
- A determination may be issued if a trade union representing the employees has consented to the variation or has had the opportunity to make representations to the Minister. A copy of any determination must be displayed by the employer at the workplace and must be made available to employees. [s 50(6)]

Chapter 8: Sectoral determinations [ss 51–58]

- The Minister of Labour may, after an investigation and acting on the advice of the Employment conditions Commission, make sectoral determinations establishing basic conditions of employment, including minimum wages for employees in unorganised sectors. [ss 51–55]

● The Commission must consider the ability of employers to carry on their businesses succesfully, the operation of small, medium and micro enterprises and new businesses, the cost of living, the alleviation of poverty and the impact of proposed conditions of employment on job creation and other factors before advising the Minister on the publication of a sectoral determination. [s 54(3)]

● A sectoral determination can regulate any matter concerning remuneration and conditions of employment. [s 55(4)]

● A sectoral determination may not cover employers and employees covered by a bargaining or statutory council agreement or a determination which is less than 12 months old. [s 55(6)]

Chapter 9: Employment Conditions Commission [ss 59–62]

● The Employment Conditions Commission is established to advise the Minister of Labour on the making of sectoral determinations and other matters arising out of the applications of the Bill. [s 59]

● In addition the Commission can advise the Minister on trends in collective bargaining which undermine the purpose of the Act. [s 59(2)(e)]

● Three members of the Commission are appointed by the Minister after consultation with NEDLAC. These members must be knowledgeable about the conditions of employment of vulnerable and underorganised workers. [s 60(1)]

● A further two members are appointed by the Minister after being nominated by the voting members of NEDLAC representing organised labour and business. [s 60(2)]

Chapter 10: Monitoring, enforcement and legal proceedings [ss 63–81]

● The Minister fo Labour may appoint labour inspectors to promote, monitor or enforce compliance with employment laws. [s 63]

● Labour inspectors must advise employees and employers on their rights and obligations in terms of employment laws. They may also conduct inspections, investigate complaints and may question persons and inspect, copy and remove records and other relevant documents. [ss 64–65]

● An inspector may serve a compliance order on an employer who is not complying with a provision of the Bill. The employer may object against the order to the Director-General: Labour, who after receiving representations, may confirm, modify or set aside an order. This decision is subject to appeal to the Labour Court. [ss 69–73]

● Maximum penalties that may be imposed for failure to comply with the Bill. [Schedule 2]

● The Labour Court has exclusive jurisdiction in all matters arising under the Bill, except where jurisdiction is given to another body and in criminal matters. The

Labour Court has concurrent jurisdiction with the civil courts to hear disputes concerning contracts of employment. [s 77]

● Employees/job applicants may not be discriminated against for exercising rights in terms of the Bill. [ss 78–81]

Chapter 11: General [ss 82–96]

The Bill includes a number of general provisions, including the following:

● A temporary employment service and the client are jointly and severally liable if the temporary employment service does not comply with the Act. [s 82]
● The Minister may, on the advice of the Commission and by notice in the Gazette, deem any category of persons to be employees for the purposes of the Act. [s 83]
● The Minister may, after consulting NEDLAC, issue Codes of Good Practice, including ones on the regulation of working time and the protection of employees during pregnancy and the birth of a child. [s 87]

Schedule 3: Transitional provisions [items 1–11]

Schedule Three contains provisions to regulate the transition from other laws to the Bill. These include the following:

● The provisions of the Bill will not apply to the public service for a period of eighteen months from its commencement date. [Item 2]
● The reduction of ordinary working hours to 45 per week will only apply to farm workers and mine workers twelve months after the Act comes into effect. [Item 5]
● The maximum ordinary weekly hours of security guards must be reduced from 60 to 45 over 30 months. [Item 5]

chapter 5 Equalising Opportunities by means of Affirmative Action

○ **STUDY OBJECTIVES**

After studying this chapter, you should be able to:

- define, and differentiate from one another, the concepts *affirmative action, reverse discrimination, equality of opportunity, formal employment equity* and *substantive employment equity*;
- describe sources of discrimination in South African society (past and present);
- explain the proposed organisational and employment equity plan;
- discuss what South Africa can learn from other countries' experience with affirmative action;
- explain how organisations could go about implementing affirmative action; and
- discuss the impact affirmative action can have on various human resource management functions.

5.1 INTRODUCTION

As can be gathered from earlier chapters, our history makes one of the most pressing issues facing South Africa today, that of how to address the vast inequalities prevalent in almost all walks of life within our multicultural society. This is not only an issue of morality. Inequalities of the magnitude encountered in the South African context (see previous chapter) not only pose a very real danger but also a daunting challenge to our society. The success of South Africa's "political miracle" will in large measure depend on our ability to face this socioeconomic challenge. The seriousness with which this country's political leaders see the problem is evidenced in many spheres (for example, one of the first public acts of the Government of National Unity (GNU) was to unveil its Reconstruction and Development Programme), and finds a niche in our society in the prominence given to "equality" in South Africa's Constitution. It is no coincidence that the drafters of the South African Constitution awarded pride of place in the Bill of Rights to the fundamental right to equality (section 9 of the Constitution).

The dilemma facing the country is thus, in other words, largely one of distributive justice and how to achieve this.

Distributive justice may be defined as the fairness of the social rules regulating how social goods (such as welfare benefits, infrastructure, fixed assets, education, jobs and income) are allocated to members and groups within the larger society.

As a student of HRM (or as HRM practitioner) you are invited to think of affirmative action in the context of employment as an effort to achieve a just distribution of a social commodity which is much sought after and is known as "jobs". In this respect employment opportunities are no different from other social goods of which all members of society wish to have their fair share, such as health care, clean water, roads, electricity, old age pensions, etc. However, from the definition of distributive justice it should be clear that, although affirmative action has historically been most closely associated with the workplace, it encompasses a much larger field. Indeed, land redistribution, reformation of the educational system, the awarding of government tenders and subsidies to companies owned by historically disadvantaged people and the distribution of radio licences, are all examples of affirmative action. Indeed, one could assert that the deep inequalities which rend our society are not wholly or even mostly attributable to employment inequity: many non-work related past policies and laws are also implicated (think, for instance, of the distributive rules that regulated the ownership of land and the distribution of the right to vote, as two obvious examples of non-work rules which unfairly discriminated against the majority of South Africans). This chapter is not intended as an exhaustive treatment of the controversial issues surrounding affirmative action. Rather the focus is on affirmative action in the workplace, bearing in mind, however, that the concept has a much wider application.

In this chapter a number of topics are covered. The American origins of the concept *affirmative action* are explored, the concept is defined and differentiated from other concepts such as *equal opportunities*, the nature of affirmative action is examined and suggestions are made as to why affirmative action is such a controversial topic. It is also argued that the real debate is not about equality as such but rather about "equality of what?". The *Green Paper on Employment and Occupational Equity*, published by the Department of Labour in 1996, as the precursor to affirmative action legislation, is discussed and affirmative action in a few other countries is also reviewed. Some practical considerations relating to the implementation of affirmative action programmes in organisations are also highlighted. The chapter concludes with some observations regarding the potential implications of affirmative action for human resource management practices such as recruitment, selection, promotion and training. (It is thus advisable to refer back to this chapter as you progress through the other chapters to follow.)

5.2   ORIGINS OF AFFIRMATIVE ACTION

Affirmative action has its roots in the earliest efforts directed against unfair discrimination. The concept *affirmative action* was first used in America in the

Wagner Act of 1935. However, it is with the passing of the Civil Rights Act in 1964 that the foundation was laid (unintentionally, because the Act's objective was only to prohibit discrimination in the private sector) for the development of affirmative action law in America as we know it today. Whatever the intent in 1964, by the time Congress enacted the Equal Opportunities Act of 1972, Congress clearly did intend to authorise preferential, results-orientated affirmative action. The most important federal legislation in the USA prohibiting discrimination in employment is Title VII of the Civil Rights Act of 1964. There were, however, several earlier efforts to make discrimination in employment unlawful. The modern history of these efforts starts in 1941 with President Roosevelt's Executive Order 8802 which prohibited discrimination based on race, creed, colour, or national origin by private employers in defence industries and by the federal government.

During and after World War II, the federal government tried to curb employment discrimination through the federal contract programme. Private employment relations, prior to the enactment of the Civil Rights Act in 1964, remained beyond the reach of federal regulation and, despite the efforts of civil rights advocates, the issue of employment discrimination stayed off the national political agenda. The change in this political situation was heralded by the Supreme Court's decision in *Brown v Board of Education* in 1954.[1] Over time the realisation grew that true equality requires more than the simple removal of existing discriminatory barriers and it was left to the courts laboriously to reconstruct Title VII of the Civil Rights Act (dealing with discrimination in the workplace) to fit the ends dictated by these new insights.

One year after Title VII was enacted, President Johnson signed Executive Order 11246, which required federal contractors to "take affirmative action to ensure that applicants, are employed, and that employees are treated during employment, without regard to their race, color, religion, sex, or national origin". The order left it to the Labour Department to define the specifics of affirmative action and its enforcement. The Labour Department's guidelines state that affirmative action applies to a wide range of minority groups and women and consists of "results-oriented actions", such as goals, timetables, back pay, and retroactive seniority, designed to ensure equal employment opportunity. By 1968 the Labour Department had developed "utilisation analysis". The underlying assumption was that, in the absence of discrimination, persons from affected classes would be hired in roughly the same proportion as they were qualified and available. Based on this assumption the Labour Department viewed disparate impact as strong evidence of discrimination. The Labour Department, the Equal Employment Opportunity Commission (EEOC) and the Office of Federal Contract Compliance (OFCCP) used such evidence to demand that goals and timetables be established to reduce the under-utilisation of affected groups. Now the government *officially* recognised discrimination as systemic (not necessarily intentional), and the results-oriented goal of proportional representation became part of US public policy.

Affirmative action in contract compliance was directed at collective social and institutional discrimination, rather than at acts of individual and/or intentional discrimination. This constituted a more direct and simpler form of promoting affirmative action in that it was based on disparate impact (and not on proof of intentional discrimination) and was thus not concerned with the legalities surrounding the meaning of unlawful discrimination, nor was proof of past discriminatory practices required to mandate affirmative action. The greater latitude to enforce affirmative action in the case of federal contracts is justified on the basis that employers are voluntarily seeking government contracts and the executive branch can impose conditions on participation which satisfy some legitimate public policy. In addition, the sanction for non-compliance could be termination of the contract based on the breach of a material term of the contract by the employer/contractor, thereby providing a strong incentive for employers to fulfil their affirmative action obligations in terms of the contract.

Title VII created a five-member EEOC, authorising it to receive complaints of discrimination from individuals, to investigate, and, upon determining that there was reasonable cause to believe that the charge was true, to seek to eliminate the alleged unlawful practice by informal negotiation, conciliation and persuasion. If EEOC conciliation failed, the complainant could bring a civil action against the employer or trade union. This commission, with its very limited powers, played a surprisingly important role in the development of the notion of disparate impact under Title VII litigation. From the start the EEOC's stance was that it had to investigate and conciliate not only individual complaints but also to investigate patterns of institutional discrimination, the effects of past discrimination and disparate impact discrimination (as opposed to disparate treatment discrimination). The EEOC viewed Title VII as remedial and retrospective in nature, rather than as simply prospective and measured its success in terms of numbers of minority group members in employment.

5.3   CLARIFYING CONCEPTS

5.3.1 Affirmative action

The concept *affirmative action* is used in many different guises and it is not readily apparent what persons mean when employing it. The following comments regarding affirmative action are reproduced here to obtain a sense of what is generally understood by the concept.

● *"Affirmative action* refers to specific steps, beyond ending discriminatory practices, that are taken to promote equal opportunity and to ensure that discrimination will not recur. The goal of affirmative action is to eliminate non-legal barriers to equal employment opportunity, including intentional discriminatory practices and unintentional (structural or systemic) discrimination. Affirmative action is best understood as a diverse continuum of more or less severe responses that attempt to overcome discrimination. Some affirmative action programmes attempt to protect the individual against intentional discrimination, others are explicitly preferential (goals): . . . it is best to be clear that affirmative action involves some degree of preferential treatment, because not to do so is to beg the question — it is to force the most crucial issue into the background: the issue of whether preferential treatment for women and nonwhites can ever be morally justifiable" (Taylor 1991: 14).

- "In its broadest meaning the phrase affirmative action is now generally understood to refer to the practice of favourably considering an individual's status as a woman, or as a member of a racial or ethnic minority group. Affirmative action is designed to aid those that have suffered historical and widespread mistreatment in the form of both de jure and de facto discrimination. Affirmative action may also be described as a temporary policy embraced by government, businesses and universities as a means of achieving true equal opportunity. Affirmative action policies are frequently used in awarding business contracts, in hiring and promotions, and in university admissions and granting of scholarships" (Starks 1992: 939).

- ". . . affirmative action is generally designed with three goals in mind: To eliminate existing discrimination against minorities and women; to remedy the lingering effect of past discrimination against these groups; and to prevent future discrimination against these groups" (Starks 1992: 940).

- "Affirmative action in the South African context has extremely broad connotations, touching, as apartheid did and still does, on every area of life . . . affirmative action covers all purposive activity designed to eliminate the effects of apartheid and to create a society where everyone has the same chance to get on in life. In terms of the ANC draft Bill of Rights, all anti-discrimination measures, as well as all anti-poverty ones, may be regarded as constituting a form of affirmative action" (Sachs 1991).

- "Affirmative action is not synonymous with quotas: 'quotas' reserve opportunities and benefits exclusively for qualified members of designated minority groups. 'Preferential treatment' on the other hand, allows an individual's status as a minority to be considered as a positive factor among other factors when allocating opportunities and benefits" (Starks 1992: 942).

- Affirmative action ". . . can be viewed as a pro-active development tool to overcome . . . constraints and more effectively mobilize latent resources in order to stimulate overall development" (Thomas, in Human 1993: 2).

- "Affirmative action programmes can be broken down into judicially imposed; voluntarily enacted; and legislatively mandated. When affirmative action is judicially imposed a court orders a party to enact affirmative action policies as a remedy for proven discrimination. Voluntarily enacted affirmative action refers to the institutional practice of implementing affirmative action policies as a means of eradicating the effects of prior discrimination against minorities without being required to do so" (Starks 1992: 947).

- "Affirmative action is thus a temporary intervention designed to achieve equal employment opportunity without lowering standards and without unduly trammelling the career aspirations or expectations of current organisational members who are competent in their jobs" (Human 1993: 3).

For the purposes of this book *affirmative action* is viewed as those proactive and remedial measures designed to bridge the gap between formal equality of employment opportunity and substantive equality of opportunity.

Viewed thus, affirmative action comes to the fore in a society in which the stage has been reached that the law does not discriminate, but societal discrimination is still prevalent. Affirmative action in the work environment is the last step towards the ideal of true employment equity. Logically and chronologically a model of the steps from a state of employment inequity to employment equity will therefore follow the following sequence:

1. discriminatory laws and societal discrimination exist (state of employment inequity);
2. anti-discriminatory laws are enacted (state of formal equity in which societal discrimination is still present);
3. affirmative action programmes and laws enacted (state of striving towards true or substantive employment equity).

5.3.2 Equality of opportunity

The title of this chapter refers to *affirmative action* and *equalising opportunities*, thus implying that there is a difference between the two.

For our purposes the phrase *equality of opportunity* is used to refer to that ideal state where everyone has an equal chance (all other things being equal, such as innate abilities) to compete with his/her peers for access to social goods, whereas *affirmative action* refers to those (fair) discriminatory interventions necessitated as a bridge between our apartheid past and our non-discriminatory future.

From this formulation it should be clear that we live in a crossover phase of our history during which discrimination and its very badges (such as gender and race) have to be employed to get past discrimination — there is no other way. This is the essential paradox inherent in affirmative action: to get past (unfair or invidious) discrimination we have to discriminate, albeit fairly, (unfair discrimination in the name of a good cause still remains just that, unfair, and exposes affirmative action to the often-heard charge of "reverse discrimination"). The progress from employment inequity to true employment equity is depicted in figure 5.1.

From figure 5.1 it can be seen that antidiscrimination laws are not enough; although they do remove legal barriers to employment, they do not eradicate the

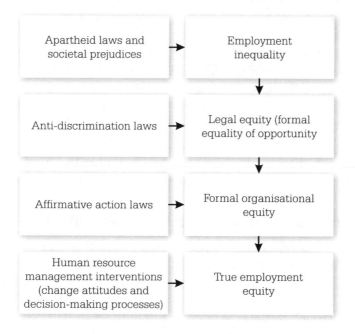

Figure 5.1

From apartheid to true or substantive employment equity

historical inequalities which are still prevalent. Furthermore, even if affirmative action laws cause organisations to hire and promote historically disadvantaged people, the law cannot in itself remove non-legal or societal barriers arising from peoples' attitudes — for this a concerted human resource management effort is needed. Thus, equality of opportunity is affirmative action in the narrow sense, that is, by prohibiting systems of legal privilege and disqualifications, thereby expanding the sphere of individual liberty. "Formal" equality of opportunity is brought about by the enactment of antidiscrimination laws and the repeal of laws which allow for discrimination. "True" or "substantive" employment equity is, however, much more difficult to achieve in that it requires a fundamental and honest change of heart among all relevant parties. This will entail, inter alia a change of attitude and an acceptance of people irrespective of their gender, cultural, ethnic or language group.

5.3.3 Reverse discrimination versus affirmative action

The difference between affirmative action and discrimination can be explained as follows: affirmative action is **not** discrimination in reverse, nor is it appropriate to apply the same requirement of neutrality, applicable in the domain of antidiscrimination regulation, to affirmative action. This is so for two reasons. First, to equate affirmative action with discrimination is fallacious as the aim of discrimination is to exclude, whereas affirmative action's aim is to include. Secondly, affirmative action requires **positive** action to overcome systemic, institutionalised discrimination, whereas antidiscrimination laws are **passive** in the sense that they proscribe someone from indulging in certain types of behaviour (as opposed to mandating certain conduct, as is the case in affirmative action initiatives). Against a background of centuries of discrimination, antidiscrimination laws are perpetuating discrimination, rather than eliminating it. However, it should be noted that, depending on the *modality* (see section 5.4.1 below) of the affirmative action programme adopted, affirmative action may be unfair and, indeed unconstitutional, irrespective of the good intentions and effectiveness of the programme. For example, an affirmative action programme amounting to "no white males need apply", will in all likelihood, be impugned as reverse discrimination.

5.3.4 Liberal, libertarian and egalitarian perspectives

In the debate surrounding affirmative action the participants are frequently labelled as falling into certain camps. Since some of this terminology is also used in this book, it may be expedient to provide a brief clarification of some of these terms.

An "egalitarian" is someone who holds that the distribution of goods in a just society shall be according to the principle of "equal shares", irrespective of differences among individuals in their respective contributions to the creation of a society's wealth (one could associate this view with communism or extreme forms of socialism).

A "libertarian" is someone who contends that the distribution of social goods should be strictly according to merit and that the state's primary task is to protect the individual's freedom to pursue his/her own goals in life (capitalists, free marketeers and individualists may be some labels associated with this school of thought).

"Liberals" are those who hold that, while individuals should be left free to pursue their divergent ends, it should be recognised that an individual owes a debt to society and consequently that it is society's duty to distribute wealth more equally (thus wealth creation is protected but the distribution of wealth is not left entirely to the individual — social democrats or capitalists with a human face could be appropriate labels for this group).

Related concepts not dealt with in this chapter are "managing diversity", "social responsibility", "black advancement" and "black empowerment".

5.4   THE NATURE OF AFFIRMATIVE ACTION

5.4.1 Modalities of affirmative action

Affirmative action can take many forms. It is important to determine the type of affirmative action contemplated by the organisation's affirmative action policy, since not all types of affirmative action programmes would be equally immune to challenges from persons who may feel aggrieved by such programmes. Another reason for this investigation of the permissible forms of affirmative action in terms of employer's objectives (as contained in an affirmative action policy document), is that if it can be shown that a form of preferential promotion was used that falls outside the ambit of the employer's objectives, such promotion could possibly be challenged as being unfair. This possibility is based on the argument that the fairness of preferential promotions is to be found in the employer's objectives.

Three modalities or forms of affirmative action can be distinguished: a *strong*, an *intermediate* and a *weak* form. In the *strong variant* a person qualifies for preferential treatment solely on the grounds that he/she possesses an immutable characteristic (for example, an employee is promoted because she is a female, without satisfying the job specifications). In the *intermediate/moderate variant* of affirmative action the person meets the minimum standards/qualification for the job and is given preference over another candidate who is better qualified, because of some immutable characteristic which he/she possesses but which the better qualified person does not (for example, the job specifies matric as a minimum qualification but preferably a bachelor's degree, and a black matriculant is promoted rather than the white male graduate candidate). In the *weak variant* of affirmative action a black/female/handicapped/etc employee is only promoted in preference to an able-bodied white male if both candidates are equally qualified for the job. While many South African employers would like to see that only the *weak modality* of affirmative action be adopted or mandated, it should be clear that such a policy will not be up to the task facing this country.

5.4.2 The controversial nature of affirmative action

"Affirmative action is a battleground for competing values, especially competing concepts of distributive justice" (Taylor 1991: xv). Libertarianism's claim that merit should be the universal principle of distributive justice can be questioned. First, there is the problem of defining merit and the influence of culture on the definer of merit which seems to make it a less than objective standard by which to allocate goods. Secondly, there is the inappropriateness of merit as a criterion of distribution in certain circumstances. Thirdly, the question should be asked whether merit is a socially desirable criterion, since it may have undesirable societal consequences. Fourthly, a further source of controversy is the criteria for defining the distributive values used to guide the allocation of social goods and resources. For some, prevailing standards are nothing more than collective, subjective preferences, and are, as such, suspect and open to the challenge that they are reflective of pervasive prejudice. Although there may be consensus about what value should serve as the basis of a distribution, there may be a considerable sense of injustice about the criteria that are used to define the value. Within a community, affirmative action may enjoy a generally high degree of acceptance, as a value in itself, on which to base job allocations, but there may exist an equally great resistance to the criteria used to identify the beneficiaries of affirmative action (for example group-based criteria versus actual victims of past discrimination).

The incommensurability of the opposing sides in the affirmative action debate is based on fundamental disagreements about the meaning of such concepts as equality and justice; both sides proclaim their allegiance to the ideal of equality. Acceptance of competing views of the relationship between individuals and society can have profound implications for our view of such fundamental concepts as property rights, employment related rights and duties, and equality. These topics are, however, so wide-ranging that no attempt will be made to deal with them here, save for giving one example. By way of contrast with the orthodox libertarian conception of property rights, the modern tendency is towards a restriction of property rights in what has been referred to as the "socialisation of property" (Jordaan, in Rycroft & Jordaan 1992: 15). Jordaan (Rycroft & Jordaan 1992: 16–17) describes this process as follows:

> "'Socialization' of law entails the adjustment of conflicting interests in society through the subordination of the individual's interests to those of society at large. In relation to property, it entails a shift away from an individualist 'and basically exploitive' perception of property rights towards the notion that property is a social responsibility. The underlying premise is that the institution of property is derived from and protected by society, i.e. it is a social institution and may be made to serve particular social objectives. This is accomplished through 'public law' regulation of the use and application of property resources. 'Absolute' rights are replaced by rights qualified to suit the needs of society best. . . . Legal rules do not exist in a vacuum but are tied to the social system within which they operate."

The preceding reasoning can therefore validly be used to justify further intrusions into managerial prerogative, for instance, to achieve the goals of affirmative action and equality.

5.5   AFFIRMATIVE ACTION AND EQUALITY

It is frequently asserted that the introduction of affirmative action is imperative in South Africa because of the vast inequalities brought about by many years of unfair discrimination. The object of affirmative action is the removal of these inequalities. This, however, leaves some questions unanswered: "equality for whom?", "equality of what?", "equality of means or equality of opportunities?" and "how shall equality be measured?". These are highly complex issues which fall beyond the scope of this book, but it may be worthwhile for the reader to reflect on these questions. For example, the bland assertion that "blacks or women should be treated equally" may be interpreted in a variety of ways, depending on what notion of equality the speaker has in mind. All normative theories of the just society that have stood the test of time have one characteristic in common, namely that they demand equality of something, that something being central to a particular theory. Utilitarians demand that equal weight be given to the utilities of all; libertarians insist on equal enjoyment of civil rights and liberties for all; income and welfare egalitarians regard equal incomes and equal welfare levels, respectively, as indispensable for the just society. Therefore, to characterise the controversy over equality as one involving those who are against equality versus those who are for equality is ". . . to miss something central to the subject" (Sen 1992: ix). For instance, a libertarian would have no objection in principle to equal incomes, given a certain set of prevailing circumstances and provided that equal enjoyment of individual rights and liberties is not compromised. Insisting on equality in respect of a particular variable that is central to a given theory of social justice of necessity entails tolerating inequalities in competing variables. For instance, a libertarian cannot demand equal enjoyment of rights and liberties and insist on the pre-eminence of the merit principle while at the same time insisting on equality of income levels. The dispute between egalitarians and libertarians in truth therefore resides not in the concept of equality but in identifying the central social variable that should be given priority over competing socially desirable arrangements. Human diversity will inevitably result in equality in one respect giving rise to inequality in another. Ethical theories typically try to justify inequalities in the peripheral variables by pointing to equality in the focal variable, which it is proposed is the most important equality in terms of a particular ethical theory.

The concept *equality* has since the earliest times been used in a variety of ways and normally in a context that implies that it is a fundamental element of justice. While justice has many manifestations, we are concerned with distributive justice when analysing the concept of equality. However, there seems to be little agreement as to what is meant by the concepts of equality and justice. One of the earliest definitions of justice holds that to treat equals equally and unequals differently encapsulates the essence of justice. But this simply begs the question, since one's system of classification of "equals" and "unequals" and the consequences of this classification will determine the fairness of the awards and punishment attached to these classifications. For instance, to classify people as "black" or "white" may not be intrinsically reprehensible, but to make the distribution of social goods and civil liberties contingent upon the classification is certainly grossly unfair.

As explained already, few countries in the world are characterised by such extremes of inequality as are prevalent in present-day South Africa. In this regard, you are referred back to chapter 4.

5.6 THE GREEN PAPER AND DRAFT BILL ON EMPLOYMENT EQUITY

5.6.1 Overview

On 1 July 1996 the Department of Labour published policy proposals for a "new employment and occupational equity statute". This was followed by a draft employment equity bill, published on 30 November 1997. In this section an overview is provided of the green paper (all page references will henceforth refer to this source), while the corresponding sections of the draft bill are summarised in endnotes.

5.6.1.1 The nature of employment equity

The *Green Paper* regards employment equity as necessary because of past discrimination (as well as the present inequalities which have emanated from past discrimination) and to ensure diversity in the workplace. Unfair discrimination based on race and gender are seen as the focal areas for rectification. In the view of the authors of the *Green Paper* (Department of Labour 1996: 6), employment equity centres on:[2]

- the eradication of unfair discrimination of any kind in hiring, promotion, training, pay, benefits and retrenchments; and
- measures to encourage employers to undertake organisational transformation to remove unjustified barriers to employment for all South Africans and to accelerate training and promotion for individuals from historically disadvantaged groups.

The objective of achieving overall social and economic equality, it is acknowledged, can only be achieved if the interventions imposed on employers will enhance productivity, democracy and diversity.

5.6.1.2 Proposals to achieve employment equity

The following proposals are put forward in the *Green Paper* (Department of Labour 1996: 10–11, 30, 32) to promote equity in the workplace.

- Employers will be required to devise non-discriminatory procedures for hiring, promoting, remunerating and selecting persons for training and retrenchment. These measures are clearly directed at ensuring equal employment opportunities (these can be called antidiscriminatory measures)[3].
- In consultation[4] with employees and other stakeholders, employers should develop an employment equity plan[5] that:
  - provides for measures to reduce barriers to historically disadvantaged groups;
  - accelerates training and promotion for people from historically disadvantaged communities; and
  - provides key indicators of success in ensuring equity.
- Measures (penalties and inducements) must be introduced to encourage institutional and cultural change by employing organisations.
- As far as possible, disputes should be resolved through mediation and arbitration, with strong legal protection against discrimination and harassment[6].
- All employers will be required to report on employment and training in terms of race and gender.
- Work organisation must be restructured to accommodate diversity and to reduce barriers to historically disadvantaged groups.

Measures to reduce nonemployment barriers to equity in the workplace include:

- the expansion of household infrastructure (for example the provision of water and electricity to individual households) and housing in historically disadvantaged communities;
- improved social services (for example community health clinics, public transport and proper roads) for historically disadvantaged communities;
- measures to foster more equal distribution of assets (for example land reform and the promotion of small and medium enterprises).

The proposals also emphasise the importance of establishing a continuous process of human resource development. Transformation of the training system must ensure that training will (Department of Labour 1996: 31–32):

- link into internal career paths that promote progression and productivity;
- bear credit in terms of the National Qualifications Framework;
- enhance employment security;
- involve adult basic education;
- build upon prior learning, whether acquired formally or informally; and
- be designated as a matter for consultation or joint decision making.

It is acknowledged that institutional change will necessitate a considerable outlay, both in time and resources, and it is therefore proposed that any policy implementation will have to take account of the more limited resources of smaller employers. Initially, the government will focus its attention on larger employers who could act as role models (for smaller employers) and whose workplace practices affect more people.

5.6.1.3 Sources of employment and social inequity in South Africa

Recognition is given to the fact that employment equity will not necessarily provide a panacea for all the evils of past discrimination. Nonemployment initiatives suggested to eradicate inequality are, inter alia, the National Qualifications Framework for education and training, improvements in education, upgrading of the infrastructure in historically disadvantaged communities, and initiatives to promote greater employment opportunities and self-employment. Some of the major sources of discrimination within and outside the labour market, as well as proposed remedial interventions, are depicted in figure 5.2.

In figure 5.3 some forms of discrimination specific to the workplace, as well as suggested general remedies, are depicted.

It is proposed that antidiscriminatory policies should be instituted which will compel employers to:

- ensure that all potential candidates, and especially those from disadvantaged groups, know about opportunities through appropriate advertising;
- define and communicate clear, nondiscriminatory criteria for their decisions regarding, for example, appointments and promotions;
- provide equal pay and benefits for equal work;
- give reasons for their decisions in terms of the aforementioned criteria; and
- establish appeal procedures to management or to representative bodies.

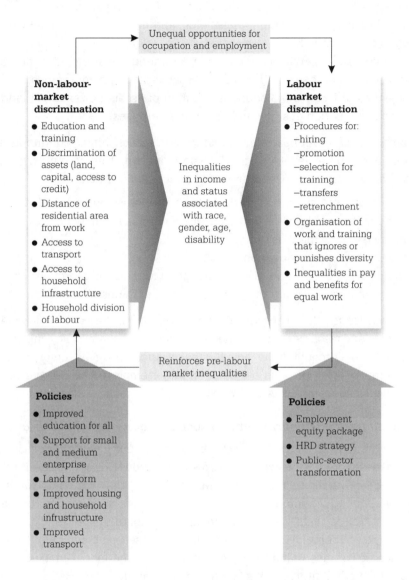

Figure 5.2

Discrimination within and outside the labour market

Source: *Government Gazette* 1 July 1996: 22

5.6.2 The organisational audit and employment equity plan

5.6.2.1 The organisational audit[7]

The *Green Paper* proposes (Department of Labour 1996: 36) that employers should be required to conduct an organisational audit to identify existing shortcomings and barriers to change. It is recommended that these audits should be conducted in cooperation with employee representative bodies (for example workplace forums and/or trade unions). It is envisaged that the audit should become a public document, unless this would harm the company's competitive advantage. These audits will have to contain information on specified key performance areas and will be used by the Department of Labour for monitoring representativeness and employment equity according to undertaking, sector and region. Exhibit A gives examples of the type of information that could be included in the organisational audit. Transformation of the workplace to make it more equitable and equal starts with the organisational audit. The information derived from the audit should serve as the basis from which to identify and devise the necessary means to eliminate barriers to historically disadvantaged groups. It should lead to a thorough review of work organisation, grading systems, career paths and training. It should also form the basis for reviewing progress towards greater employment equity. It is also suggested that, in order to foster a culture of fair and open industrial relations and respect for human rights and diversity, managers and employees should participate in training on conflict management, cultural and gender diversity and institutional change.

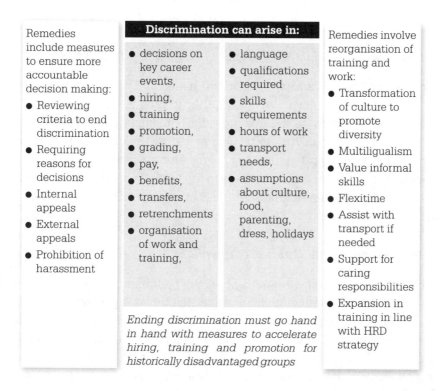

Remedies include measures to ensure more accountable decision making:	**Discrimination can arise in:**		Remedies involve reorganisation of training and work:
• Reviewing criteria to end discrimination	• decisions on key career events,	• language	• Transformation of culture to promote diversity
• Requiring reasons for decisions	• hiring,	• qualifications required	• Multiligualism
• Internal appeals	• training	• skills requirements	• Value informal skills
• External appeals	• promotion,	• hours of work	• Flexitime
• Prohibition of harassment	• grading,	• transport needs,	• Assist with transport if needed
	• pay,	• assumptions about culture, food, parenting, dress, holidays	• Support for caring responsibilities
	• benefits,		• Expansion in training in line with HRD strategy
	• transfers,		
	• retrenchments		
	• organisation of work and training,		

Ending discrimination must go hand in hand with measures to accelerate hiring, training and promotion for historically disadvantaged groups

Figure 5.3

Sources of discrimination in the labour market and some general remedies

Source: *Government Gazette* 1 July 1996: p 26

Exhibit A

Proposed organisational audit

An organisation audit should give information on:
- Employment, pay and benefits in major categories by race, gender and disability
- Programmes and policies on human resource development, including levels of expenditure, certification, and race, gender and disability status of trainees
- Organisation of work in terms of the skills and responsibilities required by different positions and hours worked
- Transport, housing and caring arrangements and preferences of employees, by race and gender, including options for hours worked
- Languages used and language competence
- Physical facilities for disabled people and women
- Procedures for hiring, training, promotion, retrenchment and transfers
- Grievance and internal appeals procedures

5.6.2.2 Employment equity plans[8]

On the basis of the organisational audit employers should develop employment equity plans.

Organisations that will have to submit employment equity plans[9]

Given the limited resources to monitor plans and to accommodate smaller employers[10], not all employers will be required to submit employment equity plans. The intention seems to be to have a gradual implementation in terms of which initially only larger employers (to be designated by the Cabinet as "organisations that belong to 'primary categories'") or maybe employers with a consistent discriminatory record, will have to submit plans to the Minister of Labour. Other employers may have to submit plans if representatives of employees or other important stakeholders formally request it.

Development and administration of the plan

The Department of Labour would support the planning process as far as possible by, for instance, developing guidelines and timetables for all employing organisations, as well as guidelines for assessing the acceptability of employment equity plans. Plans should be developed in consultation with stakeholders. It is acknowledged that employment equity will only succeed if it occurs in an atmosphere where all employees, from management to the shop floor, can freely debate specific measures. It is suggested that larger organisations should have an official responsible for all aspects of employment equity in the organisation[11]. In addition, a body representative of all employees should participate in the auditing and planning process and help to establish internal structures (such as internal appeals procedures). Where workplace forums exist, they should take on this task.

5.6.3 Responsibilities of employers

The suggested responsibilities of employing organisations are the following:

- Employers should consult with employees and possibly with other important stakeholders on employment equity measures, including the audit and plan.
- All employers should provide some key data on employment on a regular basis, as defined by the Department of Labour.
- All employers should introduce procedures to end discriminatory decision making about employees and ensure equal pay and benefits for equal work.
- All employers should review grievance systems to ensure their effectiveness in handling discriminatory behaviour or harassment.
- Employers in some categories should submit employment equity plans for approval by the Minister of Labour. Other employers might have to submit plans, if requested by employees or other stakeholders, or in order to get subsidies or tendering rights (see next section). Once approved, employers should have a legal obligation to carry the plans out and report on their implementation.
- Large and strategically placed or persistently unrepresentative employers should be asked to implement employment equity processes more rigorously and report on them in greater detail.

5.6.4 Proposed institutional framework

5.6.4.1 Introduction

In this section we look first of all at the institutions tasked with ensuring that employment equity becomes a reality and then at the proposed sanctions and incentives to promote employment equity. It should be noted that it is proposed that the statute should contain only the overall framework: the Minister of Labour will be empowered to prescribe the finer detail by regulation. In this way greater flexibility and adaptability will be built into the legislative framework. The authors of the *Green Paper* propose that the legislative framework should endeavour to strike a balance between strict administrative processes and an effort to build positive relations among the affected parties. Management will be glad to see that quotas are not proposed at this stage. It is to be expected that some unions may object to this and that, should the proposed system not produce the required results, quotas will once again be placed on the agenda. It is therefore in the interest of employers to do everything possible to promote employment equity. If the soft approach does not yield results, a harder approach is bound to follow.

5.6.4.2 Institutions

The institutions to be involved with the employment equity initiative (some established in terms of other legislation and others proposed in terms of the envisaged Employment Equity Act), are the government, the Department of Labour, the Labour Inspectorate, bargaining councils, the Commission for Conciliation, Mediation and Arbitration (CCMA), the Labour Court and the Labour Appeal Court, and the Employment Equity Advisory Council (EEAC). In addition, it is proposed that the burden of proof be reversed, that class action suits be allowed and that certain monitoring mechanisms be put into place.

The Department of Labour

The Department of Labour should be responsible for achieving compliance with the proposed legislation and codes of good practice. Within the Department, the Directorate for Equal Opportunities and the Labour Inspectorate should be tasked with the administration of the legislation[12].

The Labour Inspectorate[13]

It is proposed that the existing inspectors of the Department of Labour should undertake monitoring and enforcement activities of a routine nature in the course of general inspections of employers' premises (such as ensuring that employers make the required returns of data, and, if applicable, employment equity plans).

Bargaining Councils

Bargaining councils established in terms of the Labour Relations Act 66 of 1995 have, as part of their functions, the promotion and establishment of training and education schemes; these could be extended to include measures to promote employment equity. Bargaining councils should be required to submit regular reports to the Minister of Labour in order to establish sectoral patterns and norms relating to employment equity in a specific sector.

The Commission for Conciliation, Mediation and Arbitration (CCMA)

It is proposed that the CCMA should play a central part in both the antidiscrimination and employment equity components of the statute. Any employment equity dispute that cannot be resolved in the workplace should be referred to the CCMA. Only if the CCMA fails to settle a dispute, would a party be able to approach the Labour Court.

The Labour Court and the Labour Appeal Court

These courts were established by the Labour Relations Act 66 of 1995 as courts of law and equity that provide specialist adjudication of labour-related disputes. The power of the courts to order costs against a party will be extended to employment equity disputes. The Labour Appeal Court will be the court of final instance, except on matters that raise constitutional issues (the latter may be referred to the Constitutional Court). One may expect that almost all employment equity disputes potentially will open the door to the Constitutional Court, these disputes having to do with the important fundamental right to equality (see section 9 of the Constitution).

It is proposed that the onus of proof be reversed in cases before the courts. This will mean that, once an allegation of discrimination has been made, an employer will have to show that he/she has not discriminated against the employee concerned. Thus, an employee will not carry the burden of having to prove his/her allegations of discrimination — it will be up to the employer to prove the contrary.

Ordinarily only individuals or groups of individuals whose rights have been directly affected have standing in a court of law (that is, capacity to litigate). For example, under the old dispensation trade unions frequently appeared before the Industrial Court, not on their own behalf, but on behalf of their members whose rights had allegedly been infringed by the respondent employer. It is proposed that the law should permit class action suits by representatives of stakeholders. For example, a trade union (or employers' organisation) will have the necessary standing to approach the courts irrespective of whether a specific individual has been directly affected by alleged discriminatory practices. This broadening of the concept of capacity to litigate provides trade unions with a powerful tool to monitor employers' compliance with employment equity even in the absence of an actual aggrieved individual. For example, it may come to a trade union's attention that an employer's selection procedures have the effect of excluding a disproportionate number of women. That trade union would then have the capacity to bring the matter to court, even though there is no specific woman who alleges that her application for employment was unsuccessful due to the alleged discriminatory practices of the employer.

The Employment Equity Advisory Council (EEAC)[14]

This body is to be established in terms of the proposed legislation as an advisory council for the Minister of Labour. The EEAC should be representative of all stakeholders. It is proposed that the EEAC should give expert advice on policy and also monitor progress in the attainment of employment equity and representativeness. All codes of good practice should be tabled for consultation in the EEAC before being presented to Parliament. The latter proposal seems to infringe on the functions of NEDLAC, which is also a forum for debating legislative proposals relating to the labour market.

5.6.4.3 Incentives[15] and sanctions[16]

The proposed incentives and sanctions incorporated into the employment equity scheme contained in the *Green Paper* can be summarised as follows:

Incentives

- Government action should favour employers who promote employment equity; suggested measures include making a good record on employment equity a consideration in:
- granting tenders for government and parastatal contracts and

- providing direct or indirect subsidies, such as training grants from the Department of Labour or investment incentives from the Department of Trade and Industry.

Sanctions

- Disputes about employment equity should first go to the CCMA and then to the Labour Court. Should the relevant body decide that an employer has violated employment equity requirements, corrective action will be taken (for example, the employer may be required to appoint/promote a person who was denied employment/promotion on discriminatory grounds.
- The imposition of fines, administrative or legal sanctions could also be considered for more serious instances of non-compliance (for example where a pattern of non-compliance exists such as repeated cases of proven discrimination or continued failure to develop an acceptable employment equity plan when required to do so).

5.7 LESSONS FROM OTHER COUNTRIES

One can usefully think of state-sponsored affirmative action interventions as a kind of social experiment and investigate what has been tried in other countries to assess what works and what does not. However, a cautionary note is appropriate: the fact that a specific type of affirmative action programme has worked in one country does not guarantee success should a similar approach be adopted in another country. The argument against the uncritical importation of foreign programmes is that affirmative action has only rarely been implemented because of some abstract idea of inequality (Weiner 1993: 3). Rather, it is usually the result of a change in the power structure within a country. As such, the historical antecedents and the present dispersion of power in a society need to be taken into account before embarking on any specific affirmative action programme. Bearing these cautionary remarks in mind, we look at some other countries' experiences with affirmative action and at the potential lessons to be learnt.

5.7.1 The United States

Section 5.2 gives an overview of the origins of affirmative action in America, and you are referred to that discussion. The Americans' experience is of limited use to South Africa because their situation differs in too many important respects from ours. In the United States it was the majority and hence the politically powerful who introduced affirmative action for minorities. The future of their society is not endangered to the extent that ours is, should affirmative action fail. Possibly one important lesson that can be learnt from the American experience with affirmative action is that group-based notions of affirmative action help the least disadvantaged individuals within the disadvantaged group without doing much to relieve the plight of those at the bottom end of the socioeconomic scale. Proof of this is to be found in many studies that point out that, while the position of black Americans as a group has improved relative to their white counterparts, the socioeconomic disparity among blacks themselves has increased since the introduction of affirmative action measures. The question then arises: who should benefit from affirmative action, the least or the most downtrodden members of the historically disadvantaged groups? In recent years the gains made by affirmative action have been rolled back in the United States. Therein is possibly a further lesson, namely that fundamental to the long-term success of any affirmative action programme is the locus of power within society. This is as true for organisations as it is for societies at large (see section 5.9, where the importance of direct CEO support for the success of any organisation's affirmative action plan is emphasised). This further differentiates the American situation from our own. In South Africa the balance of power is shifting towards the majority who also happen to be the intended beneficiaries of affirmative action, making it unlikely that affirmative action gains will be relinquished, as is happening in America. Opposition to affirmative action can garner votes in America; in South Africa it will amount to political suicide. If the American experience is of limited use to us, what about countries nearer to home?

5.7.2 Zimbabwe

Discriminatory legislation introduced during the colonial period in Zimbabwe led to large disparities between whites and blacks in terms of income, employment, education, vocational training and wealth. High unemployment among blacks with almost full employment among whites was a structural feature of preindependence Zimbabwe (Castle 1995: 7). One of the first priorities of the government after independence in 1980 was to redress the vast inequalities caused by historical discrimination. A presidential directive was issued soon after independence calling upon the Public Service to follow a vigorous programme of replacing whites with blacks. No such directive was made applicable to the private sector, since it was hoped that the private sector would follow the lead taken by the public sector and embark on its own voluntary programme of affirmative action. That black advancement was effective in the public service is evidenced by the fact that a mere nine years after independence 95 % of the public service was staffed by blacks. Several writers ascribe this rapid advancement of blacks to various factors, one of these being an unbelievable growth in the size of the civil service from 40 000 posts in 1980 to 90 000 in 1989. Unfortunately, this bloated civil service gave rise to inefficiencies and allegations of nepotism, tribalism, fraud and corruption. Over the last few years the government has introduced cutbacks (prompted in no small measure by the International Monetary Fund and the World Bank). Other factors necessitating cutbacks were the shrinkage of the economy since independence and an unacceptably high budget deficit.

As was said previously, no affirmative action legislation was introduced in Zimbabwe and the presidential directive on black advancement was only made directly applicable to the public sector. What legislative intervention there was focuses on the elimination of discrimination. For example, the Labour Relations Act of 1985 focuses on instances of individual discrimination and does not address the present effects of past discriminatory practices in the workplace. Nevertheless, black advancement in the private sector has been impressive (with the exception of top managerial positions and the ownership of companies). According to government statistics, the number of blacks in professional, technical, administrative and managerial positions has increased eightfold in the seventeen years since independence (equal to 90 % of all positions). Gatherer and Erickson (Castle 1995: 11) observe that the most significant spur to black advancement in the private sector is the sustained support of top management for black advancement. In particular, the following factors are cited by Castle (1995: 11) as contributing to the success of black advancement in Zimbabwe:

● recognition by top management that it is in the organisation's own long-term interest to train black managers (educated young white people tend to emigrate, whereas educated young blacks tend to stay);

● development of precise career paths with detailed job descriptions;

● implementation of merit-based promotion criteria;

● development of management training programmes tailored to the needs of black graduates;

● early identification of persons with high potential;

● willingness of experienced white managers to provide on-the-job training to junior black colleagues.

Notwithstanding these impressive advances, social discrimination is still alleged to be a pervasive problem within Zimbabwean organisations, with blacks claiming that they are excluded from important decision-making processes and subjected to bias in promotions and pay. There also is concern that the tendency of black graduates to job-hop in pursuit of ever higher remuneration packages undermines the development of managerial talent.

According to press reports over the past few years, there are disquieting indications that the Zimbabwean government's commitment to equality is, in certain respects, suspect. To name a few instances: there seems to be deeply ingrained discrimination against women as regards land ownership and succession rights; gays are denied civil rights (if not by law or presidential decree). These discriminatory practices are fuelled by inflammatory rhetoric by the President himself and enforced by mob rule (in some instances in flagrant disregard of court orders upholding the rights of homosexuals). Women also tend to cluster around lower level jobs. The potential lessons South Africa can learn from the Zimbabwean experience are summarised in exhibit B.

Exhibit B

Lessons from Zimbabwe*

- Like Zimbabwe, South Africa will have to develop an indigenous base of skilled human resources.
- Antidiscriminatory laws are necessary, but are not sufficient to eliminate the present effects of past discrimination.
- Laws cannot by themselves eliminate societal discrimination in the workplace (for this human resource interventions aimed at organisational cultural and attitudinal change are necessary).
- If senior politicians are not seen actively to support the protection of the equality rights of certain groups (such as homosexuals and women), societal discrimination will flourish irrespective of constitutional guarantees.
- In order to absorb the increased number of black school graduates, the economy must expand dramatically; it is therefore absolutely necessary that the government's macroeconomic policy should pursue economic growth and job creation (for, without sufficient jobs, an improved educational system will create expectancies which the economy will be unable to deliver, leading to an increase in social tension).
- Broadly targeted affirmative action programmes tend to favour the already privileged members of the disadvantaged group (such as exiles trained abroad and those blacks who had access to good schooling).
- Job fragmentation and well-developed career paths are necessary for black advancement.
- The training and development of managers, regardless of their race, takes time.
- Window-dressing is not the answer.
- Ways have to be found to counter the problem of well-qualified blacks chasing ever-increasing salary packages without spending enough time with any one employer to gain substantial managerial skills. One possible solution would be to place black managers in positions of real authority (such as operational or financial manager as opposed to public relations or human resources manager).
- Black aspirations regarding black ownership of businesses must be accommodated.
- The basis for effective managerial training remains proper prior formal education.
- The problem of advancing the least advantaged among the historically disadvantaged (eg black women) needs special attention.
- Appointments and promotion based on merit should prevail over window-dressing.
- The attitude of top management to affirmative action is crucial for the success of any programme (the same holds for the attitude of political leaders and the successful eradication of discrimination in society at large).
- In the absence of private black advancement initiatives, the government will tend to impose impracticable measures.
- Decisions should be based on economic and business principles and not on political rhetoric.
- Human resources departments must take the initiative in black advancement programmes.

*Source: Adapted from Castle 1995: 12–14; Gerber, Nel & Van Dyk 1995: 197

5.7.3 Namibia

Namibia had been under colonial domination since 1884, first by Germany and, after the First World War, by South Africa (which occupied Namibia originally in terms of a mandate from the League of Nations). Although South Africa's mandate was officially terminated in 1966, South Africa continued to occupy and govern Namibia until independence in 1990. Namibia has a small economy based largely on mining and agriculture.

Parallels between Namibia, Zimbabwe and South Africa are the following: at independence white males dominated in positions of wealth and power; blacks were subjected to an inferior system of education; widespread structural unemployment among blacks; a skewed allocation of resources and services favouring whites and the urban elite; and the fear of a brain drain resulting from white emigration after independence (Castle 1995: 15). In 1995 less than 50 % of the labour force was employed in the formal sector. As in South Africa, white civil servants in Namibia were guaranteed security of employment during the negotiations leading up to independence. The new government, in the interests of reconciliation and the retention of white skills, has followed a policy of including blacks in the civil service rather than of excluding whites. This policy has largely been successful since, although the civil service has increased, there has not been a mass exodus of white skills (at least, not of the magnitude experienced by Zimbabwe). Also, the moderate stance taken by the new government, the fact that the President has refrained from castigating whites for all the ills that plague society, and the fact that the government has eschewed socialist policies in favour of the free-market ideology, have all contributed to greater racial harmony in civil society and greater willingness on the part of the international community to provide financial assistance to the Namibian government than is the case with Zimbabwe.

One of the greatest challenges facing Namibia is job creation. At entry levels, four times more school leavers enter the labour market than can be absorbed through the creation of new jobs (Castle 1995: 18). In the light of this, Swanepoel (1992: 24) emphasises the importance of employers not only promoting black advancement through affirmative action but also having to formulate total employment strategies that will create and redistribute wealth. Apart from unacceptable levels of unemployment, the high population growth is also bound to exacerbate the need for economic growth and job creation.

In 1990 Namibia adopted a new constitution, of which Article 10 guarantees equality for all persons and prohibits discrimination on the grounds of sex, race, colour, ethnicity, religion, creed or socioeconomic status. Article 23 of the Constitution declares the practice and ideology of racial discrimination a criminal offence and authorises Parliament to enact legislation and to implement policies and programmes to advance people who have been socially, economically or educationally disadvantaged by past discriminatory laws or practices. In the early 1990s draft affirmative action legislation was published, but, although there has been subsequent government activity in this regard (such as the appointment of a commission to oversee the implementation of affirmative action), at present neither a statute nor a presidential decree has materialised to establish the legislative framework for affirmative action.

Exhibit C

Lessons from Namibia

- Moderation in political and economic policies and rhetoric can go a long way in retaining white skills and attracting foreign investment.
- Measures must be found to curb population growth if the pressing problem of unemployment is to be addressed effectively.
- Economic growth and job creation are imperatives in the quest for social and employment justice and equality.
- Investment in formal education and training is essential.
- Words, however well-intentioned, will remain just that: without government initiatives (including a monitoring agency, sanctions and inducements) affirmative action in private enterprises will not be realised.

5.7.4 Zambia

Shortly after independence Zambia embarked on a very drastic process of "Zambianism" in order to eliminate all vestiges of colonialism as rapidly as possible. These included (Gerber, Nel & Van Dyk 1996: 195): partial nationalisation of large multinational companies; whites were replaced by blacks in almost all jobs; vacancies were created for blacks to fill; and black education was improved. According to Alfred (Gerber et al 1996: 195), the results of these steps were as follows: Zambia's economy was all but destroyed; education focused on academic subjects, causing a shortage in technical skills; many blacks were placed in positions for which they were ill-equipped. The lessons of the Zambian experiment in black advancement are summarised in exhibit D.

Exhibit D

Lessons from Zambia*

- Transformation should not be too rapid.
- Black employees, like whites, should not be promoted to jobs for which they have not been trained and in which they are incapable of achieving success.
- Education, especially in a developing country, should concentrate on market-related skills rather than on general, purely academic training.
- Economic policies should promote wealth and job creation.
- Redistribution of existing wealth through nationalisation and patronage may be detrimental to the economy as a whole.

*Source: Adapted from Gerber et al 1995: 195

5.7.5 Malaysia

The Malaysian experience with affirmative action is of particular importance to South Africa because that country seems to have achieved remarkable economic growth while at the same time advancing the disadvantaged majority of its citizens. In this respect Malaysia is a more applicable model for South Africa than any of the countries discussed thus far. As we have already seen, the United States is a developed country in which the politically powerful introduced affirmative action measures for the benefit of disadvantaged minorities, while the African examples have in common with the South African situation the fact that black advancement was instituted for the benefit of the political majority, the post-colonial economic histories of these countries indicating, however, that they have failed to balance the quest for social justice, employment equity and equality with the dictates of economic growth. The overview of the Malaysian experience that follows is based largely on an article by Castle (1995: 6–33).

The population of Malaysia comprises three main ethnic groups, whose major demographic characteristics at independence in 1957 can be summarised as follows. The majority (55 %) were Malays comprising a small aristocratic elite who controlled the political sphere and the administration and a majority of extremely poor persons making a living in the rural areas as subsistence farmers. The Chinese, who migrated to Malaysia in the nineteenth century, comprised 35 % of the population. Under British colonial rule the Chinese sector of the population had become relatively wealthy merchants and traders, living mostly in urban areas. The Indians, comprising 10 % of the population had, like the Chinese, prospered under colonial rule and had become powerful in commerce and finance. At independence therefore, the different ethnic groups had an unequal share in the economy as a whole.

The first government after independence was formed by an alliance party consisting of three parties, each of which represented one of the major ethnic groups. Subsequent governments followed this pattern of alliances between the parties representing the three ethnic groups. Successive governments embarked upon development plans to eradicate the economic gap between the Malay majority and the other two ethnic groups. Malays were granted political supremacy; Islam (the Malay religion) was established as the state religion; Malay was entrenched as the national language; quotas in favour of Malays in the public service were introduced. In return, citizenship requirements were relaxed and an understanding was reached that the economic interests of the advantaged ethnic groups would be protected. The original Malaysian Constitution provided that the affirmative action provisions had to be reviewed fifteen years after independence, but this sunset clause was removed from the Constitution as a result of serious civil unrest in 1969.

The civil uprising of 1969 can be attributed to a number of factors. Between 1957 and 1969 there was little government interference in the private sector and the economy grew at a healthy 5,7 % per annum, while retaining its dual character of affluent Chinese and Indians with a poor rural (Malay) majority who did not share in the spoils brought about by the economic growth. Also, impressive as the economic growth was, it failed to keep pace with an even bigger population growth which caused unemployment to rise in all ethnic groups and led to an 11 % decline in the mean household income of the bottom 40 % of the population (mostly Malays). In addition, the Chinese began to pose a political threat to the Malay majority. To summarise, despite political power and domination in government decision making, there was little evidence of the benefits of the economic boom as far as the greater majority of the Malaysian population was concerned. As a result of this violent uprising, the government instituted some drastic reform measures.

Exhibit E

Lessons from Malaysia

- Affirmative action policies based on race/ethnicity can cause great rifts along ethnic lines and undermine efforts to foster a national rather than a sectoral identity among all groups in society.
- The important role of education of the right kind in promoting equality and economic growth cannot be overemphasised.
- The "trickle-down effect", so beloved by many capitalists (ie laissez faire policies whereby the rich are left to enrich themselves in the hope that some of those riches will somehow find their way to the lower socioeconomic classes) was shown to be a chimera.
- Affirmative action plans founded on group-based notions of disadvantage do little to benefit the poor (indeed, the gap between the poor and the rich within the historically disadvantaged group tends to increase markedly subsequent to the introduction of affirmative action programmes).
- Neglecting the needs of the poor masses, even while vastly improving the number of entrants from the disadvantaged group into the bourgeoisie, may lead to social unrest and serious class conflict.
- Labour policies and measures that ensure labour market flexibility will promote foreign investment.
- Extensive government intervention in the private sphere is not necessarily irreconcilable with economic growth, provided that it does not inhibit market processes.
- Irrespective of political protestations to the contrary, once affirmative measures are introduced, it may be very difficult to remove them.

After 1970 the state started to follow an interventionist strategy to increase corporate ownership by Malays and to foster the transfer of wealth to the Malays. In this way a Malay middle class soon appeared. Affirmative action targets (previously limited to the public service) were extended to the private sector, land settlement schemes, agricultural credit and price supports were introduced, and the state enterprise sector was rapidly expanded. Special initiatives were introduced to promote Malay businesses. Trade unions' ability to organise was also strictly regulated in an effort to attract foreign investment. The importance of education (and especially of the right kind of education) was appreciated by the Malays. The government embarked on a vigorous education programme favouring Malays and concentrating on the development of managerial, technical and scientific knowledge and skills. The government also introduced and supported in-service training schemes in the private sector. All these schemes to advance the socioeconomic interests of Malays have paid off in that there has been a remarkable growth in Malay corporate ownership and wealth since 1970. However, the quota system has operated to divide Malaysian society more deeply on ethnic lines. Plaut (1992: 42) also contends that there were greater disparities in income in 1992 within the Malay group than within any other ethnic group, which once again raises the issue of affirmative action's inability to come to the aid of the least advantaged among the disadvantaged group. What can we learn from the Malaysian experience? The possible lessons are summarised in exhibit E.

5.7.6 Sri Lanka

The Sri Lankan experience is an example of an affirmative action experiment which went horribly wrong. As a direct consequence of the government's affirmative action policy, the country has been involved in a bloody civil war in which thousands have been killed and the economy adversely affected.

Sri Lanka is a country whose population is divided along linguistic and religious lines. The largest group is Sinhalese Buddhist (75 %) with a Tamil Hindu minority (18 %). During the nineteenth century missionaries built schools in the predominantly Tamil areas in the north and east of the country. As a result of this historical favouring of the Tamils, they held a disproportionate share of government jobs, had higher levels of education and were generally better off than the Sinhalese majority. In 1956 a Sinhalese Buddhist political party came into power with the promise of elevating the Sinhalese. One of the new government's interventions was to replace English as the official language of the country with Sinhalese. This policy produced dramatic results (since very few Tamils could speak Sinhalese): within a decade the Tamil composition of the civil service had dropped from 50 % to 15 % (Weiner 1993: 8). Likewise, entrance examinations for tertiary education were no longer to be in English. When the authorities saw that Tamils still represented a disproportionate share of tertiary education entrants, a directive was issued in terms of which entrance examination marks had to be standardised so as to produce Sinhalese and Tamil pass rates in strict proportion to the composition of the national population. Resentment among the Tamils grew as they saw themselves marginalised in medical and engineering schools, the universities and jobs in the public sector. Furthermore, job opportunities in the private sector decreased for Tamil school-leavers because the government had nationalised much of the private sector.

Given the above circumstances, it is not wholly surprising that young Tamils took to arms and called for the creation of an independent Tamil state. To date the Tamil liberation movement, (known as the "Tamil Tigers") and government forces have been engaged in fierce fighting with no clear winner in sight. What is especially ironic and tragic is that during the 1970s a promarket Sinhalese government took office and set out to liberalise the economy, achieving considerable success in privatisation and job creation. Sadly this came too late, since many young Tamils were already so alienated from the sociopolitical mainstream that they could not be enticed back into civil society and the armed struggle continued unabated. Weiner (1993: 9) concludes his review of the Sri Lankan failure with the following synopsis:

> " . . . a misguided affirmative action policy proved destructive for the country's political and economic development, and for relations among the country's major ethnic communities. Affirmative action had become an instrument of the majority Sinhalese for using its political power to restrict opportunities for the Tamils; it was not a policy that emerged out of consensus among the major ethnic groups in the country. Moreover special opportunities for some had in effect 'eaten up' equal opportunities for all with disastrous consequences for the country."

Exhibit F

Lessons from Sri Lanka

- In an ethnically divided society a strong modality of affirmative action may lead to serious civil unrest if it takes place in the context of slow economic growth (because each affirmative action appointment is at the cost of someone from the marginalised groups).
- Policies amounting to outcome quotas (which is what, in effect, the university entrance examinations in Sri Lanka became), may spawn deeply felt resentment.
- If a minority group feels itself excluded from sharing in the social goods on offer (such as government jobs and tertiary education opportunities), it might seek its salvation in violent means.
- The harm done by an ill-considered affirmative action policy is very difficult to undo (and may prove impossible in the case of Sri Lanka — secession of the eastern and northern regions of the country in an independent state may well be the only long-term solution to the civil war).
- A government's use of affirmative action as a political weapon to suppress minorities rather than as a way to create employment opportunities for all may backfire, with disastrous consequences for society as a whole.

5.7.7 Affirmative action in other countries: concluding remarks

As the examples from the above countries illustrate, achieving equality is extremely difficult and may well not only endanger social stability and national unity but also lead to economic decline if handled incorrectly or too quickly. Another intriguing problem is the inability of traditional group-based notions of affirmative action to assist the most disadvantaged members of society. In this respect it is interesting to note that Namibia's Constitution offers a competing vision of affirmative action based on socioeconomic criteria irrespective of race or gender. If it is considered that race or gender are indirect indicators of disadvantage, whereas criteria of individual socioeconomic disadvantage are direct indicators of the degree of actual disadvantage suffered by a person, it may well be worthwhile to explore the practical feasibility of introducing an individual-based socioeconomic model of affirmative action. Lastly, for affirmative action to be successful in promoting equality, it must be approached in a holistic way, encompassing, in addition to work-related measures, many other spheres of social and public life (such as education, corporate ownership, access to infrastructure and housing, etc), without neglecting the dictates of economic growth and restructuring.

As far as South Africa is concerned, the government has introduced a number of initiatives that incorporate much of the valuable lessons from other countries. The most noteworthy of these are the Reconstruction and Development Programme, the recently announced macroeconomic policy (GEAR) and the national qualifications legislation aimed at restructuring our educational system to make it more flexible and market related. Other positive initiatives are aspects of the new Labour Relations Act (such as workplace forums which should be involved in affirmative action measures), aspects of the proposed new employment standards legislation, as well as the proposed legislation dealing with employment and occupational equity and the proposed skills development legislation currently being debated.

The Sri Lankan experience shows us that we should never forget that equality of opportunity is the objective of affirmative action and not the establishment of majority control in all institutions and every sphere of social and public life. For instance, the demand that all universities should reflect the demographics of society would inevitably result in each and every university in South Africa having to be English and black in character, with scant regard for minority groups' cultural interests. However, if the demand is that the university sector, seen as a whole, should be broadly reflective of national demographics, this would create the necessary space to include minority groups rather than to exclude them. We end this discussion with the following sobering observations of Weiner: "No-one has developed a general theory for dealing with the most difficult task in all contemporary multi-ethnic societies; how to reduce disparities among ethnic communities and manage ethnic conflict at the same time" (Weiner 1993: 3), and "How can one have an affirmative action policy if the goal is a colour-blind and classless society?" (Weiner 1993: 4).

5.8   IMPLEMENTATION OF AN AFFIRMATIVE ACTION PROGRAMME

5.8.1 General

The challenge facing South African organisations is to develop and implement affirmative action programmes that will achieve the joint goals of employment equity and wealth creation. We have seen that in many African countries measures to redistribute wealth and impose organisational control have been implemented with scant regard for economic growth. The consequences of this approach have been disastrous for the national economies of these countries and have resulted in the impoverishment of all. In section 5.9 the implications for certain specific human resource management practices are examined and that section should be read in conjunction with this discussion. In this section we discuss how an organisation can go about developing and implementing an affirmative action programme. It should be stressed that the aim is not, and cannot be, to provide a universally applicable blueprint, since an affirmative action programme should be tailored to meet the needs of a particular organisation, taking into account, *inter alia*, its present human resource skills base and future needs, its present labour force composition and its resources.

Figure 5.1. shows how the government, through legislation, can prohibit discriminatory practices and can promote affirmative action. However, the reach of the law is limited; without organisational culture change and the transformation of individual attitudes, affirmative action cannot succeed. This is so for a number of reasons. If an employer views affirmative action as a necessary evil, he/she will embark on measures to get "the numbers right" at what he/she considers to be the least cost to the organisation; this in turn will lead to window-dressing and to a low investment in human resource development. Power will thus remain firmly in the hands of white managers and black appointees will be tolerated (rather than seen and developed as valuable representatives of the organisation's human resource assets). The appointment of blacks will tend to be clustered in the lower hierarchical levels, and those blacks who are "lucky enough" to be appointed to managerial positions will find themselves in positions of no real authority and will thus soon leave in frustration. All this will lead to a reinforcement of racial stereotypes and to the entrenchment of the view that affirmative action measures lead to increased costs, a lowering of standards and a dropping of productivity. Just as no law can ensure that a marriage will be successful and compel a couple to be happily married (although the law can (and does) provide the legal framework for the institution of marriage), no statute can force an employer and employee to make a general success of their employment relationship and of affirmative action in particular. This is where the human factor becomes all important. In similar vein Njuguna (Gerber et al 1996: 186) stresses the importance of attitudes when he defines affirmative action as " . . . adopting management styles conducive to racial integration, and developing attitudes that enhance racial coexistence, racial tolerance and racial acceptance". Similarly, Charlton and Van Niekerk (1994: xvii) put it thus:

> "The giving of money and material resources is the easier option. It does much to appease the conscience of the giver and does not demand the sacrifice of time and involvement. In short it does not require a change of heart on the part of the giver. Unless affirmative action arises from a fundamental change of heart in the giver, and boosts the psychological confidence of the receiver, it is ultimately a waste of time."

Central to the challenge facing an organisation wishing to implement a policy of affirmative action is the need to identify the various stakeholders and to address most of their fears and aspirations. The most important of the stakeholders are: the intended beneficiaries of the programme; the previously advantaged members of staff; the shareholders; and the community within which the organisation is situated. Only by addressing most of these (often divergent) groups' reasonable fears and legitimate aspirations can an organisation hope to succeed in changing the hearts and minds of its employees — an essential ingredient for employment equity really to succeed. In order to do this it must firstly be appreciated that the objectives of affirmative action do not stand in opposition to the goals of the organisation — that is, affirmative action, when implemented correctly, is not only supportive but indeed essential for the future of the organisation. Given the shortage of skilled human resources and the inability of the white group to meet this ever more pressing need, blacks simply have to be brought into the mainstream of the economy. Secondly, although blacks do want to improve their economic circumstances, this on its own is not enough. The need for psychological growth is a universal human attribute (think of Maslow's hierarchy of needs) that cannot be satisfied simply by giving people impressive titles and inflated remuneration packages. People need to be given the opportunity to develop and this can only be done by placing them in positions of real authority and responsibility (providing training support where necessary and creating well-developed career paths, so as not to set them up for failure). The present phenomenon of qualified blacks continually changing jobs in pursuit of ever higher remuneration packages may well be symptomatic of managements' failure to appreciate this. The real cause of the high turnover among qualified black employees may well be their frustration of being placed in sinecures and at being miscast: it is not as much the quest for better material rewards, but the search for meaningful employment (meaning authority and responsibility) that may be causing job-hopping by professional blacks.

Turning to the interests of the advantaged group, it must be appreciated that their fears (real or imagined) cannot simply be disregarded. First, it is an unfortunate fact that much needed skills are currently concentrated in the hands of the white minority and that organisations can ill afford to lose their expertise. Secondly, the willingness of this group to impart their skills to other employees is indispensable for the success of affirmative action. Thirdly, depending on the modality of affirmative action adopted in the organisation, it may well be that at least some of their fears are well founded. While it may be persuasive on a macro or theoretical level to point to the moral correctness of affirmative action and to stress the social, economic and political forces that render affirmative action imperative, these arguments will not sound convincing to a forty-something middle manager who has been told (a) that he has to train his (black/female) successor; or (b) that he should not expect to progress any further within the company. White employees will fear for their careers when affirmative action is first mooted, and these fears, whether imaginary or not, must be addressed. Although some reject what has been called undue pandering to white fears, it is also true that perceptions are reality and that few organisations at present can afford immediately to replace all their white staff with blacks.

How can this be done? First, the issue of affirmative action must be placed on the public agenda within the organisation right from the start. Focus groups where fears and aspirations may be freely identified and aired (and unjustified fears and misperceptions removed) could go a long way in resolving problems. Secondly, management must be honest with all its employees: the management's intentions and the affirmative action measures which are under consideration must be clearly communicated to staff. Thirdly, management should stress that, although disad-vantaged groups will be given preference, appointments and promotions will be on merit (thereby reassuring present incumbents that they will still be afforded oppor-tunities for advancement within the organisation). Keeping staff informed on a continual basis, running workshops on issues such as the organisation's new recruitment and promotion policies and practices and on attitudinal change, to name but a few, can all be strongly recommended. Lastly, it should be made clear to all staff that unfair discrimination will not be tolerated and that employees who are not prepared to accept the envisaged transformation of the organisation will have to reconsider their continued presence within the organisation. Addressing legitimate concerns and removing imaginary misperceptions and fears is abso-lutely necessary; however, pandering to the demands of people who do not accept that change is both essential and desirable, is not a feasible option.

To summarise: an affirmative action plan will only succeed if all the groups affected by the measure are involved and their interests and concerns addressed and balanced. Only then will they take ownership of and endorse the process. Without the human element an affirmative action programme is little more than a costly and self-defeating attempt at window-dressing and head-counting. We now examine obstacles to the successful implementation of affirmative action meas-ures.

5.8.2 Failure of affirmative action programmes

Companies that try a quick-fix route to affirmative action often find that their efforts are stymied by the following obstacles to success (Gerber et al 1995: 205–206; Charlton & Van Niekerk 1994: 79–82).

- Strategic planning for affirmative action does not get implemented effectively. While commitment to affirmative action from the CEO is absolutely vital, the process requires support from all the employees at all organisational levels for its successful implementation.
- People do not know how to implement affirmative action initiatives.
- Human resource planning is not carried out.
- Attitudes remain negative and rooted in the status quo. Control remains with white managers and black employees are regarded as incapable of taking responsibility and accountability.
- Concerns are not clarified and problems surrounding the programme are not addressed because of a failure to foster two-way communication.
- Formal training methods continue to be used although they are obsolete and do not equip people with the necessary skills to handle the challenges of affirma-

tive action (such as attitudinal reorientation, managing diversity and empowerment). Furthermore, trainers are not equipped with the required skills and
understanding of the issues to provide the necessary training.

- Line management eschews ownership of and responsibility for the programme.
- There is a lack of personal commitment by top management to invest sufficient
  time, effort and public support in the programme. This (modelling) behaviour
  communicates the message that the failure to reach departmental targets in
  terms of the programme will be condoned because management itself is only
  going through the motions out of necessity.
- The programme lacks a clearly communicated objective and targets with timetables which undermines its implementation and makes measurement of
  progress haphazard.
- Recruitment and selection methods are not adapted to attract and to screen
  suitable black people who can contribute to the success of the programme.
- Assumptions about the abilities and qualifications necessary to do a specific
  task are presumed to remain valid.

From the above it should be evident that the removal of substantive employment
inequalities is one problem that cannot be resolved by throwing money at it or
hoping that it will go away. Programmes that are implemented without proper
prior planning will prove to be costly, unproductive and will entrench negative stereotypes between groups. These will inevitably amount to a lose-lose outcome for
the organisation, the supposed beneficiaries of the programme, as well as for the
nonbeneficiaries. In the next section a possible strategy for the successful implementation of affirmative action is outlined.

5.8.3 A strategic approach to affirmative action

Because affirmative action forms such an integral part and key focus area of general human resource management in South Africa, it should be treated as a strategic business priority by South African organisations. Although 'strategic human
resource management' as a topic is addressed in the next two chapters, it is important to emphasise the necessity of dealing with affirmative action in a strategic
way. Figure 5.4 provides an outline of a strategic approach to the development of
an affirmative action programme within an organisation.

Any strategic plan must incorporate an assessment of where one is at present
in relation to where one wants to be. The distance between "what is" and the strategic objective should be covered by a clearly demarcated route plan consisting of
achievable, intermediate goals that are measurable and attached to time schedules and review dates. An affirmative action strategy should be an integral part of
the overall business strategy of the organisation. Figure 5.5 outlines the process to
be followed in developing an affirmative action strategy and in fostering organisational commitment.

The challenge
- Exponential change
- Commitment, credibility, productivity crisis
- World-class stress levels
- Ostrich syndrome
- Gap between strategy and implementation
- SA ranks last in the utilisation of its people and employee motivation

GAP

Quality of people: primary source of competitive advantage

Critical focus
- Developing leadership and change competence (top-down)
- The coach/mentor as leader
- Selecting and training for growth (bottom-up)
- Systematic strategic development

- Guided by business plan
- Identify competencies underpinning success
- Complementary selection, appraisal, and reward systems
- Developing a learning culture that rewards competence
- Marketing people development
- Generate commitment: personalise the need for change
- Creative training that impacts on the bottom line
- Transfer ownership

Principles and objectives
- Holistic, multi-faceted approach
- Getting the right people in the right place at the right time
- The accelerated development of people into meaningful, responsible positions, to the benefit of the individual and the organisation
- To produce competent people (many of whom will be black and/or women) to meet present/future needs
- Identifying and removing obstacles to development and providing opportunities for previously disadvantaged groups
- To create an environment conducive to learning, personal growth, and productivity

Why development?
- Bridging the gap between supply and demand of competent people
- Moral, economic, political rationale
- Human competence: cornerstone of successful organisations and nations
- Burgeoning skills shortage
- Cope with employee expectations: quality of life, personal growth, and participation
- Key to competitive advantage in the human race

Develop whom?
- Previously disadvantaged groups (blacks/women)
- Line managers, in order to facilitate trainee growth
- Organisational leadership: commitment to affirmative action

Failures of affirmative action/people development
- Lack of top management/executive support
- No two-way communication
- No clarity/vision
- Focus on trainee incompetence, ignoring self-defeating attitudes and growth-inhibiting culture (deficiency model)
- Insufficient follow-up/on-the-job application
- Ad hoc, piecemeal approach, no model of competence and success
- Lack of trainer competence
- Irrelevant material
- Focus on skills, not attitudes, producing "conditioned responders"

Figure 5.4

A strategic approach to affirmative action

(Source: Charlton & Van Niekerk 1994: 145)

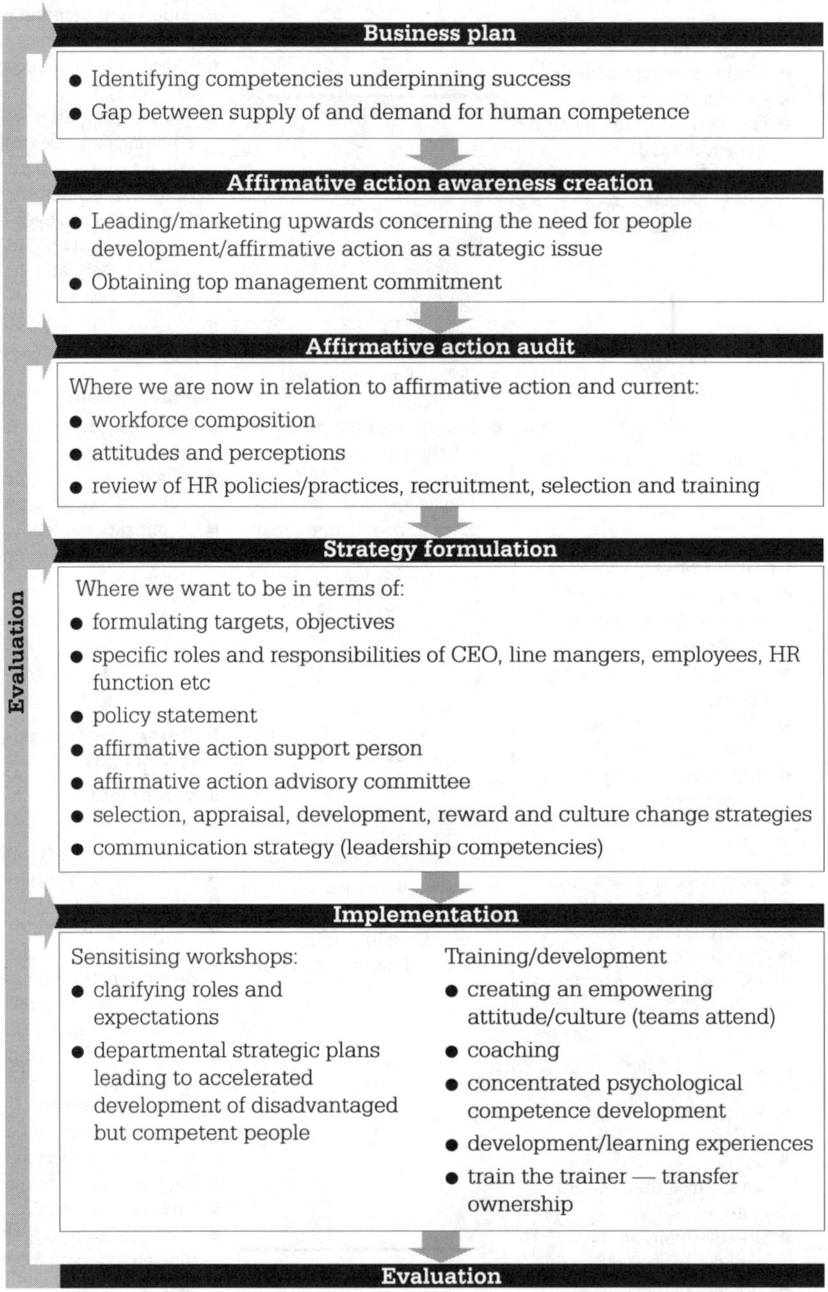

Business plan

- Identifying competencies underpinning success
- Gap between supply of and demand for human competence

Affirmative action awareness creation

- Leading/marketing upwards concerning the need for people development/affirmative action as a strategic issue
- Obtaining top management commitment

Affirmative action audit

Where we are now in relation to affirmative action and current:

- workforce composition
- attitudes and perceptions
- review of HR policies/practices, recruitment, selection and training

Strategy formulation

Where we want to be in terms of:

- formulating targets, objectives
- specific roles and responsibilities of CEO, line mangers, employees, HR function etc
- policy statement
- affirmative action support person
- affirmative action advisory committee
- selection, appraisal, development, reward and culture change strategies
- communication strategy (leadership competencies)

Implementation

Sensitising workshops:

- clarifying roles and expectations
- departmental strategic plans leading to accelerated development of disadvantaged but competent people

Training/development

- creating an empowering attitude/culture (teams attend)
- coaching
- concentrated psychological competence development
- development/learning experiences
- train the trainer — transfer ownership

Evaluation

(Evaluation — left vertical label)

Figure 5.5

The process of developing an affirmative action strategy incorporating organisational commitment

Source: Charlton & Van Niekerk 1994: 160

It will be recalled that the *Green Paper on Employment and Occupational Equity* proposes that organisations should be required to perform an organisational audit to identify existing shortcomings and barriers to change. This organisational audit can provide a picture of the present to determine the distance from the overall goal. From this audit it would be possible to develop an employment equity programme outlining the means by which the organisation proposes to close the distance between the present situation and the strategic objective of employment equity within the organisation. The process depicted in figure 5.5 highlights the need to contextualise any affirmative action programme within the overall business plan, the need to obtain commitment from all employees and the importance of developing all employees to ensure that they can cope with the demands of such a programme as well as with its outcomes.

Although personal and visible commitment from the most senior person in the organisation, as well as line ownership for its implementation, are both prerequisites for the success of any affirmative action programme, it will normally fall on human resource staff to facilitate the development of policies, procedures and practices and to provide advice on an ongoing basis to facilitate the implementation process. Human resource managers and their departments will therefore play an indispensable role in the introduction and implementation of any affirmative action programme. In the next section some human resource functions are reviewed in the context of the challenges posed by the need for affirmative action.

5.9 AFFIRMATIVE ACTION AND OTHER AREAS OF HUMAN RESOURCE MANAGEMENT*

Although the general aspects of HRM are discussed in later chapters, the importance of the impact of affirmative action on the whole spectrum of HRM activity is introduced here.

5.9.1 Job analysis

A job analysis is usually performed to ascertain what a job incumbent is supposed to do as part of the larger organisational quest to achieve the company's objectives. Job design and regulation are, however, not immutable factors and can be restructured without compromising the attainment of organisational objectives. For example, if a job currently calls for an incumbent to be an expert on financial reporting procedures, the Companies Act, tax law and strategic management, it is possible that a suitable candidate may not be found among black candidates. However, if the job were to be restructured to fit the competencies of black candidates (for example by shifting some of the required competencies to another job), a suitable candidate may well be found. This "pairing down" of a job can take place without compromising standards or the overall organisational objectives. As

*It is suggested that this section be read in conjunction with relevant other parts of the book.

regards the regulation of work, work times and job content can likewise be scrutinised and adapted to prevent discrimination against employees who have inadequate access to public transport or who carry onerous family responsibilities (such as women with young children).

5.9.2 Selection

To select is to discriminate, be it the selection from a group of applicants of a suitable candidate for appointment to the organisation, the selection from a group of employees of a suitable candidate for promotion, the choice of a person to perform a specific task, or the selection of employees for retrenchment. The issue addressed in this section is therefore not whether or not to discriminate but how to discriminate fairly and, more particularly, how to achieve this in the context of the human resource procurement process (see figure 5.6). Generally speaking, for discrimination to be fair, the criterion used to differentiate must be relevant to the business objectives of the organisation and to their achievement. Arvey (1979: 7) provides the following working definition of unfair discrimination:

"*Unfair discrimination* or bias is said to exist when members of a minority group have lower probabilities of being selected for a job when, in fact, if they had been selected, their probabilities of performing successfully in a job would have been equal to those of nonminority group members."

A simple illustration of the application of this definition would be the case where an organisation requires people employed as filing clerks to be at least 180 cm tall. As females are on average shorter than males, a much larger proportion of women would be excluded from this position. However, if this height requirement is not related to success on the job, unfair discrimination could be said to exist against female job applicants. It may, of course, also happen that a requirement was job related at the time of its adoption, but that it has since ceased to predict job performance due to technological innovation (the introduction of aluminium ladders in the illustration cited previously is an example). This illustrates the importance of reviewing selection criteria periodically to assess their fairness. South African legislation will introduce some form of monitoring agency to whom employers will have to submit returns on their selection practices (see section 5.6).

As will be explained in later chapters, the process whereby new entrants to an organisation's workforce are identified, attracted and screened takes place within the larger context of the organisation's strategies and goals. From these business strategies and goals the human resource needs of the organisation are derived (the first phase of the workforce plan). Proceeding from this analysis of the human resource needs, the question of supply is investigated. This investigation may reveal that the organisation's needs may be fully met from internal sources, external sources, or from a combination of both. The work force plan may also reveal that positions within the undertaking need to be reorganised or restructured, and/or that new positions need to be created, and/or that the task composition of existing positions needs to be reappraised. The information derived from the preceding analyses should form the basis for the development and implementation of a strategy to procure the desired quantity and quality of staff. It is useful to think of procurement as consisting of the components listed below in figure 5.6.

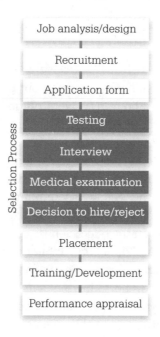

Figure 5.6
The procurement process

For the procurement process to be fair, not only must the demands of equity be met at each of the steps outlined in figure 5.6 but also the *overall consequences* must be fair. It follows that non-discriminatory overall employment statistics will not excuse the disparate impact of one of a number of selection criteria.

The importance of securing a good fit or match from the organisation's point of view is underscored by the costs associated with low productivity and low job satisfaction. Turnover costs have been estimated to be equivalent to approximately 1,2 to 2,0 (averaging about 1,5) times the annual salary of the position in question. Based on the average turnover costs estimate, this will mean that in the case of a company employing 50 workers at R 20 000 per annum each (total salary bill of R 1 000 000), with a labour turnover rate of 10 %, the costs associated with turnover will amount to about R 150 000 per annum (or 15 % of the total salary bill). A "revolving door" or "hire-and-fire" procurement policy (so dear to many South African employers) is not cheap!

As will again be explained later, the basic aim of testing job applicants during the selection process is to make predictions of job performance before making the hiring decision. This prediction can only be based on data obtained by measuring attributes of the applicants as at the time of selection. From this it is clear that at least the following two variables need to be investigated when assessing the fairness of the selection process:

1. the job-relatedness of the attributes being measured ("height" in our filing clerk example); and
2. the attributes of the measuring instrument used to assess the attributes in 1.

The position prior to the new Labour Relations Act 66 of 1995

In the years following the changes brought about by the recommendations of the Wiehahn Commission, our labour laws were purged of discriminatory provisions relating to race, gender or colour. In many instances discrimination based on these factors was prohibited. These prohibitions were, however, of limited effect, since wage-regulating measures in practice only regulate minimum conditions of employment. This has the effect that an employer would not be contravening these statutory prohibitions if he/she were to discriminate on the basis of gender, race or colour when awarding employment benefits in excess of the stipulated minima. Two further limiting factors on the effectiveness of these prohibitions were the fact that the Labour Relations Act 28 of 1956 did not cover all employees and the fact that not only had the discrimination to take place within the context of the employment relationship but it also had to have arisen out of this relationship. The net effect of these limitations was that an employer could discriminate on the grounds of race, gender or colour with impunity when employing or promoting an employee. However, on a number of occasions the Industrial Court expressed its displeasure at discriminatory practices and held that such practices can in fact constitute an unfair labour practice.

The new position (under Act 66 of 1995)

As explained in chapter 4, the new Act, in line with our Constitution, protects persons against unfair discrimination whilst at the same time allowing for affirmative action. Furthermore, the Act specifically provides for its antidiscrimination provisions to be extended to provide protection for job applicants. The Act also lists a great number of grounds which constitute unfair discrimination, such as gender and race, and proscribes direct as well as indirect discrimination. For a discussion of these issues, see chapter 4. In addition, the government has clearly indicated that it intends to introduce affirmative action legislation in the very near future (see section 5.6).

5.9.2.1 Recruitment

Care should be taken that information regarding employment opportunities reaches all sectors of society. For example, advertising in a newspaper that has a predominantly white readership will almost certainly be unfair. The same applies to the holding of recruitment interviews at the traditionally white universities, while ignoring the traditionally black universities. Recruitment by word of mouth may also constitute unfair discrimination, depending on the composition of the organisation's present workforce (because a predominantly white workforce will, in all likelihood, spread the word about job openings among their white relations and friends, thereby preventing blacks from getting to know about vacancies). Obviously advertisements will have to be purged of any racial or gender barriers. For example, an advertisement requiring fluency in Afrikaans and English may well fall foul of discriminatory laws, except if it can be shown that these are genuinely needed for the particular job (such as a position in a branch of the organisation serving the public in a neighbourhood where Afrikaans and English are the linguae francae).

It should be noted that the recruitment process can easily give rise to unfair discriminatory practices. For instance the language used in an advertisement can convey gender bias (for example "female secretary, male nurse"), while the probable readership of the newspapers in which advertisements are placed can also indicate (race) preferences (for example using the *New Nation* rather than *Die Patriot*). In an American case adverse impact was found where the company followed the practice of using its present staff as sources of recruitment. As the present staff was overwhelmingly white, this naturally resulted in mostly white prospective applicants getting to know about vacancies.

5.9.2.2 Application blanks

Human resource practitioners will have to evaluate existing application forms to ensure that these are not discriminatory. For example, questions relating to age, gender, religion, health, disability and an applicant's criminal record will have to be handled with circumspection. Only if one is confident that this information is really necessary to select a suitable person for the job in question should these be retained. For example, the presence of an item requiring an applicant to provide information regarding his/her criminal record when the position in question does not entail working with money or confidential information, may well be unfair. Likewise, should the application form require an applicant to disclose that he/she is HIV positive, and the vacancy carries no risks for other people should the incumbent be thus afflicted, this fact may form the basis of alleged unfair discrimination. This will place the organisation in a difficult position, because the onus will be on the employer to show that the information was not used to disqualify the unsuccessful HIV candidate. This heavy onus will rest on the employer even though he/she really did not take the candidate's HIV status into account. It would therefore be in the interests of the organisation to delete such items on application forms.

5.9.2.3 Selection interviews

Care should be taken to train human resource practitioners and other managers to be aware of and to disregard culturally determined characteristics during the interview situation. Interviewers must understand that cues such as body language (for example eye contact), assertiveness (women tend to phrase their responses less assertively), differences in verbal fluency, the choice of words and intonation (a universal language such as English has many acceptable forms that may differ from the "Queen's English"), may be job-irrelevant, if viewed from a cultural diversity point of view. Such factors should not be taken into account unless they can be shown to be job-related (for example pronunciation that will render the speaker unintelligible to the majority of the organisation's clients may legitimately disqualify a candidate from the position of telephonist).

5.9.2.4 Medical examination

It is important that consideration should be given to the work-relatedness of certain medical conditions and that the utmost confidentiality regarding the results of such investigations is maintained. The example of the candidate who tests positive on an HIV test is relevant. First, the fact that such a person may have many years of productive work ahead of him/her renders disqualification on these grounds unfair. A second consideration is whether the work to be performed by the prospective employee entails activities and situations where there may be a real risk to others and, if so, whether these cannot be minimised by taking simple preventative measures. For example, a medical practitioner who is HIV positive and who applies for a job at a hospital could be barred from doing surgery and could be required to wear gloves when examining patients, his/her appointment being subject to such conditions.

5.9.2.5 The decision to hire/reject

Once all the available information on applicants has been collected and transformed into comparable data, a decision will have to be made regarding whom to select from those individuals who meet or exceed the minimum job specifications for the vacant position. Of course, if their number is exceeded by the number of jobs, the employer will simply employ all of the applicants who meet or exceed the minimum job requirements. However, should there be more qualifying applicants than positions, the employer has to reject some of them, even though those persons would have been capable of doing the job. A strictly libertarian approach would dictate the appointment of the best applicant, irrespective of other considerations. Such an approach would not, however, further the organisation's affirmative action goals. Therefore it would be necessary to consider other factors, such as affirmative action plans and targets and the workforce profile (obtained from the employment equity audit) before reaching a final decision regarding whom to appoint. This approach need not result in a lowering of standards and productivity, provided that the organisation is not indulging in window-dressing by appointing incompetent people in a misguided attempt to get its numbers right. Without going into complex models of the selection process, it will suffice to say that the best candidate is not necessarily the person who obtained the highest composite score on the battery of selection devices utilised by the organisation.

5.9.3 Placement

It is also advisable to review placement practices so as to ensure that these do not give rise to allegations of discrimination. For instance, an overconcentration of employees from disadvantaged groups in departments or branches that are less sought after or are regarded as dead ends may easily be construed as discriminatory. Furthermore, any compulsory affirmative action return will in all probability also take into account the dispersion of employees by race and gender throughout the organisational hierarchy, as well as the progression of employees within the organisation from one reporting period to the next.

5.9.4 Training and development

One of the greatest iniquities of the past and a major cause of the skewed distribution of income and of senior jobs on the basis of race and gender is the fact that selection for training and the resources allocated to different forms of training were biased in favour of white males. This had the effect of disqualifying blacks and females from competing on an equal footing with white males for promotions and senior positions. Henceforth it will be necessary for employers to redirect greater resources to those previously neglected sectors of its workforce. It will also be necessary, when selecting employees for training, to reassess the set entrance qualifications, placing greater emphasis on competencies, potential and experience gained informally, and less on formal qualifications.

5.9.5 Physical arrangements

It is important that employers be able to show that they have made reasonable accommodation for people suffering from disabilities. This may include alterations to toilets and ramps for people in wheelchairs. Other considerations that may be applicable are: providing culturally diverse food (if there is a company cafeteria); the extent to which working mothers are accommodated (included here are not only facilities such as daycare centres but also aspects of work regulation such as working hours and the provision of time off to take children to the doctor).

5.9.6 Disciplinary procedures

Regular audits should be undertaken to ensure that an organisation's disciplinary code and procedures do not discriminate between different classes of people. For example, if a disproportionate number of employees from a particular group (for example blacks or women) are disciplined for particular types of misconduct (for example timekeeping related offences) it may behove the employer to investigate the underlying causes (for example distance from work, absence of proper public transport or family duties). It may also be that the penalties imposed for misconduct are relatively harsher when an offence has been committed by an employee from one particular group than is the case when exactly the same infraction is committed by an employee from another group. This will indubitably constitute unfair discrimination and must be monitored by way of an audit on a continuous basis.

5.9.7 Grievance procedure

Employers should ensure that an effective grievance procedure is put in place that will be used by employees who feel that they have been unfairly discriminated against. Such an effective internal mechanism will reduce the necessity to resolve disputes through external agencies such as the CCMA and/or the Labour Court and will further the interests of sound employee-employer relations.

5.9.8 Performance appraisals

Two of the most frequently heard objections to affirmative action are that it rides roughshod over the principle of merit and that it will lead to the lowering of standards. These claims are subjected to closer scrutiny in this section. Exhibit G contains some points to ponder regarding affirmative action and the concept of *merit*.

Exhibit G

What is merit? Some questions to ponder

- Can *merit* have a wider meaning than the narrow, traditional (Western) liberal meaning of "the employee's contribution to the bottom line"?
- Can preferential internal selection for promotion contribute to a company's productivity/profitability?
- Can being black/female themselves be job-related attributes that justify promotion based on merit as that concept is traditionally understood?
- Even in instances where being black/female is not directly related to the effective performance of a specific task/job, can the overall racial/gender mix of an employer's workforce impact positively on the profitability of the undertaking?
- Should performance appraisals be undertaken with reference to the employer's objectives as formulated in the organisation's policy statements, so that the latter embrace values other than profit maximisation? Can appraisals and promotions based on these (that is, "non-commercial" objectives) appropriately still be regarded as being based on merit?

By definition, preferential promotions can result in less than the best-qualified being promoted. However, it is equally true (although not always realised) that race/gender may themselves be job-related qualifications — for instance, in the case of service to a particular community or where role modelling is of importance (for example in the school setting) or where diversity in workforce composition may lead to greater creativity and thus to greater chances of organisational success. Focusing widely divergent perspectives on a problem (as will be the case in a culturally or ethnically mixed workforce) may very well increase the likelihood of creative problem solving. Without offering empirical evidence, it is submitted that in the case of group or team problem solving a homogeneous group may initially find it easier to become a group in the psychological sense and will thus be quicker off the mark in coming up with solutions to a problem. However, over time a heterogeneous group (once it has sorted out its roles and communication problems) will tend to produce solutions of a higher quality and originality of thought. It should be borne in mind that once race is accepted as a genuine job-related qualification, it should be applied both ways — that is, there may be situations where it can be argued that a white person, by virtue of his/her whiteness, has a qualification that gives him/her an edge over a black applicant.

In addition to those cases where race itself is a genuine job-related qualification, it is also possible that the overall efficiency of the employer's enterprise could be enhanced by a racially mixed workforce as opposed to one that is homogeneous. An example is the case where an employer serves a racially heterogeneous market where customer satisfaction is largely determined by the staff's ability to communicate with clients in their own vernacular. From this it follows that the assertion that preferential promotion will always result in lower efficiency is putting it too strongly.

A third consideration in evaluating the reduced efficiency claim against preferential hiring (or promotion at the lower levels) is the effect of the nature of the job in question: it is plausible that, if preferential promotion is applied to lower-graded jobs, the drop in efficiency could be minimal, if not zero. Lastly, in the utility calculus it may be found that the slight drop in efficiency occasioned by preferential promotion is more than justified by the social utility of such a programme. Smith (1992: 234–248), *inter alia*, sees the main justification for affirmative action in its potential to facilitate the development of a fully integrated society. As Fullinwider (1980: 90) puts it: "There is nothing sacred about efficiency that says it can never be sacrificed to justice or social peace or diminished racism." To this one may add that, in certain institutions, such as the public service, **effectiveness** and not **efficiency** should be the criterion of organisational success: Japan is sometimes quoted as a country in which a massive civil service provides a highly effective service to the public at large. Those who give absolute priority to selection for appointment and promotions based on merit are themselves prepared to sacrifice efficiency, as the preceding examples illustrate.

In conclusion, the following are guidelines for designing and managing a proper merit rating system.

- Merit rating is a continuous process and the HRM department must ensure that it is not seen by line management as an annual event that must be slogged through because "the personnel department requires their paper work".
- The merit rating system must be based on criteria that are demonstrably job related.
- The criteria must be specific and objectively verifiable (measurable); criteria such as "loyalty" will not do. The employer must be able to ward off challenges based on allegations that the criteria used are biased, open to abuse and nep-

otism, and that they are so vague that supervisors can use them to victimise trouble makers.

- The criteria should include factors that are not traditionally regarded as falling within the ambit of the concept *merit* but that will promote the achievement of affirmative action goals.
- Line management must undergo training on how to conduct the appraisal interview itself. Such training must stress the importance of empathy, active listening, future orientation, joint goal-setting, and giving accurate feedback on the interviewee's performance for the period under review (see also chapter 13).
- The performance appraisal of line managers should include criteria relating to their success in achieving departmental affirmative action targets and efforts made to train deserving candidates from disadvantaged groups.
- All performance appraisals must be recorded on a standard form and filed on the employee's personnel file as well as in a central database.
- Provision should be made for objections by employees who feel dissatisfied with their appraisals and for reevaluation by a higher level of management.
- If there is a workplace forum, the performance appraisal system must, of course, be drawn up in conjunction with that body. Even in the absence of a workplace forum, it would make good employee-relations sense (in the interests of employee participation, transparency, accountability and acceptability, and legitimacy of the system) for management not to develop and implement a performance appraisal system unilaterally.

5.9.9 Promotions

Selecting employees for promotion is, in effect, a selection issue involving the concept of *merit*; as such, this issue has much in common with the considerations raised in the previous paragraphs. The following are factors of particular importance in promotional decisions.

- All employees should be provided with information regarding promotional opportunities.
- The standards that will apply in promotions must be clearly communicated to all employees.
- Unsuccessful candidates must be provided with feedback regarding the reasons for their failure to be promoted. Furthermore, suggestions must be made regarding ways in which they can supplement deficiencies in their skills profile (for example, suggesting particular training courses).
- Employees from disadvantaged groups must be groomed for promotion.
- All employees must be provided with career paths and with the supplementary training, experience and skills necessary at each progressive stage in his/her career path in order to be considered for promotion.
- Selection must be made on the basis of actual skills and potential rather than on paper qualifications.

- Job specifications must be reassessed to determine whether these are really essential for the job.
- The use of a selection panel representative of all important decision makers (for example workplace forum, trade union, current and prospective supervisor) must be considered to make the promotional decision, rather than leaving it in the exclusive domain of managerial prerogative.
- Psychometric testing must be used carefully. This will involve not basing one's decision exclusively on psychometric results (but viewing such results only as one source of information in the decision-making process); ascertaining that the test has cross cultural validity and reliability; and giving preference to tests that measure potential and competencies rather than constructs that may be unduly influenced by differences in candidates' formal education.
- The organisation's affirmative action programme and goals must be taken into account in the final selection of candidates from the list of those who satisfy the minimum job specifications.

As regards the last point, it is suggested that the following guidelines should be adopted regarding promotional issues:

- in "same merit" situations, blacks/females must be promoted over equally qualified white males;
- unqualified blacks/females may not be promoted over qualified* white males; and
- if blacks/females are qualified,* they may/should be promoted over better qualified white males.

Lastly, a reassessment of the importance of past experience as a consideration in making promotional decisions is necessary. If in-company experience in a particular job is included in an employer's merit rating system, this may taint promotions with discrimination. In the United States of America the courts have held that in cases where employees of protected groups have only recently gained access to certain jobs and seniority gained in those jobs is regarded as a requisite for promotion, such a system will amount to discrimination. (Schlei & Grossman 1983: 587–588). This form of discrimination is called the present effects of past discrimination and it does not matter that the actual discriminatory practices which precluded protected group members from acquiring the requisite experience took place prior to the enactment of discriminatory legislation. Now that prospective employees are protected against discrimination by the Labour Relations Act 66 of 1995, employers who have experience requirements may be exposing themselves to discriminatory promotional claims. For instance, employees who were previously barred from certain jobs by job reservation or company policy or who have been appointed as temporary employees for indefinite periods, for which they have received no seniority

*The term "qualified" is used here as shorthand for "meeting the minimum job specifications".

recognition, may claim that they are being discriminated against. The employer's defence in such cases will have to be based on the "inherent requirements of the job" rationale or defence (that is, that the prescribed experience is absolutely essential for the job in question).

5.10 CONCLUSION

Many studies show that human resource development is crucial to economic growth and sustained prosperity. Therefore, extending human resource development to include all South Africans is in the long-term interests of the country as a whole. "It is acknowledged that there are significant costs in the short term, but in the long term, affirmative action will have positive returns for business and for the country in terms of improved political and business stability, higher productivity and better availability of high-level manpower" (Nkuhlu 1993: 19).

Proponents of affirmative action can claim that instead of compromising organisational effectiveness and equity norms, good affirmative action programmes promote effectiveness:

1. by expanding standards so that they can apply to individuals who deviate from the white male standard (which, after all, is a standard based on a minority of the population); and
2. by making the organisation more aware of what precisely it wishes to recognise and reward. "At the very least, affirmative action programs force us to examine the standards we use both when rewarding past performances and predicting future performances. At the most, affirmative action programs promote both true equity and effectiveness" (Blanchard & Crosby 1989: 6).

In short, the following are the **two major goals of affirmative action.**

1. To alert employers to the previously unobserved abilities of underutilised groups and to foster a critical reevaluation of standards and policies. As Asmal (1992: 14) puts it: "(t)he implementation of affirmative action in South Africa will encourage employers to reevaluate their qualifications standards so that they more accurately reflect the true requirements of a job. Employers will need to look beyond traditional criteria to those characteristics that directly impact on job performance. This will allow employers to spot black and female candidates who have the ability and potential to succeed."
2. To promote substantive equality of opportunity in the workplace (Holloway 1989: 10–19).

In this chapter you have been exposed to the origins, nature, problematics and managerial challenges related to affirmative action in South African organisations. To really make affirmative action work for the benefit of all of the country's citizens, we will have to take cognisance of aspects such as those covered by this chapter.

SELF-EVALUATION QUESTIONS

1. Briefly describe the origins of affirmative action.
2. Define the following concepts:

   ○ affirmative action
   ○ *equality of opportunity*.

3. Describe the relationship between affirmative action and equality.
4. Explain the different modalities of affirmative action.
5. What is an "organisational audit and employment equity plan"?
6. Describe developments in and experiences of affirmative action in any three other countries and draw lessons therefrom for South Africa.
7. Describe in detail how affirmative action can be implemented in South African organisations.
8. Why do affirmative action programmes often fail.
9. Explain the implications of affirmative action for other HRM practices.

ENDNOTES

1. 347 US 483 (1954)
2. **Purpose of the Act [Section 1]**: The purpose of the Act is to achieve equality in the workplace by: promoting equal opportunity and fair treatment in employment through the elimination of unfair discrimination; and implementing positive measures to redress the disadvantages in employment experienced by black people, women and people with disabilities.
3. **Prohibition of unfair discrimination [Section 5]**: No person may unfairly discriminate (or harass), directly or indirectly against an employee (or job applicant), in any employment policy or practice, on one or more grounds, including race, gender, sex, pregnancy, marital status, family responsibility, ethnic or social origin, colour, sexual orientation, age, disability, religion, conscience, belief, political opinion, culture, language and birth. Affirmative action is specifically exempted from this general prohibition, as well as differentiations, exclusions or preferences based on the inherent requirements of a job. Testing of an employee for any medical condition is prohibited, unless legislation permits or requires the testing, or it is justifiable to do so in the light of medical facts, employment conditions, social policy, the fair distribution of employee benefits or the inherent requirements of a job.
4. **Consultation with employees [Section 13]**: A designated employer must take reasonable steps to consult and attempt to reach agreement: a workplace forum; or if no workplace forum exists at the workplace, with any registered trade union representing members at the workplace and its employees or representatives nominated by them; or if no registered trade union represents members at the workplace, with its employees or representatives nominated by them. The employees or their nominated representatives with whom an

employer consults, taken as a whole, must reflect the interests of employees from across all occupational categories and levels of the employer's workforce; employees from the designated groups; and employees who are not from the designated groups.

5. **Positive measures [Section 12]**: Positive measures are measures designed to ensure that people from designated groups have equal employment opportunities and are equitably represented in all occupational categories and levels in the workforce of a designated employer. Positive measures implemented by designated employers must include: measures to identify and eliminate employment barriers, including unfair discrimination, which adversely affect people from designated groups; measures designed to further diversity in the workplace based on the equal dignity and respect of all people; making reasonable accommodation of people from designated groups in order to ensure that they enjoy equal opportunities and are equitably represented in the workforce of a designated employer: affirmative action measures, including preferential treatment, to appoint and promote suitably qualified people from designated groups to ensure their equitable representation in all occupational categories and levels in the workforce; and measures to retain, train and develop people from designated groups. Nothing in the Act requires a designated employer, in implementing employment equity, to: appoint, train or promote a fixed number of people from designated groups; appoint or promote people from designated groups who are not suitably qualified; take any decision concerning an employment policy or practice that would establish an absolute barrier to the employment prospects of people who are not from the designated groups; or create new positions in its workforce.

6. **Disputes about unfair discrimination [Section 6]**: Any party to a dispute involving unfair discrimination, may refer the dispute in writing to the CCMA. A dispute must be referred if it is a dispute about a dismissal, within 30 days after the date of dismissal; or in any other case, within 12 months after the act or omission that allegedly constitutes unfair discrimination (late referrals may be condoned by the CCMA on good cause shown). The party who refers a dispute must satisfy the CCMA that a copy of the referral has been served on every other party to the dispute and that he/she has made a reasonable attempt to resolve the dispute. The CCMA must attempt to resolve the dispute through conciliation. If the dispute remains unresolved after conciliation a party to the dispute may refer it to the Labour Court for adjudication (or arbitration by the CCMA, if all the parties consent to this).

7. **Analysis [Section 16]**: A designated employer must collect information and conduct an analysis, as prescribed, of its employment policies, practices, procedures and the working environment, to identify employment barriers which adversely affect people from designated groups. This analysis must include a profile, as prescribed, of the designated employer's workforce within each occupational category and level in order to determine the degree of under-represen-

tation of people from designated groups in various occupational categories and levels in that employer's workforce.

8. **Employment equity plan [Section 17]**: A designated employer must prepare and implement an employment equity plan which will achieve reasonable progress towards employment equity in that employer's workforce. The employment equity plan must state: the objectives to be achieved for each year of the plan; the employment barriers identified in the analysis and the steps the employer will take to eliminate those barriers; the positive measures to be implemented as required by Section 12(2); where under-representation of people from designated groups has been identified by the analysis, the numerical goals to achieve the equitable representation of people from designated groups within each occupational category and level in the workforce; the timetable with which this is to be achieved, and the strategies intended to achieve those goals; the timetable for each year of the plan for the achievement of goals and objectives other than numerical goals; the duration of the plan, which may not be shorter than one year or longer than five years; the procedures that will be used to monitor and evaluate the implementation of the plan and whether reasonable progress is being made towards implementing employment equity; the internal procedures to resolve any dispute about the interpretation or implementation of the plan; the persons in the workforce, including senior managers, responsible for monitoring and implementing the plan; and any other matter that may be prescribed.

9. **Application [Section 3]**: The Act applies to all employees and employers except to members of the National Defence Force, the National Intelligence Agency, and the South African Secret Service. The provisions of the Act prohibiting unfair discrimination (Chapter 2) applies to all employees and employers. All employers must take steps to promote equal opportunity in the workplace, and to this end, to eliminate unfair discrimination in any employment policy or practice. The provisions of the Act dealing with affirmative action (Chapter 3) only applies to designated employers and people from designated groups.

10. **Definitions [Section 61]**: "designated employer" means a person who employs 50 or more employees; . . .

11. **Designated employer must assign manager [Section 21]**: Every designated employer must: assign one or more senior managers to take responsibility for monitoring and implementing an employment equity plan: . . .

12. **Review by Director-General [Section 39]**: The Director-General may conduct a review to determine whether an employer is complying with this Act. In order to conduct the review the Director-General may: request an employer to submit to the Director-General a copy of its current analysis or employment equity plan; request an employer to submit to the Director-General any book, record, correspondence, document or information that the Director-General believes could reasonably be relevant to the review of the employer's compliance with the Act; request a meeting with an employer to discuss its employment equity plan, the implementation of its plan and any matters related to its compliance

with the Act; and request a meeting with any employee, workplace forum or trade union consulted in terms of Section 13 or any other person who may have information relevant to the review.

Assessment of compliance [Section 40]: In determining whether a designated employer is implementing employment equity in compliance with this Act, the Director-General, in addition to the factors stated in Section 12, must take into account: the extent to which people from designated groups are equitably represented within each occupational category and level in that employer's workforce in relation to the: national demographics; pool of suitably qualified people from designated groups, from which the employer may reasonably be expected to appoint or promote employees; regional demographics; economic and financial factors relevant to the sector in which the employer operates and the present and anticipated financial circumstances of its employer; progress made in implementing employment equity by other designated employers operating under comparable circumstances and within the same sector; reasonable efforts made by a designated employer to implement its employment equity plan; the extent to which the designated employer has made progress in eliminating employment barriers that adversely affect people from designated groups; and any other factor that may be prescribed.

13. **Powers of labour inspectors [Section 32]:** A labour inspector acting in terms of this Act has the authority to enter, question and inspect as provided for in Sections 64 and 65 of the Basic Conditions of Employment Act.

Undertaking to comply [Section 33]: A labour inspector must request from a designated employer a written undertaking to comply within a specified period if the inspector has reasonable grounds to believe that the employer has failed to: consult with employees as required by Section 13; conduct an analysis as required by Section 16; prepare an employment equity plan as required by Section 17; implement its employment equity plan; submit an annual report as required by Section 18; publish its report as required by Section 19; prepare a successive employment equity plan as required by Section 20; assign responsibility to one or more senior managers as required by Section 21; inform its employees as required by Section 22; keep records as required by Section 23; or comply with a request made by the Director-General in terms of Section 39(2).

Compliance order [Section 34]: A labour inspector may issue a compliance order to a designated employer if: that employer has refused to give a written undertaking in terms of Section 33, when requested to do so; or that employer has failed to comply with a written undertaking given in terms of Section 33. This compliance order must set out the prescribed information, including: any steps that the employer must take and the period within which those steps must be taken; and the maximum fine that may be imposed on that employer in terms of Schedule 1 for failing to comply with the order. A labour inspector who issues a compliance order in terms of this section must serve a copy of that order on the designated employer, who must: display a copy of that order prominently at each of its workplaces; and either: comply with that order within the period stated in it; or object to that order in terms of Section 35. If a designated employer does not comply with an order within the period stated in it, or does not object to that order in terms of Section 35, the Director-General may apply to the Labour Court to make the compliance order an order of the Labour Court.

14. **Establishment of Commission for Employment Equity [Section 25]**: The Commission for Employment Equity is established.

    Composition of Commission for Employment Equity [Section 26]: The Commission consists of a chairperson and eight other members appointed by the Minister to hold office on a part-time basis. The members of the Commission must include two people nominated by those voting members of NEDLAC who represent organised labour; two people nominated by those voting members of NEDLAC who represent organised business; two people nominated by those voting members of NEDLAC who represent the State; a woman who represents the interests of women and is nominated by those voting members of NEDLAC who represent the organisations of community and development interests; and a person with disabilities, who represents the interests of people with disabilities and is nominated by those voting members of NEDLAC who represent the organisations of community and development interests.

    Functions of Commission for Employment Equity [Section 27]: The Commission advises the Minister on: codes of good practice; regulations made by the Minister; and policy and any other matter concerning the Act. In addition to the above functions the Commission may make awards recognising achievements of employers in furthering the purpose of this Act, research and report to the Minister on any matter relating to the application of this Act, and perform any other prescribed function.

    Public hearings [Section 29]: In performing its functions, the Commission may call for written representatives from members of the public and hold public hearings at which it may permit members of the public to make oral representations.

    Report by Commission for Employment Equity [Section 30]: The Commission must prepare a written annual report to the Minister.

15. **State contracts [Section 38]**: Every employer that makes an offer to conclude an agreement with any organ of State for the furnishing of supplies or services to that organ of State or for the hiring or letting of anything, must: if it is a designated employer, comply with Chapters 2 and 3 of the Act, or if it is not a designated employer, comply with Chapter 2 (and the relevant provisions of Chapter 3). The employer may request a certificate from the Minister confirming its compliance. A failure to comply with the relevant provisions of the Act is sufficient ground for rejection of any offer to conclude an agreement or for cancellation of the agreements.

16. **Maximum permissible fines that may be imposed for contravening this Act [Schedule 1]**: Contravention of any of the provisions of: Sections 13, 14, 16, 17,

18, 19, 20, 21, 22, 23 and 39(2). Fines range from R500 000 to R900 000, depending on whether an employer is a repeat offender or not.

BIBLIOGRAPHY

Arvey, RD. 1979. *Fairness in Selecting Employees.* Reading, Massachusetts: Addison-Wesley Publishing Co.

Asmal, K. 1992. *Affirmative Action or Not?* Paper delivered at the 5th Annual Labour Law Conference, Durban, 16–18 July 1992.

Blanchard, FA & Crosby, FJ (eds). 1989. *Affirmative Action in Perspective.* New York: Springer-Verlag.

Castle, J. 1995. Affirmative action in three developing countries: Lessons from Zimbabwe, Namibia and Malaysia. *South African Journal of Labour Relations*, 19(1), Autumn 1995, 6–33.

Charlton, GD & Van Niekerk, N. 1994. *Affirming Action: Beyond 1994.* Kenwyn: Juta & Co Ltd.

Department of Labour. 1996. *Green Paper on Employment and Occupational Equity.* Pretoria: *Government Gazette* no 17303, 1 July 1996.

Fullinwider, RK. 1980. *The Reverse Discrimination Controversy: A Moral and Legal Analysis.* Totowa, New Jersey: Rowman and Littlefield.

Gerber, PD, Nel, PS & Van Dyk, PS. 1995. *Human Resources Management,* 3 ed. Halfway House: ITP/Southern.

Holloway, FA. 1989. What is affirmative action? In *Affirmative Action in Perspective,* eds FA Blanchard & FJ Crosby. New York: Springer-Verlag.

Human, L. 1993. *Affirmative Action and the Development of People: A Practical Guide.* Kenwyn: Juta & Co Ltd.

Nkuhlu, W. 1993. Affirmative action for South Africa in transition: From theory to practice. In *Affirmative Action in a Democratic South Africa,* ed C Adams, 11–20. Kenwyn: Juta & Co Ltd.

Plaut, M. 1992. Ethnic quotas — Lessons from Malaysia. *Work in Progress,* 80, 42–43.

Rycroft, A & Jordaan, B. 1992. *A Guide to South African Labour Law,* 2 ed. Kenwyn: Juta & Co Ltd.

Sachs, A. 1991. Affirmative action and good government. *Alistair Berkeley Memorial Lecture,* November, 14–15.

Schlei, BL & Grossman, P. 1983. *Employment Discrimination Law,* 2 ed. Washington, DC: American Bar Association, Section of Labour and Employment Law, The Bureau of National Affairs, Inc.

Sen, A. 1992. *Inequality Reexamined.* New York: Oxford University Press, Inc.

Smith, N. 1992. Affirmative action: Its origin and point. *South African Journal on Human Rights,* 8(2), 234–248.

Starks, SL. 1992. Understanding government affirmative action and *Metro Broadcasting Inc v FCC. Duke Law Journal,* 41, 993–975.

Swanepoel, BJ. 1992. Affirmative action and employee empowerment in Namibia: Southern African research perspective on some pieces of the jigsaw puzzle. *South African Journal of Labour Relations*, 16(3), 23–36.

Taylor, BR. 1991. *Affirmative Action at Work: Law, Politics and Ethics.* Pittsburgh, Pa: University of Pittsburgh Press.

Weiner, M. 1993. Affirmative action: The international experience. *Development and Democracy* (Urban Foundation publication), 4 May 1993, 1–15.

part two

Strategising, Structuring and Planning

chapter 6 Strategic Decisions Regarding HRM — Part 1: Formulating HRM Strategies

⊙ STUDY OBJECTIVES

After studying this chapter, you should be able to:

- explain the meaning of the concept strategy;
- discuss what "a strategic approach to human resource management" entails;
- describe the process of formulating strategy for human resource management;
- distinguish between and explain four different human resource management generic strategy options;
- differentiate and discuss the nature and content of different human resource management grand strategies;
- describe the nature of the grid or matrix outlined in this chapter that can be used to integrate strategic decisions about human resource and labour relations management;
- explain the nature and importance of human resource management *business plans*.

6.1 INTRODUCTION

In chapter 2 it was pointed out that, in our view, human resource management (HRM) ought to be managed in accordance with a strategic approach. The need for such an approach in South Africa was already being mooted in the early eighties.

Although the strategic approach to HRM is a recurrent theme throughout the book, the aim of this chapter (and the next one) is to clarify in greater detail certain aspects of a strategic approach to human resource management.

To this end key concepts are clarified and the link between the general strategic management of organisations and strategic human resource management is explained. The focus then falls on management decision making relating to the formulation of human resource strategies. This is followed by a discussion of other long-term decisions relating to HRM.

6.2   A STRATEGIC APPROACH TO HRM: WHAT THIS MEANS

In any analysis of the concept *strategic approach,* the core concept is the noun "**strategy**", from which the adjective "strategic" is derived. We therefore first have to take a closer look at the concept *strategy.*

6.2.1 Strategy as a concept: From the military to the business world

The concept *strategy* is relatively new to literature on management in general, and even more so within the context of the human dimension of management. This concept actually has its roots in military literature. Small wonder, then, that there is so little agreement in the literature on management regarding the real meaning of "strategy". As Shirley (1982: 262) points out:

> "Every emerging discipline goes through a shake-out period during which there is significant disagreement — confusion, even — over fundamental concepts."

In this regard Lewis (1988: 12–13) makes the following statement that underscores the view taken in this book:

> "Unfortunately the area of management suffers from an abundance of words that enter the managerial vocabulary on a wave of popularity and then, as a result of imprecision and overuse, quickly degenerate to having little specific meaning . . . In contemporary management parlance, there is a danger of [sic] everything, and therefore nothing, is strategic."

From a purist point of view it would thus make sense not to deviate drastically from the original meaning of the concept *strategy* — within the military context.

Franks (1987: 33) makes a similar suggestion when he states that in order " . . . to fully understand the implications of the concept strategy it is important to review its origins in the art of war". Similarly, Steiner and Miner (1982: 18) make the following acknowledgement in an effort to come to grips with the concept *strategy* within a management context: "Strategy derives from the Greek word *strategox,* which meant the general. The word strategy therefore literally meant the art of the general. It refers to that which is of major concern to top managements of organisations."

Fourie (1991: 56) also analyses the original meaning of the concept from a military perspective. He favours the definitions of Von Clauzewitz, a Prussian army general and respected military theorist, concluding that the important features of his definitions are "that they emphasise that strategy is concerned with the war as a **whole**. It is concerned with battles in so far as their outcome bears on the outcome of the war. It is used to plan the whole war to gain **the object of the war**."

From the foregoing military-based analysis it can be concluded that strategy, within the context of management, ought also to emphasise the organisation as a whole and the ultimate object, purpose or "mission" of the organisation. It relates to the primary concern of the top management of an organisation — namely to survive or be successful in an environment of competition. In management parlance "you win the war if you beat the competition". Just as generals are concerned with the war as a whole or with winding up a military campaign, and just as they use terminology such as utilising "military intelligence" and "capturing the territory" of the enemy, the top managements of organisations focus on the competitive environment and make overall "game plans" to beat the competition. It is, for instance, not uncommon to hear the use of phrases in the business world such as "it's a war out there", "use market intelligence", "plan new marketing campaigns", or "let's recapture territory from the competition".

From the above it is clear that *strategy* has the following characteristics:

- it is long-term and future orientated;
- it focuses on matching or creating the necessary fit between the organisation (its internal environment) and its external environment (which is competitive and constantly changing); and
- it is concerned with the mission and objectives of the organisation as a whole and thus with its success within this environment of competition and change.

From this it follows that decisions and actions relating to strategy will have major resource implications.

In the literature on management strategy, a differentiation is made between various so-called levels of strategy. Because the term *levels* may create the impression of lower or higher order, the approach in this book is that one should rather think of these as different *types* of strategy.

Corporate strategy **essentially revolves around the type/s or line/s of business in which an enterprise is engaged (or wishes to engage in).**

The top managements of some organisations prefer to be involved in one type or line of business only, while others decide to engage in different types or lines of business. Decisions relating to corporate strategy therefore basically entail deciding on the enterprise's business mix and portfolio of businesses. Organisations that are involved in different businesses are often referred to as *multiple-business enterprises* (Smit & Cronjé 1992: 123). Purcell and Ahlstrand (1994: 6) refer to these as "M-form companies".

Pearce and Robinson (1991: 227–243) describe *grand strategy* **as "a comprehensive general approach that guides a firm's major actions".**

They go on to describe twelve such different grand strategy options, including concentrated growth, market development, retrenchment turnaround, divestiture, joint venture, vertical integration, horizontal integration, concentric and conglomerate diversification, innovation, product development and liquidation. Each grand strategy has its own particular principles regarding how the organisation, in broad terms, should conduct its business.

Business strategy **can be described as the particular broad approach or plan which the top management of a single business organisation adopts in order to be successful — in other words, to be competitive.**

Pearce and Robinson (1991: 227–243) say that any organisation's grand strategy ought to be based on some core idea about how the particular organisation can be most competitive in a particular marketplace. This core idea they refer to as *generic strategy*. Three such core ideas or *generic strategies* are identified, namely **overall cost or price leadership, product/service differentiation** and **focus**. The latter essentially entails focusing on either product/service differentiation or overall cost leadership, depending on the particular market segment. In the case of overall cost leadership strategies, organisations try to beat the competition by cutting the prices of their products/services through cheaper operational processes (such as production). Organisations which choose product/service differentiation as a generic business strategy try to beat the competition by creating a perception in the marketplace that their services/products are unique in terms of features such as quality or after-sales customer service.

Functional strategies relate to the strategies used in functional areas such as marketing, manufacturing, product development and public relations. Because from the point of view of business management — and hence strategic business management — the primary object is to become and remain successful in a competitive environment, these functional strategies are in a sense secondary or "downstream" to corporate and business strategy. They do, however, form an integrated part of strategic management. All the different types of strategy are closely linked and interdependent. Because of this reciprocal interdependence, decisions about these different types of strategy have to be taken in a fully integrated way. This, to a large extent, forms the major challenge of strategic management.

6.2.2 Strategic management

Chapter 1 emphasises that management basically entails a process of planning, organising, leading or directing and control. Strategic management is thus the application of this management process at the top level of the organisation. At this level the focus is on the success of the organisation as a whole over the long term, within the context of a changing and competitive environment. Smith, Arnold and Bizell (1988: 5) provide the following definition:

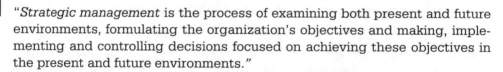

"Strategic management is the process of examining both present and future environments, formulating the organization's objectives and making, implementing and controlling decisions focused on achieving these objectives in the present and future environments."

In the same vein Pearce and Robinson (1991: 18) describe *strategic management* as "the set of decisions and actions that result in the formulation and implementation of plans designed to achieve a company's objectives. Because it involves long-term, future-orientated, complex decision making and requires considerable resources, top management participation is essential."

The process of strategic management is described by most authors as consisting of strategy formulation and strategy implementation. Although it is self-evident that the distinction between the two is not watertight and that they are interdependent, Schendel (1992) points out that there " . . . are two different types of activities here: shaping has to do with finding strategy, implementing has to do with using strategy . . . ".

In defining these two broad activities, different components or tasks in the strategic management process can be identified. It must, however, be emphasised that, although for conceptual and analytical purposes these tasks/components of the process are separated (and even treated by some as a series of discrete steps in the process), in practical reality they are often performed simultaneously or in a different order, making the whole process interactive and dynamic by nature. Nevertheless, in order to facilitate learning, most authors describe the strategic management process in terms of these different tasks, steps, components or sub-processes. The same approach is followed here.

Environmental scanning and *analysis* entails a thorough study of all the factors or variables both external and internal to the organisation. The ultimate aim is to create the necessary match or fit between the two. This is often referred to as SWOT-analysis, and involves the process of analysing and synchronising the organisation's internal strengths and weaknesses and the opportunities and threats coming from the external environment.

Developing a vision and/or mission is another facet of strategic management. This direction-setting task concerns determining exactly what business you are in and what business you want to be in. Another component or task is the formulation of long-term objectives relating to, for example, market share, profitability and competitive market positioning. Other components of strategy formulation include the formulation of different types of strategies such as generic business strategies, corporate and grand strategies as well as functional strategies, drafting policies and identifying and defining so-called critical success factors (CSFs) or key strategic issues (KSIs) within the context of the business plans that are drafted.

The implementation of a strategy entails creating the necessary structures and also establishing a culture whereby all the role-players actually work towards overall mission accomplishment. It is all about mobilising resources towards mission accomplishment.

Throughout the process it is important continuously to monitor and evaluate the extent to which strategic decisions match or fit the changing circumstances, as well as the extent to which they are actually being implemented.

Finally it must be emphasised that strategic management cannot be regarded simply as a neatly packaged set of rational decisions and related behaviour. The role of the socio-organisational side (the "political" or "softer" side of management) has become increasingly important. Aspects such as the ideologies of managers, the motivations and frames of reference that they have, their perceptions and the role of so-called cognitive maps and cognitive processes, all play a very significant part in the process of strategic management. Wood (1996: 4) says the following in this regard: "Ideological differences saturate the presumably rational organisational process of decision making . . . We need to understand how we in business organisations are guided by ideology."

6.2.3 Strategic human resource management

From the foregoing it can be concluded that by *strategic human resource management* we mean those long-term, top-level management decisions and actions regarding employment relationships that are made and performed in a way that is fully integrated with the overall general strategic management of organisations.

It thus chiefly concerns synchronising and integrating the organisation's strategic business needs and plans with the human dimension of management — or rather with all those aspects stemming from and relating to the management of employees.

Strategic human resource management is not viewed as something separate from or subordinate to the formulation and/or implementation of business or corporate strategy. It is also not seen as something which has only to do with either general strategy formulation or with strategy implementation. On the contrary, it is viewed as an integral part of general strategic management. Aspects related to or connected with the management of employment relationships permeate all facets of general management strategy formulation and implementation. Business strategy cannot be formulated without incorporating the relevant human resource related issues. If, for instance, the top management of an organisation decides to diversify (diversification strategy) into different markets, industries or lines of business, the human resource related implications that will have to be considered include peculiar labour market conditions in those sectors or lines of business (for example supply/demand of labour, skills needed, wage levels/labour costs, trade union activity/strategies, etc). Similarly, the human resource-related requirements will be quite different in an organisation that is following a strategy of innovation, from one where a strategy of retrenchment/turnaround is followed. In the case of the latter, the emphasis will be on cost reduction and/or asset reduction. If, for example, an organisation experiences a phase of decline (for instance because of an economic recession), it may decide to embark on such a strategy with the hope of recovering later. In such a case emphasis will be on strategies to reduce the size of the workforce by natural attrition and/or by means of retrenchment/redundancy packages. Should people still be required in certain critical areas because of voluntary separations in those areas, the emphasis will only be on short-term employment relationships.

On the other hand, if the strategy is one of innovation, the organisation's aim will be to beat the competition by concentrating on bringing out new or improved products/services. By doing so, product life cycles will be shortened, the new/

better products/services making the older ones obsolete. This strategy can, however, only be considered if there is the will to employ, train for and facilitate worker creativity and flexibility.

Thus, although many textbooks on general strategic management deal with the human side of things only when strategy implementation is discussed (focusing on aspects like leadership, culture and reward), it is clear that human resource issues should also be viewed and dealt with as an integral part of the strategy formulation phase. When the top management of an organisation defines the vision/mission statement of the organisation, it should be borne in mind that such a statement is not only important for the public and the market environment, but in particular also for the employees. This type of statement can go a long way in getting employees to identify with the organisation and to support it or be committed. Such a mission statement should not only outline the typical product-market orientation of the organisation but it should also be "employee friendly" and explicitly state what the organisation's stance towards the management of employee-related affairs is. Furthermore, when SWOT-analyses are executed as part of strategy formulation, it is often realised that many of the external threats/opportunities and/or the internal strengths/weaknesses are actually related to human resources.

Similarly, the design of organisational structures (the notion of "structure follows strategy") relates essentially to how the work of the organisation is organised — and this is clearly a people-related issue. The same holds true for a strategy implementation issue such as trying to elicit and maintain employee behaviour that is actually in line with what is required. Rewarding employees for behaving/performing in such a way that strategy is implemented is clearly a human resource management issue.

It is important to note, however, that although human resource related issues and decisions are dispersed throughout the process of general strategic management, the actual process of strategic human resource management can also, for the purposes of analysis and conceptualisation, be subdivided into strategy formulation, structure that follows strategy, and strategy implementation.

6.3 FORMULATING STRATEGY FOR HUMAN RESOURCE MANAGEMENT

The process of human resource strategy formulation in essence involves top-level management decisions and actions regarding appropriate generic and grand strategies for the management of employment relationships within the context of an analysis of the internal and external environments. It is all about making certain strategic choices within the context of environmental constraints, opportunities and threats. As Human and Horwitz (1992) explain: "One of the basic lessons in strategic management is that the performance of an organization is dependent upon its ability to match or fit the variety in its environment. The first task of the strategist is the art of achieving fit between the organization and its environment." With reference to the human dimension of management in particular, the same is true. Because the concept of fit or match is so central to strategic management, the point of departure must be thorough environmental scanning.

6.3.1 Scanning the environment to create the necessary fit

From a systems perspective (see chapter 1) the human resources subsystem is seen as being influenced not only by the other internal organisational subsystems (such as the operational, marketing and financial subsystems), but also by variables or factors in the external environment. In actual fact, there is a strong interconnectedness between all these systems and all of these have to be aligned with each other as well as with the overall mission of the organisation.

Human resource strategies do not exist in isolation and are essentially formulated to be used offensively or defensively to mediate between the preferences and frames of reference of management and the perceived environmental threats, opportunities and constraints. Environmental influences need not, however, be accepted passively. Really proactive managers will attempt to influence or shape their environments — even though such an approach will not necessarily make them immune to forces in the external environment.

It should be noted, however, that from a systems perspective, "external" environment does not only refer to factors or forces external to the organisation but also to those internal to the organisation but external to the organisation's human resources system. This means that when environmental scanning is done from the perspective of human resource strategy formulation, not only are the relevant factors in the political, economic, social and technological (PEST) environments explored but also those related to organisationally internal variables. This requires, first of all, the alignment of the organisation's general business strategies with the human resource strategies. As the business strategies are being formulated and the market environment of the business and other PEST-factors are scanned, particular attention should be paid to the relevant human resource related implications. Similarly, as decisions related to the pure financial side of the organisation are made within the context of certain environmental trends that are analysed, the relevant human resource implications have to be actively searched for. The reverse is also true, however. The potential financial and business strategy implications of particular human resource strategy related factors have to be seriously considered when top management does environmental analyses for the purpose of business strategy formulation. In order for the whole organisational system to be successful, all of the parts or subsystems must work together. This is why it is so important to execute an integrated environmental scanning process.

At this stage you may wonder which particular factors need to be analysed. To draw up a complete list in this regard is neither possible nor feasible. Each organisation is different and each organisation's environmental make-up differs. Some examples may, however, serve to structure your thinking. In this regard you are specifically referred to chapter 4 where the macroexternal environment of human resource management is discussed. Chapter 3 also contains categories of variables related to the broader organisational environment as well as those related to the individual as an employee. Chapter 5 examines a particular environmental factor that has to be constantly monitored in South Africa nowadays, namely affirmative action.

In the process of analysing all such environmental factors, different methodologies can be used, including interviews with experts, scenarios, the delphi technique, the nominal group technique and document reviews. Typically, the aim would thus be not only to identify the variables but also to analyse how these factors may impact on the organisation, the work that is to be done, the employees who have to do the work and especially the managerial employees who have to manage the people — including the organisation's HR department/section. Boseman and Phatak (1989: 31), however, point out that the " . . . most important element in the framework for analysing the SWOT's of a business is the accurate determination of its key success factors . . .". One of the first key success factors to be considered is an appropriate mission statement regarding the human resource subsystem of the organisation.

6.3.2 Considering the mission or ultimate goal in respect of human resource management

Typically, an organisation's mission statement will contain the scope of its operations in product and market terms. It will spell out the "who, why, what and whereto" of the organisation. In essence it refers to the domain that the organisation stakes out for itself and to its *raison d' être*. In this regard all the different stakeholders of the organisation have to be taken into account.

As mentioned before, the fundamental purpose or mission of any organisation can be found in the needs of society. If there were no need for certain products/ services, there would be no market and thus no opportunity for an organisation to be set up and maintained successfully. As Eaton (1990/91) puts it, any company " . . . may be seen as a set of resources belonging to and serving society". Thus, although the shareholders or owners of any organisation form an important stakeholder group — which has to be specifically catered for in the organisation's mission statement — there are also other important stakeholder groups such as the customers (market), the suppliers, the employees (in particular), as well as society at large. This means that not only should the organisation's mission statement reflect its attitude towards its employees but also that the purpose of human resource management must always be tied in with the purpose or mission of the organisation as a whole.

Formulating the organisation's objectives with regard to its human resources system thus requires an explicit statement outlining the means by which the organisation's management intends managing the relationship between the organisation and its employees as important stakeholders. In the process of shaping this part of the organisation's mission statement, the crucial linkup and integration between human resource and general business management is thus to be facilitated. Creating the necessary fit between the organisation's human resources subsystem, the organisation as a whole (including the other subsystems), and the macroexternal environment thus forms part and parcel of this process. It also forms the basis of the process of formulating an appropriate human resource management grand strategy.

6.3.3 Deciding on an appropriate human resource management grand strategy

In the process of strategy formulation, top management has to make certain important decisions. Before we discuss in some detail the nature of particular strategic options, it is important first to reflect briefly on what decision making in this context entails.

6.3.3.1 Decision-making dynamics

Throughout this book the centrality of decision making is emphasised. Most probably you will have already noticed that decisions regarding the management of employment relationships have to be made all the time. This is natural, simply because decision making is so central to management in general. More than two decades ago already, Dale (1965) stated that "management is decision making".

At strategic level decisions have to be made about what the organisation should do and why, how it should go about achieving its mission, what the role of the organisation's human resources subsystem should be in this regard, how it should be managed, etc. At an operational level decisions may revolve around choices about who to appoint or promote, how to deal with misconduct or with a person who is a poor performer, what type of training somebody might need, what performance bonus a specific employee should get, whether a subordinate should be allowed time off for attending to personal affairs, etc. All of these matters involve decision making.

In the literature on general management a great deal of emphasis is usually put on decision making. South African textbooks often devote separate chapters to this topic. For the most part, however, the emphasis falls on *rational* decision-making theory, with very little (if any) attention being paid to alternative aspects of decision making such as behavioural and political theories. Crous (1990: 189), for instance, describes decision making as follows:

> "It is an unavoidable rational process by which a specific plan is chosen to solve a particular problem or save a situation, taking the potential effect on enterprise activities into account, on the one hand, and established enterprise principles, on the other."

This is clearly an example of the rational theory of decision making. According to this school of thought, decision makers deliberately, consciously and rationally examine and weigh up various variables and factors and then make appropriate choices that could maximise the benefits to the organisation whilst minimising the costs. This theory emphasises the process of problem identification, situational analysis by means of gathering relevant information, the generation of possible alternative solutions, the evaluation of the various alternatives and the choice of the "best" alternative/s. In this framework there is little room for the "softer", more intangible side of decision making. Because organisations are social entities (in other words, they are made up of people), decisions are rarely, in reality, made in such a clear-cut, rational way. Aspects like gut feeling, emotions, values, intuition, ideology, the mind-sets of people, the relevant political and cognitive processes, as well as the role of the decision makers' frames of reference, are mostly underplayed and often grossly neglected in textbooks.

Lewis (1988) has the following to say in this regard:

> "A better understanding of the strategy process, and more effective management of strategic change, hinges on the development of a theoretical framework that has as central to it the cognitive structures of decision makers . . . frames of reference that are shared by the members of the social entity . . . described variously in the literature as cognitive structures, schemata, cognitive maps, . . . recipes, shared beliefs, values and attitudes, or basic assumptions . . . . "

Similarly Hirschohn (1988: 17) explains that through "its ideological filter management interprets events and develops policies and strategies to manage the organisation's interaction with the environment". All of this implies that beliefs, value systems and ideologies influence the way managers tend to think about things and will thus influence how they perceive "reality", making any rational decision making also inherently subjective and in some sense *irrational*. This is especially true when it comes to decision making about matters relating to the employees of an organisation. Strategic choices in this area are influenced by the assumptions, ideologies and frames of reference of decision makers regarding both the *individual* and *collective* dimensions of employment relationships.

With regard to the **individual dimension**, the principal issue revolves around what management's frames of reference are regarding people as employees (see chapters 11 and 12 in this regard). Various theories on motivation (what and how people are motivated) and leadership (what leaders should do and how they should do it) contain important information that makes up the building blocks of our frames of reference regarding the management of employees as individuals.

Although it is very true that people all differ and that one must be cautious not to overgeneralise when it comes to what motivates people and how they should be managed, this does not mean that managers do not, in fact, tend to generalise. The important thing is that the way managers tend to think (their assumptions and frames of reference) about people as workers in general influences the type of strategies they will decide upon to manage these people. This has been proven empirically (Swanepoel 1995).

Managers will tend to have either a relatively positive or a relatively negative mind-set about people as employees. This relates to management's beliefs or assumptions about the inherent nature of workers as individuals. A very negative frame of reference can be likened to McGregor's theory-X assumptions or Schein's characteristics of rational-economic man (see chapter 11 in this regard). This essentially includes beliefs such as that the average person dislikes work, wants to avoid it and is not interested in work for anything but the money. Because of this employees do not naturally feel committed or loyal. They also do not want to take responsibility and lack any motivation to develop themselves (no ambition). Thus, in order to deal with this "low-value production factor", a belief system is built around the assumption that workers have to be coerced, strictly controlled and directed by management. A very positive frame of reference can be likened to McGregor's theory–Y assumption: each employee has inherent potential, wants to work hard and be held responsible and accountable, is inherently creative and committed and wants to learn, grow and develop.

On the other hand, as far as the **collective dimension** is concerned, managers also have particular frames of reference regarding the need for and role of trade unions and other social groupings that represent the interests of workers within organisations and society at large. Poole (1986) refers to two such frames of reference. Managers will tend to have either *unitaristic* or *pluralistic* mind-sets. Unitaristic managers view trade unions as unnecessary because they see no real conflict between workers and their employers or organisations. Business organisations are thus viewed as social entities where unity and shared objectives and values are the natural characteristics. On the other hand, pluralists tend to believe that business organisations are made up of different subgroups of employees with some conflicting objectives and values. They view this inherent conflict to be natural to any employment relationship and therefore believe that it is natural for trade unions (and similar representative entities) to exist and to play a role in representing their members' interests. Managers will thus tend to have either a relatively positive or a relatively negative mind-set about trade unions.

It has been empirically proven that together these frames of reference regarding the individual and collective dimensions of employment relations have an important but complex influence on the preferences of South African managers, and consequently on the types of strategies that they will choose for the management of employment relationships in their organisations (Swanepoel 1995). Because managers differ from each other with regard to these frames of reference, decisions on appropriate strategies to manage the human dimension of organisations will not, as a rule, be made on a purely rational basis. Certain political processes will also be involved when the decision makers interact in the process of trying to decide which strategies to follow. In the process of formulating human resource management strategies, the role of the softer, more intangible aspects of organisational decision making should therefore not be underestimated.

6.3.3.2 Strategy options

As explained under heading 6.2.2, a *grand strategy* is essentially a *comprehensive general approach* that guides and directs all other decisions, practices and efforts toward mission accomplishment. Such a comprehensive general approach ought to be based on a certain *core idea* about how to be successful — referred to by Pearce and Robinson (1991: 224) as *generic strategy*.

The same can be said of strategies on how to manage employment relationships. It has to be decided what comprehensive general approach will be followed in managing the individual and collective dimensions of employment relationships within the organisation. This decision must be based on a certain core idea of what will work best within the context of the internal and external environments.

The individual and collective dimensions must already be **integrated** at the stage when the appropriate core idea and comprehensive general approach are evaluated. Storey's (1992: 278) research in the United Kingdom led him to reach the following conclusion:

> "If policy makers are to contribute to moving relationships forward they will need to attend in particular to the problem areas identified in this study — most especially the persistence in the lack of integration between human resource initiatives and the collective aspects which have trodden water, and the related issue of seeming lack of integration between these practices (individual and collective) and wider business strategy issues."

Similarly, Cowling and James (1994: 1) state that the modern-day practice in organisations in the United Kingdom is increasingly to integrate personnel management and industrial relations "as part of a policy of creating coherent and effective systems for the management of people".

In South Africa there seems to be a similar need. It has been established through empirical research (Swanepoel 1995) that there is a strong interconnectedness between the way managers (and human resource practitioners/specialists) think about the individual and collective dimensions of employment relationships. With regard to HR specialists in particular, it has been established that their mind-sets about the collective dimension (notably trade unions) are almost just as strongly correlated with the type of human resource strategies (individual dimension) that they prefer as are their mind-sets (frames of reference) about the individual dimension (people as individual employees). In general a strong correlation has also been found between the types of human resource strategies that will be preferred by managers and their tendency to prefer pluralistic-based labour relations (collective dimension) strategies. People who favour pro-union strategies also tend to favour more progressive human resource management strategies. It has thus been found that it is especially the South African managers' predispositions regarding the collective dimension of employment relations that influence their strategic management choices in respect of the human dimension of organisations. This is probably so because trade unions have come to play such an important role in South Africa, which is not the case in all countries.

Generic strategy options

In the light of the above it is useful to conceptualise strategic options in this field on a two-dimensional grid, as depicted in figure 6.1.

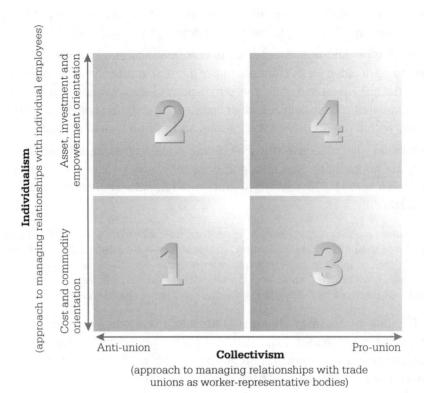

Figure 6.1

Core ideas on managing employment relationships:
Four generic strategy options

The four generic strategy options for managing employment relations within organisations are summarised below.

1. **Low individualism/low collectivism:** This involves a relatively negative (or non-positive) attitude towards trade unions and a relatively low positive (or perhaps even negative) view of the nature and potential value of the individual worker in general.

2. **High individualism/low collectivism:** Although trade unions are still viewed in a negative light, the attitude towards individual employees is generally much more positive, with a definite belief in each one's inherent value, potential and will to contribute.

3. **High collectivism/low individualism:** Here trade unions and the role that they can play are relatively highly regarded — that is, there is a generally positive attitude towards trade unions. The mind-set regarding individual workers is, however, less positive, the view being rather that employees should at best be "cared for and maintained". This can be likened to a combination of Schein's so-called rational-economic man and social man (see chapter 11 in this regard). It should be noted, however, that it is not so much a **negative** mind-set, but rather one lacking strong positive features.

4. **High collectivism/high individualism:** The core idea in this instance is that trade unions are good social institutions that may well be capable of making a constructive and positive contribution, and that each individual worker has the inherent nature and potential to contribute a great deal to the organisation — provided that he/she is managed appropriately.

Grand strategy options

On the basis of the four core ideas or generic strategies spelled out above, a decision has to be made at top management level regarding an integrated, comprehensive general approach to the management of the individual and collective dimensions of employment relations. By refining the two axes of the matrix or grid, at least eight grand strategy options may be considered. Figure 6.2 reflects ten possible grand strategy options as potential **integrated**, comprehensive, general approaches towards human resource management in South Africa.

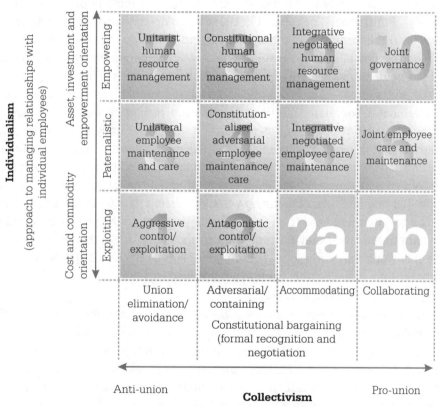

Figure 6.2

The comprehensive general approach to managing the individual and collective dimensions of employment relationships: Grand strategy options in human resource management

TWO GRAND STRATEGIES OF EMPLOYEE EXPLOITATION

Although in this day and age strategies based on antihuman attitudes will in practice be very unlikely, especially in light of the emphasis on a **human rights** culture for modern-day society, such possibilities still cannot be completely excluded. Strategies 1 and 2 (see figure 6.2) are examples — at least on a theoretical level — of such extreme low individualism approaches to HRM.

In both these strategies each worker is viewed (and preferably dealt with) as if he/she is "just another factor of production", much like a machine or money. Concerns about human dignity and the needs and rights of individuals are thus virtually nonexistent. Each employee is treated as a "commodity" (labour), and the aim is to get the most out of this commodity by means of practices like coercion and a system of command and control. Because it is a strategy based on extreme efforts to minimise the costs of labour, plans will be made to keep pay at absolute minimum levels. Because it is believed that people inherently really dislike work, and that they work purely to get money, such plans may include piecework payment systems. Furthermore, because it is believed that people are not interested in their work or in their employing organisations and that they cannot or do not want to take on responsibilities or contribute creatively, management will devise systems around rigid, narrowly defined job descriptions, with many different organisational levels and a great deal of emphasis on strict compliance with all managerial requirements. Therefore, methods to maintain discipline will be extreme, with "firing and hiring" occurring at random on an almost daily basis. After all, it is believed that this commodity is easily replaceable. If at all possible management will actually prefer to avoid long-lasting employment relationships, opting for temporary and part-time workers, even contracting out the labour component, or perhaps — if possible — mechanising work (robotising it). Any dissatisfied employee will be told that he/she is "free to go". Employees must not even try to complain — they are treated as if they have no right to speak out. All of this is combined with one of two options (see below) regarding management's broad approach to dealing with trade unions, who may want to get involved especially because of the abusive, exploitative cultures and practices.

In the case of *aggressive control and exploitation*, unions are ruthlessly avoided, resisted and opposed. Plans are made to keep unions out as far as possible. Such extreme low collectivism is built around the idea that there is absolutely no need for trade unions. If at all possible, campaigns will even be planned to wipe out or eliminate any form of unionism. Management will thus devise ways and means (even using underhand tactics and foul play), to keep out these "unnecessary, trouble-making third parties" at all costs.

In the case of *antagonistic control and exploitation* the abusive/exploitative features of the handling/treatment of individual employees are combined with a broad, general approach which aims to limit or contain the involvement of trade unions. Unions are accepted very reluctantly only because there is little else to do. Management will typically try rigidly to define the union's scope of involvement —

limiting it to collective bargaining about remuneration and working conditions only. Management will take a very adversarial stance when it comes to bargaining, defending managerial prerogative and emphasising that the unions are actually unwelcome intruders. Management will also want to codify strictly, by means of detailed agreements, the nature of the collective employment relationship. Management's approach to bargaining will be very distributive, aimed at "winning" the most and "losing" the least.

Four grand strategies built around paternalism

The comprehensive general approach towards managing the relationships between individual employees and the organisation in all four of these strategic options (boxes 3–6 in figure 6.2) is to create an atmosphere of general employee care and wellbeing within a secure environment. Management practices are supposed to reflect a caring image that cater for the social needs of employees. The aim will thus be to devise ways of making all employees feel at home and create the idea that they are members of one, big, happy family in which everybody knows what is expected and what to expect. Typical elements of these strategies are respect for seniority (like in the family) and hierarchical structures, numerous job classifications and levels, and a focus on order and stability in exchange for reasonable, sufficient and fair pay, while still emphasising the containment of labour **costs**. There is security in the work environment because jobs are narrowly defined in said job descriptions, with little (if any) scope for worker creativity and participation. Employees feel secure because they know that, as long as they do as they are told, their jobs will be quite safe. In times of economic hardship, however, workers may (in extreme cases) be required to face up to the reality of lay-offs or retrenchments unless they are prepared to make sacrifices in terms of pay and benefits, as these are viewed as major cost factors to the organisation. A great deal of emphasis is placed on the distinction between **management** (at different levels) and **labour** (as the workers). Competency for the current narrowly defined job is an important driving force and not development for higher order, future work. Strict adherence to procedures and due processes (such as discipline and grievance handling) also forms part of establishing an environment where 'all know what is expected'. Training is mostly done on-the-job and is aimed at only the minimum requirements of current jobs. Communication is mostly downward, but employees may view their opinions as and when management allows it. Management will only share limited information, and only on those aspects which they feel the workers will understand.

The differences between these four grand strategies lie in the way in which trade unions are handled or dealt with. In the case of strategies 3 and 4 (see figure 6.2), management follows a similar broad approach towards the collective dimension (trade union interaction) as those adopted in strategies 1 and 2. In the case of *unilateral employee maintenance and care*, unions are actively and aggressively avoided and kept out. However, chances are that unions will not get involved as easily as is the case with strategy 1, simply because workers are not treated as badly. In the case of *constitutionalised adversarial employee maintenance and care* (strategy 4), trade unions are dealt with reluctantly and in a very antagonistic, adversarial manner on the minimum of issues mentioned in strategy 2, in particular pay and working conditions. Once again, because the emphasis is on cost containment and unions have to be dealt with simply because they cannot be wished away or avoided, the dealings with unions will preferably be built around win-lose, distributive style negotiations. However, in this instance management's approach will rather be to show the unions that they are not needed because the "employees are well cared for" and members of a "happy family". In this way it is hoped that the workers really will not have any need for unions and that the unions will start to feel unwelcome.

However, when a switch is made to a true pluralist stance that is really more pro-union, the approach will be to engage the worker representatives constructively in certain areas. In the case of *integrative negotiated employee care and maintenance*, management's approach to interaction with the unions shifts from a pure conflict/adversarial stance to a more friendly, accommodating attitude, aimed at broadening the scope of issues over which management will engage in discussions, deliberations and consultation with the unions. The style of interaction will thus be of a more **integrative** nature, especially when it comes to issues such as job descriptions, job evaluation, employee wellbeing programmes, etc. Issues such as wages will often be dealt with at a different, higher level, such as a bargaining council, where distributive bargaining will obviously still be prominent. Thus, because trade unions may have been recognised for quite some time and because collective relationships will have matured, management will accept that more constructive relationships in general can actually help to create a happier workforce. The reluctance to deal with the unions has now generally fallen away, and management will now negotiate rather than fight. Such a strategy is viewed as a more mature means of containing costs and keeping control over employment relationships. As is the case with *constitutional employee maintenance and care*, however, a great deal of emphasis is placed on highly codified agreements which defend areas of managerial prerogative. It is believed that, in this way, stability, order and conflict are best institutionalised. Accordingly, it is hoped that both the unions and the employees will be less antagonistic.

Joint employee care and maintenance takes it one step further. The approach is still to create an image of an organisation which is orientated towards the general wellbeing of its employees, but there is an even greater shift towards pro-unionism. Trade unions are in fact welcomed as coequals with management in the efforts to create a caring environment. Trade unions are valued as true partners in the process of caring for employees and in the creation of a secure, safe working environment. Structures for union-management cooperation on all the issues related to such an environment (as spelled out earlier) are set up and an approach of extensive information sharing is followed. Similarly, joint problem solving takes place in areas such as narrowly defined job descriptions, job evaluations, career paths, pro-

motion systems, grievance and disciplinary systems, skills training and even remuneration and working conditions. Integrative (win-win) negotiation is viewed as
absolutely essential and, because this is the case, decentralised joint decision
making on all these paternalistic-type issues takes place. Shop stewards thus typically undergo joint training with supervisors to equip them in this new task of
collaborative employee care. Constructive and fully cooperative interaction is thus
preferred and trust is viewed as the cornerstone of the employment relations.
Because trust is emphasised to such an extreme extent, management will over
time move away from formalised, highly codified agreements. The emphasis, it
must be remembered, remains on creating an environment of employee care and
wellbeing to promote loyalty, while, at the same time, the aim is to limit or contain
costs. For this reason the unionists are also trained in the interpretation of cost
accounting and other financial information. In this way management tries to
ensure that the parties who cooperate actually "talk the same language" all the
time.

FOUR STRATEGIES OF EMPLOYEE EMPOWERMENT

In all four of these grand strategies (boxes 7–10 in figure 6.2) the underlying theme
is management's belief in their employees' inherent potential, value and ability to
contribute towards organisational goal accomplishment. Employees are viewed as
the most valuable **assets** of the organisation; investment in employees is seen as
a means of engendering commitment, rather than as a means of containing costs
and imbuing only loyalty. The assumptions on which these strategies are based are
essentially in line with Schein's "self-actualisation man" and McGregor's "theory-
Y" (see chapter 11). In terms of these theories individual employees are generally
seen to possess a great deal of creative and imaginative energy, ingenuity, to want
to take on more responsibility, and as ambitious and committed to organisational
goal accomplishment — as long as they can satisfy their self-actualisation needs
in the process.

With this in mind, a great deal of professional effort goes into the employee
procurement process. In order to attract and employ the right people, sophisticated
recruitment and selection techniques are adopted to attract high performers. At
the same time, however, work design is broad-based. Jobs are broadly defined with
a variety of tasks requiring multiskilling to master complexity through innovation
and creativity. Hierarchical lines become blurred with few job classifications and
few organisational layers. Management prefers teamwork and flexibility in the
internal labour market. Because in such a system management believes that
employees will easily be bored if they are not given enough freedom and leeway to
do things their own way and to experience variety and the challenge to develop
themselves fully, holistic work design (where conception is linked with task execution) is preferred. The idea is that, if the right environment is created, employees
will stay with the organisation rather than leave as soon as a new external challenge comes up. Management will also prefer elements like job rotation, job enrichment and broad (rather than narrow) career paths.

Management's approach to employee development will thus be driven by future needs and by general multiskilling. Training in areas like communication and problem solving will be important. A great deal of money will be invested in the development of all employees; this will be linked to a performance management system that has strong group and individual elements and is results- rather than behaviour-driven. In all of these aspects the long term rather than short term, and flexibility rather than rigidity, are important principles. Individual employees partake fully in decision making at various levels and, because the creative ideas and other positive values of employees are recognised, meaningful two-way communication and extensive information sharing with employees occurs. Although the traditional systems employed to handle discipline and grievances will not be abandoned, the emphasis shifts from paternalism and conformance maximisation to openness and commitment maximisation. In this context management will be prepared to opt for above average basic pay — typically in the upper quartile — extensive benefits, flexibility and increased individual and (especially) group-based incentive schemes and even aspects like employee ownership plans and gainsharing.

Because in all four of these strategies the broad approach is to create an open and free environment in which high-potential employees can excel, make contributions and suggestions, take part in problem solving at all levels, cooperate and commit themselves towards total quality, there is often a need to have more stereotyped work done by subcontractors or part-timers. This will not, however, apply to the organisation's core business functions.

These four grand strategies also differ mainly in the manner in which trade unions are dealt with. In this regard the same four options applicable to the four paternalistic-based strategies also apply here. Either unions are vigorously kept out, or they are in constant conflict with management, or they are accommodated and accepted as legitimate stakeholders in the process of creating such a high empowerment environment. In the case of the grand strategy of *joint governance*, there is maximum empowerment on both the individual and collective dimensions. Trade unions and other employee representative bodies are viewed as coequals with management in steering the organisation as a whole towards mission accomplishment. Managerial prerogative is something of the past and it is not only issues related to the employment relationship that are dealt with on a joint problem-solving basis (as is mostly the case with *integrative negotiated human resource management*), but the organisation as a whole is jointly managed. Parallel structures that coexist with ordinary organisational structures, consisting of worker representative committees at all levels throughout the organisation (which are, in any event, fewer than is the case with the paternalistic strategies), will be a natural consequence. Because trade unions may fear that such things may be regarded as cooption or as a sell-out by the rank and file, checks and balances will have to be built into the system to ensure that the trade union remains the focal point in the full-blown empowerment process. Typically, aspects like closed shop and agency

shop agreements (see chapter 20) will therefore be preferred. In such a fully integrated organisation there is little (if any) need for old-style distributive collective
bargaining over the distribution of wealth generated by the organisation. Because
the approach is so inclusive and transparent, all will know that they are getting
their fair share. However, this does not mean that there will be no conflict. Disputes
may still arise and appropriate dispute resolution processes will thus still form part
of the joint governance strategy.

The grid of grand strategy options: General remarks

In the real world few things (if any) are immutable. It must therefore not be
assumed that the grand strategies can be rigidly applied; the dotted lines exem-
plify their fluidity. It would be wishful thinking to believe that these strategy
options exist in watertight compartments and that hard and fast rules can be
applied. In the real business world things are not that simple. The grid has been
developed from a combination of empirical evidence, theoretical argumentation
and practical experience, and the various grand strategy options for the management of employment relations, should be viewed as a conceptual guide. This
matrix (and the accompanying research instrument), however, facilitates management decision making as a practical strategic planning tool to detect an organisation's current practices (emerged strategies) and desired or intended strategies.
Thus, although it can be viewed as a conceptual framework, it also forms the basis
of a practical, diagnostic management tool that is used for strategic planning in the
field of human resource and labour relations management.

It is, however, important to guard against the tendency to overgeneralise. Obviously, in practice not all employees are the same. Indeed, we must accept that
human beings are complex and that diversity is a fact of life. Although one will
tend to use some generalisations in order to formulate a *comprehensive general*
approach to guide and direct all other major decisions and practices in this area,
sufficient room will have to be left to manoeuvre and deviate when certain elements just do not fit. It is not always possible to manage all employees throughout
an entire organisation in exactly the same way. A grand strategy can only be
regarded as a strategy if it is flexible enough to accommodate changing or different
circumstances. Remember always that strategy, to a large extent, revolves around
creating a constant fit with a changing environment.

A further word of caution relates to the progression principle that is inherent in
this matrix. As one moves to the right on the horizontal axis, there is a progression
in the degree of the pro-union stance taken. There is no exact midpoint, but at
some point there will be a shift over from a unitarist to a pluralist strategy. In practice organisations may move on this axis (either to the left or to the right) incremen-
tally or gradually, without necessarily having any intention of doing so — purely as
a natural response to developments internal and/or external to the organisation. At
other times, deliberate decisions will be taken in this regard. A similar argument
holds for the vertical axis, representing the individual dimension.

Furthermore, as has already been mentioned, it is almost inconceivable in this day and age that a manager could want to pursue any strategy based on pure "theory-x" or "rational-economic-man" principles. In practice, there will be progression from a less individualistic mode to one of higher individualism. In the switch from the former mode to the latter (again finding an exact midpoint would be an oversimplification) the major difference lies in whether employees are treated well for loyalty and compliance whilst containing costs, or whether they are invested in and empowered so that they can contribute and maximise their commitment. This shift can occur unintentionally and gradually, or as a deliberate strategic effort towards change.

By now you may have wondered about the two black boxes, question marks (a) and (b) (see figure 6.2). All that can be said here is that it is extremely unlikely that individual employees would be exploited and abused, whilst management is at the same time working together with trade unions. Should any such situation be identified in practice, serious questions would have to be asked about the trade union's bona fides.

Another aspect which needs some clarification concerns the common characteristics shared by the three "adversarial containment" strategies (numbers 2, 4 and 8) and the two "accommodating" strategies (numbers 5 and 9). Although these two differ in terms of the broad way in which trade unions are dealt with, in all these cases there is a great deal of emphasis on true collective bargaining and highly codified collective agreements which create an environment of strict contract administration in order to enhance control, stability and the formal institutionalisation of conflict. This is in other words, where trade unions (or other worker representative bodies) are formally recognised and bargained with — in some cases from a more distributive adversarial stance (in the cases of boxes 2, 4 and 8) and in other cases (boxes 5 and 9) from a more accommodating, integrative stance. A move beyond this constitutional bargaining will require maturity in the collective relationship, where trust is at the optimal level and where there is a definite shared vision.

Lastly, the interconnectedness between the two axes must be pointed out. There will be a correlation between the progression on the two axes. In other words, as one moves to the right on the horizontal (collectivism) axis, there may be a corresponding (though less) move upwards on the vertical axis. This means, for instance, that even though all four paternalistic strategies share the same essential ingredients, as one moves from *unilateral employee maintenance and care* towards *joint employee care and maintenance*, the degree and quality of the individualism will progress towards the higher end of the vertical axis. In other words, not only will the quality of employee care improve but more elements of employee empowerment may also start to creep in. Although the correlation is not as evident in the reverse situation — that is, if one moves up towards the higher end of the vertical axis there will also be a move to the right on the horizontal axis — such a correlation has also in fact been proven empirically (Swanepoel 1995) to exist. It is important to note that there is indeed a very complex interrelationship between these two dimensions — and this is why it is proposed that the two dimensions be treated in a fully integrated manner at the strategic level.

6.3.4 Drafting human resource management business plans

In essence, *business plans* are documents detailing the more medium-term plans and objectives of the organisation. Typically, such business plans cover five-year periods and are redrafted annually within the context of strategic planning, which is carried out in order to ensure the necessary fit between internal and external environments on a continuous basis. Taking into account the environmental scanning information, the SWOT analysis, the strategy decided upon and the organisation's current and future strategic postures, medium-term moves are formulated to facilitate mission accomplishment. *Business plans* will thus focus in more detail on various functional areas and on what ought to be done in these areas, by whom and how, in order to get the grand strategy implemented and to thus achieve the goals of the organisation. These business plans will form the basis of the short-term, annual *action plans* which are drafted each year. On the basis of such action plans, annual budgets are integrated to allow for appropriate resource allocation. In other words, resources (such as money, people, time) are allocated so that action plans can be carried out, which in turn facilitates execution of the *business plan*, which finally leads to strategy implementation.

When drafting the HRM business plan the concept of fit is of crucial importance. Not only must the HR business plan fit the HRM strategy but it must also fit the internal and external environmental factors — most notably the organisation's general business strategy.

As explained under heading 6.2.1, *business strategy* essentially revolves around how best to compete in a specific marketplace. You were also informed of Michael Porter's three strategic options of *overall cost leadership, differentiation* and *focus* (Porter 1980: 40–41).

In the process of drafting a business plan for human resource management it is again necessary not only to ensure that the business plan fits the HRM grand strategy but also that the HRM grand strategy's fit with the business strategy will be facilitated by the execution of the HRM business plan. In other words, the HRM business plan's purpose should basically be to **operationalise** or bring about the concept of **fit** between general business strategy and HRM grand strategy. Although the selection/choice of an appropriate HRM grand strategy must itself ensure that there is an alignment between business and HRM strategy, the various elements of the business plan must now clarify how the necessary fit will be achieved.

If, for instance, the organisation's business strategy (in Porter's terms) is, one of overall cost leadership, the basic approach will be to seek cost minimisation through the construction of large-scale facilities, through strict control of overhead and fixed costs, including costs linked to marketing/sales and distribution. The focus will also be on product design that facilitates cost containment and, as result, less money will be spent on something like research and development and after-sales service. The emphasis will thus be on quantity of products/services rather than on outstanding quality. In such circumstances tight management control is more likely to be of paramount importance, requiring more strict supervisory practices and organisational structures that are hierarchically based along authority lines of "demand-and-control". The environment will be relatively more risk averse, with a strong concern for stability and order, which can facilitate efficient operational/production processes. In line with this, the focus will have to be on relatively more "mechanistically" designed jobs, work demarcation and more narrowly defined job descriptions and specifications. More emphasis will be placed on detailed work and operating procedures, and employees' training will centre more around compliance and improved "hard skills" to do their jobs more efficiently. Where there are group processes (such as, for example, quality circles), the focus will be on improving the efficiency of the organisation's delivery systems (for example production). Because control is so central, performance appraisals will focus more on behavioural norms, using this as some form of control mechanism, rewarding behaviour that conforms to the norm. Pay will be work-based rather than output based. In other words, aspects like job evaluation will be of greater importance.

On the other hand, in an organisation that follows a business strategy of **differentiation**, aspects such as creativity, innovation, top class quality, uniqueness of products/services, and customer care will be emphasised. The focus will typically be on research and development to ensure that the organisation becomes a leader in its field, and also on excellent marketing strategies, including after-sales service to ensure outstanding quality. In such circumstances, because the emphasis is not on cost containment, the HRM strategy emphasis will as a rule also not be on paternalistic or exploitative strategies (see above). Employee creativity, innovation, and commitment will be sought, rather than compliance and employee control. Rigid job descriptions will be much less important with more broad-based work classifications and broader career paths. Flexibility and team-based work design will be more common and training will be more focused on developing the person as a whole and on eliciting better thinking abilities for creativity, innovation, excellence and the achievement of self-actualisation. Making errors (within limits, of course) will be viewed as positive rather than negative because of an environment typified by ambiguity, innovation and greater risk taking. The ability to work with others and to do different jobs will be more important. An employee's remuneration will be influenced by performance in terms of outputs or results; performance appraisals as such will typically be used as instruments to facilitate development and change. Group incentives will also be more common because of a greater emphasis on the team concept. However, because "new blood" will from time to time be needed in order to ensure that the organisation remains at the cutting edge of innovations in product/service engineering, external equity in the sense of good pay will also be important.

The above should serve to clarify some links between business strategy and HRM strategy. When drafting HRM business plans, the challenge lies in identifying the **key areas** that require attention over the medium term in order to facilitate strategy implementation. It may, for instance, be necessary to redesign the work (see next chapter), to rewrite job descriptions, to recruit new employees with different characteristics, to design a new performance management system and/or to redesign the organisation's remuneration system. The emphasis thus shifts to the different functional areas of HRM, selecting the required strategic change interventions in each area and assigning responsibilities and allocating time limits in respect of each functional intervention. In this way appropriate objectives can be formulated in order to monitor progress over time.

6.4   CONCLUSION

In this chapter the focus was on, inter alia, the nature of strategy and strategic management, and on how human resource management can be linked with the general strategic management of organisations. The emphasis was on options, choices and decision making in the formulation of human resource management strategies that have to match or fit the internal and external environmental conditions of the organisation. Special attention was devoted to the necessity of streamlining the organisation's human resource strategies with its general business and grand strategies. In this respect particular emphasis was placed on the nature of different HRM grand strategy options.

It was emphasised that both vertical integration (that is, aligning general business management strategies with strategies relating to the human dimension of organisations) and horizontal integration (in other words between human resource and labour relations management) are prerequisites if any approach is to be strategic — especially in South Africa. The latter refers specifically to the integration of the management of the individual and collective dimensions of employment relationships. Because of the complex interrelationship between these two dimensions and the importance of trade unions in South Africa, strategic decisions relating to the management of employment relationships in our organisations should, as far as possible, facilitate optimal integration of what are traditionally termed *personnel management* on the one hand and *labour relations* on the other. To facilitate this important integration, the grid or matrix provided in this chapter with an accompanying research instrument can serve as both a conceptual guide and a practical tool for strategic human resource management.

In line with the notion of "structure follows strategy", stemming from strategic decisions (such as those discussed in this chapter), is the need to decide on certain structural dimensions that can facilitate strategy implementation. These decisions

— which are essentially also strategic and long term by nature (although they revolve around structural aspects) — form the focal point of the next chapter.

SELF-EVALUATION QUESTIONS

1. Explain what is meant by the concept *strategy* by illustrating how it has been transplanted from the military to the management context.
2. Describe and differentiate between the following concepts:
   - O corporate strategy;
   - O grand strategy;
   - O business and generic strategy;
   - O functional strategy.
3. Discuss briefly what "strategic management" entails.
4. Explain the nature and meaning of "strategic human resource management".
5. "Making decisions about human resource management strategies is a purely rational process."
   Critically discuss the above statement.
6. From a strategic management perspective, what can be done to integrate decisions about human resource and labour relations management?
7. What is meant by "low collectivism and high individualism"?
8. Explain any three grand strategies for human resource management that are built around paternalism.
9. "The time has come for empowerment. We have to empower the people employed by organisations!"
   In the context of the above statement, discuss the nature and potential value of the four employee empowerment strategies explained in this chapter.

BIBLIOGRAPHY

Boseman, G & Phatak, A. 1989. *Strategic Management: Text and Cases,* 2 ed. New York: Wiley

Cowling, A & James, P. 1994. *The Essence of Personnel Management and Industrial Relations.* London: Prentice Hall

Crous, MJ. 1990. Decision making. In *General Management,* ed J Kroon, 189. Pretoria: Haum

Dale, E. 1965. *Management: Theory and Practice.* New York: McGraw-Hill

Eaton, J. 1990/91. Human resource management and business policy. *Human Resource Management Journal,* 1(2), 66–67

Fourie, DFS. 1999. The conduct of war. In *Military Management II: Only Study Guide for MBII, Course 2,* by PJ Smit, BJ Erasmus & BJ Swanepoel, 56. Pretoria: Centre for Business Economics, Unisa

Franks, PE. 1987. Strategic management. *IPM Journal,* 6(1), 33

Hirschohn, PA. 1988. *Management Ideology and Environmental Turbulence: Understanding Labour Policies in the South African Gold Mining Industry*, (MSc dissertation, Oxford University)

Human, P & Horwitz, FW. 1992. *On the Edge: How South African Companies Cope with Change*. Kenwyn: Juta and Co Ltd

Lewis, G. 1988. *Corporate Strategy in Action*. London: Routledge

Pearce, JA & Robinson, RB. 1991. *Strategic Management: Formulation, Implementation and Control*. Homewood, Illinois: Irwin

Poole, M. 1986. Managerial Strategies and "styles" in industrial relations: A comparative analysis. *Journal of General Management,* **12**(1), 40–53

Porter, ME. 1980. *Competitive Strategy*. New York: Free Press

Purcell, J & Ahlstrand, B. 1994. *Human Resource Management in the Multi-dimensional Company*. Oxford: Oxford University Press

Schendel, D. 1992. Introduction to the summer 1992 special issue on "strategy process research". *Strategic Management Journal,* 13, 1–4

Shirley, RC. 1982. Limiting the scope of strategy: A decision based approach. *Academy of Management Review,* 7(2), 262

Smit, PJ & Cronje, GJ de J. 1992. *Management Principles*. Cape Town: Juta and Co Ltd

Smith, GD, Arnold, DR & Bizell, BG. 1988. *Business Strategy and Policy*, 2 ed. Boston: Houghton Mifflin

Steiner, GA & Miner, JB. 1982. *Management Policy and Strategy*, 2 ed. New York: MacMillan

Storey, J. 1992. *Developments in the Management of Human Resources*. Oxford: Blackwell

Swanepoel, BJ. 1995. *'n Strategiese Benadering tot die Bestuur van die Diensverhouding* (ongepubliseerde doktorale proefskrif, Pretoria, Universiteit van Suid-Afrika)

Wood, JD. 1996. The nature of ideology. *Business Day Supplement — Mastering Management (part 16),* 10 June, 2–4

STUDY OBJECTIVES

After studying this chapter, you should be able to:

- explain what is meant by the statement "structure follows strategy" in the context of human resource management;
- discuss the nature of and different approaches to job design;
- describe the nature and importance of the notions of *flexibility* and *high performance work systems* in South African organisations;
- outline what is meant by "group-level" considerations of work organisation;
- list and briefly explain the most important variables relating to organisation structure;
- differentiate between different types of organisation structures;
- describe different "models" and "typologies" reflecting the potential role of HR departments in organisations.

7.1 INTRODUCTION

The notion that "structure follows strategy" is generally very common in the literature dealing with strategic management. Within the context of human resource management, structure also follows strategy. Once an appropriate overall strategy has been formulated, various long-term decisions have to be made regarding certain structural dimensions relating to the management of the human dimension in the organisation.

In general management parlance these decisions revolve largely around the function of organising. To a large extent the focal point in this regard is the *work* that has to be distributed amongst employees throughout the organisation in order to achieve its objectives.

The view of Smit and Cronjé (1992: 176), quoted below, clearly illustrates that organising is all about employees and structuring the work that they have to do.

> "An enterprise comprises a group of people who work together in a co-ordinated fashion to realise the objectives of the enterprise. However, certain tasks have to be performed before these objectives can be realised and these must be carried out properly. This brings us to the organizational function, for through organization managers decide how strategies and objectives are going to be attained.

Organizing entails grouping together activities necessary to attain common objectives, as well as allocating each group of activities to a person with the necessary authority to supervise those responsible for performing the activities."

In the previous chapter the interconnection between different strategy alternatives and the manner in which work is designed was mentioned. As various external forces (such as globalisation, the information technology explosion, the trend towards democracy, etc) impact on organisations, the way that work ought to be structured in jobs and other productive units is also undergoing a fundamental rethink the world over. After all, the activities that have to be carried out in order to achieve an organisation's objectives will have to be allocated to people. There are many ways in which these tasks and roles can be structured, and the relationships between these work roles and the people concerned organised. Structuring the work and the relationships and interactions between the technical systems and the people (the sociotechnical systems), as well as between the people themselves (that is, structuring the flow of work), form important building blocks of organisations. Individual jobs cannot therefore be viewed in isolation.

Each employee is supposed to perform certain activities to achieve something (work outputs), which have certain consequences for the organisation as a whole. In order to be able to do the work, however, employees need certain things which form the inputs into the work system (for example material, equipment, resources and specifications). One of the most fundamental inputs relates to the technical systems of the organisation — the technology used. The interaction between employees and technology thus forms an important consideration in the context of designing the work of employees. Through the use of technology and through interaction with others, employees deliver their outputs. The outputs of certain employees eventually form the inputs of other employees. The specific requirements of the next employee in the process of delivering goods and services should thus form one of the main inputs into the work design process. In this sense the totality of work has its origin in the requirements of those who want to buy or use the organisation's outputs (products/services) — in other words, the customer. Through the work executed by each employee, value is supposed to be added at each point in the work-flow process. Work is thus structured into a complex system of interconnected value-creating steps from the point of the customer (who essentially initiates the need for work to be performed), to the point where the customer's needs are satisfied through appropriate, need-satisfying products/services. It is important to create the necessary fit at various levels — a fit between the technology and the job, between employee and the job or position, between the different jobs or positions, between different groups of jobs, between the organisation and the outside world, and so forth. The end result ought to be efficient and effective work operations that facilitate the achievement of the organisation's objectives through high performing, satisfied employees, with due consideration for the impact of all of this on the environment. The way in which this totality of work is organised can thus be viewed from different perspectives: from that of the *indi-*

vidual employee, of *groups* of employees, and from that of the *organisation* as a whole.

In this chapter we focus on all three of these levels. In addition, we take a look at organising the work which concerns the human resource management functions and activities of an organisation.

7.2 INDIVIDUAL-LEVEL CONSIDERATIONS: JOB DESIGN

7.2.1 What job design involves

Job design refers to the way in which work is structured into the different tasks and responsibilities required to execute a particular job.

Job design is thus how one defines a given job — what work or tasks are to be performed, how they are to be performed, and what authority goes along with the job. If the point of departure is the requirement that the organisation must perform well (be efficient and effective), the aim of job design is to ensure appropriate on-the-job performance by the individual employee. Although the basis of job design is an analysis of what work needs to be done, the important **strategic** consideration is **how** the work should be organised in order to obtain the necessary work performance from the employee.

Job analysis (which is discussed in the next chapter) is the systematic process of collecting information about a job and exploring the activities of a particular job.

Whereas job design decisions are largely strategic by nature, the task of job analysis is more operational. Job design decisions are long term and are based on certain beliefs or assumptions about what will inspire the individual employee's best performance (in this regard you are referred to chapter 6, section 6.3.3.1). On the basis of these assumptions certain strategies will be considered and this will dictate the type or form of job design adopted (see chapter 6, section 6.3.4).

In arriving at these decisions, a number of job dimensions or characteristics have to be considered within the context of the relevant strategy, for example *depth*, *range* and *relationships*.

Job depth refers to the extent to which the holder of a particular job or position will be granted the necessary discretion to influence the activities and outcomes of that job.

Job range has to do with the number of different tasks that make up a particular job.

Job relationships in this context refer to the sociotechnical aspect of relationship requirements and opportunities linked to a particular job: interpersonal work-related relationships, as well as relationships between the technical side of the job (the technology) and the jobholder.

The greater the job depth, the more autonomy the jobholder will have; the greater the job range, the wider the range of activities, tasks or decisions a jobholder will be expected to perform — that is, the greater the variety. Other important job characteristics relate to *task identity*, *feedback* and the *social* dimensions of the work. The latter aspect takes job relationships (see above) one step further and refers to the opportunities provided by the job to establish and maintain informal relationships with people (other than employees) in and outside the organisation. *Task identity* refers in essence to the extent to which the conception, execution and results of a job are integrated and whether the jobholder can identify him/herself with these. *Feedback* is related to this aspect in the sense that it refers to the extent that jobholders actually see/experience the end results of their work.

7.2.2 The traditional mechanistic approach to job design: Simplification and specialisation

Decisions about job design have long been profoundly influenced by the principles of scientific management, laying the foundation for a very mechanistic form of work design. The key figure in this movement was Frederick Winslow Taylor. Taylor believed that mental and manual work ought to be separated. He also believed in work specialisation. Management, according to him, should specialise in the planning, organisation and control of the work, while workers should actually do the work. He also proposed that complex jobs performed by individual workers should be broken down and fragmented into their most simple component parts. He argued that, in this way, workers would become more efficient and productive in their performance of a limited range of simple, repetitive and, routinised task activities — if they knew exactly what to do, how to do it ("one best way"), if the workplace/shopfloor and the tools and equipment layout were such that unnecessary movements were minimised, and if they were given above average rewards for their performance.

A clear-cut division of labour and the fragmentation and simplification of jobs were thus proposed. A split between conception and execution of work was advocated, with management monopolising the conception work and with the emphasis falling on simplifying the execution part that is left to the workers.

This form of work organisation can be contextualised in the rise of the era of mass production and so-called Fordism. Taylorist narrow job descriptions and the division of labour are often associated with Fordist mass-production setups characterised by assembly lines, short-cycle jobs and standardised products. Taylorism or scientific management principles and Fordism or mass-production systems are thus often seen to go hand in hand. In these mass-production systems an important requirement is consistent, disciplined performance by workers in the execution of their repetitive, simple tasks. The work efforts and behaviour of individual employees are thus closely monitored. Management clearly specifies work performance requirements, leaving little scope for workers to make decisions related to their work; because the tasks are simple and repetitive, little skill and discretion are required. The main emphasis is on the monitoring activities of managers or supervisors, with centralisation and concentration of authority and decision making, leaving very little scope for job flexibility.

Although such forms of work design may be appropriate from certain perspectives in certain circumstances (such as when large amounts of standardised products are manufactured), a great deal of criticism has been levelled against this type of work design over the years. Specialisation facilitates faster work and requires fewer skilled people to do the work. This means that fewer resources have to be devoted to expensive and time-consuming training, which results in lower paid work and greater ease in replacing workers. In the case of assembly work, specialisation may reduce work in progress and transformation time, it may require less space and it can simplify control over the production process. All of this may facilitate cost savings and greater profitability — especially over the short term. From the perspective of the employee, however (and, over the longer term, probably also the organisation), many potential negative aspects can be identified. Work can become pretty meaningless, boring and monotonous. This can lead to feelings of apathy, carelessness and overall dissatisfaction. Extreme fragmentation and simplification of work may lead to de-skilling and to the so-called degradation and dehumanisation of work. Work alienation may follow — an experience of estrangement from one's work or job — which, in the long run, may mean uncommitted, disloyal and disinterested workers. This may impact adversely on labour productivity, with symptoms such as tardiness, poor timekeeping and high absenteeism and labour turnover rates. All sorts of measures to ensure that workers *comply* with the requirements of the job and to regulate and control the labour process may thus become necessary — instead of eliciting *commitment*.

These and other criticisms have caused management and behavioural scientists to experiment and search for new, more modern approaches to job design, often referred to in general terms as job "redesign".

7.2.3 Horizontal work redesign

The concept of work redesign can be interpreted from a general or specific perspective. Generally speaking it refers to the trend towards new forms of work organisation. In this regard reference is often made to the so-called post-Fordist era or new-Fordism in the manufacturing world.

 In specific terms *work redesign* may be taken to refer to those instances where management reconsiders the fundamental way in which the labour process is organised or structured in an organisation.

Work redesign does not simply mean altering the job description of an employee: it involves a large-scale, fundamental re-engineering of the labour process or of a substantial component thereof. Whereas job design in the true sense of the word refers to the first instance when a job is created by management, work redesign means the reshaping of the way people (employees) have to work. In this sense work redesign can be thought of as changing job design patterns on a large scale.

From the perspective of strategic decision making, the switch from one human resource management strategy to another may in all probability require decisions about the redesigning of work; in other words, work restructuring. One form of work restructuring aims at broadening the range of the tasks undertaken by a particular jobholder whilst not tampering with the complexity and level of difficulty of the activities involved. In this way the requisite activities relating to a particular job are increased, with a concomitant increase in the range of skills required by job-holders. Two of these forms of work redesign are *job rotation* and *job enlargement*, both essentially aimed at reducing boredom and fatigue. Both of these approaches entail some form of multiskilling in the sense that jobholders will require an increasing number of different skills — although not higher-level skills.

7.2.3.1 *Job rotation*

This is the practice of rotating workers from job to job without disturbing workflow, whilst the different jobs are still narrowly defined. Since the jobs include different tasks and activities, jobholders are exposed to a greater variety of job content, which should lead to a reduction in boredom, fatigue and errors, thus improving job satisfaction and, hopefully, productivity. Rather than redesigning a particular job's content, work is restructured in such a way that workers move from job to job. This is why some critics of this form of work restructuring refer to job rotation as little more than the performance of several monotonous and boring jobs instead of only one — calling it "pseudo-job redesign".

7.2.3.2 *Job enlargement*

Another form of work reorganisation where job depth remains unchanged but which involves an increase in job range, is the practice of expanding the job descriptions of workers to include an increased number of different tasks and duties which are not more complex but which remain very basic and simple. This is, in effect, almost the opposite of dividing work or fragmenting it. The number of tasks, activities and duties is increased and it can thus be seen as a form of de-specialisation in the sense that a job that used to consist of, say, six tasks is rede-signed by adding five more tasks (which were previously grouped with other jobs) at the same level of depth. Job enlargement is often equated to multi tasking.

7.2.4 **Vertical work redesign: Increasing job depth through job enrichment**

Much of the traditional criticism against scientific management was born out of the human relations movement. It was alleged that mass-production techniques and associated efforts towards job fragmentation did not pay enough attention to the sociopsychological needs of workers. Scientific management was deemed to lack the human focus in that it was said to be focused solely on the technicalities of production systems with the aim of creating efficient ways of working. The human relationists alerted management scientists to the fact that the focus should be shifted to human needs, to the employee, employee behaviour and human relations in the work environment. Focusing only on money and sufficient rest was deemed not to be enough. It was argued that work had become meaningless for those who had to execute it and that the humanisation of work was necessary. This required, inter alia, a focus on the worker as a social being.

Elton Mayo was probably one of the first of the leading figures in the human relations movement to draw attention towards workers' social needs. In his view it was important for those who designed work to pay thorough attention to the individual worker's need to experience a sense of belonging, to be able to interact meaningfully with others and to engage in social processes of worthwhile information exchange. It was regarded as important to show employees that management cares by listening to their personal problems and by emphasising the importance of each individual employee in the organisational community or family.

What followed was an era in which the focus of management science research shifted to the needs of human beings and how they could be motivated in the work situation by designing work environments to address their needs. One prominent researcher in this field was the American psychologist, Abraham Maslow, who came up with his hierarchy of human needs (see chapter 11). Another prominent figure was Fred Herzberg who devised the so-called two-factor theory of motivation. According to Herzberg (see chapter 11 for more details in this regard), one had to distinguish between *hygiene* and *motivational* factors. The former, if attended to in work design, prevent the worker from being unhappy, whereas the motivators, if present, actually enhance satisfaction, better work performance, etc. This led to the conclusion that work had to be redesigned in such a way that "motivators" were built into jobs, and this meant that jobs had to be *enriched*.

 Job enrichment thus focuses on increasing job depth by giving employees more discretion, autonomy, responsibility and control over their work.

The foundation of this form of work design is the individual's need for psychological growth, taking into account aspects (such as challenging work) that can facilitate a sense of achievement in the worker. This could be facilitated by redesigning jobs so that tasks and task elements (which had previously been fragmented) could be combined into whole and meaningful pieces of work. In this way, the employee would receive direct feedback regarding work performance through his/her work itself.

Building on Herzberg's job enrichment approach to work redesign, Hackman and Oldham (1975) developed an approach called the "job characteristics model". (See also Hackman, Oldham, Jansom & Purdy 1975.)

7.2.5 The job characteristics model of job design

Hackman and Oldham developed the "Job Diagnostic Survey", containing measures of core job characteristics or dimensions, linked to the critical psychological states of workers which are in turn linked to certain personal and work outcomes. The model recognises that the relationships between the core job characteristics and the psychological states of individuals are moderated by each individual worker's "growth-need strength" — in other words, each person's need for accomplishment, to learn, grow, develop and be challenged by work content.

The core job characteristics are *skill variety, task identity, task significance, autonomy* and *feedback* (see Exhibit A below).

Exhibit A

The core job characteristics

- *Skill variety* refers to the extent to which a job requires the jobholder to possess a number of different skills, talents, abilities, competencies, etc.
- *Task significance* refers to the extent to which a job can be viewed as important and as having an impact on others within as well as outside the organisational environment.
- *Task identity* refers to the extent to which a job requires the jobholder to complete a whole piece of work from beginning to end with a visible outcome.
- *Autonomy* is essentially the extent to which a job allows or requires the jobholder to control his/her own work. Discretion and freedom to make decisions independently with regard to the way work is to be carried out thus form a part of this characteristic.
- *Feedback* is the extent to which a job itself provides the jobholder with clear, unambiguous information about work performance and its outcomes.

The three critical psychological states are *experienced meaningfulness, responsibility* and *knowledge of results*. The first state has to do with the degree to which the jobholder experiences the work as worthwhile, important and valuable. Responsibility is the extent to which jobholders feel responsible and accountable for the outcomes of their work. The last psychological state refers to the extent to which the jobholder knows and understands how well he/she is performing the job on a regular basis.

According to this model, a job which is designed in such a way as to allow the jobholder to experience all three of the critical psychological states will lead to high internal work motivation, high work satisfaction, high quality work and low absenteeism and turnover — but only if there is also adequate satisfaction with the work environment (for example working conditions and supervision) and if the job characteristics and the jobholder's abilities and needs are matched.

With regard to the work environment, it is also particularly important to take note of the biological aspects of job design.

7.2.6 A note on ergonomic considerations in work design

Noe, Hollenbeck, Gerhart and Wright (1994: 225–226) discuss this topic by drawing on the work of Campion and Thayer (1985). According to these authors, *ergonomics* is derived primarily from the sciences of occupational medicine, biomechanics (the study of body movements) and work physiology.

Ergonomics concerns the interface between an individual jobholder's physiological and psychological features and the physical work environment.

The basic idea is to structure the physical work environment around the way in which human bodies work.

Ergonomics is especially useful in the process of redesigning aspects of work like furniture, equipment, machinery and other technological features. In short, it can be said that principles of ergonomics can be used as sets of interventions to design and redesign the physical work environment on the basis of the human characteristics that employees possess. In this sense it is thus not a particular approach to job design but rather an aspect that form an important component of job design and redesign. In the light of the current drive towards all sorts of organisational flexibility, work designs are required also to include elements of flexibility in furnishings and adaptability of space (Harder 1996). Reference has been made, for example, to the "virtual office". Harder (1996: 5) makes the following observations:

> "A building is, we hope, a fairly stable thing. Certain features, such as load-bearing walls, foundations and mechanical systems lend an air of permanence, and somewhat constrain changes that organisational designers might like to make. But at the same time, new ways of designing work are requiring flexibility of furnishings and adaptability of space.
>
> As an example, whether it is referred to as hotelling, hot desking, just-in-time space or non-territorial offices, the idea that people no longer have their "own" desk but must use whatever is available at the time means that furnishings and equipment must be suitable for several individuals of potentially different heights, sizes and weights.
>
> This includes chairs that can be customised, articulated keyboard holders and adjustable lighting, so that each user can adjust the environment for his or her best usage. Flexible and easily assembled furniture systems are becoming more important, so that physical space can be adapted for either individual or team work."

From the above one can only deduce that the quest for flexibility is putting an increasing demand on designing or structuring work in a manner that can facilitate fast-moving, quick-response and high-performance organisations.

7.2.7 The quest for flexibility and high-performance work systems

The first real efforts to restructure work, as we have mentioned, were founded in classical, industrial-engineering thinking. Taylor was concerned with production or operational efficiency — the aim was to make work as simple as possible so that people could be quickly and easily trained to perform the work the one best way (for maximisation of operational efficiency). This "way" was engineered by making use of time and motion studies to determine the most efficient worker movements. The focus was on the mechanical side of things and not the human side.

The next efforts to reorganise work developed from the fact that Fordist mass production and Taylorist work techniques did not take into account the needs of workers. The focus thus shifted to the employee as a human being with needs and to behavioural aspects, as opposed to the production or operational system.

In the light of current external pressures on organisations to become more adaptive, flexible and quick to respond to the world of global business and competition, the trend today is towards focusing on **both** the human and the operational side of organisations. The idea is to identify high-performance work systems that have built-in features of innovation, creativity, teamwork and flexibility to facilitate high-performance or "lean" production.

Anstey (1995) points out the differences between lean production and mass production. The production focus has shifted from "producer-pushed" to "consumer-pulled" and "customer-choice", to low waste, zero defect, continuous improvement, reduced inventories and other buffers, speed in production and rapid product development. All of this requires new ways of work organisation of which flexibility makes up a core factor.

Cappelli and Rogovsky (1996: 2) summarise the work design implications as shown in exhibit B.

Exhibit B

Work design implications of high performance work systems
"The contemporary debate in the US began by identifying "high-performance" work systems in the context of new production systems. "Lean" or high-performance production systems were identified and the work systems demanded by them were identified — by definition — as high-performance work. These production systems are most clearly seen with Japanese manufacturing, and include techniques such as statistical process control, just-in-time inventory systems, continuous improvement and total quality management. The models of lean production basically argue that increased quality, productivity and flexibility can be obtained by making better use of employees. In particular, responsibility and decision making are transferred from administrative structures directly to employees or to their teams. These arrangements demand significantly more from employees than do work systems associated with scientific management, where tasks are narrowed and virtually all decision making is in the hands of management. But it appears that they may demand less than the work systems associated with the behavioural models of work reform. Lean production work systems appear to demand more from workers in the way of stress and effort/work pace than do the behavioural models. They also offer workers substantially less autonomy. Employee decision making, when it occurs, happens in an aggregated, inter-team setting. The highly regimented tasks of lean production limit individual autonomy, and while they may offer more variety than do work systems governed by scientific management, it is substantially less than that associated with behaviourally based models."

The approach of "lean production" is, therefore, not without its critics — especially as far as trade unions in South Africa are concerned. Lloyd's work (1994) is a case in point. As Cappelli and Rogovsky admit, these high-performance systems are aimed at "speed-ups". Lloyd (1994: 7) (like other critics) refers to it as "management by stress". Lloyd (1994: 7) goes on to say that those who are proponents of such work systems surely cannot then say that their organisations are fundamentally better places to work at. Rather, it is argued, such work systems impact adversely on occupational health and safety and overall quality of working life. Lloyd quotes Taiichi Ohno, the "father" of lean production systems, as follows: "There is an old Japanese saying 'the last fart of the ferret'. When a ferret is cornered and about to die, it will let out a terrible smell to repel its attacker. Now that's real nous, and it's the same with human beings. When they're under so much pressure that they feel it's a matter of life or death, they will come up with all kinds of ingenuity."

In the redesign of work, a host of factors must thus be taken into account. The crucial consideration, as mentioned already, and one which forms part of so-called best practice (Lloyd 1994: 35), relates to the notion of organisational and workforce flexibility.

Anthony, Perrewe and Kacmar (1996: 292) specifically call work flexibility a "current strategic issue in job design", while Horwitz and Franklin (1996) say that "flexibility is the name of the game". Flexibility within the context of work can take on various forms (Horwitz & Franklin 1996). These include functional, temporal and numerical flexibility (see definitions below).

Functional flexibility refers to multiskilling so that workers can be more mobile and adaptable in order to undertake a much broader range of tasks.

Temporal flexibility has to do with various patterns of work hours. Work can be structured in such a way that employees are required to work shifts. Provision can also be made to allow for part-time work, temporary work, job sharing or even homeworking.

Flexitime is a generic concept to capture the idea of arranging for flexible work hours.

Numerical flexibility concerns allowing for variety with regard to the size and structure of the workforce. Making use of temporary staff or subcontracting or outsourcing work are forms of numerical flexibility.

The extent to which South African organisations make use of flexibility in structuring or organising their work is reflected in the recent research findings outlined in the appendix to this chapter (page 261).

7.3   GROUP-LEVEL CONSIDERATIONS OF WORK ORGANISATION

As has been indicated already, teams and teamwork form important features of modern approaches to work design. In the process of organising work, consideration must thus also be given to the possibility of creating structures where groups of employees can work in **teams**.

The modern trend to focus on teams was largely inspired by Japanese forms of work organisation. Very early efforts to structure work along group lines can, however, be traced back to experiential work undertaken by the Tavistock Institute for Human Relations in London, United Kingdom, during the late 1940s and early 1950s. This Institute's researchers found that, by emphasising social interaction and communication through the clustering of jobs into work teams, rather than through traditional functional divisions of labour, better work results were achieved. The research that led to these conclusions was conducted in the coal mining, electronics and textile industries.

Before we proceed with a brief overview of different types of teams that can be found in the workplace, it is important to clarify what we mean by "work team".

A *work team* can be regarded as a group of two or more employees with different but complementary competencies who are interdependent and who work together towards the achievement of a common goal.

Harris (1986: 229) describes a team as "a workgroup or unit with a common purpose through which members develop mutual relationships for the achievement of goals/tasks. Teamwork, then, implies cooperative and coordinated efforts by individuals working together in the interests of their common cause. It requires the sharing of talent and leadership, the playing of multiple roles."

As can be seen, it is not easy to provide a definitive definition. Part of the underlying reason for this is probably the fact that many different types of teams can be structured within organisations.

7.3.1 Different types of teams

There are different ways of categorising different types of teams. One can, for instance, focus on levels in the organisational structure to distinguish between top management teams, middle-management teams and worker teams. Then there are, for example, project teams, task forces and committees. Problem-solving teams and quality circles can be seen as types of special-purpose teams which aim to improve the quality of production or operations.

Quality circles are groups that consist of a number of workers who meet regularly with their superiors to discuss quality problems and to find joint solutions through the process of group problem solving. They are thus essentially "off-line" in the sense that they do not operate as a team all the time on a daily basis. They take time out periodically to address quality issues.

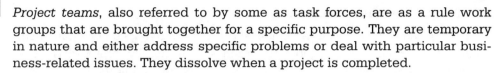

Project teams, also referred to by some as task forces, are as a rule work groups that are brought together for a specific purpose. They are temporary in nature and either address specific problems or deal with particular business-related issues. They dissolve when a project is completed.

Project teams also typically comprise employees who together cover the broad range of competencies and experience necessary to plan, execute and complete a project. Because a project, per definition, has a cut-off date for completion, the project team is temporary in that it dissolves at the point of project completion.

A self-directed work team (SDWT), also known as an autonomous work group or a self-managed work team, is usually a relatively small group (6–18) of well-trained employees that is fully responsible for achieving complex goals such as producing an entire product.

The SDWT team functions autonomously and the team members themselves decide over control issues like production planning, setting priorities and assigning work and rest breaks. The members thus also share responsibility for the level of the team's performance.

Within SDWTs, job rotation is usually very common. Because members of SDWTs are required to perform a variety of cross-functional tasks, multiskilling is usually a prerequisite. The team members normally all take part in all decision making and there is a very high degree of information exchange. Interpersonal dynamics are intended to be very open and, in cases of team member problems (such as the poor performance of an individual team member, or excessive absenteeism or poor timekeeping) the rest of the team ensure that the behaviour of an individual team member does not deviate from agreed-upon norms.

As mentioned above, job rotation is usually a very common feature of self-directed work teams. As Vecchio (1996: 242) puts it:

> "By rotating assignments, members gain knowledge of a broader range of tasks and are able to help out other team members who may need assistance. The team thus gains in versatility and flexibility. Because members become, in a sense, interchangeable as a result of shared knowledge, there is less 'downtime' due to a single member lacking the know-how to remedy problems. Mandatory job rotation, which usually occurs at 6- or 12-month intervals, has the added advantage of eliminating 'turf wars' that sometimes develop in work units. That is, no one 'owns' a particularly enjoyable, or cushy, job, and everyone eventually spends some time doing the least enjoyable job in the unit. Because of rotation, no employee can obtain a permanent position that is removed from the work flow or that would provide a form of 'early retirement with pay'."

As can be gathered, SDWTs are a very democratic and participative form of work organisation. A great deal of emphasis is also placed on on-the-job training because of the job rotation and accompanying focus on multiskilling. Because there is job rotation and multiskilling, the remuneration system is often also skills- rather than position-based.

7.3.2 Implications of teamwork

Teams are viewed by most as a form of work structuring that can facilitate greater task flexibility, cooperation, job satisfaction and eventually improved work performance and quality. It does, however, involve a cost factor as well.

Structuring work more along the lines of teamwork means that a great deal of emphasis must be put on training and retraining. This in itself may be a good thing, especially if the appropriate strategy has to be investment orientated, but training costs money and trained people who leave the company may have to be replaced, which may also prove costly. Furthermore, team-based work organisation cannot be executed in isolation: it has implications for broader organisational structuring decisions (see section 7.4). Traditional hierarchical structures cannot easily accommodate work structuring along team lines. It is commonly accepted that the jobs of supervisors will be eliminated, or at least redefined to that of team leaders, in cases of team-based work organisation. The retraining of supervisors to fulfil more the role of facilitators rather than overseers will thus be required.

The benefits of a team-based approach, however (so it is asserted by proponents of this approach), usually far outweigh the costs. Johnson (1986: 48) explains the potential benefits that flow from such an approach:

> "Improve the way team members interact, and you improve their ability to solve problems. Better problem solving means better efficiency in general. Increased efficiency tends to boost morale and productivity. It also helps to decrease stress, turnover and operating costs. And all of these improvements bolster the organization's public image."

Stott and Walker (1995: 55) discuss the potential benefits of teams, and conclude that, if correctly used, such an approach may be able to provide both the organisation and the individuals involved with the benefits listed in exhibit C.

Exhibit C

Potential benefits of teams*
• Reduced duplication of effort.
• Increased cooperation.
• Innovative ideas.
• Better, wiser and more complete decisions.
• Motivated colleagues.
• Improved product and service quality.
• Increased productivity and profits.
• Added flexibility to allow easier adaption to changing circumstances.
• Increased commitment to implementation.
• Reduced destructive conflict.
• Improved interpersonal and interunit relations and communication.
• Higher standards of performance.

*Source: Stott & Walker (1995: 55).

7.4 ORGANISATIONAL-LEVEL CONSIDERATIONS: ORGANISATION DESIGN

Structuring the flow of work also involves decisions about how the organisation as a whole is to be structured. Organisation design essentially means choosing an organisational structure that is appropriate for strategy implementation and mission accomplishment. Although it still concerns how the work of the organisation is organised, it is quite removed from the employees as such, since it revolves around the way the **organisation as a whole** is structured. This holds specific implications for reporting lines and these decisions thus hold important implications for the management of employment relationships. Thus, although a comprehensive discussion of organisation structure and design is beyond the scope of this book, a brief look at some of the relevant issues is necessary.

7.4.1 Variables of organisation structure

Different structural variables come into play in the process of designing organisations.

- *Configuration* concerns the nature and form of the role structures within the organisation. It thus involves aspects such as the number of levels in the hierarchy, the horizontal and vertical span of control of different levels of management jobs, etc.
- *Formalisation* concerns the extent to which use is made of procedures, policy manuals, written job descriptions and similar written documentation.
- *Standardisation* is in some way linked to formalisation and refers to the degree to which activities or work processes have to be executed in a uniform manner. Reliance on aspects like rules and regulations is therefore relevant. In the case of high standardisation there is little scope for discretion.
- *Specialisation* refers to the extent to which specific functions and tasks are identified and earmarked for one specific individual or group to execute.
- *Centralisation* refers to the extent to which the power and authority to make decisions is delegated throughout the various levels of the organisational structure.

As can be seen, all of these variables hold important implications for individual as well as group perspectives of work organisation. However, they also play an important role in the choices that have to be made in respect of different types of organisation structures.

7.4.2 Different types of organisation structures

There are many ways of categorising different types of organisation structures. We will briefly mention a few examples.

Bureaucratic organisation structures result from what is known as the mechanistic approach to organisation design. This approach or model is described by

Gibson, Ivancevich and Donnelly (1994) as an "organizational design emphasizing the importance of achieving high levels of production and efficiency through extensive use of rules and procedures, centralized authority, and high specialization of labor." Typically this will lead to a tall, pyramid-shaped structure with a hierarchy of many different levels. A top-down, "command-and-control", military-like organisation structure flows from such an approach. A great deal of emphasis is placed on departmentalisation (due to specialisation) and work is often structured in rigid, functional work units, with definite boundaries between different jobs, different sections, different departments, different divisions and other work units. Figure 7.1 depicts a typical tall, bureaucratic organisation structure.

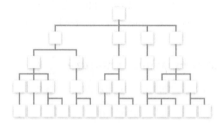

Figure 7.1
Bureaucratic organisation structure

Flat organisation structures are essentially the result of following the organic model or approach to organisation design. According to Gibson et al (1994: 538), this entails organisational design that emphasises aspects like the importance of high levels of adaptiveness, responsiveness and development through limiting the use of rules, regulations and procedures. It emphasises decentralisation of authority and lower degrees of specialisation. The flat organisation structure thus develops from the fact that there is a great deal of decentralisation with resultingly few layers of management levels. In contrast to the bureaucratic organisation structure, flat structures mean wide spans of control. Jobs will generally be more broadly defined with greater overlaps and flexible boundaries between different work units, such as different jobs and sections. Teams are often also part of flat structures and are likely to be organised around different customers, services or products rather than functions. Figure 7.2 is an example of a flat structure.

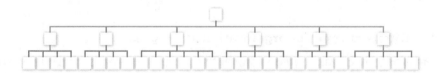

Figure 7.2
Flat organisation structure

Apart from these two types of organisation structures, there are other designs such as project and matrix designs, while more modern designs such as network designs and even the boundaryless organisation are also emerging.

A few remarks about the latter two, more modern, approaches are necessary.

With regard to the *network* organisation, Shani and Lau (1995: 13–18) say that "the network structure blends traditional management concepts . . . with market concepts such as exchange agreements. Network forms of structure rely heavily on contracting out and outsourcing . . . Companies downsize to their core areas of competence and establish alliances with independent suppliers and distributors." According to Tapscott and Caston (1993: 75), such organisations are "based on cooperative, multidisciplinary teams and businesses networked together across the enterprise. Rather than a rigid structure, it is a modular organizational architecture in which business teams operate as a network of what we call client and server functions."

Boundaryless organisations share with flat organisation structures the idea that boundaries between units ought to be broken down. However, they go a step further in the sense that, as in the case of network organisation designs, boundaries between organisations and their customers, suppliers and competitors are also broken down to some extent. In this way relationships are formed that allow these organisations to pool and share resources such as employees, information and distribution channels. Typically, in cases of joint ventures cross-organisational teams are set up so that they can work together.

7.5 STRUCTURAL CONSIDERATIONS REGARDING HUMAN RESOURCE MANAGEMENT FUNCTIONS

Just as decisions have to be made regarding the structuring of the work of an organisation's employees in general, all the work of those personnel engaged in human resource management must likewise be organised. Questions relating to who is going to do what in the field of human resource management have to be answered. This will include decisions regarding the extent to which there will be *specialisation* in this area of management in an organisation. In other words, it will have to be decided what role line management will play in the management of employment relationships, and what the role of the human resource specialists or departments will be. Furthermore, it will have to be decided at what organisational level certain human resource management decisions will be taken — that is, will human resource management decisions be centralised or decentralised?

The answers to such questions must be left to top management to decide. In this regard, different researchers/authors have come up with different HRM models or typologies.

7.5.1 The role of the HR department/specialist: Three models or typologies

Within the context of this complex question, various theorists/researchers have endeavoured to come up with typologies to present models conceptualising the potential roles which HR departments or specialists can play in HRM. One such typology has been devised by Brewster and Holt Larsen (1992).

7.5.1.1 Model/Typology 1

Brewster and Holt Larsen see the role of the HR department/specialists vis-à-vis line management as one involving two dimensions plotted on a matrix. The horizontal axis depicts *devolvement*, described as the degree to which the line managers, rather than personnel specialists, are involved in and responsible for HRM. On the vertical axis the second dimension, referred to as *integration*, represents the degree to which HRM issues are considered to be an integral part of the formulation and execution of the organisation's business strategies.

From the matrix, four HRM 'models' can be identified, in terms of the two dimensions (see figure 7.3).

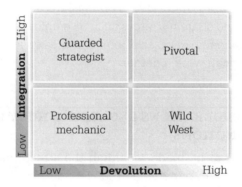

Figure 7.3
Brewster & Holt Larsen's models of human resource management
Source: Adapted from Brewster & Holt Larsen (1992: 414)

These models allow one to analyse the role of the HR department and also the nature of HRM as a general management function.

The "professional mechanics"

The bottom left-hand corner of the matrix depicts a model of HRM where the integration of HR issues with business strategy is low and little devolvement of HRM to line management takes place. In this case the HR manager is termed the professional mechanic. The HR specialist is viewed as a professional in the same way as in other professions (for example an engineer). Here the HR specialists see themselves as having higher imperatives, beyond those of organisations. They believe that many or most areas of HRM are beyond the understanding of other managers.

As a result, the interests of the HR department diverge more and more from the strategic interests of the business, and there is an increasing concern with the technical details of the HR profession. The consequence of this is "an ever-greater isolation from other members of the management team" (Brewster & Holt Larsen 1992: 414).

The "wild wests"

In the wild-west model the integration of HR issues with the business aspects of the organisation is still low, but HRM is substantially devolved to line managers. Managers are thus almost free to develop their own styles of HRM. They sometimes even have the power to reward and to hire and fire employees as they deem fit. In this model, inconsistency, incoherence and even strong employee reaction could quite easily result.

The "guarded strategists"

In the guarded-strategist model, HRM is highly integrated with business strategy, the HR department retains authority and the HR specialists are viewed as very powerful people in the organisation. They work with senior management when corporate strategy is formulated. The HR departments are influential and control the number of employees, who is employed and developed, and how they are rewarded — all in line with the business objectives. For line management this can create a situation of considerable frustration. They often find that most aspects of their relationships with their subordinate employees are practically "abrogated by the personnel function: the weaker managers will welcome the chance to slough off their responsibilities, while simultaneously having someone else to blame for all failures; the better managers will be frustrated" (Brewster & Holt Larsen 1992: 416).

The "pivotals"

In the pivotal model all HRM issues are integrated with business strategy and the devolvement of HRM to line management is extensive. Here the senior personnel specialists act as facilitators, catalysts and coordinators of all the HR issues at the top level of the organisation. Human resource departments are thus small, but competent and powerful, fulfilling the functions of monitoring and advising on HRM-related issues. Line and human resource specialists are often exchangeable. Furthermore, as Brewster and Holt Larsen (1992: 415) point out: "the concentration on the development and monitoring of policy is correlated with the devolution of responsibility and authority to carry out the policy to line management". In these organisations difficulties can arise in staffing the HR department with competent HR specialists of a high quality, who can understand the business of the organisation and who can also train and develop line managers to perform operational level HRM successfully.

7.5.1.2 Model/Typology 2

The works of Tyson and Fell (1986), Tyson (1987) and Sisson (1989) provide details of another such typology of models.

The "clerks of works"

In the clerk-of-works model the key role of the HR department is that of adminis-trative support. The emphasis falls on the routine tasks of correspondence and record keeping about absenteeism and staff turnover. The HR department may also sometimes fulfil a supportive role in staffing functions (such as employment inter-views), as well as a welfare role (for example in visiting the sick). The staff of these HR departments will have little specialised training, there will be a lack of sophis-ticated HRM systems and the specialists will not have any real clout.

The "contracts managers"

In the contracts-manager model the emphasis falls on meeting all events with sys-tems (Tyson 1987: 526). The key role of this type of HR department is thus most likely to be "the making and interpretation of procedures and agreements . . . (to) resolve day-to-day problems" (Sisson 1989: 12). This type of HR department is typ-ically staffed with highly skilled and experienced labour relations specialists whose role will be primarily reactive by nature. However, these specialists may possess considerable power and authority due to their abilities to solve personnel and labour relations related problems.

The "architects"

According to the architect model, the HR department plays a constructive role in the organisation's striving towards success in a competitive business environ-ment. Their role is thus comprehensive and extends beyond pure personnel issues in that these specialists often view themselves as "'business managers' first and 'personnel managers' second" (Sisson 1989: 12). The head of the HR department is typically a member of the top management team and he/she fulfils a strategic role in helping the organisation to achieve business success, for example through the design of organisational structures and the formulation of policies which seek to give effect to corporate and/or business plans. Right from top management level downwards, there is an integrated system of cooperation between line managers and human resource specialists, the latter as a rule being highly qualified, trained and competent in their specialist areas while simultaneously having a broad-based business and general management background. It is thus almost an internal con-sultant type of role which is highly valued by all of those involved in HRM in gen-eral. According to Storey (1992: 167), recent research findings suggest an apparent gradual move towards this type of model in HR departments in the United Kingdom.

7.5.1.3 Model/Typology 3

Storey's research (1992: 166–185) leads him to another typology of the role which HR departments can play in organisations. Two dimensions are utilised to form another matrix with four typical 'models' of the role of the HR department (see figure 7.4).

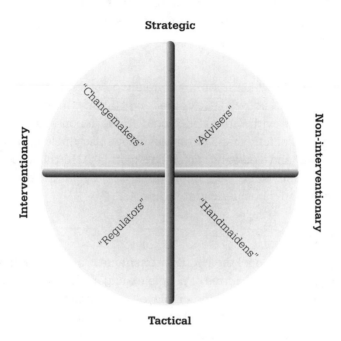

Figure 7.4
Storey's types of personnel management
Source: Adapted from Storey (1992: 168)

The "advisers"

In terms of the advisers role, the HR practitioners act as internal consultants or advisers upon request from line management (being quite reactive or non-interventionary). Devolution is thus high and the HR department leaves HRM largely over to the other managers although, when it comes to strategic (or policy) issues (even broader business/strategic), the small group of competent HR specialists are often approached for their advice.

The "handmaidens"

In the handmaiden model, the HR department's role is also relatively non-interventionary or reactive (acting when approached), but their role is actually limited to pure HR issues such as looking after the welfare of employees and performing clerical functions such as record keeping, collating information on the payroll, monitoring absenteeism statistics, headcounts, and so forth. Furthermore, in terms of this role type, the HR department's function is to help line in the area of labour relations when such assistance is requested. The term *handmaiden* is used pre-cisely to signal a type of attendant, subservient relationship between the HR spe-cialists and line management with regard to HRM. Storey (1992: 75) notes that the major difference between this role and the advisers role is that "the service offered was of a more routine administrative, or at best tactical kind, rather than being in the nature of strategic advice". Devolution is thus still high, while the specialists are mostly engaged in servicing line's routine requirements upon request.

The "regulators"

The HR departments which fall into the role type of regulators are referred to as "managers of discontent" who seek order and stability, inter alia through tempo-rary, tactical truces with organised labour (trade unions) and the formulation, promulgation and enforcement of employment rules (including union-manage-ment agreements and personnel procedure manuals). In this case, although the role of the specialists is interventionary (proactive) by nature, the specialists very rarely engage in wider business strategy issues.

The "changemakers"

In the changemakers model the HR department plays an interventionary and stra-tegic role by initiating new forms of people management in line with the needs of the business and aimed at eliciting employee commitment and the willingness to "go the extra mile". Storey (1992: 180) says of this role that: "the orientation is away from bargaining, away from ad hocery, and away from 'humble advice' . . . The dual forms of integration . . . (integration of the different aspects of resourcing, planning, appraising, rewarding and developing; and the further integration of all of this into the business plan) are characteristics of this type. . . ." Furthermore, Storey indi-cates that within this role type there are two further variations — the hard and soft roles. In the former the emphasis falls on the business language of numbers and hence the quantification of input/output ratios. An extreme profit orientation is thus emphasised where the HR department and specialists constantly concentrate on the value they add to the bottom line of the organisation. The HR specialists thus become business thinkers — to the extent that they are eventually not even typified as specialists any longer and line and personnel managers often exchange roles. In the soft role type, the focus is on the distinctive nature of the specialist's inputs to the management of the organisation in inventing and displaying unique techniques to tap the creativity and commitment of resourceful humans.

From the above it should be clear that the nature of human resource manage-ment — and particularly the role of HR departments in this regard — can vary from situation to situation, especially as far as the role differentiation in HRM between the HR department/specialists vis-à-vis the general/line managers is concerned. Structuring all HR related work in organisations thus entails making important strategic decisions in conjunction with decisions on generic and grand strategy (see the previous chapter). Another strategic decision relates to the actual structuring of the organisation's HR department.

7.5.2 The place and organisation of HR departments

The human resource departments of different organisations can vary considerably in terms of aspects such as size (staff numbers), services rendered or functions performed, and how they are structured and managed. Much of this will depend upon circumstantial factors related to the HR department's specific type of role within the organisation, which will again be influenced by factors such as the kind of industry, organisational strategy, size, structure and top management philosophy. It will obviously also be influenced strongly by the kinds of HRM strategies decided upon.

In the case of a relatively small or medium sized manufacturing organisation with only one establishment and, say, 400 employees, a human resource department might, for example, be one of the usual functional areas, such as the financial department, the operations/production department and the marketing department (see figure 7.5.)

Figure 7.5
Placing the HR department within the organisational structure

In such a case the HR department, headed by an HR manager, can, for example, be structured as in figure 7.6, with different sections responsible for certain activities and functions. The structure of such a department will therefore also be strongly influenced by the relative importance of the various functions or tasks to be performed by the HR department.

In larger organisations with more complex organisational structures the structuring and positioning of the HR department will naturally be different and likewise more complex. Organisations with more than one plant/establishment might, for example, have corporate level HR departments, as well as HR departments at the plant or establishment levels. The HR departments at the various organisational levels will thus most likely have specific roles to fulfil. In such cases decisions will therefore also have to be made about the centralisation/decentralisation of HRM functions — in other words about the *organisational level* (corporate/plant) at which various HRM decisions are to be made.

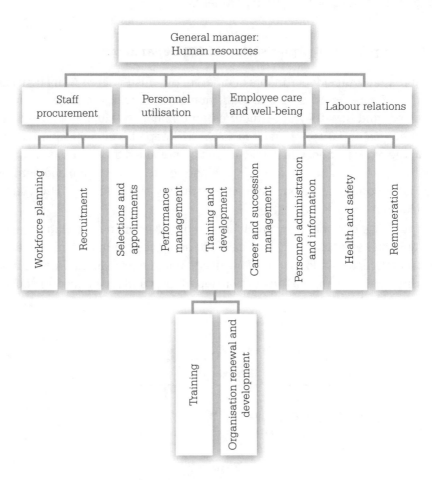

Figure 7.6

Structuring the human resource department

7.6 CONCLUSION

In this chapter we focused on human resource management decisions that relate to structure. We looked at structural decisions at the level of individual jobs, from a group-level perspective, as well as from the perspective of workflow in the organisation as a whole. In addition, particular emphasis was placed on structuring the work relating to the human resource management functions as such. All decisions regarding these aspects are long term, hold serious resource implications and require top management attention. This is why they are regarded as strategic decisions.

SELF-EVALUATION QUESTIONS

1. Define the concept *job design.*
2. Differentiate between *job analysis, job redesign, job depth* and *job range.*
3. What is horizontal work redesign? Describe two forms of this type of work redesign.
4. Explain the job characteristics model of job design.
5. "Flexibility within the context of work can take on various forms."
   Explain the meaning of this statement and discuss its application in South Africa.
6. Define the concept *team* within the context of organisations and discuss the nature, potential and pitfalls relating to teamwork in South African organisations.
7. Write an essay briefly outlining certain organisational level considerations of work organisation.
8. "Different options and possibilities exist with regard to the type of role that human resource departments can play within South African organisations: it's a matter of strategic choice."
   Discuss this statement by describing three different models or typologies.
9. Explain how the organisation of HR departments can differ within the context of different organisational circumstances.

ENDNOTE

1. This section is based on the various sources quoted.

BIBLIOGRAPHY

Anstey, M. 1995. Can South African industrial relations move beyond adversarialism? Some comparative perspectives on the prospects of workplace forums in South Africa. *South African Journal of Labour Relations,* 19(4), 13

Anthony, WP, Perrewe, PL & Kacmar, KM. 1996. *Strategic Human Resource Management.* Orlando: The Dryden Press

Brewster, C & Holt Larsen H. 1992. Human resource management in Europe: Evidence from ten countries. *The International Journal of Human Resource Management,* 3(3), 409–434

Campion, M & Thayer, P. 1985. Development and field evaluation of an interdisciplinary measure of job design. *Journal of Applied Psychology,* 70, 29–34

Cappelli, P & Rogovsky, N. 1996. What do new systems demand of employees? *Business Day Supplement: Mastering Management Series,* Part 5, 1 April, 2

Gibson, JL, Ivancevich, JM & Donnelly, JH. 1994. *Organizations: Behavior, Structure, Processes,* 8 ed. Burr Ridge, Illinois: Irwin

Hackman, JR & Oldham, GR. 1975. Development of the Job Diagnostic Survey. *Journal of Applied Psychology,* 60, 159–170

Hackman, JR, Oldham, GR, Jansom, R & Purdy, K. 1975. A new strategy for job enrichment. *California Management Review,* Summer, 57–71

Harder, JW. 1996. Search for the virtual water cooler. *Business Day Supplement: Mastering Management Series,* Part 4, 25 March, 5

Harris, P. 1986. Building a high performance team. *Training and Development Journal,* 40 (April), 229

Horwitz, FM & Franklin, E. 1996. Flexibility is the name of the game. *Business Day Supplement: Mastering Management Series,* Part 7, 15 April, 15

Johnson, C. 1986. An outline for team building: Cooperation, collaboration and communication are the key ingredients of an effective team. *Training: The Magazine of Human Resource Development,* 23 (January), 48

Lloyd, C. 1994. *Work Organisation and World Class Management: A Critical Guide.* Senderwood: Red Earth Publications

Noe, RA, Hollenbeck, JR, Gerhart, B & Wright, PM. 1994. *Human Resource Management: Gaining a Competitive Advantage.* Illinois: Irwin

Shani, AB & Lau, JB. 1995. *Behavior in Organizations: An Experiential Approach,* 6 ed. Chicago: Irwin

Sisson, K. 1989. Personnel management in perspective. In *Personnel Management in Britain,* ed K Sisson, 3–21. Oxford: Basil Blackwell

Smit, PJ & Cronje, GJ de J. 1992. *Management Principles.* Kenwyn: Juta & Co Ltd

Storey, J. 1992. *Developments in the Management of Human Resources.* London: Blackwell

Stott, K & Walker, A. 1995. *Team, Teamwork & Teambuilding.* New York: Prentice Hall

Tapscott, D & Caston, A. 1993. *Paradigm Shift.* New York: McGraw-Hill

Tyson, S. 1987. The management of the personnel function. *Journal of Management Studies,* 24(5), 523–532

Tyson, S & Fell, A. 1986. *Evaluating the Personnel Function.* London: Hutchinson

Vecchio, RP. 1996. *Organizational Behavior,* 3 ed. Orlando: The Dryden Press

APPENDIX: FLEXIBILITY IS THE NAME OF THE GAME — SOME SOUTH AFRICAN RESEARCH FINDINGS*

At the end of 1995, the extent to which workplace flexibility has been implemented in 626 mostly manufacturing organisations in SA was investigated. Thirteen key areas were looked at: workplace information, use of contractors, part-time and temporary workers, consultants and homeworkers. Sections also covered labour cost reduction measures, workforce changes, shift working and work hours and trade union participation in workplace flexibility. Some of the findings include the following.

Emphasis on numerical flexibility

Flexibility in South African organisations occurs most commonly in the numerical category, specifically through reductions in workforce size. This is indicative of recent economic conditions in South Africa. Other elements of numerical flexibility practised are the use of temporary agencies, contractors and consultants. Home-workers and job sharing are not commonly used. Despite the claims of positive consequences for employers and employees, job sharing is rare, possibly due to lack of managerial interest and indifference from trade unions.

Temporal flexibility

The next most common type of flexibility is the temporal category, specifically in the use of shifts, part-time and temporary staff. Overtime is still heavily relied on in South Africa. Just as in the case of shift work, the impact on people's quality of life appears to be significant.

Functional flexibility

The use of functional flexibility is evident in methods to save labour costs, such as training, new technologies and work reorganisation. But functional flexibility does not often replace numerical flexibility.

Contractors and consultants

Most organisations have increased their use of contractors and consultants. This is expected to continue, following global trends. The use of subcontractors in South Africa has shown a steady expansion of about 20 % since the mid-1970s. Reasons include avoidance of non-wage benefits, greater flexibility by passing costs of fluctuating demand on to the contractor, greater flexibility in hiring and firing, organisational restructuring, usage in high-risk areas, lean manufacturing and scab labour.

*Source: Extracted and adapted from Horwitz and Franklin 1996.

But 16 % of employers, particularly in manufacturing, have insourced functions previously outsourced, due to efficiency, delivery, quality and labour problems in subcontracting firms.

Influence of unions

The introduction of flexible work practices is not strongly associated with the presence (or absence) of unions. Although unionised companies generally make greater use of flexible work practices, they show little difference in their pattern of usage. While relative usage of flexible work practices is similar between unionised and non-unionised companies, unions may influence the success of implementation.

Organisation size

There is a relationship between organisation size and use of flexible work practices. Larger organisations may be more attuned to international developments and best practices. There may be pressure from employees within larger organisations for the implementation of certain flexible work practices.

Economic imperatives

Given the country's rapid reintroduction to the global economy and foreign competition, use of flexible work practices is important for international competitiveness in the local industry.

Employers and unions cannot ignore flexible forms of employment, but they need to minimise their adverse impact and develop constructive practices to benefit workers and the enterprise.

STUDY OBJECTIVES

After studying this chapter, you should be able to:

- define the concept *job analysis*;
- explain the stages in the job analysis process;
- list the different uses of job analysis;
- apply the different job analysis methods;
- demonstrate, with the aid of an example, the principles of job analysis;
- explain how to write a job description and a job specification;
- explain the concept *workforce planning*;
- explain who is responsible for workforce planning;
- explain the purpose and importance of workforce planning;
- explain, with the aid of a diagram, the workforce planning process;
- list the various phases in step 1 of the workforce planning process;
- discuss the importance of the workforce implementation and evaluation steps in the workforce planning process.

8.1   INTRODUCTION

The outcome of work design is an organisation structure made up of various work units such as individual positions, sections, teams, etc. When an organisation has been operating for some time, the work to be performed by these units will already have been structured. However, even if work is not redesigned, it is still important to plan who will do the work, when, and how. It is necessary to know what kinds of positions, what types of work and what numbers of people with what kinds of competencies will be needed to ensure the successful operation of the organisation over the long term. When one starts to do a detailed analysis of these types of issues, the management process that has been put into motion can be termed *workforce planning* (traditionally also known as *manpower planning*). The basis of such workforce planning is information about what work is being or may need to be done, and this information comes from job analysis.

In order to staff the organisation with suitable employees, jobs will have to be analysed, potential employees will have to be identified and encouraged to apply for positions and the selection and appointment of employees will have to take place. To do this it is important to plan in advance what work needs to be done and what positions may become vacant. One must also project and profile the need to fill these positions. Effective human resource management in an organisation cannot take place without proper *workforce planning*, of which job analysis is an important part.

8.2   JOB ANALYSIS

The most basic component of an organisation's structure is (as we pointed out in the previous chapter) the work and the different work units, such as positions created to facilitate the carrying out of that work. Objectives are achieved by means of people performing their work in the various jobs; it is therefore essential that when jobs are designed utmost care be taken with respect to the quantity and quality of people needed to execute the work. The cornerstone of this process is job analysis.

Job analysis is a technical procedure which systematically explores the activities within a job (De Cenzo & Robbins 1994: 135).

In the job analysis process the duties, responsibilities and accountabilities of a job are analysed. The information gathered from a job analysis generates two outcomes — namely job descriptions and job specifications (see figure 8.1).

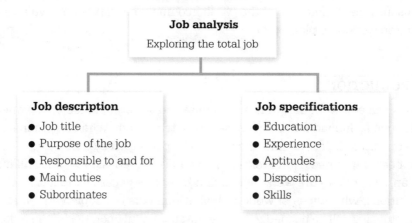

Job analysis
Exploring the total job

Job description	**Job specifications**
● Job title	● Education
● Purpose of the job	● Experience
● Responsible to and for	● Aptitudes
● Main duties	● Disposition
● Subordinates	● Skills

Figure 8.1
Job analysis

Job descriptions define the nature of the job content, the environment, and the conditions under which employment is carried out. A job description is a written statement of the content of a job which is derived from the analysis of the job. It states what the jobholder does, how it is done, under what conditions it is done and why it is done.

Job specifications stipulate the minimum acceptable characteristics a job-holder must possess as a requisite to be able to perform the job. A job specification describes the attributes that an employee requires to carry out the job — that is, it identifies the knowledge, skills, level of education, experience, and abilities needed to do the job effectively.

8.2.1 Stages in the job analysis process

The job analysis process can follow various stages (see figure 8.2).

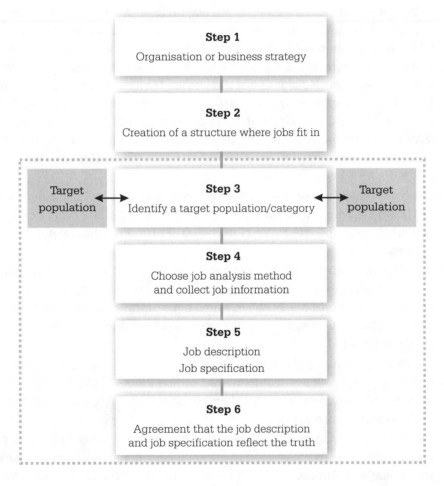

Figure 8.2
Stages in the job analysis process

It is suggested that the following procedure be adopted:

- determine the organisation's general business strategy;
- create a structure to identify the various jobs;
- identify a target population to be analysed;
- decide on a job analysis method to collect and verify job information;

- compile the job descriptions and job specifications;
- the group must agree that the job descriptions and job specifications accurately reflect the jobs concerned.

8.2.2 What job analysis can be used for

Job analysis can be used for a number of purposes (Cushway 1994: 41):

- *Workforce planning* ensures that the right number of employees, with the right skills, knowledge and experience, are available in the right places at the right time in an organisation. Objectives are set based on the business strategy, whereafter a plan must be devised to acquire the human resources necessary to meet the stated objectives. Organisational outputs required are derived from the objectives, and decisions must then be made on how many jobs are required to achieve the various outputs. The implications of this may be that certain jobs should remain as they are, or that certain jobs should be slightly changed, or that completely new jobs should be designed. Workforce planning cannot be accurately undertaken without information about the different jobs (see section 8.3).

- *Selection* can only take place if the job requirements have been clearly identified. With a job description and a job specification available it will be clear what qualifications, experience and personal attributes a potential candidate must possess.

- *Training and development inputs* based on a proper training-needs analysis can only take place once the job standards have been determined and the individual's performance has been measured against the set standards. With accurate job information available, discrepancies in individual performance can easily be detected.

- *Job redesign* requires job analysis. With organisations changing rapidly to realign themselves as a result of increased competition and other external forces, responsibilities and duties must often be reallocated. This makes accurate job analysis information essential.

- *Performance management* cannot take place without proper job information (see chapter 13). To measure job performance it is necessary to compare the incumbent's performance with the standards set by the job. Without clear job objectives, proper performance management cannot take place.

- *Organisational restructuring* can only take place with accurate information about the various jobs available. Duplication of responsibilities can be eliminated to ensure more smooth operations through better work flow processes.

- *Labour relations* may improve if every individual in an organisation knows as far as possible what his/her responsibilities and reporting lines are. Proper job analysis helps to ensure that the chances of communication gaps are minimised.

- *Job evaluations* and remuneration decisions require job related information that stems from the job analysis process (see chapter 17).

8.2.3 Information to be obtained through a job analysis

- One of the first tasks in the process of job analysis is to identify the job clearly; the job title, the department and the number of employees doing the job.
- The reporting relationships must be identified. It is essential to provide the title of the job immediately superior to the job in question and to indicate clearly the coordination links and functional relationships between jobs.
- The job content must be defined; this includes the main purpose of the job, its boundaries, responsibilities and accountabilities, and the tasks and activities to be undertaken.
- The required performance standards and how these are to be measured must be determined. The key performance areas (KPAs) or outputs of the job must be established and the standard to which they should be performed must also be clearly indicated.
- Any constraints must be identified: the limits of authority and decision making must be established.
- Those aspects of the job for which the incumbent is responsible (such as budget, equipment, material) must be determined.
- The working conditions under which the incumbent must perform the job must be established.
- The necessary personal characteristics must be identified; this includes the knowledge, skills and experience required of the incumbent to meet the requirements of the job.
- Any other relevant information (for example training requirements or aspects of a temporary nature) must be included.

8.2.4 Job analysis methods

The following methods can be used to obtain the necessary job information (De Cenzo & Robbins 1994: 135):

8.2.4.1 Individual interviews

Jobholders are identified and interviewed with the purpose of determining what the job entails. This will usually result in the preparation of a job description which will be confirmed by the supervisor. This is a time-consuming but effective method and is commonly used. An important drawback of this method is that people can inflate the importance of their jobs. It is also important that the interviewer pre-pares him/herself properly for the interview.

8.2.4.2 Group interviews

Some similar principles that apply to individual interviews apply to group interviews; the difference is that a number of jobholders are interviewed simultaneously. Group dynamics may increase or decrease the effectiveness of this method; job assessments may be more accurate and time-effective but one has to be able to manage and utilise the group process properly.

8.2.4.3 Observations

Observation involves watching employees while they perform their duties. This can be done by means of direct observation or through videos. A negative aspect of this method may be that employees do not perform as they normally do while knowing that they are being observed. A further problem is that certain aspects of jobs cannot always be observed all the time — for example, in the case of certain categories of managers and sales people.

8.2.4.4 Structured questionnaires

One of the methods most widely used to obtain information about jobs is the questionnaire. Employees are given a structured questionnaire on which they check or rate duties which they perform in the course of their work. This method is less time consuming and less costly than interviews, but exceptions may be overlooked and follow-up questions may not be asked or vague points clarified. The most common systems used are the Position Analysis Questionnaire (PAQ) and the Saville and Holdsworth Work Profiling System, which is a consulting service. The details of these methods, which are used worldwide as well as in South Africa, fall beyond the scope of this book.

8.2.4.5 Self-reports

In the case of self-reports jobholders are required to write their own job descriptions. It is, however, essential to provide the required training beforehand. Without the necessary guidance, the quality of the information received may be of no use. The success of this method also depends on the report writing skills of the jobholder.

8.2.4.6 Conference method

In this method, the information about a job is obtained from the jobholder's supervisor. The supervisor acts as expert and one of the aspects which may be overlooked is the jobholder's own perceptions of what he/she actually does on the job. Subject matter experts can also be drawn from other organisations. This method is also very useful if a new job is to be created — for example when a new operator is appointed after a computer network has been installed.

8.2.4.7 Diaries and logs

Jobholders must record their daily activities in a diary or a log. This can be very time consuming and must take place over a long period to ensure that all the activities are recorded. This method is better suited to higher managerial levels.

8.2.4.8 Critical incident methods

Jobholders are required to recall critical incidents that have occurred in the course of their work. This process has as its ultimate aim the identification of critical aspects of the job that are related to failure or success. The incumbent is required to write down all relevant issues; this could, however, result in the omission of important mundane aspects of the job.

8.2.4.9 Hierarchical task analysis

This method requires that the job be broken down into a hierarchical set of tasks and subtasks. Clearly identified objectives are defined as well as their means of execution. The standards which must be achieved and the conditions applicable to the job must be identified.

8.2.4.10 Competence assessment

Assessments of competence are undertaken by the steps outlined below:

- The performance effectiveness criteria (for example profits and customer satisfaction) must be defined.
- A sample of superior performers must be defined (for example the top five or ten performers achieving targets).
- Using expert panels or focus groups, information must be collected regarding the competencies of both the superior and the average jobholder. Competencies can also be obtained from the 360 degree performance ratings (jobholders, peers, supervisors and clients are involved in such ratings).
- Once the competencies of an average and an above average performer have been identified, the last step is to validate the predictive validity of the competency model using a second sample of jobholders.

8.2.4.11 Checklists

This method requires that a checklist of items that might be applicable to the job be drawn up. The jobholder and supervisor must then indicate which items are applicable to the job or to part of the job. Checklists are quick to complete and make it easy to obtain information about a large number of jobs. The items or tasks must, however, be carefully formulated and all relevant items or tasks must be included. This method is especially useful in determining the less well-defined aspects of a job, for example the labour relations responsibilities of a certain level of managers.

Exhibit A

Core competencies for senior managers

Core competencies for senior managers at a large engineering firm in South Africa
- Business acumen
- Participative approach to human resources
- Client service
- Teamwork
- Leadership
- Managerial skills
- Resilience
- Drive and flexibility
- Communication

8.2.4.12 Other job analysis methods

- Management Position Description Questionnaire (MPDQ)

  This method analyses managerial job activities in terms of responsibilities, instructions, activities and demands.
- Positional Analysis Questionnaire (PAQ)

  This analyses jobs in terms of information input, mental processes, work output, relationship with others, job context in both physical and social terms.
- Job Element Inventory (JEI)

  This is an adaptation of the PAQ, but presented at a much lower reading level.
- Occupational Analysis Inventory (OAI)

  This provides vocational guidance and occupational exploration.

8.2.5 Principles of job analysis

The following principles are applicable to job analysis (Cushway 1994: 43).

8.2.5.1 Analyse the job, not the person

The focus area is the job and not the job incumbent. The requirements of the job in terms of skills, knowledge and experience are analysed. The incumbent's skills, knowledge and experience may in fact be far different from what the job requires. The job content may also be affected by a variety of aspects such as superior's expectations, individual abilities, other jobs, colleagues, attitudes of managers and organisational structure.

8.2.5.2 Analyse the full ambit of the job

An analysis of the job is not simply a list of tasks; the job should be broken down into its different components. All the aspects of the job should be fully described to give a complete picture of what the job entails. An indication of how the job is linked with other jobs, and what the complexities and the challenges of the job are should be clearly spelled out. Lastly, what the job contributes to the ultimate success of the organisation must be clearly stated.

8.2.5.3 Do not be judgemental

Consideration should be given only to the job content; how appropriate and how logical the job content is, is not relevant.

8.2.5.4 Focus on the present status of the job

The job must only be analysed as it is presently structured and the focus should be on the job content. Future changes or changes which occurred in the past must not be included.

8.2.6 Writing job descriptions

When writing a job description it must always be borne in mind why it is being written. The content of a job description will depend on the nature of the job, the organisation and the environment. Job descriptions should contain information (also see example of a job description below) such as:

- Job title
- Job identification details
- Name of the current jobholder
- Reporting lines
- Main purpose of the job
- Tasks and responsibilities (key performance areas)
- Context (optional)
- Relation to other positions
- Subordinate positions
- Financial and statistical data required to do the job
- Working conditions
- Knowledge, skills and experience required
- Competencies
- Other relevant information
- Signature and date

8.2.7 Job specifications

The information necessary to compile a job specification is normally obtained during the process of job analysis and is often described as part of the job description document (see section 8.2.3).

Job specifications are used primarily to facilitate the recruitment and selection process. Without a job specification the characteristics of the ideal job incumbent are unknown and comparisons between job applicants cannot be made. The job specification should be related to the actual job requirements and must be consistent with the particular activities and duties of the job.

Exhibit B

Job description and specification

Job title:	Senior Human Resource Officer
Department:	Human Resources
Jobholder:	Joseph Molatse
Reports to:	General Manager: Human Resources
Prepared by:	N Nonembe
Approved by:	G Bobhese
Approved date:	15 August 1997

Summary of the job
Plans and carries out policies relating to all phases of human resources activity by performing the following duties personally or through subordinates.

Essential duties and responsibilities
These include the following (other duties may be assigned).
- Recruits, interviews, and selects employees to fill vacant positions.
- Plans and conducts new employee orientation to foster positive attitude toward company goals.
- Keeps record of insurance coverage, pension plan, and personnel transactions such as appointments, promotions, transfers, performance reviews, and terminations. Investigates accidents and prepares reports for insurance carrier.
- Conducts wage survey within labour market to determine competitive wage rate.
- Prepares budget of human resource operations.
- Prepares employee separation notices and related documentation, and conducts exit interviews to determine reasons behind separations.
- Prepares reports and recommends procedures to reduce absenteeism and staff turnover.
- Represents organisation at personnel-related hearings and investigations.
- Contracts with outside suppliers to provide employee services, such as canteen, transportation, or relocation service.
- Keeps records of hired employee characteristics for governmental reporting purposes.
- Administers manual and dexterity tests to applicants.

Supervisory responsibilities
Supervises 12 full-time employees.

Qualifications
To perform this job successfully, the incumbent must have the following knowledge, skill, and/or ability. Reasonable accommodation may be made to enable individuals with physical disabilities to perform the essential functions.
- *Education and/or experience:* B degree or equivalent and 5 years' experience at a managerial level
- *Language skills:* English
- *Mathematical skills:* Adequate comprehension of basic mathematics and accounting skills
- *Reasoning ability:* Persuasive, logical and the ability to make presentations
- *Physical demands:* The physical demands are those required for an office position. Reasonable accommodation may be made to enable individuals with disabilities to perform the essential functions.
- *Work environment:* Office job. The work environment characteristics described here are those an employee encounters in a typical office. Reasonable accommodation may be made to enable individuals with disabilities to perform the essential functions.

Signature. . . . .   *Date* . . . .

When a qualification is attached to a job, utmost care must be taken to determine whether that qualification is indeed necessary. Job specifications should be constantly monitored to determine whether the specifications are not too high or too low or whether the incumbent possesses the right profile. Cognisance must be taken of the possibility of indirect discrimination in job specifications due to preconceived and entrenched attitudes, prejudices and assumptions (see also chapter 5).

All the information that flows from job analyses efforts is eventually used for the purposes of workforce planning, recruitment and selection, training, and so forth. The first area, however, is workforce planning.

8.3 THE NATURE OF WORKFORCE PLANNING

workforce planning can be viewed as the process of developing and implementing plans and programmes to ensure that the right number and types of individuals are available at the right time and place to perform the work necessary to achieve the organisation's objectives (Dolan & Schuler 1987: 41). Workforce planning must be directly linked to strategic business planning — it addresses the major objectives of the organisation in that it spells out what types of people will in future be needed to execute the work in order to accomplish the business goals of the organisation. In this sense it is thus directly linked to and flows from strategic human resource management decisions (see chapters 6 and 7).

To ensure effective workforce planning the starting point is the organisation's mission statement and the strategic business plan. As mentioned before, part of strategic planning is the formulation of strategies, goals and objectives (goals being long-term broad purposes or aims and an objective being short term and much more detailed). According to French, workforce planning is an ongoing process within the context of overall strategic planning and the changing conditions both within and outside an organisation (French 1994: 131).

This has the implication that the structure of the organisation, the particular jobs to be performed, the financial and technological resources needed and the qualifications and numbers of people employed, must always reflect the general organisational strategies and goals, and also the HRM strategies and structural dimensions.

Hercus (1993: 405) summarises workforce planning by stating that it is a management process involving the following elements:

- forecasting workforce requirements for an organisation to execute its business plan;
- forecasting human resources available for meeting these needs and doing a scan of the internal and external environments of the organisation;
- identifying the gaps between what will be needed and what will be available and developing the necessary action plans;
- implementing and monitoring these action plans.

The following are typical issues that a workforce planning section will have to address (O'Doherty 1995: 119):

- How many employees does the organisation employ?
- Where are these employees to be found?
- What is the age profile of employees by department?
- What skills do these employees possess?
- Which are the biggest departments?
- How many employees leave the organisation per year and in which job categories?
- In which departments are we likely to lose more employees?

Proper workforce planning ought to play the dominant role in answering questions such as these.

8.3.1 The purpose and importance of workforce planning

As stated earlier, the main purpose of workforce planning is to identify future human resource requirements and to develop action plans to eliminate any discrepancies between the demand and supply of labour that may be foreseen. Excessive turnover and absenteeism, low labour productivity and ineffective training programmes can be reduced and expenses lowered if workforce planning is executed properly. According to Dolan and Schuler (1987: 42), the purposes of workforce planning are more specifically to:

- reduce labour costs by helping management to anticipate shortages or surpluses of human resources, and to correct these imbalances before they become unmanageable and expensive;
- provide a basis for planning employee development that makes optimum use of workers' aptitudes;
- improve the overall business planning process;
- provide more opportunities for minority groups in future and to identify the specific skills available (affirmative action);
- promote greater awareness of the importance of sound human resource management throughout all levels of the organisation;
- provide an instrument for evaluating the effect of alternative human resource planning actions and policies.

With the aid of computer technology all these aims are now more easily attainable than ever before. Computers allow for vast numbers of job-related records to be maintained on each job and employee, thereby creating a human resource information system (this is discussed in chapter 23). Records could include information on employees' job preferences, qualifications, work experiences, performance evaluations, the job history of each employee in an organisation and a complete set of information on the jobs or positions held in the organisation and/or elsewhere. This can be used to facilitate workforce planning in the interests of the individual as well as the organisation.

Workforce planning is thus important to organisations for the following reasons (Anderson 1994: 36).

- Labour is a significant cost to an organisation and planning allows greater control.
- Business planning is a key ingredient of organisational success, and financial, marketing and corporate planning must be augmented by workforce planning.
- The labour supply is neither constant nor flexible and people's social aspirations must be considered, especially in South Africa.
- Environmental changes (technological, political, social and economic) mean that HRM is becoming more complex and challenging, which makes planning essential.
- Changing product demands have social implications for labour (ranging from redundancy to retraining) and planning can help to accommodate these demands.

8.3.2 The responsibility for workforce planning

The responsibility for workforce planning will depend to a large extent on variables such as the size of the organisation and the extent to which HRM is handled by specialists or has been devolved to other levels of management (see previous chapter). For example, in very large organisations overall workforce planning will normally be undertaken by a specialist section in the human resource department, with the necessary inputs from line management, whilst in smaller organisations it may be carried out largely by the line managers of the particular organisation.

Large organisations in South Africa, such as Eskom, Transnet, Anglo American and Telkom, will probably have separate sections staffed by workforce planning specialists, at a centralised level, focusing on the process of reconciling the number of available employees with the present and future demand for employees. One important issue to be considered in this process of reconciliation is the budget requirements of the organisation concerned. The organisation's budget will to a large extent determine whether decisions will be made on a centralised or decentralised level. In large organisations the usual practice is to monitor the workforce planning process (once it has been designed by all the stakeholders) according to an approved plan. This may help ensure that head office keeps control over activities and that the organisation as a whole continues to move towards stated goals. Different business units and departments can then carry out the necessary workforce planning, using the standard methods of deploying the workforce (for example introducing flexible working hours, engaging contract employees and seasonal workers), to ensure the optimal utilisation of employees. In smaller organisations a centralised process of workforce planning is recommended due to the number of employees. The workforce planning process could be decentralised should centralisation prove to be unsuccessful.

A general approach to workforce planning would be to include all affected by the process. In the South African context, for example, it would be advisable to include employee representatives in this process. This could prove to be invaluable when the organisation is in a process of restructuring or re-engineering. Because South African organisations are facing increasing international competition, organisations may face downsizing to be able to compete better. A proper workforce plan will not only assist in the smooth running of any necessary downsizing or adjustment in the organisation but the inclusion of employee representatives in the workforce planning process could also assist in planning expansion and affirmative action programmes. The requirement that the staff composition of organisations should reflect our demographics is a long-term goal that can be effectively addressed only if it is an integral part of proper workforce planning efforts (as explained in chapter 5).

The role that the line manager plays in the workforce planning process is crucial. It is accepted that the business plan and long-term strategic goals determine the direction of the organisation. As explained in chapter 7, the nature of the market and the product or service to be delivered will influence the organisational structure of the organisation. It is, therefore, the line manager who must manage the employees who have been recruited to fill the identified posts within the structure. It is on the shop floor that the plan must come together, where the success or otherwise of the plan will be demonstrated. The input of line managers into the workforce planning process is therefore essential; they can provide feedback on issues such as:

- whether there are enough and appropriate jobs to ensure the output;
- whether there are enough and appropriate job categories;
- whether the incumbents are performing in accordance with accepted standards;
- whether there is a high labour turnover;
- whether more or different product output will necessitate more or different jobs;
- whether a change in product technology will change the job content with a concomitant change in training or recruitment requirements.

We believe, however, that, although workforce planning specialists in large organisations may be responsible for driving the overall process, all those affected (for example line managers and employee representatives) should be included. In smaller organisations, the same approach holds true, should there be any HR specialists.

8.4　THE WORKFORCE PLANNING PROCESS[1]

As stressed before, the first and most fundamental task in the process of planning the workforce, is to ensure that there is a clear link between the organisation's general strategic plans, the formulated human resource management strategies and structures and the workforce plans as such. Cognisance must thus be taken of the organisational goals and, more particularly, of the human resource implications. Once the external and internal factors have been considered, the supply and demand of current and new employees can be analysed.

The external factors include issues such as labour market conditions, government policies and educational trends, whilst the internal factors refer to issues such as the number of employees leaving the organisation who will have to be replaced, the number of employees retiring in the future and the career progression of employees remaining in the organisation (see figure 8.3). Other factors to consider include organisational reward systems, current work practices, the labour relations climate, the technology, turnover targets, production processes and profit targets. All of these issues are identified and analysed with the purpose of drafting a plan that can best utilise the implications these factors may have for the organisation. In other words, these factors must be incorporated into the workforce plan to ensure that their influence on the organisation is properly managed, as the programme or plan is implemented.

8.4.1 Step 1: Gathering, analysing, and forecasting workforce supply and demand data

Step 1 outlines the various important phases to be followed and methods and techniques to be used to ensure the successful implementation of workforce planning and programming.

8.4.1.1 Phase 1: Forecasting

When personnel forecasting is undertaken, the workforce planner attempts to ascertain estimates of the supply and demand of various types of personnel in terms of the key performance areas that flow from business plans. The primary goal is to predict areas in the organisation where there may be labour surpluses or shortages. Forecasting on both the demand and supply side can be done by judgemental and/or statistical methods (see phases 3 and 5 below). Statistical methods are used mainly to capture historic trends in an organisation's demand for labour and can, given the right conditions, provide much more accurate predictions than judgemental processes. In other circumstances the judgemental approach is more appropriate, for example in the absence of historical data regarding events occurring in the marketplace or in an organisation. To achieve an appropriate and balanced result, workforce planners should ideally combine statistical and judgemental approaches when forecasting. Although many sophisticated forecasting techniques have been developed, forecasting is often informal and judgemental. Forecasting in stable organisations is more accurate than in organisations in volatile environments. The value of a forecast should, however, be judged not so much on its accuracy but on the extent to which it forced managers to think and consider alternatives.

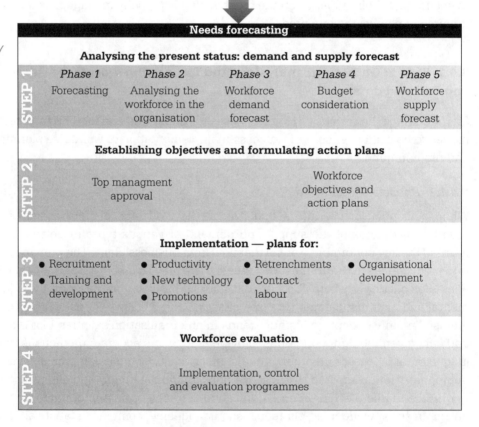

Figure 8.3

The workforce planning and programming process

Source: Adapted from Dolan & Schuler (1987: 47) and French (1994: 132)

8.4.1.2 Phase 2: Analysing the existing workforce in the organisation

This phase begins with an analysis of the **inventory** of the current workforce and the current jobs in the organisation. Questions that need to be asked include: Who are our employees? What skills do they have? How good are they? How are they developed? These are but a few of the questions that need to be answered. To know what the skills, abilities, interests, and preferences of the current workforce are forms only one part of the inventory. It is also important to determine the **characteristics of present jobs**, how they are organised and structured, and the skills required to fill them. Organisational charts could, for example, be useful in this regard. Proper job analysis facilitates this part of the inventory. Much of the information in larger organisations can be stored, adapted and retrieved from a human resource information system (see chapter 23). The importance of having updated records of all the jobs in an organisation cannot be overemphasised. Lately there seems to be some trend to regard rigid job descriptions and job specifications as outdated methods of determining the required skill levels in organisations. The important issue, however, is not the method used but that the competency requirements at all levels in the organisation should be known and determined by the requirements of the jobs and not by the characteristics of current incumbents. Many organisations fail to produce credible workforce plans because of the lack of accurate information on job requirements — in other words, job descriptions and specifications.

An analysis of the flows or patterns of employees through the organisation is important because it not only provides supply data but also identifies any changes in human resource flow patterns. Such an analysis illustrates the availability of employees who are ready to advance to new jobs and it identifies those ready to retire, as well as the average rate at which employees progress through jobs (McBeath 1992: 31).

Another key aspect to be considered when workforce planning is done, is the probable future national composition of the labour force. Data from the **external** analysis on labour force composition, current demographic and economic data are used to make labour force projections. Most often these projections are very general in nature. They do, however, provide an organisation with information for its workforce plans, particularly regarding its long-term needs. In this regard, as explained in chapter 5, affirmative action is currently of paramount importance in the process of workforce planning in South Africa.

Another aspect to analyse is **organisational labour productivity** and how it will change in the future. Projected employee turnover, absenteeism, and retrenchments, for example, influence the productivity of an organisation's workforce and its future workforce needs. These issues must be analysed so that plans can be developed to address them. It is suggested that a one-off productivity improvement approach be avoided and that an attempt be made to develop long-term productivity plans for the organisation (Sibson 1992: 60).

Another aspect of this phase is the examination and projection of an **organisational structure** for the organisation. The probable size of the top, middle, and lower levels of the organisation, including both managers and non-managers, must be determined. Information about changes in the organisation's workforce needs and about specific activities or functional areas is crucial to the workforce planning process. Determining the type of organisational structure which will be required in the future is obviously essential to forecast workforce needs (see previous chapter).

8.4.1.3 Phase 3: Workforce demand forecast

The demand for employees can be determined by a number of forecasting methods. It should, however, always be borne in mind that at best, forecasting results in approximations. The accuracy of forecasts depends on the information available and on the predictability of events. In the short term events are more predictable and information will usually be more accurate. Dolan and Schuler (1987: 50) distinguish between two classes of forecasting techniques to project an organisation's demand for employees, namely *judgemental forecasts* and *conventional statistical projections*; these are briefly discussed below.

Judgemental forecasts

● The *Delphi technique* is most commonly used in judgemental forecasts. This technique requires a large number of experts to take turns presenting forecast statements and assumptions (Schuler, Dowling, Smart & Huber 1993: 64). Each expert makes forecasts and the forecasts are then routed to the other experts, who then revise their own forecasts until a viable composite forecast emerges. Specific projections or a range of projections may be developed, depending on the positions and experience levels of the experts.

This technique has produced better short-term forecasts than linear regression analysis, but problems are sometimes experienced, for example in integrating the opinions of experts. This technique is, however, very useful for generating ideas about unstructured or relatively less developed subject areas, such as workforce planning.

● *The nominal group technique* also entails using multiple inputs from several persons. The information can be obtained in a structured format and it is a structured variation of small-group discussion methods (Newstrom & Scannel 1980: 107). People sit around a conference table and independently list their ideas regarding the forecast on a sheet of paper. After a period of time they take turns expressing their ideas to the group. Each member's ideas are recorded so that everyone can see all of the ideas and refer to them later on in the session. For example, a group of managers from different departments may get together with the purpose of determining the number of employees who will be required in two years' time due to a change from the traditional, labour intensive production method to a semi-automated approach. Each manager will have the opportunity to state his/her case. This process prevents the domination of discussion by a single person and encourages the more passive persons to participate. Eventually all the ideas of the managers are prioritised and integrated.

- The *managerial judgement technique* involves managers deciding, possibly in consultation with other staff, what their future activities are likely to be and what types of staff they will need to ensure success. This approach can be top-down or bottom-up (lower-level managers who make estimates and pass them up) or a combination of the two. The biggest problem with this technique is that it is judgemental in nature and is focused on the managers' experience only. It is, however, straightforward and can be implemented easily (Cushway 1994).

Statistical techniques

- *Linear regression analysis* can best be explained by the case of a perfect linear association between two variables, for example production and employment (Babbie 1995). If a relationship can be established between the level of production and the level of employment, predictions of future production can be used to make predictions of future employment. Although there may be a relationship between production and employment, however, the relationship is often influenced by a number of factors; for example, if production doubles it does not mean that employment must be doubled — it could be achieved by better productivity arrangements.

- *Multiple linear regression analysis* is used to analyse those situations where a given dependent variable is affected simultaneously by several independent variables. For example, instead of using only production to predict employment demand, productivity data and equipment-use data also may be used. The reason why this method is used is because it incorporates several variables related to employment, and may produce more accurate demand forecasts than linear regression analysis. It seems that only relatively large organisations use multiple regression analysis (Schuler et al 1993: 65).

- The *unit demand forecasting* technique is a method whereby departmental or functional managers provide certain labour estimates because they know what business activity will be performed by their units/departments in the future. When the estimates for all departments are added up, they form an overall forecast for the organisation; this often differs from the organisation forecasted demands (as prepared by the workforce specialist). An example of this is where an organisation finds that ten salespeople will retire in twenty-four months and that a radical product expansion will probably exacerbate the shortage. By anticipating the problem, a plan can be drafted for new salespeople to be recruited. This will make department managers more aware of the skills, abilities, and desires of their employees and may reveal a discrepancy in respect of the aggregate organisational forecast. The broad organisational forecast may not, for example, take into account certain losses of personnel due to a lack of intimate knowledge about employees' performance. A compromise will then have to be reached to establish the real organisational demand. This exercise will probably produce a higher-quality forecast. An obvious advantage is that the unit/department manager knows how many new positions will be needed to achieve output and is therefore the right person to participate. A disadvantage is, however, the fact that a large group of people have to be organised and that they could work on different assumptions.

Other statistical methods

According to Schuler et al (1993: 66) other statistical methods may be helpful too:

- Productivity ratios
  Historical data are used to examine past levels of a productivity index (P):

$$P = \frac{\text{Workload}}{\text{Number of people}}$$

  Where constant or systematic relationships are found, human resource requirements can be computed by dividing predicted workloads by P.

- Personnel ratios
  Past personnel data are examined to determine historical relationships among the employees in various jobs or job categories. Regression analysis or productivity ratios are then used to project either total or key group human resource requirements and ratios are used to allocate total requirements to various job categories or to estimate requirements for non-key groups.

- Time series analysis
  Past staffing levels (instead of workload indicators) are used to project future human resource requirements. Past staffing levels are examined to isolate seasonal and cyclical variations, long-term trends and random movement. Long-term trends are then extrapolated or projected using a moving average, exponential smoothing or regression techniques.

- Stochastic analysis
  The likelihood of landing a series of contracts is combined with the personnel requirements of each contract to estimate expected staffing requirements. This has potential application in government contracts and construction industries.

8.4.1.4 Phase 4: Budget agreement

A budget is a plan for controlling the use of funds over a period of time (Jarrell 1993: 86). By reconciling workforce planning and budgeting, the whole exercise is placed into a financial perspective. Managers have to indicate the need for additional personnel to fill posts in the future. This whole process is based on managers making accurate estimates. This forecasting method is highly judgemental, varying from a bottom-up approach (where the manager determines his/her own needs) to a top-down approach where top managers place constraints either in terms of budget allocations or numbers of employees. Unit/department managers are then required to plan these objectives within this framework (Cherrington 1995: 160). The workforce forecast must be expressed in terms of rands, and must be compatible with the organisation's monetary objectives and overall budget limitations. The budget reconciliation process may also indicate that the budget has to be adjusted to accommodate the workforce plan. This step provides the opportunity to align the objectives regarding the personnel of the organisation with those of the organisation as a whole.

8.4.1.5 Phase 5: Forecasting workforce supply

Forecasting supply can be derived from internal and external sources. The internal source is generally most important and readily available. There are basically two categories of techniques to help forecast internal labour supply, namely judgemental and statistical.

Judgemental techniques

● *Replacement planning* is a shorter-term technique which uses replacement charts to show the names of the current incumbents of positions in the organisation together with the names of likely replacements. Replacement charts make it clear where potential vacancies may occur, based on the performance levels of the employees in the current jobs.

   It is important to note that aspects such as gender, race and age should be omitted from these replacement charts to prevent these criteria from being used in making promotion decisions; this will avoid possible violations of the Labour Relations Act of 1995.

● *Succession planning* is a longer-term, more flexible method, which focuses on the development of managers or leaders (see figure 8.4).

Management succession plan				
Organisation:			Date:	
Probability of vacancy: A = within 1 year B = after 1–3 years C = beyond 3 years				
Position incumbent	Readiness			Continency plan
	A Now	B 1–3 years	C 3 years +	
J Cocker				

Figure 8.4

Succession planning

Adapted from French (1994: 133)

This technique is widely practised, especially in large organisations like Eskom and ABSA. There is a tendency to emphasise the characteristics of the managers themselves and to downplay the characteristics of the job to which employees may eventually be promoted. This approach is flawed as both aspects have to be emphasised.

The following differences between succession planning and replacement planning can be identified.

- Replacement planning covers a short time span (for example, up to 12 months) and the best candidate is chosen, whilst succession planning is more long term and the candidate with the best potential development is chosen.
- Replacement planning is very flexible but can be limited by the structure of the plan, whilst succession planning is perceived as being flexible but is intended to promote development and thinking about alternative candidates.
- In the case of replacement planning the experience base of those managers to be considered is based on the judgement and observation of candidates and this forms the basis of the plan; in the case of succession planning the results of the plan are based on inputs and discussion involving a number of other managers and is thus a group effort.
- The development planning for managers in replacement planning is normally informal, whilst for succession planning it is more formal and extensive. Specific long-term personal development plans for individuals are developed as part of succession planning.
- With replacement planning the identified candidate will fill a vacant post, whilst with succession planning all candidates are considered to fill the post because a pool of candidates have been identified.

Statistical techniques

When statistical techniques are not widely used it is usually because of inadequate databases, lack of software computer programs and a shortage of trained professionals.

The following are examples of a few statistical methods (Schuler et al 1993: 69).

- *Markov analysis* This type of analysis projects future flows to obtain availability estimates through a straightforward application of historical transition rates. Historical transition rates are derived from analyses of personnel data concerning losses, promotions, transfers, demotions and, perhaps, recruitment.
- *Simulation* (based on Markov analysis) Alternative (rather than historical) flows are examined for effects of future human resource availabilities. Alternative flows reflect the anticipated results of policy or programme changes relating to voluntary and involuntary turnover, retirement, promotion, etc.
- *Renewal analysis* Renewal analysis estimates future flows and availabilities by calculating vacancies as created by organisational growth, personnel losses and internal movements, and the results of decision rules governing the filling

of vacancies. Alternative models may assess the effects of changes in growth estimates, turnover, promotions or decision rules.

- *Goal programming* This type of programming focuses on optimising goals. Desired staffing patterns are established, given a set of constraints concerning such things as the upper limits on staff flows, the percentage of new recruits and total salary budgets.

The last stage in Step 1 focuses on the process of reconciliation necessitated by the mismatch between the quantitative and qualitative demand for employees based on the future plans of the organisation and on current projections of employee availability — that is, the supply of employees. At first this imbalance will be portrayed by a numerical shortfall or surplus in employees that is likely to occur in the future. Shortfalls in the organisation may result in departments running at overcapacity due to employee shortages, overtime work — with concomitant long-term problems. Surpluses of employees may, on the other hand, lead to low productivity, financial losses and, if employees are not transferred or retrenched, to the eventual closing of the organisation. Proper workforce planning is thus essential to maintain a proper balance in the number of employees required by the organisation and to avoid the ill effects of employee problems or organisational readjustments. The supply forecast, once complete, can be compared with the workforce demand forecast to help determine action programming necessary to identify workforce talent and balance the supply and demand forecast. It must, however, be borne in mind that most current forecasting of labour supply and demand is short range and used for the purpose of budgeting and cost control.

8.4.2 Step 2: Establishing objectives and formulating plans

As we have stressed many times, workforce objectives are directly related to general organisational objectives and strategies. The impact of the organisation's objectives, policies, and plans on workforce planning is difficult to ignore. However, according to a survey in the USA, only about 25 % of organisations achieve a substantial link between their general institutional planning and their workforce planning (Dolan & Schuler 1987: 53). Step 2 focuses on the desired end result and on providing a target to measure the achievement of success in addressing the labour surplus or shortages in the organisation. Definite objectives (including a timetable for their achievement) should be set to measure effectiveness (for example, that the number of miners in a particular mine should be increased by 35 % within the next year).

Once the objectives have been set, action plans must be formulated to facilitate their achievement. Responsibilities must also be assigned to different persons for the execution of the action plans. There are a number of options that can be considered to reduce an expected labour surplus in an organisation, for example retrenchments, demotions and transfers. Such decisions can be put into effect quickly, but the possible consequences and impact on employees can be harsh.

Other options which are slow to take effect but which can still be considered are normal retirement, resignations and the retraining of staff.

A possible labour shortage can be quickly remedied by, for example, taking on temporary employees (bearing in mind that the Labour Relations Act of 1995 prohibits the use of temporary employees under certain circumstances), subcontracting and working overtime. Other possible options are to reduce resignations, to retrain employees for new jobs and to recruit new employees. This is, however, a slow process.

8.4.3 Step 3: Implementation

Once the goals have been set, individuals must be held accountable for the planned actions and the necessary resources must be made available. Plans relating to recruitment, training and development, increasing labour productivity, retirements, and retrenchments must be executed with the necessary professionalism. For example, a retrenchment decision must follow the specified procedure (see chapter 24). It can be expected that certain affirmative action programmes will be challenged in the courts and organisations can avoid such negative publicity by ensuring that programmes are professionally developed and implemented.

8.4.4 Step 4: Workforce plan evaluation

It is important to determine the success of workforce planning through thorough evaluation of the plans and programmes being implemented.

Possible criteria or standards for evaluating workforce planning include the measurement of (Dolan & Schuler 1987:59):

- actual staffing levels against established staffing requirements;
- productivity levels against established goals;
- actual personnel flow rates against desired rates;
- programmes implemented against action plans;
- programme results against expected outcomes (for example improved applicant flows, reduced quit rates, improved replacement ratios);
- labour and programme costs against budgets;
- ratios of programme results (benefits) to programme costs.

8.5 CONCLUSION

In this chapter workforce planning and the job analysis process was discussed. Job analysis is an integral part of workforce planning, work and organisation design in that the total organisational structure and the different role responsibilities to govern work are established. The different stages in job analysis were highlighted, as were various uses of this type of analysis, for example workforce planning, recruitment and selection, training and development, compensation and labour relations. Methods used by job analysts were also explained. Principles underlying job analysis were discussed and the nature of job descriptions and job specifications were explained.

The concept of workforce planning was defined, followed by a discussion of its purpose and importance and of the persons responsible for the process. The four phases of the workforce planning process were also described.

SELF-EVALUATION QUESTIONS

1. What is job analysis and how does it relate to workforce planning?
2. Explain the differences between a job description and a job specification.
3. Describe the principles of job analysis and indicate how these principles contribute to organisational success.
4. Explain the different job analysis methods. What method would you recommend if approached to analyse (a) the jobs of accountants who work in all the major cities in South Africa; and (b) ten computer analysts working in Johannesburg? Why?
5. How would you draw up a job description and a job specification?
6. How does job analysis relate to labour relations, affirmative action plans, training and development, recruitment and selection?
7. Explain the role of workforce planning in attaining business objectives. Substantiate each argument.
8. Who is responsible for workforce planning in an organisation? Give reasons for your suggestions.
9. Describe the workforce planning process to a group of engineers who have just joined your organisation. They are very interested in the various steps of the forecasting process.
10. Explain the role of the budget in the workforce planning process.
11. Discuss possible plans that can be developed to address both shortages and a surplus of employees in an organisation.

ENDNOTES

1. This section is based partly on Dolan & Schuler (1987: 45–58); French (1994: 132–137); Schuler, Dowling, Smart & Huber (1993: 60–66); and O'Doherty (1995: 134–136).

BIBLIOGRAPHY

Anderson, AH. 1994. *Effective Personnel Management: A Skills and Activity-based Approach.* Oxford: Blackwell

Babbie, E. 1995. *The Practice of Social Research,* 7 ed. Harmsonburg, Virginia: Wadsworth

Cherrington, DJ. 1995. *The Management of Human Resources,* 4 ed. New Jersey: Prentice-Hall

Cushway, B. 1994. *Human Resource Management.* London: Kogan Page

De Cenzo, DA & Robbins, SP. 1994. *Human Resource Management: Concepts and Practices.* New York: John Wiley & Sons

Dolan, SL & Schuler, RS. 1987. *Personnel and Human Resource Management in Canada.* New York: West Publishing Company

French, W. 1994. *Human Resource Management,* 3 ed. Boston: Houghton Mifflin

Hercus, T. 1993. Workforce planning in eight British organisations: A Canadian perspective. In *Handbook of Workforce Management,* ed Bran Towers, 405. Oxford: Blackwell

Jarrell, DW. 1993. *Human Resource Planning: Business Planning Approach.* New Jersey: Prentice-Hall

McBeath, G. 1992. *The Handbook of Human Resource Planning: Practical Manpower Analysis Techniques for HR Professionals.* Oxford: Blackwell Business

Newstrom, JW & Scannel, EE. 1980. *Games Trainers Play: Experiential Learning Exercises.* New York: McGraw-Hill

Noe, R, Hollenbeck, JR, Gerhart, B & Wright, PM. 1994. *Human Resource Management: Gaining a Competitive Advantage.* Boston: Irwin

O'Doherty, D. 1995. Towards human resource planning? In *Human Resource Management: A Contemporary Perspective,* eds I Beardwell & L Holden, 119. London: Pitman

Schuler, RD, Dowling, PJ, Smart, JP & Huber, VL. 1993. *Human Resource Management in Australia,* 2 ed. Melbourne, Australia: Harper Educational

Sibson, RE. 1992. *Strategic Planning for Human Resources Management.* New York: AMACO

part three

Establishing employment relationships

◉ STUDY OBJECTIVES

After studying this chapter, you should be able to:

- explain what a recruitment policy and procedure entail;
- discuss the internal and external factors influencing recruitment decisions;
- describe the aspects that play a role in job choice;
- list and explain the different recruitment sources;
- explain the factors involved in drawing up a recruitment advertisement;
- discuss the recruitment process;
- describe the evaluation of the recruitment process.

9.1 INTRODUCTION

Once the work has been designed and structured and workforce planning has been carried out, it may from time to time become necessary to recruit new employees. In order to do this, certain activities must be performed to attract the necessary job applicants from which selection (dealt with in chapter 10) will take place.

Recruitment can be described as those activities in human resource management which are undertaken in order to attract sufficient job candidates who have the necessary potential, competencies and traits to fill job needs and to assist the organisation in achieving its objectives.

By means of the recruitment process the organisation aims to attract and to retain the interest of suitable applicants and to project a positive image of the organisation to outsiders.

The recruitment process may be set in motion by the recognition of a need arising out of the workforce planning process. It may also happen that vacancies arise from resignations, promotions or transfers. From time to time the organisation needs to attract job candidates with the required competencies and traits for the tasks to be performed. The response of potential employees depends on their attitude towards both the work to be performed and the organisation, as well as their perception of whether the necessary fit can possibly be established between them and the organisation trying to recruit them.

JUTA

This chapter deals with recruitment policy and procedures, the job choice a potential employee has to make, the sources and methods of recruitment, and the recruitment process in general. Lastly, a strategic approach to recruitment is briefly examined.

9.2 RECRUITMENT POLICY AND PROCEDURES

The recruitment policy stipulates broad guidelines on how an organisation intends to deal with recruitment. The answers to the following questions may be of assistance when formalising a recruitment policy:

- What legal prescriptions regarding fairness and discrimination should be taken into account? (For example the Labour Relations Act of 1995.)
- Which clauses in collective agreements with trade unions are applicable? (For example recognition agreements and bargaining council agreements.)
- How can recruitment be carried out within budget limitations?
- How urgently should vacancies be filled?
- What are the prescriptions of the workforce planning and succession planning documents? For example:
  - Will promotions from within the organisation take preference?
  - May relatives of existing employees be employed?
  - Will handicapped persons be employed?
  - May part-time employees be employed?
  - May minors be employed?
- Which department or person (designated title) will be responsible for the execution of the policy and procedure?

A recruitment policy is developed largely to provide broad guidelines, and the procedures to provide more detailed guidelines to assist in attracting qualified candidates at minimum cost and time and to help managers to make the correct decisions. A properly planned and executed recruitment policy and procedure will normally allow managers to use a variety of recruitment sources and methods which will help to avoid discriminatory recruitment practices (see section 9.4). An example of a recruitment policy and procedure is provided in exhibit A.

Various factors influence recruitment policy. These may be divided into two broad categories, namely external and internal factors (Gerber, Nel & Van Dyk 1992: 176). External factors are factors outside the organisation, such as labour market conditions, government and trade union influences. Internal factors are those decided by the organisation, such as its selection criteria and organisational image. These are briefly discussed below.

Exhibit A

Example of a recruitment policy and procedure

Africa Limited
Policy: It is the policy of Africa Limited to use a variety of cost-effective employee recruitment resources to attract a qualified applicant pool to be considered for employment.
Applies to: All positions, except temporary workers.

Procedure:

1. Each department manager is responsible for recommending department staffing levels when preparing the annual budget. Upon receipt of the approved department budget, the department manager can authorise the filling of new or replacement positions. Exceptions to budgeted staffing must be authorised by the human resource manager.

2. When a job opening occurs, the department manager and supervisor shall confer to identify job duties, skills, and requirements for the job. The human resource officer can provide assistance in defining job specifications if requested. The department supervisor shall then prepare a job description or revise the existing job description.

3. The supervisor shall prepare a recruiting requisition. The requisition, together with the job description, shall be approved by the department manager and then routed to the Human Resource Department.

4. Consideration shall be given to qualified employees available through transfer or promotion. The human resource manager shall confer with line managers and check employee files to identify possible candidates. (See "Policies on Promotions and Transfers".) In the event that no current employee is selected for the vacant position, the human resource officer shall initiate the recruitment process.

5. The human resource officer is responsible for developing and maintaining effective recruiting contacts. Recruiting methods and sources may include:
   - Newspaper advertisements
   - Referrals from employees
   - "Help wanted" sign on building or premises
   - Applications on file
   - Walk-in applicants
   - Local schools or colleges
   - Public employment referral/training services or other similar resources.

6. Should recruiting costs exceed R2 000 (for example to meet the costs of a large advertisement or employment agency fee), the cost must be approved by the General Manager.

7. The human resource officer is responsible for contacting recruitment sources and for providing information on the job opening. Refer to the job description and job specification and other job information. Advise the recruiting agency of the organisation's policy of affirmative action and equal employment opportunities.

8. Except in cases of a confidential search, the human resource officer is responsible for notifying current employees of the job opening by a bulletin board posting and for notifying the switchboard/receptionist so that enquiries can be properly routed.

9. In the event of unsolicited enquires from job seekers or employment agencies to supervisors or managers, such enquiries shall be referred to the Human Resource Department.

9.2.1 External factors influencing recruitment

9.2.1.1 Labour market conditions

If there is an abundance of qualified candidates who meet the job specification requirements, a small recruiting effort may generate many applications. If the job market is tight, more creative and expensive efforts will be necessary. Skills shortages will require larger compensation packages to attract the right candidates. The Department of Labour has statistics available for different sectors of the labour market. Human resource specialists should remain abreast of current trends in the labour market to employ the right recruitment policy.

9.2.1.2 Government policy and legislation

Government policy will play an increasing role in the determination of recruitment practice in the future. As explained in chapter 5, the South African government will introduce legislation governing affirmative action. (See the proposed legislation on Employment and Occupational Equity in Chapter 5.) Wingrove (1993: 11) states that the African Management Forum, the National African Federated Chamber of Commerce (NAFCOC) and COSATU have all declared strong support for affirmative action and will lobby government in the future for its enforcement.

The following guidelines from the Labour Relations Act 66 of 1995 regarding discrimination should also be considered before embarking on the recruitment of potential employees.

The Act stipulates that an unfair labour practice could be committed in cases where an employer/recruiter unfairly discriminates against a potential employee — that is, for reasons other than bona fide job requirements and affirmative action. The following instances may be viewed as possible unfair discriminatory recruitment practices:

● Discrimination against a potential employee on the grounds of pregnancy, intended pregnancy, or any reason related to pregnancy.
● Discrimination against a potential employee, directly or indirectly, on any arbitrary ground, including, but not limited to race, gender, ethnic or social origin, colour, sexual orientation, age, disability, religion, conscience, belief, political opinion, culture, language, marital status or family responsibility.
● Section 5 of the Labour Relations Act of 1995 provides protection of the rights of persons seeking employment, and expressly prohibits an employer from advantaging, or promising to advantage a person seeking employment in exchange for that person's undertaking not to exercise any right conferred by the Act (for example, joining a trade union, participating in strike action, participating in workplace forums or in other procedures provided for in the Act).

9.2.1.3 Trade unions

Many unions seek to persuade employers to enter into agreements stipulating that only union members will be employed by the enterprise concerned; such agreements are referred to as closed shop agreements. Increasingly also, unions seek greater participation in recruitment processes and decision making, and they make known their approval or otherwise of selection criteria. Management should take cognisance of the influence of unions and adopt recruitment practices which are acceptable to both parties.

9.2.2 Internal factors influencing recruitment

9.2.2.1 Strategic plans

Recruitment must not be seen as an isolated activity. The organisation's broad long-term plans are the basis for the detailed shorter-term plans on which the recruitment efforts are based. It is essential that the human resource department use the business plans of the organisation to ensure strategic recruitment. A recruitment policy must be developed in line with the human resource strategy decided upon (see chapter 6). The required number of vacancies and job titles for recruitment purposes are normally an outflow from the workforce planning process (see chapter 8).

9.2.2.2 Organisation policy

The organisation's recruitment policy must be clarified as soon as possible. If preference is given, for example, to affirmative action candidates or to promotion from within or employment of the handicapped, the policy must state this clearly and certain procedures must be implemented to ensure the execution of the policy. It is, however, recommended that all the stakeholders in the organisation be included in the process of determining the organisational recruitment policy.

9.2.2.3 Recruitment criteria

Abnormally stringent criteria will hamper recruitment efforts. Accurate job descriptions and specifications will help to set realistic requirements to facilitate effective recruitment. Criteria must also be drawn up to avoid any discriminatory practices.

9.2.2.4 Costs

Smaller organisations do not always have the resources to allow for expensive recruitment drives, and often substandard compensation packages are offered. In larger organisations the human resource department will probably have a recruitment budget based on forecast employee losses and future personnel requirements (see chapter 8 which deals with workforce planning). In larger organisations, budgets play an important role in determining the number of people to be recruited. In many organisations, however, there is a trend to minimise appointments to ensure organisational survival rather than to appoint personnel simply because a vacancy has arisen.

9.3   THE POTENTIAL EMPLOYEE

Both the employer and the person considering employment have a lot at stake in the employment process. The applicant can be viewed as a person seeking a position that will provide him/her with both material and psychological rewards. As explained in chapter 3, potential employees have different perceptions, expectations, needs, etcetera, and managers trying to employ a person are expected to take note of these differences. For most people the process of job choice begins long before they become aware of any recruitment efforts by organisations. Recruiters must be aware of the factors influencing job choice, as this will enable them to give better advice and to make better choices when recruiting candidates. Job choice for most people consists of three components, namely occupational choice, job search and organisational commitment.

9.3.1 Occupational choice

During early childhood, an individual starts making choices about an occupation. This process continues through adolescence and adulthood and involves a number of decisions until an initial choice is made. During this process, psychological, economic and sociological factors influence the occupational interests of the individual. As occupational interests become more focused, the individual begins to seek employment that will best satisfy his/her particular interests.

9.3.2 Job search

When designing a specific recruitment programme, one must consider the most preferred methods of job seeking used by candidates. There are both informal and formal methods, an example of the latter being the use of employment agencies. However, many candidates may prefer more informal recruitment methods, such as asking friends or responding to newspaper advertisements.

With this in mind, management should design the recruitment drive around these preferred methods. One word of caution, however: should an employer decide to encourage existing employees to refer friends and family, this could result in nepotism. This may influence other plans to redress the current cultural mix within an organisation and hence it may lead to unfair discrimination.

9.3.3 Organisational commitment

The recruiter plays a major role in gaining the prospective employee's commitment to the organisation right from the outset. Recruitment can play an important role in marrying the candidate's vocational and job-related needs with the organisation's ability to satisfy them. Greenhaus (1987: 127) suggests that the recruiter should display the following desirable qualities in the initial interaction between candidates and the organisation:

● ensure that you are perceived as both knowledgeable and well-prepared;

- ask relevant questions;
- discuss career paths;
- produce positive responses from candidates;
- display warmth, enthusiasm and perceptiveness.

The recruiter must not be afraid of providing realistic information, both positive and negative, as this will enhance commitment. Realistic information serves to:

- prevent the formation of unrealistic expectations;
- facilitate balanced and improved decisions regarding careers;
- allow individuals to feel that they have greater freedom of choice.

Other factors affecting organisational commitment are salary, type of work and fringe benefits. However, personality type also plays a major role in commitment as a mismatch will result in feelings of inadequacy and fatigue and thus a resultant lack of productivity (Myers & McCaulley 1992: 78).

The following basic questions may be asked by job seekers before making a final decision on a particular position (Ivancevich & Glueck 1983: 163), (since questions of this type are almost unlimited, the following should be viewed simply as examples):

- How hard do I like to work?
- Do I like to be my own boss or would I rather work for someone else?
- Do I like to work in a group or on my own?
- Do I like to work at an even pace or with bursts of energy?
- Do I like to work near home?
- How much money do I want? Would I prefer a more interesting job for less money?
- Do I like to work in one place or many? Indoors or outdoors?
- How much variety do I want in work?
- Does the organisation have a good future?
- Do I want to work in a small or large organisation?

9.4   RECRUITMENT SOURCES

Once it has been decided that additional employees are needed, the recruiter is faced with the decision of where to search for applicants. Two basic sources of applicants can be used: internal (current employees) and external (those not presently in the employ of the enterprise).

9.4.1   Internal sources

- *Skills inventories:* If the employee shortage is for higher-level employees, a skills inventory system may be used to search for appropriate candidates. A skills inventory is simply a record system listing employees with specific skills (Singer 1990: 166).

- *Job posting:* Vacancies within the organisation are placed on notice boards or in information bulletins. Details of the job are provided and employees may apply.
- *Inside moonlighting:* In the case of a short-term need or a small job which does not involve a great deal of additional work, the organisation could offer to pay bonuses of various types to people not on a time payroll.

9.4.2 External sources

- *Employment agencies:* The organisation instructs the agency to recruit suitable candidates. The agency advertises or uses its placement database — that is, a database of persons who have provided curriculum vitae to the agency which then seeks employment for them. The organisation may elect to do its own selection or can leave this in the hands of the agency.
- *Walk-ins:* Often prospective employees will apply directly to the organisation in the hope that a vacancy exists or will complete application forms and send them to the enterprise concerned. One-third of employees obtain their first jobs in this manner (Singer 1990: 168).
- *Referrals:* This is a word-of-mouth technique in which present employees refer candidates from outside the organisation. This is an inexpensive technique which is effective in finding candidates with specific skills quickly.
- *Professional bodies:* Accounting, engineering and scientific institutes look after the interests of their members by allowing vacancy advertisements in their publications. Opportunities for networking are also afforded through conventions.
- *Head-hunting:* Top professional people are "hunted" through specialised agencies. The persons are approached personally with an offer to fill a vacancy. Alternatively, an advertisement is written with the specific person's CV in mind.
- *Educational institutions:* Schools, colleges, technikons and universities provide grass-roots level opportunities for recruiters to pick the "best of the crop". This is especially important in areas of skills shortages and professional appointments. The recruiter normally makes a presentation to final-year students and invites desirable candidates to visit the company concerned.
- *Consultants:* Recruitment consultants or placement agencies have a broad network base and are exposed to management in action. They often offer a placement service to client companies. It is important to make use of the following guidelines to ensure efficiency and sensitivity when dealing with consultants.
    - All applicants' personal details should be treated confidentially and accepted professional recruitment procedures should be followed at all times. Professional bodies (such as the SABPP) may take disciplinary action if breaches occur among consultants/professionals. To ensure client protection, a contract should be established with the agency or consultant. The client should also determine whether the consultant is experienced and is

an expert in recruiting for a particular vacancy. Complete details of the job description should be ascertained before the recruitment process begins. The consultant and client should agree on all the terms of business and the fee structure so that both parties can fully understand all the terms and what takes place in the recruitment process.

O The *recruitment procedure* may be established between the consultant and the client. This includes the number of required interviews, checking references and how best to advise unsuccessful candidates. A consultant communicates the agreed procedure to candidates; the client is expected to adhere closely to the agreed procedure. Candidates will be continuously briefed on the progress of their applications. Unsuccessful candidates will be advised as quickly as possible. A candidate's current employers will not be contacted unless the candidate agrees.

9.5 RECRUITING METHODS

Various recruitment methods can be used and some of the more important ones are discussed in this section.

9.5.1 Advertisements

The most popular method of recruitment is the advertisement. Whether in the daily newspaper, weekend job supplement or periodicals, organisations often advertise their vacancies in a carefully worded manner to attract as many as possible right applicants. Other media used are billboards, radio, Internet and television. Professional publications are also used effectively to attract those in their respective professional fields.

Advertising has one basic underlying principle and that is communication. The purpose of an advertisement is to gain the right person's interest and attention; this must then lead to action. The AIDA formula may be used to structure an advertisement:

Attention
Interest
Desire
Action

9.5.1.1 *Attention*

An advertisement must attract attention. The following aspects are important for this purpose.

Headings

A meaningful heading can describe a potential job by making use of specific subject areas or by naming particular posts. Headings should be large and readable, and should also describe what is expected by the employer. Headings should be specific, not ambiguous or misleading.

Visual outlay

The visual outlay should have immediate impact on a potential applicant. The size and form of the advertisement may influence the extent of the reaction which it evokes. Where the advertisement is positioned on a page is also important.

Variety

Potential applicants may be attracted by various factors which make the advertisement stand out.

● Background differences
  The use of a dark background can serve to draw readers' attention.
● Colour
  Because of the high costs involved, only some newspapers make use of colour in recruitment advertisements. Research should be conducted to determine the influence of colour in attracting attention to advertisements.
● Outline
  Outlining is used to make an advertisement more prominent. The use of outlining may draw attention to an advertisement by emphasising it and contrasting it with competing advertisements. Neatness and unity are also emphasised.
● Imagery
  The use of imagery can serve to attract attention. Images may consist of people and faces, enlarged emblems, background images and work situations.
● Types of letters
  Different letter types may be used to make an advertisement easier to read and to differentiate it from other advertisements. Eye-catchers are especially black, broad letter types. The position which is being advertised is usually clear and large. Smaller letter types are usually used in subheadings and in the general content areas.

9.5.1.2 Interest

One of the most important elements of the interest factor is the organisation itself. Information about the organisation may include a short description of its line of business, its activities and goals, its growth potential and its expectations for the future.

Information about the position being offered is also important and should be short, describing the responsibilities involved and what is expected of the successful applicant.

Lastly, the relevant requirements of candidates should also be included, limited only to information such as educational qualifications, experience and other job-relevant attributes.

9.5.1.3 Desire/urge

In this context, *desire* refers to the wish of the reader of an advertisement to work for a particular organisation, but is not limited to a formal request for a post. The proposed salary may or may not be named; it may, however, serve as an important screening device.

Advantages of mentioning a salary

If a salary is very attractive and competitive, this will be in the organisation's favour. Possible candidates may desire such financial advantages and may thus be more eager to apply for the post.

Disadvantages of mentioning a salary

Some potential applicants may resist applying for a post because they are receiving a lower salary at present. This will mean that the organisation will not come into contact with such potentially successful candidates. Another disadvantage of advertising the salary being offered is that other organisations may raise their current salary levels in order to remain competitive. Employees may also feel dissatisfied if they are being paid less than the advertised salary.

9.5.1.4 Action

The placement of advertisements will be successful if it leads to applications from many 'right' candidates for the job. Each applicant should receive an indication of what is expected of him/her. The applicant should write his/her address clearly on the letter of application and should also include a telephone number so that more detailed information can be obtained if necessary. Immediate arrangements may in this way be made for an initial interview.

Sometimes applicants are required to fill in coupons or short job request forms so that basic details can be obtained and a larger number of responses elicited by the advertisement.

9.5.2 Special-event recruiting

Some companies stage open houses and visits to headquarters and even son and daughter days. Others address specific groups of students on campuses.

9.5.3 Vacation work

Many organisations hire students during their vacations. This allows the organisation to get specialised piecework completed and simultaneously to identify prospective permanent employees. Students are also afforded an opportunity to experience working life, thereby eliminating unrealistic expectations. Sometimes students take up a great deal of supervisory time and the work done is not always of the highest standard. Students may however become disillusioned when their initial expectations are not met. Upon return to their educational institutions, they may then actually become reverse recruiters, having a negative effect on the company's recruitment drive.

9.6   THE RECRUITMENT PROCESS

The following steps in the recruitment process (see figure 9.1) are usually followed in larger organisations, and can be used as a model approach to recruitment. It should, however, be noted that, since organisations have different needs, the recruitment process will have to be adapted to suit each organisation's specific requirements.

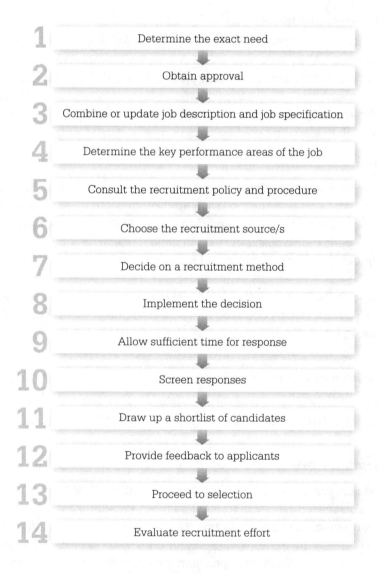

1   Determine the exact need

2   Obtain approval

3   Combine or update job description and job specification

4   Determine the key performance areas of the job

5   Consult the recruitment policy and procedure

6   Choose the recruitment source/s

7   Decide on a recruitment method

8   Implement the decision

9   Allow sufficient time for response

10   Screen responses

11   Draw up a shortlist of candidates

12   Provide feedback to applicants

13   Proceed to selection

14   Evaluate recruitment effort

Figure 9.1

The recruitment process

Step 1: Determine the exact need

Consider the circumstances under which the need for recruitment arose. Make sure that the decision can be substantiated with facts obtained from objective measurements or available valid management information. The need for recruitment would often be an outflow of the workforce planning process. It is very important that departmental heads (line managers) be full partners in the process to verify the need for recruitment in cases where it has not been initiated by them.

Step 2: Obtain approval to recruit in terms of the human resource budget and level of appointment

Since employing a person is a major expenditure to an organisation (for example, an employee who is employed for ten years at an average salary of R100 000 per annum will cost the organisation one million rand), the budget of the organisation as well as strategic plans and guidelines for recruitment, should be taken into account. Approval must be obtained from senior management. This will ensure that the recruitment is compatible with the broad organisational and human resource plans. This step will also create the opportunity to reconsider the overall recruitment strategy and to consider alternatives to recruitment, for example overtime and outsourcing. Managers must be aware of the fact that a possible ad hoc restructuring may harm certain departments in the organisation and that recruitment must therefore be executed with utmost care.

Step 3: Compile or update job description and job specification

We have already explained the role and nature of job descriptions and specifications. A job description and job specification comprise the point of departure for all recruitment activities; it is thus essential that the job description should provide an accurate reflection of job activities. A job description will enable the recruiter to determine the exact nature of the vacant job — that is, the purpose, duties, responsibilities and position of the relevant job in the organisational structure. The job specification, on the other hand, helps the recruiter to profile the required jobholder, for example the necessary experience, qualifications, motivation and communication abilities. Problems arise when job descriptions and job specifications have not been compiled and when job content have not been updated. As explained, the writing of job descriptions and specifications is often a cumbersome process which is often neglected in organisations. The recruiter must, however, ensure that the correct job information is obtained.

Step 4: Determine the key performance areas for the job

This step is a natural outflow of the previous step. Key performance areas refer to those aspects of the job which are crucial for the success of the job and normally focus on outputs and not on job activities. This needs to be done objectively to provide the recruiter and person responsible for interviewing and selection with insight into actual job requirements. This may form part of a job description.

Step 5: Consult the recruitment policy and procedure

The recruitment policy and procedure document will contain specific guidelines for recruitment, and should be consulted in the interest of consistency and to ensure the long-term efficiency of recruitment in the organisation. This document reflects the organisation's views regarding the approach and procedures to be followed in the organisation and could include steps in the recruitment process (as explained in this section). The policy and procedures document will indicate, for example, whether recruitment should be done internally or externally and will specify the cost limitations. This document is, however, a dynamic document and must be amended as and when required.

Step 6: Choose the source/s

When the recruiter knows what type of person must be recruited for the job, the recruitment source can be selected. Historical data on the success rate of certain sources could be very useful in this regard. As mentioned in step 5, the recruitment policy may give an indication of whether the person(s) should be recruited internally or externally, and once this has been ascertained, the recruiter will make a choice of one or more sources (depending on the group or person required). It is good policy to try to recruit internally first of all and then, if a suitable candidate cannot be identified, to channel the recruitment effort externally. In certain cases recruitment will have to be done externally — for example when a pool of new employees is required (such as new apprentices for possible technical training at a later stage or a specialised computer expert).

Step 7: Decide on a method of recruitment

Recruitment methods which have traditionally proved successful must always be used, for example newspaper advertisements (which are very common) and internal succession planning. It is also important to consider previous experience with different methods, as well as factual data on the effectiveness of different methods in various geographical areas and in different job categories. The recruiter must, however, select the best method or methods for recruitment. The possible source of recruitment may also be an indication of the methods to be used. Recruiters must also guard against being accused of discrimination through using one particular recruitment method to the exclusion of others. This could be the totally unintentional result of a traditional practice in the organisation — for example advertising in only one newspaper which is circulated in only one particular area and in the process excluding potential employees from other areas in which the newspaper is not circulated.

Step 8: Implement the decision (apply the recruitment method)

In this step the chosen recruitment method(s) must be applied. For example, in the case of a newspaper advertisement the planned advertisement must be screened to prevent embarrassment to the organisation and to potential employees. When a recruitment agency is used, clear parameters of what is expected must be communicated well in advance. Advertisements, for example, must provide a clear indication of the tasks to be performed and the job specifications required. Other aspects to be specified are the location, pay, allowances, application procedures, deadlines, telephone numbers, contact numbers and facsimile numbers. Steps must be taken not to allow any discrimination other than those issues inherent in the job requirements and in affirmative action appointments.

Step 9: Allow sufficient time for response

The method used will dictate the time that should be allowed for responses. Set clear deadlines, but remain flexible to ensure the maximum number of responses.

Step 10: Screen responses

Potential employees will respond to the recruitment method used and the majority of the applicants will not be successful. Initial screening could be done telephonically (see exhibit B).

Exhibit B

Example of a telephonic screening form

Africa Limited
Telephone screening

Position:. . . . .
Name: . . . .
Address: . . . .
Contact telephone no: . . . .

Qualifications:
— Schooling:. . . . .
— Tertiary: . . . .
Experience and skills: . . . .
. . . .
. . . .

Current position:. . . . .
From: . . . .   To:. . . . .
Company: . . . .
Job title:. . . . .

Previous employment: . . . .
From: . . . .   To . . . .
Company: . . . .
Job title:. . . . .

Forward details. . . . .
Interviewed by:. . . . .   Date: . . . .
Signature: . . . .

The applicants' particulars must at this stage be compared with what has been stipulated in the job description and specification. The unsuccessful candidates must be separated from those who may be considered for possible appointment. Screening should take place according to the initial criteria set for the job. Recruiters should guard against prejudice and subjective opinions that could lead to discrimination against applicants. Sometimes initial screening will lead to only some people receiving application forms. During this step the recruiter may also screen applicants on the grounds of already completed application forms and/or CVs.

Step 11: Draw up an initial short list of candidates

During this step a short list of possible successful candidates is drawn up. Also here telephonic screening can often help the recruiter to obtain important information which can further eliminate unsuitable candidates. The short list of potentially suitable applicants must be forwarded and discussed with the relevant department or section head before proceeding to the selection interviews.

Step 12: Advise applicants of the outcome

It is important to advise all applicants as soon as possible of the outcome of their applications. This will include those who were unsuccessful and those who may be invited for interviews. Great care must be taken to respond as soon as possible to ensure that the reputation of the organisation remains unblemished.

Step 13: Proceed to selection

Qualifying applicants are now invited for interviews. The selection process is discussed in more detail in chapter 10.

Step 14: Evaluate the success of recruitment

Following the appointment of a recruited employee, the success of the recruitment process can be evaluated. Several methods can be used for evaluating the effectiveness of recruitment. The size of an organisation will usually dictate the method and intensity of evaluation (see section 9.7 and chapter 23).

9.7   EVALUATION OF RECRUITMENT

It should be borne in mind that recruitment is a costly process that includes costs such as the recruiter's salary, advertising costs, managers' salaries and other direct and indirect costs. Thus it is essential that the recruitment process be evaluated.

It is relatively easy to evaluate the cost effectiveness of the recruiter in terms of whether the recruitment target was reached. Another method of evaluation is to decide the number of interviews required per successful placement.

However, it is essential to evaluate the cost/benefit ratio of each or a combination of recruitment methods employed. When weighing up their cost effectiveness, factors such as external conditions in the labour market, time taken to fill the vacancy and the nature of the job must be considered. Finally, the effectiveness of the recruitment strategy will impact on employee turnover statistics.

Figure 9.2 outlines a general framework in terms of which a recruitment programme may be evaluated. The framework can produce useful information on the strengths and weaknesses of a specific programme as well as useful ideas for improving the programme. It does not, however, provide a rands-and-cents evaluation.

Stage of entry	Type of criteria
Pre-entry	
	Ability of the organisation to recruit newcomers
Entry	
	Initial expectations of newcomers
Post-entry	

	• Choice of organisation by the individual
	 • Initial job attitudes such as:
	   • Satisfaction with the job
	   • Commitment to the organisation
	   • Discriptive statements about job expectations (to be compared with those held as an outsider)
	   • Thoughts about quitting
	 • Job performance
	 • Job tenure and voluntary turnover rates

Figure 9.2
A framework for the evaluation of an overall recruitment programme

It is also important that an assessment be made of the equal opportunity situation. The different applicants can, for example, be categorised in terms of their race, gender, religion and disability status. A further list can be compiled in terms of the number of applicants for a particular position, the number who were unsuccessful and the number of successful candidates, including the reasons for their success.

It is very important that the recruitment department should keep accurate records of each step in the recruitment process, including the relevant documents. This will enable the organisation to answer any possible questions which interested parties may have at any time during the selection process.

9.8 STRATEGIC RECRUITMENT: A NOTE

Recruitment approaches will have to change significantly to enable organisations to move into a new era of international competition. There are various problems with the traditional recruitment methods because they are past and present orientated. It must, however, be emphasised that, if the workforce planning process has been executed properly the reactive approach to recruitment will be largely eliminated. It is, however, important that recruiters maintain a strategic approach to recruitment, which implies that job descriptions and job specifications, among other things, must be in line with the general strategic direction of the organisation. If, for instance, it is of strategic importance to implement affirmative action more vigorously, recruitment efforts should support this.

According to Rothwell and Kazanas (1994), the following strategic approach to recruitment can be adopted.

- **Step 1:** Reconsider the purpose of the recruitment function in the context of the organisational strategy and human resource management strategy. What is it at present? What should it be in the future?
- **Step 2:** What are the present strengths and weaknesses of the organisation's recruitment approach? Can present strengths be built on? Can present weaknesses be rectified?
- **Step 3:** What trends in the external and internal environments are likely to affect the recruitment function? Answer the following questions: To what extent will economic conditions make it easier to recruit certain kinds of talent in the future? To what extent will economic trends affect future labour supply outside the organisation? Inside the organisation? To what extent will technological change influence the kinds of talent needed? The appropriate sources to look for that talent? To what extent will market conditions in the industry influence labour supply? To what extent will social changes affect public views about employer recruitment methods? How will those changes affect state-of-the-art practices?
- **Step 4:** What range of recruitment strategies are available?
- **Step 5:** What choice of recruitment strategy is appropriate considering other human resource management practices and strategies?
- **Step 6:** How is a new recruitment strategy implemented? Consider: What skills will be needed by recruiters? Managers? What rewards can be given to those who act in a manner consistent with new recruitment strategy?
- **Step 7:** What criteria should be used to evaluate recruitment?

9.9   CONCLUSION

We initiated our discussion by stating that human resource management activities cannot be effective unless suitable employees have been recruited. This process begins with the employee's occupational choice and job search, and culminates in his/her commitment to join the organisation.

Before the organisation can start recruiting it must decide on a recruitment policy, taking various external and internal factors into consideration. Once these factors have been considered, the organisation can utilise various employment sources such as skills inventories, job postings, employment agencies and professional bodies. The second major decision that the recruiter must make is which method of recruiting to employ, such as placing an advertisement above a special event promotion or whether to use a combination of methods.

The steps in the recruitment process were discussed as well as the evaluation of recruitment. This was followed by a brief discussion on a strategic approach to recruitment.

SELF-EVALUATION QUESTIONS

1. Advise your human resource manager how to draw up a recruitment policy. Provide a step-by-step procedure.
2. Discuss how both internal and external factors can influence the recruitment policy in an organisation of your choice.
3. Describe the recruitment procedure you will follow to recruit a:

   O cleaner;
   O typist;
   O store manager.

4. Draw up a recruitment advertisement for an adult basic education trainer.
5. Compare the recruitment process discussed in this chapter with the recruitment process followed in an organisation of your choice. Explain why the steps differ.
6. Discuss the influence of the Labour Relations Act 66 of 1995 on recruitment procedures in organisations.

BIBLIOGRAPHY

Dessler, G. 1984. *Personnel Management*, 3 ed. Boston: Prentice-Hall International
Gerber, PD, Nel, PS & Van Dyk, PS. 1992. *Human Resources Management*, 2 ed. Halfway House: Southern Books
Greenhaus, JH. 1987. *Career Management*. Orlando, Florida: Dryden Press
Hubbart, WS. 1993. *Personnel Policy Handbook: How to Develop a Manual that Works*. New York: McGraw-Hill
Ivancevich, JM & Glueck, WF. 1983. *Foundations of Personnel/Human Resource Management* rev ed. Plano, Texas: Business Publication
Myers, IB & McCaulley, MH. 1992. *A Guide to the Development and Use of the Myers-Briggs Type Indicator*. Palo Alto, California: Consulting Psychologists Press, Inc
People Dynamics, Johannesburg, May 1994, 10
Rothwell, WJ & Kazanas, HC. 1994. *Planning and Managing Human Resources: Strategic Planning for Personnel Management*. Amherst: HRD Press
Singer, MG. 1990. *Human Resource Management*. Boston: PWS Kent

Wanous, JP. 1980. *Organizational Entry: Recruitment Selection and Socialization of Newcomers.* Massachusetts: Addison-Wesley

Wingrove, T. 1993. *Affirmative Action.* Randburg: Knowledge Resources

Employees

STUDY OBJECTIVES

After studying this chapter, you should be able to:

- describe selection;
- distinguish between a criterion and a predictor;
- define reliability and describe the different types of reliability;
- define validity and describe the different types of validity;
- discuss the selection process in detail;
- distinguish between different types of selection tests;
- explain the nature and importance of the employment interview and give guidelines in this regard;
- discuss the assessment centre as a method of personnel selection;
- describe the nature and importance of fairness in selection decisions within the South African context;
- discuss the process of appointing and socialising new employees.

10.1 INTRODUCTION

The purpose of recruitment is to gather together a body of good quality applicants from whom to select and appoint suitable employees. The next important facet of human resource management is therefore to select, appoint and orientate or socialise employees.

It is not always possible to draw a distinct line between the steps of the recruitment and the selection process. This is the case because selection flows naturally from the recruitment process.

Personnel selection is based on individual differences between human beings — that is, on the fact that attributes differ greatly from person to person, each individual possessing unique traits and abilities (as explained in chapter 3).

Selection can be defined as the process of trying to determine which individuals will best match particular jobs in the organisational context, taking into account individual differences, the requirements of the job and the organisation's internal and external environments.

Essentially thus, selection is the prediction of future performance in terms of individual differences. Before selection, information about the job or work in question is gathered, the knowledge, skills and abilities needed to do the job successfully are identified, and it is determined how such knowledge, skills and abilities can be assessed.

This chapter focuses on differences between predictors (selection instruments) and criteria, the requirements of predictors, the selection process, the value of the different selection devices, assessment centres and on the importance of fairness in selection decisions. A brief overview of the appointment and induction or socialisation of newly appointed employees makes up the final part of this chapter.

10.2 PREDICTORS AND CRITERIA

In order to make a valid selection decision, the decision maker should know what distinguishes successful performance from unsuccessful performance in a specific job. In this regard, the relevance of job analysis (see chapter 8) must again be emphasised. Job analysis provides the necessary information to develop relevant criteria and make good judgements about predictors.

A *predictor* is a selection instrument (such as an interview, test, or application blank) that assists organisations in making selection decisions. A *criterion* is a standard to be attained, for example above average job performance. A predictor is thus any variable that can be used to forecast a criterion.

The information needed to select a meaningful predictor is contained in the job specification expounded in a job analysis. The job description, on the other hand, facilitates the development of criteria for job success.

Choosing a criterion measure is difficult, as it could be influenced, for example by a supervisor who might be biased when carrying out a performance appraisal. Criteria that can be used include performance appraisals, objective production data (items produced, sales volume) and personnel record data (absenteeism, tardiness, accident rates, promotions) (Scarpello & Ledvinka 1988: 298).

Exhibit A

Preferred predictors

In a study that was conducted in 1974, the percentage of applicants for which the different predictors were used also indicated that application forms and interviews, with 93 % and 60 % respectively, were also amongst the more preferred predictors (Momberg & Langenhoven 1974: 18). A study undertaken in 1989 indicated that interviews (98 %), application forms (67 %), and tests (60 %) were most frequently used by the respondents (Holburn 1992). A recent study indicated that 95 % of organisations use the interview as selection method, 60 % use the structured interview, 67 % the panel interview, and 34 % the unstructured interview (Kriek & Van der Ohe 1996).

Some predictors and criteria are used more frequently than others. A recent study to determine the frequency with which various measures are used indicated that application forms and interviews are the most frequently used predictors in Europe and the USA (Nyfield, Gibbons, Baron & Robertson 1995: 2). Performance appraisals are more frequently used than, for example, production rates, which is a much more objective method (Scarpello & Ledvinka 1988: 298). The results obtained from three South African studies are indicated in exhibit A.

10.3 ASSESSING THE QUALITY OF PREDICTORS (SELECTION INSTRUMENTS)

The success of a predictor is judged by its *reliability* and *validity*. If a predictor is not both reliable and valid, it is worthless.

10.3.1 Reliability

Reliability can be defined as the consistency of a measure.

Consistent results must be obtained at various times to ensure that a specific predictor (selection instrument) can be confidently applied. Widely diverging results achieved by the same candidate on different days under the same conditions would serve as an indication to the employer that the test being applied is not reliable. This renders the test in question useless to the employer.

Various methods may be used to assess the reliability of a measure. One of these is the *test-retest method* in terms of which subjects are required to take the same test twice, at different times. The results are correlated and the degree of correlation between the two sets of scores indicates the reliability of the test.

Another approach to assessing the reliability of a test is the *parallel forms method.* Two versions of the same test are compiled and both tests are taken by the same group of people. The correlation between the two scores achieved indicates the reliability of the test. It is assumed that both tests measure the same qualities.

The *split-half method* is a third way of assessing the reliability of a test. The test is divided into two equal parts, with a score being calculated for each; the correlation between the two sets of scores serves as an indicator of reliability.

A final approach used to determine reliability is *internal consistency*. This is the degree to which a score obtained from one item in a test can be generalised to the scores obtained from the other items in the same test. The more homogeneous the items in a test, the higher the reliability with which one score on a test item may be generalised to scores on the rest of the test items. Internal consistency could therefore be regarded as an aspect of test reliability.

10.3.2 Validity

A selection instrument does not only need to be reliable: it also has to measure certain attributes that are essential for success in a job

The term *validity* may be defined as the "agreement between a test score or measure and the quality it is believed to measure" (Kaplan & Saccuzzo 1993: 133).

Various approaches may be used to assess the validity of a measure. The criterion-related validity method compares the test score achieved by an individual with a measure of job performance. Criterion-related validity may be divided into *predictive* and *concurrent validity*.

Predictive validity is the preferred measure used in personnel selection. The relationship between a predictor (test score) and the criterion (job performance) is established. The test is given to all applicants, but is not used as a selection instrument. Data on job performance are subsequently collected and the original test scores are then compared to the actual job performance. If they correlate well, the test can be used for purposes of personnel selection in future.

Concurrent validity is determined by giving the test to current employees as opposed to job applicants. The job performance data are therefore collected at the same time as the test scores. The degree of the relationship between the predictor (test) and the criterion (job performance) determines the validity of the predictor (test). This method is also known as the "present-employee" method.

In addition to the criterion-related validity method, the methods of content validity and construct validity may be used.

Content validity raises the question of whether a predictor (test) is a fair representation of the entire job content or at least of the most important tasks involved. The ability of the applicants to perform actual job tasks is evaluated. A definition of content validity would thus be the degree to which the tasks included in the test are representative of the total set of tasks or job goals.

Construct validity refers primarily to the degree to which a specific test measures the construct that it is designed to measure. Furthermore, it must be established to what extent the construct corresponds to the job requirements. Job analysis can be used to prove the relevance of the construct to the job. It is difficult to determine the construct validity because theoretical constructs may be abstract.

10.4 THE SELECTION PROCESS

The selection process consists of several phases, which should include at least those indicated in figure 10.1. These steps are typical of most organisational selection procedures. After each step the applicant can either be rejected or accepted. As can be seen, there may — in practice — be an overlap between the recruitment and selection processes. Already, especially during the latter phases or steps of the recruiting process, selection starts to take place. This also happens when screening takes place (see chapter 9).

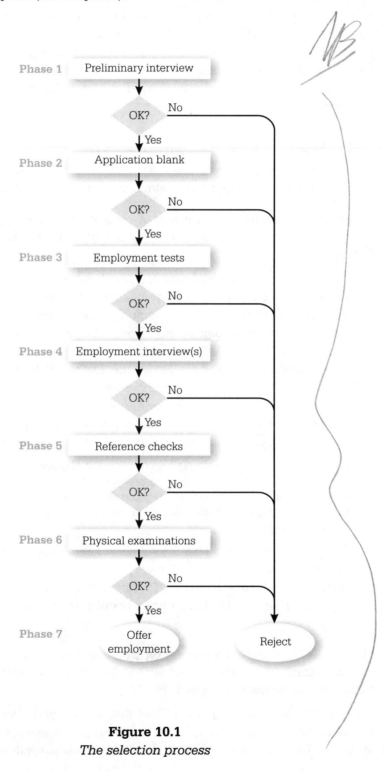

Figure 10.1
The selection process

10.4.1 Preliminary interview

The selection process starts with the preliminary interview which is short and concise. The main purpose is preselection and the elimination of applicants who are obviously not qualified for the job. Straightforward questions around areas such as qualifications, experience, and salary are asked. This is normally done once people have responded to initial recruitment efforts. It usually happens over the telephone and can in a certain sense also be viewed as part of the recruitment process (see chapter 9).

10.4.2 Application blank

The next step in the selection process would be to request those applicants who were successful in the preliminary interview to complete an application blank.

An *application blank* is a form that is completed by the applicant providing information such as education, work history, some personal data, medical history, hobbies, etc.

This information gives an indication of an applicant's suitability for a job. The use of past behaviour to predict future performance continues to form part of the selection process and, as a result of research, application blanks have become more scientific, and, to some extent, more predictive because of the refinements.

Studies have shown that the application blank is a valid predictor of job performance and of length of service (Heneman, Schwab, Fossum & Dyer 1986: 315).

The accuracy of the information is, however, often a problem. To improve accuracy, reference checking, which will be discussed later, can be used to verify some of the information. Another way of ensuring the accuracy of the information is to require the applicant to sign a statement similar to the following:

> "I hereby certify that the answers given by me to the foregoing questions and statements made are true and correct, without reservations of any kind whatsoever and that no attempt has been made by me to conceal pertinent information. Falsification of any information on this application can lead to immediate discharge at the time of disclosure." (Byars & Rue 1987: 169).

An example of an application blank for Vodacom is provided in the appendix to this chapter on page 331.

A significant advance in the use of biographical data for selection has been the development of the weighted application blank. Singer defines this type of instrument as follows:

"*Weighted application blanks* are written forms completed by candidates in which each item is weighted and scored, based on its importance as a determinant of job success" (Singer 1990: 136).

For example, an organisation may find that its successful salesmen were very active in social activities at school and technikon but average in academic performance. These items are given a definite score when applicants are evaluated.

To develop weighted application forms is very time consuming and should be restricted only to the key positions within an organisation.

10.4.3 Employment tests

Once the applicants have been screened by means of the application blank, the next step is for the successful candidates to undergo employment tests.

 An *employment test* is an instrument which is used to obtain information about personal characteristics.

Constructs such as ability, aptitude, interest and personality are usually measured. The purpose of selection tests is mainly to predict job success among a number of applicants.

Psychological tests are used in different walks of life. In schools intelligence, aptitude and interest tests are used to assist pupils in making subject choices and career choices. In organisations, tests are used to select employees at all levels. Tests are also administered to current employees to identify personnel with the potential for promotion. Psychometric assessment can play a key role in placing people in the right kinds of careers and ensuring that they receive the right kind of training.

10.4.3.1 Types of tests

 Cognitive ability (intelligence)

The measurement of intelligence has always been a popular ability test for selection. An intelligence test gives an indication of general intelligence by means of a single score.

The following intelligence tests are used in South Africa:

- the South African Wechsler Individual Intelligence Scale for Adults;
- the Mental Alertness Scale of the National Institute for Personnel Research (NIPR);
- the New South African Group test;
- the senior and junior South African Individual Intelligence Scale (for use with children).

 Aptitude

Aptitude measurement is used, inter alia, for the selection of job applicants. Most aptitude tests, such as the High Level Scales and the Senior Aptitude Test (SAT), are based on Thurstone's primary group factors like verbal ability, word fluency, memory, deductive reasoning, inductive reasoning, numerical ability, perceptual speed, form perception, spatial aptitude, coordination.

Personality tests

The majority of authors agree that people's personality has an influence on work performance. The aim of personality questionnaires is to identify personality traits. People are aware of their own behaviour and are able to make valid assessments of themselves.

The following are examples of personality tests used in South Africa.
● Projective techniques
  ○ The Thematic Apperception Test (TAT)
  ○ The Rorschach Test
  ○ The Structured Objective Rorschach Test (SORT)
● Self-report questionnaires
  ○ The 16 Personality Factor Questionnaire (16PF)
  ○ The Jung Personality Questionnaire (JPQ)
  ○ The South African Personality Questionnaire (SAPQ)
  ○ The Occupational Personality Questionnaire (OPQ).

Performance tests

The purpose of performance tests is to assess the applicant's performance on specific tasks that are representative of the actual job. As performance tests are designed for a specific job, there are many different versions. Examples would be a typing test (for typists), mechanic tool identification, editing skills, etc.

Performance tests appear to be good predictors of job success and studies have revealed that these tests are more valid than written tests (Scarpello & Ledvinka 1988: 340).

Interest

Interest is also regarded as an important determinant in choosing an occupation. Interest is related to an individual's motivation and satisfaction. The basic premise in measuring interest, is that people will be happy in a job if they like the activities involved. The following are examples of tests:
● Strong Vocational Interest Blank
● Kuder Interest Questionnaires
● Field Interest Inventory
● Self-Directed Search

10.4.4 Employment interview

One of the most common instruments for selecting employees is the employment interview. The aim of the interview is to determine an applicant's degree of suitability for a job by matching the information given by the applicant to the job requirements. The applicant may be interviewed by a combination of human resource specialists, executives or senior management within the organisation, a potential supervisor, worker representatives (such as shop stewards), and special affirmative action committee members.

10.4.4.1 Types of interviews

Interviews usually range from unstructured to structured. The unstructured interview refers to the coincidental, poorly organised type of interview where there is no attempt to explore specific areas for information about the applicant. It is usually left to the interviewer to mention topics which he or she considers to be important. Although it is not necessarily detrimental to concede such freedom to an interviewer, this method can give rise to a lack of validity if the interviewer has no training in conducting interviews. In the hands of an untrained and incompetent person, this method might not differentiate accurately between applicants with either a high or low potential.

Structured interviews are characterised by two essential features: careful, systematic planning of the interview and exclusive use of technically skilled interviewers. It is to be expected that a systematic approach to any problem would normally produce better results than coincidental, random procedures. Naturally an interview is planned according to the requirements of the job for which the selection is taking place. The reason for conducting the interview is therefore to obtain precise job related information about the applicant.

A systematic analysis leads to clear statements of objectives, a plan for obtaining the necessary information and procedures according to which this information can be assessed. A structured interview provides for a more organised approach and a more stable basis for assessment of the different candidates. The procedure of the structured interview provides guidelines for the general framework of the questions. The specific questions that will be asked remain the responsibility of the interviewer and develop from the interview situation. In organisations you will find that most interviews fall between structured and unstructured.

10.4.4.2 Problems with the employment interview

Research has shown, however, that an interview may not be the most suitable selection instrument after all. It has been found that interviews may be an unreliable and even invalid method of selection because interviewers tend to compare applicants with their own perception of the ideal employee. In addition, interviewers often base their decisions on first impressions rather than on the information gleaned during the interview, or even make up their minds about applicants during the first few minutes of the interview. It has also been shown that females are often rated lower than males and that traditional sex roles tend to predominate. Most interviewers also do not improve with training because their inborn social prejudices distort any new insight that they may have gained (Smither 1988).

Despite all these problems, there is still a need to meet the applicant face to face to ensure that the applicant will fit in with the organisation. The interview is therefore here to stay. The onus is on the manager to improve the success of the interview. No organisation can really afford to appoint the wrong people. In spite of this, very few interviewers are really capable of obtaining adequate information to ensure a proper fit between the worker and the work. The value of the interview can be increased by well-trained and skilled interviewers. Below are some guidelines that can be used to improve the skills of the interviewers.

10.4.4.3 Guidelines for interviewing

Preparing for an interview

One of the major reasons for ineffective interviewing is the fact that the interviewer is often unprepared. The following steps can be followed by the interviewer to prepare himself/herself better (Weitzul 1992: 70–82).

- Establish what the job requirements are with regard to skills, knowledge, aptitudes and personal characteristics. Study the job description and job specification carefully in this regard.
- Study all written material such as application forms, résumés and reference checks.
- Make note of any incomplete questions.
- State preliminary ideas for further exploration in the interview.
- Be careful not to ask discriminatory questions.
- Remind yourself about your own prejudices and not to use yourself as a model. Think about the job requirements and try to evaluate the person's strengths and weaknesses as objectively as possible.
- Plan the areas that you want to cover, for example background, education, work history, etc in a logical manner.
- Questions analysing topics like planning, organising, problem analysis, risk taking, judgement, self-esteem, adaptability and persuasiveness should be considered.

Opening the interview

If a panel interview is used, the introduction should include the name and job title of each interviewer. A nameplate can also be put in front of the interviewers. The interviewer should also give an idea of the degree of formality expected by using (or not using) first names.

- Establishing rapport
  The atmosphere must be friendly and relaxed. Most people experience the employment interview as stressful. The interviewer is primarily responsible for putting the applicant at ease. This process is called establishing rapport. Establishing rapport can be seen as the process of creating a harmonious relationship between the interviewer and the applicant so as to develop the applicant's confidence in the interviewer to such an extent that he/she begins to talk spontaneously (Fear & Chiron 1990: 46).
- Purpose of the interview
  Once rapport has been established, the purpose of the interview should be explained. In this regard the applicant should be told that you want to find out

more about his/her previous experience, training, background, interests, goals and values, the applicant, in turn, will be told more about the job in question and the organisation. The applicant should also be invited to ask questions.

NB

Obtaining information

The main purpose of the employment interview is to obtain the required job-related information in order to enable the interviewer to make a decision. The following guidelines with regard to questioning can be followed (Fear & Chiron 1990: 57–68).

● Make use of open-ended questions. This will enable the applicant to talk freely. Use phrases like "to what extent", "how do you feel about" etc to make questions open-ended.

● Questions must be work related. To avoid issues which may be regarded as unfairly discriminatory, interviewers must ensure that the questions that they ask are job related. Try to obtain only the necessary information which is required to determine whether or not the applicant will be successful on the job.

● The interviewer must make use of follow-up questions in order to ensure that the applicant meets critical job requirements.

● The interviewer should clarify the true meaning of the applicant's casual remarks. Where the interviewer is concerned about an applicant's remarks, for example his/her dislikes, the interviewer should establish the extent of these dislikes by means of further questioning.

● The interviewer must search for evidence which substantiates hypotheses established earlier. Interviewers often observe clues to an applicant's behaviour early on in the discussion a hypothesis is then established. Further questions should be asked to determine whether or not there is support for such a conclusion.

● Emphasise the present rather than the past and concentrate on real job experiences.

● The interviewer should also be careful not to be too direct in the questioning: it is important not to lose rapport.

In order to avoid accusations of unfair discrimination (see chapter 5 as well), the interviewer should bear the following in mind (Fear & Chiron 1990: 69).

● Questions must be job related.
● Ask all the different groups of people the same questions.
● Avoid asking questions out of curiosity.
● Avoid asking females questions such as their plans for marriage, plans for children.
● Do not ask questions that can be seen as unfairly discriminatory against older people, the disabled, etc.

Closing the interview

Interviewers must remember that the applicant will also have to ask certain questions in order to make sure that this is the right job for him/her. The interviewer should at least give the applicant enough information to make an informed decision. The applicant should also be given an indication of when an answer can be expected from the organisation regarding the outcome of the application.

10.4.4.4 *Other ways of improving the effectiveness of the interview*

As indicated earlier, the interview is not rated highly as a selection instrument because of its low validity. Recent research findings have, however, revealed a more optimistic view of the predictive capability of the interview — two studies found average validities in the 0,40 to 0,50 range (Landy, Shankster-Cawley & Moran 1995).

It appears that structured and panel interviews make a significant difference (Smith, Gregg & Andrews 1989: 46). Validity of structured interviews can reach the same level as that of ability tests (Huffaitt & Woehr 1995: 10). Two types of structured interviews, namely the situational interview and the patterned behavioural description interview (PBDI), will be referred to. The situational interview deals with samples of work behaviour. The applicant's response to situations which are typical of the job and crucial to the successful performance of the job is tested. It has been found that the predictive validity of the situational interview is around 0,30 and 0,46 (Singer 1993: 26).

In the PBDI the applicant is expected to recall an incident similar to the situation described and to relate how he/she reacted in that situation. The predictive validity of the PBDI is around 0,45 and 0,72 (Singer 1993: 26).

The panel interview gives more people the chance to assess the applicant. The fact that more people are involved in the selection process leads to a fairer assessment. Not too many interviewers must be involved, only for instance a chairperson, the line manager and the human resource practitioner.

To summarise, the effectiveness of the interview can be improved by doing the following:

- train interviewers in the skill of interviewing;
- change to more structured and situational interviews;
- use job-related questions;
- use the panel interview.

10.4.5 Reference checks

Reference checks are conducted after the employment interview to find out more about an applicant's employment record, education and training, and behavioural patterns.

These details are used to predict the expected competence of a particular applicant for the job in question.

Exhibit B

Reference check form

Name of applicant: ....

Reference: .... Date: ....

Relationship to applicant: ....

  1. Period of employment: ....

  2. Positions and duties held: ....

    ....

    ....

    ....

    ....

  3. Reason for resignation: ....

    ....

    ....

    ....

  4. Would the candidate be re-employed? ....

  5. Job performance: ....

    ....

    ....

  6. Managerial ability: ....

  7. Communication skills: ....

  8. Influencing skills: ....

  9. Strengths and weaknesses: ....

 10. General comments: ....

Reference checking is important for the following reasons (Kieffer 1991):

- input is obtained from a number of people;
- there is useful feedback on the strengths and weaknesses, achievements and failures of individuals;
- the organisation receives a verbal report on an individual's performance.

10.4.5.1 Guidelines for checking references

A popular way of checking references is by telephone. Candidates are required to furnish the names and contact numbers of previous employers and other people.

References are useful if they satisfy the following four requirements (McCormick & Ilgen 1987: 195):

- the person providing the reference must have observed the candidate in a relevant situation (for example during work);
- the person providing the reference must be capable of assessing the candidate's performance;
- the person must be prepared to express his or her forthright opinion;
- the person must express himself or herself in such a way that his/her opinion is not misinterpreted.

Although all of the above-mentioned points are of importance, the honesty with which an opinion is expressed is probably the point on which most references fail, as people are often reluctant to state a negative opinion.

The person following up references may also ask about the candidate's job title, employment period, salary and whether his/her old company would consider rehiring him/her. As a general guideline, only the references of serious candidates are worth checking. The validity of the information provided must be checked, the candidate should be informed that the references he/she provided will be checked, and the questions to be asked should be formulated in such a way that information about the candidate's qualifications, skills, work habits, sense of judgement and performance level will be obtained.

10.4.6 Physical examination

Before the successful applicant is appointed, he/she may be required to undergo a physical examination. The purpose is to determine the applicant's physical suitability for the position for which he/she has been selected. Organisations must also be careful when specifying a physical qualification to ensure that it is job related and that the employee would not otherwise be able to do the job properly.

10.5 ASSESSMENT CENTRES

Another well-known selection method is the assessment centre, where applicants are asked to perform within a simulated work environment. Trained assessors then measure the applicants' job behaviour with the aid of various instruments. Assessment centres are most often used in the selection of managers or other personnel required to plan, guide, control and make decisions about operations.

The first step is to carry out a job analysis to establish the evaluation criteria. This is followed by the assessment itself, during which several assessors rate the applicants' behaviour to eliminate subjectivity and standardise methods. As Cascio points out: "By using multiple assessment techniques, by standardizing methods of making inferences from such techniques, and by pooling the judgment of multiple assessors in rating each candidate's behavior, it is felt that the likelihood of successfully predicting future performance is enhanced considerably." (Cascio 1991: 327).

10.5.1 Value of the assessment centre

The assessment centre is regarded as a valid indicator of job suitability, a finding which has been confirmed by research conducted in South Africa (Kriek 1991: 34–37). Research has shown that the assessment centre can be used as a valid predictor of supervisory performance across all groups (Kriek, Hurst & Charoux 1994). Furthermore, in various decisions our courts have found the assessment centre to be superior to other traditional selection instruments (Arvey & Faley 1988). Assessment centres have thus come to be regarded as both reliable and fair, the use of several assessors reducing the possibility of unfair discrimination (Smith, Gregg & Andrews 1989: 62).

Particularly in South Africa, where organisations are under pressure to introduce fair human resource management practices, assessment centres appear to be an option for the future. In a recent study on the use of assessment centres, almost half of all respondents were found to be making use of them already (Kriek & Van der Ohe 1996).

10.6 FAIRNESS IN SELECTION DECISIONS

This aspect has already been discussed in chapter 5. Just to reiterate, fairness in selection has been the focus of much important research, particularly with regard to employment tests and interviews (Singer 1993: 16). The meaning of fairness in the context of selection has been dealt with in chapter 5, but here is a non-South African vierw: "Unfair discrimination exists when persons with equal probabilities of success on the job have unequal probabilities of being hired for the job."(Guion 1966: 26).

As we've explained, in the future South African organisations will be increasingly expected to prove the scientific basis and/or fairness of their selection decisions. It is important to realise that selection decisions are more likely to be regarded as fair if the links between the requirements of the job and the personal characteristics required to do the job can be proved and specified. Once these links have been established, a selection technique to identify personal characteristics can be considered. This emphasises, once again, the need for proper job analysis.

Managers of South African organisations must therefore realise the need for proper job analysis processes as well as the potential usefulness of valid predictors of job performance. They have to ensure that they are in a position to defend all such decisions with scientific proof. Selection techniques and decisions must be proved to be job related if they are to be considered fair. A more scientific approach to selection is therefore essential.

10.7 APPOINTING AND SOCIALISING NEW EMPLOYEES

As soon as the selection process has been completed and a final decision has been made, it is usual practice to discuss a provisional offer with the prospective employee. It may happen that an applicant withdraws or that the parties cannot agree on certain terms and conditions of employment. As soon as agreement is reached, however, a letter of appointment is given to the successful candidate. Sometimes the person is contacted telephonically and requested to come to the organisation, in order to finalise the offer. However, this is not always the method used, except if it has perhaps been preceded by a verbal agreement between the parties that the offer would be accepted. It is advisable that the person should accept the job offer in principle (and conditions of service) before the letter of appointment is sent out.

As soon as the person has accepted the offer in writing, all the other applicants must be informed in writing that their applications have been unsuccessful. Such a letter must, of course, be of a high standard and must always be politely worded. After all, this is the beginning of another recruitment process, as it is yet another way of portraying the image of the organisation externally.

Once the employment relationship has been formally established, the new employee's first few days and weeks in his/her new working environment form the next important facet of human resource management.

"First impressions last!" This statement has been proven countless times in practice. If a person is negatively disposed towards an organisation during his/her first days or weeks in its employ, this may have a lasting influence on that employee's orientation and attitude towards the organisation in the long term. The opposite is equally true.

For this reason it is essential that newly appointed employees be positively disposed towards the organisation, towards the section in which they are working, towards their jobs and towards other employees.

The organisation's socialisation programme (induction or orientation programme) is thus a formal attempt at changing this potential threat into an opportunity for better human resource utilisation.

The socialisation or orientation programme is aimed at gradually (but as soon as possible) introducing the new employee to the organisation, the work unit in which he/she will be working, the particular work and the people and things with which he/she has to work.

It is basically a structured process involving welcoming, receiving and introducing the newly appointed employees, providing them with the necessary information, and making them feel at ease so that they can settle down as soon as possible. This helps to ensure that they will be happy as soon as possible and become productive at work.

The process is thus aimed essentially at making the newcomer feel at ease and involves the following:

- reducing anxiety/tension;
- creating a feeling of security as soon as possible;
- creating realistic expectations on the part of the employee;
- creating a foundation for the integration of personal and organisational objectives (creating the match or fit);
- making the employee productive as soon as possible.

One aspect of orientation involves introducing the employee to the organisation itself. This entails providing the employee with information about aspects such as the following:

- a brief overview of the company — its history, market, industry, products, organisation structure and the top management team;
- conditions of employment and benefits — such as normal hours of work, holidays, medical and pension schemes, group life insurance;
- remuneration policy, pay scales, when paid and how, payroll administration;
- work rules and standard procedures;
- human resource and labour relations management policy;
- disciplinary code and procedure;
- grievance procedure;
- relationships with employer organisations;
- trade union related arrangements (for example which unions, recognition agreements, consultative structures);
- training and development policy and facilities;
- employee wellness policy;
- medical and first-aid infrastructure;
- restaurant facilities;
- social responsibility policy;
- community involvement policy;
- procedures for internal and external telephone system and correspondence;
- procedures relating to travelling and subsistence expenses;
- issues relating to confidentiality of certain company information.

The other important component relates to departmental and actual work orientation. In this case the focus is on the work in the department or work unit of which the employee will be part and on the people with whom he/she will have to work. In the process the newly appointed employee will obtain a brief introductory overview of the workflow process, the nature of his/her specific work role and on how his/her department and job fits in with the rest of the organisation.

The initial socialisation or induction of an employee is thus a shared responsibility. The HR specialists or department will be primarily responsible for the general organisation-level orientation, while line management takes primary responsibility for introducing the employee to his/her more immediate work environment. These role players should liaise and work together to help the new employee to feel at ease and to become productive as soon as possible.

10.8 CONCLUSION

Selection is the process of making decisions about the matching of individuals to jobs, taking into account individual differences and the requirements of the job. The selection process consists of different steps and the success of the whole process can be improved by continuously improving each step. The first step is the preliminary interview, the purpose of which is to eliminate the obviously unqualified applicants. Then the applicant completes an application blank and the employer makes an initial attempt to establish a match between the applicant and the job. Another step is to use employment tests, by means of which information concerning personal characteristics is obtained. These tests must be reliable and valid. The employment interview is the next step whereby the information obtained is related to the requirements of the job in order to determine suitability for employment.

The purpose of the reference check is to gather information about an applicant's past history from people with whom he/she has been associated. Once an applicant has successfully completed all the steps in the selection procedure, a physical examination may be required as a prerequisite for employment.

Assessment centres are used more often because employees attach a high value to the results obtained by such centres. To improve the fairness of selection decisions, the whole selection process should be based on job relatedness and on specific links between the requirements of the job and the personal characteristics required to do the job. When the selection process has been completed and a final decision has been made, a provisional offer is discussed with the prospective employee. Once an agreement is reached, the successful candidate is appointed. When the successful employee starts with the organisation, he/she is supposed to be orientated, during which period the newly appointed employee is introduced to the work environment and the organisation. The idea of socialisation is to ensure that the employee is as happy and productive as possible, as soon as possible.

 SELF-EVALUATION QUESTIONS

1. What is personnel selection? Explain how it may differ between a small and a large organisation.
2. Distinguish between a predictor and a criterion. Give examples of each.
3. Which method to determine validity is preferred in personnel selection? Explain the method.
4. What is an application blank? How would you improve on the accuracy of the data obtained by the application blank?
5. Distinguish between ability, aptitude and personality tests.
6. How would you improve on the validity of the employment interview? Explain in detail.
7. What is a reference check? What is the underlying principle of a reference check? Should it be used for all jobs? Substantiate your answer.
8. What is an assessment centre? How would you evaluate an assessment centre?
9. What would you do to improve on the fairness of selection decisions in your organisation?
10. How would you go about appointing and socialising a new employee who has been selected for a particular position?

BIBLIOGRAPHY

Arvey, RD & Faley, RH. 1988. *Fairness in selecting employees.* New York: Addison-Wesley Publishing Company

Bragg, A. 1990. Checking references. *Sales and Marketing Management*, 142, 68–70

Byars, LL & Rue, LW. 1987. *Human Resource Management.* Homewood, Illinois: Irwin

Cascio, WF. 1987. *Applied Psychology in Personnel Management.* Englewood Cliffs, New Jersey: Prentice-Hall, Inc

Cascio, WF. 1991. *Applied Psychology in Personnel Management.* Englewood Cliffs, New Jersey: Prentice-Hall

Cooke, R. 1988. Human resource management : A case for reference-checking. *Credit Union Management,* 11(10), 28–29

Einhorn, LJ, Bradley, HP & Baird, JE. 1982. *Effective Employment Interviewing.* Illinois: Scott Foresman and Company

Falcone, P. 1992. Reference checking: Revitalize a critical selection tool. *HR Focus*, Dec. 1992, 19

Fear, RA & Chiron, RJ. 1990. *The Evaluation Interview.* New York: McGraw-Hill Publishing Company

Gatewood, RD & Feild, HS. 1987. *Human Resources Selection.* New York: The Dryden Press

Guion, RM. 1966. Employment tests and discriminatory hiring. *Industrial Relations,* 5, 20–37.

Heneman, HG, Schwab, DP, Fossum, JA & Dyer, LD. 1986. *Personnel/Human Resource Management.* Homewood, Illinois: Irwin Inc

Holburn, P. 1992. *Psychometric Assessment — Identify Appropriate Assessment Techniques for Specific Jobs to ensure that the Right Person is Elected.* Johannesburg: Congress on Culture, Fair Assessment Techniques. International Executive Communications

Huffcutt, AI & Woehr, DJ. 1995. *A Further Analysis of Employment Interview Validity.* Paper presented at the 10th Annual Meeting of the Society for Industrial and Organisational Psychology, Orlando

Kaplan, RM & Saccuzzo, DP. 1993. *Psychological Testing.* Belmont, California: Wadsworth Inc

Kieffer, M. 1991. The reference check: What you need to know. *Health Care Executive,* 6(6), 18–19

Kriek, HJ. 1991. Die bruikbaarheid van die takseersentrum: 'n Oorsig van resente literatuur. *Tydskrif vir Bedryfsielkunde*, 17(3), 34–37

Kriek, HJ. 1993. *Fair Assessment Techniques: General Remarks and Conclusions.* Johannesburg: Conference on Culture-Fair Assessment Techniques. International Executive Communications

Kriek, HJ, Hurst, DN & Charoux, JAE. 1994. The assessment centre: Testing the fairness hypothesis. *Journal of Industrial Psychology*, 20(2), 21–25

Kriek, HJ & Van der Ohe, H. 1996. *Managerial Assessment Methods Survey* (in press)

Landy, FJ, Shankster-Cawley, L & Moran, SK. 1995. Advancing personnel selection and placement methods. In *The Changing Nature of Work*, ed A Howard, 252–281. San Francisco: Jossey-Bass Publishers

McCormick, EJ & Ilgen, D. 1987. *Industrial and Organizational Psychology*. Englewood Cliffs, New Jersey: Prentice-Hall Inc

Momberg, JP & Langenhoven, HP. 1974. *Die Indiensnemingsonderhoud in die Suid-Afrikaanse Bedryf*. Universiteit van die Oranje-Vrystaat, Bloemfontein

Munchus, G. 1992. Check references for safer selection. *HR Magazine,* 1992, 75–77

Nyfield, G, Gibbons, PJ, Baron, H & Robertson, I. 1995. *The Cross-cultural Validity of Management Assessment Methods*. Paper presented at the 5th Annual Conference on Fairness in Personnel Decisions of the Department of Industrial Psychology, Pretoria

Owens, WA. 1976. Background data. *In Handbook of Industrial and Organizational Psychology,* ed MD Dunnette. Chicago: Rand McNally

Peel, M. 1988. *Ready made Interview Questions*. London: Kogan Page Limited

Plug, C, Meyer, WF, Louw, DA & Gouws, LA. 1986. *Psigologiewoordeboek*. Johannesburg: McGraw-Hill

Plumbley, P. 1991. *Recruitment and Selection*. Worcester: Billing and Sons Ltd

Scarpello, VG & Ledvinka, J. 1988. *Personnel/Human Resource Management*. Boston: PWS-Kent Publishing Company

Schultz, DP & Schultz, SE. 1986. *Psychology and Industry Today*. New York: Mac-Millan Publishing Company

Schultz, DP & Schultz, SE. 1994. *Psychology and Industry Today: An Introduction to Industrial and Organisational Psychology*. New York: Macmillan Publishing Company

Singer, MC. 1990. *Human Resource Management*. Boston: PWS-Kent Publishing Company

Singer, M. 1993. *Fairness in Personnel Selection*. Aldershot: Avebury

Smith, M, Gregg, M & Andrews, D. 1989. *Selection and Assessment: A New Appraisal*. London: Pitman Publishing

Smither, RD. 1988. *The Psychology of Work and Human Performance*. New York: Harper & Row Publishers

Taylor, HC & Russell, JT. 1939. The relationship of validity coefficients to the practical effectiveness of tests in selection: Discussion and tables. *Journal of Applied Psychology,* 23, 565–578

Weitzul, JB. 1992. *Evaluating Interpersonal skills in the Job Interview*. New York: Quorum Books

APPENDIX: VODACOM APPLICATION BLANK

1.0 Personal particulars

ID Number

Surname _____

Full first names _____

Preferred name _____

Maiden name (If applicable) _____

Age_____ Nationality _____

Sex	Male	Female	Marital state	Married	Unmarried	Widower Widow	Divorced

Husband's initials_____

Occupation of spouse_____

Dependants — Number _____

Residential address _____   Postal address_____

_____   _____

_____   _____

_____   _____

_____ Postal code:_____   _____ Postal code:_____

Telephone number(s)   Home (   ) _____   Work (   ) _____

Spouse (   ) _____

Home language _____

How proficient are you in the following languages?

	Fair	Good	Totally fluent
Afrikaans	☐	☐	☐
English	☐	☐	☐
Others (please specify)	☐	☐	☐

_____

Extra-mural activities _____

_____

_____

_____

_____

_____

2.0 Qualifications

Highest school standard passed _____ Year 19 _____

Type of school | Academic | Technical | Commercial | Other_____

Name of school _____

Place (city/town) _____

Post-school qualifications:

Qualification	Year attained	University/Technikon	Full-time/Part-time
1.			
2.			
3.			

Current studies: _____

3.0 Previous work experience (if this space is insufficient, attach a complete CV)

Employer (name and address) and name of superior	From	To	Position held	Nature of work	Reason for leaving

4.0 Military training

Called up for national service   Commencing date   Y   M ☐☐☐☐|☐☐

Exempted – Reason _____

_____

or

Postponed to   Y   M   D ☐☐☐|☐☐|☐☐

or

Training undergone (period)   Y   M   D ☐☐☐☐|☐☐|☐☐ to   Y   M   D ☐☐☐☐|☐☐|☐☐

Military rank _____

5.0 Contractual commitments (military, bursary, training, etc)

Organisation	Amount	Specify particulars of commitment

6.0 References

Name	Occupation/Rank	Work address	Tel. no.	Code

May we contact your previous/present employer? ☐ Yes ☐ No

7.0 General

Have you ever been found guilty of a criminal offence? ☐ Yes ☐ No

If yes, furnish full details _____

_____

_____

_____

_____

Which source(s) led to your application? _____

Any information you wish to supply in support of your application? _____

_____

_____

Give brief reasons why you are interested in employment in the Company _____

_____

_____

_____

_____

_____

_____

_____

On what date can you assume duty?   Y □□□□ M □□ D □□

To the best of my knowledge, the above information is correct. I fully realise that the furnishing of false or incorrect information will disqualify me from employment or subject me to discharge.

_____   _____
Signature   Date

Office use

Approval of appointment

Initials and surname [   ]

Division [   ]

Designation [   ]

Salary [R   ] p.a.

Date of appointment   Y □□ M □□ D □□

Recommendation

_____   _____
Name   Signature

_____   _____
Designation   Date

Health questionnaire

Are you suffering or have you ever suffered from	Mark with a cross in the appropriate column	If any answer is yes, give details of the nature, severity, date and duration of the illness
1. Any skin disease?	Yes No	
2. Any affection of the skeleton and/or joints?	Yes No	
3. Any affection of the eyes, ears, nose or teeth?	Yes No	
4. Any affection of the chest or respiratory system?	Yes No	
5. Any affection of the heart or circulatory system?	Yes No	
6. Any affection of the digestive system?	Yes No	
7. Any affection of the urinary system and/or genital organs?	Yes No	
8. Any nervous affection or mental abnormality?	Yes No	
9. Any other illness?	Yes No	

1. Do you suffer from any defect of hearing, speech or sight?   Yes No

2. Are you physically disabled and do you use artificial limbs?   Yes No

Give details of the nature and severity of the disability

1. Have you undergone any operation(s)?   Yes No

Give details of the nature and date of the operation(s)

I declare that the above information is true and correct and that I have not withheld any information regarding my health.

Signature   Date

part four

Utilising and Developing employees

STUDY OBJECTIVES

After studying this chapter, you should be able to:

● discuss fully the implications of the different assumptions about the nature of organisational man, for HRM in general and motivation in particular;

● describe in detail the basic motivational process and its relationship to anxiety and performance;

● list and explain the different motivational theories classified as *content theories, process theories,* and *reinforcement theories* respectively; and

● compare and critically analyse the different motivational theories in terms of their relative strengths and weaknesses.

11.1 INTRODUCTION

As soon as a person is employed, management's main concern is to get the new employee to do his or her work as well as possible. This is why people are employed. It is therefore essential to understand why people work and why some people want to perform better than others. In order to elicit the best performance from employees it is necessary to understand what motivates them in general and, more particularly, what the implications of motivation are for management.

In our modern, technological society work is a very complex phenomenon and, as explained in chapter 1, it is central to most people's lives in that they are dependent on it for their very livelihood. In South Africa, with our high rate of unemployment, having a job has become a highly desirable goal. We therefore find people competing fiercely for jobs and companies even have to enter into agreements with job seekers as to how jobs will be awarded. Work takes on different meanings for different individuals and thus a person's performance in a job cannot be separated from the individual who performs it. An employee's motives, socioeconomic background and value system will all interact with how he/she performs the work and reacts to efforts to influence his/her performance. It is this latter aspect that interests us in this chapter. Management naturally aims to make optimum use of employees' abilities. It is well established that the manner in which employees are treated has a profound influence on their work performance. However, given the complexity of work itself, the different shades of meaning that can be attached to the concept of work in modern life, as well as the inherent complexity of the human psyche, the link between managerial efforts to motivate employees to higher levels of performance and the actual performance realised by these efforts is highly complex and only partially understood. Compounding this complexity in the South African situation is our sociopolitical heritage, the great disparities in living standards and, of course our great cultural and ethnic diversity. These uniquely South African aspects of the problem of developing, utilising and maintaining a high-performance workforce make it risky to import concepts and theories from other countries without trying to place these in the South African context.

Nevertheless, given the dearth of basic research on the topic of motivation in South Africa, we are forced to start our enquiry with the traditional (Western) literature on these topics. A second warning is apposite: given that it is the whole individual (bringing along his/her cultural and psychological make-up to the workplace) who reports for work (and not just that dehumanised fraction of the person typically regarded by many managers as a "factor of production"), it is impossible even to begin to do justice to this topic in the course of one chapter. For this we would have to explore the realms of psychology and anthropology, to name just two fields of study that fall outside the scope of this book.

11.2 OUR ASSUMPTIONS ABOUT PEOPLE AND MOTIVATION

If good management includes the ability to motivate people to do things in such a way that they are actually inspired to achieve the goals identified by the leader, a central attribute of good management is the ability to create an environment in which people are motivated to act in a goal-directed way. When a manager considers ways of motivating subordinates, that manager brings to the situation his/her own socioeconomic and psychological complexities (remember that the manager is also an employee with his/her own unique psychological make-up). Therefore, the way in which a manager tries to motivate subordinates is strongly influenced by his/her own assumptions about others. The degree to which the manager will succeed in motivating his/her subordinates depends to a large extent on the closeness of fit between his/her assumptions about people and empirical reality.

Schein (1972: 55–79) has formulated a useful classification of managerial assumptions about people, based on the chronology in which these assumptions held sway in the history of industrial psychology. The four sets of assumptions about the nature of "man" — and "organisational man"* in particular — are the following: (i) rational-economic man; (ii) social man; (iii) self-actualising man; and (iv) complex man. These four sets of assumptions find expression in specific managerial practices and thus have a very real impact on how businesses are run and

*This includes females as well!

on human resource management practice. Schein's historical classification of management's assumptions about people is still one of the most useful ways of introducing you to motivation as it provides an overview of theories of motivation (and their concomitant managerial implications). Before dealing with the different theories of motivation in more detail (and with leadership in the next chapter), we thus start with Schein's classification by way of an overview.

11.2.1 Rational-economic man

The assumptions underlying the rational-economic man theory is the proposition that people are motivated by avoidance of unpleasantness and attraction towards that which gives pleasure. The rational-economic man can be described as a rational computer programmed to maximise self-gratification and interest. In terms of this hedonistic view of man, combined with McGregor's Theory X assumptions (see section 11.3.10), the characteristics of employees are those listed in exhibit A.

Exhibit A

Employees — a rational-economic man perspective

- Employees are motivated primarily by money and will always do that which will result in the greatest material gain.
- Since economic incentives are under managerial control, employees are passive pawns to be manipulated, moved and controlled by management.
- Employees' feelings are irrational and must be prevented from interfering with their pursuit of self-interest. This can be achieved through appropriate organisational design and managerial control mechanisms.
- Employees are inherently lazy and must thus be motivated by external incentives.
- Employees' natural objectives run counter to organisational objectives; employees must thus be subjected to external controls to ensure that they work towards (and not against) organisational objectives.
- Because of their irrational feelings, employees are inherently incapable of self-discipline and self-control.

Not surprisingly, this denigrating view of employees presupposes that there are other human beings who possess superior attributes: the managers! Managers are people who are self-motivated, self-controlled and less victim of their feelings. Schein (1972: 56) summarises this as follows:

"Ultimately, then, the doctrine of rational-economic man classified human beings into two groups — the untrustworthy, money-motivated, calculative mass, and the trustworthy, more broadly motivated, moral elite who must organize and manage the mass. As we shall see, the main problem with this theory is not that it fits no one, but rather that it overgeneralizes grossly and oversimplifies in painting man as either black or white."

11.2.1.1 *Managerial implications*

Given South Africa's apartheid legacy, there is an uncomfortable parallel between Schein's summary and some of the assumptions which underpinned Grand Apartheid (think of the Verwoerdian notion of black education as opposed to white education). Unfortunately, the structural and social inequities resulting from apartheid were also tainted with the self-fulfilling prophecy that if a group of people are continually told that they are inferior and cannot aspire to anything but the lowest of stations in life, many of them may come to believe it. Therefore, one could plausibly hypothesise that in South African business some of the victims as well as the beneficiaries of apartheid hold views that approximate those of the rational-economic man model; both groups are thus in need of re-education.

If a manager holds the assumptions associated with the rational-economic-man model, his/her managerial style will typically be grounded upon the following elements.

- Since employees are motivated by money and are inherently irresponsible, management should take a paternalistic attitude towards them and control them strictly: there should be minimal delegation of authority, a very formal hierarchy of power must be enforced, and people must be rewarded extrinsically. Management must be task orientated and the emotional aspect of people (managers and employees alike) must be suppressed.
- If work performance is unsatisfactory the solution lies in the redesign of jobs and organisational structure, as well as in restructuring the reward system and controls. One could typify this as a "scientific management" approach to the management of people.
- The onus for organisational performance rests exclusively with management. Workers are expected to do no more than that which the reward and control systems encourage and permit.

As Schein correctly points out, the great danger for an organisation operating under these assumptions " . . . is that they tend to be self-fulfilling. If employees are expected to be indifferent, hostile, motivated only by economic incentives, and the like, the managerial strategies used to deal with them are very likely to train them to behave in precisely this fashion" (Schein 1972: 57). Another way of putting this is that, if management treats its workforce like irresponsible children, the workforce will quickly conform to this notion and live up to managerial expectations. It could plausibly be conjectured that in the early post-industrialised world this paternalistic approach to the management of employees led to the rise of trade unions, and that, while the assembly line mode of production proved its efficiency as work became more complex, management found that workers-as-mindless-automata were not up to the task demanded by modern production methods. A different type of worker was thus needed: one who wanted to exercise his/her own discretion and judgement and who was motivated by non-financial incentives. An economy based on simple products and production methods could run on the lines proposed by the rational-economic model (pay human robots for doing simple, repetitive tasks). However, an economy based on the provision of complex services and production methods cannot. For this type of economy a more autonomous and self-directed workforce is needed: one that is not satisfied by mere money and that will not tolerate the external and formal strictures placed upon it by a paternalistic management intent on keeping tight control. As jobs became more demanding (and hence management's expectations of their employees became more exacting) so the expectations of employees grew in terms of what they wanted to get out of the employment relationship (see figures 11.1 and 11.2).

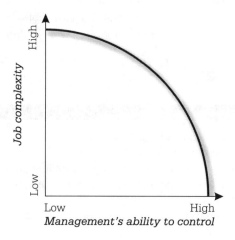

Figure 11.1

Relationship between job complexity and ability to manage by means of external controls

Figure 11.2

Relationship between job complexity and employee's expectations

11.2.2 Social man

The second stage in the development of our understanding of the human side of organisations is identified by Schein as being that of the "social-man model" (1972: 58–65). The notion that workers are at least, if not more, motivated by social factors present in their work environment, rather than by monetary rewards, can be traced to the seminal research done in the 1920s at the Hawthorne Plant in the USA. The "Hawthorne Studies", as they came to be called, dramatically drew attention to the fact that people's need to be accepted by co-workers is at least as important as monetary incentives in determining their performance. On the basis of his Hawthorne studies, Elton Mayo developed assumptions about the nature of man in the context of the world of work that are diametrically opposed to the assumptions derived from the rational-economic model of man. These are summarised in exhibit B.

Exhibit B

Employees — the social-man view*

- Employees are fundamentally motivated by social needs and develop their self-identity through relationships with others.
- The Industrial Revolution and the consequent fragmentation of work removed the meaning from the work itself and meaning must therefore be sought in the social relationships at work.
- Employees are more responsive to their peer group than to the incentives and controls of management.
- Employees are responsive to management to the extent that management can meet their social needs and needs for acceptance.

*Source: (Adapted from Schein 1972: 59)

11.2.2.1 Managerial implications

As observed above, the assumptions underlying the social-man model are almost the direct opposite of those identified as belonging to the rational-economic-man model. Likewise, a manager operating under the social man set of assumptions will be a totally different type of manager from his/her more "scientific" counterpart. More specifically, the "social-man manager" will tend to be associated with the following characteristics.

- The manager will not concern himself/herself exclusively with the task at hand — the needs of the people who must perform the task will also be taken into account.

- Instead of focusing on motivating (by manipulating external incentives) and controlling subordinates, the manager will pay much more attention to subordinates' feelings (especially those relating to the need for acceptance and identity).

- Since employees want to belong, the manager will accept the reality of informal groups within the organisation and thus concentrate on group incentives rather than on individual incentives.
- The manager's role shifts from the traditional generic managerial functions (planning, controlling, etc) to becoming a conduit between his/her subordinates and higher levels of management and being sensitive to their needs and feelings.
- The burden for organisational performance shifts from the manager to all employees. As Schein puts it (1972: 59): "The manager instead of being the creator of work, the motivator, and the controller, becomes the facilitator and sympathetic supporter."
- The manager still sets goals for the group, but leaves them much discretion in deciding how they will accomplish these goals.

The expected payoff of this type of employment relationship is that a more loyal and committed employee will result (because of his/her greater identification with the organisation through his/her greater need satisfaction — this goes beyond the mere instrumental value of getting money to embrace more fundamental needs such as the need for affiliation and a positive self-identity). In terms of this model, the great danger resulting from management's failure to look after the social needs of its workforce lies in the fact that employees will nevertheless seek to satisfy these needs by creating and joining informal groups whose objectives will run counter to those of the formal organisation. For instance, employees may join a trade union to satisfy their social needs and to channel their frustration at the formal organisation's failure to satisfy these needs into industrial action "to punish management".

Although it is tempting to view the "social-man manager" as the "good guy" and to cast his/her opposite, the "rational-economic-man manager", into the role of the "bad guy", this would be incorrect, for the simple reason that both amount to unjustified overgeneralisation and, perhaps more fundamentally, because people differ in their needs structure (the latter being a function of a multitude of factors).

11.2.3 Self-actualising man

According to this view, modern work has become meaningless; this meaninglessness, however, is related not so much to people's social needs as to man's inherent need to develop and utilise his potentialities to the full. Job specialisation, job fragmentation and the resultant de-skilling of jobs have caused work to become unchallenging and alienating in the sense that employees are no longer permitted to use and develop their abilities to the full or to see a clear connection between their activities and the total organisational goals. For instance, a worker in a cottage industry busies himself/herself with a wide range of activities that are intimately involved with the ultimate goal of his/her endeavours. (Think, for example, of a family unit who all work together to produce clothing to sell on the local market — tending to the sheep, shearing, spinning yarn, making garments and finally taking them to the market to sell; all of these activities are clearly and meaningfully related to the ultimate goal of the family as an economic unit, thereby giving meaning to each of the family member's activities. Compare this with a modern production worker whose job may involve the monotonous repetition of the same movement (the author once worked twelve-hour shifts on an assembly line fastening the left-hand front wheel of a relentless procession of lawnmowers) — it is difficult to see this activity as meaningful or to relate it to any organisational objectives!

Maslow's hierarchy of needs is probably the best known version of the self-actualising-man model of human behaviour as a function of motivational states. An application of Maslow's model in the employment relationship is depicted in exhibit C.

Exhibit C

Employees — the self-actualising model*
• Employees' needs (which can act as motivators) fall into five sequential classes. These are (from the bottom to the top): basic needs for survival, safety and security; social needs; self-esteem needs; autonomy and independence needs; and self-actualisation needs. • Employees want to grow in their jobs (which implies that they expect some autonomy and independence); to adopt a long-term perspective; to develop their skills; and have some flexibility in adapting to work circumstances. • Employees are primarily self-motivated and self-controlled; external controls are seen as threats to their need to grow to maturity in their jobs. • There is no inherent disparity between organisational goals and the self-actualising goals of the individual employee; given the opportunity an employee will integrate his/her own life goals with those of the organisation.

*Source: (Adapted from Schein 1972: 66)

11.2.3.1 Managerial implications

There are similarities but also differences between the way in which the self-actualising man manager and the social-man manager will approach the task of managing subordinates.

- The manager will place less emphasis on showing consideration for employees' feelings and more emphasis on making the job intrinsically more challenging and meaningful. Employees will be given the scope and freedom in their jobs to achieve and obtain a sense of pride and self-esteem. Take note that, should the manager assess an employee's level of need-fulfilment to be at the level of social needs, he/she will respond appropriately (see the next point).

- The manager will have to be an accomplished diagnostician to determine which of the five levels of needs a particular employee will respond to in order to delegate responsibility to employees in accordance with to their differing levels of need-fulfilment.

- Relating to the manager's role as diagnostician, the manager also will have to be flexible enough to adapt his managerial style to match the different need levels of each of his/her subordinates.

- Most importantly, the basis of motivation shifts from being extrinsic (that is, control that lies outside the job content) to being intrinsic, in the sense that management must provide the opportunity (through job design, job enrichment, delegation of authority, etc) for the employee's innate motivation (aroused by the ultimate need for self-actualisation) to be unleashed by jobs characterised by challenge, autonomy and scope for growth towards maturity.

- In order to allow for greater subordinate autonomy, the manager will be prepared to divest himself/herself of much of the traditional managerial power or managerial prerogative; the organisation will thus be characterised by greater delegation of authority to lower levels and a more equal distribution of power throughout all levels of the organisation.

To summarise: the self-actualising model of man holds that people have inherent needs and are thus self-motivated, provided that they are given the opportunity to strive towards whatever will result in fulfilling that level of need that is hierarchically above the need(s) that has already been satisfied (for a more complete discussion of this topic, see section below). In the words of Schein (1972: 69):

> " . . . the assumptions underlying the concept of self-actualizing man place emphasis on higher-order needs for autonomy, challenge, and, self-actualization, and imply that such needs exist in all men and become active as lower-order security and social needs come to be satisfied. There is clear evidence that such needs are important in the higher levels of organizational members like managers and professionals on the staff. It is not clear how characteristic these needs are of the lower-level employee, although many of the problems which were interpreted to be examples of thwarted social needs could as easily be reinterpreted to be instances of thwarted needs for challenge and meaning."

Perhaps this quote from Schein is a bit slanted towards the higher-level needs, which only come to the fore once the lower-level needs have been substantially satisfied; the challenge for the manager is to determine what will be need-fulfilling and thus act as a powerful motivator of a specific individual at a specific time. For the masses of poor and unskilled workers in South Africa it may well be their security and safety needs (such as job security and a reasonable income). In the South African context it could also be argued that, due to the greater prevalence of the extended family and involvement in community issues (as compared with the situation in Western developed countries), as well as the existence of powerful trade unions, social, independence and autonomy needs are at this stage satisfied to some extent by other social institutions (the family, the community and the trade union), so that the work context is relied upon primarily to satisfy the need for material wellbeing.

11.2.4 Complex man

After reviewing the preceding models of man, Schein (1972: 69) comes to the conclusion that these models all contain elements of truth, but that they suffer from the defect of being generalisations which do not reflect the complexities of reality. He comes to the conclusion that:

> "Man is a more complex individual than rational-economic, social, or self-actualizing man. Not only is he more complex within himself, being possessed of many needs and potentials, but he is also likely to differ from his neighbour in the patterns of his own complexity. It has always been difficult to generalize about man, and it is becoming more difficult as society and organisations within society are themselves becoming more complex and differentiated." (Schein 1972: 69–70.)

Schein (1972: 70–76) suggests that the assumptions summarised in exhibit D will do justice to this complexity.

Exhibit D

Employees — the complex-man perspective*
• Employees are not only complex but also very variable; many motives operate at different levels of importance to the employee, with this hierarchy of needs and motives changing from time to time and situation to situation.
• Employees learn new needs and motives through their organisational experiences; motivational patterns are thus partly a function of the interaction between initial needs and organisational experiences.
• An employee's needs and motives may differ, depending on the type of organisation in which he/she is employed or on the suborganisation within the larger organisation. A person who is in an alienating formal position may find fulfilment of his/her social and self-actualising needs in the informal organisation, social groups, or even the trade union. If the job itself is complex and challenging, some aspects of the job may fulfil some needs while other aspects will fulfil other needs, with much less reliance on factors external to the job for need-fulfilment.
• Organisational effectiveness is also dependent on factors other than motivation; for instance, a highly skilled but unmotivated employee's contribution to organisational performance may equal that of a very unskilled but highly motivated employee.
• There is no one managerial approach based on one set of assumptions about the nature of man that will be appropriate for all employees at all times under all circumstances.

*Source: (Adapted from Schein 1972: 70)

11.2.4.1 Managerial implications:

The complex-man model presents the manager with the following two challenges.

● The manager must be a good diagnostician in that he/she must be able to determine what motivates different individuals under different circumstances.

● The manager must value difference and possess the personal flexibility and range of skills to vary the approach appropriately, depending on his/her assessment of the differential needs of each of his/her subordinates, as explained under point 1.

These two core competencies, namely **diagnostic ability** and the ability to adopt a **flexible leadership style**, are specifically apposite for a multicultural society characterised by great disparities in the development of its human resources. For the South African manager who must acquire the skills to manage a diverse work-force effectively, the complex man model probably provides a more realistic representation of reality than the other models discussed and is particularly instructive in that it brings to the fore the daunting tasks facing management as our country approaches the twenty-first century.

Having examined Schein's perspectives on the nature of man and what motivates him, we now turn to an overview of the best-known motivation theories.

11.3 THEORIES OF MOTIVATION

What is motivation? Why do people act in the way that they do? Why do others refrain from doing certain things? And can we in a predictable and systematic way influence people to act in the way we want them to? At best we have partial answers to these questions. In this section we introduce some of the theories developed to answer the above questions in the organisational context. Without attempting to answer the first question (there are a multitude of potential answers), the following working definition of motivation will suffice:

" . . . *(M)otivation* **is the willingness to do something, and is conditioned by this action's ability to satisfy some need of the individual.**" (Robbins 1994: 42)

The basic motivational process is shown in figure 11.3.

Figure 11.3
Basic motivational process

Another preliminary aspect of motivated behaviour that needs some clarification is the role of anxiety in the effectiveness of behaviour. In terms of our basic motivational process model, we see that needs give rise to tension, which in turn spurs behaviour directed at a specific goal which is perceived as being desirable in that it will lead to need-fulfilment. However, what figure 11.3 does not show is the possibility that anxiety as a by-product of the tension, or arising from some other source (for example due to some form of psychopathology), may impact negatively on the person's performance. The correlation between anxiety levels and effectiveness of performance is illustrated in figure 11.4.

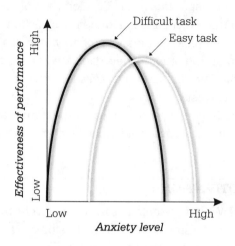

Figure 11.4

Relationship between anxiety and performance: Easy versus difficult task

Exhibit E

Anxiety and performance

- Anxiety facilitates performance on easy tasks.
- Anxiety debilitates performance on difficult or demanding tasks.
- For any task an upside-down bell curve can be plotted that will show that, up to a certain point, anxiety will increase effectiveness of performance, but, beyond that point, increased anxiety will decrease the effectiveness of performance.
- For easy tasks the level of anxiety can be increased considerably before it will become debilitating; for more difficult tasks only a slight increase in the absolute level of anxiety may prove to be debilitating.

Recognition of the role of anxiety in effective performance may lead to the following implication for management (Korman 1977: 40–41): in the case of employees who perform relatively simple jobs it may be effective to use anxiety as a means of stimulating more effective performance; for subordinates who perform complex tasks the reverse will apply.

A popular taxonomy of motivational theories divides the various theories into *content, process,* and *reinforcement theories. Content theories* focus on factors that allegedly motivate people, for example "needs" (they try to answer the question: **what** motivates people?). *Process theories,* on the other hand, try to analyse the process or manner in which people get motivated (they focus on the question: **how** are people motivated?). *Reinforcement theories* focus on how people can be conditioned to exhibit the desired behaviour (these try to answer the question: how do people **learn** to exhibit desirable behaviour?). The *content* theories discussed in this book are Maslow's needs hierarchy, Alderfer's ERG theory, Herzberg's two-factor motivation theory, McClelland's achievement motivation theory and Locke's goal-setting theory. The *process* theories which are examined include cognitive dissonance theory, Stacey Adams' equity theory and Vroom's expectancy theory. Reinforcement theory and McGregor's theory X and theory Y are also briefly discussed.

11.3.1 Hierarchy of needs theory

It can safely be stated that probably the best-known theory of motivation is Abraham Maslow's theory of hierarchy of needs. Maslow's theory, which postulates that within every person there exists a hierarchy of five need levels, is depicted in figure 11.5 (see also section 11.2.3).

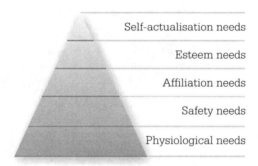

Figure 11.5
Maslow's hierarchy of needs

The self-actualisation model (of which Maslow's hierarchy is the best-known example) is based on the work of existential philosophers who postulate that man has the innate drive to achieve his full potential, but that it is the conditions of everyday life that place constraints on this "instinct for self-actualisation" and cause him to perform suboptimally. Maslow's five levels of "needs" (or "motives" — motives simply being the other side of the same coin, as can be seen from figure 11.3) are:

● **Physiological:** These include hunger, thirst, shelter, sex and other physiological needs associated with the biological survival of the individual and the species.

● **Safety:** These include security and protection from physical and emotional harm.

● **Social:** These include the needs to belong, to be liked and for friendship.

- **Self-esteem:** These include internal mental states such as self-liking, autonomy, achievement, as well as external factors such as needs relating to status, recognition and attention.
- **Self-actualisation:** This concerns the need to become what one is capable of becoming and includes needs relating to growth and development, achieving one's potential and self-fulfilment.

The key to an understanding of Maslow's schemata is the concept of "prepotency". This simply means that as a lower-level need(s) becomes substantially fulfilled the next higher-order need(s) increases in strength and thus becomes a powerful motivator(s). A person fighting for his/her very survival (that is, a person whose safety needs are unfulfilled) will not be motivated by opportunities to fulfil his/her status needs, because safety as a lower-order need must first be satisfied before the higher-order esteem needs. However, once that person's physiological, safety and

Table 11.1

How status symbols vary at different levels of the organisational hierarchy*

Visible appurtenances	Top dogs	VIPs	Brass	No 2s	Eager beavers	Hoi polloi
Briefcases	None — they ask the questions	Use backs of envelopes	Someone goes along to carry theirs	Carry their own — empty	Daily — carry their own — filled with work	Too poor to own one
Desks, office	Custom made (to order)	Executive style (to order)	Type A (Director)	Type B (Manager)	Castoffs from No 2s	Yellow oak — or castoffs from eager beavers
Tables, office	Coffee tables	End tables or decorative wall tables	Matching tables, type A	Matching tables, type B	Plain work table	None — lucky to have own desk
Carpeting	Nylon — one inch pile	Nylon — one inch pile	Wool-twist (twist pad)	Wool-twist (without pad)	Used wool pieces — sewed	Asphalt tile
Plant stands	Several — kept filled with strange, exotic plants	Several — kept filled with strange, exotic plants	Two — repotted whenever they take a trip	One medium-sized — repotted annually during vacation	Small — repotted when plant dies	May have one in the department or bring their own from home.
Vacuum water bottles	Silver	Silver	Chromium	Plain painted	Coke machine	Water fountain
Library	Private collection	Autographed or complimentary books and reports	Selected references	Impressive titles on covers	Books everywhere	Dictionary
Parking space	Private — in front of office	In plant garage	In company garage — if enough seniority	In company properties — somewhere	On the parking lot	Anywhere they can find a space — if they can afford a car

*Source: Certo, 1994: 419

social needs have substantially been met, he/she will become aware of his/her esteem needs. A person who is barely able to provide for his/her own sustenance would not be motivated, for example, by the chance to acquire a better office, while a person who earns an above average wage would be motivated by status symbols such as a better type of carpet or a bigger desk in his/her office. Companies do in fact pay a great deal of attention to the motivational value of status symbols at different levels within the organisational hierarchy (see table 11.1).

Although Maslow's theory enjoys wide support, this in all probability is due more to its intuitive appeal than to its empirical validation. Possibly the greatest practical virtue of the theory lies in the fact that it draws attention to the fact that people have different needs and are therefore motivated by different things: what acts as a motivator for one person may be totally ineffectual for another, or what is an effective motivator for a person at one time may not be effective on another occasion.

11.3.2 ERG theory

Alderfer adapted Maslow's need hierarchy on the basis of empirical research (Robbins 1996: 218–219). According to Alderfer, there are three core needs, namely "Existence", "Relatedness" and "Growth" — hence the name ERG theory. These needs are summarised in exhibit F.

Exhibit F

ERG hierarchy of needs
• **Existence needs:** These needs relate to our basic material existence needs (similar to Maslow's physiological and safety needs)
• **Relatedness needs:** These needs relate to our desire for interpersonal relationships and interaction (similar to Maslow's affiliation/social needs and the external aspect of Maslow's esteem needs)
• **Growth needs:** This grouping of needs relates to our inherent desire for personal development (this includes the internal aspects of Maslow's esteem needs and his self-actualisation needs category)

Apart from conflating Maslow's five-level hierarchy of needs into three levels, ERG theory represents a refinement on Maslow's theory in that it more closely relates to our everyday observations about people and is thus regarded as a more valid version of the needs theory of motivation. Alderfer's ERG theory differs from Maslow's hierarchy of needs theory in the following important respects:

● ERG theory does not postulate a rigid hierarchy of needs where a higher-order need only becomes operative once a lower-order need has been satisfied substantially; therefore, in terms of ERG theory, two or even all three needs categories can influence behaviour simultaneously.

● ERG theory also suggests that, should one level of needs remain unsatisfied for a period, the person may regress to a lower-order needs category. Whereas Maslow held that a person will remain fixed on a particular need level until that need has been satisfied, ERG theory postulates that continued frustration of a need may cause an exaggerated desire to have a lower-order need satisfied. For example, a person who does not experience personal growth in his/her job (frustration of the growth needs) may develop an inordinate need to earn a lot of money (an existence need).

Two important inferences can be derived from ERG theory. First, an exaggerated need for something may indicate that the employee is experiencing frustration in satisfying a higher-order need. The implication of this would be that to provide that individual with more of what he/she professes to want may not be enough, since the higher-order need that gave rise to the regression and exaggerated perceived lower-order need will remain unsatisfied. For example, workers' demands for higher salaries may in truth be caused by unsatisfied needs for recognition and/or growth in their jobs. Secondly, needs fulfilment is not a unidimensional process as more than one level of needs can be operative in the same person at the same time. Managers should therefore attend to different levels of needs simultaneously. In other words, needs do not present themselves in a neat, linear, chronological order from lower to higher levels.

11.3.3 Motivation-hygiene theory

Frederick Herzberg investigated the question, "What do people want from their jobs?" From his research Herzberg concluded that all variables that make people feel either good or bad about their jobs can be grouped into one of two factors or categories (hence the appellation "Herzberg's two-factor theory of motivation"). The more *intrinsic* factors, such as achievement, recognition, the work itself, responsibility, growth and advancement, seem to be related to job satisfaction; *extrinsic* factors, such as status, security, company policy, administration, remuneration, supervision, interpersonal relations with subordinates, peers and supervisors and working conditions, on the other hand, tend to be associated with job dissatisfaction. Herzberg suggests that the opposite of satisfaction is not dissatisfaction. Removing dissatisfying aspects (the hygiene factors) from a job does not necessarily make the job satisfying. According to Herzberg, job satisfaction is a function of challenging, stimulating activities or work content (these variables he calls "motivators"). On the other hand, dissatisfaction is a function of the environment, supervision, co-workers and general job context (these he calls "hygiene factors"). The presence of hygiene factors will not lead to a state of job satisfaction but simply to a state of "no dissatisfaction". This in itself is, however, not sufficient to motivate employees; in order to do that, the motivators must also be present. Conversely, for motivators to operate as motivators, the hygiene factors must be present. In other words, hygiene factors are a necessary but insufficient prerequisite for a motivated workforce.

It is only in the fourth quadrant that both hygiene factors and motivators are present, leading to a state of satisfaction and motivation. In the third quadrant, the presence of hygiene factors leads to a state of "no dissatisfaction", which, in the absence of motivators, is in itself insufficient to produce a motivated workforce.

Table 11.2

Herzberg's two-factor theory of motivation*

		Motivators	
		Not present	Present
Hygiene factors	Not present	Dissatisfied **1**	Not satisfied **2**
	Present	Not dissatisied **3**	Satisfied & motivated **4**

*Source: Herzberg, Frederick. 1968. One more time: How do you motivate employees? *Harvard Business Review*, Jan-Feb 1968, 57.

Unfortunately, Herzberg's theory has received scant empirical support, and, most damning of all, other researchers have failed to replicate his results in follow-up studies, leading to the conclusion that the original research results are suspect and/or that the research design was flawed (see Blum & Naylor 1968: 376–378; Korman 1977: 140–143).

11.3.4 The three needs theory

David McClelland (Robbins 1996: 219–222) proposes that the following three basic needs are operative in the workplace.

- **The need for achievement (nAch):** This is the desire to exceed some standard of behaviour; the need to excel; the need to be successful.
- **The need for power (nPow):** The need to make others behave in a way in which they would not otherwise have behaved; the need to control others; to be influential.
- **The need for affiliation (nAff):** The need for warm and close interpersonal relationships; to be liked and accepted by others.

If the above listed needs constitute the totality of needs, it remains for the manager to determine his/her subordinates' dominant need and to offer opportunities whereby the individual's needs and the organisation's goals can simultaneously be met. For example, a person with a high nAff can be placed in a job situation where the need for affiliation can be satisfied. Remember: a good rule of thumb definition of a motivated employee is a person who realises that his/her personal or life goals can be achieved by promoting organisational goals! McClelland's theory holds some interesting implications for the selection of personnel (see point 4 below).

Research undertaken by McClelland and other researchers has revealed the following factors which tend to support his theory.

- People with a **high nAch** prefer the following work situations and will work harder in them than individuals with a low nAch:
  - **Situations of moderate risk:** In situations of low or high risk feelings of achievement are absent.
  - **Situations where knowledge of results is provided:** People with a high nAch want to know whether they have achieved or not; they want feedback.
  - **Situations where individual responsibility is provided:** The high nAch person wants to take personal responsibility for achieving (and also wants to take the credit, of course!).

  Therefore, a person with a high nAch prefers jobs with moderate risk, feedback and personal responsibility. Under these conditions high achievers will be strongly motivated. Since these types of situations are typically present in entrepreneurial roles, it is not surprising that people with a high need to achieve are successful entrepreneurs.
- Interestingly, individuals with a high nAch generally do not make good managers, especially in large organisations. For instance, the hyperenthusiastic salesperson does not generally make a good sales manager.
- The best managers are people with a **high need for power** (nPow) and a **low need for affiliation** (nAff).
- One can think of some jobs which pose interesting contradictions in terms of McClelland's taxonomy of needs. For instance, think of the work of a life insurance representative. To be successful in this job one needs to have a high need to achieve, but in order to be successful one will have to project a caring attitude, which is typically a high nAff attribute! This may explain why retired sport stars are frequently very successful insurance (and other types of) representatives. In order to achieve in sport one presumably needs a high nAch but, especially in team sports, the person's ability to be part of a team (nAff) should be highly developed — exactly the attributes one is looking for in a sales representative!

11.3.5 Goal-setting theory

Edwin Locke suggests that, all other things being equal, people will perform better if they strive towards a definite goal than if they are expected to perform without a specific objective in mind (Robbins 1996: 224–225). Therefore, the crux of this theory is that specific goals operate as powerful motivators in that they tell the individual what needs to be done and how much effort is likely to be required in the process. For example, to give a person an amorphous goal such as "to work harder" is much less likely to motivate the individual than to have him/her work towards a specific goal such as a "20 % increase in units produced next month". All things being equal (such as ability and acceptance of goals,) goal-setting theory postulates that the more difficult the goal, the higher the level of performance, provided that the person believes that he/she is capable of achieving that goal. Other important contingency factors associated with goal-setting theory are the following.

- Persons will perform better when they receive continuous feedback on how well they are progressing towards the goal, because feedback provides information regarding gaps between what they have done so far and what they wish to achieve.
- At present there is little unambiguous, empirical evidence to suggest that goals that have been set by the individual himself/herself enjoy any inherent superiority over goals that have been set by someone else. It has been found, however, that goal-setting by the individual for himself/herself or jointly by the individual and the supervisor will increase the likelihood that the individual will accept the goals as legitimate and be committed to achieving them. In the South African context the latter consideration may be of decisive importance in opting for participative goal-setting rather than unilaterally imposed goals, given our general low levels of trust between management and workers. The failure to gain legitimacy and acceptance of goals by workers may render the fact that workers are capable of achieving these goals irrelevant.
- Goal-setting theory presupposes that the person is *committed* to the goal. Research suggests that commitment is most likely to be present if goals are made public, if the person has an internal locus of control, and when the goals are self-set rather than unilaterally assigned.

11.3.6 Cognitive dissonance theory

A discussion of this theory is included for two reasons: first, it provides explanations for results which cannot be explained by expectancy-value theories (discussed later), and secondly, the theory of Stacey Adams (discussed in section 11.3.7) is an important derivative of the more general cognitive dissonance theory. The general theory of cognitive dissonance was first proposed by Festinger (Korman 1977: 59–63) and is summarised in exhibit G.

Cognitive dissonance theory presumes that, if a person did poorly a number of times in a task, he/she will do poorly again, even if he/she can do better, in order to be consistent with his/her cognitions (self-perception) of incompetency developed in the preceding tasks. Employees with low self-esteem will forfeit the oppor-

Exhibit G

Cognitive dissonance theory

- An individual's cognitions (ideas, attitudes, opinions, etc) may have the following three types of relations to one another.
  - **Consonant:** When cognition A follows from cognition B. For instance, if a person works for an organisation and says (and feels) that that organisation is a good place to work (the cognition of liking the company is consonant with the cognition gained from experience).
  - **Dissonant:** When cognition A does not follow from cognition B. For instance, if the same person says that he/she dislikes working for that organisation.
  - **Irrelevant:** If cognition A has no relation to cognition B. For example, the same person decides to buy himself/herself a cat.
- From the above-listed possible cognitive relations it is postulated that a dissonant set of cognitions constitutes a negative motivational state that the person finds unpleasant and is motivated to reduce. The way in which this negative motivational state can be eliminated is by changing one's cognitions and/or the behaviour leading to these cognitions so that they become consonant.

tunity to achieve in order to be consistent with their self-perceptions. This surprising result is difficult to explain in terms of an expectancy model of motivation. In the words of Korman (1977: 61–66) "If individuals have negative self-cognitions, they need, according to the consistency model, negative outcomes in order to achieve a consistent result, and this is what happens in a good many cases." Korman (1977: 61–66) cites the following findings in support of the latter assertion (references omitted).

- When a person is paid by piecework, his/her productivity will be greater when the piecework rate is perceived as being deserved than when it is regarded as undeserved.
- Women with high self-esteem who want to go to college are more likely to engage in behaviours designed to achieve this goal than women with low self-esteem who want to go to college.
- People who, on the basis of past experience, expect that they will have to do something unpleasant, choose to perform the unpleasant task, even when they could perform a more pleasant one.
- People who, on the basis of past experience, perceive that they are getting a higher piece rate than they deserve, decrease their performance, whereas people who are getting less than they perceive they deserve increase their performance.

One can summarise cognitive dissonance theory by the old saying that "nothing succeeds like success" (and add that "nothing fails like failure"). One obvious managerial implication of the theory is that, if a manager always finds fault with a subordinate's work and accordingly corrects it, this will result in the subordinate's seeking failure since this will be the only outcome consonant with his/her self-perception. In other words, for this individual success will create cognitive dissonance which he/she will be motivated to reduce, and this can be done by failing. Therefore, even if the boss can improve marginally on the subordinate's report for the board, the manager should have the wisdom to allow the report to be submitted to the board, minor warts and all (provided, of course, that it is of an acceptable standard).

11.3.7 Equity theory

Stacey Adams' equity model is an important theory of motivation which has its roots in cognitive dissonance theory. People do not work in a vacuum: they work alongside others and they make comparisons between their perceived efforts and concomitant rewards and the exertions of others and their rewards. Equity theory asserts that the employee compares his/her input-outcome ratio with the input-outcome ratio of relevant others. If these ratios are equal, a state of equity is said to exist. Since the employee perceives the situation to be fair, he/she will not be motivated to change anything. On the other hand, if the input-outcome ratio comparison yields an unequal equation, inequity is said to exist and the individual perceives this to be unfair and is thus motivated to do something to equalise the equation. Inputs, according to Adams, are anything that the person may invest in a task, such as effort, education, time, money. Outcomes are anything he/she might receive, such as money, praise, recognition, etc. The motivational hypothesis is that unequal ratios lead to negative motivational states which the person tries to reduce.

The equity model can be expressed by the equation in exhibit H.

Exhibit H

The equity model
$$\frac{\text{Perception of own inputs}}{\text{Perception of own outcomes}} = \frac{\text{Perception of others' inputs}}{\text{Perception of others' outcomes}}$$

If the depicted equality does not obtain (because the left-hand ratio is either bigger or smaller than the right-hand ratio), inequity and unfairness exist and the person is motivated to restore the equilibrium by either one or more of the following means:

- distorting the perception of one's own or the other's inputs and/or outcomes;
- withdrawing from the situation (for example by resigning from one's job);
- behaving in a certain way so as to cause others to change their inputs and/or outcomes;
- changing one's own actual inputs and/or outcomes; and/or
- changing the comparator (that is, selecting a different person with whom to compare oneself).

There is an impressive body of research that supports predictions of work behaviour based on equity theory. Some of these predictions which have been verified by research are summarised in exhibit I.

Exhibit I

Predictions based on equity theory

- Overpaid employees who are paid for hours worked, will produce more than equitably paid employees (salaried/hourly paid employees will maintain a high quality and/or quantity of production in order to increase the input side of their ratio and so bring about equity).
- Overpaid employees who are paid on a piece-rate basis (that is, per unit produced), will produce fewer but higher quality units than equitably paid employees (employees paid on a piece-rate basis will increase their effort to achieve equity by increasing the quality of their inputs, but they will not increase the number of units produced since this will only increase the inequity; therefore effort is expended in increasing quality rather than quantity).
- Underpaid hourly employees will produce less or their output will be of a poorer quality (inputs will be decreased, which will cause fewer units to be produced or production of a lower quantity, in an effort to decrease the inequitable ratios).
- Underpaid piece-rate employees will increase the quantity of their production, even if this results in the production of a large number of low quality units (the employees reduce the inequity by producing more units and by trading off quantity of output for quality; the increase in their rewards is achieved at little increased effort on their part).

These are indeed interesting findings that suggest that in certain situations the following reward systems could be appropriate.

- **If quantity of output is more important than the quality:** Pay per unit produced (that is, piece-rate reward system) and slightly underpay employees.
- **If quality is more important than quantity:** Employees could be paid either on a piece-rate or an hourly basis, but should be slightly overpaid.

Of course, in reality, things are not quite as simple as the above propositions would suggest. First, remember that outcome can consist of things other than monetary rewards (for example recognition and/or status); secondly, there is the problem of whom the employee chooses as comparator. With regard to the latter, one must also bear in mind the fact that the person may pick himself/herself as his/her own comparator, in which case the individual's present situation will be compared with situations in which he/she had been in the past. This would suggest, inter alia, that it would not be wise to offer a job applicant a smaller salary to do the same work that he did in the past (in his previous employment), even if he/she is desperate to have the job and insists that he/she is prepared to work for less. Inequity would soon come into play when the employee compares his/her present input-outcome ratio with previous ratios. (For instance, during a recession one may be able to employ a highly qualified and experienced retrenched manager for a fraction of what he/she had earned before.) Other things being equal, equity theory would seem to suggest that this course of action would not be prudent because the person would in time perceive the situation to be unfair and might reduce the inequity by reducing output.

One last word about equity theory. Despite the research findings which support this model, most people will recognise intuitively that the absolute value of rewards for performance is pretty meaningless unless one has a standard with which to compare it and that most people tend to seek a comparator. You may be quite happy to do task X for R y until you hear that I am paying another person R y + z for doing the same work. Your unhappiness upon hearing this cannot derive from any reduction in your rewards (there is no question of reducing your income), it can only result from your feeling that, compared with the other person, you are being treated unfairly.

11.3.8 Expectancy theory

Vroom's expectancy theory of motivation holds that the tendency to act in a certain way depends on the strength of the expectation that the act will be followed by a given outcome, and on the degree to which the person desires that outcome. The expectancy theory is illustrated in exhibit J.

Exhibit J

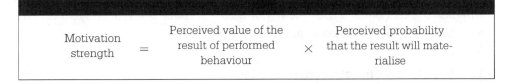

| Motivation strength | = | Perceived value of the result of performed behaviour | × | Perceived probability that the result will materialise |

Motivational strength is therefore dependent on the following three variables.

- **Attractiveness:** The importance that the person attaches to the rewards that can be achieved by performing a task.
- **Performance-reward link:** The degree to which the person believes that performance at a given level will result in the desired outcome.
- **Effort-performance link:** The degree to which the person believes that his/her efforts will lead to the performance necessary to achieve the desired result.

For example: a certain employee may greatly desire a promotion, but may still not be motivated to work hard for any one or more of the following reasons:

- he may believe that, however hard he is capable of working, he will never be able to perform at the level necessary to get the promotion (absence of the individual effort-performance linkage);
- he may believe that he is capable of performing at the required level, but may nevertheless be of the opinion that in the company he works for promotions are

based on whom you know and that he would not be promoted (absence of per-formance-rewards linkage).

It could, of course, also be that the employee's life goal is to start up his own busi-ness and that he does not value the organisational reward (that is, promotion) because he does not think that it will bring him any nearer to achieving his ulti-mate goal of being self-employed.

Once again, the expectancy theory holds some important implications for man-agement, some of which are listed below.

- Set attainable performance standards for employees and provide the necessary support (for example training) to assist them in achieving these standards.
- Ensure that rewards are clearly linked to set performance standards (for example merit increases directly linked to objectively assessed performance).
- Try to ascertain the personal goals of subordinates and to link these to organi-sational rewards. For instance, one may expect that a young workforce would more easily perceive monetary rewards as contributing to personal goals, whereas in the case of an older workforce, security or status needs may be more prominent (the implication being that rewards should be structured to satisfy these needs).

With regard to points 1 and 2 above, it is important to remember that it is not the actual attainability (or the manager's perception of this) that determines the employee's motivation to exert himself/herself: it is the subordinate's perceptions that are important. Therefore, it is crucial that management should ascertain whether workers believe that the performance standards are attainable and that rewards will follow upon performance.

11.3.9 Reinforcement theory

In contrast with goal-setting theory which is a cognitive theory (it postulates that a person directs his/her conduct wilfully and in a purposeful manner towards the achievement of a goal that has been explicitly identified), reinforcement theory is a behavioural approach. Behavioural theories of personality hold that the mental processes that determine behaviour are unfathomable — the human mind is a "black box" in which certain inputs are made which in turn cause certain reac-tions. We can study the relationship between inputs and outputs in an effort to predict and manipulate behaviour, but the mediating processes between these two events (that is, the internal cognitive processes) are not capable of being studied scientifically (and indeed we do not need to concern ourselves with these). In its simplest form reinforcement theory holds that consequences shape subsequent behaviour. This principle is also known as operant conditioning and is most closely associated with the work of BF Skinner. For example, if a worker who has exhibited certain behaviour is rewarded for it, the probability that this behaviour will be repeated increases (the behaviour is "reinforced"). Conversely, behaviour that is not rewarded or that is punished leads to a decrease in the likelihood that this behaviour will be repeated in future (the behaviour is "extinguished"). Without going into any detail it should be noted that withholding rewards for behaviour is not the same as punishing behaviour and that these two types of "negative reinforcement" have different behavioural implications. Suffice it to say that as a general rule it is better to employ strategies that amount to the withholding of rewards than those that amount to punishment. In the work environment performance bonuses can serve as an example of the application of reinforcement theory: if workers exhibit certain behaviour that results in desirable outcomes, that behaviour is rewarded by the payment of monetary rewards. On the other hand, undesirable behaviour is extinguished by withholding the reinforcement (bonuses are not paid). Giving a worker a warning for behaviour that constitutes misconduct could be an example of punishment following behaviour that management wishes to extinguish in the workplace.

Reinforcement or conditioning is undoubtedly an important variable in determining behaviour and can be used to great effect both in and outside the workplace. Space unfortunately prohibits us from going into this fascinating subject in any further detail, save to say that reinforcement and extinguishing of behaviour exert an influence on all of us from the day we are born (and even in the prenatal phase of development) and that the ubiquitous nature of these influences on our subsequent behaviour is frequently the result of unintended responses from those who stand in a relationship of authority to us (such as parents, teachers and supervisors). Thus, it may be useful for managers who are confronted with behavioural problems exhibited by subordinates to reflect on their reactions to these: they may discover that they are themselves partially responsible for this undesirable state of affairs in that they are quite unintentionally reinforcing the inappropriate behaviour!

11.3.10 Theory X and theory Y

Although McGregor's theory is typically regarded as a theory of leadership and is thus also discussed in the next chapter, his theory is included in this chapter because, as was shown in section 11.2, our assumptions about man fundamentally influence our motivational strategies. McGregor's greatest contribution to the study of working man is precisely his focus on the importance of underlying assumptions about man in directing our behaviour towards co-workers, peers and especially subordinates. Douglas McGregor, in his seminal work, *The Human Side of Enterprise* (1960), proposed that managers hold one of two diametrically opposed views of the nature of man and that these implicit philosophies are determinative of managerial style: "Behind every managerial decision or action are assumptions about human nature and human behavior. A few of these are remarkably pervasive" (McGregor 1960: 33).

These two theories are designated as "theory X" and "theory Y" and are also discussed in chapter 12.

Relating McGregor's theory to that of Maslow, it should be apparent that theory X assumes that lower-order needs dominate individuals, whereas theory Y assumes that higher-order needs are prevalently dominant in persons. McGregor himself argued for the adoption of theory Y and therefore proposed ideas such as participative management, responsible and challenging jobs and good group relations as strategies that would optimise employees' motivational levels. Once again, as is the case with Maslow's theory, there is little empirical validation of McGregor's theory, but its singular virtue is that it draws our attention to the fact that our implicit (and frequently unconscious) assumptions of our fellow man direct our behaviour towards others. The following example should be familiar to students. When given the choice between doing an assignment together with another student (and thus sharing the mark for their collective efforts) and submitting an individual assignment, students frequently prefer the latter option. When questioned on their choice they frequently say that they are worried that a partner will not do his/her fair share and that they therefore prefer to rely on their own efforts rather than on those of others, even if only to a limited extent. When it is pointed out that this is a very good example of theory X reasoning, this comes as a complete surprise!

11.4 SOME IMPLICATIONS FOR THE MANAGEMENT OF SUBORDINATE EMPLOYEES

Figure 11.6 provides a graphic summary in which the theories of Maslow, Herzberg, McGregor and Alderfer are compared with one another and with intrinsic versus extrinsic needs (as explained in the discussion of Schein's classification in section 11.2). A few managerial implications are also provided.

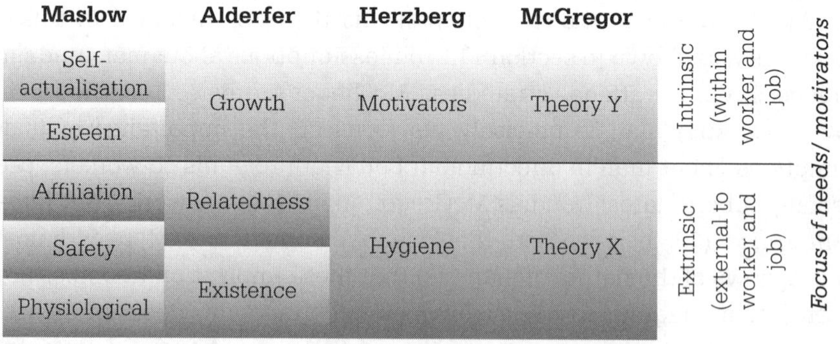

Maslow	Alderfer	Herzberg	McGregor		
Self-actualisation	Growth	Motivators	Theory Y	Intrinsic (within worker and job)	Focus of needs/ motivators
Esteem					
Affiliation	Relatedness			Extrinsic (external to worker and job)	
Safety		Hygiene	Theory X		
Physiological	Existence				

Figure 11.6

Comparison between the theories of Maslow, Herzberg, McGregor and Alderfer

In this chapter some of the best known and important theories of motivation were discussed and compared. But what are some of the general overall implications for managers? Some implications associated with specific theories have already been pointed out. Without discussing this in any further detail, the following pointers for managing people can be inferred from the various theories discussed (Robbins 1994: 56–58):

- Recognise individual differences in employees.
- Place people in jobs which suit their personalities.
- Set specific goals for employees.
- Provide employees with immediate feedback on how they are performing.
- Ensure that employees perceive goals as attainable.
- Individualise rewards in recognition of the fact that employees have different needs and are therefore motivated by different types of rewards.
- Link rewards clearly to performance.
- Ensure that the principle of internal equity is honoured in the company's reward system.
- Although the modern trend is to place great emphasis on "intrinsic motivators", one should not forget the fact that most people work for money and that one's system of monetary rewards therefore remains of the greatest importance. As Robbins (1994: 44) has pointed out:

  "Maybe the best case for 'money as a motivator' is a recent review of eighty studies evaluating motivational methods and their impacts on employee productivity. Goal setting alone produced, on average, a 16 percent increase in productivity; efforts to redesign jobs in order to make them more interesting and challenging yielded 8 to 16 percent increases; employee participation in decision making produced a median increase of less than one percent; while monetary incentives led to an average increase of 30 percent." In figure 11.7 this research finding is illustrated.

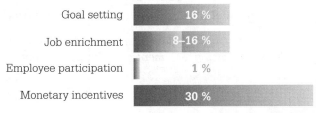

Goal setting	16 %
Job enrichment	8–16 %
Employee participation	1 %
Monetary incentives	30 %

Increase in employee productivity

Figure 11.7
Effectiveness of motivators

- Always remember that motivation theories are culture bound. Especially in South Africa, with our great cultural and ethnic diversity, a manager from one group will assume at his/her own risk that what he/she regards as self-evident motivators also hold for his/her subordinates, especially if they are from another cultural or ethnic group. Many of these theories assume the presence of universal variables, such as the so-called Protestant Work Ethic and the individualistic concept of man that is so prevalent in Western society. For example, Morris (1996: 235–236) points out that in Japan, Greece and Mexico security needs would be placed at the top of Maslow's hierarchy of needs. It may well be that in the African context socialisation needs would occupy a different position from that proposed by Maslow. These uncertainties regarding the applicability of foreign theories of motivation in South Africa once again underscore the need for local scientific research to develop and validate theories of motivation applicable to our national culture and circumstances. This is, of course, not to imply that there are not any cross-cultural consistencies; the point is that we, as South African managers, simply do not know!

11.5 CONCLUSION

In conclusion, research has revealed some interesting comparisons between the ability of various motivational theories to explain and predict outcomes on four important organisational variables (namely: productivity, absenteeism, labour turnover and job satisfaction) which are commonly believed to be dependent on levels of motivation. The results of these comparisons are shown in table 11.3 (Robbins 1996: 237). For the purposes of table 11.3 the theories are grouped together as follows: "need" refers to those theories that focus on needs, namely Maslow's hierarchy, Herzberg's motivation-hygiene theory, Alderfer's ERG theory and McClelland's needs theory; "goal-setting" refers to Locke's theory; "reinforcement" refers to "cognitive dissonance theory" and "equity" refers to Stacey Adams' theory.

Table 11.3
Power[1] of motivational theories to explain and predict*

Variable	Need	Goal-setting	Reinforcement	Equity	Expectancy
Productivity	3[2]	5	3	3	4[3]
Absenteeism			4	4	4
Turnover				4	5
Satisfaction	2			2	

[1]Theories are rated on a scale of 1–5 (five being highest).

[2]Applies to individuals with a high need to achieve.

[3]Limited value in jobs where employees have little discretionary choice/

*Source: Based on Landy, FJ & Becker, W S. 1978. Motivation theory reconsidered. In *Research in Organizational Behaviour*, eds LL Cummings & BW Staw, vol 9, 33. Greenwich, CT: JAI Press

It is therefore essential to have knowledge of various theoretical perspectives concerning the motivation of people in the context of the work environment. It is not advisable to regard any single theory as most or least correct. Rather — one should study all theories and learn by trial-and-error in practice. The fact that all of us, managers included, tend to adopt that theory that is most congenial to our own personalities, also indicates the necessity of preferring an eclectic approach, rather than promoting one specific theory of motivation.

SELF-EVALUATION QUESTIONS

1. Explain how our assumptions about people and motivation can hold implications for the ways in which we manage people in employment situations.
2. Differentiate between the basic assumptions underlying Edgar Schein's "rational economic man" and "social man" theories.
3. List and briefly describe the content theories of motivation as discussed in this chapter.
4. Explain briefly Stacey Adams' cognitive dissonance theory of motivation as well as his equity theory. Also evaluate the potential implications thereof for South African managers, specifically keeping in mind South Africa's challenges with regard to affirmative action.
5. Write an essay on the following topic: "Motivating employees in South African organisations: An evaluation of the nature, relevance and value of different motivational theories."

BIBLIOGRAPHY

Blum, ML & Naylor, JC. 1968. *Industrial Psychology: Theoretical and Social Foundations.* New York: Harper & Row Publishers

Certo, SC. 1994 *Modern Management: Diversity, Quality, Ethics and the Global Environment,* 6 ed. Boston: Allyn & Bacon

Korman, AK. 1979. *Organizational Behaviour.* Englewood Cliffs, New Jersey: Prentice-Hall, Inc

McGregor, D. 1960. *The Human Side of Enterprise.* New York: McGraw-Hill Brook Company, Inc.

Robbins, SP. 1994. *Essentials of Organizational Behavior,* 4 ed. New Jersey: Prentice-Hall, Inc

Robbins, SP. 1996. *Organizational Behavior,* 7 ed. Englewood Cliffs, New Jersey: Prentice-Hall Inc

Schein, EH. 1972. *Organizational Psychology,* 2 ed. Englewood Cliffs, New Jersey: Prentice-Hall, Inc

STUDY OBJECTIVES

After studying this chapter, you should be able to:

- describe the general nature of leadership in organisations;
- explain the early or industrial approaches to leadership;
- discuss the postindustrial approaches to leadership;
- describe business leadership;
- identify and explain contemporary issues in leadership;
- debate the leadership challenges facing South Africa.

12.1 INTRODUCTION

All employees in an organisation need to be led in some or other way. Once they are employed, their behaviour and actions have to be channelled and directed towards the achievement of the organisation's objectives. This calls for leadership.

Throughout the twentieth century the concept *leadership* has been attributed with a variety of meanings. Over the past eighty years, more than 3 000 studies concerning leadership have been conducted. Some of the most heavily researched populations are students, military personnel, and business people. This research has yielded a small number of theories concerning the behaviours that distinguish between effective and ineffective leaders. While none of these theories is definitive, there is solid empirical evidence in support of each of them.

However, according to House (1993), current research findings and theories are not very helpful in the design of educational programmes for potential leaders of diverse ethnic groups, or of international organisations, or for those who will be interacting with individuals from nations and cultures other than the United States; this is because we have little knowledge of the diverse demands placed on leaders in cultures other than the North American culture. Almost all of the prevailing theories of leadership, (and about 98 % of the empirical evidence available) is distinctly North American in character: individualistic rather than collectivistic; emphasising assumptions of rationality rather than ascetics, religion, or superstition; stated in terms of individual rather than group incentives, stressing follower responsibilities rather than rights; assuming hedonistic rather than altruistic motivation; and assuming centrality of work and democratic value orientation.

Given the increased globalisation of markets, and the increased interdependence of nations over the past two decades, there is a significant need for a better understanding of cultural influences on leader behaviour and effectiveness. This chapter therefore not only focuses on traditional leadership research and theory, but also on more contemporary issues such as diversity's influence on leadership.

House (1993) has analysed a number of American textbook leadership definitions and has come to this conclusion:

> "Despite the fact that all (of the above) definitions come from US scholars, they vary in terms of emphasis on leader abilities, personality traits, influence or power relationships, perceptions of followers versus communication of leaders, cognitive versus emotional orientation, individual versus group orientation, and appeal to self versus collective interests."

He argues that, if leadership is defined in such a varied way within the United States culture, it will surely be defined in different ways across cultures. He then lists some interesting examples of how different cultures see leadership.

- The Dutch culture places emphasis on an egalitarian society and is sceptical about the value of leadership. Terms like leader and manager carry a stigma. If a father is employed as a manager, Dutch children will not admit it to their schoolmates.
- The Arabs worship their leaders — as long as they are in power!
- The Iranians seek power and strength in their leaders.
- The Oriental leader is expected to behave in a manner that is humble, modest and dignified, and to speak infrequently and only on critical occasions.
- The French appreciate two kinds of leaders: De Gaulle and Mitterand are examples. De Gaulle is an example of a strong charismatic leader, while Mitterand is an example of a consensus builder, coalition former and effective negotiator.
- The Americans appreciate two kinds of leaders. They seek empowerment from a leader who grants autonomy and delegates with confidence. They also respect the bold, forceful, confident and risk-taking leader as personified by John Wayne and the robber barons.

Booysen and Van Wyk (1994) analysed focus group discussions carried out involving 430 first-year Unisa Masters of Business Leadership degree students and twenty middle managers in South Africa, and came up with distinct definitions of an effective leader in the South African context (see exhibit A).

Given that there is no consensually agreed upon definition of leadership, and given that cultural-semantic and evaluative interpretations of leadership vary widely, leadership can be defined differentially according the culture studied, and the type of preferred leadership can vary across culture and over time and within different contexts.

Exhibit A

The effective leader: a South African view

- A leader is an accepted person who displays a natural ability in a given situation to inspire others to willingly follow an ideal or vision.
- A leader is a person who leads followers to believe in themselves, their own strengths, abilities and worth, who inspires followers to commitment, motivation and self-confidence.
- A leader is a person who is capable of paradigm shifts, who takes risks, is a facilitator of people and empowers people, and who is perceived to be a trustworthy person with high moral values.

Robbins (1996) states that there are almost as many definitions of leadership as there are persons who have attempted to define the concept. He continues by giving a very broad definition of leadership, one that encompasses most of the current approaches to the subject: *"Leadership is the ability to influence a group toward the achievement of goals."* Kreitner and Kinicki (1993) give a more specific definition by stating ". . . leadership is . . . a social influence process in which the leader seeks the voluntary participation of subordinates in an effort to reach organizational goals".

This chapter provides a brief overview of existing leadership theory and the perennial debate of leadership versus management. The concept *business leadership* is also examined, after which new emerging trends and contemporary issues in leadership are discussed.

12.2 EARLY APPROACHES TO LEADERSHIP

12.2.1 The trait theories

The earliest research conducted on the concept of leadership found that great leaders possess a unique set of qualities or traits that distinguish effective leaders from non-leaders. Until the late 1940s theorists concentrated on identifying the traits associated with leadership in an effort to develop a universal set of characteristics common to all leaders. The media usually describe leaders in terms of the trait theory: Margaret Thatcher is usually described as confident, iron-willed, determined, and decisive. Nelson Mandela, on the other hand, is described as charismatic, courageous, diplomatic, democratic and calm.

Rost and Smith (1992) assert that conceptions of leadership based purely on individual differences began to fall out of vogue in the late 1940s and 1950s, primarily as a result of two major reviews of the leader trait literature by Stogill (1948) and Mann (1959). These researchers concluded that no single trait or constellation of traits clearly and consistently differentiates leaders from non-leaders. Robbins (1996) argues that the main reasons why this approach did not prove to be successful in explaining leadership are the following:

- it overlooks the needs of the followers;
- it generally fails to clarify the relative importance of various traits;
- it does not separate cause from effect (for example, are leaders self-confident or does success as a leader build self-confidence?); and
- it is difficult to specify traits without taking situational factors into account.

In recent years there has been a distinct re-emergence of interest in individual differences research, most significantly as it applies to understanding leaders' performance. Researchers are now attempting to identify the set of traits that people implicitly refer to when they characterise someone as a leader. Robbins (1996) argues that this line of thinking proposes that leadership is as much style — projecting the appearance of being a leader — as it is substance.

Table 12.1 provides a summary of some of the research findings in this field.

Table 12.1

*Leadership traits and skills**

Personality	Abilities and intelligence
<ul><li>Adaptability</li><li>Alertness</li><li>Ambition</li><li>Independent</li><li>Assertive</li><li>Responsible</li><li>Persuasive</li><li>Organised</li><li>Dependable</li><li>Energetic</li><li>Persistent</li><li>Self-confident</li><li>Tolerant of stress</li><li>Emotional stability</li><li>Honesty and integrity</li></ul>	<ul><li>Ability to enlist cooperation, and to cooperate</li><li>Interpersonally skilled</li><li>Diplomatic and tactful</li><li>Socially skilled</li><li>Fluency in speech</li><li>Good judgement and concept formation</li><li>Creativity</li><li>Decisiveness</li><li>Knowledgeable</li><li>Courage</li><li>Competence</li></ul>

*Source: Adapted from Darling (1992); Kreitner & Kinicki (1993); Greenberg & Baron (1993); and Robbins (1996)

12.2.2 Behavioural theories

Several alternative approaches to leadership emerged in line with the behavioural movement in the late 1950s. The first of these approaches was the move to delineate characteristic patterns or styles of leadership behaviour such as Lewin's (1939) "Three Classic Styles of Leader Behaviour", the "Michigan and Ohio State Studies", and the managerial grid of Blake and Mouton (1964).

Table 12.2 summarises Lewin's three classical styles of leader behaviour.

The Michigan studies defined job-centred and employee-centred leadership as opposite ends of a single leadership continuum. A leader could exhibit either one of these two behaviours, but not both.

Table 12.2

Lewin's three classical styles of leadership*

	Authoritarian	Democratic	Laissez-faire
Nature	• Leader retains all authority and responsibility • Leader assigns people to clearly defined tasks • Primarily a downward flow of communication	• Leader delegates a great deal of authority, while retaining ultimate responsibility • Work is divided and assigned on the basis of participatory decision making • Active two-way flow of upward and downward communication	• Leader denies responsibility and abdicates authority to group • Group members are told to work things out themselves and to do the best they can • Primarily horizontal communication among peers
Primary strength	• Stresses prompt, orderly, and predictable performance	• Enhances personal commitment through participation	• Permits self-starters to do things as they see fit without leader interference
Primary weakness	• Approach tends to stifle individual initiative	• Democratic process is time-consuming	• Group may drift aimlessly in the absence of direction from leader

*Source: Kreitner & Kinicki (1993)

The Ohio State leadership studies defined consideration and initiating structure behaviours as independent dimensions of leadership, for example low or high consideration behaviour and low or high initiating structure behaviour. These dimensions are set out in figure 12.1.

The managerial/leadership grid was developed by Blake and Mouton, and evaluates leader behaviour along two dimensions, namely concern for production and concern for people, which essentially represent the Ohio State dimensions of consideration and initiating structure or the Michigan dimensions of employee-centred and job-centred. It also suggests that effective leadership styles include high levels of both behaviours (see figure 12.2).

The grid has nine possible positions along each axis, creating eighty-one different positions in which the leader's style may fall. Based on the findings of Blake and Mouton, managers were found to perform best under a 9,9 style, as contrasted, for example with a 9,1 (authority type) or 1,9 (country club) style.

The grid, like the other behavioural theories of leadership, offers a better framework for conceptualising leadership styles rather than presenting tangible new information to clarify the leadership quandary, since there is little substantial evidence to support the conclusion that one style is most effective in all situations.

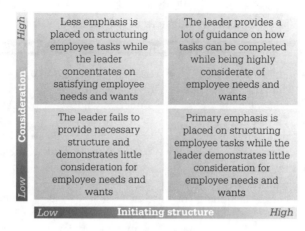

Figure 12.1

Four leadership styles derived from the Ohio State studies

Source:Kreitner & Kinicki (1993)

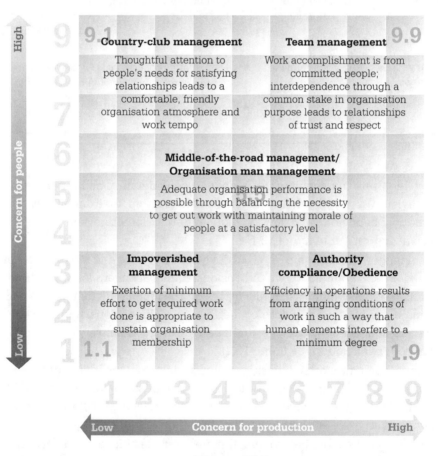

Figure 12.2

The leadership grid

Source: Adapted from Kreitner & Kinicki (1993) and Robbins (1996)

Hersey and Blanchard (1992) support the contention that there is no one best leadership style, and point out that successful and effective leaders are able to adapt their style to fit the requirements of the situation.

12.2.3 Contingency theories

A third school of thought focuses on situational factors that determine the pattern of leadership. This approach assumes that effective leadership depends on the particular situation and involves a fit between personality, task, power, attitudes and perceptions. Effective managers diagnose the situation, identify the leadership style that will be most effective, and then determine whether they can implement the required style. Gordon (1993) argues that early situational research suggested that subordinate, supervisor and task considerations affect the appropriate leadership style in a given situation. Variants of this approach emphasised situational contingencies that constrained or heightened the operations of particular individual qualities and leadership styles.

12.2.3.1 McGregor's theory X and theory Y formulation

You have already encountered this theory in the previous chapter. As explained, according to theory X and theory Y, leadership styles are based on the individual's assumptions about other individuals, together with characteristics of the individual, the task, the organisation and the environment. McGregor compiled two sets of assumptions which leaders may have concerning employees and which may affect the leader's behaviour towards subordinates. These two sets of assumptions are summarised in table 12.3.

Table 12.3
Theory X and theory Y assumptions*

Theory X assumptions	Theory Y assumptions
• People are inherently lazy, and will avoid work if possible	• People are not inherently lazy and mental or physical effort associated with work is as natural as relaxation.
• People are extrinsically motivated and rate security above any other need.	• People are intrinsically motivated and seeks self-actualisation
• People are incapable of self-discipline and self-control, prefer to be controlled and avoid responsibility, and have little ambition.	• People exert self-control and seek responsibility
• Most people have limited creativity when solving organisational problems.	• Creativity in the solving of organisational problems is a general phenomenon.

*Source: Adapted from Robbins (1996)

12.2.3.2 Fiedler's contingency model

Fiedler's theory proposes that effective group performance depends on the proper match between the leader's style of interacting with his or her subordinates and the favourableness of the situation or, in other words, the degree to which situations give control and influence to the leader. Fiedler suggests that leaders have a natural tendency towards either a task-oriented or a relationship-oriented leadership style. He developed a measuring instrument called "least preferred co-worker", which purports to measure whether a person is task or relationship oriented. He argues further that, because of this natural tendency towards a specific style, an individual leader's style is rather inflexible and difficult to change, but that organisations must put individuals in situations that fit with their style. From this assumption it also follows that if a given situation requires a task-oriented leader and the person in the leadership position is relationship oriented, either the situation has to be modified or the leader removed and replaced if optimum effectiveness is to be achieved.

Fiedler also identified three situational factors or contingency dimensions in the organisation that influence the favourableness of the situation, which in turn influences the effectiveness of the leader, namely *leader-member relations*, *task structure* and *position power*.

- The *leader-member relationship* can be either good or poor, and depends on factors such as the degree of confidence, trust and respect subordinates have in their leader.
- *Task-structure* can be either high or low and depends on whether the task is relatively structured or unstructured.
- *Position power* can be either strong or weak and depends on the degree of influence the leader has over rewards (such as promotion and salary increases) or punishments (such as disciplinary steps).

After a person's leadership style and the favourableness of situations have been identified, it is necessary to match the leader with the situation to achieve maximum leadership effectiveness.

Robbins (1996) has examined Fiedler's research on 1200 groups in which he compared relationship- versus task-oriented leadership styles in each of the eight situational categories. Fiedler concluded that task-oriented leaders tend to perform better in situations that are very favourable to them and in situations that are very unfavourable to them. Relationship-oriented leaders, however, perform better in moderately favourable situations. Fiedler's research findings are summarised in figure 12.3.

Fiedler's model in essence concerns the fit between leader and situation, but because he sees leadership style as fixed, there are only two ways to fit the leader and the situation — either by selecting the right leader for a given situation or by changing the situation to fit the leader. Cherrington (1994) points out that, rather than changing the leader to fit the situation, Fiedler recommends changing the situation to fit the leader through what he calls *job engineering*. Job engineering consists of changing one or more of the situational factors to increase or decrease the favourability of the situation.

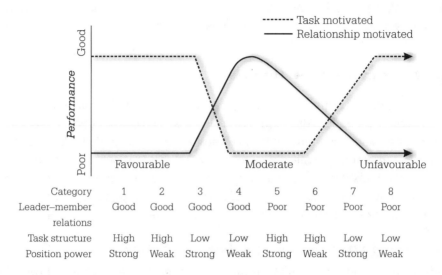

Figure 12.3

Findings from Fiedler model

Source: Robbins (1996: 423) and Cherrington (1994: 641)

12.2.3.3 The revised Vroom-Jetton-Jago leadership-participation model

The leadership-participation model of Vroom-Jetton-Jago is both a decision-making model and a theory of leadership. It provides a set of rules to determine the form and amount of participative decision making in different situations. To be able to handle different situations the model identifies five leadership or decision-making styles on a continuum from autocratic, through consultative, to group decision making, along with a series of diagnostic questions on contingency variables, which are answered on a five-point scale, to determine which style is most appropriate. The five leadership/decision-making styles can be described as follows.

● The leader decides alone without soliciting any input from members.

● The leader decides alone after obtaining the necessary information from members.

● The leader makes the decision after consulting with group members individually. The leader shares the problem with them and obtains information, ideas, suggested alternatives, and evaluation.

● The leader makes the decision after meeting with the members as a group to collect their information, ideas, suggested alternatives, and evaluation.

● The leader and members arrive at a group decision through consensus decision making. The leader may chair the group, but is simply one of the group and does not try to influence the group to adopt a particular solution.

This model assumes that leadership behaviour is flexible, that no single leadership style is appropriate for all situations and furthermore that leader behaviour must adjust to reflect the task structure. Robbins (1996: 431) argues that, according to this model, it probably makes more sense to refer to autocratic and participative *situations* than to autocratic and participative *leaders*.

12.2.4 The transactional theories

From the late 1970s until the mid-eighties a transactional approach was adopted by leadership theorists. Although it was also based on contingencies, the emphasis was on the social exchange occurring between leaders and followers. As a result, increased importance was given to followers' perceptions of leaders and their behaviour. Subsequent extensions of the social exchange or transactional approach have emphasised the role of leaders in elevating the motivation, competence, and collective responsibilities of their followers.

12.2.4.1 The situational theory of Hersey and Blanchard

Hersey and Blanchard's (1982) situational theory focuses on the follower. It proposes that effective leader behaviour depends on the readiness or maturity level of the leader's followers. Readiness is defined as the extent to which a follower possesses the *ability* and *willingness* to complete a task. The emphasis on the followers in this leadership theory reflects the reality that it is they who either accept or reject the leader. Regardless of what the leader does, effectiveness depends on the actions of his/her followers. Robbins points out that this is an important dimension that has been overlooked or underemphasised in most earlier leadership theories.

Situational leadership uses the same two leadership dimensions that Fiedler identified: task and relationship behaviours. However, Hersey and Blanchard go a step further by considering each as either high or low and then combining them into the following four specific leader behaviours.

- **Telling** (high task-low relationship). The leader defines roles and tells people what, how, when, and where to do various tasks. Directive behaviour is emphasised.
- **Selling** (high task-high relationship). The leader provides both directive and supportive behaviour.
- **Participating** (low task-high relationship). The leader and follower share in decision making, with the main role of the leader being facilitating and communicating.
- **Delegating** (low task-low relationship). The leader provides little direction or support.

The final component in Hersey and Blanchard's theory is defining four stages of follower readiness.

- People are both unable and unwilling to take responsibility to do something. They are neither competent nor confident.
- People are unable but willing to do the necessary job tasks. They are motivated, but currently lack the appropriate skills.
- People are able but unwilling to do what the leader wants.
- People are both able and willing to do what is asked of them.

The situational theory of leadership is summarised in figure 12.4.

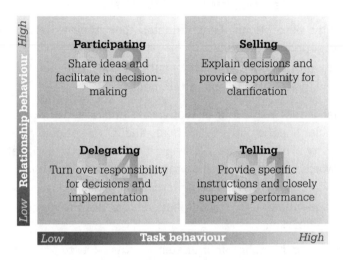

Figure 12.4

Situational leadership behaviour

Source: Kreitner & Kinicki (1993) & Robbins (1996)

Figure 12.4 integrates the various components and suggests that as the followers mature, they may require different styles of leadership from their managers. Inexperienced subordinates may require a high level of structuring by their leaders. Those who are moderately mature may require a high level of social and emotional support (showing consideration). However, those who are fully mature may require low levels of both types of behaviour on the part of their leaders.

Actually there is a high similarity between Hersey and Blanchard's four leadership styles and the four extreme corners in Blake and Mouton's managerial grid. The telling style equates to the 9,1 leader, selling equals 9,9, participating is equivalent to 1,9 and delegating is the same as the 1,1 leader. Hersey and Blanchard (1993), however, claim that the grid emphasises concern for production and people, which are attitudinal dimensions, whereas situational leadership, in contrast, emphasises task and relationship behaviour. Robbins argues that, despite Hersey and Blanchard's claim, it is a pretty small difference, and the question can very well be asked whether situational leadership is then not merely the managerial grid with one major difference — the replacement of the 9,9 contention — one style for all occasions — with the recommendation that the "right" style should align with the readiness of the followers.

12.2.4.2 House's path-goal theory

The path-goal theory is a situational theory developed by Robert House (Robbins 1996). This theory extracts key elements from the Ohio State leadership research on initiating structure and consideration, and the expectancy theory of motivation. The theory explains how leaders can facilitate task performance by showing subordinates how their performance can be instrumental in achieving desired rewards or goals.

Essentially this theory explains what leaders should do to:

- influence the perceptions of subordinates about their work, through coaching, guidance, support or rewards;
- identify important personal goals for subordinates; and
- clarify the various paths to goal attainment.

It claims that leader behaviour is motivating and satisfying or accepted to the extent that it clarifies the paths to the goals and increases goal attainment. House has identified two basic leader behaviours, namely path clarification and gatekeeper of rewards, (that is, increasing the number of rewards available to subordinates by being supportive and looking after their needs).

House has identified four distinct leadership styles that enable leaders to perform these two functions.

- *Directive leadership* tells subordinates what is expected of them and provides specific guidance, standards, and schedules of work.
- *Supportive leadership* treats subordinates as equals and shows concern for their wellbeing, status, and personal needs, and seeks to develop pleasant interpersonal relationships among group members.
- *Achievement-oriented leadership* sets challenging goals, expects subordinates to perform at their highest level, and continually seeks improvement in performance.
- *Participative leadership* means consulting with subordinates and using their suggestions and ideas in decision making.

Unlike Fiedler's model, which implies that leadership style is resistant to change, the path-goal theory maintains that the four styles of leadership can be displayed by one manager at different times in different situations; for example, if a directive leader discovers that the situation has changed and now requires a participative style, it is possible to change.

Cherrington (1994) points out that a fifth leadership style, the punitive leader, ought to be added to this theory. He argues that the path-goal model focuses almost exclusively on the leader's ability to administer positive reinforcement and ignores the powerful impact of carefully administered punishment.

Although the path-goal theory does not explain how to identify the appropriate leadership style, the theory does identify two types of situational factors: *subordinate contingency factors,* which include locus of control, authoritarianism and abilities, and *environmental contingency factors,* which include the nature of the task, the formal authority system within the organisation, and the group norms and dynamics that need to be considered.

12.2.4.3 Evaluation of transactional leadership theories

The transactional leadership theories emphasise the transactions between leaders and their followers. Transactional leaders manage the transactions between the organisation and its members; they get things done by giving contingent rewards, such as recognition, pay increases, and advancement for employees who perform well. Transactional leaders usually use the management by exception principle to monitor the performance of employees and take corrective action when performance deviates from standards. Leaders of this kind guide or motivate their followers in the direction of established goals by clarifying role and task requirements.

The main characteristics of transactional leadership are summarised in exhibit B.

Exhibit B

> **The main characteristics of transactional leadership**
>
> - The main concern is with the accomplishment of organisational goals in the short term.
> - These leaders are good at defining and communicating the work that must be done.
> - They make clear the rewards for expected performance.
> - They practise situational leadership.
> - They understand the strengths and the weaknesses of their subordinates.
> - They are effective at maintaining the status quo.

There is, however, another kind of leader who inspires followers to be committed to the organisation, to transcend their own interests for the good of the organisation, by focusing on employees' changing attitudes and assumptions. Leadership theories focusing on this kind of leadership are discussed in section 12.3 below.

12.3 A POSTINDUSTRIAL APPROACH TO LEADERSHIP

Rost and Smith (1992) propose that in order to understand the concept of leadership, leadership theory must move away from the industrial school of leadership, which is noted for emphasising what is peripheral to the nature and content of leadership. These peripheral aspects are issues such as traits, personality characteristics, nature or nurture, greatness, group facilitation, goal attainment, effectiveness, contingencies, situations, goodness, style and, above all, how to manage an organisation better.

In the book *Leadership for the Twenty-first Century,* Rost and Smith (1992) give a new definition of leadership:

"Leadership is an influence relationship among leaders and followers who intend real changes that reflect the purposes mutually held by both leaders and followers."

This section therefore centres on relatively more recent approaches that do in fact look at the leadership/follower relationship, emphasising interactions and mutual aims. More recent literature highlighting the latest approaches to leadership includes the work of, for example, Darling (1992); Greenberg & Baron (1993); Hersey & Blanchard (1993); Kreitner & Kinicki (1993); Moorhead & Griffins (1992); Nanus (1992); Robbins (1993, 1996); and Rost & Smith (1992).

12.3.1 Charismatic leadership

The charismatic leadership theory emerged in the late 1980s and is an extension of the attribution theory; like the trait theories, it assumes that charisma is an individual characteristic of the leader. Although traits may well play a role in charismatic leadership, there is a growing belief that it makes more sense to view such leadership as involving a special type of relationship with followers.

Several studies have been conducted to identify the personal characteristics of the charismatic leader; one very comprehensive analysis in this regard is the study undertaken by Conger and Kanungo (1988). Conger and Kanungo propose that charismatic leaders possess the characteristics, set out in exhibit C.

Exhibit C

Key characteristics of charismatic leaders*

Charismatic leaders:
- have an idealised goal or vision that they want to achieve;
- have a strong personal commitment to their goal;
- are perceived as unconventional;
- are assertive and self-confident; and
- are perceived as agents of radical change, rather than as managers of the status quo.

The charismatic leader has the following relationship with his/her followers.
- The leader has a strong need to influence his/her followers.
- The leader communicates high expectations about follower performance.
- The leader expresses confidence in followers.
- The followers trust the correctness of the leader's beliefs.
- The followers' beliefs are similar to the leader's beliefs.
- The followers accept the leader unquestioningly.
- The followers feel affection for the leader.
- The followers obey the leader willingly, in other words, they are motivated.
- The followers have an emotional involvement in the organisation's mission.
- The followers have heightened performance goals.
- The followers believe that they can contribute to the success of the group's mission.

*Source: Conger and Kanungo (1988)

Charismatic leadership may not always be needed to achieve high levels of employee performance. It may be most appropriate when the follower's task has an ideological component. That is why charismatic leaders are most likely to emerge when an organisation is introducing a radically new product or facing a life-threatening crisis — in other words, in times of dramatic change.

Gordon (1993) points out that there will, however, also be a dark side to charismatic leadership, if the leader overemphasises devotion to him- or herself, makes personal needs paramount or uses highly effective communication skills to mislead or manipulate others. Such leaders may be so driven to achieve their own vision that they ignore the costly implications of their goals.

12.3.2 Transformational leadership

Transformational leadership emerged in the 1990s and is closely related to charismatic leadership. Transformational leadership is the set of abilities that allows the leader to recognise the need for change, to create a vision to guide that change, and to execute the change effectively. This type of leader can influence in every direction — downward with subordinates, laterally with colleagues, upward with superiors, and outward with clients and customers. Thus, transformational leaders can change the culture of the organisation.

Transformational leaders are also charismatic and possess all the above-mentioned characteristics associated with charismatic leaders, but they have got more than charisma. Avolio and Bass (in Robbins 1993) describe the difference between these two leaders as follows:

> "The charismatic leader may want followers to adopt the charismatic's world view and go no further; the transformational leader will attempt to instill in followers the ability to question not only established views but eventually those established by the leader."

From this it follows that the transformational leader empowers followers. Charismatic leadership, which results in compliance, keeps followers dependent on the leader. Transformational leadership is aimed at creating follower independence.

Apart from being charismatic, transformational leaders also have the following characteristics:

- they identify themselves as change agents;
- they are value-driven;
- they believe in people;
- they take risks and are courageous individuals;
- they have the ability to deal with:
  - complexity;
  - ambiguity; and
  - uncertainty;
- they are life-long learners;

- they engage in impression management — using tactics and techniques designed to enhance their attractiveness and appeal to others;
- they are visionaries, and engage in framing — defining their vision or purpose in a way that gives meaning and purpose to whatever actions they are requesting from followers.

It is clear from the above characteristics that their influence does not stem from the possession of semi-magical traits, but is rather a logical result of a complex cluster of behaviours and techniques.

Exhibit D lists the differences between transactional and transformational leadership.

Exhibit D

Transactional and transformational leaders — a comparison*
Transactional leader
• Establishes goals and objectives
• Designs workflow and delegates task assignments
• Negotiates exchange of rewards for effort
• Rewards performance and recognises accomplishments
• Searches for deviations from standards and takes corrective actions
• Contingent reward: Contracts exchange of rewards for effort, promises rewards for good performance, recognises accomplishments
• Management by exception (active): Watches and searches for deviations from rules and standards, takes corrective action
• Management by exception (passive): Intervenes only if standards are not met
• Laissez-faire: Abdicates responsibilities, avoids making decisions
Transformational leader
• Charismatic: Provides vision and a sense of mission, gains respect and trust, instills pride
• Individualised consideration: Gives personal attention, and treats each person individually, coaches
• Intellectually stimulating: Promotes learning, encourages rationality, uses careful problem solving
• Inspirational: Communicates high performance expectations, uses symbols to focus efforts, distils essential purposes

*Source: Adapted from Cherrington (1994) and Robbins (1996)

The industrial (transactional) and postindustrial (transformational) leadership views should not, however, be seen as opposing approaches to getting things done. Transformational leadership is built on top of transactional leadership.

Exhibit E compares the industrial and postindustrial views on leadership as identified by Rost and Smith (1992).

Exhibit E

The traditional vs the emerging view on leadership	
• Good management • Leader behaviour/traits • Comply with the leader's wishes • Pursue any organisational goals • Use any legitimate behaviours	• Process distinct from management • Leaders and followers interacting in a relationship • Do what both leaders and followers wish • Pursue proposals that intend real change • Use influence

From exhibit E it is clear that there is a paradigm shift. In the emerging, postindustrial view, leadership now appears to be:

- a process distinct from management;
- a process in which other people besides managers can be leaders;
- a relationship in which the focus is on the interactions of both leaders and followers, instead of focusing on only the behaviours and/or traits of the leader;
- a relationship that aims at mutual purposes rather than at just those of the leader;
- a process in which people intend real changes as opposed to a process in which they achieve any goal; and
- a relationship in which only influence behaviours are acceptable rather than one wherein all legitimate behaviours (authority and other forms of coercion included) are acceptable.

In a way transactional leadership can be compared to good management and transformational leadership to good leadership — and we need both in organisations. This distinction brings us to the perennial debate of leadership versus management.

12.4 MANAGEMENT AND LEADERSHIP

The debate concerning management versus leadership continues to rage. Darling (1992) and Capowski (1994) for instance, point out that the primary factor which prevents organisations from growing and changing is that they tend to be overmanaged and underled.

It is argued that managers within these organisations may excel in handling the daily routine, yet never question whether that routine should be followed at all. From such a perspective there is a profound difference between management and leadership.

Darling asserts that to manage means to bring about, to accomplish, to have charge of or responsibility for, or to conduct. Thus, the activities involved in mastering routines facilitate effectiveness as a manager. Leading involves influencing, guiding in direction, course, action, opinion. Thus, activities of vision and judgement facilitate our effectiveness as leaders.

Exhibit F summarises the differences between managers and leaders as identified by Darling (1992) and Nanus (1992).

Exhibit F

Management vs leadership*	
A manager:	*A leader:*
• Administers	• Innovates
• Is a copy	• Is an original
• Focuses on systems and structure	• Focuses on people
• Relies on control	
• Has a short-range view	• Inspires trust
	• Has a long-range perspective
• Asks how? and when?	• Asks what? and why?
• Has his/her eye on the bottom line	• Has his/her eye on the horizon
• Imitates	• Originates
• Accepts the status quo	• Challenges the status quo
• Is the classic good soldier	• Is his/her own person
• Does things right	• Does the right thing

*Sources: Darling (1992) and Nanus (1992)

We do not, however, totally concur with these authors. Our opinion is that leadership is one particular (albeit extremely important) function of management. The view taken by these authors of what management is all about tends to be oversimplistic and quite subjective. Our view is that management has more to it than providing leadership to people (refer again to chapter 1). For the sake of completeness, however, we provide you with the views of these authors.

Booysen and Van Wyk (1994) found that some South African respondents were of the opinion that South Africa breeds managers, not leaders. The following are some of the reasons offered by the respondents for this view.

● Formal learning inhibits creativity.
● External insignia of leadership are regarded as important.
● Ours is a confirmative and rule-bound society.
● Society values technical managerial skills (the "good" employee is promoted to management).
● Development of leadership is limited by finances and economics.
● Bureaucracy plays an important role.
● South African society does not value humanities/soft sciences.
● The South African schooling system is inadequate: it does not stimulate the development of intellect, creativity and self-confidence; it does not identify children with natural leadership abilities and does not develop such skills.

Most of the obstacles to leadership mentioned by the respondents related to South Africa's cultural and linguistic diversity and lack of transcultural empathy, interaction and accommodation.

Although managers are not always good leaders and leaders are not always good managers, the distinction is, in our view, somewhat overstated. There are managers who are also good leaders and leaders who are also good managers. Because we view leadership as part of management, we believe that, although one can be a good leader without necessarily being a good manager, one can never be a good manager if one is not a good leader. Some refer to managerial leaders or business leaders. Grobler (1996) argues that the real challenge is to combine strong leadership with strong management and to use the one to balance the other.

12.4.1 Business leaders

Tait (1996) quotes the findings of a study involving in-depth interviews of eighteen successful business leaders, focusing on the qualities and skills they regarded as essential for success in directing and guiding a large organisation. These qualities include:

- the ability to make sense of a complicated pattern of events and from this to formulate clear goals for the organisation — in other words, to create a clear vision;
- people/interpersonal and communication skills;
- integrity or character, and
- drive and ambition.

Darling (1992) discusses a study conducted by Warren Bennis (1989) on several different types of major US business firms, where he interviewed over 100 successful managerial leaders. Four characteristic leadership strategies emerged from this study.

- **Attention through vision**
  The ability to draw others to them, not just because they have a vision, but because they communicate an extraordinary focus of commitment. Leaders manage attention through a compelling vision or picture that provides focus for people.

- **Meaning through communication**
  Leaders make their vision and ideas tangible, real and meaningful to others through effective communication, so that they can support them. In other words, they constantly communicate the vision in creative, understandable ways, which motivates followers to go that extra mile and provides synergy and coordination of effort.

  An important aspect of communication is empathy. Successful leaders are open and sensitive to the needs and differences of others, and look at relative viewpoints rather than at absolutes. Empathy includes understanding that skin colour, nationality, birthplace, gender, political belief, financial status and intelligence are not measures of worth or worthiness.

The pathway to effective communication is acceptance of the fact that every human being is a distinctly unique individual.

● **Trust through positioning**

This concerns inspiring trust in the leader as well as trusting the followers to do what needs to be done. Trust is a facilitator which helps to make it possible for an organisation to function effectively. Trust implies accountability, predictability, reliability, and provides the foundation which maintains organisational integrity. Integrity in the leadership position leads to trust within those individuals counted on to facilitate the achievements of the organisation.

● **Confidence through respect**

A key factor in building confidence through respect focuses on the creative deployment of self, which has as a prerequisite a positive self-regard. A positive self-regard seems to consist of three major components:
○ knowledge of one's own strengths;
○ the capacity to nurture and develop those strengths; and
○ the ability to discern the fit between one's strengths and weaknesses and the organisation's needs.

Darling (1992) also argues that "[a] real test of successful leadership in management lies in giving, to the greatest extent possible, opportunities to others within the situational context of the firm. One does not have to be brilliant to be a good leader, but you have to understand people — how they feel, what makes them tick, and the most effective ways to influence them."

12.4.2 South African perspectives on business leadership

Charlton (1996) points out that studies conducted in South Africa have supported the findings of Bennis. He adds that the above strategies are dependent on the leader's ability to manage himself/herself. This involves diagnosing inappropriate or ineffective behaviour, and assuming personal responsibility for learning, productive growth and change. He also argues that a business leader needs to create an empowering environment where followers are motivated, able and allowed, (that is, having the responsibility and authority) to perform to their potential. Charlton (1996) concludes by saying that "[e]mpowerment is both a consequence (indication) and competence of effective leadership".

Preliminary research undertaken by Booysen and Van Wyk (Booysen 1994) on the preferred leadership style of effective leaders in South Africa has found that outstanding leaders in South Africa are perceived to show a strong and direct, but democratic and participative leadership style.They are perceived as agents of change, visionaries and individualists. This indicates a preference for a transformational leadership style. Although they are seen as being moderately charismatic, they are also seen as responsible, not as agitators.

The preliminary results also indicate that South African leaders are perceived as being sensitive to followers' needs and are expected to reflect followers' ideas, to satisfy their needs and to be respectful and understanding. South African leaders are expected to be pragmatic and creative; by utilising their interpersonal skills and knowledge they must act reactively as well as proactively, depending on their analysis of a situation.

12.5 CONTEMPORARY ISSUES IN LEADERSHIP

12.5.1 Leadership and diversity

Prior to the 1960s the study of leadership was limited largely to the study of white men occupying leadership positions in business organisations. In the 1970s and 1980s there was a surge of interest in the experiences of women and minority men in management (Berry & Houston 1993). Moss-Kanter and Corn (1994) point out that as economies globalise and organisations increasingly form cross-border rela- tionships, there is a resurgence of interest in the management problems caused by national cultural differences — in values, ideologies, organisational assumptions, work practices and behavioural styles — spawning research into cross-cultural leadership.

The idea of the world as a global village is already a reality. Communication networks such as telephone conferences, interactive visual links and Internet have made it possible to transact business as quickly between Johannesburg and New York as between two organisations in Johannesburg. The increasing multination- alism and multiculturalism pose significant challenges for any leader or manager. In South Africa we do not only experience the influences of globalisation and inter- nationalisation, but internally, in our own country, we are faced with numerous diversity issues, such as cultural diversity, diverse languages and religion, and race and gender inequities. Not only are more women, blacks, coloured and Indian people entering the labour market but they are also entering more management/ leadership positions. In order for South African organisations to survive, it is of utmost importance to understand and manage diversity effectively.

In the following sections gender and cultural issues in leadership are discussed.

12.5.1.1 Gender issues: Feminisation of leadership

Betters-Reed and Moore (1995) argue that, although the (American) workforce is becoming increasingly diverse, the predominant paradigm for educating and man- aging this new labour force has remained rooted in an exclusively Anglo-American male mind-set. Even management development programmes designed to focus on females have suffered from the tendency to encourage women to "think manager, think male". They assert that the implicit (and sometimes explicit) assumption has been that women will succeed if they adopt the characteristics of effective white male managers. The constantly reinforced message is that women can succeed only if they become more assertive, competitive, "dressed for success" and more politically and socially astute. This is unfortunately also the case in South Africa. Because of the above-mentioned assumptions and because they were breaking new ground, the first female executives adhered to many of the rules of conduct that spelled success for men.

Rosener (1990) points out that a second wave of women is making their way into top management, not by adopting the style and habits that have proved successful for men but by drawing on the skills and attitudes that they have developed from their shared experience as women. She adds:

> "These second generation of managerial women are drawing on what is unique to their socialisation as women and creating a different path to the top. They are seeking and finding opportunities in fast-changing and growing organisations to show that they can achieve results — in a different way. They are succeeding because of — not in spite of — certain characteristics generally considered to be 'feminine' and inappropriate in leaders."

This second wave of women leaders is equipped with a leadership style that is more based on consensus-building, more open and inclusive (power and information sharing), more likely to encourage participation by others, to enhance the self-worth of others and to energise them, and that tends to be more caring than the style adopted by many of their male counterparts. Rosener (1990) refers to this approach to management as an interactive leadership style.

Betters-Reed and Moore (1995) argue that as a result of competitive pressures and strategic rethinking which has brought about flatter organisational structures and more decentralised authority and decision making, the trend is towards more collaborative styles of management — working across organisational departments to create an environment where teamwork encourages innovation and creative problem solving. They point out that Senge (1990), in Betters-Reed and Moore (1995), has spurred interest in the importance of understanding open models of communication among all employees for the purpose of improved learning and performance, and that total quality management also demands that these principles be adopted. It is clear from the above that these trends are in line with what Betters-Reed and Moore (1995) refer to as a feminist or women-centred approach.

Robbins (1993) points out that the research suggests two conclusions regarding gender and leadership. First, the similarities between women and men tend to outweigh the differences, and secondly, the differences suggest that male managers feel more comfortable with a directive style, whereas female managers prefer a more democratic style. Appelbaum and Shapiro (1993) argue that since men have occupied most executive positions, their leadership style is defined as traditional — and thus, because the female leadership style contradicts the traditional, it is seen as non-traditional. Table 12.4 compares the feminine leadership model with the traditional masculine model.

From table 12.4 it is evident that generally women tend to follow a more transformational leadership style, with the emphasis on the followers, consensus, and the use of charisma, personal reference and personal contact to enhance interper-

Table 12.4

Comparison of masculine and feminine leadership styles*

Variables	Masculine	Feminine
Operative style	● Competitive	● Cooperative
Organisational structure	● Vertical and hierar-chical	● Horizontal, network, egalitarian
Objective	● Winning	● Quality
Problem-solving approach	● Rational and objective	● Intuitive and subjective
Key characteristics	● High control ● Cling to power ● Strategic ● Unemotional ● Analytical	● Low control ● Power sharing/empowerment ● Empathetic ● Collaborative ● High performance
Perceived power base	● Organisational position and formal authority concentrated at the top	● Personal characteristics shared within a group
Perspective on leadership	● Social exchange in terms of transactions	● Follower-leader commitment relationship

*Source: Applebaum & Sharpiro (1993); Govender & Bayat (1993); Smith & Smits (1994); Wilkenson (1995) and Rosener (1990)

sonal relations and to influence followers. Men in general, on the other hand, tend to follow a more directive style where job performance is seen as a series of transactions with subordinates, where rewards are exchanged for services and punishments for inadequate performance — that is, more of a transactional approach. Men seem to be more inclined to use formal position, power and authority to control people.

It is, however, very important to emphasise that the above are genererelisations and that many men possess certain attributes that are linked mainly to the female model as set out in table 12.4, and vice versa.

In conclusion, even though men have historically held the great majority of senior positions in organisations, and some people therefore still think that the noted differences between men and women will automatically work in favour of men, this is no longer the case. In today's flatter organisations, flexibility, networking, teamwork, trust, and information sharing, empowerment and self-leadership are replacing rigid and hierarchical structures, competitive individualism, control, and secrecy. The better managers listen, motivate, empower and provide support to their people. We need a new brand of managers, who can develop and use feminine skills and attitudes in conjunction with the skills used by traditional managers.

"Optimally, what would emerge from this transformation is neither a masculine nor a 'feminine' model of leadership, but a synergistic model that enables people to work together to maximize their collective strengths and avoid their individual weaknesses." (Smith & Smits (1994.))

12.5.1.2 Cultural issues: Eurocentric vs Afrocentric leadership

"Europeans would be crazy to behave as though they were not European; Americans and Japanese would come across as both funny and phoney if they tried to be anything other than American and Japanese respectively. Similarly Africans, in our particular case, South Africans, had better stop behaving as though they were an outpost of Europe or somebody else (or a state of America). We have to get to know ourselves and begin to use our existential reality as a departure point." (Khoza 1994). In previous sections Euro-American approaches were discussed. The aim of this section is not to discuss the merits and demerits of the Eurocentric and Afrocentric leadership or management approaches, nor is the aim to discuss Afrocentric leadership in detail, but simply to explore some of the implications of Afrocentric views on leadership.

Khoza (1994) argues that it is a fallacy to believe that a business culture can be imposed on people, and that it can work perfectly, without taking into account the cultural archetypes of the people in question. Yet, he adds, corporate South Africa is guilty of just this: "Corporate culture as experienced in South Africa is very Eurocentric. Business practice as currently conceptualized in most South African corporations is generally cast in a Eurocentric mould, in fact, worse, an Anglo-Saxon mould." Avolio (1995) points out that in South Africa there appears to be both an individualistic and communalistic orientation, depending on whether the group is white, black, Asian or coloured. Koopman (1994) espouses the view that whites have primarily designed exclusive institutions which give primacy to the individual, his/her development and self-fulfilment, which serve to foster liberal democracy. He further says that blacks, on the other hand, believe that man is very much part of the societal fabric and see the need for each individual to find his/her place in a societal structure, to play his/her particular role in it and, to a large extent, to subordinate himself/herself to the societal needs — which leads to inclusive organisations.

South Africans have to come to terms with each others' differences, acknowledge them, put them in perspective, discover the strengths and weaknesses in different ideologies and resolve them, in order to improve the aggregate potential of South African organisations — to create the best prospects of unity through diversity (Koopman (1994); Khoza (1994); Avolio (1995)).

Central to Afrocentric management is *Ubuntu* — the community concept of management. *Ubuntu* is not a management style or a business technique, but it is an epistemology, a humanistic philosophy — African humanism — which focuses on people and puts down some guidelines for leadership style and management practices. *Ubuntu*, literally translated, means: "I am because we are"; it is an expression of our collective personhood and collective morality. Simply put, it implies encouraging individuals to express themselves through the group — through group support and commitment, acceptance and respect, cooperation and consensus, caring and sharing and solidarity. Khoza (1994) points out that *Ubuntu* is opposed to individualism and insensitive competitiveness, but is not comfortable with the kind of collectivism that stresses the importance of the social unit to the point of depersonalising the individual.

Ubuntu places a great emphasis on concern for people, as well as being good and working for the common good (Khoza (1994); Mbigi (1995a, 1995b, 1995c)). Mbigi (1995b) argues: "[t]he heart and soul of *Ubuntu* is the solidarity principle, group conformity and care in the face of survival challenges, based on unconditional group compassion, respect, dignity, trust, openness and cooperation".

Avolio (1995) draws a clear parallel between the Eurocentric or individualistic models (discussed in the previous sections) and *transactional leadership*, and continues by saying that African humanism or *ubuntu* is much more closely tied to *transformational leadership*. Specifically, transformational leaders work to create a climate and culture where each individual and the group can achieve their full potential. In doing so, transformational leaders can facilitate the Africanisation of South African organisations."

The implications of an *ubuntu*-oriented leadership style do not only include teamwork down to grass-roots level but also the encouragement of the team members or followers to sacrifice their personal gains/goals for the gains/goals of the group. This style includes creative cooperation, open communication, teamwork and reciprocal moral obligations (Khoza (1994); Avolio (1995); Mbigi (1995b).

In agreement with Madi (1995) and Beaty (1996), it can be said that managers in this country need to extract the best management tools from camps representing a variety of cultural management orientations both within and outside South Africa, and that managers who understand and value the cultural diversity of the South African workforce, and who are flexible in using what works from a cultural perspective, will more likely have the competitive edge.

Madi (1995) concludes by saying that "[t]he issue is not that there should be an Africanisation of the corporate culture in South Africa, but there should be *South Africanisation* of the corporate culture", and cites the following as example: instead of giving a tie or watch to Mr Mhlongo for his thirty years of loyal service, it is possibly just more South African to slaughter a goat and invite his friends and relatives to come and feast with him.

Professor David Beaty offers some of the recent applications and thoughts in the debate on Afrocentric versus Eurocentric management styles. This article is quoted in the appendix to this chapter.

One cannot but observe the striking parallels between and the complementary nature of the feminine and the Afrocentric leadership approaches, which are already reflected in the South African situation. This just emphasises the dictum: Unity in diversity. Only a diverse leadership team that includes both feminine and masculine and Eurocentric and Afrocentric strengths will be strong and flexible enough to help South African organisations to compete in today's highly competitive, global marketplace.

12.6 CONCLUSION: LEADERSHIP CHALLENGES FACING SOUTHERN AFRICAN ORGANISATIONS

Throughout this chapter it has been emphasised that leadership is important, and that the styles, actions, attributes, orientations, and approaches of leaders all have a major effect on subordinates and ultimately on the success of organisations. In South Africa we have very specific limitations, constraints, issues and dilemmas that influence leadership and organisational success.

The increasing multinationalism and multiculturalism of workforces pose significant challenges for leaders in South African organisations. South Africa is experiencing not only the influences of globalisation and internationalisation but also numerous challenges related to cultural diversity, such as language, religion, race and gender issues. Now, more than ever before, with the implementation of affirmative action and equal opportunity programmes, change in workplace values and in people's values and norms is taking place, which impacts on styles of management and leadership.

Some authors point out, however, that there is still a value system of old conventions and traditions to be overcome — that of the traditional white South African male manager. White male managers also continue to comprise the majority group in management, especially senior management (Govender & Bayat 1993; Fischer 1995; Madi 1995; Grobler 1996).

There is no doubt, however, that affirmative action programmes will lead to more cultural and gender diversity in the South African workforce. By-products of diverse workplaces may also, however, include aspects like distrust, negative attitudes towards diversity and perceived barriers to successful careers for newly disaffected groups. While the resistance, resentment and aggression shown towards management by a certain faction of workers must be taken into account on the one hand, the fears and uncertainties of others must also be considered (Makwana 1994; Booysen 1996). These are among the critical human resource management issues that South African business leaders must confront in the future.

 SELF-EVALUATION QUESTIONS

1. What has South African research revealed regarding the views on effective leaders?
2. Explain and differentiate between trait and behavioural theories of leadership.
3. What do you understand by transactional theories of leadership?

4. Explain and differentiate between charismatic and transformational leadership.

5. "Management is less important than leadership." Critically discuss this statement.

6. Write an elaborate essay on the following topic:

   "What we need in South Africa is an approach towards leadership that recognises, values and nurtures diversity."

BIBLIOGRAPHY

Appelbaum, SH & Shapiro, BT. 1993. Why can't men lead like women? *Leadership & Organization Development Journal,* 14 7, 28–34

Avolio, BJ. 1995. Integrating transformational leadership and Afro-centric management. *Human Resource Management*, 11 (6), 17–21

Beaty, DT. 1996. Eurocentric or Afrocentric? *Business Day: Mastering Management Series* Part 2, 11 March 1996.

Bennis, W, & Nanus, B. 1985. *Leaders: The Strategies for Taking Charge.* New York: Harper and Row

Berry, LM & Houston, JP. 1993. *Psychology at Work*. Dubeque: WCB Brown & Benchmark Publishers

Betters-Reed, BL & Moore, LL. 1995. Shifting the management development paradigm for women. *Journal of Management Development*, 14(2), 24–38

Booysen, AE. 1994. *An Introduction to a Multination Study on Leadership and Organisational Practices.* Paper delivered at the Congress on Psychometrics for Psychologists and Personnel Practitioners: Evaluation in Diversity — New Challenges, 13–14 June 1994 at Escom College, Midrand

Booysen, AE & Van Wyk, MW. 1994. *Globe-Research First Qualitative Report* March 1994. SBL Unisa Midrand.

Booysen, AE. 1996. Doctorate in Business Leadership. *An examination of race and gender influences on the leadership attributes of SA managers.* Proposal presented at DBL Colloquy. 16 Mei 1996. Midrand SBL.

Burns, JM. (1978). *Leadership*. New York: Harper & Row

Capowski, G. 1994. Anatomy of a leader: Where are the leaders of tomorrow? *Management Review*, March, 10–17

Charlton, Guy. 1996. Beyond change — Doing the extraordinary. *People Dynamics*, 13(12), 22–25

Cherrington, DJ. 1994. *Organizational Behaviour: The Management of Individual and Organizational Performance*, 2 ed. Massachusetts: Allyn & Bacon

Conger, JA & Kanungo RN 1987. Toward a behavioural theory of charismatic leadership in organisational settings. *Academy of Management Review*, **12**, 637–647

Darling, JR. 1992. Total quality management: The key role of leadership strategy. *Leadership and Organization Development Journal* 13(4), 3–7

Fischer, Sarah. 1995. Placing women on the affirmative action agenda. *People Dynamics*, 13(5), 23–25

Fleishman, EA, Zaccaro, SJ & Mumford, MD. 1992. Individual differences and leadership: An overview, part 1. *Leadership Quarterly: Industrial Differences and Leadership*, 2(4), 238–243

Gordon, JR. 1993. *A Diagnostic Approach to Organizational Behaviour*, 4 ed. Boston: Allyn & Bacon

Govender, Devi & Bayat, Saheed. 1993. Leadership styles. The gender issues. *Industrial and Social Relations*, 13(314), 139–144

Greenberg, J & Baron, RB. 1993. *Behaviour in Organizations: Understanding and Managing the Human Side of Work*, 4 ed. Boston: Allyn and Bacon

Grobler, PA. 1996. *Leadership Challenges facing Companies in the New South Africa*. Inaugural lecture, Department of Business Management, University of South Africa, Pretoria

Hersey, P. & Blanchard, K.H. 1993. *Management of Organizational Behaviour: Utilizing Human Resources*, 6 ed. Englewood Cliffs: Prentice-Hall, Inc

House, RJA Proposal to Conduct a Multi-nation Study of Leadership and Organizational Practices. Pennsylvania: Unpublished

Human, Linda & Bowmaker-Falconer, Angus. 1992. Managing diversity: Just another way of avoiding the issues? *People Dynamics*, 10(12), 25–31

Khoza, R. 1994. The need of an Afro-centric approach to management. In *African Management Philosophies, Concepts and Applications,* ed P Christie, R Lessem & L Mbigi, 117–124. Pretoria: Sigma Press

Koopman, A. 1994. Transcultural management. In *African Management Philosophies, Concepts and Applications,* ed. P Christie, R Lessem & L Mbigi, 117–124: Pretoria: Sigma Press

Kreitner, R. & Kinicki, A. 1993. *Organizational Behavior.* 3 ed. Homewood: Richard D Irwin, Inc.

Lord, R & Maher, KJ. 1991. *Leadership and Information Processing: Linking Perceptions and Performance.* Boston: Unwin: Everyman Maddi

Madi, Phinda. 1995. Moving the centre. *People Dynamics,* 13(3),

Makwana, Mpho. 1994. Growing real talent: Implementing authentic affirmative action. *People Dynamics*, July, 22–25

Matthews, R. 1995. African dream. *Financial Times*, 6 October 1995

Mbigi, L. 1995a. The roots of Ubuntu in business: A definitive perspective. In *Ubuntu: The Spirit of South African Transformation Management.* Johannesburg: Knowledge Resources

Mbigi, L. 1995b. A new dimension for business. *Enterprise,* November

Mbigi, L. 1995c. Towards a rainbow management style. *Enterprise,* December

Mbigi, L. 1997. *Ubuntu: The African Dream in Management.* Johannesburg: Knowledge Resources

Moorhead, G & Griffin, TW. 1992. *Organizational Behavior,* 3 ed. Boston: Houghton Mifflin Company.

Moss Kanter, R, & Corn, RI. 1994. Do cultural differences make a business difference? *Journal of Management Development*, 14(2), 5–23

Nanus, B. 1992. *Visionary Leadership*. San Francisco: Jossey-Bass, Inc

Robbins, SP. 1993. *Organizational Behavior: Concepts, Controversies and Applications*, 6 ed. Englewood Cliffs, New Jersey: Prentice-Hall

Robbins, SP. 1996. *Organizational Behavior: Concepts, Controversies and Applications*, 7 ed. New Jersey: Prentice Hall

Rosener, JB. 1990. Ways women lead. *Harvard Business Review*, **Nov/Dec**, 119–125

Rost, J & Smith, A. 1992. Leadership: A postindustrial approach. *Leading European Management Journal*, (10)(2), 193–201

Senge, PM. 1990. *The Fifth discipline*. New York: Doubleday

Smith, PL & Smith, SJ. 1994. The feminisation of leadership. *Training and Development*, February, 43–46

South African Statistical Release PO317. 1995. *October Household Survey 1994*. Pretoria: Central Statistical Services

South African Statistical Release PO317. 1996. *October Household Survey 1995*. Pretoria: Central Statistical Services

Tait, Ruth. 1996. The attributes of leadership. *The Leadership and Organizational Development Journal*, 17 (1), 27–31

APPENDIX: EUROCENTRIC OR AFROCENTRIC MANAGEMENT —
DO SOUTH AFRICAN MANAGERS HAVE TO CHOOSE?

Professor David Beaty, University of South Africa Graduate School of Business Leadership.

South African managers face a dilemma that concerns two different management approaches in this country. On the one hand, some people argue that "Eurocentric Management" (unlike "Afrocentric Management") has proven value in improving organisational performance worldwide. And they assert that this management approach has made significant positive contributions to South African work and organisation.

On the other hand, supporters of "Afrocentric Management" (using terms that include "Ubuntu" and "Nhorowondo") argue that for managers to be relevant in South Africa, they must accept concepts embodied in such terms as "solidarity", "conformity" and "relationships". They argue with their critics by claiming that those in opposition do not understand Afrocentric Management and suggest that critics misrepresent the approach as just another "oversimplified" and "bastardised" business technique.

This article is not written to explore the merits and demerits of both management approaches. Indeed, a number of recent books, articles, speeches, media reports, and even television programmes have devoted adequate time and space to this issue. And each camp has marshalled what each believes are the "right" facts to support their conclusions. Both sides argue for understanding and acceptance of their opinions by managers in a new South Africa.

It's no wonder that managers listening and watching this debate are confused about "who's right" and "who's wrong". Anyone? Everyone? Indeed, each camp presents a list of logical points in hopes of persuading the opposition (and any observers) to their point of view. However, while academically intriguing, the debate has become divisive. In fact, emotional temperatures have risen as supporters from both camps rally around their viewpoints. What's more, the real problems facing South Africa of low productivity and poor international competitiveness have become obscured in the desire to prove who's right and who's wrong.

This article is written to offer a different perspective on the debate. I believe that managers do not, and should not, choose between Eurocentric and Afrocentric management approaches in South Africa. What's more, placing these two approaches on two ends of a continuum is not the current reality facing most managers in South Africa. South African managers don't face a "melting pot" of people from one or two cultures. In fact, the South African workplace reflects many diverse cultures — including European, African, Asian, Indian, Middle Eastern and others. What's more, people from the same culture in South Africa frequently differ along regional and ethnic lines and reflect a workplace that I describe as a cultural "fruit-cocktail".

So the debate between supporters of Eurocentric and Afrocentric management is, I contend, mined with pitfalls and not unlike to common practice of business firms presenting elaborate marketing and strategic plans without listening to real live customers and staying reality-based. Bandying around survey data, business techniques, models, opinions from political, literary and trade union leaders — like supporters in both Eurocentric and Afrocentric camps do — is no substitute for "on the ground"— eye-ball to eye-ball — contact with people from diverse cultures. In fact, I believe that managers in this country need to extract the best management tools from camps representing a variety of cultural management orientations within and outside of South Africa. Managers in this country need to use "whatever works" to improve management and worker performance.

How will South African managers know "what works"? The answer — simple in concept but requiring great diligence to carry out — is found, I believe, in "naive listening".

Naive listening is just what its name implies: active, nonjudgemental listening to a target person(s) with no rebuttals, arguments, or debates. The concept grew from the discovery that senior managers are frequently out of touch with customers' and employees' needs and desires because they don't regularly interact with them. Getting out of the office regularly (not "whenever I have some time"), daily (not my "once-a-quarter visit to the troops"), informally (not the typical adversarial negotiating sessions or the occasional regal visit with employees) for the purposes of listening and learning as well as for monitoring and educating will be a significant step in the direction of addressing the productivity and competitive dilemmas facing managers in this country.

People who have succeeded in international business emphasise the importance of knowing the language, culture and norms of those in the host country in order to conduct naive listening. This advice is sound within South Africa itself, since this is a rainbow nation of multiple languages and cultures. For managers, it pays to know the language and culture of the different peoples from which one's labour force and customers are drawn. For example, when Sony opened a plant in San Diego, an American city near the Mexican border, one of the first things that the new plant manager (a Japanese) did was to learn Spanish, since the majority of his workforce was Mexican and Chicano.

The following true case example is given to illustrate the need to use "what works" in South Africa, and to avoid being constrained by one or two "cultural" management approaches.

A firm, with operations in a medium-size Eastern Transvaal city, had major problems in the theft of goods from one of its plants. In fact, the Managing Director suspected that the culprits were employees (including managers and workers). So he implemented a system in which a sum of R50 000,00 was deposited into a bank account. Then, all employees were informed that whenever an item was stolen, the value of that item would be deducted from the money deposited. At the end of a six month period, the outstanding amount left in the kitty would be divided equally among all employees. The MD's objective was to get employees to police themselves since all stood to gain by having the full amount available at the end of the period. This, he believed, would lead to a decrease in company theft.

Two months into the scheme, the theft of goods continued unabated. What's more, a company bakkie had been stolen and the MD suspected it was an inside job. So he brought in the police to question and fingerprint all employees. Nothing turned up. Frustrated, the MD considered what some might find to be a strange strategy in identifying the culprit and locating the bakkie.

The MD called in a Sangoma and all employees were told by the Sangoma that whoever had stolen the bakkie would be given 24 hours to confess the crime. If the culprit did not confess, the individual(s) would die from a spell that had been cast on all employees. The result — within 8 hours the Managing Director received a knock on the door of his home and an employee confessed to having stolen the bakkie as well as other items in the plant.

This case is not written to suggest that Sangomas are the only solution to workplace theft. Rather, the case is used to illustrate how a variety of different management approaches were used to solve a business problem. These strategies reflected different cultural values. For example, peer-based control systems reflected practices consistent with Asiancentric management; police investigations and finger-printing reflected Eurocentric practices; and calling on the services of a Sangoma reflected African cultural practices.

South African managers who understand and value the cultural diversity of all South Africans and are flexible in using "what works" from a cultural perspective will have a competitive edge over their foreign counterparts. As Clive Barker said in a newspaper interview while discussing the remarkable victory of Bafana Bafana in the Africa Nations

Cup: "I keep saying to the players: If we play like Germany we'll never beat Germany; if we play like the Dutch we'll never beat them either. But if we play like South Africa, there are no limits."

What lessons can managers learn from this article. First, managers in South Africa should have a healthy scepticism of so-called gurus who preach one (or even two) management solutions to South Africa's productivity malaise. Second, managers need to use "what works" in solving work performance problems. Knowledge of many culturally diverse management approaches combined with a heavy dose of naive listening to those we say we are trying to lead, is an important step forward in improving organisational performance. Finally, South African managers are beginning to explore a "home-grown" management recipe. But our need to learn from the rest of the world and adopt a best practices approach to management must be central in our drive for world class competitiveness.

Source: *Business Day. Mastering Management Supplement*, Part 2, 11 March 1996, p 15

chapter 13 Appraising and Managing Work Performance

⊚ STUDY OBJECTIVES

After studying this chapter, you should be able to:

- list the various purposes of performance appraisal;
- explain the difference between performance appraisal and performance management;
- discuss the basic requirements for effective appraisal systems;
- describe the typical problems that may be experienced with performance appraisal systems and identify possible solutions;
- explain the basic steps in the development of an appraisal system;
- distinguish various appraisal techniques and discuss the limitations of each;
- outline the requirements for conducting effective appraisal interviews.

13.1 INTRODUCTION

In previous chapters it was emphasised that measuring and assessing is an activity that finds application in virtually all the human resource management functions. Naturally, therefore, individual performance as the outcome of work activities must also be subject to measurement. In the course of their daily managerial activities, supervisors and managers ought to continuously assess on an informal basis how well their subordinates are doing their work. Such informal assessment enables the individual manager to make the necessary decisions regarding the most effective utilisation of staff, motivating those who perform well and rectifying substandard performance.

Informal appraisal, which usually results in an overall impression of worker efficiency and effectiveness, often operates satisfactorily in small organisations where the management knows and interacts with all employees. However, even though it may be argued that effective supervisors continually provide informal feedback to their subordinates (Robbins 1995: 229), the information generated through an unsystematic, informal evaluation has limited value for making valid and justifiable human resource management decisions in a large organisational context. In such a context accurate performance data obtained through standard processes is required for activities such as workforce planning, training and development, compensation, career development and succession planning. Most organisations therefore have a need for a formal performance appraisal system and it is in the areas of the development, implementation, maintenance and utilisation of such systems that the human resource specialist has to play a leading role.

In this chapter we shall explore this role together with the current human resource management technology available for providing organisations with meaningful formal appraisal systems.

13.2 DEFINITION AND ROLE OF PERFORMANCE APPRAISAL IN HUMAN RESOURCE MANAGEMENT

Performance appraisal may be defined as a formal and systematic process by means of which the job-relevant strengths and weaknesses of employees are identified, observed, measured, recorded and developed.

The above definition captures the essential components of what the process of performance appraisal should ideally entail (Cardy & Dobbins 1994: 2):

- *identification* refers to the determination of the performance dimensions to be examined;
- *observation* indicates that all appraisal aspects should be observed sufficiently for accurate and fair judgements to be made;
- *measurement* refers to the appraiser's translation of the observations into value judgements about the ratee's performance;
- *recording* concerns the documentation of the performance appraisal process outcomes; and
- the *development* component indicates that appraisal is not simply on assessment of the past but that it should also focus on the future and on the improvement of individual performance.

It may be stated that performance appraisal finds its true definition only by its application, or the purpose it serves in the attainment of organisational goals. This contention will be further expanded upon in later sections of this chapter.

In establishing the role of performance appraisal within human resource management, we need to consider the typical purposes for which appraisals can be used and the relationships that may exist between the appraisal system and other human resource management functions in an organisation.

13.2.1 Purposes of performance appraisal

Many uses and purposes of performance appraisal have been advanced, but generally these can be categorised under the headings of *administrative purposes* and *development purposes*.

Administrative purposes concern the use of performance data as bases for personnel decision making, including:

- human resource planning, for example compiling skills inventories, obtaining information regarding new positions to be created, and developing succession plans;
- reward decisions, including salary and wage increases (or the withholding thereof), merit bonuses, etc;
- placement decisions such as promotions, transfers, dismissals and retrenchments;
- personnel research, for example validating selection procedures by using appraisals as criteria or evaluating the effectiveness of training programmes.

Developmental purposes of performance appraisal can focus on developmental functions on the individual as well as the organisational level.

- Appraisals can serve individual development purposes by:
  - O providing employees with feedback on their strengths and weaknesses and on how to improve future performance;
  - O aiding career planning and development;
  - O providing inputs for personal remedial interventions, for example referral to an Employee Assistance Programme (performance impairments may be due to factors outside the work environment).
- Organisational development purposes may include:
  - O facilitating organisational diagnosis and development by specifying performance levels and suggesting overall training needs (Cascio 1991);
  - O providing essential information for affirmative action programmes, job redesign efforts, multiskilling programmes, etc;
  - O promoting effective communication within the organisation through ongoing interaction between superiors and subordinates.

Figure 13.1 illustrates diagrammatically the centrality of performance within some of the different functional HR areas and the role of appraisal in an integrated human resource cycle.

13.2.2 Performance appraisal versus performance management

Since it is the performance of individual employees which primarily determines the attainment of the goals and objectives of an organisation, the measurement or appraisal of performance rightfully deserves a central position in any HRM programme (refer to figure 13.1).

Performance appraisal, (often referred to as *performance evaluation, merit rating, staff assessment, performance review,* etc) is also the HR function most often criticised and whose systems carry the greatest risk of either failing, falling into disuse or degenerating towards a meaningless, paperwork exercise.

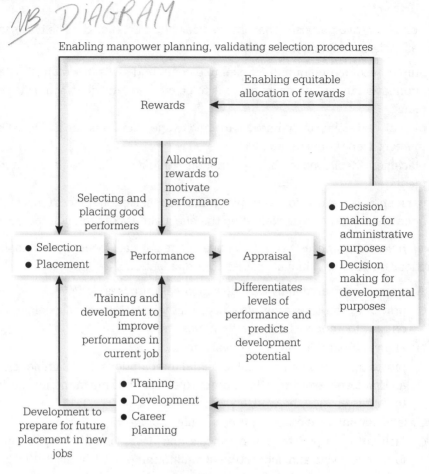

Figure 13.1

Performance appraisal in the human resource cycle

Source: Adapted and expanded from Fombrun, CJ, Devanna MA & Tichy NM. 1988. The human resource management audit. In *The Strategic Human Resource Management Source-book*, eds LS Baird, CE Schneier & RW Beatty, 252. Amherst, Mass: HRD Press.

The typical problems associated with performance appraisal will be explored in greater depth in a later section. At this stage suffice it to say that increasingly competitive business environments, criticism of traditional approaches to perform-ance appraisal and the emergence of the concept of total quality management have led to a shift in emphasis from *performance appraisal* to *performance man-agement* (Butler, Ferris & Napier 1991; Lockett 1992; Spangenberg 1994).

Spangenberg (1994) describes performance management as:

"an approach to managing people that entails planning employee perform-ance, facilitating the achievement of work-related goals, and reviewing performance as a way of motivating employees to achieve their full potential in line with the organisation's objectives".

Figure 13.2

An integrated performance management cycle

Source: Adapted and expanded from Mitrani, A Dalziel M & Fitt, D. 1992. *Competency Based Human Resource Management*, 97. London: Kogan Page

As such performance management can be regarded as an ongoing process that involves the planning, managing, reviewing, rewarding and development of performance (Spangenberg 1994: 29).

While performance appraisal systems are often no more than a system of measurement (that is, a specific form together with certain written rules and procedures controlling its use), the concept of performance management signifies an attempt to entrench performance appraisal as a legitimate and integral part of a manager's job of getting subordinates effectively to achieve the results and goals expected of them. Swan (1991: 11) expresses this idea as follows:

"Performance management means more than assessing an employee's performance at regular intervals (ie performance appraisal). It unites a number of related tasks: monitoring, coaching, giving feedback, gathering information, and yes, assessing an employee's work. It accomplishes those tasks in the context of objectives — the immediate objectives of the department and the overall goals of the organisation. And it carries them out systematically, throughout the year. For different organisations the actual means may differ, but regardless of the procedures used to implement it, the basic strategy is the same and the benefits are the same."

The theoretical foundations of the performance management approach may be operationalised within an integrated cycle of separate but related managerial processes, as illustrated in figure 13.2.

13.3 FUNDAMENTAL REQUIREMENTS FOR SUCCESSFUL PERFORMANCE APPRAISAL SYSTEMS

Specific requirements for an appraisal system as a criterion for judging the work performance of individuals are: *relevance, reliability, discriminability or sensitivity, freedom from contamination, practicality* and *acceptability*.

Relevance

The requirement of relevance refers to the question: "What is really important for success in this job and this organisation?" The appraisal system must therefore be directly related to the objectives of the job and the goals of the organisation. Cascio (1989: 312) suggests three necessary processes to ensure relevance:

1. establishing clear links between the performance standards of all jobs and the organisational goals;
2. establishing clear links between the critical job elements of each job (as determined through job analysis) and the performance dimensions to be rated on the appraisal form; and
3. ensuring the regular maintenance and updating of job descriptions, performance standards and appraisal systems.

Reliability

The system must produce evaluations or ratings that are consistent and repeatable. The requirement of reliability does not only refer to the psychometric properties of the measuring instrument itself, but also to the need for judges who carry out the rating process both competently and consistently and who have the opportunity to observe the behaviour that is to be rated.

Discriminability/sensitivity

Despite being highly relevant and reliable, a system will still be of no use if it is unable to distinguish between good performers and poor performers. If the system gives rise to similar ratings for both effective and ineffective employees through either design deficiencies (for example insufficient performance categories) or rating errors (for example central tendency), results cannot be used for developmental or administrative decisions.

Freedom from contamination

The system should be able to measure individual performance without being contaminated by extraneous factors that are outside the employee's control, for example material shortages, inappropriate equipment or procedures.

Practicality

This requirement implies that an appraisal system should be easy to understand and to use by managers and subordinates alike. It should thus be "user friendly" and manageable in terms of the amount of administration (time and paperwork) it requires and in terms of its cost-effectiveness.

In making design decisions relating to the practicality and utility of an envisaged system, the practitioner may have to make some compromises, since an increase in practicality usually comes at the expense of measurement precision. Conversely, technically advanced systems, such as behaviourally anchored rating scales (BARS), may perhaps be superior in meeting requirements of relevance, reliability and discriminability, but they are also complex and expensive to develop and implement.

Acceptability

The acceptability of a system is an extremely important prerequisite, since the support and perceived legitimacy a system receives from both managers and employees will probably carry more weight in determining its success than its inherent technical soundness.

In order to establish a positive attitude towards the system, it would be prudent to utilise all possible means of involving the eventual end users in its development, implementation and maintenance; they must also be made to feel that they are the actual owners of the appraisal system.

13.4 GENERAL PROBLEMS IN PERFORMANCE APPRAISAL AND POSSIBLE REMEDIES

In a previous section reference was made to the so-called inherent problematic nature of performance appraisal. Since McGregor first took a "uneasy look at performance appraisal" in his famous 1957 article, a vast amount of research has focused on identifying the shortcomings of the performance appraisal process and on finding possible solutions to these problems. The literature abounds with lists of reasons why appraisal systems fail, and in practice many problems are experienced. This is clearly indicated by a survey of some leading South African organisations conducted by Spangenberg in 1993 (see exhibit A).

Exhibit A

Performance management problems in South Africa

Some of the major problems highlighted by Spangenberg's research (1993: 30–34) are:
- a lack of a culture of productivity and quality;
- insufficient line management support;
- employee mistrust of the real goals of performance review;
- performance management systems becoming mechanistic and control orientated;
- dwindling enthusiasm due to long implementation periods; and
- difficulties in linking other systems, for example the reward system to the performance management system.

Problems in performance appraisal typically stem from:
- technical issues in the system itself (choice of format and administrative procedures; purposes for which it is designed); and
- human issues related to the interaction process between supervisor and subordinate.

13.4.1 Problems related to appraisal system design

It would be safe to state that there is not a single method or format of performance appraisal that is not subject to some limitations. Indeed, the very fact that there are so many different formats of varying complexity from which to choose, is a direct result of trying to overcome deficiencies of previously conceived formats. Such deficiencies in the design of performance appraisal instruments are mostly related to concerns regarding their **reliability and validity** as basic psychometric requirements for any measuring instrument.

Reliability in assessment refers to the consistency and stability of the measurement process. Szilagy and Wallace (1990: 535) suggest four approaches for improving reliability in performance measures:

- increasing the number of items in the rating instrument that measure the same performance dimension;
- using more than one evaluator in order to obtain multiple observations;
- increasing the frequency of observations;
- standardising the administration of the appraisal process.

The question of *validity* addresses the "what" and "how well" an instrument measures and whether it really measures what it is supposed to measure.

In terms of format design the use of irrelevant performance criteria or reliance on personality trait measures may compromise validity, whilst certain rater biases may detract from validity during the evaluation process. (The most common of these biases or errors are discussed separately in section 13.4.3 on page 410.)

With research pointing towards the limited impact a specific format or technique may have on the actual ratings (Kreitner & Kinicki 1995: 404), HR practitioners must bear in mind that the technical soundness of an appraisal system alone does not ensure its success.

In practice frustrations resulting from the imperfect nature of appraisal systems often prompt organisations to modify or totally redevelop their current systems. Naturally this is more often than not a futile exercise which does little for establishing the credibility of the appraisal process or convincing line management of its essential purposes. Consequently, HR practitioners faced with demands for more effective appraisal should not approach the dilemma purely by adopting more technically advanced and complex techniques, but by focusing on the proper implementation and improvement of the process as such — that is, by taking a **performance management** perspective.

A case at hand . . .

Performance management example*

In Foodcorp, a company which employs a highly diverse workforce of 18 000 employees in a large number of separate businesses, little emphasis is placed on any particular standardised appraisal format. Instead, the HR division is making a concerted effort to get supervisors and subordinates committed to an ongoing process of effective interpersonal communication.

*I Lätti, Foodcorp,1993

13.4.2 Problems related to conflicting purposes and roles

If we refer back to the many possible purposes that performance appraisal may serve (see section 13.2.1 on page 402), it should be clear that no single general method can be appropriate for all of them. Within the two general categories of purposes which were distinguished (namely administrative (or judgemental) and developmental), the basic objectives are in direct conflict.

Administrative objectives focus on the evaluation of the past performance of employees to enable managers to make decisions regarding the differential award of pay increases, candidates for promotion, etc. To allow supervisors to make comparisons between employees, an appropriate system will have to utilise some *relative* rating format such as ranking procedures (that is, listing employees in some order of merit). However, the nature of such employee-to-employee comparison methods does not only make the process of appraisal feedback difficult but also provides little information for the identification of individual performance deficiencies and how to address them in terms of training and development interventions.

To address the developmental objective, an appraisal system needs to focus on *absolute* rating formats where each individual is evaluated against several specified performance standards, for example rating scales, or against specific objectives, for example MBO. Since these formats require the rater to evaluate the employee without direct reference to other employees, valid comparisons across individuals or groups are not possible and administrative purposes cannot thus be effectively served.

The two general purposes also force managers into fulfilling conflicting roles during appraisal interviews — that is, simultaneously serving as both judge and counsellor. Naturally managers feel uncomfortable about first criticising an employee (and possibly having to justify an unpopular decision about salary increases or other employee expectations that have not been met) and then trying to set a positive tone for constructively discussing future improvement and setting new performance goals. It is generally accepted that single interviews attempting to serve both purposes of informing and justifying administrative decisions and then providing feedback and counselling are less effective than interviews addressing these purposes separately. In keeping with the philosophy of the performance management approach, the best way to resolve the judgement-versus-development dilemma would probably be the emphasis on developing effective and ongoing supervisor-subordinate interaction. If a supervisor manages performance on a daily basis, all subordinates will have a reasonable idea of where they have succeeded and where they have failed and no formal appraisal session will hold unexpected surprises. However, if this is not done, the supervisor will have to lump together all the praise, criticism, blame and advice into one mixed bundle, the annual delivery of which will hold little joy for either the supervisor or his/her subordinates. Therefore any formal annual appraisal interview should essentially be a summary of previous formal and informal discussions.

13.4.3 Rating errors/judgemental biases

Performance appraisal requires the supervisor to **observe** and **judge** behaviour as objectively as possible. Since both these processes are conducted by humans, the appraisal process is necessarily prone to distortions and biases which confound any attempts at total objectivity.

In order to evaluate the effectiveness of an employee's behaviour, the supervisor must first have observed such behaviour. Unless the rater is able to observe his/her subordinates continuously and to provide regular evaluative feedback, annual appraisal judgements will have to be based on a limited sample of observed performance events (those which the supervisor still remembers). Since many managers may simply not have the time or the inclination to practice "management by walking around" and observing their subordinates at work, sampling errors such as the *recency effect* and *infrequent observations* may lead to invalid and subjective evaluations (Aamodt 1991: 255–257).

● The *recency effect* refers to the tendency to emphasise recent behaviours rather than the individual's performance over the entire review period. Good performers who may have slacked towards the end of the rating period may thus be penalised unfairly.

- The error of *infrequent observations* usually manifests itself in ratings based on non-representative samples of behaviour and unsubstantiated inferences.

   Apart from the obvious advantages that continuous performance management may hold in this regard, the utilisation of multiple raters may alleviate the problem somewhat.

   Some commonly encountered judgemental biases or so-called rater errors are outlined below.

- *Leniency and strictness error.* This is the tendency of some evaluators to assign either mostly favourable ratings or mostly very harsh ratings to all employees.

- *Central tendency.* This is the tendency to assign all ratings towards the centre of all scales, thus evaluating all workers as "average".

- *Halo error.* This is the tendency to allow the rating assigned to one performance dimension to excessively influence, either positively or negatively, the ratings on all subsequent dimensions.

- *Same-as-me and different-from-me error.* This refers to the tendency to assign more favourable ratings to employees who are perceived by the rater to be similar to or to behave in a similar way to the rater or, alternatively, to rate less favourably those workers who demonstrate traits or behaviours different from those of the rater.

- *Contrast error.* This is the tendency to allow the rating of an individual to be positively or negatively influenced by the relative evaluation of the preceding ratee. Thus an average performer may receive a poorer rating than would otherwise have been the case if his/her appraisal follows that of the company's star performer.

13.4.3.1 Overcoming rating errors

Three basic approaches can typically be followed in trying to combat rating errors (Birkenbach 1984).

- The first strategy focuses on the statistical correction of ratings by, for instance, converting all ratings to some type of standard score or by using a forced distribution of ratings in terms of the requirements of a normal curve. In the latter case, the assumption of a normal distribution of employee performance ratings (that is, that there are certain percentages of excellent, average and poor employees in every group) may be a fallacy, since star performers and underperformers may already have been promoted or fired out of the group. Similarly, a group may, for example, consist entirely of top performers due to excellent selection and training.

- The second approach follows the traditional route of addressing appraisal problems, namely that of developing new, more sophisticated techniques and formats that incorporate design features and procedures aimed at minimising the risk of subjectivity.

- Finally, the third approach comprises the training of raters in three important areas (Latham & Wexley 1994: 137–167)
  - O training aimed at eliminating or at least lessening rating errors and biases;
  - O training aimed at promoting better observational skills amongst raters;
  - O training aimed at improved interpersonal and communication skills during appraisal interviews.

Reviews of the effects of rater training generally support the effectiveness of this approach (Cascio 1995: 291).

13.4.4 Problems related to the human interaction process

The very notion of evaluation — as well as the appraisal process itself — may often be a highly emotional issue for both raters and ratees alike.

Raters who feel uncomfortable about any confrontation with subordinates may, for instance, assign average ratings where poor ratings would have been appropriate; ratees facing even the most accurate and objective criticism may resist or trivialise findings if they perceive the assessment as a blow to their self-esteem.

In addition, many situational factors (such as stress, sexual and racial biases, leadership style, etc) have been implicated in contaminating accurate and valid ratings (Cascio 1991: 97–91).

Clearly not even the most advanced and complex technique could possibly hope to control all such possible interactional problems. The importance of fostering effective supervisor-employee relations in the daily performance management process cannot be overemphasised.

13.5 STEPS IN THE DEVELOPMENT OF A SUCCESSFUL PERFORMANCE MANAGEMENT AND APPRAISAL SYSTEM

Whilst the foremost requirement for any effective appraisal system would be a tailor-made design and process that fits the specific needs, business environment, culture, etc of the organisation, there are a number of basic steps common to any successful system.

13.5.1 Planning the system

An effective performance management system should enable and empower line management to implement the strategy and objectives of the organisation successfully. If a manufacturing company, for example, changes the emphasis of its strategy from growth to product quality, the focus of its existing systems and criteria should likewise be changed from high daily outputs to the encouragement, development, reinforcement and reward of those behaviours that contribute to the elimination of errors, wastage and comebacks.

The pertinent questions to be addressed during the planning phase relate directly to the typical problems and fundamental system requirements discussed previously, for example:

- Who will be involved in appraisals (direct supervisor, peers etc)?
- What will the overriding purpose be (developmental or judgemental)?
- How will the results be used?
- What organisational factors need to be taken into account (size, dispersion of branch offices, prevalent culture or management style, etc)?

13.5.2 Developing the system

During this phase appropriate solutions need to be found to design questions such as:

- What is to be appraised (quantitative outputs, traits, etc)?
- How is it to be appraised (choice of format)? (See section 13.6.)
- Who is to appraise whom?
- How often must it be appraised?
- How will the results be linked to improving, developing and rewarding performance?

These questions translate into the following essential activities to be performed by the HR department.

Obtaining basic job information

The gathering of job-related information is done through appropriate job analysis techniques and results in the writing of job descriptions. Analysing job duties and responsibilities should be part of supervisor-employee interaction and HR practitioners should only provide expert advice and the necessary training in writing job descriptions in the style or format chosen by the organisation. Agreement must be reached between supervisor and subordinate on the job requirements.

Establishing performance standards and performance criteria

Performance standards describe the conditions for totally satisfactory performance. Performance standards should be mutually agreed upon and provide details as to:

- the worker action or output that will be assessed;
- the criteria to be used for the assessment; and
- how performance will be measured.

Setting appropriate criteria that meet the requirements discussed in section 13.3 on page 406 is a crucial component of the entire system and a key determinant of its success. Criteria are the measures of "what a person has to do to be successful at performing his/her job" and may be obvious in certain jobs (for example, the number of arrests and number of cases solved for policemen).

(Note that these criteria may not be appropriate if the strategic emphasis of the policeman's job is on community relations and involvement.)

Choosing the format and the sources of appraisal information

Decisions on the format of the appraisal instrument and the sources that should generate the ratings (that is, the direct supervisor, peers, subordinates, consultants, etc) must again be the outcome of thorough deliberation on many factors such as the overall objectives, potential advantages and disadvantages, organisation-specific circumstances, etc.

Preparing documentation

Once the above-mentioned decisions have been made, the appraisal forms have to be designed and a user guide or policies and procedures manual for managers must be prepared.

13.5.3 Implementing the system

Procedures related to the implementation phase focus mainly on various training sessions and introductory exercises. The contents of such training may be determined by the level of involvement of users during the development phase, the complexity of the specific system and the existing competence in performance management of the supervisors.

Although familiarisation and rater training may take on many forms, ranging from mere information provision to "dry-run" conferences and intensive workshops, a few basic aspects need to be covered to ensure its success. The following are some of the important components of effective rater training:

- a training format which allows for the active involvement of raters in the training process, for example modelling, role-play, group discussions;
- thorough familiarisation with the measurement instrument and scales;
- developing rater consensus regarding the interpretation of performance standards and relative levels of behaviour effectiveness (for example, how does "superior" effort differ from "good" effort?);
- encouraging the recording of specific examples of behaviour;
- allowing for experiential exercises and practice;
- providing raters with feedback regarding their own rating behaviour (for example, comparison with expert ratings);
- reinforcing desirable rater behaviour through periodic follow-up training.

13.5.4 Maintaining the system

The maintenance of an appraisal system entails activities such as:

- monitoring the consistent application of performance ratings;
- reviewing pay decisions and recommended disciplinary actions;

- devising and arranging training and development interventions indicated by review results;
- monitoring the internal and external environment for changing circumstances that may necessitate a review or adjustment of current practices;
- auditing and evaluating the effectiveness of the programme on an annual basis.

The case study on page 416 shows how a South African organisation has used the concepts of performance management to develop a workable system geared to its own specific needs.

13.6 APPRAISAL TECHNIQUES

Appraisal techniques may be categorised according to the **type of criteria** utilised namely:

- trait-oriented methods (for example trait scales);
- behaviour-oriented methods (for example critical incidents, BARS);
- results-oriented methods (for example MBO).

Alternatively, techniques may be classified according to the **main purpose** that the procedure serves, namely:

- comparative purposes (relative standards);
- developmental purposes (absolute standards).

In keeping with the dictum that the specific objectives of an appraisal system should determine the choice of format, the second classification approach will be used for distinguishing various appraisal methods.

13.6.1 Relative rating techniques

13.6.1.1 Ranking

Straight ranking entails simply the rank ordering of individuals, according to overall merit or according to other performance factors, from the best performer through to the worst performer.

Clearly this is a very basic evaluation procedure and it is suggested that its use should be limited to cases where:

- only small numbers of individuals are to be rated;
- only the "better than" is important and not the "how much better than";
- employees will not be compared across groups;
- the evaluation is not aimed at feedback to employees (Singer 1990: 213).

13.6.1.2 Paired comparisons

This procedure requires the evaluator to compare each worker separately with each other worker. The eventual ranking of an individual is then determined by the number of times he/she was judged to be better than the other worker.

A case at hand . . .

Performance management at the SA Reserve Bank*

In accordance with the human resource philosophy articulated in the strategic mission statement of the South African Reserve Bank, its human resource department has developed and launched a comprehensive performance management system which provides line management with an integrative framework and powerful tools for managing individual and team performance effectively.

The system essentially follows the different steps in the performance management cycle — that is, planning, managing, reviewing, rewarding and developing performance — and its process comprises the following elements.

Planning for performance: developing a performance plan
The performance plan is a comprehensive document generated jointly by the team leader (manager) and the job incumbent by means of the following steps:
- formulating a job mission comprising the fundamental purpose of the job;
- formulating key result areas, describing tasks and outputs;
- developing performance standards in terms of processes and outputs;
- identifying and describing task requirements in terms of KSAs (knowledge, skills and other attributes);
- mutually agreeing on the appropriate management style in accordance with situational leadership technology.

Managing performance: facilitating team members' performance
The role of the team leader in managing individual performance essentially comprises the creation of a working environment most suited to enabling each team member to achieve the objectives of his or her unique performance plan in accordance with the performance standards mutually agreed upon. A wide variety of resources and management techniques may be applied in this process and essential management training is provided; however, the key element is always **continuous, effective, job-related communication between the manager and the subordinate**. Within the performance management system specific managerial behaviour is required (and also forms part of the individual manager's performance plan).

Rewarding and developing performance
Although not entirely performance based, the Bank's remuneration practices allow performance appraisal results to impact significantly on the allocation of pay increases and other rewards. The performance management system also includes specific procedures on the effective management of substandard performance, ranging from the revision of performance plans to disciplinary action.

Similarly, the information generated by the performance management system provides a direct and integral input for the formal succession planning, management development, and career management programmes in operation at the Reserve Bank. The central and integrative position of the performance management system within the total HRM function is further reinforced by practices such as, for example, the fact that no recruitment for new positions is allowed unless a full performance plan has been developed and the fact that selection procedures focus exclusively on the task requirements (KSAs) specified in the performance plan.

*Source: Human Resources Department, South African Reserve Bank

The number of comparisons required may be calculated by the formula N(N-1)/2, where N refers to the number of individuals to be ranked. The more workers to be ranked, the more unwieldy the method becomes. Limitations are similar to those identified for ranking (see exhibit B).

Exhibit B

Example of paired comparisons

1. Employees to be rated: John, Sipho, Mary, Portia, Peter
2. Paired comparisons: Indicate the better performer in each pair

John ✓	Sipho
John ✓	Mary
John ✓	Portia
John ✓	Peter
Sipho ✓	Mary
Sipho ✓	Portia
Sipho ✓	Peter
Mary	Portia ✓
Mary ✓	Peter
Portia ✓	Peter

Scoring:	Employee	Number of times chosen	Rank
	John	4	1
	Sipho	3	2
	Mary	1	4
	Portia	2	3
	Peter	0	5

13.6.1.3 *Forced distribution*

When using this technique, the evaluator is required to assign certain portions of his/her workers to each of a number of specified categories on each performance factor.

The forced distribution chosen can specify any percentage per category and need not necessarily comply with the requirements of a normal curve. Whilst this format controls rating errors such as leniency and central tendency, the forced distribution chosen may differ substantially from the performance characteristics of the ratees as a group.

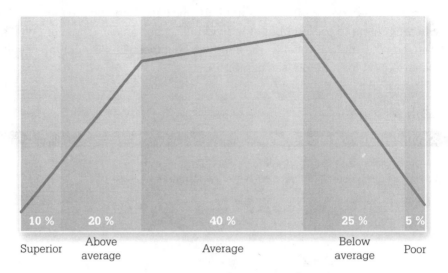

| 10 % | 20 % | 40 % | 25 % | 5 % |
| Superior | Above average | Average | Below average | Poor |

Figure 13.3

Example of a forced distribution

13.6.2 Absolute rating techniques

13.6.2.1 *Essay method*

The rater is required to write a report on each employee, describing individual strengths and weaknesses. The format of the report may be left entirely to the discretion of the rater, or certain specific points of discussion may have to be addressed. This is generally a time-consuming method, the success of which is very much dependent on the writing skills of the raters. If done well, however, it may prove valuable as a feedback tool for the ratees.

13.6.2.2 *Critical incidents*

This technique requires the supervisor to record continuously actual job behaviours that are typical of success or failure, as they occur. Whilst this method focuses on behaviour rather than on traits as a basis of appraisal and thus has the potential for meaningful feedback, the recording of incidents is both time consuming and burdensome for supervisors. This obstacle may often lead supervisors to try to recall and document incidents only towards the end of the review period, thus confounding objectivity and opportunities for timely feedback.

13.6.2.3 *Behavioural checklists*

This format provides the rater with a list of descriptions of job-related behaviours which have to be marked if they are descriptive of the individual being rated. In a variant of this format, the *summated ratings* method, the behavioural statements are followed by a Likert-type scale of response categories, each of which is weighted, for example "strongly agree" = 5 to "strongly disagree" = 1. The weights of the checked response for each item are then summed and represent the overall performance score of the individual.

Exhibit C

Example of a portion of a summated rating scale*					
Knowledge	Strongly agree	Agree	Neutral	Disagree	Strongly disagree
Makes effective use of developments in his/her field of specialisation					
Interprets user's requirements accurately					
Can explain specialist knowledge to non-specialists					
Obtains all relevant information before making decisions					
Keeps abreast of latest developments in his/her field					

*Source: Adapted extract from a Nedbank format

Although this format does not really lend itself to diagnostic feedback, it has the advantage of being behaviourally rather than trait based and has acceptable reliability and controls for some rating errors, for example the halo error.

13.6.2.4 Graphic rating scales

As this is a very popular format, many variations of graphic rating scales can be found. Basically, a scale for a specific trait or characteristic consists of a continuum between two poles on which the rater indicates to what degree the ratee possesses that characteristic. The variations on this basic format stem from:

1. the dimensions on which individuals are to be rated;
2. the degree to which the dimensions are defined; and
3. the degree to which the points on the scale are defined.

The popularity of graphic rating scales is due to advantages such as the fact that they are easy to understand, they allow for comparisons across individuals because they are standardised, they are acceptable to users and they are less time consuming to develop and administer than some other formats.

13.6.2.5 Behaviourally anchored rating scales (BARS)

In essence BARS are a variation of graphic rating scales with the difference that performance dimensions are defined in behavioural terms and the various levels of performance are anchored by examples of critical incidents. Behaviourally anchored rating scales are job specific and require a high level of participation from

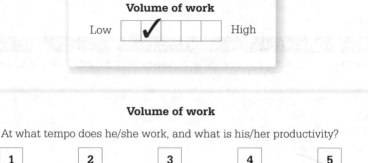

Figure 13.4
Examples of graphic rating scales

Self-confidence

He is realistic and has a positive self-image; acts confidently in a variety of situations

7 — Actively participates in discussions at all levels and in diverse situations; makes suggestions and proposals

6 —

5 — Has a realistic self-image and displays a positive approach to life

4 — He is confident in one-to-one or small discussions, but finds it difficult to participate in groups of six or more people

3 — Shows signs of low self-confidence in unknown or unfamiliar situations

2 —

1 — Too much self-confidence; gives an opinion where it is not wanted; arrogant, conceited, bombastic

Figure 13.5
Example of a Behaviourally Anchored Rating Scale
Source: Adapted from Spangenberg, Esterhuyse, Visser, Briedenhann & Calitz 1989: 23

supervisors. The development of BARS is a complex process, the details of which are beyond the scope of this chapter. Only rudimentary details regarding the different steps in the construction of BARS are provided.

Steps in the development of BARS

1. Behavioural statements/incidents describing effective, average and ineffective behaviour are gathered from job knowledgeable employees and supervisors.
2. Supervisors classify the statements in terms of performance dimensions (for example motivation, know-how) and reject those that are ambiguous.
3. A different group of judges then **retranslates** each statement by rating it on a scale ranging from outstanding to poor performance.
4. Specific statements are then chosen as anchors on the final scale, with the calculated average of the judges' ratings determining where on the scale the statement will feature.

These scales have the advantage of behavioural emphasis, job relevance and a high level of user participation. On the other hand, the complex development procedure makes it a relatively time-consuming and expensive method (Rice 1996: 245).

In addition, their job relatedness does not allow them to be used across dissimilar jobs and, if job requirements should change, new BARS have to be constructed.

13.6.3 Other appraisal methods

There are other performance appraisal methods as well. Two appraisal methods referred to in this section — management by objectives (MBO) and assessment centres — did not originate as appraisal techniques, although they may be utilised as such.

13.6.3.1 *Management by objectives (MBO)*

Management by objectives (MBO) is a management philosophy that focuses on the motivation of individual performance, but due to its process can also be used for evaluating performance. This method typically entails:

- supervisors and employees mutually establishing and discussing specific goals and formulating action plans;
- supervisors aiding their employees to reach their set goals;
- each supervisor and employee reviewing at a preset time the extent to which objectives have been attained.

As a results-based method of appraisal, MBO does not address the **how** of performance and is therefore unable to appraise whether achievements are really the outcome of individual excellence or of external factors.

Since its heyday when MBO was (unfortunately) hailed as the panacea for all management ills, its popularity has declined to the extent that it has largely been relegated to just another planning exercise. However, its emphasis on mutual goal setting, opportunities for participation and regular supervisor-employee interaction are valuable components that are applied in many performance management systems.·

13.6.3.2 Assessment centres

An assessment centre is a procedure originally adopted to assess managerial potential. It is an assessment method that consists of a standardised evaluation of behaviour based on multiple raters and multiple measures such as in-basket excercises, paper and pencil ability tests, leaderless group discussions, simulations and personality questionnaires.

Vecchio (1991) correctly points out that, strictly speaking, an assessment centre is designed to appraise individuals' current managerial ability, rather than their past performance. This future orientation would therefore make the method quite suitable for developmental purposes; this realisation has led to the evolution of assessment centre technology ranging from early selection orientation to the current developmental centres which focus on diagnosing development needs, making development recommendations and providing participants with comprehensive feedback.

In the South African context assessment centres enjoy a relatively high level of popularity. The application of the technology is monitored through an Assessment Centre Study Group in terms of professional guidelines adapted from international standards (Spangenberg 1991: 29–32), and already a substantial body of evidence has been amassed to confirm the value and utility of the technique (Kriek 1991: 34–37).

Despite its potential advantages, the assessment centre has fundamental shortcomings as a practical performance appraisal technique for all levels of employees. Such limitations emanate from the inherently costly nature of the procedure, its overwhelming emphasis on managerial jobs and its exclusive future orientation.

13.6.3.3 360-degree appraisals

Another approach that has gained increasing popularity is the so-called 360-degree performance appraisal technique. Essentially this is a multiple rater/multiple source approach to the assessment of an individual's work performance. In South Africa more and more organisations are making use of (or considering switching to) this method. One example is Fedsure.

The essence of the process revolves around gathering and processing performance assessments on individual employees involving persons such as customers (both internal and external to the organisation), suppliers, peers and team members, superiors, subordinates as well as the person assessed. The data collection process normally includes aspects like formal and stuctured interviews as well as informal discussions, surveys and observations. The assessment information is used as feedback to the employee and serves as important inputs for career development and management and training development. Because of the use of multiple sources, a broader perspective can be developed of an individual's strengths and weaknesses. This enhances self-insight in the process of developing to one's full potential.

This approach fits more comfortably with the latest trends in leadership thinking (see chapter 12) and with strategies emphasising aspects like empowerment, self-responsibility and teamwork. Using multiple data sources can also go a long way in helping to make performance appraisal more fair, simply because elements of subjectivity are lessened and a more balanced view of a person's actual work performance can be created. This can hence also lead to more accurate training needs analyses and to draft more realistic personal development plans (PDPs). It also provides a rich source on which to base one-to-one developmental processes like mentoring and coaching. It furthermore serves the purpose of opening up communication and information flows in the organisation, and in this way it supports more transparent and democratic management. Because it involves customers it is also a valuable means to demonstrate to the customers that the organisation is really customer-focused.

13.7 THE APPRAISAL INTERVIEW

Although a continuous or at least regular interaction process is advocated by the performance management process, the formal appraisal interview at the end of a review period remains a prominent feature of most performance appraisal systems. Irrespective of the appraisal techniques or methods used, appraisal results need to be communicated to employees in a constructive way in order to achieve the aims of providing feedback, motivating and counselling the individuals and also rectifying poor performance.

Despite the fact that the interviews are the responsibility of line management, it will most probably be the HR practitioner's job to ensure the effectiveness of this process by training supervisors how to plan and conduct appraisal interviews properly.

Three types of appraisal interviews are usually distinguished: *tell and sell, tell and listen,* and *problem solving* (Nankervis, Compton & Mc Carthy 1996: 349).

- *Tell and sell approach:* The supervisor acts as judge and jury and needs to persuade the ratee to change his/her behaviour in a prescribed way.
- *Tell and listen approach:* During the first part of the interview the employee's strong and weak areas of performance are addressed; during the second part the focus falls on the employee's feelings about the appraisal.
- *Problem-solving approach:* The supervisor acts as helper and facilitator and discusses the problems, needs, innovations, dissatisfactions, etc that the employee may have experienced since the last performance interview. The main focus is on growth and development.

Job-specific and employee-specific factors may exert a moderating influence on the effectiveness of the interview process, thus implying that there cannot be one single "best approach" for conducting all appraisal interviews. The supervisor should be knowledgeable about such variables and be trained in the neccessary skills for a flexible and situational approach towards appraisal interviews.

It should also be noted that the skills and requirements for effective appraisal interviews correspond with those applicable to other types of interviews, for example selection interview, and general aspects such as as pre-interview preparations, active listening, questioning and feedback techniques should therefore not be excluded from rater training programmes.

In the South African context, with its characteristic racial imbalance in managerial positions, it may also be prudent to focus training efforts on intercultural aspects of communication and interaction.

13.8 CONCLUSION

The effective management of individual performance is the central requirement for the attainment of organisational goals. If line managers are to achieve strategic objectives, accurate information regarding the performance levels of their team members is essential. This is the reason why most organisations insist on a formal and systematic process whereby such information may be gathered and recorded.

An effective performance assessment procedure is the hub of any integrated human resource management system and the information that it generates is utilised for a multitude of purposes. However, despite its extreme importance as a human resource function, the effectiveness of appraisal systems has traditionally been plagued by a variety of knotty problems related to technical as well as human obstacles. On a macrolevel the continuous performance management approach has been advanced as a potentially promising solution, whilst on the microlevel several categories of general problems and their possible remedies have been identified. These may serve as the basic background against which the HR practitioner can proceed to develop and implement a performance appraisal system which is most likely to achieve its stated purpose and is least likely to flounder on the many possible obstacles.

Fundamental requirements for effective appraisals may sometimes be mutually exclusive and decision making during the development process may therefore require trade-offs regarding the utility of the many available choices of appraisal techniques and procedures. The importance of proper implementation procedures and evaluator training has been stressed throughout, since even the best conceived systems and techniques will be ineffective in the hands of an incompetent manager.

Performance evaluation is a vital component of the process of managing human resources with the aim of achieving employee and organisational goals and will remain a key concern for South African HR practitioners and managers alike.

SELF-EVALUATION QUESTIONS

1. Explain the nature (definition), role and value of performance appraisal in human resource management.
2. Differentiate between performance appraisal and performance management.
3. "There are certain fundamental requirements underlying successful performance appraisal systems." Discuss this statement.
4. What are some of the common problems related to designing performance appraisal systems?
5. Explain the problem of "rating errors/judgemental biases" within the context of performance appraisal.
6. Write an essay detailing the process of developing, implementing and maintaining a successful performance appraisal and management system.
7. Explain various performance appraisal techniques.
8. What is "MBO"?
9. What guidelines can you provide regarding the successful conduct of a performance appraisal interview?

BIBLIOGRAPHY

Aamodt, MG. 1991. *Applied Industrial/Organizational Psychology*. Belmont, California: Wadsworth

Birkenbach, RC. 1984. Halo, central tendency and leniency in performance appraisal: A comparison between a graphic rating scale and a behaviourally based measure. *Perspectives in Industrial Psychology*, 10(1), 15–34

Butler, JE, Ferris, GR & Napier, NK. 1991. *Strategy and Human Resource Management* Cincinnati, OH: South Western

Cardy, R & Dobbins, G. 1994. *Performance Appraisal: Alternative Perspectives.* Cincinnati, OH: South Western

Cascio, WF. 1989. *Managing Human Resources: Productivity, Quality of Work Life, Profits*, 2 ed. New York: McGraw-Hill

Cascio, WF. 1991. *Applied Psychology in Personnel Management*, 4 ed. Englewood Cliffs, NJ: Pretice-Hall

Cascio, WF. 1995. *Managing Human Resources: Productivity, Quality of Work Life, Profits*, 4 ed. New York. McGraw-Hill

Kreitner, R & Kinicki, A. 1995. *Organizational Behavior*, 3 ed. Homewood, Ill: Irwin

Kriek, H. 1991. Die bruikbaarheid van die takseersentrum: 'n Oorsig van resente literatuur. *Journal of Industrial Psychology*, 17(3), 34–37

Latham, GP & Wexley, KN. 1994. *Increasing Productivity through Performance Appraisal*, 2 ed. Reading, Mass: Addison-Wesley

Lockett, J. 1992. *Effective Performance Management*. London: Kogan Page

McGregor, D. 1957. An uneasy look at performance appraisal. *Harvard Business Review*, 35(3), 89–94

Nankervis, AR, Compton, RL & McCarthy, TE. 1996. *Strategic Human Resource Management*, 2 ed. Melbourne: Thomson

Rice, B. 1996. Performance review: The job nobody likes. In *Human Resources Management*, eds GR Ferris & MR Buckley, 3 ed, 245. Englewood Cliffs, NJ: Prentice-Hall

Robbins, SP. 1995. *Supervision Today*. Englewood Cliffs, NJ: Prentice-Hall

Singer, MG. 1990. *Human Resource Management*. Boston: PWS-Kent

Spangenberg, H. 1991. New guidelines and ethical considerations for assessment centre operations. *IPM Journal*, June, 29–32

Spangenberg, H. 1993. A managerial view on performance management. *People Dynamics*, 11(12), 30–34

Spangenberg, H. 1994. *Understanding and Implementing Performance Management*. Kenwyn: Juta

Spangenberg, HH, Esterhuyse, JJ, Visser, JH, Briedenhann, JE & Calitz, CJ. 1989. Construction of behaviourally anchored rating scales (BARS) for the measurement of managerial performance. *Journal of Industrial Psychology*, 15(1), 22–27

Swan, WS. 1991. *How to do a Superior Performance Appraisal*. New York: Wiley

Szilagyi, AD & Wallace, MJ. 1990. *Organizational Performance and Behavior*, 5 ed. Glenview, Ill: Scott Foresman

Vecchio, RP. 1991. *Organizational Behavior*, 2 ed. Chicago: Dryden

STUDY OBJECTIVES

After studying this chapter, you should be able to:

- describe the concepts *career, career development, career planning* and *career management;*
- discuss the career choice theories of Holland and Super;
- define the term *career anchor* and discuss the different anchors;
- describe the different career patterns;
- describe the different kinds of plateaued performers;
- discuss possible solutions to career plateauing;
- define "obsolescence" and explain the "worker obsolescence model";
- name certain actions that can be taken by organisations to prevent obsolescence;
- define "job loss" and explain how employees who have lost their jobs can be assisted;
- define a "working couple";
- define work–family conflict;
- explain three types of work–family conflict;
- discuss possible organisational actions to balance work–family needs;
- discuss different career development support methods.

14.1 INTRODUCTION

As we have mentioned time and again, organisations worldwide are in a state of flux. They are changing in terms of structure, labour composition, size and technological make-up. The global economy and technological revolution bring new international competition which imposes new demands on organisations. Organisations are under pressure to do more with less, to be more flexible, efficient and effective. Organisations are adapting by, among other things, designing flatter structures, organising around processes rather than functions, using self-directed work teams, and by being more knowledge based, with less emphasis on command and control and narrowly defined jobs.

These organisational changes have wide-ranging implications for careers. The following trends are becoming increasingly apparent.

- Careers are becoming more cyclical, and lateral rather than upward career moves are becoming more widespread (Hall & Mervis 1995: 333).

- Individuals take ownership of their careers while the organisation plays a supportive role (Hall & Mervis 1995: 334).

- Continuous learning and development are essential in order to live up to the new expectations (Schein 1993: 54).

- New kinds of employment relationships are emerging as more and more people are becoming freelance providers of skills and services (Rousseau & Wade-Benzoni 1995).

- Employability rather than employment becomes a source of security (Kanter 1990: 322).

- The traditional role of the manager is changing (Harris 1993).

In the light of the above, the individual is expected to take control of his/her career, while the organisation plays more of a supportive role in this self-management process. Information about opportunities in the organisation and the provision of techniques to facilitate the career planning process are two important sources of assistance in this process.

In this chapter a career is defined in the context of present demands, and other important elements of the career management process are examined and discussed.

14.2 CAREER CONCEPTS

An indication of the changes currently taking place in organisations is that, according to Hall & Mervis (1995), careers should become more *protean*. The term *protean* is taken from the name of the Greek god Proteus who could change shape at will (Hall & Mervis 1995: 322).

A *protean career* is defined as "a process which the person, not the organisation, is managing. It consists of all the person's varied experiences in education, training, work in several organisations, changes in occupational field and so forth. The protean career is not what happens to the person in any one organisation. In short, the protean career is shaped more by the individual than by the organisation and may be redirected from time to time to meet the needs of the person" (Hall & Mervis 1995: 332).

Career development can be defined as an "ongoing process by which individuals progress through a series of stages, each of which is characterized by a relatively unique set of issues, themes or tasks" (Greenhaus & Callanan 1994: 7).

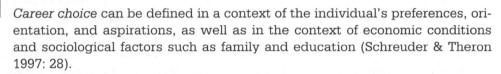

Career planning can be described as "the process by which employees obtain knowledge about themselves (their values, personality, preferences, interests, abilities, etc) and information about the working environment, and then making an effort to achieve a proper match" (Schreuder & Theron 1997: 15).

Career management is described as an "ongoing process in which an individual (1) gathers relevant information about himself/herself and the world of work (2) develops an accurate picture of his/her talents, interests, values and preferred life-style as well as alternative occupations, jobs and organisations (3) develops realistic career goals based on this information and picture (4) develops and implements a strategy designed to achieve the goals (5) obtains feedback regarding the effectiveness of the strategy and the relevance of the goals. " (Greenhaus & Callanan 1994: 7).

14.3 CAREER CHOICE

Career choice can be defined in a context of the individual's preferences, orientation, and aspirations, as well as in the context of economic conditions and sociological factors such as family and education (Schreuder & Theron 1997: 28).

Over the last fifty years many different theories of career choice have been formulated to explain how individuals choose careers. These theories can be divided into the so-called **content theories**, which describe career choice in terms of specific factors, such as individual characteristics or the psychological phenomena that are involved in choice, and the so-called **process theories** which describe career choice as a dynamic process that evolves over stages of development (Schreuder & Theron 1997: 28). Career choice is now described in terms of a process theory (Super) and a content theory (Holland).

14.3.1 Super's theory

According to Super, career choice refers to a whole series of related decisions which are made during a development process covering five life stages from childhood to old age. The following career stages are identified (Super 1992).

1. **Growth** (from birth until the beginning of puberty, that is from about 0 to 14 years)

   Although during childhood careers have not yet become a relevant factor, it is now generally believed that the instinct of curiosity makes children explore their environment, all the while gathering information, particularly through contact with adults whom they adopt as role models. During this time, they ought to develop certain concepts of their future roles as adults, their autonomy, self-esteem, a perspective on the future and a feeling of being in charge of their lives. Once they have developed interests through fantasy, experience and feedback, they are able to plan for the future. As they gradually become aware of the opportunities that life offers them, their interests become more closely linked to reality.

2. **Exploration** (adolescence, that is, from about 14 to 25 years)

   While the only type of systematic exploration during this stage is provided by schools and other organisations, an adolescent's social exploration is stimulated by his or her parents and/or peer group. This may lead to the first tentative attempts at career exploration, which later become more focused. If, however, an adult has set an adolescent career goal, his or her career exploration may be too focused, which may lead to unhappiness and frustration later in life.

3. **Establishment** (early adulthood, that is, from about 25 to 45 years)

   As early adulthood is reached, some individuals stabilise as far as their career exploration is concerned, while others continue to change careers, their field of activity and their level of employment throughout their lives. It was found, however, that children of well-educated parents tend to be well-educated themselves and to be employed at higher levels than the children of people with a low level of education. Young adults also tend to pass through a stage of trying out various careers in their late twenties, followed by stabilisation in their thirties and early forties. This is in turn followed by a period of consolidation and advancement, without which the individual usually becomes frustrated, causing him or her either to stagnate in a career or to change careers.

4. **Maintenance** (middle age, from about 45 to 65 years)

   Those adults who had previously stabilised in a career now attempt to maintain their position in the workplace in the face of competition from younger people, whose more up-to-date training may pose a threat to the career advancement of their older counterparts. Those who fail to advance tend to stagnate and become disillusioned. They now avoid opportunities to learn new skills and develop a passive approach to their work instead of actively acquiring and applying new knowledge. The more motivated keep up to date in their career fields, while the innovators are constantly exploring new avenues.

5. **Decline** (old age, from about 65 years onwards)

   As people age, they often grow to resent their physical and mental decline and the implications that this has for their future. In fact, the process of decline already begins around the age of 25. This is particularly apparent in physically-oriented careers, such as in sports. As older people become aware of their declining powers, they tend to slow down, sometimes disengaging themselves from some areas of life. Others continue to work long past retirement age. Indeed, for many people retirement is a negative experience, while for some it means a wealth of new opportunities, a feeling of being wanted and the excitement of returning to the explorative stage.

14.3.2 Holland's theory

One of the most widely used approaches to guide career choices is the theory of John L Holland. According to Holland (1985), personality (including values, driving forces and needs) is an important determinant of career choice. Holland (1985) says that the choice of career is in fact an expression of personality. He states that there is an interaction between personality and the environment, so that individuals are drawn towards environments which correlate with their personal orientation. Holland found it necessary to categorise people according to their personality types, and to associate these personality types with specific environmental models. He identified six basic personality types and according to him, each person shows a degree of similarity to one of these types. The greater the degree of similarity, the more an individual will exhibit behaviour patterns typical of a certain personality type. With regard to the environmental models, he distinguishes between six similar types, and by integrating the individual and the environment, conclusions can be made regarding career choice, career stability, career performance, personal capabilities and social behaviour. Holland (1973) based his theory on four primary points of departure:

- In our culture most people can be categorised as one of six types — realistic, investigative, social, conventional, enterprising and artistic. Each type is established through a unique interaction between various sociocultural, personal and physical environmental factors. Each individual belongs primarily to one of these personality types, but may also exhibit characteristics of the other types. In this way profile is derived which could indicate that individual's personality pattern.
- There are six similar environmental types: realistic, investigative, social, conventional, enterprising and artistic. In each environment there are individuals of similar personality types. Each environment also has certain limitations, and individuals of the same personality type group together according to the same environmental models.
- People seek out environments which will allow them to practise their capabilities and abilities, to express their attitudes and values and to accept problems and roles. This pursuit takes place in various ways, and has the result that a realistic person will, for example, find the biggest potential for self-expression in a realistic environment, and the social person in a social environment.
- A person's behaviour is determined by the interaction between a personality and an environment. Being aware of an individual's personality pattern and the type of environment he/she prefers could facilitate a prediction with regard to career choice, career stability and career performance, as well as educational and social behaviour.

14.3.2.1 Personality types

Holland (1973: 14–17) describes the characteristics of the personality types as follows.

- The preferences of the *realistic personality type* include the clear and orderly manipulation of aspects such as tools, machinery and animals, through which, amongst others mechanical, electrical, technical and manual skills could be acquired. This personality type prefers realistic careers, such as craftsman, farmer, and so forth, and avoids socially oriented careers such as barman, social worker, etc. This person values concrete things, such as money, and personal characteristics such as status and power.

- The *investigative personality type* develops a preference for the observation and creative investigation of physical, biological and cultural phenomena, with the aim of understanding and controlling these phenomena. This personality type prefers investigative careers in fields such as economics, engineering, psychology, veterinary science, computer programming, toolmaking, and so forth, and avoids situations of an enterprising nature. This person regards himself/herself as learned and has a high regard for scientific knowledge.

- The *social personality type* develops a pattern of behaviour preferences which includes the manipulation of people by means of activities such as training and assistance. This type of person usually prefers socially oriented careers, such as social worker, teacher, and so forth, and avoids realistic careers, such as mechanical engineer, plumber etc. This person regards himself/herself as being well equipped to help other people, to understand and to educate them, and he/she also places a high priority on social and ethical matters.

- The *conventional personality type* displays a pattern of preference for orderly, systematic jobs, such as keeping records, filing, and so forth, through which clerical and accountancy skills, for example are acquired. This type of person prefers conventional careers such as record keeper and typist and avoids careers in the arts such as photographer, musician, etc. This individual sees himself/herself as conforming and orderly, and as having clerical and numerical skills, and has a high regard for business and economic achievements.

- The *enterprising personality type* develops a pattern of preference for activities which entail the manipulation of people in the pursuit of organisational objectives or economic advantages, through which leadership and interpersonal and persuasive skills are acquired. This type of person prefers careers and situations which demand an enterprising nature, such as a banker, estate agent and so forth, and avoids careers requiring analytical skills such as economist, actuary, etc. This personality type regards himself/herself as aggressive, popular, full of self-confidence and blessed with leadership and communicative skills, and has a high regard for economic achievements.

- The *artistic personality type* develops a pattern of preference for free, unsystemised activities which involves the manipulation of human, physical and verbal material, and the acquisition of skills in the fields of language, art, music, drama and writing. This type of person prefers a career in the arts such as language teacher, dramatist, etc, and avoids conventional activities such as typist, accountant, and so forth. This individual regards himself/herself as creative, nonconforming, independent, organised and blessed with artistic and verbal skills such as writing, communicating, acting, having a high regard for the aesthetic.

14.3.2.2 Environmental types

Holland (1973: 29–33) describes the characteristics of the six corresponding environmental types as follows.

- The *realistic environment* is characterised by the domination of environmental demands and opportunities, involving the orderly and systematic use of tools, machinery and animals, and is also marked by a population consisting mainly of realistic personality types.
- The *investigative environment* has dominant characteristics such as the observation and symbolical, systematic and creative investigation of physical, biological or cultural phenomena.
- The *social environment* is distinguished by a population consisting mainly of social personality types.
- The *conventional environment* is characterised by the dominance of environmental demands and opportunities involving the orderly and systematic manipulation of data, such as record keeping, filing, reproducing documents, compiling data according to a prescribed plan, and working with business machines and data processors. This environment is dominated mainly by conventional personality types.
- The *enterprising environment* is characterised by demands and opportunities from the environment regarding the manipulation of other persons in order to achieve personal and/or organisational goals, and is also marked by the presence of especially enterprising personality types.
- The *artistic environment* is dominated by demands and opportunities which include ambiguous, free and unsystemised activities and skills for the creation of art and art products, and consists mainly of a population of artistic personality types.

When an individual is faced with a career choice, his/her characteristics are compared with the above-mentioned types, with the aim of determining with which type he/she displays the most similarities. A person's personality type is the primary determinant of career choice in that an enterprising type would thus most probably select an enterprising career. The first and second subpersonality types will determine the individual's second and third choices. The vocational guidance tutor who works according to this approach will concentrate on determining the individual's personality style and on the selection of a suitable career environment.

14.3.3 Environmental influences on career choice

Thus far we have only discussed individual differences which influence career choice. There are, however, also a number of environmental influences which play a role in career choice. These are described as nonpsychological factors (Crites 1969: 79).

The **family** undoubtedly plays an important role in career choice, as even at an early age children identify with their parents and often prefer the careers which their parents hold in high esteem. It is often believed that the family, through its economic interests, affiliations and values, determine the careers of family members. A South African study by Van Rooyen (1969: 180) indicated that the higher the career structure and educational level of the parents, the higher the aspirations of their children. Hall (1976: 22) asserts that the background and attitudes of the parents have a greater influence than those of friends, teachers and other influential people in society. According to Crites (1969: 88) the **school**, second to the family, exerts the biggest influence on career choice.

Sometimes an individual finds himself/herself in a career which he/she did not purposefully pursue, but is appointed in a position due to coincidence, unplanned and unforeseeable circumstances. These are normally referred to as the **chance factors** which influence a person's career choice (accident theory) (Crites 1969: 79).

14.4 CAREER MANAGEMENT STEPS

Various steps in career management according to Greenhaus and Callanan (1994: 18) are discussed below.

Career exploration (step one) is the collection and analysis of information to enable the individual to become aware of himself/herself (values, interests, talents) and his/her environment (occupations, jobs, organisations). This information will create an **awareness of self and of the environment (step two)** so that more informed decisions can be made. Because of this greater awareness a **career goal, (step three)** that is, what the individual decides he/she wants to accomplish **(step four)** can then be formulated. Once the career goal has been decided on, a **career strategy**, which will enable the individual to attain his/her career goal, can then be **developed (step five)** and **implemented (step six)**. Once a strategy has been implemented **progress toward the career goal (step seven)** can be made and useful **feedback (step eight)** can also be provided to the individual. The feedback will enable the individual to do **career appraisal (step nine)** which is the process that enables the individual to determine whether his/her goals and strategies are still relevant. The information obtained from the career appraisal can be used for **career exploration (step one)** and so the career management cycle is continued.

14.5 RELATED CAREER ISSUES

14.5.1 Career anchors

Career anchors are developed during the early stages of an individual's career, that is, during the establishment and achievement stages although it is quite possible for an individual only to become aware of his or her career anchors much later.

14.5.1.1 Definition of career anchor

Although new employees may be appointed to a position for which he or she has been trained, this does not mean that he or she will be able to meet the present and future requirements of his/her job and potential career. The new employee will not know whether he/she will like the new work or whether his/her values will fit those of the organisation. During the initial period of employment, the organisation and the employee get to know each other. This allows the person to acquire more information about the career he or she has embarked on. The new employee gradually gains more knowledge about him/herself and develops a clearer self-concept. This self-concept comprises the following three components, which, according to Schein (1978), together form the employee's career anchor.

Schein (1978: 125) describes a career anchor as follows:

- self-perceived *talents* and abilities based on actual successes in a variety of work settings;
- self-perceived *motives* based on opportunities for self-testing and self-diagnoses in real situations and on feedback from others;
- self-perceived *values* based on actual encounters between self and the norms and values of the employing organisation and work setting.

According to Schein (1978, 1990), a career anchor consists of the individual's talents, motives and values, as perceived by him- or herself, which the individual uses to delimit motives and stabilise his or her career. If an employee is not aware of his/her career anchor, he/she could land up in a work situation in which he/she lacks job satisfaction. As an individual is likely to make job selections that are consistent with his or her self-image, career anchors can serve as a basis for career choices (Schein 1990).

14.5.1.2 Types of career anchors

Schein (1990: 58–60) identified the following career anchors.

Technical/functional competence

Employees for whom technical/functional competence is a career anchor, attempt to find ways in which they can use skills to improve their competence. They are self-confident and enjoy challenges. Such employees are usually competent leaders in their own fields of specialisation, but tend to avoid general management because this usually involves leaving their field of expertise. As the working environment becomes increasingly technologically complex, the need for technical/functional expertise will grow. However, the rapid advances in technological development means that such experts must constantly keep up to date and abreast of the progress being made in their particular fields (Schein 1996: 83).

Managerial competence

Employees for whom general managerial competence is a career anchor like to coordinate the activities of other employees and want to be seen to be making a positive contribution to the success of the company or department for which they work. A person with this type of anchor "needs to be" a manager as he/she must give expression to interpersonal skills (influencing and controlling people), analytical skills (identifying and solving problems in uncertain situations), and emotional stability (stimulation by emotional and interpersonal crises, rather than experiencing them as tiresome). Schein (1996) foresees that the need for general management will increase and will permeate the lower levels of organisations. Greater coordination and integration at lower levels will be required as work becomes more technically complex.

Autonomy/independence

Employees for whom autonomy/independence is a career anchor like to carry out their work in their own way. They enjoy variety and flexibility, but are unsuited to strictly regulated jobs or jobs that require them to exercise control over others. If forced into such position, they may well decide to start a business of their own. As the working environment is changing rapidly, such employees often find the world an easier place to negotiate. Schein (1996: 820) puts it as follows: "The autonomy anchored is aligned, at least for the present, with most organisational policies of promising only employability." Self-reliance, which is important for future career survival, is already part of these employees and they may become the role models of others in future (Schein 1996).

Security/stability

Employees for whom security/stability is a career anchor consider both financial and job security to be important. They like to settle at a company and are prepared to employ their skills in any manner required of them. If such an employee changes form one organisation to another, he/she always chooses a similar type of organisation and a similar type of work. At present these employees are experiencing the most severe problems due to the current shift from "employment security" to "employability security" which is taking place in organisations. This means that employees can only expect from employers the opportunity to learn and the employee should become dependent on himself/herself (Schein 1996).

Entrepreneurial creativity

Employees for whom entrepreneurial creativity is a career anchor would jump at the opportunity of creating a business of their own. They want to show the world that they can create a business that is the result of their own efforts. These people often work for a company initially to gain the experience that they need to go out on their own. Current developments in the working environment are convincing more and more people that they can develop their own business. The opportunities for people who are anchored in entrepreneurial creativity will probably greatly increase in future.

Lifestyle

Employees for whom lifestyle is a career anchor like to find a compromise between their personal needs, family needs and the requirements of their career. Schein (1990: 60) explains this as follows: "You want to make all of the major sectors of your life work together toward an integrated whole, and you therefore need a career situation that provides enough flexibility to achieve such integration. " Sometimes such employees have to sacrifice certain aspects of their career (for example, they are often reluctant to accept transfer to another city or country). They define success in broader terms than simply career success and their identity is dependant more on how they live their total life. Schein (1996: 82) states that, since his original research of the 1960s and 1970s, this anchor has shown the most change. As social values are moving towards more autonomy and concern for self, people are becoming more preoccupied with lifestyle. Just as in the United States, the current trend in South Africa is for executives to shift from the technical/functional or general management category or career anchor.

Sense of service/dedication to a cause

Employees for whom service/dedication is a career anchor, are always prepared to do something to improve life in general, whether to upgrade the state of the environment, to promote peace, etc. These employees may even change employers in order to carry on doing this kind of job and do not accept any promotion unless the new position meets the requirements of their value system. Schein (1996: 85) reports that the number of people with this anchor is increasing. He states that not only young people but people of middle age are expressing this need to do something meaningful in a larger context.

Challenge

Employees for whom pure challenge is a career anchor enjoy undertaking difficult tasks and solving complex problems. They never choose the easy way out of a problem and like to "achieve the impossible". They tend to grow bored quickly when the job holds no challenge for them. Schein (1996: 85) is of the opinion that the number of people with this career anchor is growing. However, he is uncertain whether this is the result of more people with this predisposition entering the labour market or the result of an adaptation to the present-day changing and challenging working environment.

14.5.2 Career patterns

Just as career success and advancement can indicate whether or not an individual's career is oriented around a specific career anchor (Schein 1993), so too can these factors be indicative of the career patterns that individuals follow (Brousseau 1990).

For some success may mean promotion, for others recognition in a field of expertise, while others seek to live a life of social contribution or to move frequently from one challenge to another. Driver (1979) has developed a model that suggests that individuals possess unique views about how their careers should develop. This model can be used to identify an individual's preferred career pattern and also to provide a basis for career decisions. The following four career patterns describe different types of careers and are ways of describing the ideal career. Each career pattern is based on underlying motives (Brousseau 1990).

The linear career pattern

Employees who prefer a linear career pattern like to progress within the organisational hierarchy and be rewarded with promotion and instant recognition, as well as financial rewards such as high salaries, perks and incentives schemes. They are usually in managerial positions and hold power, achievement, status and money in high regard.

The expert career pattern

These employees work within their chosen career field for their entire careers. They identify themselves with their fields of expertise, and aspects such as expertise, security and stability are strongly correlated with this pattern. Their emphasis is on the acquisition of special skills. Examples of this career pattern are medical practitioners, engineers and lawyers. These people prefer to be rewarded by speciality assignments and skills training. They prefer recognition for their expertise in a specific field.

The spiral career pattern

Employees who prefer a spiral career pattern tend to change their career fields periodically. These changes are major and entail a change from one field to another, thus allowing them to acquire new skills and capabilities while using their previous experience. Motives such as self-development and creativity are highly regarded by the spiral career person.

The transitory career pattern

Employees with a transitory career pattern tend to change careers fields as often as every two to four years. This pattern has been referred to as a "consistent pattern of inconsistency". They are independent and like variety in life. Their most favoured rewards are immediate financial rewards, flexible working hours, job rotation and autonomy.

14.5.3 Career plateaus

A career plateau is defined as "the point in a person's career when there is no longer any opportunity to progress in the organisational hierarchy" (Leibowitz, Kaye & Farren 1990: 28).

A distinction can be made between structural and content plateauing. *Structural* plateauing refers to a situation in which opportunities for promotion are restricted by the structure (pyramid) of the organisation. Only a few employees can make it to the top. *Content* plateauing occurs when an employee knows the job too well and no challenges are left. The challenge for managers is at least to address the problems of content plateauing, as it is the easier one to avoid (Leibowitz et al 1990: 28).

14.5.3.1 Plateaued performers

Four kinds of plateaued performers are identified by Leibowitz et al (1990: 30), namely productively plateaued, partially plateaued, passively plateaued and pleasantly plateaued.

Kinds of plateaued performers

1. Productively plateaued

   These employees experience job satisfaction because they feel that they have achieved their ambitions. They are loyal to the organisation because they feel that the organisation supports them in achieving their personal goals, and recognises their contributions. They are productive high performers, but occasionally require motivation.

2. Partially plateaued

   Employees who are partially plateaued feel that the organisation does not do much for them, but they usually have an interest that maintains their involvement in the job. These people are usually specialist in a certain field, but feel that their jobs lack excitement and that their organisation does not support them enough in acquiring new skills. They value any opportunity to acquire new skills.

3. Pleasantly plateaued

   These employees who are pleasantly plateaued do not aim for promotion and change, but prefer to remain where they are. They are unlikely to be innovative, and usually stay with one organisation.

4. Passively plateaued

   Employees who are passively plateaued feel that they have been in their jobs for too long and know them too well. They lack challenge and display no interest in additional training in their fields. However, they also feel unable to change their situations.

14.5.3.2 Organisational actions

Certain actions can be followed by organisations to address the problem of plateauing.

The following are possible solutions (Allen, Poteet, Russel & Dobbins 1995: 15–18; Leibowitz et al 1990: 32):

- change the structure of the organisation;
- pay for performance;
- set up job rotation programmes to create lateral movement and broaden skills;
- give candid feedback;
- establish a career plan and goals;
- provide individual career planning opportunities (for example career planning workshops, self-assessment of skills);
- encourage career exploration;
- encourage further education.

14.5.4 Obsolescence

"Obsolescence is the degree to which professionals lack the up-to-date knowledge or skills necessary to maintain effective performance in either their current or future work roles" (Kaufman 1974: 24). This simply means that an individual is becoming outmoded and outdated.

14.5.4.1 Dealing with worker obsolescence

Worker obsolescence illustrates the continuous process in which the balance between the employee and the job is upset, either by technological factors such as computerisation or by organisational factors such as restructuring, or even by an action on the part of the employee. Once the balance has been upset, symptoms such as frustration, hostility or resistance to change may result. Once the symptoms have been identified, treatment in the form of training courses, organisational changes or career counselling may follow to restore the balance between the worker and the job, until the cycle is repeated (Bracker & Pearson 1986).

Managers can take certain actions to prevent worker obsolescence and to reduce feelings of obsolescence. These include the following:

- providing training and education;

- encouraging continuous learning;

- providing challenging initial work;

- encouraging people to attend conferences and to subscribe to professional journals;

- stimulating employees to stay up to date with new techniques;

- creating a culture of growth and development.

14.5.5 Job loss

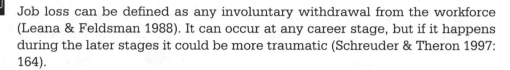

Job loss can be defined as any involuntary withdrawal from the workforce (Leana & Feldsman 1988). It can occur at any career stage, but if it happens during the later stages it could be more traumatic (Schreuder & Theron 1997: 164).

It is well known that an individual's emotional well-being can be extremely adversely affected by the loss of a job. It is even more traumatic if any of the following conditions are present (McKnight 1991):

- if it appears unlikely that the individual will find alternative employment;
- if the individual lacks multiple skills;
- if the individual has worked for only one employer;
- if the employee perceives himself/herself is to be unemployable.

Managers can take the following steps to assist people who have lost their jobs:

- introducing training programmes which teach workers who have been laid off how to manage stress and take control of the future;
- helping people to overcome the initial shock of job loss and providing advice on career moves (professionals can be used in this regard).

14.5.6 Working couples and work–family conflict

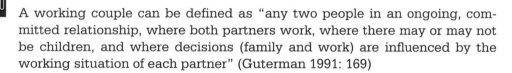

A working couple can be defined as "any two people in an ongoing, committed relationship, where both partners work, where there may or may not be children, and where decisions (family and work) are influenced by the working situation of each partner" (Guterman 1991: 169)

Working couples are more likely to experience work–family conflict than couples in which only one partner works

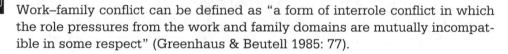

Work–family conflict can be defined as "a form of interrole conflict in which the role pressures from the work and family domains are mutually incompatible in some respect" (Greenhaus & Beutell 1985: 77).

Three types of work–family conflict have been identified (Greenhaus & Beutell 1985: 88):

- *Time-based* conflict develops when time that is devoted to one role cannot be devoted to another. Time-based conflict would occur when time pressures in one role makes it impossible to satisfy the expectations of the other role. Inflexible work schedules, excessive overtime and work involvement can be related to work–family conflict.

- *Strain-based* conflict occurs when performance in one role is adversely affected by the stress that is experienced in another. For example, a crisis in the family can cause fatigue which results in poor performance at work.

- *Behaviour-based* conflict occurs when certain patterns of role behaviour are in conflict with expectations of behaviour in other roles. For example, a male manager is expected to be self-reliant, emotionally stable, and somewhat aggressive, while the manager's family expects him to be warm and caring.

Conflict between work and family roles can, for instance, be created by the following work-related factors:

- number of hours worked;
- lack of control over the decision to work overtime;
- an inflexible work schedule;
- irregular starting time;
- psychologically demanding work.

On the basis of current research, Schreuder and Theron (1997: 152) suggest, *inter alia* the following action to balance family and work needs:

- more organisational sensitivity for home life;
- the introduction of flexible benefits to assist employees with family needs such as child care and the care of sick children;
- the introduction of flexible work hours and work-at-home programmes;
- the revision of relocation policies to make provision for the needs of the modern worker;
- the introduction of alternative career paths: not all employees want to climb the corporate ladder.

The diversity of today's workforce underscores the need for flexible policies to accommodate the personal responsibilities, aspirations and needs of employees.

14.6 CAREER DEVELOPMENT SUPPORT METHODS

While the employee is primarily responsible for career planning, the organisation's management can do a great deal to support employees in managing their careers and in making more realistic career decisions (Schreuder & Theron 1997: 126).

The following are methods that can be used by organisations to support career development.

14.6.1 Career planning workshops

Career planning workshops are widely used by organisations as part of their career development systems. In such a workshop people obtain self-knowledge (that is, insight in their strengths and weaknesses) and are introduced to work opportunities. An action plan usually results.

Such workshops should cover the following aspects (Otte & Hutcheson 1992: 19–20):

- individual assessment (information about self);
- environmental assessment (information about work);

- comparison of self-perceptions with those of others (reality testing);
- establishing long- and short-term career goals (goal setting);
- choosing among alternatives (decision making);
- establishing and implementing plans (action planning).

14.6.2 Career discussion

"A career discussion is a planned discussion between a manager and an employee who are attempting jointly to clarify developmental options in the employee's current job, examine career issues in light of current job performance and goals of the organisation, and/or clarify future career options for that employee" (Otte & Hutcheson 1992: 46).

Conducting career discussions is one of the most important HRM tasks of the manager. In this way managers support career planning. The manager should act as an adviser and facilitate the career development process.

14.6.3 Career centres

A *career centre* is a repository of the relevant material to assist employees in career planning. The information provided can not only inform the employee of career opportunities within the organisation but also avail him/her of self-knowledge.

14.6.4 Career planning workbooks

Facilities such as career centres and workshops are not always available to all employees. A well-designed workbook can fill this need. The individual works alone through a series of assessment exercises and thereby obtains valuable self-knowledge. In this way a workbook can achieve some of the objectives of a workshop.

14.7 CONCLUSION

This chapter examined various factors related to the management of employees' careers and the implications of recent developments taking place in organisations worldwide were briefly discussed. The concept *career* was defined within the context of the adaptive organisation. "The new career is about experience, skill, flexibility and personal development. It does not involve predefined career paths, routine ticket punching, stability or security" (Hall & Mervis 1995: 330). A model was used to depict career management as an ongoing process whereby the individual develops realistic career goals and develops a strategy for achieving these goals. The process of career choice is illustrated by different theories.

Although career management is primarily the responsibility of the individual, the organisation has a role to play in helping the individual to make better career decisions. This can be achieved through in-house career workshops, career centres, the provision of career workbooks and counselling.

Career issues such as plateauing, job loss and working couples are the order of the day. Suggestions were put forward regarding the actions that organisations can take to manage these issues.

SELF-EVALUATION QUESTIONS

1. Do individuals have a responsibility to manage their own careers? Explain.
2. How would you describe the employer's responsibility in career management?
3. Would you agree that career choice is a single event which usually occurs in the early twenties? Motivate.
4. What is a career anchor? With which anchor do you associate best?
5. How would you utilise career anchors in career management?
6. Describe briefly what appears to you to be the ideal career.
7. How would you distinguish between structural and content career plateau?
8. Define a "working couple".
9. How can employers help employees to manage their careers?

BIBLIOGRAPHY

Allen, TD, Poteet, ML, Russel, JEA & Dobbins, GH. 1995. *Influence of Learning and Development factors on Perceptions of Plateauing.* Paper presented at the Tenth Annual Meeting of the Society for Industrial and Organisational Psychology, Orlando

Bracker, JS & Pearson, JN. 1986. Worker obsolescence: The human resource dilemma of the 80s. *Personal Administrator*, 31(12), 113

Brousseau, KR. 1990. Career dynamics in the baby boom and baby bust era. *Journal of Organizational Change Management*, 3(3), 47–58

Crites, JO. 1969. *Vocational Psychology.* New York: McGraw-Hill

Cronbach, LJ. 1970. *Essentials of Psychological Testing.* New York: Harper & Row Publishers

Dalton, GW, Thompson, PH & Price, RL. 1986. *Innovations: Strategies for Career Management.* Glenview, Illinois: Scott, Foresman and Company

Dessler, G. 1988. *Personnel Management.* New Jersey: Prentice-Hall, Inc

Erwee, R. 1991. Accommodating dual-career couples. *IPM Journal,* 9, 29–34

Feldman, DC. 1988. *Managing Careers in Organisations.* Boston: Scott Foresman and Company

Ginzberg, E, Ginsberg, SW, Axelrad, S & Herman, JL. 1951. *Occupational choice: An approach to a General Theory.* New York: Columbia University Press

Ginzberg, E. 1984. Career development. In *Career Choice and Development;* edited by D. Brown & L. Brooks, 169–191 Washington: Jossey Bass Publishers

Greenhaus, JH & Beutell, NJ. 1985. Sources of conflict between work and family roles. *Academy of Managemnet Review,* 10, 77

Greenhaus, JH. & Callanan, GA. 1994. *Career Management*. New York: The Dryden Press

Guterman, M. 1991. Working couples: Findings a balance between family and career. In *New Directions in Career Planning and the Workplace,* ed JM Kummerow, 167–193. Palo Alto, California: Davies Black Publishing

Gutteridge, TG, Leibowitz, ZB, Shore, JE. 1993. When careers flower, organizations flourish. *Training and Development*, 47(1), 14–29

Hall, DT. 1976. *Careers in Organisations*. California: Goodyear Publishing Company, Inc.

Hall, DT & Mervis, PH. 1995. Careers as lifelong learning. In *The Changing Nature of Work,* San Francisco: Jossey Bass Publishers

Harris, TG. 1993. The post-capitalist executive: An interview with Peter F Drucker. *Haward Business Review*, May/June, 115–122

Holland, JL. 1973. *Making Vocational Choices: A Theory of Careers*. Englewood Cliffs, New Jersey: Prentice-Hall, Inc

Holland, JL. 1985. *Making Vocational Choices: A Theory of Careers*. Englewood Cliffs, New Jersey: Prentice-Hall, Inc

Kanter, RM. 1990. *When Giants Learn to Dance*. New York: Simon & Schuster

Kaufman, HG. 1974. *Obsolescence and Professional Career Development*. New York: AMACON

Leana, CR & Feldsman, DC. 1988. Individual responses to job loss. Perceptions, reactions and coping behaviours. *Journal of Management,* 14 (3),

Leibowitz, ZB, Kaye, BL & Farren, C. 1990. Career gridlock. *Training and Development Journal*, April 1990, 29–35

Mcknight, R. 1991. Creating the future after job loss. *Training and Development,* 45, 69–72

Otte, FL & Hutcheson, PG. 1992. *Helping Employees Manage Careers*. Englewood Cliffs, New Jersey: Prentice-Hall

Rousseau, PM & Wade-Benzoni, KA. 1995. Changing individual–organisational attachments: A two-way street. In *The Changing Nature of Work,* ed A Haward, 305. San Fransico: Jossey-Bass Publishers

Schein, EH. 1978. *Career Dynamics: Matching Individual and Organisational Needs*. Phillippnes: Addison Wesley Publishing Co

Schein, EH. 1990. *Career Anchors : Discover Your Real Values*. San Diego: University Associates

Schein, EH. 1993. *Career Survival: Srategic Job and Role Planning*. California: Pfeifer & Company

Schein, EH. 1996. Career anchors/revisited: Implications for career development in the 21st century. *Academy of Management Executive,* 80–88

Schreuder, AMG & Theron, AL. 1997. Careers: An Organisational Perspective. Kenwyn: Juta & Co, Ltd

Super, DE. 1992. Toward a comprehensive theory of career development, 35–61. In: *Career Development : Theory and Practice*, ed DH Montross & CJ Shinkman. Illinois: Charles C. Thomas Publisher

Uys, JS. 1993. *The Organisation of the Future.* Paper presented at the SATBT Congress, Grahamstown

Van der Walt, S. 1982. *Work Motives of Women in the Retail Business.* Pretoria: Raad vir Geesteswetenskaplike Navorsing

Van Rooyen, MS. 1969. *Aspekte van die Beroepskeuse struktuur van 'n Generasie St X-leerlinge.* Onge publiseerde MA-verhandeling, Universiteit van Port Elizabeth, Port Elizabeth

chapter 15 Training and Developing Employees: Macrolevel Perspectives

STUDY OBJECTIVES

After studying this chapter, you should be able to:

- describe the principles on which the National Training Strategy is based;
- discuss briefly the problems relating to education and training in South Africa;
- explain the essential elements of the proposed National Training Strategy;
- discuss the role to be played by the National Qualifications Framework in the proposed National Training Strategy;
- describe the role and functions of the South African Qualifications Authority (SAQA);
- explain the proposed structure of the bodies formed to govern training and development in South Africa;
- discuss the importance of Adult Basic Education and the role of training and development practitioners in South Africa;
- discuss the training and development aspects which must be addressed by the labour market strategy;
- outline briefly the contents of the Manpower Training Act.

15.1 INTRODUCTION

It is common knowledge that South Africa lacks highly skilled human resources. The state is constantly seeking ways to alleviate one of our most important national problems — illiteracy. It is estimated that of the total 1994 population of 41,5 million people, 12,5 million could be described as illiterate (that is, having little or inadequate formal schooling — below standard eight) (National Training Board 1994). The percentage of the population with primary schooling or less varies considerably according to age group. For example, 13 % of the population between the ages of 18 to 24 years have primary school education or less, while the figures are 28 % for the age group 25 to 34 years and 46 % for the age group 35 to 50 years. The percentage of illiteracy is the highest in the agricultural sector, namely 85 %, followed by the mining sector with 62 %, transport and communication 40 % and manufacturing 24 %. The lowest level of illiteracy is in the financial business services sector with 7 %. The focus of human resource development at the macrolevel is therefore crucial for the economic prosperity of all South Africans. Human resource development embraces a wide range of areas, and it is therefore essential to understand the broader national developments in training and development — these form the parameters within which organisations can train and develop their employees.

While the next chapter focuses on the training process in an organisational context, this chapter deals with human resource development from a macro or national level, the emphasis being on the development and status of the national training initiative, the national qualifications framework and the Manpower Training Act.

15.2 THE NATIONAL TRAINING STRATEGY INITIATIVE

The National Training Board (NTB) published a provisional national training strategy in 1991. This report contained valuable and important information but the Board failed to include all the relevant stakeholders in its compilation. In 1993 a representative task team was set up comprising members of the National Training Board and representatives of the main stakeholders, namely employers, employee organisations, the state and the providers of education and training.

In April 1994 a document entitled *A National Training Strategy Initiative* was published (Eberlein 1995:1). This document proposed an integrated approach to education and training for the future and also emphasised the centrality of training in the quest to ensure international competitiveness.

The national training strategy provided a new vision for education and training, namely that "it must meet South Africa's need for a human resources development system in which there is an integrated approach to education and training which meets the economic and social needs of the country and the development need of the individual".

The NTB task team indicated that this new approach means that we must no longer think about education and training as separate entities but rather view them as an integrated system. Education and training must therefore be dealt with as a whole, but this does not, however, imply that each aspect cannot be dealt with in its own unique manner. Learning must be considered a lifelong process and this culture must be instilled as soon as possible and maintained for as long as possible.

15.2.1 Principles

Twelve principles form the basis of the national training strategy. These principles are outlined below.

- Education and training should form part of a system of human resources development which provides for the establishment of an integrated approach to education and training.
- Such a strategy should be and remain relevant to national development needs.
- The strategy should have international and national credibility.

- It should adhere to a coherent framework of principles and certification.
- It should be expressed in terms of a nationally agreed framework and internationally accepted outcomes standards.
- The strategy should provide for participation in planning and coordination by all significant stakeholders and should be legitimate.
- Access to appropriate levels of education and training should be provided for all prospective learners in a manner which facilitates progression.
- The national training strategy should provide for learners, on successful completion of accredited prerequisites, to move between components of the delivery system.
- It should ensure that the framework of qualifications permits individuals to progress through the levels of national qualifications via different appropriate combinations of the components of the delivery system.
- It should provide for learners to transfer their credits or qualifications from one learning institution and/or employer to another (portability).
- It should through assessment give credit to prior learning.
- It should provide for the guidance of learners by persons who meet nationally recognised standards for educators and trainers.

Exhibit A

Bodies responsible for training in South Africa: 1994

- Department of Labour
- National Training Board
- Nine autonomous regional training centres with 62 satellite campuses and 65 mobile centres
- 1 417 private training centres established by employers
- 26 industry training boards, mostly with predominantly employer representation

15.2.2 International training systems

Research conducted by the NTB found that worldwide education and training systems have been developed in countries where a common sense of identity exists in the population, and have often followed unrest which led to or threatened large-scale impoverishment or economic depression. These international systems have nurtured those competencies which are prerequisites for success in industry, small business and the informal sector and which encourage the development of a partnership between business, trade unions and the state in education and training. Strong links and a culture of cooperation have also been developed between the education and training systems and organisations to act as champions for the development of these systems. Those education and training systems which achieved success were seen as credible by all relevant stakeholders. In contrast with the above, the South African education system faces serious problems, for example:

- large-scale inconsistency in standards;
- the breakdown of the culture of learning;
- imbalances in funding qualifications, the provision of facilities and teacher/pupil ratios;
- the legacy of illiteracy;
- too few graduates in mathematics and science to sustain economic growth in a modern, technologically advanced economy.

There is thus no doubt that an integrated system for training and development needs to be created and that various lessons can be learnt from international systems.

15.2.3 Education and training problems in South Africa

According to the NTB report, technical and skills training has historically never been a priority in South Africa and there is a lack of coordination between the different components of the training system. For example, in the workplace many forms of technical training take place but, apart from artisan training, these are not recognised. There are many other causes for concern.

- In the education and training field the basic assumption is that teachers and trainers should be more highly qualified than their students before being allowed to teach or to train. These requirements are increasingly being met within the education system, but such requirements do not apply when trainers are appointed to train in organisations.
- The unemployment training programmes of the Department of Education and Training and the Department of Labour lack legitimacy because they do not deliver.
- Educators and trainers are not developed to meet South Africa's needs.
- There is only limited provision for formal and informal organisational links between education, training, business, labour and the state. An example of this is the fact that school-leavers cannot find jobs.
- There is no nationally recognised framework of qualifications.
- The existing career counselling system is inadequate. The limited range of occupations for which education and training currently caters does not provide for progression within recognised career paths.
- The methods used to provide access and the recognition of prior learning do not cater for the effects on individuals of the inadequacies of existing education and training programmes.

According to the NTB task team in 1994 there was an imbalance between the amounts spent by the state on education and on training (R3,1bn versus R300 million). The private sector spends approximately R3,5 billion on training. From this it can be deduced that South Africa's total spending on training is less than 1 % of total employment costs. This 1 % compares unfavourably with the 5 % spent by South Africa's major trading partners and the 10 % spent by the Japanese. It must, however, be pointed out that certain parastatal and other larger organisations in South Africa spend up to 10 % of total employment costs.

A case at hand . . .

The financing of training: A study by Nedlac

It would be impossible, after considering the situation in eight widely differing countries (United Kingdom, New Zealand, Brazil, Australia, Mauritius, Malaysia, South Korea) around the world, to provide a neat formula as to what constitutes the ideal system of vocational training and the best way of financing it. There are too many variables. Each country has a different starting point, different strengths and weaknesses, and different social and economic circumstances in which the training system is required to operate and by which sooner or later it will be judged. Nevertheless, a comparative examination of the eight countries does provide certain insights which could usefully be brought to the South African training debate.

With regard to the financing of training it becomes immediately apparent that all the countries examined used a combination of funding sources for their vocational training programmes, but usually place most reliance on one and sometimes two of the following main sources: levies (usually on company payrolls), tax incentives for approved training, state expenditure, and voluntary private sector expenditure.

Brazil and South Korea rely heavily on levy systems. Mauritius and Malaysia also operate levy systems, but rely equally on state expenditure. Chile is the only country which operates a successful tax incentive scheme, while Australia is alone in relying largely on government expenditure from general tax revenue. New Zealand relies equally on state and private sector expenditure. The United Kingdom, on the other hand, relies mostly on voluntary spending in the private sector.

A further source of financing is fees charged for training at both public and private training institutions. All the countries examined take revenue from this source. This suggests that training systems are evolving in the direction of greater levels of costs recovery for training at both public and private training institutions. All the countries examined take revenue from this source. This suggests that training systems are evolving in the direction of greater levels of costs recovery for training provided.

*Source: *Financing of Training: The International Experience* (1996:19). A Nedlac Publication: IR Network.

15.3 A PROPOSED NATIONAL TRAINING STRATEGY

Based on a discussion of the above section, a core set of principles for the development of a new national training strategy was developed, namely that "education and training must empower the individual, improve quality of life and contribute towards development targets in the national economic plan through a national qualification framework".

Certain essential elements were derived from the strategy and are depicted in figure 15.1. The National Qualification Framework (NQF) forms the starting point of the strategy which specifies learning in terms of nationally and internationally accepted outcomes. This will make it possible to adopt an integrated approach to education and training and will empower the individual.

Exhibit B

Factors influencing a national training strategy *

- South Africa's heterogeneous population of 37,7 million (1991) has no sense of common identity, is growing at a rate of 2,06 % per annum and will reach nearly 54 million in 2011.
- The unemployed, those in the informal sector and the youth make up a large percentage of the economically active population and merit special attention.
- There is no integrated approach to or structure for education and training, or provision for linkages between education, training, business and labour, although there are elements of the structure which, suitably modified, could be used to develop an integrated approach.
- Approximately 1,6 million South Africans between the ages of 6 and 13 do not attend school.
- 11,5 million adults have not achieved an adequate level of literacy.
- Only 29 % of all learners leave school with a matriculation exemption; 33 % with Std 10.
- Approximately 50 % of African and a minority of students of other races in Standard 10 are 20 years old or older.
- The level of education of the workforce is unknown but assumed to be low.
- The level of education in mathematics and science is totally inadequate for a modern economy.
- Using conventional teaching methods and educational technology, and assuming the 15:1 learner to teacher ratio of developed countries, the number of high-level persons in South Africa would not be able to support the numbers of teachers and trainers (about 900 000) needed to serve and maintain the education and training systems at the standard expected of developed countries.
- The environment in which the majority of South Africans find themselves is not conducive to learning or to the conventional use of modern educational technology.
- For a large part of the population, the learning environment is unable to support modern educational technology adequately.
- For a large part of the population no culture of learning exists, the education and training systems have no credibility, and are the target of violence and disruption.
- South Africa is going through a period of massive change in the political arena, accompanied by instability and violence.
- Change is occurring in a number of fields, fostered and supported by democratic and representative bodies such a forums.
- The possibility of the acceptance of change in the education and training systems, if an acceptable process is followed, is good.
- The expected limited growth in the economy will not be enough to accommodate those entering the labour market (approximately 30 000 per annum); therefore priorities for education, training and employment will need to be determined.
- These priorities should take into account the need for growth and development in specific sectors of the economy.
- In general terms, South Africa has ample unskilled labour, energy and material resources, while capital, skilled labour and technology are in short supply.
- The factors hindering technological advance, including dependence on licensing and a reluctance to engage in long-term challenges, need to be addressed.
- There is a need to develop all workers in technology, and not merely to focus on selected groups such as engineers and scientists.
- Investment in research and development needs to be increased dramatically in a planned manner to about 2,7 % of Gross Domestic Product.
- Articulation between schooling and other levels of learning; assessment of the performance of the system would be based upon measures such as the Principles which are an integral part of the strategy; the tangible and visible indicators of performance of all elements of the strategy, by some form of national award.

*Source: Adapted from: National Training Board. 1994. *Discussion Document on a National Training Strategy Initiative*, 55–57

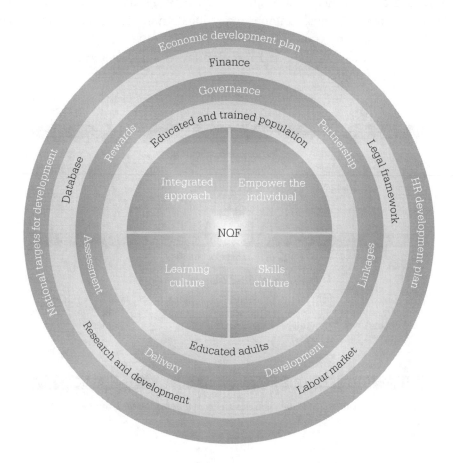

Figure 15.1
Essential elements of a National Training Strategy
Source: National Training Board (1994: 90)

15.3.1 A national qualification framework

The National Qualification Framework (NQF) (see figure 15.2) will provide a means to meet the needs of the key stakeholders, namely the state, the community, the business sector, labour organisations and the providers of training (Eberlein 1995: 1).

As illustrated in figure 15.2, the NQF could provide the integrating factor for education and training. The various levels defined in figure 15.2 are the following.

● **Level 1**. Two ways of reaching level one are possible. The Adult Basic Education and Training sublevels, A, B and C, comprise the one route to the General Certificate of Education and the other is the compulsory 9 to 10 years of schooling.

- **Levels 2 to 4.** National and Higher Certificates of schooling could be acquired in any number of ways, ranging from education at senior secondary schools, technical community colleges, private providers, etc.
- **Levels 5 to 8.** At tertiary and research levels study would lead to national diplomas and degrees.

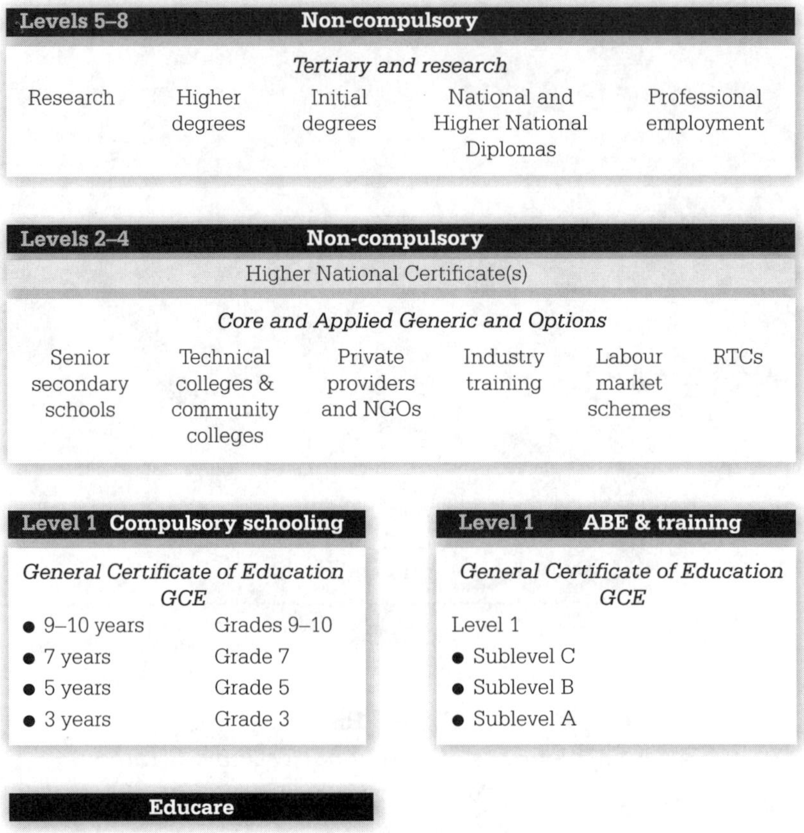

Levels 5–8	Non-compulsory			
Tertiary and research				
Research	Higher degrees	Initial degrees	National and Higher National Diplomas	Professional employment

Levels 2–4	Non-compulsory			
Higher National Certificate(s)				
Core and Applied Generic and Options				
Senior secondary schools	Technical colleges & community colleges	Private providers and NGOs	Industry training	Labour market schemes	RTCs

Level 1 Compulsory schooling
General Certificate of Education GCE
● 9–10 years   Grades 9–10
● 7 years   Grade 7
● 5 years   Grade 5
● 3 years   Grade 3

Level 1   ABE & training
General Certificate of Education GCE
Level 1
● Sublevel C
● Sublevel B
● Sublevel A

Educare

Figure 15.2
National Qualification Framework
Source: National Training Board (1994: 96)

It is envisaged that the NQF will ensure the development of partnerships between the state, business, labour and other stakeholders and the linking of national structures for employment and labour to education and training with regional structures.

Subsequent to the suggestions made by the NTB task team, the South African Qualifications Authority Act 58 of 1995 was published. The aim of the Act is to provide for the development and implementation of a National Qualification

Framework and to establish the South African Qualifications Authority (Republic of South Africa 1995).

15.3.1.1 Objectives of the NQF

In terms of the Act the objectives of the NQF are as follows:

- to create an integrated national framework for learning achievements;
- to facilitate access to and mobility and progression within education, training and career paths;
- to enhance the quality of education and training;
- to accelerate the reparation of past unfair discrimination in education, training and employment opportunities; and
- to contribute to the full personal development of each learner and the social and economic development of the nation at large.

15.3.1.2 South African Qualification Authority (SAQA)

Section 3 of the Act provides for the establishment of a juristic person called the South African Qualifications Authority, which will consist of a chairperson appointed by the Minister of Education, various members and an executive officer. A nomination procedure is prescribed in section 4(4) of the Act for the appointment of 28 members representing various stakeholders. The formation of the SAQA Board was announced in the Government Gazette on 31 May 1996.

15.3.1.3 Functions of the Qualifications Authority

The various functions of the SAQA are to:

- oversee the development of the NQF;
- formulate and publish policies and criteria for
  - the registration of bodies responsible for establishing education and training standards or qualifications; and
  - the accreditation of bodies responsible for monitoring and auditing achievements in terms of the standards and qualifications;
- oversee the implementation of the NQF, namely;
  - the registration or accreditation of training standards or qualification bodies and the assignment of their functions;
  - the registration of national standards and qualifications;
  - ensuring that steps comply with the provisions of accreditation; and
  - taking steps to ensure that standards and registered qualifications are internationally comparable;
- accept responsibility for the control of the authority's finances;
- advise the Minister on matters affecting the registration of standards and qualifications.

Figure 15.3 outlines the framework of the SAQA.

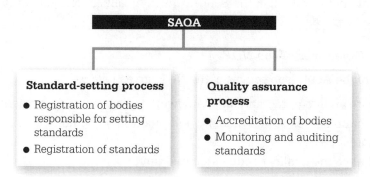

Figure 15.3
South African Qualifications Authority (SAQA) framework

15.3.1.4 Committees of SAQA

Committees may be established by the Qualifications Authority and persons who are not members of the Authority may be appointed. The chairperson of a committee may be appointed and committees may be dissolved. The Authority may further delegate any of its powers to any of its committees, excluding those powers prescribed in section 7 (powers of authority). Meetings of the Authority and committees must be held regularly and it is the Authority's responsibility to determine its own rules.

15.3.1.5 Units of learning and qualifications

In terms of the NQF, qualifications should be based on a credit system comprising two fundamental building blocks, namely *units* of learning (called "units") defined in terms of learning outcomes and *modules* of learning describing the length, form or mode of delivery (for example, the use of distance study/open learning, structured work experience, and/or assignments).

According to the NTB report, the key characteristics of a unit of learning could include:

- statements of outcomes of learning to be achieved by the learner;
- outcomes aligned with endorsed standards;
- outcomes presented in a statement of learner capability reflecting an appropriate integration of knowledge and skill which can be understood, applied and transferred to different contexts;
- the assignment of a credit value at different levels based on agreed nominal learning time according to a common system (the suggested norm is 40 hours or multiples thereof); and
- registered units with the same credit value, regardless of the provider used to access them.

Exhibit C

Criticism of the NQF *

- It imposes a single viewpoint on all education and training.
- It is a system to introduce standardised curricula for all levels and learners.
- It is a way of lowering standards by forcing the vocationalisation of education.
- It may bring chaos through the ad hoc selection of unrelated bits of learning to make up qualifications.
- It could end up as a nightmare of bureaucratic red-tape.
- It could devalue the *standard* of learning to the lowest common denominator in the field.
- It is a plot by labour to collapse the difference between mental and manual labour.
- It could rob any institutional sector of its identity or "academic freedom".
- It will be a straitjacket to force all qualifications to look the same.
- It is another "good" idea invented by government which provides the opportunity for countless scams and the exploitation of learners and their parents.
- It means that only the government will issue qualifications with the invention of national qualifications.
- Quality assurance is another term for "thought policing".
- It is not relevant to higher education, especially to the universities who are concerned with generating new knowledge and not just transmitting existing knowledge.

*Source: Adapted from: Ways of seeing the NQF. Human Sciences Research Council, September 1995, 29–33.

A number of credits achieved through agreed clusters of units at specific levels would form a qualification. It is further envisaged that units should be sufficiently self-contained to enable learners to take a module and be assessed for a unit without necessarily completing all the units required for a particular qualification (provided that specified prerequisites are met). Qualifications would have a total credit rating and these may differ from level to level.

According to the NTB report: "A modular approach does not mean that traditional programmes are simply divided up into small segments while all else remains the same." Units of learning are therefore clearly distinguished from modules for the delivery of learning. The development of modules could occur through national, regional, sectoral or local sponsorship in which curriculum development agencies (both state and private) at the local and regional/sectoral levels could support institutions and consortia of institutions (together with employers and community groups) in developing modular courses and the materials and resources to support them.

It is further envisaged that all qualifications would have the following components:

- core units required for any qualification at a particular level (for example units in language and mathematics or social, economic and scientific understanding);

- optional units (for example engineering, specialist skills such as welding, performing arts);
- core units which are generic and may form part of several curricula.

The NQF will apply to all qualifications and will be based on accredited units of learning in agreed clusters of learning outcomes, defined according to national criteria established for the different levels.

It will further recognise, through assessment against national standards, on-the-job learning and prior learning on an equal basis to skills and knowledge acquired in formal courses through national certification.

The NQF will also require all national certificates issued, regardless of level, to be endorsed by a South African Qualification Authority. The name of the awarding body, as well as the fields of learning, will be stipulated in the certificate. It is further suggested that certificates could carry not only the names of "subjects" but also the units that were completed as clusters within the subject area.

The next aspect to be considered is the structure of governance.

15.4 STRUCTURES FOR GOVERNANCE

The recommended governance structure is illustrated in figure 15.4 and is discussed briefly.

A single integrated Ministry of Education and Training, headed by a Minister accountable to Parliament, is suggested.

A National Council for Learning (NCL), representative of the key stakeholders, is required to formulate national policy on education and training.

Statutory councils, representative of specific sectors of education and training and subordinate to the NCL, are required to advise on, develop and monitor the implementation of specific policy guidelines for the four sectors:

- National Educare Council (EC)
- National Education Council (NEC) (covering compulsory schooling)
- National Education and Training Council (NETC)
- National Tertiary Council (NTC)

A regional level executive department of education and training, supported by representative committees similar to the representative councils established at national level, needs to be introduced.

As mentioned earlier, a South African Qualifications Authority (SAQA) must be introduced as part of the NQF. Serving as a national accreditation and certification authority, this statutory body will have jurisdiction extending over the four sectors of education and training to enable them to set up a coherent integrated system of assessment, accreditation and registration for all national qualifications offered in South Africa. (This was discussed in section 15.3.)

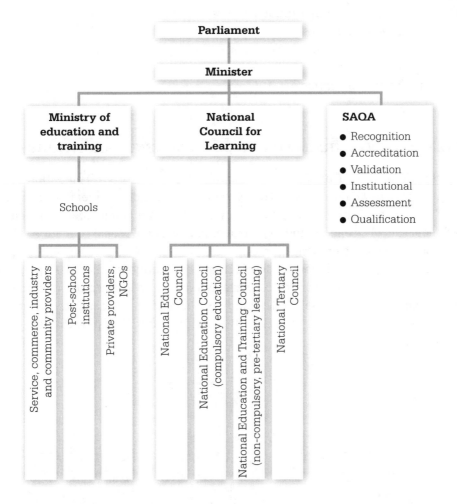

Figure 15.4

Suggested structures for governance

Source: National Training Board (1994: 106)

The establishment of Sector Education and Training Organisations (SETOs) is envisaged; these will serve essentially as representative service-, commerce-, and industry-based education and training organisations. They will be responsible for identifying and specifying development and ensuring the achievement of the desired level of education and training in a specific sector. It is envisaged that through a process of negotiation and evolution Industry Training Boards (see section 15.10.3) will change their structure, role and name to Sector Education and Training Organisations.

Education and training programmes in the non-compulsory pretertiary sector are presently provided by a wide range of organisations, such as:

● secondary schools
● technical colleges

- non-governmental organisations (NGOs)
- regional training centres
- private colleges and training centres
- private companies
- industry training centres

15.5 THE EDUCATION, TRAINING AND DEVELOPMENT PRACTITIONER

The term *Education, Training and Development Practitioner* (ETD practitioner) was adopted by the NTB task team. This was done to include "trainers" who are normally associated with training offered by industry and commerce; "teachers" in technical schools, colleges and technikons; trainers, adult basic education (ABEs); and community development trainers.

A model (see figure 15.5) for the development of practitioners has been proposed. This model makes provision for compulsory core competencies to build occupational expertise, contextual understanding, facilitating of learning and for the further specialisation of the ETD practitioner. It also makes provision for career progression.

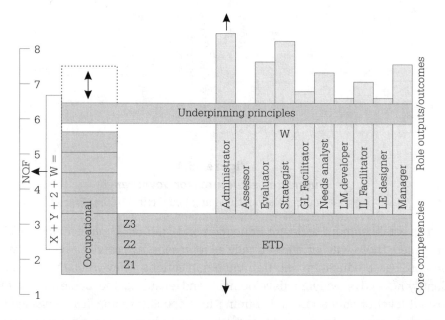

Figure 15.5
The practitioner development model

The intention is that no practitioner should be allowed to practise unless competence in the core aspects can be demonstrated, through a combination of formal qualifications, in-house training and development, or prior self-acquired learning accredited within the National Qualification Framework.

Ten roles for the ETD are proposed, namely: (i) Administrator; (ii) Assessor; (iii) Evaluator; (iv) Group Learning Facilitator; (v) Individual Learning Facilitator; (vi) Learning Experience Designer, (vii) Learning Materials Developer; (viii) Manager; (ix) Needs Analyst; (x) Strategist.

In practice many practitioners perform many or all of these roles to a greater or lesser extent; the roles should therefore be seen as integrated and interrelated.

15.6 ADULT BASIC EDUCATION (ABE)

Research has shown that millions of adult South Africans have received no education at all. Millions more have received little formal education and what they have received has been of low quality. The NTB report proposes to solve this problem by improving access to learning by greatly increasing the resources devoted to Adult Basic Education (ABE). This will be done by addressing the quality of learning and by integrating ABE into the National Qualification Framework. Adult Basic Education is the basic phase in the provision of lifelong learning and consists of levels along a continuum of learning aimed at adults who have very little or no formal schooling and who do not have the equivalent of a compulsory school-leaving certificate. The final exit point from ABE should be equivalent to the exit point from compulsory education. Adult Basic Education has the potential to embrace all aspects of training which enable learners to demonstrate technical and practical competencies.

Adult basic education (ABE)*

"The providers of ABE in South Africa are: the private sector, NGOs and the state. The private sector is currently providing about 100 000 adults with ABE classes, NGOs are reaching some 10 000 learners per year and the state, through a complex network of adult education centres and departmental projects, is reaching some 110 000 ABE learners per year. The expenditure, some R200 million per year, comes from the private sector.

Only 1 % of adults who may need ABE classes are presently taking them. The key to a more effective system in future lies in the development of a policy framework to enable step by step transition from the present small-scale inefficient provision of ABE, to large-scale effective and coherent provision of ABE.

South Africa does not have the capacity to provide ABE to 12 million people at the same time. A set of priorities should therefore be developed in order to begin to tackle the problem. Proposed criteria for selection include:
- the most disadvantaged sectors of society;
- groups involved in key economic and development projects; and
- those in whom an investment in ABE is likely to bring the greatest advantage."

---

*Source: National Training Board (1994: 159–160)

According to the NTB report, the basic aims of ABE are to enable individuals to:

1. develop their full potential;
2. participate actively in society as a whole;

3. develop communication skills in their mother tongue and in English;
4. develop skills in mathematics;
5. shape and develop economic policies, to build a democratic society and enhance job creation schemes;
6. develop a critical understanding of their society; and
7. take development initiatives and understand the world of science and technology.

15.7 LABOUR MARKET STRATEGY

There is a strong relationship between a future labour market strategy and the proposed national training strategy (see also chapter 4). During 1997 a *Green Paper* focusing on a labour market strategy was published by the government for comment.

The following problem areas have been identified in the labour market:

- lack of a learning culture;
- noncompetitive skills base;
- lack of linkage between industries;
- lack of linkage between the education and training sectors;
- lack of linkage between education/training and labour market planning;
- an unacceptable product of education (school-leavers);
- limited recognition of prior learning;
- no financial incentives for training;
- insufficient Adult Basic Education and education in technical subjects;
- legislation which does not cater formally for training and recognition of qualifications below that of the artisan;
- limited state funds allocated for training in the micro-enterprise sector;
- inadequate funds for training the unemployed;
- no meaningful role played by the state in retraining the displaced and retrenched;
- inadequate levels of language, numeracy, mathematics, science, technology and broad life skills among school-leavers;
- unrealistic expectations of school-leavers;
- entry levels which form barriers for those leaving school before attaining a standard 8 (grade 10) certificate;
- an increase in the number of students who have no access to the compulsory practical components of their courses;
- apprentice training criteria beyond the reach of small business; and
- inadequate career guidance which lacks national and regional databases and appropriately qualified career guidance educators/officers.

In the light of the above, the NTB report recommends that the following important aspects should be addressed.

- **The development of a culture of learning** and skills development commencing at primary school level. Programmes to assist in this development should be multifaceted and, wherever possible, have short-term effects.
- The formation of an organisation or coordinating body to facilitate **linkage between formal and micro-enterprise** sectors, to act as an organised voice for the micro-enterprise sector and to facilitate the obtaining of capital.
- The development of targeted programmes for different categories of the **unemployed**, such as unemployed youth, women, etc, through appropriate agencies is one of the most important aspects.
- The state should encourage and support the development of service/commerce/industry plans for industries undergoing a process of restructuring so that **retrenched** people can be accommodated.
- The state should ensure the development of an integrated approach to education and training to allow school-leavers more structured access.
- The state should develop funding programmes to provide incentives to employers to support practical training.
- Provision must be made for the training needs of small business and small businesses must be encouraged to identify the outcomes that they require and for which they can provide training within the structure of the National Qualification Framework.
- Affirmative action policies should be an integral part of development programmes.
- A large number of career guidance and placement centres should be established and these should aim at becoming high profile services within the communities they serve. They should be responsible for the development of their own databases reflecting vacancies and the range of available education and training courses. The centres should be linked to both the regional and national databases.

15.8 INFORMATION DATABASE SYSTEM AND LEGISLATION

The NTB report recommends that other interested stakeholders should join in the establishment of a project to develop a suitable "Education and Training Information System" for the management of the National Training Strategy and that this become part of the functioning of the proposed National Education and Training Council.

15.9 DEVELOPMENTS SINCE THE PUBLICATION OF THE PROPOSED NATIONAL TRAINING STRATEGY

The following developments have taken place since the publication of the proposed National Training Strategy (see Eberlein 1995: 10–14; Nel 1996).

15.9.1 Governance structures

15.9.1.1 Interministerial working group

The Ministers of Education and Labour agreed to the establishment of an Intermin-isterial Working Group (IMWG) to address the National Training Strategy and other aspects. The IMWG consists of members from the Departments of Education and Labour, organised business and labour, the teacher organisations and the office of the Reconstruction and Development Programme. Its terms of reference include the development and establishment of the South African Qualification Authority and the coordination of activities leading to the development of the NQF.

15.9.1.2 Restructured National Training Board (NTB)

The NTB was not adequately representative of all the stakeholders and in April 1994 the term of office of the Board was extended. Members of the national task team who were not members of the Board were then made members (see section 15.10.2). This was seen as an interim measure to make the Board more represent-ative. The Cabinet had in the meantime authorised a change to the structure of the Board and this process was put into motion. The Cabinet appointed the restruc-tured Board in February 1996; it now consists of:

- 5 representatives from business;
- representatives from labour;
- representatives from government;
- representatives from training providers;
- representatives from the community;
- specialists.

15.9.1.3 Other structures

Other structures have been developed or are in the process of being developed. These include:

- a Committee comprising the heads of education departments;
- a Committee of education ministers drawing together the provincial authorities of education;
- committees covering the universities and technikons, the technical colleges and other colleges;
- an association of regional and other training providers;
- the Association of Industry Training Boards; and
- emerging coordination structures from provincial departments of education and labour structures.

15.9.2 Implementation research

A consolidated programme of implementation research has been initiated. Areas in which work is being carried out with both local and international assistance and expertise include the following:

- pilot projects for the development of the NQF in specified areas;
- a national project on the recognition of prior learning in the building industry;
- the development of the education training development practitioner;
- the development of governance structures for the integrated approach to education and training, and for the management of the National Training Strategy Initiative;
- the execution of a national skills audit in terms of the NQF;
- the development of a funding mechanism;
- the development of an active labour market strategy; and
- several crosscutting projects such as the development of a skills culture, revision of the apprentice system, pre-employment and unemployment training.

Several new activities aimed at the engagement of the education authorities in the process of developing an integrated approach to education and training are also under way. They are:

- the establishment of an NQF Committee and reference group;
- the development of a basic framework to be applied to the NQF process;
- research into the need for the development of a National Institute of Curriculum Development; and
- the extension of the implementation research to include aspects of particular significance to educational interests, including facilities and the field of education.

15.9.3 Discussion documents on the NQF

In October 1995 the Human Sciences Research Council (HSRC) published a document entitled *Ways of Seeing the National Qualification Framework* which was developed by an independent group of interested persons as a document to stimulate further discussion on and development of the NQF. This document indicates how the development and setting of standards could be initiated and describes the possible functions of National Standards Bodies, Education Training Qualification Authorities and other structures necessitated by the integrated approach.

A similar discussion document entitled *Lifelong Learning through a National Qualifications Framework* was published by the Department of Education in February 1996. A workshop was held on standard setting in April 1996 under the auspices of the International Working Group.

15.9.4 NQF pilot projects

A goal-orientated Project Planning workshop (GOPP) was held for organisations wishing to share in the pilot projects. The aim of the projects was to learn about the NQF and standard setting and about the development of the necessary structures and capacity to handle these aspects.

Various pilot projects under development include aspects related to Information Technology; Management and Supervision; Transport; Hospitality and

Tourism. The Engineering and Manufacturing processes pilot project was launched on 4 June 1996.

15.9.5 Recognition of prior learning

This project was carried out jointly by the Building Industry Training Board and the Irish National Training Authority in Bloemfontein. It assessed more than 200 casual builders against the artisan standards of the bricklayer and carpenter, providing the necessary top-up training and issuing nationally recognised certificates to successful candidates. The project was completed in December 1995. It is intended to extend the assessment nationally and to commence a similar project to assess the prior learning of students wishing to enter university, using a selected faculty in the University of the Free State as a pilot.

15.9.6 Education, training and development practitioner

The education, training development practitioner project, sponsored by the German government, aims at developing the standards for the new "educator-trainer" — the "Education Training Development Practitioner" — to meet South Africa's needs. Its actions are based upon the roles depicted in the NTB document and the intention is to produce key standards and guidelines.

15.9.7 Structures

Assistance from the Canadian and German governments will help the SAQA to develop the necessary structures. Up to the time of writing, no further information has become available.

15.9.8 Skills audit

A skills audit became necessary to establish the types and quantities of skills upon which the education and training system should concentrate. As was the case with the development of the NQF, the Irish National Training Authority and others assisted in developing a state-of-the art form of skills audit to meet the needs of South Africa. The audit has been developed and the funding of the project must be approved.

15.9.9 Green Paper on a skills development strategy

A Green Paper on the skills development strategy for economic and employment growth in South Africa was published in March 1997 for comments. The objectives of the strategy according to the Green Paper are (Republic of South Africa 1992: 2):

● to increase the skills profile of the population through accredited high quality education and training limited to the NQF;
● to increase the quality and quantity of intermediate level skills in the country;

- to facilitate more efficient social and infrastructural delivery;
- to raise the quality, relevance and cost-effectiveness of skills development;
- to facilitate more structured and targeted skills development within enterprises;
- to increase access by workers to education and training;
- to support target groups to enter regular employment;
- to support the establishment of viable small micro enterprises;
- to increase access to entry-level education and training.

The six core components of the strategy are the collection of information for strategic planning, a system of leadership, a new employment service, the enhancement of provision, skills-development intermediaries and natural coordination and the funding of skills development.

15.10 THE MANPOWER TRAINING ACT

The aim of the Manpower Training Act is "to provide for the promotion and regulation of training of manpower and for that purpose to provide for the establishment of a National Training Board, a Manpower Development Fund and a Fund for the Training of Unemployed Persons; to provide for the establishment, accreditation, functions and powers of training boards; the registration of regional training centres, private training centres and industry training centres; and the imposition on certain employers of a levy in aid of training; and to provide for matters connected therewith".

The Act does not apply to:

- anyone who is a registered student or pupil at any educational institution, and who is not
  - O an apprentice;
  - O a trainee;
  - O receiving training in terms of the Act;
- any work performed in or in connection with any educational institution which is part of the education or training of the person performing the work concerned;
- any person who, having obtained a degree, certificate or diploma at any educational institution, performs work in a designated trade in order to obtain practical experience; or
- service or training in the South African Defence Force.

15.10.1 Definitions

The following important definitions are quoted directly from section 1 of the Act.

- **Employee** means "any person employed by or who performs work for an employer in any industry and who receives or is entitled to receive remuneration from such employer".

- **Labour relations** means "all aspects of and matters connected with the relationship between employer and employee, including matters relating to negotiations in respect of the remuneration and other conditions of employment of the employee, the prevention and settlement of disputes between employer and employee, the application, interpretation and effect of laws administered by the Department (of Labour) and the management of the affairs of trade unions, employers' organisations, federations and industrial councils".
- **Industry** "includes any class of undertaking or activity, any division or part of an industry or any group of industries, as well as work in private households".
- **Trade** "includes any branch of a trade, or any group of trades or branches of trades".
- **Training** means "any training which has as its special aim the improvement of the proficiency of any person for any work performed in or in connection with any industry, and includes training in labour relations".
- **Workseeker** means "a person over the age of fifteen years who is unemployed, is not required by law to attend school, is not a pupil or a student at an educational institution, is not awaiting admission to an educational institution and who is seeking work".

15.10.2 The National Training Board

The Minister of Labour appoints members of the National Training Board taking into consideration the proper representation of the interests of the state, employers and employees regarding workforce training. The Minister also appoints as members people who, in his/her opinion, possess expert or special knowledge or experience of workforce training or development.

The functions of the Board are to:

- advise the Minister regarding:
  - matters of policy arising out of, or connected with, the application and provisions of the Act;
  - any matter relating to training;
- perform the other functions assigned to it by the Act or by the Minister.

The Board may also undertake research and make rules concerning its meetings and for the effective performance of its functions. The Board has to submit a report annually to the Minister outlining its activities and "the general state of affairs as regards training in the Republic", and the Minister can, if he/she so decides, table the report in Parliament. The Board may also establish committees for a specific period and a particular purpose.

15.10.3 Training boards

Training boards may be established in respect of an industry by:

- an employer, if the registrar so approves; or

- an employers' organisation; or
- a group of employers; or
- a group of employers' organisations; or
- a group of one employer and one or more employers' organisations; or
- a group of employers and one or more employers' organisations; or
- one or more industrial councils; or
- a trade union; or
- a group of trade unions; or
- a group of employees.

Any group of employees has the right to negotiate with the employer regarding the establishment of a training board.

Training boards require accreditation and must submit a constitution and an application for accreditation to the registrar.

The functions of training boards are as follows:

"an accredited training board shall, unless the registrar determines otherwise, perform in the industry and in the area in respect of which it has been accredited, the following functions:

- carry out the duties and exercise the powers which are by this Act imposed on or conferred upon it, with due consideration of the training needs of the Republic;
- frame conditions of apprenticeship and other formalised training schemes which will best serve the training needs of the industry in respect of which the training board has been accredited;
- accept responsibility for the administration of apprenticeship training;
- on request of the registrar inquire into and make recommendations to him with regard to any matter which in terms of the provisions of this Act falls within the functions of the registrar;
- inquire into any dispute arising out of:
  (i) any contract of apprenticeship;
  (ii) the application of the proviso to section 13 (11)
  (note: this concerns the deduction of an apprentice's pay for periods when he has been absent without good reason) and which has been referred to it by a party to the dispute or by the registrar or a training adviser, and endeavour to settle the dispute.
- appoint persons whom it may authorise to perform any of its functions in terms of this Act;
- in consultation with the registrar evaluate trade qualifications obtained outside the Republic;
- in consultation with the registrar establish a system for the governing and controlling of trade testing;
- make available training in the principles and techniques of evaluation to trade test officers and all persons evaluating the training and conducting the testing of apprentices;
- by a continuous process of training and retraining upgrade the work proficiencies of qualified artisans;
- counter any limiting factors on the flow of sufficient candidates for training as artisans;

- in collaboration with the Department frame guidelines on the selection of candidates for apprenticeship and encourage employers to provide persons doing the selection with the necessary training;
- in collaboration with the Department furnish prospective apprentices with vocational guidance on career selection and career content;
- furnish the Department on a continuous basis with information regarding technical professions and the career opportunities which they offer;
- in consultation with the board promote closer cooperation between formal education and training in respect of the design and content of curricula;
- take the necessary steps, especially during downswings in the economy, for the promotion of training, including the training of apprentices;
- initiate and monitor training programmes;
- provide out of its own funds financial incentives for the training of apprentices and where applicable of other employees;
- furnish the registrar with such statistics as he may require from time to time and may accredit training centres as contemplated in sections 31 (Regional Training Centres), 32 (Private Training Centres) and 34 (Industry Training Centres) to provide training on behalf of employees in the industry and area concerned."

15.10.4 Apprenticeship training

The Minister may, on the recommendation of the training board concerned, designate trades for the purpose of apprenticeship training. The Minister has the power to prescribe the conditions of apprenticeship, including such matters as the qualifications for apprenticeship, conditions concerning hours of work, overtime and holidays, and "the standard of proficiency, including the level of theoretical training and the minimum period of practical training in actual production and maintenance circumstances, which is required before an apprentice is permitted to undergo a trade test".

Certain of the conditions of apprenticeship which the Minister may lay down do not apply to apprentices employed by the state.

Any person who

- has the prescribed qualifications;
- has a certificate of physical fitness;
- is over fifteen years of age; and
- is not required by law to attend school,

can bind himself or herself as an apprentice.

A contract of apprenticeship will not be valid unless:

- the time it was entered into, it was reduced to writing; and
- it has been signed by or on behalf of the employer and by the apprentice and, in the case of an apprentice who is a minor, by his/her guardian; and
- it has been registered by the relevant training board.

The Act contains a great deal of detail concerning apprentices and their training which is too lengthy to be even summarised here. Everyone involved in apprentice-ship and training should become well acquainted with the Act.

15.10.5 Employment of minors in designated trades

If an employer employs a minor in a designated trade in a capacity other than that of an apprentice or a trainee, he/she must inform the relevant training board and must also inform the board if the employment of the minor is terminated. A employer may not employ a minor in a designated trade unless the minor con-cerned is qualified to bind himself/herself as an apprentice, and the minor may not be employed on conditions less favourable, as far as pay and hours of work are concerned, than those which apply to apprentices in the trade in question.

15.10.6 Training of persons who are not apprentices or minors

Section 30 of the Act which makes provision for the training of persons other than apprentices or minors, reads as follows:

"Whenever the Minister is satisfied that it is necessary in the public interest to do so, he may after consultation with the board and any other Minister which in his opinion has an interest therein, and with the concurrence of the Minister of Finance, make such arrange-ments as he may deem expedient to provide for the training in a particular trade or occupation of persons who are not apprentices or minors, and he may for that purpose by notice in the *Gazette* issue such directives as he may deem necessary for such training; Provided that the Minister may after consultation with the board provide, in terms of the foregoing provisions of this section, for the training of persons who are minors but who have completed a first period of training or service in terms of the provisions of the Defence Act, 1957 or section 34A of the Police Act, 1958."

15.10.7 Training centres and schemes

Any group or association of employers who have established or intend to establish a centre for the training of employees and other persons may apply for registration as a regional training centre. The registrar can set conditions concerning:

- the courses of training which may be provided;
- the nature, duration and standard of such courses;
- the standards of education or practical experience which have to be achieved or gained by employees or other persons before they may be permitted to undergo the training;
- the requirements relating to the qualifications and experience of the instructors;
- the premises, equipment, facilities and materials which will be used or pro-vided for the purposes of training; and
- any other matter connected with the training centre or the training provided.

The Advisory Committee for Regional Training Centres, established by the Minister, comprises:

- one person nominated by each regional training centre;
- one person nominated by the National Training Board; and
- one person nominated by the Department of Labour.

The Advisory Committee will advise the registrar on the conditions which he/she may set (listed above), and on any other matter relating to the training of employees or other persons which has been referred to the Committee by the registrar.

15.10.8 Private training centres

Private training centres may also be established through the efforts of an individual employer or other person.

15.10.9 Industry training centres

Industry training centres are centres established by training boards. Just as is the case with regional training centres, the registrar has the power to set conditions pertaining to industry training centres, but in the latter case conditions regarding the fees to be charged may also be set.

15.10.10 Labour relations training

It is important to note the requirements in respect of labour relations training which are set out in section 33:

> "No person, excluding a trade union, employers' organisation, federation, industrial council or educational institution, may conduct labour relations training at a regional, private or industry training centre unless the centre has been registered and the courses are in accordance with courses approved by the registrar."

This does not apply to employers who provide labour relations training to their own employees. Labour relations is defined in section 1 of the Act (see above).

15.10.11 Grants-in-aid

Grants-in-aid may be granted on conditions determined by the Minister to:

- registered trade unions or employers' organisations which provide training in labour relations to office bearers, employees or members, or in the case of employers' organisations, to the employees of members;
- registered federations which provide training in labour relations to office bearers, employees or members of affiliated unions or organisations, or in the case of a federation of employers' organisations, to employees of members of affiliated organisations.

A grant-in-aid must be used exclusively to defray the costs arising from the presentation of the training concerned.

15.10.12 The fund for the training of unemployed persons

The Act provides for the establishment of a "Fund for the Training of Unemployed Persons" which must be used "for financing training whereby unemployed persons are equipped with working skills to facilitate their entry into the labour market". The funds will emanate from:

- money appropriated by Parliament;
- money appropriated by interest groups in the private sector;
- money from any other source; and
- interest

Control of the fund is vested with the Director-General: Labour, who is to be advised by a committee comprising:

- the Director-General or other officer of the Department, who will be the Chairperson;
- seven members representing the private sector;
- two officers from the Department; and
- the Chairperson of the National Training Board.

The committee is to advise the Director-General on:

- work categories in which unemployed persons should be trained;
- the granting of contracts for the training of unemployed persons;
- the standards that should apply to the training of unemployed persons;
- the placement in employment of trained unemployed persons; and
- any other matter connected with the training of unemployed persons and their placement in lucrative employment in the labour market.

15.10.13 Manpower Development Fund

A Manpower Development Fund under the control of the Director-General has been established in terms of the Act. The money in this fund is used to make loans to regional, private and industry training centres, and also to training schemes which may have been established under section 48 of the Labour Relations Act. (This section was repealed in terms of the Manpower Training Act, but any schemes established under it which continue will be eligible for a loan from the Manpower Development Fund.)

15.10.14 Training levies

The Minister, after consultation with the National Training Board, may impose a levy on all or on any category of employers. Money raised in this way will be used "for the purposes of the achievement of any of the objects" of the Act, or for the financing of a training scheme for which no other provision has been made in the Act.

Groups or associations of employers who have established training schemes may also request the Minister to make binding the payment of contributions to finance the scheme in their industry, or area of industry.

15.10.15 Training advisers

The Minister may appoint suitably qualified training advisers whose duties will include:

- assisting employers, or others, in determining training needs;
- Giving advice in connection with:
  - the development of training programmes;
  - improving the quality of any training provided;
  - the selection of training of employees, workseekers or other persons;
- the testing of employees, workseekers or other persons during or after completion of their training;
- giving advice in connection with any aspect of instruction.

15.11 CONCLUSION

In this chapter the focus was on some national-level trends regarding the development and training of employees. Attention was given to the most important aspects of the National Training Strategy Initiative which was developed by a task team under the auspices of the National Training Board. The background to the development of the National Training Strategy and the problems related to training and development in South Africa were briefly discussed. The National Qualification Framework and the various structures associated with it were described. An update was provided on the developments which have taken place since the publication of the NTB report. The last section of this chapter focused on the Manpower Training Act.

In the next chapter we focus on organisational-level aspects of the training and development of employees.

✓ SELF-EVALUATION QUESTIONS

1. Discuss the problems associated with the training and development of human resources in South Africa.
2. Describe how the knowledge and experience of the international community can assist in the development of a national training strategy.
3. Explain the main elements of the proposed national training strategy. Discuss the elements involved and the role that the NQF will play.

4. Explain how the NQF will impact on training and development in your organisation.
5. Discuss the influence of a coordinated and well-developed National Training Strategy on the competitiveness of South African organisations.
6. Analyse the role of ABE in your organisation and discuss the role that it can play in the improvement of knowledge and skills in South Africa.
7. Explain the importance and appropriateness of the structures of the Manpower Training Act to meet South Africa's training and development needs.

 BIBLIOGRAPHY

Eberlein, R. 1995. *The National Training Strategy Initiative of South Africa: Update October 1995*. Pretoria.

National Training Board. 1994. *A Discussion Document on a National Training Strategy Initiative*. Pretoria: NTB.

Nel, J. 1996. Personal Discussion on the Future Development of the National Training Initiative.

Republic of South Africa. 1981. The Manpower Training Act 56 of 1981. Pretoria: Government Printer.

Republic of South Africa. 1995. The South African Qualifications Act 58 of 1995. Pretoria: Government Printer.

Republic of South Africa. 1997. *Green Paper: Skills Development Strategy for Economic and Employment Growth in South Africa*. Department of Labour, March 1997. Pretoria: Department of Labour.

chapter 16 Training and Developing Employees: Organisational-Level Perspectives

STUDY OBJECTIVES

After studying this chapter, you should be able to:

- explain the concept *human resource development*
- distinguish between "training", "education" and "development"
- list the reasons for human resource development in organisations;
- illustrate the training process with the aid of a sketch;
- discuss the training needs assessment phase and training phase of training;
- explain how the effectiveness of training will be evaluated.

16.1 INTRODUCTION

All organisations engage employees to execute certain activities in order to achieve their goals and objectives. It has been emphasised a number of times that, irrespective of the nature of these goals and objectives, organisations must have competent employees to perform the tasks to accomplish them. Although well-thought-out strategies and efficient human resource planning, recruitment and selection initially provide an organisation with the required employees, additional training is normally necessary to provide them with job-specific skills which enable them to survive over time.

As mentioned in chapter 4, according to the *World Competitiveness Report*, when compared with other developing countries, South Africa usually ranks among the last countries in the people category. Aspects such as literacy and education are critical in this regard. For a very long time organisations in South Africa have neglected to invest in their employees to equip them for the challenges of our modern, globally competitive world. According to a report by SPA Consultants (1994), industry invests, on average, 0,5–1,0 % of its payroll in education and training. Comparative figures in Europe are 4–6 % and in Japan 10 %. It is therefore essential that human resource development should play a prominent role in South African organisations

In this chapter the focus is on training and development efforts within the organisation. The training process starts with assessing training needs and formulating objectives for training programmes. The next step is to design and deliver the necessary training programmes using those methods and procedures most likely to ensure that they achieve their desired ends. The training programmes are then evaluated to ensure that objectives are met.

16.2 HUMAN RESOURCE DEVELOPMENT (HRD): CONCEPTS AND IMPORTANCE

The importance of HRD as a means of ensuring that organisations maintain their competitiveness in an ever-changing environment cannot be overemphasised. The country's history, technological innovations, competitive pressures, restructuring and downsizing, the low level of literacy and numeracy, (especially in the South African context),and the increasing diversity of the workforce are some of the important issues which force organisations to retrain employees and to provide basic literacy training, thus ensuring that employees are ready to face present challenges and to prepare themselves for the future.

16.2.1 What is human resource development (HRD)?

Human resource development can be defined as a learning experience organised mainly by an employer, usually within a specified period of time, to bring about the possibility of performance improvement and/or personal growth (Nadler & Nadler 1989: 6).

The main focus of HRD is learning and its principal aim is to attain the objectives of both the organisation and the individual. Human resource development takes place over a particular period of time; it is therefore essential to notify planners of the time scale involved so that not only can replacements be found for those who have to attend courses but the cost-effectiveness of the programme can also be determined.

As mentioned above, the chief focus of HRD is the possibility of performance improvement and/or personal growth. Learning can take place without producing any improvement in performance and it is therefore important to focus on the word "possibility" in the definition (Nadler & Nadler 1989: 4). Performance improvement can be widely interpreted but in the context of HRD it refers to how employees perform their work after the HRD intervention. It is not always possible to distinguish between personal growth and performance improvement; that is why the word "and" is included in the definition of HRD (Nadler & Nadler 1989: 12). Some people are of the opinion that personal growth falls outside the ambit of the organisation, while others believe that the organisation has a responsibility for the personal growth of employees. The latter belief is commonly held in the Asian-Pacific basin and has spread to other parts of the world (Anderson 1994: 123). Some organisations introduce HRD programmes with the sole purpose of personal growth, while others do not. The question now is: when conducting a course aimed at performance improvement, how do you prepare employees for inevitable changes in the organisation when it is not known when these changes will take place? Performance improvement concerns how individuals do their jobs in relation to other employees and in terms of the set standard. It is, however, important to remember that HRD should focus on all the employees in an organisation because every employee contributes to organisational goals.

Generally, learning can be viewed as a relatively permanent change in behaviour and HRD focuses on intentional rather than incidental learning. The learner focuses on a learning experience with the express purpose of learning something. Although a person can learn something incidentally by watching TV, reading the newspaper or having a discussion with friends, the main purpose of such activities is not to learn. Intentional learning can be formal or informal. Broadly speaking, formal learning refers to the situation where an employee is taken out of the normal working environment to attend a course or lecture or to do a practical course. Informal learning, on the other hand, includes on-the-job training which is provided by the supervisor or by a person designated to do the training.

16.2.2 The concepts "training", "education" and "development"

Employee *training* is job-related learning that is provided by employers for their employees. The main aim is the improvement of employees' skills, knowledge and attitudes so that they can perform their duties according to set standards.

Employee *education* in the organisational context concerns the preparation of an individual for a job different from the one he/she currently holds. In this case the outcome of performance is clearly defined. (Nadler & Nadler 1989: 5). Employee education usually refers to the preparation of managers for higher-level jobs or for possible changes in the future. In many organisations it is also termed *management development*. Education in the general sense refers to the broad educational process covering preschool, primary, secondary and tertiary education; this usually occurs outside the organisation (except for adult literacy, life skills and numeracy training which normally occur within the organisational context). In contrast to training (which is job-related) and education (which is the preparation of an employee for a different job) employee *development* is a broad term which relates to training, education and other intentional or unintentional learning and which refers to general growth through learning. It is important to note that "training", "education" and "development" do not form part of a continuum. Employee development can also take place through the process of training and education; it must, however, be emphasised that, in this case, it does not refer to the job context but that its activities vary widely and are not constrained by the relationship to a present or future job.

16.2.3 Importance of HRD

The following are a few of the many reasons why organisations train and educate employees.

- To improve the performance of employees who do not meet the required standards of performance, once their training needs have been identified.
- To prepare employees for future positions.
- To prepare employees for forthcoming organisational restructuring or for changes in technology.
- To ensure competitiveness in the marketplace by retraining employees.
- To increase the literacy levels of employees.
- To benefit the individual employee. For example, HRD, helps the individual to make better decisions and increases job satisfaction; this in turn should benefit the organisation.
- To improve interpersonal skills and to make the organisation a better place to work.

It is of utmost importance that HRD should be tailored to fit the organisation's strategy and structure.

16.2.4 The relationship of HRD to other human resource management functions

Human resource development is linked to many other human resource subfunctions in an organisation. Workforce planners identify the quality and quantity of employees required by the organisation. Projected workforce needs enable the HRD subfunction to plan the training of both current and newly recruited employees. The recruiting and selection subfunctions locate candidates with the required skills in the market.

The need for formal training depends on the level of the job in the organisation. For example, high entry requirements will diminish the need for intensive formal training, while a good in-house training course may reduce the need to recruit highly skilled candidates.

Performance assessments and career planning are also two subfunctions which are directly related to HRD. Performance assessments allow a supervisor to identify possible training requirements and possible career opportunities in an organisation.

16.3 A MODEL FOR SYSTEMATIC TRAINING

One of the main reasons why training fails in an organisation is the lack of a systematically developed training model. The principal aim of training is to contribute to an organisation's overall objectives; however, in many instances such objectives have not been clearly formulated, training programmes are never evaluated and it seems that behaviour changes do not form part of the HRD effort. A systematic approach to the development of training is essential. In figure 16.1 a systematic approach to training is outlined. Three phases are shown in this model, namely: the needs assessment phase, the training phase and the training evaluation phase.

The rest of the chapter is devoted mainly to a discussion of each of these phases of the training model.

16.3.1 The training needs assessment phase

Successful training begins with a *needs assessment* to determine **which employees** need to be trained and **what** they need to be trained to do. The training needs analysis phase culminates in the formulation of a set of objectives which clearly state the purpose of the training and the competencies required of trainees once they have completed the programme.

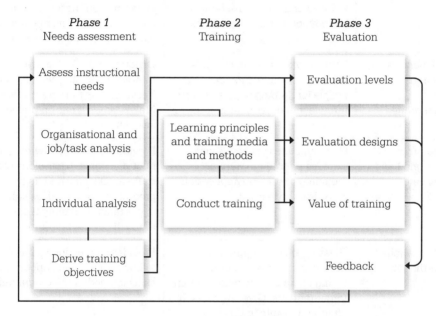

Figure 16.1
General systems model for training
Source: Adapted from Cascio, W.F. (1992: 236).

Needs analysis requires time, money and expertise. Unfortunately, many organisations undertake training without making this essential preliminary investment. Often there is no systematic plan to predict future training needs or to determine whether perceived needs and problems can be addressed by training. Training which is undertaken without a careful analysis of requirements is likely to be ineffective and to reduce the motivation of employees to attend future programmes.

16.3.1.1 What is training needs assessment?

Training needs assessment is an investigation which is undertaken to determine the nature of performance problems in order to establish the underlying causes and how these can be addressed by training. A training gap is usually defined as the

Table 16.1

*Example of the training cycle in an organisation**

Steps	Management actions	Training department actions
Management goals	Management decides that it wants to reach specified target markets using radio marketing techniques.	No decision making. Should actively pursue up-to-date knowledge of management direction and key goals.
Training needs identified	Makes a decision that a segment of the new agent orientation programme should cover target markets and how to use radio marketing techniques to reach those markets.	Suggests and recommends ways that training might best be used. May identify areas that could best be learned on the job, recommends ways for line managers to support desired performance.
Audience and training content determined	Hires new agents. Determines training schedule. Provides key people for training departments to interview to determine training content.	Conducts a content analysis using interview and observation data. Recommends training content. Makes suggestions on prerequisite skills.
Training designed and delivered	Communicates expectations to trainees prior to programme, including on-the-job application of skills to be learned.	Provides advice on how to conduct precourse discussions with trainees. Designs and delivers a programme that enables students to use radio-marketing techniques to reach certain target markets.
Skills applied on-the-job	Gives specific assignments for new agents to use radio-marketing techniques to reach certain target markets. Gives rewards for effort and results in this area.	Provides suggestions on how to follow through and support the skills learned in the programme.
Training outcomes evaluated	Determines if new agents are using the radio-marketing techniques and if their performance shows that the techniques are helping them reach target markets.	Gathers specific data on the application of new skills. Provides feedback to management on revisions to training content, audience, precourse preparation and/or supervision for application on the job.

*Source: Adapted from Fisher, Schoenfelt & Shaw (1993: 371).

difference between the required standard of the job (normally specified in a job description) and the performance of the incumbent. The ultimate aim of needs analysis is to establish (Institute of Personal Management (IPM) 1991: 17):

● what needs actually exist;
● whether they are important;
● how the needs became apparent;

- how they were identified;
- how they may best be addressed;
- what the priorities are.

There are several sources of information which can be used for needs analysis and many ways of gathering such information. The choice of methods and sources depends partly on the nature of the problem and the purpose of the training. If the purpose is to improve an employee's present job performance, the trainer must start by identifying performance deficiencies or areas where improvement is necessary.

Information on performance deficiencies can be obtained, *inter alia*, through supervisors' and clients' complaints, performance appraisal feedback, measures of output and/or quality, and performance tests given to employees to establish their current knowledge and level of skills (Fisher et al 1993: 372). Specialists in HRD can also collect critical incidents of poor job performance and obtain reports to identify skill or knowledge problem areas.

The following are examples of methods of gathering data for training needs analysis:

- Searching existing records by studying performance appraisals, performance records, productivity records and training records;
- individual interviews with job incumbents, supervisors and clients;
- group interviews;
- assessment centres;
- Delphi technique;
- observation;
- nominal group technique;
- collection of critical incidents;
- questionnaires;
- job analysis; and
- performance tests.

Once the performance deficiency or training needs have been identified, the next step is to determine whether the deficiency or need should be addressed by training. Sometimes employee motivation, organisational constraints, or poor task design may cause the deficiency and, in these situations, training in job skills will not solve the performance problem.

Robert F Mager and Peter Pipe (1970) have developed a flow chart to determine if training can correct a performance deficiency; a quick reference checklist (Institute of Personnel Management 1991: 19) is provided in exhibit A.

Exhibit A

Can training correct a performance deficiency?

Quick reference checklist

What is the performance discrepancy?
- What is the difference between what is being done and what should be done?
- What is the evidence and is it reliable?

Is the discrepancy important?
- What is it costing?
- Will the problem grow?
- Is it worth fixing?

Is it a skill/knowledge lack?
- Could they do it if their lives depended on it?

Did they know how to do it in the past?
- Have they forgotten?
- Is the skill used often?
- Do they get regular feedback on how they are doing?

Is there a simpler way?
- Can the job be simplified?
- Could job aids be used?
- Can they learn by being shown instead of training?

Do they have the potential to do the job well?
- Are they physically fit?
- Have they the mental potential?
- Are they over/underqualified?

Is the correct performance being punished?
- Do they perceive performing correctly as penalising?
- Is not doing the job rewarding?
- Is there some reward for non-performance (less work, worry, tiredness, more attention)?

Does correct performance really matter?
- Is there a favourable outcome for performance?
- Is there any status/job satisfaction connected with the job?

Are there any obstacles to performing?
- Are the resources available (time, equipment, tools, space)?
- Are there any other barriers (policy, culture, ego, systems, authority, conflicting time demands)?

What is the best solution?
- Are there any solutions which are unacceptable to the organisation?
- Are the solutions beyond the resources of the organisation?

16.3.1.2 Levels of needs analysis

Any thorough needs assessment effort must address three key areas: the organisation, the job and the individual.

In the first place **organisational assessment** considers the proposed training within the context of the rest of the organisation. The following questions may be asked in the organisational analysis portion of the needs assessment to highlight problem areas (Fisher et al 1993: 376).

- What are the training implications of the organisation's strategy?
- What will the result be if we do not train?
- How does this training programme fit in with the organisation's future plans and goals?
- Where in the organisation is training needed?
- How are various departments performing in relation to expectations or goals?
- In which departments is training most likely to succeed?
- Which departments should be trained first?
- Can the organisation afford this training?
- Which training programmes should have priority?
- Will this training adversely affect untrained people or departments?
- Is this training consistent with the organisation's culture?
- Will this training be accepted and reinforced by others in the organisation, such as the trainees' superiors, subordinates and clients?

An important consideration, however, is whether or not the proposed training will be compatible with the organisation's mission, strategy, goals, and culture. Corporate culture compatibility is of utmost importance for training and management education in an organisation. Possible factors that can create a need for future training are:

- **product changes:** an increase or decrease in demand as a result of population shifts;
- **economic changes:** availability of credit and loan facilities which could jeopardise small business;
- **political changes:** examples are affirmative action and creation of new regional structures in South Africa with the integration of the former homelands;
- **sociological changes:** demographic changes, for example high urbanisation;
- **technological changes:** more efficient machinery and methods.

The impact that the training of one department has on other departments must also be considered in an organisational assessment.

The second crucial aspect is the **job** and its concomitant duties and responsibilities. This phase is called *task analysis* and different methods are used, for example, the critical incident method and the Delphi technique. A training practitioner can use any or a combination of methods.

Once the duties or tasks in which training is needed are identified, the detailed analysis of each task may begin. The purpose of this step is to find out if the task is important and if training is essential and to determine the procedures that should be taught. *Subject-matter experts* such as superiors and high-performing employees could be used to generate this information. Examples of questions to be asked by the experts are the following (Fisher et al 1993: 376):

- How difficult is this task?
- Should it be taught in training or can it be learned on the job?
- How important is it that incumbents should be able to do the task from the very first day on the job?
- What knowledge, skills, information, equipment, materials, and work aids are needed to do this task?
- What signals the need to perform this task?
- What are the steps in performing this task?
- Can the incumbent explain if the task has been performed correctly?

The final level of analysis focuses on the individuals to be trained. Here it must be determined which employees should receive training and what their current levels of skill and knowledge are. Individuals may be nominated on the basis of their past performance, an entire work group may be identified, or all incumbents with a specific job title. The trainer should assess, or at least estimate, the skill and knowledge levels of the chosen trainees, so that the training fits their needs.

If individual assessment indicates that a wide range of skills and knowledge are required, it is advisable to group employees together into basic and advanced groups. Alternatively, a training method that allows for self-paced learning or individualised instruction should be developed. This kind of flexibility should be planned for before the training commences to ensure that all trainees can have a satisfying learning experience and contribute to organisational goals.

16.3.1.3 *Identifying training objectives*

The last step in the assessment phase of training is to translate the needs identified by the organisational, task and individual analyses into measurable objectives that can guide the training process. Behavioural training objectives state what the person will be able to do, under what conditions, and how well the person will be able to do it.

Training objectives should focus on a behaviour component which describes in clear terms what a learner has to do to demonstrate that he/she has learned. Words which are open to few interpretations should be used such as "compare", "construct" and "identify". Avoid vague words such as "to know" and "to understand". The conditions or limitations under which performance should take place must also be clearly stated. The tools or equipment needed to perform the task must also be specified, for example: "without help", "using a calculator", "given a list of". A criterion component which provides the standard of performance, for example how well the learner has to perform to be considered successful, must also be included. The standard can focus, for example, on speed (within ten minutes), accuracy, sequence and quality.

Exhibit B

Example: learning objective

With the aid of a pair of scissors, cut from a sheet of paper the shape of a tree within *five minutes.*

- with the aid of a pair of scissors — **condition**
- cut out — **behaviour**
- within five minutes — **criterion**

Writing training objectives is more difficult than it may appear. The following guidelines must be considered.

- Write objectives as concisely as possible and avoid being long-winded.
- Do not use vague language.
- Avoid using descriptions that are linked to instructor satisfaction, for example "to perform to the satisfaction of the instructor".
- When describing the condition required for learning, avoid producing a long list of necessary equipment.

Once the training objectives have been identified, training practitioners can begin to plan both the training and evaluation phases of the training cycle (Fisher et al 1993: 379).

16.3.2 The training phase

Once the training needs have been determined and behavioural objectives stated, a training programme can be developed to achieve the stated objectives. In order to ensure the success of the training programme, appropriate training methods must be selected and suitable training materials developed to convey the required knowledge and skills identified in the training objectives. The necessity of understanding how people learn in order to design an effective training programme cannot be overemphasised; this aspect will be dealt with first.

16.3.2.1 Learning principles

A number of principles which can facilitate the learning process have been identified; these will be discussed briefly. However, attention must first be devoted to the preconditions for learning which are in themselves also learning principles.

Preconditions

There are two preconditions for learning: *readiness* and *motivation.*

Trainee readiness concerns the situation where trainees possess the background skills and knowledge necessary to master the material that will be presented to them in the new training programme. For example, a basic knowledge of mathematics is a prerequisite for learning statistical quality control techniques. *Trainee motivation* requires trainees to experience a need to learn new skills and therefore to understand the need for training. Learning that takes place without motivation is not as successful as learning with motivation. Learner motivation can be improved by (Anderson 1994: 125):

- trainees who attend courses voluntarily;
- trainees who are involved in needs analysis;
- trainees who are given a short summary of the benefits of the training and how it will influence their careers;
- trainees who set their own ideas on how they will approach the training;
- enhancement of self-efficacy by **persuasion** (telling the trainees that they can do it), by **modelling** (showing the trainees others like themselves who have succeeded) or by **enactive mastery** (allowing the trainees to experience success in the early stages of training).

In addition to the preconditions for learning, other relevant learning principles include:

- conditions for practice,
- knowledge of results,
- overcoming interference,
- transfer of training, and
- adult learning principles.

Conditions for practice*

Actively practising the skill or task being learned can increase learning. An important condition in designing training is to decide whether to have the **whole** task learned and practised as one unit or whether to break down the task into separately learned and practised **parts.** A second condition of practice is to determine whether the practice should be divided into spaced segments or scheduled in one long session. A last condition of practice is to decide how much practice is enough. Overlearning is practising beyond the point at which the trainee has mastered and performed the task correctly. Overlearning should be used in those circumstances where the trainee is learning a task which demands that the first reactions be absolutely correct. It is important because it increases retention over time, makes the behaviour more automatic, increases the quality of performance under stress and helps trainees to transfer what they have learned to the job setting.

*This section is based on Fisher et al (1993: 382–386).

Knowledge of results

Effective learning requires that trainees receive **feedback**, or **knowledge of results**, on how they are performing. Feedback is critical for both learning and motivation and, if feedback is not provided, trainees may learn a technique incorrectly or lose the motivation to learn. Feedback maximises trainees' willingness to learn and is also necessary if goals for maintaining or improving performance have been set. (See also the preconditions for learning.)

Overcoming interference

A trainee experiences **interference** when habits and/or learning acquired before the start of training make it difficult for the trainee to absorb new material. High interference occurs when the trainee has learned a strong stimulus-response connection in the past and now has to learn a totally different response to the same or similar stimulus. To overcome interference, the trainer should teach the principles underlying the new response and provide support and sufficient practice to increase the strength of the new stimulus-response connection.

Transfer of training

If learning that has taken place during training is not transferred to the job situation, the training programme has been ineffective.

Learning theorists recommend the following traditional ways of maximising the transfer of training.

- Maximise the similarity between the training situation and the job situation.
- Provide as much experience as possible with the task being taught.
- Provide a variety of examples when teaching concepts of skills.
- Label or identify important features of the task.
- Make sure that general principles are understood before expecting any transfer.
- Make certain that the training behaviours and ideas are rewarded in the job situation.
- Design the training content so that the trainees can see its applicability.
- During the training, the trainer should emphasise the usefulness of the new material, drawing on illustrations from the work environment.
- The trainer should ask trainees to set specific and measurable goals for performing the new behaviours back on the job.

After the training, trainees should be encouraged to assess themselves against these personal goals on a regular basis. Trainers should also plan as carefully for the transfer of training as for the classroom presentation. If the above suggestions are implemented in a training programme, the more likely it is that positive transfer to the job will take place and that job satisfaction will result.

Learning principles for adults

Most employees in organisations are adults. The science of teaching adults is known as *andragogy* whilst the science of teaching children is termed *pedagogy*. There are several differences that adult educators consider important, for example:

● adults already possess a great deal of knowledge and experience on which they can rely;

● adults normally take responsibility for themselves and their learning;

● adults focus on present problems and want to learn things that have immediate use.

Andragogy is based on the premise that learning should be active and student-centred, that training should focus on real-world problems and on applying techniques such as case studies and role-playing, and that the experience and knowledge of adults can be used productively.

When a trainer assumes that adults know very little and that their experience is irrelevant, thus treating them as children, adults do not learn effectively. Particularly in South Africa, where a large majority of adults need to be trained, this could have disastrous consequences.

16.3.2.2 Teaching style

The way in which training practitioners approach teaching may influence the effectiveness of learning. Training practitioners must take particular note of the following characteristics that may affect optimal teaching style.

● **Instrumentality** is the extent to which the trainee is concerned with the immediate applicability of the concepts and skills being taught.

● **Scepticism** is the extent to which the trainee exhibits a questioning attitude and demands logic, evidence, and examples.

● **Resistance to change** refers to the extent to which the trainee fears the process of moving in to the unknown, or the effect which that process may have on him/her.

● **Attention span** is the length of time for which the trainee can focus attention before substantial attentiveness diminishes.

● **Expectation level** is the quality and quantity of training that the trainee requires from the trainer.

● **Absorption level** is the pace at which the trainee expects and can accept new information.

● **Topical interest** is the degree to which the trainee can be expected to have personal (job-relevant) interest in the topic.

● **Self-confidence** is the degree to which the trainee independently and positively views him- or herself; this determines the trainee's need for feedback, reinforcement, and success experiences.

- **Locus of control** is the degree to which the trainee perceives that he or she can implement the training successfully back on the job with or without organisational support.

16.3.2.3 Training methods for nonmanagerial employees

The term *training* has historically been used to describe technical or job skill training for nonmanagerial employees. *Development,* on the other hand, is the term which has traditionally been used for the education of managers. In some cases, because of the different learning content, different methods have been used. As we move into the twenty-first century, the distinction between training managerial and nonmanagerial employees is becoming less clear. Organisational structures are changing rapidly and more emphasis is being placed on self-managed work teams, while the fact that first-line supervisors should also be trained in managerial skills such as planning, organising, leading and control is being increasingly acknowledged.

However, the distinction between the training of nonmanagerial and managerial employees is still made. This section discusses the training methods more commonly used for technical training, while the next section focuses on methods used for developing management skills.

Once clearly defined training objectives have been formulated and cognisance has been taken of the learning principles, the appropriate training method can be chosen. Some of the methods can be used on the job, while others can be more appropriately used off the job.

On-the-job training

On-the-job training (OJT) is conducted at the work site and focuses on the actual job. The advantages of OJT are (Bird McCord 1987: 356; French 1994: 290; Piskyrich 1993: 262):

- the transfer of training to the job is maximised;
- a full-time trainer and separate training facilities are avoided;
- trainee motivation remains high because what employees are learning is relevant to the job and provides a sense of satisfaction;
- the employee is assimilated more quickly into the organisation.

An OJT training programme should be planned as carefully as any other training programme (see figure 16.2). On-the-job training should be designed to form part of the total training effort in an organisation. Classroom training normally forms an important part of OJT as it will cover the orientation part of the training programme. In the classroom, trainees will be informed of the equipment involved, the function each performs, the total production process will be explained, and this will be followed by a tour of the department. Knowledge gained in the classroom can now be transferred to the job; the procedure explained in figure 16.2 would then be of value. Avoid the following when conducting OJT programmes:

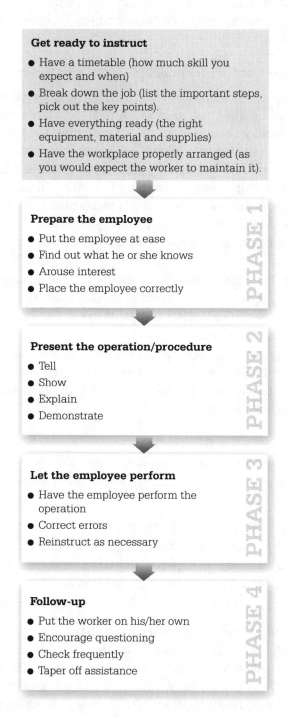

Get ready to instruct

- Have a timetable (how much skill you expect and when)
- Break down the job (list the important steps, pick out the key points).
- Have everything ready (the right equipment, material and supplies)
- Have the workplace properly arranged (as you would expect the worker to maintain it).

Prepare the employee

- Put the employee at ease
- Find out what he or she knows
- Arouse interest
- Place the employee correctly

PHASE 1

Present the operation/procedure

- Tell
- Show
- Explain
- Demonstrate

PHASE 2

Let the employee perform

- Have the employee perform the operation
- Correct errors
- Reinstruct as necessary

PHASE 3

Follow-up

- Put the worker on his/her own
- Encourage questioning
- Check frequently
- Taper off assistance

PHASE 4

Figure 16.2

A job instruction procedure which could be of value for OJT

Source: Adapted from Fisher et al 1993: 387

- frequent interruptions as the trainer or trainee is called away to perform other duties;
- abandoning employees busy with OJT and expecting them to pick up necessary skills when they can;
- not informing employees about important but infrequent events;
- allowing co-workers to teach them bad habits.

Off-the-job training

Training offered at locations away from the job is designated off-the-job-training (for example locations near the workplace or away from work, at a special training centre or at a resort). Training which is conducted away from the workplace minimises distractions and allows employees to devote their full attention to the training offered.

Methods and materials often used are: lectures, group discussions, role-playing, assigned reading, case studies, video tapes and *vestibule training*. Vestibule training requires trainees to do the whole job with the same tools and machines that are required on the job. (For a more detailed discussion of these methods, see section 16.3.2.3 on page 491.)

Computer training

This section deals with the various training approaches which use a computer as a tool (This section is based on Hart 1987: 470–485; Fisher et al 1993: 387–391; and Wills 1993: 91–95.)

- Computer-assisted instruction (CAI)

  Computer-assisted instruction uses the computer as a self-contained teaching machine to present individual lessons. The trainee is requested to respond to the questions and, if the answer is correct, the computer indicates that the student can proceed to the next level of information. These instructional units replace/supplement more traditional classroom activities and include aspects like drill and practices, tutorials, simulations and games, and problem-solving exercises.

- Computer-managed instruction (CMI)

  Here the computer determines the employee's initial level of competence and then provides a customised set of learning modules and exercises. Computer-managed instruction uses the computer to organise instruction and to track student records and progress. The instruction does not have to be delivered via computer, but very often CAI is combined with CMI. Performance is assessed frequently, and the content is modified continuously to suit the learner.

- Computer-based training (CBT)

  Computer-based training includes both CAI and CMI. It is very expensive to introduce CBT training because each trainee needs access to a computer and there is no interaction among trainees. It is therefore not suitable for developing interpersonal skills.

- Computer-mediated education (CME)

  Computer-mediated education describes computer applications that facilitate the delivery of instruction, for example fax, electronic mail (E-mail) and computer conferencing.

- Computer-based multimedia (CBM)

  The aim with CBM is to integrate various voice, video and computer technologies in a single accessible system. An example of CBM is CD-Rom. Computer-based multimedia will allow the instructional designer to focus on content requirements and students need a relatively constraint free technological environment.

- Interactive video training (IVT)

  This involves CBT with the addition of a videodisc or video cassette player and a monitor. It has the advantages of CBT and the ability to use sound and high-quality moving pictures to demonstrate learning content and to provide problems for trainees to solve.

Which method should the trainer select? Aspects that the organisation must consider are the cost of the method, the number of individuals to be trained, their location, the availability of skilled trainers and, most important, the fact that the method must be consistent with the training content.

Advantages and disadvantages of using computers as training tools

The following advantages and disadvantages are applicable when using computers:

Advantages

- Self-pace learning is facilitated and immediate feedback and reinforcement are provided.
- Computers are interactive which makes learning very flexible and allows for learner control.
- Computer-assisted instruction can be conducted at remote sites, on all shifts. It can be fitted into lulls in the work schedule that would otherwise be unproductive.
- Managers and supervisors can be trained in their offices so that they are available to deal with job-related problems if necessary.
- Transportation and lodging costs for trainees are nonexistent and overall training costs can be reduced once the system has been developed.
- There is consistent quality of instruction over time and from group to group and subjectivity is eliminated.
- Disruptions during instruction due to unexpected trainer problems (for example illness) are excluded.
- Updates and changes can be made to all points very quickly.

- Retention of learning content is at least as good as with other instructional methods.
- Slow learners have a greater chance of success than with classroom training.
- Customised instruction according to each learner's needs can be developed.

Disadvantages

- Computers require motivated learners and students must be *au fait* with computer operations before they can learn.
- Systems are costly to develop.
- Computer technology is changing rapidly and an effort will have to be made to keep abreast with the latest changes.
- There is still widespread computer illiteracy and an effort has to be made to help employees overcome blocks.

16.3.2.4 Management education methods

This section deals with management education and focuses on the different methods used to educate employees. Because managerial work is important, complex, and challenging, many organisations provide regular management training. In South Africa where there is a critical shortage of high-level management expertise it is essential that organisations should identify potential candidates and educate them accordingly.

On-the-job methods *

Managerial education normally takes place off the job but a great deal of learning takes place on the job. According to Fisher et al (1993: 395), there have been several recent studies of managerial learning and skill development in the USA as a result of on-the-job experience. This research suggests that managers learn the most from assignments that are very difficult and challenging. A program of management education should include assignments and job rotating plans that stretch managers to their limits. The general on-the-job management education methods will be discussed briefly.

- Coaching

  In coaching experienced managers guide the actions of less experienced managers to help them develop their delivery. The advantage of coaching is that it provides immediate feedback on performance. A possible disadvantage is that it maintains the present values since the less experienced manager may adopt the same values and approaches as the coach (Fisher et al 1993: 395).

- Committee assignments

  Junior executives are assigned to committees where they can observe more experienced managers in action because a lot of organisational work takes

*This section as well as section on page 496 are based on Fisher et al 1993: 395–402; French 1994: 313–314; and De Cenzo & Robbins 1994: 268–273.

place in committees. The purpose of this method is to use normal committees as training instruments, one which will also help the inexperienced manager to participate. The major reason for his or her presence is, however, to observe the proceedings, for example, the interpersonal processes, agreements and disagreements, decision-making processes, negotiations, and successes and failures of the committee.

- Job rotation

This method entails moving from one job assignment to another within the same organisation and can take four to six months. The inexperienced manager will gain insight and broad understanding of the organisation and allow specialists to turn to generalists. This is true for senior management who must obtain an overall perspective of the organisation especially, and who must spend more and more of their time managing the total organisation and less and less time managing on the micro level. Job rotation is a method for broadening individuals' exposure to company operations, reducing boredom and stimulating new ideas. A further advantage of job rotation is that people are prepared to assume greater responsibility in the higher levels. A disadvantage, however, is that it can demotivate intelligent and aggressive employees who seek specific responsibilities and can eventually produce a number of employees with limited job knowledge (De Cenzo & Robbins 1994: 272). (See also chapter 7.)

- Understudy assignments

A person who acts as an assistant to someone else may be termed an understudy. Understudying is similar to coaching, but this method is a full-time mentor-understudy arrangement where coaching is only periodic. The understudy works with the mentor on a daily basis to learn how the job is done. In the manager's absence, the understudy performs the role of the manager on non-critical activities and develops valuable managerial skills. A disadvantage of this method is that managers may feel threatened by understudies and may not assist them as they should.

Off-the-job methods

Managerial education programmes often occur off the job and away from the place of work. An important reason for the off-site location is to remove the manager from the daily environment of the organisation and thereby minimise interruptions and distractions. Organisations conduct their own management education programmes or send managers to universities or consulting firms. Commonly used off-the-job methods are discussed below.

- Sensitivity training

Sensitivity training includes techniques such as laboratory, T-group training communication workshops and outward board trips (Ronen 1989:438). The purpose of sensitivity training is to make employees more aware of their own behaviour and how their behaviour is perceived by others. It also increases the participants' awareness and acceptance of the differences between them. Small groups of eight to fourteen individuals who are strangers to each other are normally grouped together and assisted by a trainer. During the discussion employees discuss themselves, their feelings, and the group process.

The most frequent changes derived from this training include a more favourable self-perception, reduced prejudice, improved scores on tests of interpersonal relations, and changed interpersonal behaviour as observed by others, all of which are particularly relevant in South Africa.

● Team building

Team building focuses on intact work groups and strives to develop the ability of managers to work together with them on the types of tasks they face each day. Team building is also an important organisational development technique.

The first phase is normally a data collection phase, followed by questionnaires or interviews with team members. Information about how the group works together, what problems exist and what norms are followed are sought. Typical activities in a team building exercise include goal setting, development of interpersonal relations, role analysis to clarify roles and responsibilities. A summarised version of the information is fed back to the group so that an objective look can be taken at their functioning. The facilitator helps the team understand the feedback and develop action plans for improving group processes. Team building attempts to use high interaction among group members to increase trust and openness.

● Behavioural-modelling training

Behavioural-modelling training holds that most human behaviour is learned by observing others and then modelling their behaviour when appropriate. Learning from others reduces the need for failure.

A fixed sequence of steps are normally followed (Latham 1989; 269–273). First, the trainer introduces a single interpersonal skill. Second, trainees view a video-tape of a supervisor performing the skill correctly. During this process the *learning points* should be highlighted. Third, trainees practice the skill by role-playing with other trainees. Lastly trainees get feedback on the effectiveness of their role-playing behaviour.

● Case study

With a case study a trainee is presented with a written description of an actual or hypothetical problem in an organisational setting. The trainee is required to read the case, identify and discuss the problem, and recommend possible solutions. The purposes of a case study are as follows.

O It shows trainees that there is usually no easy solution to complex organisational problems.

O Trainees realise that different perspectives and solutions to the same case may be equally valid

O Case studies help managerial trainees develop their problem-solving skills.

The case study provides stimulating, discussion and opportunities for individuals to defend their analytical and problem-solving abilities. It is an effective method of improving decision-making abilities within the given contracts (De Cenzo & Robbins 1994: 269).

● Simulation methods

By using simulation methods the work setting in which the trainee will have to perform is replicated for the trainee to try out different behaviours or strategies. The objective is for trainees to learn from their own actions, and from the group discussion that follows the simulation. Various forms of simulation are used, for example:

O in-basket exercises;
O role plays;
O leaderless group discussions;
O large-scale behavioural simulations;
O computerised business decision-making games.

The aim of the in-basket exercise simulation is to provide practice in aspects like setting priorities, making decisions, managing time and delegating. Participants individually play the role of a manager who has a certain period of time to deal with certain items in the in-basket within set conditions and constrains (Pfeiffer 1994: 58).

Role-playing allows the participant an opportunity to practice new behaviours in a controlled environment. They can be coached and receive feedback on interpersonal skills such as active listening, problem solving, communication and information sharing.

In *two-person role-playing*, trainees and, at times, trainers assume the roles of characters and act a simulated situation. The success of this method depends largely on the trainees' willingness to adopt the roles and to react as if they are really in the work environment.

The *leaderless group discussion*, also used in assessment centres, is a larger-group simulation consisting out of four to eight trainees working together to solve a problem. Group members are assigned different roles to play in the simulation and given information unique to that role.

Large-scale behavioural simulations can get very complex and involve simulated organisations of up to twenty people in different roles, lasting from six hours to several days. Simulations at this level of complexity are used with executives rather than lower-level supervisors.

Computerised business decision-making games may be defined as sequential decision-making exercises structured on a model of a business operation, in which the trainee assumes the role of managing the simulated operation (Pfeiffer 1994: 58).

One of the objectives of the business games is to teach general management skills such as decision making, setting priorities, long-range planning, and effective use of time, personnel, and equipment. Trainees also develop an appreciation of the complexity of organisations and the many factors that must be considered before making a decision.

Action learning

One of the best ways to educate managers is to give them challenging jobs with support systems to help them learn. Action learning is the study of real-life problems and then solutions within a real-life environment (Reid, Barrington & Kenny 1992: 119). This approach provides challenges and demands the transformation of problems into opportunities for managers.

Table 16.2

*Comparing action learning with traditional learning**

Traditional learning	Action Learning
• Individual based	• Group based
• Knowledge emphasis	• Skills emphasis
• Input orientated	• Output orientated
• Classroom based	• Work based
• Passive	• Active
• Memory tested	• Competence test
• Focus on past	• Focus on present and future
• Standard cases	• Real cases
• One way	• Interactive
• Teacher lead	• Student lead

*Source: Morgerison (1991: 40)

Action learning has been developed by Revans (Morgerison 1991:38) on the basis of the following principles.

● Management development must be based on real work projects.
● Identified projects must be owned and defined by senior managers as having significant impact on the future success of the company.
● Managers must aim to make a real return on investment.
● Managers must work in a team and learn from each other; crossing departmental and functional boundaries.
● Real action and change must be the end result.
● The content (knowledge) and the process (questions and methods) of change must be studied.
● Managers must publicly commit themselves to action and report on outcomes.

16.3.2.5 Conduct the training

An important aspect which needs to be finalised before training can be conducted is a proper analysis of the learner group. This could entail an analysis of their past experience, qualifications, job titles, reason for training and supervisors' reasons for nominating the trainee.

The choice of a training method to a large extent also determines how the training should be conducted. Apart from the above, a curriculum should be planned and the course content should be set out in a logical order. Part of the introduction would include the purpose of the lesson, the time duration, other sources to facilitate the learning process, learning objectives, possible problem areas which might be experienced by the trainer and possible questions to stimulate discussion if required.

Apart from the fact that the appropriate facility must be chosen and that pre-course material must be available, the trainer must be fully prepared to present the content. Although this phase of the training process represents only the tip of the iceberg, it is essential that it is executed successfully.

16.4 THE EVALUATION PHASE

The last phase is the evaluation phase. The purpose of this phase is to determine the extent to which the training activities have met the stated objectives and is the last phase in the training process. Evaluation of training is often done poorly or not done at all. One reason for this is that there is a general assumption that training will work and that a fear exists by those who initiated the training that an objective evaluation of the effectiveness of the training will prove otherwise.

The basic approach to evaluation should be to determine the extent to which the training programme has met the learning objectives identified prior to the training. Planning for the evaluation should commence at the same time that planning for the training programme begins.

16.4.1 Evaluation levels and measures

Kirkpatrick suggests four levels of evaluation (Cascio 1992: 253–254).

16.4.1.1 Level 1: Reaction

The first level is the *reaction* level, or the participants' feelings about the programme. If trainees enjoyed a programme it does not imply that the programme was useful to the organisation, but unpopular programmes may be cancelled due to a lack of interest. A questionnaire is normally used to obtain the information during or immediately after the programme. Typical questions to be answered are "Are you satisfied with the programme arrangements?" "Are the learning objectives clear to you?"

16.4.1.2 Level 2: Learning

Learning measures the degree trainees have mastered the concepts, information, and skills that the training intended to impart. Learning is assessed continually, for example during and/or at the end of the training programme with paper-and-pencil tests, performance tests and examinations.

16.4.1.3 Level 3: Behaviour

Once the training has been completed on-the-job training can be assessed by any of the performance evaluation techniques discussed in chapter 13. Behaviour ratings can be collected from the superior, peers, subordinates, or clients of the trained employees. The training practitioner should visit the worksite for example, two to three months after the training has be completed and objectively assess the change in behaviour.

16.4.1.4 Level 4: Results

The impact of the training programme on the work group or organisation as a whole is assessed objectively. The appropriate objective measures to use depend on the content and objectives of the training and includes cost savings, profit, productivity, quality, accidents, turnover, and employee attitudes. A cost–benefit analysis could be executed to determine the benefit derived from training from a cost point of view. It should be remembered that all three levels should be considered to assess the overall effectiveness of the training programme.

So how can we evaluate training? Well, we can apply the evaluation model shown below in table 16.3.

Table 16.3
Evaluation matrix

Degree	I	II	III	IV
What we want to know	Are the trainees happy? If not, why not?	Do the materials teach the concepts? If not, why not?	Are the concepts used? If not, why not?	Does application of the concepts positively affect the organisation? If not, why not?
What might be measured	Trainee reaction during workshop.	Trainee performance during workshop.	Trainee performance at end of workshop.	Assignments. Ongoing management support
Measurement dimensions	Relevance. Ease of learning.	Perceived "Worth".	Understanding. Application.	Analysis. Results.
Sources of data	Trainee comments. Questions about exercises. Questions about concepts.	Learning time. Performance on exercises. Presentation. Use of tools on exercises.	Results. Discussions.	Results. Discussions.
Data gathering methodology	Observation. Interview. Questionnaire.	Observation. Review. Questionnaire.	Questionnaire (critical incid.). Interview	Interview questionnaire (critical incid.).

16.4.2 Evaluation designs

Apart from Kirkpatrick's four levels of evaluating training, other complex and effective designs for evaluating training also exist. These designs focus mainly on the effectiveness of the training phase and a few of the commonly used ones will be discussed below (Fisher et al 1993:409).

16.4.2.1 One-off post-test design

This evaluation design is not planned prior to training but only half-way through the training. The trainer decides to collect data but because there is no pretraining measure and no untrained group to compare the results with, this exercise could prove to be worthless. This ad-hoc approach, if not done for a specific reason, should be avoided.

16.4.2.2 One-group pretest-posttest design

This is a simple evaluation design. A group of trainees is assessed both before and after the training. This design allows the trainer to identify a change in behaviour due to training but it cannot necessarily be concluded that the change was due to the training input. The reason why the change in behaviour cannot directly be attributed to training is because a number of factors might influence behaviour by chance during or after the training period. It nevertheless remains a useful indicator to establish whether knowledge has been gained.

16.4.2.3 Multiple-baseline design

Certain shortcomings of the above designs are overcome by the multiple baseline design. The training group is measured several times both before and after the training. The trainer probably should not use an obtrusive measure, such as a questionnaire or learning test. Trainees could improve over time because they are gaining practice with the measure. Objective measures of behaviour or results are less obtrusive, and they are easy to collect repeatedly.

This design allows the trainer to observe trends in performance and to see if there is a change in the trend immediately after the training.

16.4.2.4 Pretest-posttest control-group design

This design uses a control group of employees who are very similar to the training group except that they do not receive the training. Here both the groups to receive the training and the control group are measured at least once before and once after the training. This allows the trainer to draw quite firm conclusions about whether any change has occurred and if it has, whether the change is a result of the training and will benefit the organisation in the short and long term.

16.4.3 The value of training in monetary terms

The value of training in this context is determined by the net rand gain realised by an organisation as a result of adopting a given human resource development approach. (Also see level 4 of Kirkpatricks approach in section 16.4.1)

Calculating the value requires both assessing the cost of the training and putting a rand value on the benefits of the training. Some cost categories associated with training are:

- One-off-costs
  - Needs assessment
  - Salaries of training developers, consultants and instructional designers
  - Evaluation of the programme when first offered
- Presentation costs
  - Salaries, travel, and lodging costs of trainers
  - Facilities rental
  - Purchase of training equipment and materials
- Trainee costs
  - Transportation and lodging for trainees during training
  - Trainee wages or salary during training
  - Training materials and handouts

By determining the value of training in rand terms an employer can build a solid justification for a training programme on purely economic grounds. It must, however, be emphasised that the evaluation of training is a complex process and that a change in human behaviour and its benefits to an organisation cannot only be expressed in rand terms and it is therefore suggested that all the results from the evaluation exercise must be considered before definite conclusions can be drawn. Finally, feedback should be given throughout the process.

16.5 CONCLUSION

In this chapter human resource development as concept has been discussed. Attention was given to the concepts training, education and development. The complete training process, from the assessment of training needs to the training phase and the evaluation phase, have been discussed. It is apparent that the importance of HRD in South Africa, and the complexity of the process of HRD, make this aspect of South African HRM an immense challenge.

SELF-EVALUATION QUESTIONS

1. What is the relationship between the HRD and other HRM functions?
2. What are addressed at the organisational analysis phase of training needs assessment?

3. What are the purposes of the individual analysis phase of training needs assessment?

4. Write a behavioural objective for your learning from this chapter.

5. Explain three preconditions for learning.

6. What is overlearning?

7. How can a trainer facilitate transfer of training?

8. Explain why adult learners may need to be treated differently from child learners.

9. What are the advantages and disadvantages of on-the-job training?

10. Do computers play a role in training? Discuss

11. Explain the levels at which training can be evaluated.

12. Describe the most useful designs for evaluating training, and substantiate your reasons.

13. You are to develop a training programme to teach reading and writing to adults with no more than grade five education. The objective of the training programme is to teach the trainees how to master reading and writing skills at basic level (grammar, vocabulary, handwriting etc). The trainees must learn the skills to be able to write a basic letter and read one page of simple language.

   (a) How will your training programme incorporate or deal with each of the following learning principles or conditions? Are there any that will not concern you?
      (i) Readiness
      (ii) Motivation
      (iii) Interference
      (iv) Feedback
      (v) Overlearning
      (vi) Distributed versus massed practice
      (vii) Whole versus part learning
      (viii) Transfer of training
   (b) What training methods will you use? In what order?
   (c) How will the success of your programme be evaluated?

 BIBLIOGRAPHY

Anderson, AH. 1994. *Effective Personnel Management: A Skills and Activity-based Approach*. London: Blackwell

Bird McCord, A. 1987. Job training. In: *Training and Development Handbook*, Ed RL Craig. 3 ed. New York: McGraw-Hill

Cascio, WF. 1992. *Managing Human Resources: Productivity, Quality of Worklife, Profits*. New York: McGraw-Hill

De Cenzo, DA & Robbins, SP. 1994. *Human Resource Management: Concepts and Practices*. Canada: John Wiley

Fisher, CD, Schoenfelt, LF & Shaw, JB. 1993. *Human Resource Management*. Boston: Houghton Mifflin

French, WL. 1994. *Human resource Management*. Boston: Houghton Mifflin

Hart, FA. 1987. Computer-based training. In: *Training and Development Handbook*, Ed RL Craig. 3 ed. New York: McGraw-Hill

IPM. 1991. *Human Resource Management Kits: Analysing Training Needs*. Braamfontein: IPM

Latham, GP. 1989. Behavioral approaches to the learning process. In: *Training and Development in Organizations*, Ed IL Goldstein. San Francisco: Jossey-Bass

Nadler, L & Nadler, Z. 1989. *Developing Human Resources*. 3 ed. San Francisco: Jossey-Bass

Pfeiffer, JW. 1994. *Pfeiffer and Company on Experiental Learning Activities. Training Technologies*, vol 21. San Diego: Pfeiffer Company

Piskyrich, GM. 1993. *ASTD Handbook of Instructional Technology*. New York: McGraw-Hill

Reid, MA, Barrington, H & Kenney, J. 1992. *Training Interventions: Managing Employee Development*. 3 ed. London: IPM

Ronen, S. 1989. Training the international assignee. In: *Training and Development in Organizations*, Ed IL Goldstein. San Francisco: Jossey-Bass

Ryan, C. 1993. By comparison, SA lags behind on most counts. *Sunday Times*. Johannesburg. 18 July 1993.

Sanderson, G. 1992. Objectives and evaluation. In: *Handbook of Training and Development*, Ed S Truclove. Massachusetts: Fielden House

SPA Consultants. *Literacy Training in South Africa: A Critical Ingredient for World-Class Performance*. Johannesburg

Wills, B. 1993. *Distance Education: A Practical Guide*. New Jersey: Educational Technology

part five

Compensating and caring for employees

◎ STUDY OBJECTIVES

After studying this chapter, you should be able to:

- define compensation and distinguish between different types of organisational rewards;
- explain the objectives of compensation systems;
- distinguish between the external and internal factors influencing the design of compensation systems;
- discuss the various quantitative and nonquantitative methods of job evaluation;
- demonstrate your understanding of the fundamental mechanics of the major job evaluation systems in use in South Africa;
- explain how to design a basic pay structure;
- discuss some process issues affecting the implementation of compensation systems.

17.1 INTRODUCTION

We explained in chapter 1 that the most basic dimension of any employment relationship is the economic dimension. This dimension revolves around the exchange transaction between employees and the organisation which employs them. An important part of human resource management is therefore concerned with this economic dimension, relating specifically to the remuneration of employees as part of the exchange transaction.

Compensation has thus always stood at the heart of any employment relationship. As explained, in its simplest form this relationship is usually based on an economically motivated process where certain *inputs* (physical and mental work behaviour) are *exchanged* for some *outputs* (rewards) that are considered to be desirable in satisfying individual needs or goals. The utilisation of rewards can therefore be a very important and powerful tool for shaping and determining work behaviour aimed at attaining the strategic objectives of an organisation.

Rewards such as pay and benefits which people gain from an employment relationship are highly important to individuals since they can meet many needs. Satisfaction of needs can range from the most basic human needs for food and shelter to those signs of achievement, status and power (for example luxury cars, overseas vacations, etc) that may be bought if sufficiently high levels of compensation are received. Self-esteem needs may also be addressed, because levels of pay usually indicate an individual's worth to the organisation.

From the organisation's perspective compensation is of equally critical importance, since employee compensation is often the single largest cost item to an organisation. The total cost of the overall remuneration and reward system can have a decisive bearing on an organisation's competitive position; effective management of the cost, nature and distribution of rewards therefore demands careful attention.

A multitude of possible rewards can be included in an overall reward system and various categories exist according to which these rewards may be classified.

Common categories include extrinsic versus intrinsic rewards, financial versus nonfinancial rewards and performance-related versus membership-related rewards. Naturally, rewards may be classified in other ways and certain rewards can fit equally well in more than one category.

17.1.1 Compensation defined

The extrinsic-intrinsic typology used in figure 17.1 is especially useful for defining the domain of compensation management.

Intrinsic rewards are self-administered rewards that are associated with the job itself, such as the opportunity to perform meaningful work, experience variety and receive feedback on work results.

Although certain human resource management related decisions may focus on intrinsic rewards (for example flexible working schedules, job enrichment and job rotation), the fact that these rewards have to be given by employees to themselves leaves little scope for direct control by management. As Bernardin and Russell (1993: 420) rightly point out: if you feel little or no satisfaction from completing a challenging assignment, there is not much that the organisation can do about it.

Extrinsic rewards, on the other hand, include all those rewards an employee gets from sources other than the job itself. An organisation has a large degree of control over the nature and monetary cost of the extrinsic rewards with which it intends to compensate the efforts of its employees and can therefore manipulate the use of these external rewards to affect employee behaviour.

In the light of the above, compensation may therefore be defined as the financial and nonfinancial extrinsic rewards provided by an employer for the time, skills and effort made available by the employee in fulfilling job requirements aimed at achieving organisational objectives.

Concepts that are sometimes used as more or less equivalent to compensation management are *reward management*, *remuneration management*, *salary and wage administration* or *pay administration*.

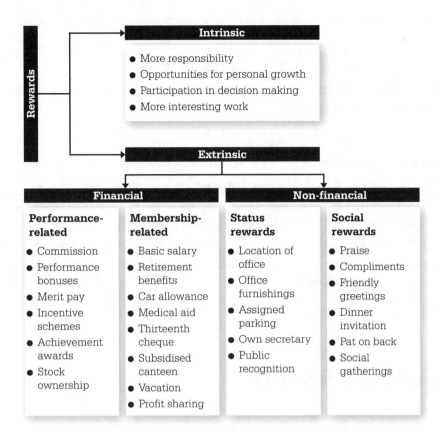

Figure 17.1

Types and structure of rewards

Source: Adapted and expanded from De Cenzo, DA & Robbins, SP. 1994. *Personnel/Human Resource Management*, 414 Englewood Cliffs, NJ: Prentice-Hall.

17.1.2 Compensation management: An overview

Compensation management has become a complex and specialised HR function and it must be emphasised from the outset that there is no one "best" reward system that will work for every organisation.

Organisations must tailor their systems to meet their own specific needs, strategies and objectives. Compensation is furthermore a dynamic function and, as an organisation grows or responds to environmental change with new strategies, certain components of the reward system may have to be modified to continue serving the needs of the organisation. (Butler, Ferris & Napier 1991: 111–113)

In choosing between the large variety of available design options, the compensation manager has continuously to keep in mind the overall reward strategy, in order to assure that design features are congruent and fit well with other human resource practices and with the organisation's business strategy (Lawler 1987: 270; McNally 1996: 312).

The following three issues have to be addressed in this design planning process.

- What should be the overall objectives of the system?
- What external and internal influences exist and what impact may they have on specific design decisions?
- What policies should govern the system?

The consideration of these issues constitutes the first part of the chapter.

The second set of design issues focuses on the essential elements or "nuts and bolts" of a compensation system. Aspects such as job evaluation, pay surveys and pay structure are examined in the second part of the chapter.

As Steers and Porter (1991: 487) note, even the best-designed reward systems can go awry in producing their intended results because of the manner in which they are implemented. In view of this, the final part of the chapter reviews some important implementation or process issues such as communication policies and decision-making practices.

17.2 COMPENSATION OBJECTIVES

Compensation objectives are those guidelines that determine the nature of a reward system. They also serve as standards against which the effectiveness of the system is evaluated (Cascio 1991: 42).

The classical objectives of any compensation system are to *attract*, *retain* and *motivate* employees. In addition, many more objectives may be formulated to ensure that the compensation system contributes to the organisation's overall objectives. The following are some common objectives of an effective reward system (Biesheuvel 1985).

Attracting the right quality of applicants

Generally organisations that give the greatest rewards tend to attract the most applicants and can therefore recruit the best qualified staff. In order to maintain a competitive pay-level strategy, an organisation needs some knowledge of the going rate in the labour market. Salary surveys are typically utilised for this purpose.

Retaining suitable employees

To encourage valuable staff members to remain, the compensation system must provide sufficient rewards for these employees to feel satisfied when they compare their rewards with those received by individuals performing similar jobs in other organisations.

Maintaining equity among employees

In compensation management the concept of equity relates to perceptions of fairness in the distribution of rewards. It is generally considered to be the most important objective of any compensation programme.

Different types of equity can be distinguished: *external*, *internal* and *individual*.

- *External equity* concerns comparisons of rewards across similar jobs in the labour market. Pay surveys are usually used for information regarding external equity.

- *Internal equity* deals with comparisons of rewards across different jobs within the same organisation. It addresses the issue of the relative worth of, for example, an engineer versus an accountant working for the same employer. The techniques of job evaluation and pay structuring are to establish internal equity.

- *Individual (or procedural) equity* is concerned with the extent to which an employee's compensation is reflective of his or her contribution and the fairness with which pay changes such as raises are made. Changes may be based, for example, on individual performance, on skills, or according to fixed increments or seniority (Cherrington 1995: 412; Leap & Crino 1993: 376).

Rewarding good performance and providing incentives for desired behaviour

An organisation can structure its reward system to encourage employee behaviour directed towards improving corporate performance and achieving specific aims. (See the case study that follows.)

A case at hand . . .

Pep links bonuses to stock losses*

Having to contend with stock losses that run into several million rand annually, Pep Stores negotiated a bonus scheme with its employees whereby each worker's Christmas bonus is linked to the level of the national stock losses of the company. A bonus of 65 % of the monthly basic salary is paid irrespective of stock losses, but the remaining 35 % is linked to the level of stock losses by means of a specific formula. In addition a quarterly bonus scheme linked to sales targets and stock losses at individual shops has been implemented.

*Source: *Finansies en Tegniek*, 11 June 1993

Maintaining cost-effectiveness

The compensation system often constitutes the single largest operating cost of an organisation and should therefore be designed and assessed from a cost-benefit perspective. A systematic pay structure is therefore needed to prevent undue expense and possible over- or underpayment of employees.

A case at hand . . .

Important factors for motivating reward systems

Research involving 150 South African companies identified 10 factors that appear to be essential in designing an effective, motivating reward system in the current South African context (Horwitz & Frost 1992: 27–33):

- consistency through external and internal equity;
- fostering entrepreneurship;
- linkage to performance assessment;
- linkage to organisational strategy and goals;
- measuring performance in terms of realistic goals;
- establishing fairness of reward for effort;
- flexibility in meeting individual motivational needs;
- timing of rewards as close as possible to goal achievement;
- appropriateness to the nature of work done;
- appropriateness in terms of the stage of organisational development.

Complying with legal requirements

Compensation design faces certain legal constraints and needs to comply with legislative regulations, collectively bargained agreements, etc.

Providing for flexibility and administrative efficiency

Design should be flexible enough to prevent bureaucratic rigidity and allow for dealing with alterations in relative market rates and individual differences in terms of merit. In addition, it should be simple enough to explain, understand and operate.

17.3 COMPENSATION POLICIES

Compensation policies are formalised guidelines for compensation-related decision making by management.

Armstrong and Murlis (1988: 24) identify eight main areas in which policies need to be formulated.

- **Levels of reward:** This concerns external competitiveness and therefore the rate of pay within the organisation. The policy question will be: Should the level of pay be above, below or at the prevailing market rate?
- **Equity**: To what degree is the organisation going to strive for internal equity and by what means are internal relativities between jobs to be established?
- **Performance-related rewards:** How should achievement be rewarded and what role should incentive and bonus schemes play?
- **Market rate policy:** To what extent should market rate pressures (for example scarce, highly regarded skills) be allowed to affect or possibly distort the salary structure?

- **Salary structure**: Is a formal structure required and, if it is, what type of structure is necessary to ensure consistent and equitable, yet flexible administration of salaries? (See section 17.9 on page 528 for a definition and discussion of this aspect.)
- **Control**: What is the amount of freedom given to individual managers to influence the salaries of their staff?
- **Total package**: What is the best reward mix of basic pay, benefits and incentives for the different categories of employees?
- **Communication**: How much information about the compensation system should be made freely available to employees?

A further important design decision concerns the *relative emphasis* that is to be placed *on the different policy areas* (Milkovich & Boudreau 1991: 459). For example, the aims of pursuing internal equity may be compromised if external competitiveness takes precedence in certain cases where job offers exceed the pay ranges stipulated by the organisation's internal pay structure. This could lead to a problem of *compression*, that is, the reduction of pay differentials between jobs or levels of jobs due to, for instance, the pay rate for jobs filled from outside the organisation increasing faster than the pay rate for job incumbents within the organisation.

(There may be other causes for pay rate compression, but the problem typically occurs when employees in a particular job grade perceive that there is not a sufficient difference between their level of compensation and that of the employees in the next lower job grade.)

17.4 INFLUENCES ON COMPENSATION POLICIES

There are various interacting factors that have an impact on the design of the compensation system. Some of these are external forces, while others are a function of the internal conditions of the organisation.

Figure 17.2
Major influences on compensation systems

17.4.1 External factors

Government legislation

South African legislation impacting directly on compensation policies includes:

- The Labour Relations Act 66 of 1995;
- The Wage Act 5 of 1957;
- The Basic Conditions of Employment Act 3 of 1983 (this Act and the Wage Act are to be consolidated and superseded by a new Basic conditions of Employment Act — see chapter 4);
- The Income Tax Act 58 of 1962, as amended.

  Provisions in the Income Tax Act which pertain to fringe benefit taxation impact primarily on reward mix design (that is, composition of total package).

Economy

Broad economic conditions such as high levels of inflation, recessionary periods, differences in the cost of living in different parts of the country, general level of employment and competitiveness in the local or international product market can greatly affect the general level of compensation.

Labour market

Compensation levels often may vary according to the forces of supply and demand in terms of general labour or specific skills.

Unions

Organised labour can have a significant impact on the determination of wage levels and benefits by means of collective bargaining and other mechanisms.

17.4.2 Internal factors

Ability to pay

An organisation's ability to pay has a big impact on its general level of compensation. The level of productivity, its profitability, its size and its competitors are all determinants of its ability to generate revenues for paying its human resources (Sherman & Bohlander 1992: 314).

Employee needs

Employees differ in terms of what they prefer to receive as compensation. Younger employees may have a higher cash need than older employees, highly compensated executives' needs differ from those of general workers, etc. There may thus be a need to build choices into the system.

Job requirements

Requirements regarding the average skill level of employees may impact on the pay level that the organisation can set and still be able to obtain sufficient numbers of qualified employees.

Strategy, culture and values

As previously emphasised, pay policies should be supportive of the organisation's strategic objectives. In addition, organisational values such as decision-making style, openness regarding communication and social responsibility may have a bearing on compensation policies (Milkovich & Boudreau 1991: 447). (For example, organisations valuing a competitive, achievement-driven climate will probably opt for performance-related rather than fixed increment pay increases; companies that are sensitive to the needs of female employees may adopt policies of fully paid extended maternity leave, etc.)

17.5 ESSENTIAL ELEMENTS OF A COMPENSATION SYSTEM

Having planned and established the overall objectives, desired design features and guiding policies of the compensation system, the compensation manager can now set out to put the plans into practice and construct the system. To achieve this aim, four basic tools or technical elements of the compensation system design should be utilised:

- Job analysis
- Job evaluation
- Pay surveys
- Pay structuring

Due to the complexity of some of these elements, each will be discussed in a separate section (that is, in sections 17.6 to 17.8 below).

17.6 JOB ANALYSIS

As with so many other human resource management functions, the process of job analysis and the resulting job descriptions constitute the basic building blocks for compensation system design. Job analysis was discussed fully in chapter 8. In the context of compensation system design, its purpose is twofold (Cascio 1991: 429):

- to identify the important characteristics of each job so that job evaluation can be carried out, and
- to identify, define and weigh the compensable factors, that is, all those shared characteristics of jobs that provide a basis for judging job value. These factors are typically linked to the specific job evaluation plan, for example, decision making (Paterson) or know-how, problem solving and accountability (Hay) (see section 17.7.2 on page 521).

17.7 JOB EVALUATION

Job evaluation may be defined as a systematic process of determining the value of each job in relation to other jobs in the organisation.

The purpose of this process is to rank jobs within a hierarchy that reflects the relative importance or worth of each job within the organisation.

Job evaluation is concerned with the relative worth of jobs as such and not with the worth of the job incumbents. The latter issue is addressed by performance appraisal, which has already been discussed in chapter 13.

Job evaluation is essentially a process of comparisons (comparisons with other jobs, comparisons against defined standards, or comparisons of the extent to which common factors are present in different jobs) and it is these different comparisons which form the foundation of the different job evaluation methods (Armstrong & Murlis 1988: 74).

17.7.1 Job evaluation methods

17.7.1.1 Job ranking

The job ranking method is the simplest but least used job evaluation method. It involves judging each job as a whole and determining its place in the job hierarchy by comparing it with all other jobs and arranging them in order of importance. Whilst its simplicity and inexpensiveness may be attractive characteristics, the method has major drawbacks that make it an unsuitable option for all but the smallest of organisations. Disadvantages are:

● cumbersomeness and unreliability with increasing numbers of jobs;
● a lack of specific criteria for the ranking process; and
● an inability to indicate the extent of differences between job levels.

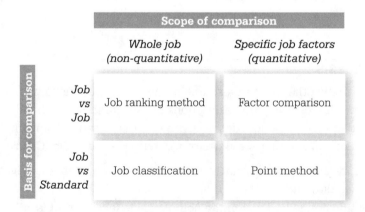

Figure 17.3

Basic job evaluation methods

Source: Adapted from Sherman, AW & Bohlander, GW, 1992. *Managing Human Resources*, 315. Cincinnati: South-Western

17.7.1.2 Job classification

The job classification method entails the placing of groups of jobs into a number of job grades or classes. The job grades and grade descriptions are established first and then individual jobs are fitted into the grade with the most appropriate description. Grade definitions are based on discernable differences regarding certain criteria such as level of decision making (for example Paterson method) or a number of factors such as decision making, controls and contact with people (for example "Q" method) (Biesheuvel 1985: 45–49).

Jobs are allotted to grades by comparing the whole job description with the grade definition. (The Paterson and Q-methods differ from this general rule in that jobs are analysed in terms of component parts and these parts are individually allotted to the appropriate grade. The highest graded tasks will determine the overall grading of the job.) (See section 17.7.2 on page 521.)

Job classification methods have the advantage of being quite simple to understand and operate, and relatively expedient and inexpensive to implement. However, major criticisms have been expressed regarding the oversimplification of using single job factors to establish compensation differentials (Biesheuvel 1985: 64), higher levels of subjectivity than for the points method, and the inability to cope with complex jobs which will not fit neatly into one grade.

17.7.1.3 Factor comparison

The factor comparison method is a complex ranking method where jobs are ranked against a number of compensable factors. Four basic steps are used in developing and using a factor comparison scale.

- **Step1:** selecting and ranking a number of **key jobs/benchmark jobs** (important jobs that are widely known and have a relatively stable job content)
- **Step2:** allocating monetary values to the compensable factors for each key job
- **Step3:** setting up the factor comparison scale where the results from step 2 are displayed
- **Step4:** evaluating non-key jobs against the key jobs

This method is very cumbersome, difficult to explain to employees and lacks flexibility. As with any other jobs, key jobs change over time and each time that this occurs the whole exercise will have to be repeated.

17.7.1.4 Point method

The point method is the most frequently used system in job evaluation plans. Although many variations exist, point systems essentially comprise a mathematical (quantitative) method whereby point values are assigned to the degree to which certain identified compensable factors are required for a particular job. The following are the typical steps followed by point systems. (The boxed portions provide a step-by-step practical illustration of the point method.)

Step 1: Selecting compensable job factors

A number of factors which are considered to be common to all jobs in the organisation are selected and clearly defined.

> **Example:** skills required, responsibility, degree of effort, working conditions

Step 2: Dividing factors into degrees

The chosen factors are divided into different degrees that describe the extent to which the factor exists in a given job.

Each degree has to be defined clearly, for example.

> **Example:** working conditions
> - Degree 1: job performed in air-conditioned private office from 09:00 to 16:30; no overtime or weekend work requirements
> - Degree 4: shift-work with unstable, long working hours; stressful, noisy conditions; weekend work required

Step 3: Allocating weights (points) to factors and degrees

The total number of points that can be allocated (for example 1 000) and the percentage of this total that will be assigned to each factor has to be decided upon. The more important the factor, the higher its point total will be. Points are assigned to each degree within the factors to provide a system of weighting each factor within the point system.

Example

Factor	1st	2nd	3rd	4th	Factor weights %
Skill	90	175	260	350	35 %
Responsibility	60	125	180	250	25 %
Effort	75	150	225	300	30 %
Working conditions	25	50	75	100	10 %
				1000	100 %

In our example the assumption was made that skill requirements are the most important and working conditions the least important compensable factors. A relative weight allocation of 35 %, 25 %, 30 % and 10 % between the respective factors was decided upon. The points allocation to each degree represents a proportionally equal progression up to the maximum points total for each factor. Note therefore that the maximum points for each factor add up to the maximum points total for the system, that is, 1000.

Step 4: Rating jobs on each factor and totalling points

Jobs are evaluated by an evaluation committee which determines for each factor the degree that best defines the level required for the job. Once each factor has been rated, points are added to give the total points value of the job.

> For example, a general labourer's job evaluated in terms of our example at the 1st degree of skill and responsibility, 2nd degree of effort and 3rd degree of working conditions, will be worth a total of 90 + 60 + 150 + 75 = 375 points.

The conversion of points to pay is a separate exercise that is independent of the evaluation process.

Whilst the point method has the major disadvantage of being complex and time consuming to develop and maintain, it does provide a higher level of objectivity and face validity than especially the nonquantitative methods. Another advantage is its ability to assess relative differences between jobs. Organisations often avoid the difficulties involved in the development of a tailor-made point-based system by sub-scribing to ready-made plans such as the Peromnes, Task and Castellion systems.

17.7.2 Major job evaluation systems in use in South Africa

A large variety of job evaluation systems, based on some of the methods discussed in section 17.7.1 on page 518 are currently in use in South Africa. Many companies and industries utilise in-house systems that have been developed as tailor-made systems taking into account the specific situation and requirements of these organisations. On the other hand, extensive use is also made of standardised, ready-made systems that have been developed locally or abroad. The most domi-nant systems in this category are the Paterson Decision Band Method, the Peromnes system and the Hay guide-chart profile system. Despite lacking perhaps the tailor-made nature of in-house systems, these systems have the important advantage that they are all supported by major consultancies and provide their users with access to the data of regular and comprehensive salary surveys. The underlying principles of the dominant systems are outlined below.

17.7.2.1 Paterson Decision Band Method

The Paterson Decision Band Method (which is often called the Paterson plan), is a job evaluation system that is essentially based on the job classification method. It was developed by Professor TT Paterson in Scotland primarily as an alternative to time consuming point systems which were at that time using a large number of factors. His research led him to the conclusion that a single factor, "decision making", was present in all jobs and could be used on its own to measure job level.

Six bands of decision making are defined in terms of the level of complexity of decisions required from job incumbents. The levels range from the completely defined decisions at Band A to policy-making decisions at Band F. Each of the bands (except Band A) is divided into an upper and a lower grade, with the upper grade coordinating or supervising the work performed at the lower grade.

There are thus eleven grades which can be further divided into subgrades according to the specific needs of the company. Typically twenty-eight subgrades are utilised, with upper grades and lower grades having two and three subgrades respectively. Table 17.1 on page 522 provides an outline of the Paterson plan.

Table 17.1

*Paterson's decision and grading structure**

Band	Type of decision	Skill level	Title	Grade and typical subgrade		Characteristics of decision
F	Policy-making	Top management	President Managing director	Upper F (Coord)	F5 F4	Creating the policy affecting the whole enterprise in terms of parameters which are limited only by legislation, by labour practices and by economic considerations.
			Vice President Executive director	Lower F	F3 F1	
E	Pro-gramming	Senior management	General manager	Upper E (Coord)	E5 E4	Programming the policy laid by the board. Concerned with long-term plan-ning in major functions such as production, sales, finance, human resources.
			Works manager	Lower E	E3 E1	
D	Interpre-tive	Middle management	Dept manager	Upper D (Coord)	D5 D4	Making the rules and establishing the precedents that enable employees in Bands C, B & A to produce. Interpreting the programmes laid down by senior management by applying material and human resources to achieve the objec-tives outlined in the programme and specific to a minor organisational function.
			Superin-tendent Section manager	Lower D	D3 D1	
C	Routine	Skilled	General foreman	Upper C (Coord)	C5 C4	Decisions are based upon a knowledge of theory and systems. Choosing the appropriate routine from a limited array of routines or rules. Working within rules or standards laid down (eg mechanic).
			Artisan	Lower C	C3 C1	
B	Auto-matic	Semi-skilled	Charge-hand	Upper B (Co-ord)	B5 B4	To become competent in the job, workers need to be trained and be given practice or experience in the work. They have to be trained to make decisions of a more general routine nature from which they can make a specific judgment to meet new situations not yet encoun-tered (eg driver).
			Appren-tice Machine operator	Lower B	B3 B1	
A	Defined	Unskilled	Labourer	Lower A	A3 A1	Workers can be taught the complete job in a short time. The job is quite specific and defined. No decisions additional to those taught to the worker are required to perform the job (eg cleaner).

*Source: Adapted and expanded from IPM Fact Sheet 172, *IPM Journal*, July 1988

When the Paterson plan is applied, jobs are first classified under the specific band (A to F) with the definition that agrees most closely with the job requirements. Jobs are then sorted into the lower and upper grades in terms of the coordinating principle — that is, where a job includes coordination of other jobs in the same band, it is placed in the upper grade.

Subgrading is generally done according to the principle that in any one grade those jobs which require more decisions of that grade are deemed to be more important and difficult and are therefore placed in a higher subgrade (Anglo American Corporation 1984).

The Paterson system is used in various European countries, Canada, Australia, India and Southern Africa. In South Africa it covers more employees than any other system due to its almost exclusive use in the mining, forestry, sugar, pharmaceutical and paint industries. (Cogill 1988: 32–34).

The Paterson method is simple and easy to understand and implement, internationally recognised and cost-effective. Its major disadvantages are, however, its reliance on a single factor to measure all jobs, lack of uniformity regarding subgrading procedures and difficulties in grading complex management hierarchies (for example in a conglomerate where the corporate structure is made up of a large number of separate companies).

A Paterson plan derivative, the TASK system, that uses a point system with a number of factors for subgrading (skill level, knowledge, complexity, influence, pressure), was developed by FSA-Contact consultancy in the early 1980s to address the problem of subgrading. Some 180 companies are currently using the TASK system. (FSA-Contact 1995)

17.7.2.2 Peromnes system

The Peromnes system has its roots in the Castellion Job Evaluation Method that was developed for South African Breweries by Professor Simon Biesheuvel (the latter system derives its name from the SAB's Castle and Lion products). The Peromnes system is essentially a simplification of the Castellion method which uses eleven factors and subfactors. Since the late 1960s when the Peromnes system was developed, it has been adopted by over 400 organisations and it is currently solely marketed and supported by FSA-Contact Pty (Ltd) who are the copyright holders.

The Peromnes system (the Latin words *per omnes* mean "for all") is based on the point method and evaluates jobs on the basis of eight factors, of which the first six are job *content* factors and the remaining two job *requirement* factors. The eight factors are listed in exhibit A.

During the evaluation process, each factor is evaluated according to comprehensive definitions on a progressive scale of complexity. The evaluation committee examines these definitions to arrive at the one which most satisfactorily describes the highest level of activity or the highest requirements of the job on the given factor. Each definition has certain point values which are added up for each factor to provide a total point value for the job. By means of a conversion table, the job is then graded into one of 21 grades, varying from 1 (the highest possible) to 19 (the lowest possible). The grades correspond approximately to the job levels listed in table 17.2.

Exhibit A

The eight factors on which the Peromnes system is based*

1. **Problem solving**: The nature and complexity of decision processes (including those required in formulating recommendations).
2. **Consequences of judgement (limits of discretion)**: The consequences of firm decisions on the organisation or any of its parts, taking account of controls and checks that may exist to prevent the implementation of judgements, especially those which are adverse.
3. **Pressure of work (division of attention)**: The pressure inherent in a job, as reflected in the variety and type of work to be achieved in the available time, the need to set effective priorities and the interruptions and distractions due to interaction with other jobs.
4. **Knowledge**: The level of knowledge required, in operational (NOT formal) qualification terms, to perform the job competently.
5. **Job impact**: The extent of influence that the job has on other activities, both within and outside the organization.
6. **Comprehension**: The level of understanding of written and spoken communications expected continuously in the regular course of the job.
7. **Educational qualifications required in the post**: The minimum essential requirements are considered, NOT the merely desirable ones.
8. **Subsequent training/experience required**: The period necessary to achieve competence in the job by the shortest possible reasonable route.

*Reproduced by the kind permission of FSA-Contact, Pty (Ltd)

Table 17.2

Peromnes grades and approximate job levels

Example of job level	Job grades
● Top management and most senior specialists and professionals	1++–3
● Senior management and specialists	4–6
● Middle management, superintendents and lower-level specialists	7–9
● Junior management, supervisors and higher-level skilled and clerical positions	10–12
● Skilled and semiskilled workers and clerical personnel	13–16
● Low-skilled and unskilled workers	17–19

The popularity of the Peromnes system may largely be attributed to advantages such as:

● its application value regarding all types and levels of posts in any type of organisation;

● its relative simplicity of terminology and application (not requiring any complex calculations or the use of any formal job description); and

● the direct comparability of the job grades between different organisations.

The system's nondependency on formal written job analyses may, however, compromise the quality of the description of job content to be evaluated. The system has also been criticised because of its choice of factors and its assignment of the same weight to all the factors (Biesheuvel, 1985: 55); because the same elements may be evaluated more than once under different headings; and because, in assigning the same points range (35) for all factors, it does not allow for differences in their relative importance as determinants of job performance.

17.7.2.3 Hay Guide-chart method

The Guide-chart method was developed by the Hay Group in the early 1950s and introduced into the South African market during 1978. The system is used extensively overseas (more than 4 000 users in 30 countries) (Armstrong & Murlis 1988: 459) and is marketed and supported in South Africa by Hay Management Consultants. Whilst the roots of the system are in the factor comparison methods, the current form of the Hay system also has strong elements of the point method.

The Hay system measures three common factors along eight dimensions (see exhibit B).

Exhibit B

The Hay system

1. Know-how
   This is the sum total of all expertise needed for acceptable job performance, eg knowledge, experience, training, education and intellectual ability. Know-how is measured against the dimensions of:
   - depth according to skill, education and training requirements;
   - breadth of management know-how; and
   - human relations skills.
2. Problem solving
   This entails the thinking challenge required by the job for problem solving (eg analysing, evaluating, reasoning and drawing conclusions). Mental processes involved in problem solving are considered to be based on existing knowledge of facts and principles and therefore problem solving is treated as a percentage utilisation of "know-how". Two dimensions are measured:
   - the environment in which the thinking takes place;
   - the challenge presented by the required thinking.
3. Accountability
   Accountability for action and the resultant consequences of action underlies this factor. Three dimensions are distinguished:
   - the freedom to act;
   - the impact on end results;
   - the magnitude of impact (usually in financial terms).

Each of the three factors is measured as a matrix and the evaluation of the involvement of these factors in a particular job is done according to a rather complex quantitative system, the details of which are subject to copyright.

Essentially point scores for each factor are derived from the guide-charts and a profile for the job is drawn up which indicates its level and nature. The total point score places the job in an organisation-specific evaluation hierarchy ranging between 0 to 4000 points. The point score for each job is used to obtain a monetary value for the job by means of the regular Hay market surveys from which the number of rands paid per Hay point may be ascertained. Guide-charts are adapted to specific client company circumstances and jobs are typically not divided into grades, thus making salary survey comparisons with other evaluation systems impracticable.

Whilst the conceptual merits of the system and the thoroughness and reliability of the evaluation process are well established, these very same advantages also make the system complex and time consuming to implement.

Table 17.3 provides an approximate correlation between some of the major job evaluation systems mentioned in the preceding section.

17.7.3 Job evaluation in a changing environment

Traditional job evaluation systems as described in the previous section have, over the past few years, been subject to a debate about their continued relevance in a changing business and employment environment. The essence of the criticism lies in the argument that the traditional methodology for evaluating the relative worth of the workforce has its roots in the Taylorist/Fordist production methods flowing from the scientific management movement (Retief 1995: 28–34). A movement from bureaucratic, hierarchical organisational structures to flatter, more flexible organisations employing a more technically oriented workforce will also necessitate more flexible job evaluation and compensation schemes.

In the South African context, for example, COSATU has formulated a policy stipulating job grading mechanisms that should provide for team-based production runs and skills-based career paths and succession opportunities.

Concepts such as broadbanding and knowledge- or skills-based remuneration are often utilised as attempts to increase skills flexibility, flatter organisational structures and greater workforce mobility in an increasingly competitive business environment.

Whilst the concept of broadbanding is explained in section 17.9 on page 528, knowledge- or skills-based pay needs to be briefly highlighted since the concept is becoming more common in compensation practice.

Whereas traditional job-evaluation based compensation uses the *job* as the basis for level of pay, in the case of the knowledge- or skills-based pay system the *person* provides the basis for pay. In the latter approach, jobs or job families are grouped according to the kinds of related skills or knowledge required to perform them. New employees are paid at the entry level pay rate and they receive pay increases as they acquire additional skills or knowledge. Employees receive added pay for the mastery of additional skills or knowledge, even when they are not using them currently.

Table 17.3

Approximate relationships among some major job evaluation systems*

Job Level	Paterson Band	Paterson Subgrade	TASK grades	Peromnes grades	Castellion grades
Unskilled	A	A1	1	19/18	1
Paterson (defined)		A2	2	17	2
TASK (basic)		A3	3	16	3
Semiskilled	B	B1	4	15	4
Paterson (automatic)		B2	5		
TASK (discretionary)		B3	6	14	5
		B4	7	13	6
		B5	8	12	7
Skilled	C	C1	9	11	
Paterson (routine)		C2	10		8
TASK (specialised)		C3	11	10	
		C4	12	9	9
		C5	13	8	
Lower/middle management	D	D1	14	7	10
Paterson (interpretive)		D2	15		
TASK (tactical)		D3	16	6	11
		D4	17		
		D5	18	5	12
Senior management	E	E1	19	4	
Paterson (programming)		E2	20		
TASK (tact./strategic)		E3	21	3	13
		E4	22		
		E5	23	2	
Top management	F	F1	24	2	
Paterson (policy-making)		F2	25		
TASK (strategic)		F3	26	1	14
		F4	27	1+	
		F5	28	1++	

*Source: Adapted from TASK Remuneration Survey, FSA-Contact Pty (Ltd) & Barling, J, Fullager, C & Bluen, S (eds). 1986. *Behaviour in Organizations*, 230. Jhb: McGraw-Hill

Despite the above trends, both local and international analysts appear to agree that present job evaluation systems will remain an essential element of compensation practices for some time to come. (Incomes Data Services 1994: 1–32; Lundy & Cowling 1996: 305).

17.8 PAY SURVEYS

Once jobs have been graded by means of job evaluation, the next step in the development of a compensation system is the determination of a pay rate for the grades. The compensation tool used to set the monetary worth of jobs or grades of jobs is the pay/remuneration survey. A pay survey provides information on how other employers compensate similar jobs and skills in an organisation's labour market. The *labour market* for a specific job category may be defined as that area where employees are drawn from or lost to (Auld 1991: 17–21). Having identified the appropriate labour markets in which he/she is competing for human resources, the survey user can determine the relative position of his/her own pay rates against those of competitors. Pay surveys therefore enable an organisation to maintain external equity.

An organisation can obtain pay survey data by conducting or commissioning its own pay survey that is designed according to its specific informational needs, or it can subscribe to any of various comprehensive external surveys that are conducted on a regular basis by large consultancies such as FSA-Contact, P-E Remuneration Services, International Compensation or Hay Management Consultants. Access to the data of these surveys is usually limited to subscribing companies who pay a fee and are obliged to submit input details for the surveys in order to receive the resulting survey reports.

17.9 PAY STRUCTURING

Pay structuring refers to the process whereby the information obtained from the job evaluation exercise (that is, the relative worth of jobs within the organisation) is combined with the information obtained from the pay surveys (that is, market values of jobs) to establish a pay structure.

A pay structure consists of an organisation's pay scales relating to single jobs, groups of jobs or grades. Among the various types of salary structures (see, for example, Armstrong & Murlis 1988: 117), the graded salary structures are probably the most common and will be used as an example to illustrate the process of pay structuring. The development of a pay structure is determined by considerations of the organisation's *pay slope*, the number of *pay grades*, the *range of each pay grade* and the *degree of overlap* between pay grades. The meanings of these terms are illustrated in figure 17.4 which represents a simple salary structure.

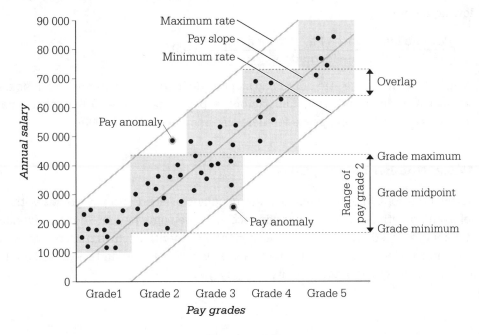

Figure 17.4

A basic pay structure

17.9.1 Pay slope

The pay slope refers to the angle or steepness of the pay curve. The pay curve (which is a curve due to pay being exponential) can be straightened by transforming the pay data (that is, the dispersion of job salaries in all the pay grades) into logarithmic form. The pay slope can be expressed quantitatively in ratio form as indicated in figure 17.5.

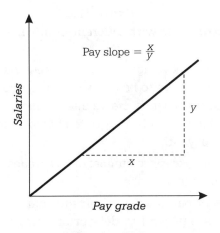

Figure 17.5

The pay slope percentage between two grades may be calculated by the following formula:

$$\frac{\text{Pay rate for grade 2} - \text{Pay rate for grade 1}}{\text{Pay rate for grade 1}} \times 100$$

Whilst the percentage size of the pay slope is dependent on variables such as the number of grades and economic factors, a pay slope of 15–20 % between pay grades is generally appropriate for most circumstances. (Auld 1990).

17.9.2 Number of pay grades

The various jobs in an organisation are usually classified into pay grades with all jobs falling within a given pay grade receiving the same pay rate (with individual differences based on factors such as seniority or merit). A pay structure based on the Paterson job evaluation plan will have eleven pay grades and one based on the Peromnes system will have twenty-one pay grades.

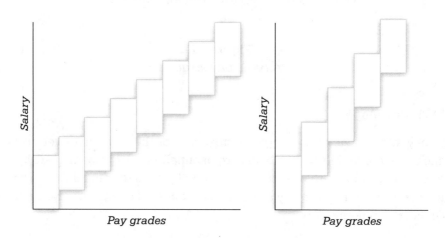

Figure 17.6

Pay structures with different numbers of grades

As can be seen from the above figure, the fewer pay grades a structure has, the steeper the pay slope will have to be and vice versa. Too few pay grades (with a resulting very steep pay slope), may create internal inequity and employee morale problems because jobs with significantly different job content and responsibilities may be paid the same pay rate.

On the other hand, an excessive number of pay grades will result in very similar pay differentials among different jobs.

Reduced numbers of pay grades may result from changes in organisational design, such as the recent trend to delayer organisational hierarchies to yield flatter structures (Hay Management Consultants 1993).

The latter problem (that is, too many grades) may arise, for example, from practices such as multiskilling and skill-based compensation systems where the assigning of subgrades for each group of skills would result in severe difficulties in differentiating between the many categories and maintaining internal equity (Bussin 1993: 26–27).

A method of compensation administration that has emerged as a tool for determining the optimum numbers of grades in changing organisational circumstances is the concept of *broadbanding*. Essentially this is a process aimed at decreasing the number of job grades by collapsing the number of original grades into broader bands, but without compromising accurate job measurements within these broad bands. The concept is illustrated in figure 17.7.

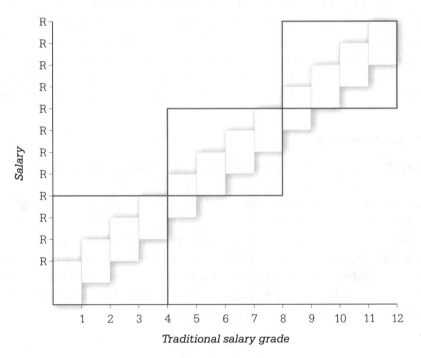

Figure 17.7
A broadbanded salary structure

The 3 "bands" (that is, the large boxes) in a broadbanded pay structure replace 4 or more traditional salary grades.

17.9.3 Pay ranges

The pay range refers to the difference between the minimum and maximum for each pay grade. It therefore reflects the width of a pay scale.

In determining the optimum width of a pay range, two factors need to be considered (Lewis 1980: 22):

- the relative emphasis to be placed on promotion and performance;
- and the nature of the jobs within a particular grade.

A narrow pay range is appropriate if the company wishes to encourage employees to seek promotion. In order to increase his/her basic pay, an employee is obliged to vie for promotion to the next grade.

A wide pay range, on the other hand, is appropriate if performance is to be encouraged within the context of the employee's current job. A wide range allows for the accommodation of greater variations in employee performance.

The width of a pay range is also determined by the nature of jobs, that is, the length of the learning phase before a job can be performed at an acceptable standard and the extent of variation in individual performance.

For instance, for routine, well-defined jobs that can be mastered in a short period of time and have little flexibility regarding how the job is done, a narrower pay range is justified. Similarly, for managerial jobs where the learning phase is longer due to the many tasks to be mastered and the wide variations that can exist between good and poor performance, a wider pay range would be appropriate.

17.9.4 Grade overlap

Grade overlap refers to the extent to which the minimum pay of the higher pay grade is overlapped by the maximum pay of the lower grade.

Such overlap acknowledges the fact that an inexperienced newcomer to the higher job grade may initially be of lesser value to the organisation than an experienced, well-performing employee in the next lower job grade.

Once the pay structure has been fully developed, only a small number of implementation considerations or process issues need to be addressed before we have our fully operationalised compensation system in place (apart from the benefits component, which is discussed in the next chapter).

17.10 PROCESS ISSUES IN COMPENSATION ADMINISTRATION

The processes by which compensation systems are implemented and administered in organisations is often considered to be just as important as the technical soundness of the design itself (Steers & Porter 1991: 482).

Lawler (1990: 221) contends that process issues are closely linked to the perceptions that employees have about a compensation plan. Irrespective of whether these perceptions are justified or not, they may have a powerful influence on the effectiveness of the pay system.

Some of the more important process issues that will be discussed briefly, are:

- performance appraisal and its link to reward administration;

- decision-making practices;
- communication policies.

17.10.1 Performance appraisal

If a compensation system is designed to distribute rewards in relation to differences in performance, it is absolutely essential that the organisation should have an effective system in place for assessing the relative quality and quantity of employee performance. If such an appraisal system is unreliable or is perceived to lack validity, it is unlikely that the rewards distributed on the basis of that system will have any positive effect on levels of performance and productivity.

The profound influence exerted by this issue is illustrated by the research of Spangenberg (1994) into South African performance management practices, which led the researcher to question the expediency of actually linking performance appraisal results to the reward system. Spangenberg states that it is not advisable to establish such a direct linkage, unless a strong supportive culture, good job designs, and adequate manager-employee relationships exist in the organisation (Spangenberg 1994: 233).

17.10.2 Decision-making practices

Traditionally compensation design and administration decisions have been made in a top-down manner with no input from line management or other employees. No doubt this approach is still valid for organisations where the management style suits the hierarchical decision-making process, but it would appear that higher levels of employee participation in compensation design and administration can result in significant benefits for organisations that have a culture of open communication and employee involvement (Lawler 1990: 221–242).

Such participation can include aspects such as codetermining compensable factors and choosing their own mix of benefits in a flexible compensation system.

Although employee involvement is an obvious way of ensuring that rewards take greater cognisance of specific employee needs, indications are that this approach is not practised widely in the South African context (Horwitz & Frost 1992: 32).

17.10.3 Communication policy

The question of how much information about the compensation system should be communicated to employees is not an easy matter to resolve. Whilst the practice of pay secrecy is probably more the rule than the exception, it is generally a matter of degree of how open pay policies are. The organisation may, for instance, provide full disclosure of how pay rates are set, but divulge no information on individual pay levels. Relevant stipulations in labour legislation regarding information disclosure are obviously very important in this regard.

A case at hand . . .

Pay secrecy for senior executives in SA*

Should the general public have a statutory right to know how much money is earned by senior executives in SA? The actual position in SA is, of course, quite simple. Executive pay excites a great deal of public debate — but precious little in the way of detailed figures. It is a much tighter secret than almost all of what passes for military or political intelligence. The bottom line is that SA business essentially believes, as it should be said does business almost anywhere else, that

1. executive pay involves personal privacy and
2. that it is "not in the best interests of the company" to make disclosure.

*Source: Other people's money. *Finance Week*, 1994, May 20–26, 19

Singer (1990: 318) points out that research on the issue has produced mixed findings and outlines the following factors that appear to be necessary for an open system to succeed:

- measures of performance must be objective;
- the pay-performance link must be apparent to employees;
- workers' attitudes towards pay secrecy must be established;
- there should be no blatant pay inconsistencies between employees with comparable jobs.

17.11 CONCLUSION

Sound compensation programmes are of critical importance to organisations because the way they are designed and administered can have a significant influence on employee behaviour and on their commitment to achieving organisational objectives. Of the many types of rewards available to an organization for compensating the productive efforts of its employees, pay remains to be the most important extrinsic reward. Therefore, the effective utilisation of monetary resources for rewarding and motivating workers constitutes a major part of the manager's role to "manage his/her people".

Compensation systems can be designed in many ways and the challenge for the organisation lies in the development of a system that is best suited to its own particular objectives with regard to factors such as cost-effectiveness, motivational ability, equitable distribution of rewards and administrative efficiency. This chapter identified the various external and internal influences that may impact on the design options and policies an organisation may wish to implement.

The compensation system mechanics of job analysis, job evaluation, pay surveys and pay structuring were explored in some detail with the aim of systematically leading up to a fully operational pay structure. Finally, performance appraisal linkages, communication policies and decision-making practices were briefly addressed as important considerations in the implementation and administration of pay systems.

Compensation management involves some complex topics, not all of which could be adequately explored within the scope of this chapter. Two important aspects that form an integral part of a comprehensive compensation system are benefits administration and incentive compensation practices; these topics are discussed in the next chapter.

SELF-EVALUATION QUESTIONS

1. "Compensation has always stood at the heart of any employment relationship." Discuss this statement critically.
2. By making use of a diagram, differentiate between different types of rewards.
3. Explain the objectives of compensation management
4. Write brief notes on compensation policies and aspects that influence them.
5. Describe the basic elements of a compensation system.
6. Write an essay on the topic of job evaluation. Pay particular attention to major job evaluation systems used in South Africa. What are some recent trends regarding job evaluation within the context of new approaches to work design?
7. Explain what 'pay structuring' entails.
8. Describe the role of the following process issues in compensation administration:

   O performance appraisal
   O decision-making processes
   O communication and information disclosure

BIBLIOGRAPHY

Anglo American Corporation. 1984. *Paterson Job Evaluation Handbook*. Johannesburg: Personnel Systems Department

Armstrong, M & Murlis, H. 1988. *Reward Management: A Handbook of Salary Administration*. London: Kogan Page

Auld, D. 1990. Remuneration. In *Managing Industrial Relations in South Africa*, eds JA Slabbert, JJ Prinsloo & W Backer, 10–36. Pretoria: Digma

Auld, D. 1991. Remuneration surveys. *IPM Journal*, October, 17–21

Barling, J, Fullagar, C & Bluen, S (eds). 1986. *Behaviour in Organisations*. Johannesburg: McGraw-Hill

Bernadin, HJ & Russell, JE. 1993. *Human Resource Management: An Experiential Approach*. New York: McGraw-Hill

Biesheuvel, S. 1985. *Work Motivation and Compensation*, vol 1 & 2. Johannesburg: McGraw-Hill

Bussin, M. 1993. Broadbanding, multiskilling, skill-based pay: Any correlation? *HRM*, July, 26–27

Butler, JE, Ferris, GR & Napier, NK. 1991. *Strategy and Human Resource Management*. Cincinnati: South-Western

Cascio, WF. 1991. *Applied Psychology in Personnel Management*, 4 ed. Englewood Cliffs, NJ: Prentice-Hall

Cherrington, DJ. 1995. *The Management of Human Resources*, 4 ed. Englewood Cliffs, NJ: Prentice-Hall

Cogill, C. 1988. The Paterson way: Does it pay? *HRM*, September, 32–34

FSA-Contact Pty Ltd. 1995. *TASK Remuneration Survey*. Johannesburg

Hay Management Consultants. 1993. *Organisational Broadbanding Report*, June

Horwitz, F & Frost, P. 1992. Flexible rewards: Critical success factors. *People Dynamics* June, 27–33

Incomes Data Services. 1994. Multiskilling: Study 558, 1–32

Lawler, EE. 1987. The design of effective reward systems. In *Handbook of Organisation Behaviour*, ed JW Lorsch. Englewood Cliffs, NJ: Prentice-Hall

Lawler, EE. 1990. *Strategic Pay: Aligning Organisational Strategy and Pay Systems*. San Francisco: Jossey-Bass

Leap, JL & Crino, MD. 1993. *Personnel: Human Resource Management*, 2 ed. New York: Macmillan

Lewis, WM. 1980. *The Design of Basic Pay Structures*. National Institute for Personnel Research, Special Report Pers 315

Lundy, O & Cowling, A. 1996. *Strategic Human Resource Management*. London: Routledge

McNally, KA. 1996. Compensation as a strategic tool. In *Human Resource Management: Perspectives, Context, Functions and Outcomes*, eds GR Ferris & RM Buckley. Englewood Cliffs, NJ: Prentice-Hall

Milkovich, GT & Boudreau, JW. 1991. *Human Resource Management*, 6 ed. Homewood, Ill: Irwin

Retief, A. 1995. Job evaluation: The heat is on. *Human Resource Management*, 10(10), 28–34

Sherman, W & Bohlander, GW. 1992. *Managing Human Resources*, 9 ed. Cincinnati: South-Western

Singer, MG. 1990. *Human Resource Management*. Boston: PWS-Kent

Spangenberg, H. 1994. *Understanding and Implementing Performance Management*. Kenwyn: Juta

Steers, RM & Porter, LW. 1991. *Motivation and Work Behaviour*, 5 ed. New York: McGraw-Hill

chapter 18 Providing Incentives and Benefits to Employees

STUDY OBJECTIVES

After studying this chapter, you should be able to:

- explain why it is often difficult to relate pay to performance;
- discuss the basic principles for establishing effective incentive systems;
- distinguish between various types of incentive schemes and discuss their relative merits;
- explain the importance of benefits in the overall compensation system;
- describe different benefit arrangement strategies and explain the principles guiding the choice of strategy;
- discuss the importance of the elements of choice, flexibility and administrative delivery for succ essful benefits programmes.

18.1 INTRODUCTION

In the previous chapter we explored the development of a fundamental compensation system and it was noted that, apart from a basic wage and salary structure, the typical overall compensation system also comprises an incentive and a benefits component.

Incentive compensation differs from other forms of compensation in that it constitutes an additional reward for outstanding efforts aimed at achieving organisational goals. It is usually monetarily based and its widespread use stems from the general belief that pay is able to motivate individuals or groups of employees to exceed minimum performance requirements and increase organisational effectiveness.

Benefits, on the other hand, are linked to employment rather than to performance and may be described as an indirect form of compensation that is mainly intended to improve the quality of work life for an organisation's employees (Sherman & Bohlander 1992: 380). A wide array of possible benefits may be incorporated in a total compensation package. Whilst the provision of some of these benefits (such as a retirement plan and accident and death insurance) are required by law, the possible range of employer-provided benefits is bound only by the limits of creativity of compensation specialists.

18.2 INCENTIVE COMPENSATION

The generally recognised problem of low productivity rates in South Africa continuously challenges managers and compensation specialists to devise compensation structures that will motivate employees towards increased levels of performance. Although the basic salary structure discussed in the previous chapter can motivate and reward superior work effort by increasing an individual's pay within the salary range or by promoting the individual into a higher pay grade, such rewards are usually only provided on an annual basis. Due to such delays, the recipients of such rewards often do not perceive them to be directly linked to performance.

Incentive compensation schemes are devised essentially as an attempt to link rewards to superior performance in a direct and prompt way. They usually function in addition to basic pay and are specifically targeted at the achievement of specified results, outputs or productivity targets (Biesheuvel 1985: 232; Burgess 1989: 278).

In this section we explore the nature, requirements, types and applications of incentive compensation schemes within the South African context.

18.2.1 Linking pay to performance

Over the past few years South African compensation specialists have consistently reported a trend towards relating rewards to performance (Stacey 1991; Gathercole 1992; Bussin 1992). This "paying for performance" trend has also been confirmed by recent national surveys of South African compensation practices (FSA-Contact 1993; 1995). From such surveys it would appear that many South African organisations are designing reward systems that reduce the guaranteed component of pay packages and increase the portion of pay at risk by means of the introduction of incentive systems.

Exhibit A

Reasons for implementing incentive schemes

In a 1995 survey FSA-Contact found that 62 % of the respondents employed incentive schemes. The most common reasons for implementing such schemes were:
- motivating staff (75 % of respondents);
- enhancing bottom-line results (45 % of respondents);
- encouraging staff to take greater accountability for their actions (44 % of respondents);
- increasing productivity (42 % of respondents);
- linking pay policies to strategic business goals (34 % of respondents)

*Source: FSA-Contact (Pty) Ltd, 1995

However, despite the widespread support for and the intuitive appeal of linking pay to performance, there is also extensive evidence of many performance-related pay systems more often than not failing to produce the expected positive effects (Horwitz & Frost 1992; Spangenberg 1993). Even strong proponents of performance-related compensation such as Edward Lawler, agree that the design of an effective pay for performance programme is a difficult undertaking that should be approached with circumspection (Lawler 1990: 70–131).

18.2.1.1 Problems with pay for performance

In chapter 10 the problematic nature of performance appraisal was discussed. This very same set of problems can generally be said to represent many of the underlying obstacles in effectively relating pay to performance. The often subjective nature of performance assessment and the difficulties in eradicating the resulting inconsistencies, create the risk of pay differences that cannot be justified.

The following common problems are often responsible for the failure of performance-related pay systems:

● the lack of objective, quantitative performance measures for many jobs and the resulting reliance on subjective performance ratings;

● poorly perceived link between performance and pay, usually due to systems ignoring the principle of immediate reinforcement by linking performance to the reward only at the end of the year;

● aspects of performance that are rewarded are not related to the overall strategic performance objectives, thus encouraging "wrong" kinds of behaviour (for example, a production bonus scheme that rewards according to levels of output, could encourage workers to take short cuts with quality assurance procedures);

● inadequate communications about the objectives, procedures and benefits of the scheme;

● the level of the performance-based portion of pay not being perceived as proportionate to the additional efforts required;

● union resistance to performance-based schemes and resistance to change in general.

18.2.2 Requirements for effective incentive compensation plans

Whilst the literature on compensation management is replete with lists of "success criteria" for incentive systems, it should be borne in mind that each organisation considering the implementation of pay-for-performance plans will be faced with a unique set of issues and problems for which it will have to find its own specific solutions.

However, although there is no single recipe for selecting the most appropriate design and implementation procedure for a successful incentive scheme, there are a number of generally accepted guiding principles that are relevant to all schemes (see, for example, Armstrong 1993: 79–82; Armstrong & Murlis 1988: 206–209;

Sherman & Bohlander 1992: 347–349; Lidstone 1992: 164–174; Brehm 1988: 10–13; Bussin 1994: 19–26; Spangenberg 1994: 233–241; Lundy & Cowling 1996: 313–314).

18.2.2.1 *Establish a pay-for-performance work culture*

The effectiveness of compensation systems is linked to the extent to which such systems are appropriately matched to their organisational context. In order for an incentive scheme to achieve its desired results, the organisational culture must therefore be generally conducive to the principles of individual merit and performance. Given that so many South African attempts at comprehensive performance management are thwarted by a lack of a work culture of productivity and quality, this requirement probably poses the biggest challenge to South African managers and compensation specialists (Spangenberg 1993: 30–34).

Two considerations are of importance in creating an appropriate performance-oriented work culture, namely the measurement of performance, and establishing determinants of performance (Bernadin & Russell 1993: 480–481; Ivancevich 1992: 35).

- The first consideration entails the development of performance evaluation systems that are regarded as meaningful and equitable by both management and employees (see chapter 11 for guidelines). Spangenberg (1994: 233) cautions that the link between a newly designed performance appraisal system and the pay system should not be established until such time as employees and managers have developed the trust needed to conduct participative performance discussions.

- Secondly, it is important to establish an environment or climate that is conducive to the following worker-related determinants of performance:

  O employees' views regarding the value of money relative to other rewards;

  O employees must be able to control the rate of performance;

  O employees must be capable of increasing their performance;

  O employees must believe that increased performance will be rewarded;

  O employees must perceive the size of the reward as sufficient to warrant increased effort.

18.2.2.2 *Ensure employee acceptance*

Employees and their representatives such as trade unions must accept the incentive scheme and it should be welcomed by all those employees covered by it. Employee acceptance may be fostered by means of effectively communicating the benefits of the scheme, establishing a highly visible and clear connection between employees' incentive payments and their performance, and by encouraging employees to participate in administering the scheme.

18.2.2.3 *Set high but attainable standards of performance*

Performance targets should be attainable, but not too easily. They should become progressively more difficult to achieve as the levels of potential reward increase. Incentive payments should never be permitted to be seen as virtually guaranteed.

18.2.2.4 *Establish clearly defined and accepted performance standards*

Performance standards or output targets should be based on objective, preferably quantified, measures and should be agreed upon with each individual or group.

18.2.2.5 *Ensure a simple and understandable design*

The incentive scheme should be sufficiently simple to enable all employees to understand its operation so that they can easily calculate what their rewards will be.

18.2.2.6 *Provide for flexibility and review*

Schemes should be sufficiently flexible to allow for adjustments that may be called for by changes in the business environment. The effectiveness of the scheme should be monitored on an ongoing basis. Typical areas that need regular review are:

- whether the performance factors that determine the level of payments still reflect the organisation's operational realities and are still relevant to the strategic business objectives;
- whether the scheme is losing motivational value due to employees taking the incentive payments for granted;
- whether the scheme needs recommunicating and repackaging to revitalise interest and improve performance.

18.2.2.7 *Ensure effective administration*

The ongoing success of an incentive scheme is often determined by the efficiency of the administrative support structures and procedures associated with the scheme. Some vital administrative issues are:

- effective ongoing communication and procedures for addressing questions and complaints;
- consistent and fair application of the rules within each group and across groups;
- sufficient budget provision and full and timeous payment in accordance with the rules;
- congruence with the overall compensation system, for example incentive schemes should not be used to make up for deficiencies in the basic salary structure.

18.2.3 Types of incentive schemes

Incentive schemes are usually categorised according to whether the system is applied on an individual, group or organisation-wide level. Further distinctions are sometimes made according to the category of employees involved, for example sales personnel, nonmanagerial workers and executives.

Exhibit B

Types of incentive schemes*

Individual schemes

Production
- Piece-rate plans
- Standard-hour systems
- Individual bonuses
- Suggestion systems

Sales
- Commission plans
- Merit awards
- Merchandise & travel incentives

Management
- Bonuses based on work unit performance
- Deferred compensation
- Share options
- Supplementary benefits

Group/organisational schemes
- Bonuses based on group performance
- Gainsharing, for example Scanlon & Rucker plans
- Profit-sharing
- ESOPs (Employee share ownership plans)
- Suggestion systems

*Adapted and expanded from Singer, MG. 1990. Human Resource Management, 314. Boston: PWS-Kent and Byars, LL & Rue, LW. 1991. Human Resource Management, 3 ed, 352. Homewood, IL: Irwin.

In general the choice between individual or group-based incentive plans is dictated by whether performance is a function of individualised or collective effort and whether the organisation can readily evaluate individual versus group performance. It is, however, not uncommon for the same employee or group of employees to be covered by various types of incentive schemes at any given time. For example, a miner at an Anglo-American gold mine may, for instance, currently receive a drilling bonus based on individual performance and also be covered by organisation-wide profit-sharing and employee share ownership schemes.

18.2.3.1 Individual incentive schemes

Individual incentive schemes can take several forms, but they all share one primary advantage — employees can distinctly see the relationship between what and how much they do and what they get.

This advantage is, however, often the cause of some unwanted effects.

For example, an organisation may "only get what it pays for", since employees will be likely to concentrate their efforts only on those activities of their total job outcome that are being measured and rewarded (for example, a commission system that is only based on sales volumes may encourage employees to neglect the customer care aspect of their jobs). Furthermore, the increased competition among employees may become dysfunctional due to workers becoming reluctant to share knowledge or ideas that can lead to overall improved productivity, or due to work groups imposing informal ceilings on outputs and enforcing these less than optimal productivity levels by means of peer pressure.

Popular individual incentive approaches include piece-rate plans, standard-hour plans, commission plans and individual bonuses.

Piece-rate plans

Under piece-rate plans individual pay is directly linked to the number of units produced.

Straight piece-rate plans usually pay an employee a set wage (for example minimum wage) for an expected minimum level of output (the standard) and a piece-rate incentive for all production above the standard. This standard is determined by job analysis and workstudy techniques and is often adjusted by collective bargaining.

Differential piece-rate plans are a common variation, according to which the employer pays a smaller piece-rate up to the standard and a higher piece-rate for production above the standard.

Standard-hour Plans

Standard-hour plans are similar to piece-rate plans, with the exception that the productivity standard is not measured in terms of output units, but is set in terms of time units needed to complete a particular task. Employees who complete such tasks in less than the standard time qualify for incentive payments on the basis of the time saved.

By way of illustration, suppose that at Louis Motors an oil change has been calculated as requiring 30 minutes to complete (standard time). A mechanic earning R50 an hour will earn R25 to complete the job, irrespective of whether he used more or less time than the allotted 30 minutes (0,5 standard hour x R50). Should he manage to complete three oil changes within one hour, he would consequently be paid R75 (1,5 x R50) under a time-bonus system where the full benefit of the time saved goes to the employee.

Commission plans

The competitive and largely independent nature of sales work demands a sustained high level of motivation and enthusiasm from salespersons and makes financial incentives therefore well suited to this category of employees. Most salespersons are usually rewarded according to some form of commission plan based at least partially on their sales volume.

Types of plans range from a straight commission to various combinations of salary, plus commission and/or sales bonuses. Under a *straight commission plan* pay is entirely determined by volume of sales, whereas under *combination plans* the salesperson is paid a guaranteed basic salary plus a (usually smaller) commission on sales. In addition to or sometimes instead of commission, companies often also pay *sales bonuses* for sales that exceed a specific predetermined quota. Another variant is the *draw plan* which is often implemented to counter the negative effect of fluctuating earnings caused by periodic changes in business climate and typically associated with straight commission plans. Essentially this involves the payment of a basic salary which is deducted from future commissions.

Exhibit C

Examples of commission plans*		
	Straight commission plan	*Salary plus commission*
Formula	1 % of total monthly sales	R 300 per week + 0,7 % of total monthly sales
		4 × R300 = R1 200
Pay	1 % × R400 000 = R4 000	0,7 % × R400 000 = R2 800
		= R4 000
	Draw plan	*Salary plus bonus*
Formula	1 % of total monthly sales less R400 weekly draw	R300 per week + 2 % of sales in excess of quota of 2 600 units
Pay	total draw already advanced: R1 600	4 × R300 = R1 200
	commission still owing:[1] R2 400	2 % × R140 000[2] = R2 800
	R4 000	R4 000

[1] R4 000 – R1 600
[2] 1 400 excess units @ R100

*Based on sales of 4 000 units at R100 each.

Individual bonuses

A bonus is an additional one-off reward for high performance. It is a discretionary payment — that is, it is not guaranteed and it does not become part of the recipients basic salary as in the case of a merit pay increase. Bonuses may be based on a variety of performance measures, for example the achievement of specific objectives, performance ratings or, in the case of executives, a percentage of total profits or return on shareholders' investments.

Care should be taken not to allow a bonus to become a virtual extension of basic salary due to the payment thereof becoming practically guaranteed, as has happened in the case of the typical South African annual bonus (13th cheque). During 1993 an FSA-Contact survey indicated that 92 % of respondent companies offered a general annual bonus and that almost all these respondents (95 %) had paid all their employees the bonus, despite the prevailing recessionary climate (FSA-Contact 1993).

In the case of executives, a bonus payment may sometimes take the form of shares or options to buy shares in the organisation. A bonus payment may also be deferred until a set future date (for example retirement) in order to realise income tax savings. Deferred bonus payments may also serve as "golden handcuffs" with which an organisation may attempt to retain the services of valuable senior personnel and sustain managerial performance (Horwitz & Frost 1992: 32).

18.2.3.2 Group and organisation-wide incentive schemes

Group or team-based incentive schemes provide incentive pay to all group members, based on the performance of the entire group. Such schemes are most applicable in situations where:

- jobs are interdependent (for example assembly lines)
- cooperation is needed to complete a task or project; and
- the measurement of individual output is difficult.

In most instances individually based schemes such as piecework, production bonuses and commission plans can also be used to pay groups of individuals (Ivancevich 1992: 395).

In the South African context indications are that at the operational level team-based incentive schemes are more applicable than individual-based schemes. Trade union positions on pay linked to productivity and collective bargaining agreements no doubt exert some influence in this regard (Cherrington 1995: 453).

Organisation-wide incentive schemes are generally aimed at involving employees in a common effort to achieve overall organisational effectiveness. Specific objectives of such schemes may be:

- to encourage economic or financial participation of employees;
- to foster improved productivity or reduced production costs; and
- to increase worker commitment (Horwitz 1988: 27; Snelgar 1988: 4–8).

The most common organisation-wide schemes are gainsharing and profit-sharing schemes, employee share ownership plans (ESOPs) and suggestion systems.

A case at hand . . .

Example of an incentive bonus scheme*

The Genmin incentive bonus scheme

The incentive bonus scheme devised by Genmin comprises two components based on organisation-wide and individual objectives.

1. At the macrolevel the overall pool of money to be made available for payment of individual bonuses is based on the overall financial performance of the organisation: 15 % to be allocated on the basis of financial performance measures to be transacted between the chairman of the board and the managing director.

    Examples of such measures are: cost saving (actual year-end cost as a percentage of the budget), profit, earnings per share, and return on capital employed.

2. At the individual level a maximum of 15 % of basic salary package can be allocated for the achievement of mutually agreed objectives that focus on strategic issues in the business plan.

    For the evaluation period a minimum of 3 and a maximum of 7 major objectives are contracted between superior and subordinate and ranked in order of priority. The objectives in order of importance are weighted as follows:

Priority count out of	\multicolumn{5}{c}{Number of objectives}
	7	6	5	4	3
1st	26	28	30	35	40
2nd	22	23	25	30	35
3rd	17	18	20	20	25
4th	12	14	15	15	
5th	10	10	10		
6th	7	7			
7th	6				
TOTAL	100	100'	100	100	100

Only employees reaching a score above 75 in the achievement of their individual objectives are eligible to receive a bonus. The size of the bonus is determined by converting the performance scores to a percentage of basic package in accordance with the following table:

Score	75	76	77	78	79	80	81	82
Percentage earned	0	0,6	0,9	1,2	1,5	1,8	2,4	3,0

Score	83	84	85	86	87	88	89	90 & up
Percentage earned	4,2	5,4	6,61	7,8	9,6	11,4	13,2	15,0

*Source: D. Groenewald Genmin

UP TO HERE

Gainsharing plans

Gainsharing plans are organisational systems for sharing the benefit (gains) of cost reductions or improved productivity and quality in the form of cash awards. They are generally based on the assumption that better cooperation between workers and management and among workers themselves will result in greater effectiveness.

Well-known examples of such plans are the Scanlon, Rucker and Improshare plans, which find wide application in the North American context. Key features of gainsharing plans are (Bernadin & Russell 1993: 488).

- a philosophy of participatory management;

- rewarding groups for suggestions by individuals in the group;

- joint worker/management committees administering the plan and evaluating suggestions;

- reward allocations to all participants according to some formula determining the contributions of specific groups of employees in defined areas of performance.

Exhibit D

Gainsharing in South Africa*

Remuneration consultants Bussin and Thomson (1995) report as follows on their study on gainsharing practices:

"In 1992, when we realised that employers were looking for a breakthrough in labour productivity, we decided to research eight companies who had reputedly achieved success in this direction. Rather surprisingly, we found that three out of the eight companies already practised gainsharing (Con Roux Construction, Golden Lay Farms and Cadac). Of the other five companies, three were under pressure from their trade unions to adopt some formula of profit-sharing.

Reliable statistics on the extent of this movement in South Africa are, however, difficult to come by as the movement is still in its infancy. We believe that many employers have developed plans during the last year to introduce gainsharing, but are holding back — perhaps waiting to see what other employers do and so conceivably learn a little from reported experiences."

*Source: Extracted from Gaining pace with Gainsharing. *People Dynamics*, June 1995, pp 22–25

Profit-sharing plans

Profit-sharing plans essentially allow employees to share in the financial success of an organisation by distributing a portion of the profits back to the employees. The underlying assumption of such schemes is that they increase commitment and identification with the organisation and its profit goal and, consequently, lead to increased productivity and cost savings.

A case at hand . . .

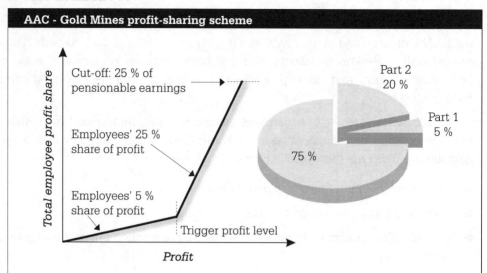

AAC - Gold Mines profit-sharing scheme

- Every three months the mines calculate their total profit and deduct capital expenditure
- The rest is divided into two parts:
  - Part 1 is money up to a trigger profit level. Five per cent of all profits below the trigger level are put into the employees profit-sharing pool.
  - Part 2 is money in excess of the trigger profit level. Twenty per cent of these extra profits are put into the profit-sharing pool.
- The trigger profit target is based on the mine's average quarterly profit for the previous year and differs from mine to mine.
- The employees profit-sharing pool has a maximum size of 25 % of the pensionable earnings of all employees of the mine.
- Profit-sharing bonuses are paid out each quarter in two portions. The first portion is divided equally among all employees and the rest is paid as a percentage of salary.

*Source: Fanie Ernst, Anglo American Corporation Gold and Uranium Division

An added advantage, especially to companies and industries with unstable markets and proportionately high labour costs (for example the South African gold mining industry), is that wage or salary supplements can be provided that do not add to the fixed cost element and therefore need not be perpetuated for years to come when adverse business conditions may prevail.

The downside for employees, however, is that they have to share in both the good times and the bad times and therefore their total income is often prone to fluctuations.

It is also often difficult for employees to see the link between their own individual effort and its result on the overall performance of the organisation. In addition, external factors outside the control of the employees (for example economic conditions) may have a far greater impact on the organisation's profitability than any actions of the employees themselves (De Cenzo & Robbins 1994: 427).

In the South African context profit-sharing schemes have become fairly well entrenched in the gold mining industry, with the scheme negotiated between ERGO and the National Union of Mineworkers probably being the best known.[1]

The Anglo American gold mines profit-sharing scheme, which covers about 150 000 employees, is briefly illustrated on page 548.

Beaker (1995: 22–23) notes that profit-sharing has had a chequered career in South Africa and cautions that issues such as income security and the planning of such incentive systems should be discussed with labour from the outset if the system is to succeed.

Employee share ownership plans (ESOPs)

Whilst share ownership in the employer organisation has been a well-established compensation principle for quite some time, in the South African context it has only relatively recently been extended beyond the executive and managerial levels. During 1987, for example, only about twenty-four ESOPs were operated by South African companies, a number of which had originated as a result of the disinvestment drive by foreign companies (Moller 1987: 50–59).

Initially such schemes were strongly opposed by especially the black trade union movement, but indications are that a more favourable attitude towards the concept of ESOPs is evolving (Bird 1988: 40–50; Mohamed 1989: 93–100; Booyens 1991: 26).

Although many variations exist, an ESOP is essentially an employee trust which buys shares in an organisation and then gradually distributes those shares to the organisation's employees. Normally the trust's share purchases are funded by grants or loans from the organisation itself, or by external loans guaranteed by the organisation (Bekker 1995: 22–23; Grenblo 1989: 4).

According to Innes (Boyens 1991: 26), it would appear that ESOPs are usually successful in situations:

- where meaningful participation by employees in decision making is practised;
- where workers derive real benefits from share ownership;
- where it is not simply seen by management as a symbolic sharing of power; and
- where organised labour perceives the scheme as a real way of cooperating with management.

Suggestion systems

A suggestion system is an incentive scheme under which employees receive rewards (usually cash) for useful ideas on reducing costs, improving safety or product quality or generally increasing organisational effectiveness. Typically such systems utilise forms that employees can use to write out their suggestions and deposit them in conveniently placed boxes for submission and evaluation by management or a special committee.

A case at hand . . .

What happened to ESOPs?*

When Anglo American and a number of other blue-chip companies implemented ESOPs for their workers during the late '80s, it was hoped that a new era of productivity and worker participation was ushered in. Since then ESOPs have unfortunately not met all such expectations. It appears as if they now have run aground on the twin rocks of union opposition and taxes.

ESOPs have been classified as attempts by management to co-opt workers and thus were rejected. Whilst many companies operate a variety of stock ownership schemes for their management, the perception exists among workers that such schemes do not really empower workers and that there is no real commitment towards worker participation.

It is, however, especially the tax dispensation that discourages companies from implementing ESOPs. The Katz Commission has also recommended that the current dispensation should remain and that the prerequisites of ESOPs should continue to be taxable.

Nevertheless, there is a resurging interest in ESOPs as a mechanism to effect particularly black empowerment via black controlled enterprises. Cosatu and Nactu for instance have significant share holdings in New African Investments (Nail) and Real African Investments (Rail).

*Source: Extracted from Wat het van ESOPs geword? *Finansies & Tegniek*, 19 April 1996

Exhibit E

Incentive compensation in South Africa*

In their comprehensive salary survey for September 1993 FSA-Contact found that 30 % of respondent companies operate formal incentive bonus schemes (other than general annual bonuses, ad hoc performance bonuses or commission schemes). Where such incentive schemes exist, they are applicable to different staff categories as follows:

- Executive and mid-managerial staff: 98 %
- General staff: 53 %
- Lower-skilled staff: 45 %

The most popular performance measure bases on which performance incentives are calculated are in descending order:

1. Profit
2. Personal performance in quantitative terms
3. Personal performance in qualitative terms
4. Team performance
5. Combination of group and individual performance.

Regarding **management reward schemes**, Horwitz and Frost (1992) found the following managerial pay elements to be most common:

1. Deferred compensation
2. Individual performance bonuses
3. Profit-sharing
4. Share-option schemes and team-based bonuses.

*Source: FSA-Contact 1993; Horwitz & Frost 1992: 32

Marx (1992: 3) cautions against the informality of suggestion boxes and sets the following criteria for a formal suggestion scheme.

- Accepted suggestions must relate to specific or potential problems or opportunities to improve processes or situations.
- A suggestion must provide a solution or possible strategy; complaints do not qualify.
- Suggestions should be in writing and must be signed by the employee.
- Written suggestions must be received and registered by the suggestion office.
- The scheme must be recognised and accepted by top management.

In the South African context a National Association of Suggestion Systems (SANASS) has been active since 1990 in the promotion of this type of incentive scheme.

18.3 EMPLOYEE BENEFITS

18.3.1 Introduction

Benefits are indirect forms of compensation that, like direct compensation, are intended to aid the achievement of the human resource objective of attracting, retaining and motivating employees.

Both locally in South Africa and abroad, benefits form a very substantial portion of total compensation expenditure. In the first place this section examines the major reasons behind the existence of benefits, as opposed to direct cash remuneration. Secondly, a benefits classification is provided and the most common benefits offered by South African organisations are detailed in terms of this classification.

The degree to which the benefit arrangement offered by an organisation aids the achievement of the human resource objectives of attracting, retaining and motivating employees is largely determined by the benefit arrangement strategy followed by the organisation. This section, therefore, also deals with different benefit arrangement strategies, and the merits of providing the elements of choice and flexibility within such strategies.

Well-structured and appropriate benefits are, however, not enough to ensure the success of an organisation's benefit programme. This section therefore concludes by detailing a number of important considerations aimed at ensuring the successful administrative delivery of benefits to an organisation's employees.

18.3.2 Reasons for providing employee benefits

The extent and nature of the benefits commonly offered by organisations within a particular country are largely determined by the country's specific circumstances and the country's laws. In South Africa, for example, the need to travel long distances together with the lack of adequate public transport has contributed significantly to the fact that company cars are a very common benefit.

A country's laws also exert a profound influence. A number of the benefits offered by South African organisations are mandated by law. Probably the most common is the minimum annual leave requirement stipulated by the Basic Conditions of Employment Act. Compulsory insurance for unemployment and disability or death caused by an event or by circumstances at work also exists for certain categories of South African employees.

The tax laws of a country, in particular, contribute very significantly to the extent and nature of benefits commonly offered. In a country like the United States, where the marginal tax rates are relatively low, most of the compensation package is given directly as cash. In South Africa, on the other hand, marginal tax rates are relatively high and benefits, despite the introduction of benefit taxation, are still generally conservatively taxed. This results in a significant portion of compensation packages being given indirectly in the form of benefits. This practice is particularly common at managerial levels in South Africa.

18.3.3 Types of benefits

South African organisations, like many organisations elsewhere in the world, provide a truly amazing range of benefits. They are available to employees while on the job (for example shift allowances, coffee breaks) as well as off the job (for example private use of company cars, vacation payments). In addition, benefits are also provided to the families and/or dependants of employees (for example medical aid, life insurance).

Benefits can be categorised in a number of ways. A popular way is to categorise benefits into cash and non-cash benefits. Non-cash benefits are then typically further subdivided into current benefits (that is, those enjoyed immediately) and deferred benefits (that is, those enjoyed at some future date). A list of the most common benefits offered in South Africa is provided in exhibit F in terms of this benefit classification.

The exact nature of most of the benefits listed in exhibit F will be determined by the benefit arrangement strategy followed by a particular organisation. For example, the nature of a company car or car allowance benefit offered under an add-on benefit arrangement strategy will differ very significantly from a company car or car allowance benefit offered under a flexible benefit arrangement strategy.

These benefit arrangement strategies are discussed in section 18.3.4 on page 553.

Exhibit F

Classification of common benefits offered in South Africa*

CASH BENEFITS

Bonuses
- Fixed annual bonus
- Incentive/performance bonus

Allowances
- Entertainment allowance
- Car allowance
- Shift allowance
- Stand-by allowance
- Tool allowance

Allowances (continued)
- Abnormal working conditions allowance
- Acting allowance

Other
- Overtime pay
- Call-out pay
- Commission
- Payment for time not worked (leave)

NON-CASH BENEFITS

Current

Transport/travel
- Company car
- Second company car
- Free or subsidised transport to and from work
- Free or subsidised rail/bus/sea/air fares
- Free or subsidised parking
- Overseas travel

Accommodation
- Housing subsidy
- Housing loan
- Free or low rental accommodation
- Holiday accommodation

Other
- Interest-free or low interest loan
- Free or cheap services
- Free or cheap company products
- Educational assistance
- Telephone account payment
- Newspapers and periodicals
- Meals and refreshments
- Club feesProfessional fees
- Medical Aid/Health care benefits
- Encashable leave
- Incentive award
- Long-service award
- Share purchase
- Computer and faxes at home
- Cellular phones

Deferred
- Pension fund
- Deferred compensation
- Provident fund
- Group life cover

- Disability cover
- Accident insurance
- Accumulated leave
- Share options

*Source: Adapted from *IPM Fact Sheet* No 176

18.3.4 Benefit arrangement strategies

18.3.4.1 Strategy alternatives

In return for their services, South African organisations typically offer their employees a basic salary to which a number of benefits are added. Eligibility for such benefits generally tends to be based on an employee's length of service and/or job level. There is also a tendency for the value of such benefits to increase with increase in length of service and/or job level.

Typically these benefits are also managed and reviewed in relative isolation to each other (and basic salary) and the employee is tied to a cash/benefit mix as defined by the organisation. This relatively isolated management of benefits very often results in employees not being aware of their total earnings, inclusive of the organisation's expenditure on benefits.

The benefit arrangement strategy described above is often referred to as the *add-on benefit arrangement strategy*. The term "add-on" refers to the nature of the employment agreement between employer and employee which, as described above, offers the employee a basic salary to which a number of benefits are added.

The local opposite of the add-on benefit arrangement strategy is the *pure flexible benefit arrangement strategy* (Greene 1990: 26–28).

Instead of a basic salary plus benefits, the employee now receives a total package value in return for his/her services. Each employee's compensation is managed and reviewed in terms of a single entity, namely *total package value*, as opposed to the relatively isolated management and review of basic salary and individual benefits.

Under the pure flexible benefit arrangement strategy, individual employees also have full discretion over the cash/benefit mix of their own total package value. Essentially an organisation will determine the total package cost it is prepared to spend in employing each of its different employees. It will then compile a list of types of benefits that it is prepared to offer an employee. From this "menu" of benefits each employee can choose those benefits which best suit his/her individual needs. The cost to the organisation of providing the particular mix of benefits is then added up and is deducted from the total package value in order to calculate the net cash salary of the employee.

Although the pure flexible benefit arrangement strategy serves a very useful purpose as a theoretical opposite to the add-on benefit arrangement strategy, it is seldom implemented in its pure form. The most important reasons for this is that organisations wish to safeguard themselves from possible adverse consequences arising from particular employee choices.

An example would be where the organisation has to inform the widow of an employee that no funds will be payable to her, as her late husband opted out of group life cover and pension benefits and converted these into improved company car benefits.

One can obviously argue that employees and their families have to live with the consequences of their own decisions. Many, if not the majority of organisations would, however, prefer to design their benefit arrangements in a way that precludes the possibility of events similar to the above example. This is achieved through a flexible benefit arrangement that includes so-called core benefits. As opposed to the other benefits under a flexible benefit arrangement strategy, which are optional, employee participation in so-called core benefits is compulsory. In practice employees are obliged to channel specified minimum portions of the total packages offered to them into these defined core benefits. The range of core benefits should ideally include basic retirement, death, disability and major medical expense (for example surgery, hospitalisation) benefits.

The most common advantages and disadvantages of flexible benefit arrangements are summarised below.

Advantages of flexible benefit arrangements

- Flexible benefits promote a clearer understanding for employers and employees of the real costs associated with benefits and how they contribute to the total package values.

- Employers have improved control over the predictability of compensation expenditure, since package values are not driven by changing external factors or fluctuations in employee utilisation of specific benefits (for example medical aid).

- Fairness and internal equity are enhanced, since differences in total package values typically only result from differences in performance and job complexity, and not from differences in personal circumstances.

   (For example: under a non-flexible system two employees with the same entitlement regarding a housing subsidy benefit and a fully maintained company car benefit may end up with substantial differences in the value of the benefits, if the one person rents a flat and lives close to work, whilst the other has a large bond on his house and travels a long distance to and from work.)

- Employees are permitted to choose benefits most suited to their individual needs and also to structure their package in the most tax efficient way.

Disadvantages of flexible benefit arrangements

- Flexible systems are more complex to set up and to administer. Despite the availability of computer software that can address the complexities of the payroll administration and the financial modelling of optimum package mixes, additional resources are usually needed for providing individual advisory and counselling services for each employee in the system.

- The problem of adverse choice may sometimes be encountered.

   This relates to the situation where those employees who have a specific and immediate need for a particular benefit select that option more often than the average employee, thus causing an inordinate rise in the cost of such benefit. (For example: employees close to retirement may attempt to buy as much additional retirement benefits as possible, or an employee with a serious medical condition, as much medical and group life insurance as possible.) The inclusion of compulsory core benefits can, however, often address this problem.

- Unions may sometimes offer resistance to flexible benefit schemes if previously negotiated benefit improvements or the loss of control over a benefit programme are at stake.

18.3.4.2 Choosing a suitable benefit arrangement

The choice between particular arrangement strategies should take account of certain fundamental compensation principles in order to ensure a benefits system that not only addresses particular organisational needs and circumstances, but will also be in line with the objectives of the overall compensation strategy. These principles are detailed in exhibit G.

Exhibit G

Compensation principles

The following compensation principles should be considered when choosing a benefit arrangement strategy:
- **Cost control.** Limit the exposure of compensation packages to unpredictable cost factors over which the organisation has very little or no control.
- **External equity.** The positioning of compensation levels inside the organisation relative to comparable remuneration levels in the broader labour market should be done on the basis of **total package values.**
- **Internal equity.** Differences in the **total** package values of individual employees should only be due to differences in **job complexity** (as measured by the job evaluation process), **skill premiums** payable to certain occupational groupings (as measured by remuneration surveys) and differences in **job performance** (as measured by a performance appraisal system).
- **Flexibility.** Individual employees should be given the opportunity to select a cash/benefit mix that satisfies their personal needs without adding to the total compensation expenditure of the organisation.
- **Simplicity.** Benefit arrangements should be simple to administer and easily understood by the employees to whom they apply.

*Source: Old Mutual Remuneration Consulting Division

Generally, it would appear that a flexible benefit arrangement strategy has a greater potential for satisfying the fundamental compensation principles mentioned above, and it is therefore not surprising to find an ever-increasing number of South African organisations of all sizes following the international trend towards greater flexibility in benefit agreements (see the case study on page 557).

18.3.5 Successful delivery of benefit arrangements

Well-structured and appropriate benefits are not enough to ensure the success of an organisation's benefit programme. The administrative delivery of the benefits to the organisation's employees must also be on time and as contracted before the benefits programme can be regarded as a success. Of particular importance in this regard is the integration of effort across functional lines within the organisation and the issue of benefit programme communication.

A case at hand . . .

Example of a flexible benefit arrangement*

John X is employed by an organisation which is prepared to spend a total package value of R120 000 per year on him.

He could either receive the full R120 000 in cash **or** part thereof in cash and part in benefits. The menu of available benefits is as follows:

- Low interest housing loan up to R100 000 at 4 %
- Company car valued at R70 000
- Holiday accommodation for 3 weeks a year hired by the employer
- Entertainment allowance of R2 500 for business-related expenses
- Occasional services of up to R500 per year
- Payment of R900 towards his annual telephone account

The package cost to the employer could be as follows:

	R
R100 000 loan at market rate (say 15 % less 4 % actual)	11 000
Lease of R70 000 car by company for 48-month period	30 000
Rental paid by employer for holiday accommodation	3 000
Entertainment allowance	2 500
Air fare (an occasional service)	480
Telephone account	900
Compulsory core benefits — pension, group life assurance, medical aid	20 000
Total benefits	67 880
Balance paid as cash salary	52 120
Total package value	120 000

*Source: Adapted from *The Ernst & Young Practical Guide to Fringe Benefits*, 3 ed, 1993, Juta Tax Library

18.3.5.1 Integration of effort

The administrative delivery of a benefits programme seldom involves only one functional area within the organisation. Responsibility for this delivery often spans the human resources, financial and information technology functions. Given the diversity of these functions, a significant potential exists for important responsibilities to "get lost" between these areas.

Where more than one functional area is responsible for the administrative delivery of a benefits programme (which is almost always the case), it is advisable for these areas to clarify and document their respective responsibilities. A coordination committee with representation from all the functional areas responsible for the administrative delivery of the benefit programme is also advisable. Benefit arrangements are seldom, if ever, static and such a body can play a very important role in realigning the administrative infrastructure whenever changes are made to the organisation's benefit arrangement.

18.3.5.2 Benefit programme communication

Compensation affects employees directly and personally. It is therefore imperative that they fully understand the processes and personal responsibilities associated with the organisation's benefit programme. The proper communication of this is of the utmost importance. Inadequate communication could quite easily result in employer and employee having different perceptions as to what has been contracted.

Under a flexible benefit arrangement strategy, benefit programme communication becomes even more vital. A flexible benefit arrangement always means transferring at least some responsibility for the structuring of individual compensation packages from the employer to the employee. The employee has to know and accept this responsibility.

Booklets, presentations, workshops and videos are among the most popular means for ensuring understanding and acceptance of the processes and personal responsibilities of the organisation's benefit programme.

18.4 CONCLUSION

Incentive systems and benefit programmes usually form an integral part of an overall compensation system. A wide variety of financial incentive plans are used in an effort to link the pay of employees more closely to their performance. This link is not always easily established, since the success of an incentive system not only depends on the sound mechanics of the plan but also on a variety of determinants such as the organisational climate, employee acceptance, effective administration and suitability to particular organisational needs and circumstances.

In achieving the common goal of fostering increased performance or output, incentive schemes utilise a variety of approaches in terms of the class of employees to be covered, the measures of performance utilised, the types of behaviour or areas of performance to be encouraged, the organisational level of performance to be rewarded and the nature of the rewards themselves. These differences in options must be carefully considered when deciding what type of incentive plan will be the most appropriate in addressing the particular needs and compensation objectives of an organisation.

Benefits usually comprise a substantial component of employees' total compensation. Other than incentive payments, however, benefits are not normally linked to performance, but are mostly regarded as entitlements, that is, they are seen as part of the conditions of employment. Whilst some benefits are mandated by labour legislation, most of the wide array of possible benefits are provided by employers in an attempt to attract and retain employees and thus remain competitive in the labour market. In devising a suitable benefits programme, various benefit arrangement strategies may be utilised, the most common of which are the add-on strategy and the flexible benefit strategy. The latter has become increasingly popular in the South African context in line with a trend towards greater choice and flexibility in accommodating differing employee needs.

Efficient administration plays a major role in ensuring the success of a benefits programme.

Incentive compensation and benefits programmes, together with the basic salary structure, are equally important components of an overall compensation system. The challenge for effective reward management lies in finding the optimal balance between these components and their congruence with the strategic objectives of the organisation, and in particular also the human resource management strategies decided upon.

SELF-EVALUATION QUESTIONS

1. What is incentive compensation?
2. List at least five reasons why it is important to have incentive schemes.
3. Discuss the important principles that underlie the process of establishing incentive systems.
4. Differentiate between and compare the merits of individual- and organisation-based incentive systems.
5. Discuss the nature and potential of "ESOPs".
6. Explain the rationale for and different types of benefits that can be provided to employees.
7. Briefly explain the compensation principles to be considered when a benefit arrangement strategy has to be chosen.
8. How can one go about successfully delivering benefit arrangements?

ENDNOTES

1. For 1993–94 ERGO and NUM entered into a new profit-sharing scheme which retains the basic original structure, but which reflects a "lower-risk-lower-yield" character. Essentially the 5 % share of profit portion is increased to 9 %, but the 20 % share of profit portion is only activated once 12 % total employee profit share is reached, and also the cutoff is lowered to 15 % of pensionable earnings.

BIBLIOGRAPHY

Armstrong, M. 1993. *Managing Reward Systems*. Buckingham: Open University Press

Armstrong, M & Murlis, H. 1988. *Reward Management*. London: Kogan Page

Bekker, D. 1995. Profit-sharing: Friend or foe? *HRM,* 11(4), 22–23

Bernadin, JH & Russell, JE. 1993. *Human Resource Management: An Experiential Approach.* New York: McGraw-Hill

Biesheuvel, S. 1985. *Work Motivation and Compensation,* vol 2. Johannesburg: McGraw-Hill

Bird, A. 1988. ESOPs: Part of a strategy to smash democracy. *SA Labour Bulletin,* 13(6), 44–50

Boyens, A. 1991. Vakbonde verander deuntjie oor ESOPs. *Finansies & Tegniek,* March, 26

Brehm, N. 1988. Incentive schemes: Taking over from fringe benefits. *HRM,* May, 10–13

Burgess, LR. 1989. *Compensation Administration,* 2 ed. Columbus, Ohio: Merrill

Bussin, M. 1992. Performance appraisal, remuneration and strategic performance management. *People Dynamics,* March, 23–28

Bussin, M. 1994. Incentives as a strategic lever. *People Dynamics,* April, 19–26

Cherrington, DJ. 1995. *The Management of Human Resources,* 4 ed. Englewood Cliffs, NJ: Prentice-Hall

De Cenzo, DA & Robbins, SP. 1994. *Human Resource Management: Concepts and Practices,* 4 ed. New York: Wiley

FSA-Contact. 1993. *Peromnes Remuneration Survey, September 1993*

FSA-Contact. 1995. *Peromnes Remuneration Survey, September 1995*

Gathercole, J. 1992. Flexibility in organisational and employment practices. *People Dynamics,* February, 8–12

Greenblo, A. 1989. In praise of ESOPs. *Finance Week,* March 23–29, 4

Greene, MH. 1990. Flexible benefits. *Superfunds,* August, 26–28

Horwitz, F. 1988. Ownership issues: How employee share participation schemes can be made to work. *Finance Week,* February, 4–10, 27

Horwitz, F & Frost, P. 1992. Flexible rewards: Critical success factors. *People Dynamics,* June, 27–33

Ivancevich, JM. 1992. *Human Resource Management,* 5 ed. Homewood, Ill: Irwin

Lawler, EE. 1990. *Strategic Pay.* San Francisco: Jossey-Bass

Lidstone, J. 1992. *Beyond the Pay Packet.* London: McGraw-Hill

Lundy, O & Cowling, A. 1996. *Strategic Human Resource Management.* London: Routledge

Maller, J. 1987. Employee share-ownership: South Africa's new capitalists? *SA Labour Bulletin,* 12(8), 59–59

Marx, AE. 1992. *A Practical Guide on Implementing Suggestion Systems.* Kenwyn: Juta

Mohamed, Y. 1989. Worker participation: A Trojan horse? *SA Labour Bulletin,* 14(5), 93–100

Sherman, AW & Bohlander, GW. 1992. *Managing Human Resources,* 9 ed. Cincinnati, Ohio: South-Western

Snelgar, RJ. 1988. Rewarding participation. *IPM Journal,* July, 4–8

Spangenberg, H. 1993. A managerial view on performance management. *People Dynamics,* October, 30–34

Spangenberg, H. 1994. *Understanding and Implementing Performance Management.* Kenwyn: Juta

Stacey, K. 1991. Remuneration trends: 1991 and onwards. *IPM Journal,* February, 21–26

◎ STUDY OBJECTIVES

After studying this chapter, you should be able to:

- briefly describe what is meant by *employee wellness*;
- give a brief overview of the statutory regulations governing occupational health and safety in South Africa;
- explain what is meant by "a proactive and holistic approach" to employee wellness;
- list and describe the nature and importance of at least seven specific issues in proactive, holistic health and safety management;
- explain what is meant by *occupational mental health;*
- discuss the issue of work-related stress;
- describe the nature and importance of employee assistance;
- write a short essay on the topic of "Occupational diseases, hazards, accidents and injuries";
- explain the challenges facing South African organisations as a result of the AIDS/HIV threat;
- describe how to deal with employees who are HIV positive or who have AIDS;
- name the different stakeholders or role-players in occupational health and safety and briefly describe the role of each.

19.1 INTRODUCTION

Management's efforts should be directed at eliciting from employees the behaviour and performance that will best achieve the organisation's mission and objectives. Apart from attracting and appointing high quality staff and deploying strategies and practices that unlock the potential of employees, management may also need to show that they care for or look after their employees. In addition to the provision of remuneration and fringe benefits, it is important also to promote and maintain the overall general state of wellbeing of the organisation's employees. All other things being equal, an employee who is generally well will usually perform better than one who is generally not well. The idea is thus to improve and maintain employee "wellness".

According to Jensen (1987: 2), "wellness" in this context refers to "the state of optimised physical and mental health and wellbeing". This therefore entails a holistic approach to looking after the physical and psychological state of health and wellbeing of each employee in the organisation. The absolute minimum requirement in this respect is to provide a working environment that is safe.

Although some types of work are generally more dangerous than others, a common-law duty rests on all employers to provide their employees with safe working conditions. South African courts have often endorsed the common-law principle that requires employers to take reasonable care for the health and safety of their employees. Apart from the common-law requirements, legislation has also been passed in South Africa which focuses specifically on the health and safety of employees (see chapter 4 and below).

Although legislation is only a very basic starting point when it comes to promoting and maintaining employee wellness in the workplace, this chapter begins with a brief introduction to some of the important aspects relating to health and safety legislation in South Africa. Of course, taking good care of an organisation's employees goes far beyond simply keeping within the requirements of the law. A much more constructive and proactive approach is required to elicit, enhance and maintain optimal states of wellness that are beneficial to both the employees and the organisation. This chapter therefore focuses largely on the elements of such a holistic approach which fall, to a large extent, beyond the scope of the law.

19.2 THE LEGISLATIVE FRAMEWORK GOVERNING HEALTH AND SAFETY AT WORK

19.2.1 General

Apart from the common law and the Bill of Rights (in the Constitution), there are two pieces of legislation with refined legal requirements regarding employee health and safety, namely the Occupational Health and Safety Act (OHSA) 85 of 1993 and the Mine Health and Safety Act 29 of 1996.

The overall aim of the OHSA (also see chapter 4) is to provide for the health and safety of employees at work (including aspects like health and safety hazards and the safety of plant machinery and equipment). Certain employers and employees are, however, specifically excluded from the ambit of the OHSA. These include parties covered by the Merchant Shipping Act and people employed in mines, mining areas or any works as defined in the Mine Health and Safety Act 29 of 1996.

Because the mining industry still forms the bedrock of the South African economy, and because it is in mining in particular that major health and safety problems occur, it is important to take note of health and safety regulations in terms of the Mine Health and Safety Act. Before taking a brief look at this legislation, let us illustrate why we regard this as such an important topic in the mining industry.

Hermanus (1991: 17) points out that, between 1900 and 1991, over 68 000 mine-workers died through accidents on South African mines, and more than one million workers were permanently disabled. Statistics generally bear testimony to the fact that mining is a very hazardous occupation: in 1989 alone, 735 workers died in accidents on mines and a further 10 000 were injured; in 1993, 578 miners died in accidents; in 1994 there were 483 deaths due to mining accidents and 7 852 injuries (Hermanus 1991: 17; Brase 1995: 24; Spearing 1996: 21). In 1986 a fire at Kinross mine near Secunda in Gauteng claimed the lives of 177 workers, and in 1995, 104 workers died due to an accident involving a locomotive that fell down a mine shaft at Vaal Reefs gold mine (Jones 1996). Gleason (1996) declares:

> "SA gold mines have always been deep, dark and dangerous places. More than 80 000 lives have been taken in accidents since the discovery of gold in 1886. The men who work in them accept a precarious working lifestyle as part of the deal."

19.2.2 The Mine Health and Safety Act: A few comments

Historically in South Africa the concern for the health and safety of workers arose from the dangers inherent in mining. This is not surprising if we consider the statistics revealed in the following quote (Lewis & Jeebhay 1996: 431 (footnotes and references omitted)):

> "As a result of this legal and political system, 69 000 mineworkers died in the first 93 years of this century, and more than a million were seriously injured. In 1993 the government mining engineer's statistics showed that there were 1,54 mineworkers killed and 25,8 seriously injured for every 1 000 workers exposed to underground risk in all sectors of the industry. The vast majority of injuries and deaths occurred at or in underground mines (99 %). Of these, the gold mines were the most dangerous, accounting in 1993 for 85,6 % of all reported injuries and 72,7 % of all reported fatalities. 61,7 % of gold mining fatalities (263 lives in 1993) were due to underground rockbursts or rockfalls. The next most dangerous subsector in 1993, the coal industry, was responsible for 15,4 % of all mining fatalities."

Apart from the common-law right to work in a safe environment, safety in the mining industry was regulated by industry-specific statutes, the earliest of which was the Mines and Works Act of 1911. The latest statute in this regard is the Mine Health and Safety Act 29 of 1996. The objects of the Act are summarised in exhibit A.

Apart from placing appropriately onerous duties on the owners and managers of mines to provide for health and safety, the Act also grants employees wide-ranging powers to be involved in health and safety issues and decisions. The pre-eminent body established in terms of the Act to regulate health and safety issues in the mining industry is a tripartite body, called the Mine Health and Safety Council, which must advise the Minister of Mineral and Energy Affairs on health and safety at mines. The Council consists of five members representing owners in the mining industry; five members representing employees in the mining industry; four members representing departments of the state; and the Chief Inspector, who must chair the Council.

Exhibit A

> **Objects of the Mine Health and Safety Act***
>
> The objects of this Act are:
> - to protect the health and safety of persons at mines;
> - to require employers and employees to identify hazards and eliminate, control and minimise the risks relating to health and safety at mines;
> - to give effect to the public international law obligations of the Republic that concern health and safety at mines;
> - to provide for employee participation in matters of health and safety through health and safety representatives and the health and safety committees at mines;
> - to provide for effective monitoring of health and safety conditions at mines;
> - to provide for enforcement of health and safety measures at mines;
> - to provide for investigations and inquiries to improve health and safety at mines; and
> - to promote: (i) a culture of health and safety in the mining industry; (ii) training in health and safety in the mining industry; and (iii) co-operation and consultation on health and safety between the State, employers, employees and their representatives.

*Section 1 of Act 29 of 1996

As is the case with the Occupational Health and Safety Act (see below), the Mine Health and Safety Act provides for the reporting of incidents and accidents and for the appointment of health and safety representatives and committees. Considerations of space do not allow further discussion of this Act, but it is important to note in conclusion that in the mining industry the Occupational Health and Safety Act 85 of 1993 is not applicable to any matter in respect of which any provision of the former Act is applicable (this means, in effect, that only in a case where the Mine Health and Safety Act is silent on any specific issue would one turn to the Occupational Health and Safety Act for statutory guidance).

19.2.3 The OHSA: Some important aspects

19.2.3.1 General

As we indicated earlier, the Occupational Health and Safety Act 85 of 1993 (OHSA) forms the legislative framework in respect of health and safety issues in most South African organisations. The overall aim of the OHSA was spelled out in chapter 4.

The OHSA makes the following provisions for the achievement of its objectives.

- The establishment of an Advisory Council for Occupational Health and Safety.
- Every employer must provide and maintain, as far as is reasonably practicable, a working environment that is safe and without risk to the health of his/her employees, as well as other people affected by the operations of the business.
- Every supplier or manufacturer of items used in a workplace must ensure that such items do not pose a safety or health risk.

- Every employer must inform his/her workforce (and the appointed health and safety representatives) of hazards at the workplace.
- Every employee must:
  - take reasonable care for the health and safety of himself/herself and of other persons who may be affected by his/her acts or omissions;
  - carry out any lawful order given to him/her, and obey the health and safety rules and procedures laid down by his/her employer;
  - report any unsafe or unhealthy situation which comes to his/her attention; and
  - report any incident which may affect his/her health or which has caused an injury to himself/herself.
- The appointment of health and safety representatives. The Act provides that every employer who employs more than twenty employees at any workplace must appoint health and safety representatives. The functions of health and safety representatives are summarised in exhibit B.
- The establishment of one or more health and safety committees in respect of each workplace where two or more health and safety representatives have been designated. The functions of health and safety committees are summarised in exhibit B.
- Certain incidents must be reported to an inspector (see exhibit C).
- Occupational diseases must be reported to the chief inspector.
- Wide powers of inspection, entry, enquiry and seizure are conferred on inspectors.
- A wide range of acts of omission and commission are declared offences and can incur criminal penalties.

19.2.3.2 Health and safety representatives and committees

(See exhibit B for the functions of health and safety representatives, and exhibit C for the functions of health and safety committees.) An employer must provide the agreed-upon facilities, assistance and training that the health and safety representative reasonably requires for the performance of his/her functions. A health and safety representative shall not incur any civil liability by reason of the fact only that he/she failed to do anything which he/she may do or is required to do in terms of the Act.

19.2.3.3 Reporting duties

In the event of an incident in which a person died, or was injured to such an extent that he/she is likely to die, or suffered the loss of a limb or part of a limb, no person may, without the consent of an inspector, disturb the site at which the incident occurred or remove any article or substance involved in the incident. This provision, as well as the provisions relating to the reporting of incidents (exhibit D) do not apply in respect of a traffic accident on a public road, an incident occurring in a private household (provided that the householder reports the incident to the South African Police), or an aviation accident.

Exhibit B

Functions of health and safety representatives

A health and safety representative may perform the following functions in respect of the workplace or section of the workplace for which he/she has been designated:

- review the effectiveness of health and safety measures;
- identify potential hazards and potential major incidents at the workplace;
- in collaboration with his/her employer, examine the causes of incidents at the workplace;
- investigate complaints by any employee relating to that employee's health or safety at work;
- make representations to the employer or a health and safety committee on matters arising from his/her performance of the preceding functions;
- make representations to the employer on general matters affecting the health or safety of the employees at the workplace;
- inspect the workplace with a view to the health and safety of employees, at such intervals as may be agreed upon with the employer;
- participate in consultations with inspectors at the workplace and accompany inspectors on inspections of the workplace;
- receive certain information from inspectors; and
- in his/her capacity as a health and safety representative attend meetings of the health and safety committee of which he/she is a member, in connection with any of the above functions.

In order to perform the above functions a health and safety representative is entitled to, in respect of the workplace or section of the workplace for which he/she has been designated:

- visit the site of an incident at all reasonable times and attend any inspection *in loco*;
- attend any investigation or formal inquiry held in terms of this Act;
- in so far as it is reasonably necessary for performing his/her functions, inspect any document which the employer is required to keep in terms of this Act;
- accompany an inspector on any inspection;
- with the approval of the employer (which approval shall not be unreasonably withheld), be accompanied by a technical adviser, on any inspection; and
- participate in any internal health or safety audit.

Exhibit C

Functions of health and safety committees

A health and safety committee:

- may make recommendations to the employer or, where the recommendations fail to resolve the matter, to an inspector, regarding health or safety matters;
- shall discuss any incident at the workplace in which any person was injured, became ill or died, and may in writing report on the incident to an inspector; and
- shall perform such other functions as may be prescribed.

Exhibit D

> **Reporting of certain incidents to an inspector**
>
> The following must be reported to an inspector: each work-related incident or incident in connection with the use of plant or machinery, in which, or in consequence of which:
> - any person dies, becomes unconscious, suffers the loss of a limb or part of a limb or is otherwise injured or becomes ill to such a degree that he/she is likely either to die or to suffer a permanent physical defect or likely to be unable for a period of at least 14 days either to work or to continue with the activity for which he/she was employed or is usually employed;
> - a major incident occurred; or
> - the health or safety of any person was endangered and where a dangerous substance was spilled, the uncontrolled release of any substance under pressure took place, machinery or any part thereof fractured or failed resulting in flying, falling or uncontrolled moving objects, or
> - machinery ran out of control.

19.3 PROMOTING AND MAINTAINING EMPLOYEE WELLNESS: A PROACTIVE AND HOLISTIC APPROACH TO THE MANAGEMENT OF HEALTH AND SAFETY

19.3.1 General

Traditionally management has not always been proactively altruistic: if it is anticipated that there is no real benefit to be derived from a particular investment of resources (in other words, to offset the outlay), the investment may well be made elsewhere. Management has thus tended to adopt a follow-the-rulebook policy in matters of health and safety.

In more recent times, however, with the spiralling costs of medical care, as well as the growing realisation that absenteeism costs a lot of money and that labour productivity must be improved, management has been considering alternatives that may yield results superior to the reactive, minimum-legalistic approach. There has thus been an increasing awareness of the direct and indirect costs that can be associated with such a negative approach. According to one expert (Human Resource Management 1993), the "direct costs of healthcare financing through medical aid have been escalating at 50 % above the CPI for several years". Santhey (1993: 14–15) indicates that medical costs rose beyond control over the period 1985–1990, with medical aid premiums having risen by 34 %. Organisations have thus begun to realise that the costs linked to maintaining their medical schemes (some estimate it at more than 7 % of their monthly wage bills) can no longer be afforded.

As Taylor (1992) points out: "If every employee takes 10 days paid sick leave per year, the cost to the company is just over 4 % of payroll." Obviously, not all absenteeism cases are related to poor physical health — some are also attitudinal.

Attitudinal problems — although the whole spectrum of human resource management activities and practices and a host of other external factors can play a role — can also, however, often be related somehow to the psychological or mental wellbeing of a person.

It has therefore become increasingly common for managers to consider the potential benefits of a system focused on proactively promoting and maintaining the mental and physical wellbeing of employees rather than dealing with health and safety problems as they occur. Such an approach has various characteristics.

19.3.2 A strategic and holistic focus

It has already been stated that a holistic approach requires that care be taken of the "whole person or employee. This means that the focus is not only on safety or on the provision of medical aid assistance but also on the acknowledgement that any person coming to work comes there as a whole person. One cannot detach the worker from the human being. It can almost be said that what needs to be taken care of proactively, is thus "body, mind and soul. This means that even the broader social and domestic dynamics of employees, such as those related to personal and family lives, must be taken into account. In this respect attention must, for instance, be paid to a well-balanced work and family life.

In addition, and linked to such a holistic approach, is the strategic focus that is required. Part of a strategic approach to managing employment relationships will be the need for functional strategies (see chapter 6). One particular substrategy relates to drawing up some kind of organisational employee wellness strategy, plan and programme. A policy document (based on the strategy) should therefore ideally be drawn up, spelling out at least what the organisation's philosophy is in respect of promoting and maintaining the physical, mental and social wellbeing of employees. Formulating such a strategy and policy should obviously be developed as part of an inclusive process in which all the stakeholders are involved and take ownership. The plan should contain a vision and mission statement, some general principles, as well as specific objectives in respect of employee wellness.

19.3.3 Towards employee wellness: Specific issues in proactive, holistic health and safety management

The old adage that prevention is better than cure can be taken one step further in the context of employee wellness: it has been proven that not only is prevention better than cure, it is also cheaper than cure (Jensen 1987: 4). A preventative approach entails a number of factors to be incorporated in the strategies, policies and action plans or programmes.

19.3.3.1 Ergonomics and workplace design

As explained in chapters 3 and 7, ergonomics have to do with matching the physical work environment to the worker. If the work environment is ergonomically satisfactory, it will enhance the general state of health and safety as well. Hattingh (1992: 55) puts it as follows: "The purpose of ergonomics is to ensure that a person's abilities are utilized efficiently and that the equipment being used will not endanger his health or safety . . . if the job is ergonomically satisfactory, then the worker will work and apply safety measures." Care should thus be taken right from the outset at the point of workplace design — including the design of buildings and infrastructure (see exhibit E).

Exhibit E

Sick-building syndrome in South Africa*

In 1992 an opinion survey conducted in South Africa under the auspices of the American organisation, Healthy Buildings International, showed that South African employers cannot afford to be complacent about the "sick-building syndrome".

The researchers visited 800 office buildings and interviewed 500 office workers from Johannesburg and Cape Town. Of those interviewed, 66 % were of the opinion that there was scope for improving their office environments. More than 80 % were dissatisfied with the temperature control in their offices and would have preferred to control it themselves. Sixty-five per cent indicated that they regularly stayed away from work to recover from symptoms that can be related to sick-building-syndrome. The symptoms most commonly experienced by these people included fatigue or tardiness (42 %), listlessness (26 %), headache (39 %), itchy and tired eyes (26 %), dry eyes (22 %), runny nose (22 %) and dry throat (24 %). According to the Director of Healthy Buildings International, 75 % of these sick-building-syndrome symptoms in South African office buildings can be ascribed to polluted air, poor ventilation, and insufficient filter-systems in air conditioners. The research showed that almost 50 % of the office buildings had filters that were dirty and contaminated.

*Source: Erwee 1993

In 1989 research conducted in the USA indicated that 30 % of all buildings in America suffer from what is known as the *sick-building syndrome* (Erwee 1993). In 1982 the World Health Organisation officially accepted this concept which they define as *a building in which a significant percentage of workers show symptoms such as headaches, fatigue and eye, nose and throat irritations.*

19.3.3.2 Health screening and safety auditing

Traditionally health screening was often viewed as a perk earmarked for senior management and especially executive employees. This situation is, however, gradually changing, with some organisations offering such a service to all levels of employees. Health screening or assessment tests are basically medical investigations that do not arise from an employee's request to be assessed with regard to a specific health-related complaint. It is a proactive intervention to make an early identification of any diseases from which an employee may be suffering and to diagnose an employee's general state of health.

By conducting such assessments, health-related problems can be detected at early stages and a health status baseline can be developed; from this a programme of lifestyle improvement can be designed. Comprehensive health screening interventions may furthermore go beyond assessing concrete health measures (such as coronary heart disease, respiratory disease, blood pressure, cholesterol levels, etc). Aspects such as habits, knowledge and attitudes may also be screened in such comprehensive health screening interventions. Other tests may include stress-level tests, hearing and vision tests, urine tests, blood tests and fitness tests. Nutritional assessments can also be conducted to collect information on aspects such as food intake and eating patterns to detect how healthy an employee's lifestyle is. Determining the nutritional status of employees should be an important component of holistic health assessment interventions in South African organisations.

Safety audits, on the other hand, are aimed at establishing the quality of an organisation's safety policies, programmes, procedures and practices. This may include conducting safety attitude surveys to determine the extent to which workers are sensitive and knowledgeable about a safety-driven environment.

These assessments and audits are necessary to identify and detect timeously potential threats to the establishment of an environment conducive to employee wellness. These evaluations therefore have to be conducted on a regular basis.

19.3.3.3 Sensitisation and education

If an organisation wishes to establish a work environment of employee wellness, it is essential to launch aggressive campaigns to promote the philosophy that employee health, safety and general wellbeing are important and beneficial to both the employee and the organisation.

This begins with a process of awareness creation by means of methods such as posters, leaflets, talks, competitions, videos, demonstrations, or advertisements in internal/in-company newspapers. The idea is, however, not only to sensitise employees or to create an awareness. At the end of the day, the efforts to promote such an environment require employees to be proactive and to do something about their own health and safety. The idea is to import information to explain the importance of health and safety and to persuade employees to become more serious about these aspects in their day-to-day lives and in the workplace. Such efforts should thus include workshops where employees can learn from others (co-employees preferably) how to go about being more safety conscious and leading a more healthy lifestyle. An important component of a more healthy lifestyle is looking after fitness and relaxation.

19.3.3.4 Fitness programmes and recreation facilities

Research has shown that proper physical exercise and general fitness can not only enhance a person's quality of life but also prolong it. Promoting exercise and the improvement of the fitness of employees is therefore an important component of a holistic, proactive approach to the establishment of employee wellness. Being fit is important for the healthy functioning of the cardiovascular system, the endocrine system, as well as the musculoskeletal system. It helps to control weight and to reduce stress, thereby making a positive contribution to a person's general feeling of wellbeing — and thus to his/her state of mental health. Fit employees are generally regarded as being more energetic and as better workers. Such employees will usually be happier and more productive and absenteeism will, in all likelihood, decrease.

There are various ways of promoting exercise and fitness. Sport as a recreational activity often forms part of the lifestyle of fit people. As Jensen (1987: 58) points out: "Many people get their exercise from participating in sports, so recreational activities can form an important component of a complete wellness system . . . Sports can be an effective release valve for stress that originates with the individual or the organization."

Organised recreational activities like sports events can have the additional benefit of enhancing the social dimension of the work environment. Some informal gatherings lead to constructive interaction and communication which can create a sense of togetherness and team spirit among employees.

Improving physical fitness through organised recreation and sports events (like soccer, cricket, tennis, golf, etc) can thus improve morale and cooperation among employees. Apart from team sports, there are also outdoor activities like hiking, backpacking, sightseeing and fishing and cultural activities like going to art and musical festivals. Obviously not all of these contribute positively to physical fitness, but they do have the potential to act as stress relief valves. Exercise can take various forms, such as gymnasium work, aerobics, jogging, cycling, squash, swimming, tennis, walking, etc.

It is up to the management of an organisation to decide what premium they put on the physical fitness of their employees. If fitness is seen as beneficial, free fitness assessments may be offered and it may be decided to provide recreation and exercising facilities on the organisation's own premises.

19.3.3.5 Work and family life interactions

Research has shown that conflicts between family and working life are related to aspects such as increased health risks for parents, poor morale, depression, reduced life satisfaction, absenteeism, poorer work performance and decreased productivity (Covin & Brush 1993).

Work–family conflict is becoming an increasingly important issue within the context of human resource management. Because our workforces are becoming more and more diverse, with the female/male ratio increasing and with an increasing number of two-career couples, the chances of employing individuals who experience job–family conflict are greater. This phenomenon is, however, not limited to female employees. Any employee who experiences the dual pressure of having to comply with the competing requirements and expectations of work and family life may suffer from the conflict.

Various options are available to organisations to prevent job–family conflict levels which are so high that they impact adversely on employee mind-sets and on performance and productivity. These range from providing child and elder (parent) care facilities, to more flexibility in terms of time, working place and leave, and the involvement of spouses and children in certain recreational, fitness and other social activities and facilities of the organisation. An organisation may even, as part of their management development initiatives for instance, occasionally involve the spouse of the trainee in the development programme. Part of the performance incentive scheme of an organisation may be to award "family breakaways" for high achievers. Some refer to these efforts holistically as work-life programmes (Martinez 1993).

It seems that one of the most popular and feasible options is *flexibility*. This may include different possibilities like workschedule adaptations, flexitime, job sharing, flexiplace and telecommuting. Such arrangements may provide employees with the necessary scope and flexibility to attend to family-related issues like caring for sick children or attending school activities like sport (such as an athletics meeting or a rugby or soccer match).

An increasingly important aspect is the need for employers to show concern about childcare (Bryant 1990). Options in this area are also quite diverse. One option is that of providing *resource and referral services*. An official is appointed or an agency is contracted to provide employees with consultation on childcare and to make lists available regarding childcare options. The employer may even establish an on-site daycare facility or it may purchase slots in existing community facilities which are then reserved for the children of the organisation's employees. Other options are to enter into some joint venture with other nearby organisations or to appoint an official of the organisation to organise and supervise a daycare network of caregivers in the neighbourhood.

Irrespective of the way in which organisations go about dealing with potential work-family conflict it is essential that they should be fully aware of the importance and potential value of this aspect of human resource management. As the human resource director of one company points out (Martinez 1993: 38): "When companies are willing to recognize that blood is thicker than water, it shows employees that their employer really cares about them — and that galvanizes loyalty."

19.3.3.6 *Nutrition programmes*

An essential component of a healthy lifestyle is a good, balanced diet. Unfortunately, we live in an era in which junk food is extremely popular. Many of the health problems plaguing our society, such as cancer and cardiovascular disorders, can possibly be linked to unhealthy lifestyles and poor eating habits. It is estimated, for instance, that 35 % of the risk of developing cancer is related to diet (Wheeler 1984: 294). In addition, many people today are overweight, which can sometimes be a threat to a person's health and can also be linked to diet deficiencies and poor eating habits. Nutrition programmes are basically aimed at improving the eating habits of individuals and at encouraging them to follow a more balanced diet.

Some workplace nutrition programmes are very basic and aim simply at informing employees about the potential disadvantages and risks associated with poor nutritional habits and the potential benefits of following a good diet. This may include increasing staff awareness by means of leaflets, booklets and posters or even group sessions involving short presentations using visual aids such as videos or films. Other programmes are much more interventionary by nature and aim at preventing or even treating diet-related health problems through weight control and diet modification. Such interventions will normally form part of a holistic well-ness programme that includes fitness exercises (see above), stress control elements and antismoking programmes (see below). In such nutrition programmes which involve behaviour change, assessments will be done to identify the employee's eating habits and the quality of his/her diet. This may include physical examinations (for example weight, height, blood pressure) and screening the usual intake of fats, carbohydrates, protein, vitamins, minerals, sugar, etc. It may also include an investigation into the perceptions and attitudes of the employee regarding eating and nutrition. After determining the employee's dietary habits and particular needs, an individualised programme is worked out that may include food choice combinations, meal planning guidelines, as well as guidelines regarding meal preparation and general eating habits. These programmes will typically also be longer term, including some kind of ongoing monitoring, feedback and support systems.

Although such comprehensive interventionary workplace nutrition programmes may be very expensive and not entirely appropriate for many smaller South African organisations, larger organisations may well find them worth considering as part of their promotion of holistic employee wellness.

19.3.3.7 Smoking policies

It is common knowledge today that smoking causes health problems. These problems can basically be categorised into two groups:

1. the health implications for the employee who smokes; and
2. the health and other implications for nonsmoking employees who become passive smokers as a result of their colleagues' smoking habits.

The health risks associated with smoking are generally well known. Smoking is, for instance, a major contributing factor in chronic respiratory diseases: it is estimated, for example, that nine out of ten lung cancer deaths are attributable to smoking (Humphrey & Smith 1991: 137). In addition to this, research has shown that smoking is an important contributory factor in coronary heart disease. With regard to the latter, Jones and Kleiner (1990: 29) state that "Recent studies have shown that approximately 46 percent of total coronary disease and 54 percent of non-fatal heart attacks in women are attributed to cigarette use."

The implications of smoking for organisations are thus abundantly clear. According to American Lung Association reports, each year smokers are absent from work more than 81 million more days than nonsmokers (Jones & Kleiner 1990:

29) (bearing in mind, of course, the size of the total American workforce). Jones and Kleiner (1990: 29) make the following assertion:

> "Since the employer directly, through paying sick leave, or indirectly through lost production, pays for the cost of absenteeism, employers are becoming increasingly aware of the cost of having employees who smoke. In addition, with company paid medical plans, the cost of increased illnesses among smokers is ultimately borne by the business."

Apart from the implications for the smoker, there are also major implications for nonsmoking employees and for the organisation as a whole (as illustrated above). It follows that, if cigarette smoke is a health risk for the smoker, it must also be so for the nonsmoker. The breathed-out smoke contains the same harmful ingredients (such as carbon monoxide and recognised carcinogens — in other words, chemicals that cause cancer) to which the smoker is exposed. In addition, smoking often bothers nonsmokers, causing conflict, hostility, negative feelings, deteriorating interpersonal relations — all of which may impact negatively on workforce morale and productivity.

Smoking is thus an issue affecting health in the holistic sense: physical, mental and social wellbeing. It is therefore essential for organisations to tackle the issue of smoking in the workplace. In this regard Araujo (1996: 39) gives the following general advice:

> "There is no single approach and policy for all organisations. The general principles, however, are that a working party should be established, the issue should be raised, the workforce should be consulted and the policy must then be formulated and implemented. One should try to avoid allowing this to become a management/subordinate issue and turn it into a health matter. It is in the interest of good industrial relations to work out an agreed policy between the company, employees and their representative trade union (if any), taking into account the interests of smokers and nonsmokers, rather than merely imposing an immediate and total ban."

With regard to balancing the interests of smokers and nonsmokers, one of the areas in which smoking causes the most discomfort is that of open-plan offices. While unrestricted and uncontrolled smoking can cause a great deal of discomfort to nonsmokers in open-plan areas, it is also true that a complete ban on smoking in such areas could be counterproductive — especially if smokers leave their work station every now and again to go and smoke. A more meaningful approach would thus be to take into consideration the interests of both groups of employees.

As explained, smoking imposes certain costs on an organisation, such as those linked to absenteeism and productivity, as well as cleaning costs and medical retirements. The control of smoking in the workplace through a professional process of formulating and implementing an appropriate nonsmoking policy will enhance the healthiness or wellness of both smoking and nonsmoking employees. This, in turn, can result in major positive benefits for the organisation. It may even be possible for the organisation to negotiate an improved benefit premium deal with its medical aid company.

A case at hand . . .

Towards the formulation of a smoking policy at Unisa

In 1993 the University of South Africa engaged in the process of formulating the organisation's smoking policy. To begin with, on 27 April 1993, the University's Occupational Health Service section involved the whole workforce by means of an "Employee Survey on Smoking in the Workplace". A questionnaire was sent out to 3 500 Unisa staff members, of whom 35 % completed and returned it. Of these, 78 % indicated that smoking in the workplace was offensive or slightly bothersome. Only 22 % did not find it troublesome — probably predominantly the smokers themselves. As a result of these findings, and at the invitation of the Occupational Health and Safety Committee of Unisa, an investigatory committee was formed to do further research into the problematics and dynamics surrounding smoking in the workplace "with a view to promoting a healthier, safer and calmer working environment".

After some time, another follow-up survey was conducted during September/October 1993. The following questions were posed:

1. Which of the following methods relating to smoking in the workplace would you choose? (Select one only.)

   1.1 The University's top management should quite simply take a decision, lay down its policy and enforce it.

   1.2 A committee, such as the present one, should, through consultation and discussion with personnel, formulate a policy.

   1.3 Individual departments and sections should formulate and enforce their own individual policy.

   1.4 The status quo should be maintained — employees may smoke where and when they wish.

2. Are you at all aware of the fact that smoking in certain areas at work (for example lifts, laboratories, certain workshops, the Film Auditorium, etc) is forbidden by law?

3. Do you work in an open-plan office or do you share an office?

4. If your answer to the previous question was 'Yes', are there both smokers and non-smokers in the office?

5. If your answers to the previous questions were both 'Yes', is there central air-conditioning (ie the windows cannot be opened)?

6. If your answers to the previous three questions were 'Yes', then which of the following would you regard as the best possible solution? (Select only one.)

   6.1 Retain the status quo (ie each person smokes where and when he/she wishes).

   6.2 Forbid smoking in all open-plan or shared offices.

   6.3 Provide separate smoking areas and forbid smoking outside these areas.

   6.4 Demarcate separate smoking and nonsmoking areas within open-plan offices and only allow smoking in the area demarcated for smoking.

   6.5 Allow smoking only at specified times (smoke breaks).

   6.6 May smoke where and when they wish.

   6.7 Other alternatives (please specify).

Subsequent to this the parties (through the committee) recommended certain policy decisions which culminated in a formal smoking policy for the University.

In summary, as Araujo (1996: 40) asserts: "Because implementation of a non-smoking policy is relatively inexpensive, it represents a good investment for health promotion."

19.3.3.8 Being prepared for emergencies

Part of a proactive approach to managing employee health and safety at work is to draw up contingency plans and to have the necessary infrastructure to deal with any emergencies. There are many types of emergency situations that can arise in the work situation and that can threaten the life, safety or general wellbeing of employees. A distinction can be made between natural and man-made disasters. The former refer to situations like floods, storms, earthquakes and epidemics, while the latter include riots and serious labour unrest, bomb threats and fires.

Apart from constantly ensuring that all the necessary emergency equipment like fire appliances and equipment (fire extinguishers and fire alarms) are at the right places and in working order, it is important to ensure that adequate emergency escape routes exist and that these are easily visible and clearly marked. Although all employees should be trained to observe the housekeeping rules so that emergency situations like fire outbreaks can be prevented, emergency procedures covering all kinds of eventuality should be well established and all employees should be thoroughly drilled in how to deal with any kind of emergency situation.

The emergency infrastructure should include the necessary first-aid facilities such as a first-aid room and first-aid equipment and material. Certain employees, who are specifically designated as first-aiders, should receive special training in first aid. Often these employees are trained by outside experts — especially if the organisation does not have the necessary internal expertise. Furthermore, all employees should receive at least some very basic, introductory first-aid training.

As already mentioned, one of the most important elements of a proactive attitude towards employee safety and health is to establish adequate contingency or emergency plans and procedures that can cater for a variety of eventualities such as fires, bomb scares or explosions. Obviously, contingency plans will depend largely on the nature of the workplace. The evacuation process would, for instance, differ radically in a gold mine, an open core coal mine, a chemical factory or an Edgars or other retail store. Regardless of the exact nature of these infrastructural elements, plans and procedures, it is essential not to neglect these aspects, as they form an essential component of also proving to employees that the organisation's management values employee safety and health.

Part of any such emergency plan is to appoint a person who will be the emergency controller. This person will have the responsibility of drafting the emergency plan and organising the emergency training. In order to do this, he/she will require the following (Acutt 1992: 168–169):
- a plan of the whole site together with a floor plan of the buildings indicating all entrances and the different areas;

- the floor plan must indicate main electricity boards, hazardous substances, inflammable materials, gas cylinders, etc;
- all fire extinguishers, first-aid boxes and emergency equipment, including rescue equipment, must be indicated on this chart;
- updated lists of names, addresses and telephone numbers of all emergency personnel, senior management and local emergency services;
- an effective communication system;
- an identification system for emergency personnel;
- an emergency transport system; and
- an efficient evacuation system.

Other aspects to be catered for relate to security, an emergency command centre, the structuring and framing of rescue, fire control and first-aid teams, transport and detailed plans to protect buildings, material, plant, equipment, stock and especially the employees of the organisation.

19.3.4 Other special issues regarding health and safety in the work environment

19.3.4.1 Occupational mental health

Occupational mental health (OMH) as an applied field of clinical and abnormal psychology deals with the maladjustment or adjustment of employees in the work or organisational context (Bergh 1992: 194). This is an extremely important and very specialised topic, to the extent that it is a separate branch of Industrial Psychology as field of study. For the purposes of this chapter a brief introduction to some of the issues (and topics) which fall within the field of OMH will suffice.

The first question one may wish to ask relates to what constitutes an adjusted or maladjusted employee. In other words, what criteria are used to evaluate psychological adjustment (or maladjustment) in the work environment? In this regard there are many relevant criteria and these can be classified in many different ways. It must be emphasised, however, that a person's behaviour at work, and the meaning of that behaviour, must always be compared with certain criteria in the **context** of his/her actions (Bergh 1992: 197). Some of the general categories of criteria, within which more specific criteria can be set, include the following (Bergh 1992: 201):

- attitudes towards and observations of one's own personality (self), which include accurate observation of one's self-image, attitudes towards one's own personality (self), and an understanding of one's identity;
- growth, development and self-actualisation, where the level of development and the person's usefulness in a role are evaluated;
- integration, which refers to the individual's ability to assimilate and handle influences from the environment;
- autonomy, which implies the ability to act effectively by means of internal powers (needs, etc) without the unnecessary domination of external influences;

- the observation of reality, which implies the accurate assessment of the external environment in terms of internal psychological needs;
- interpersonal efficiency, which refers to the establishment of interpersonal relationships;
- affective conditions, which include emotional manifestations such as manic-depression, anxiety, fear, etc;
- specific pathological conditions, both physical and psychological, for instance schizophrenia, neuroses, brain syndromes, etc;
- adjustment and adaptability — in other words, the person's ability to meet the demands of the environment in terms of his/her personal capabilities.

A complex web of potential factors may separately or in various combinations influence the state of OMH of an employee either positively or negatively. Before we briefly look at these, it is important to take note of certain types of psychological work adjustment problems that may be encountered by employees in organisations.

Some psychopathological conditions relate to stress-based disorders, others to anxiety, some to personality disorders or to psychosomatic, narcotic and organic conditions, and still others to mental retardation.

Stress-related adjustment problems can, for instance, occur immediately or some time after a very traumatic experience such as a disaster, for example after an explosion in a factory or a rock slide in a mine. Emotional disorders such as fear, anger or depression may follow, which may in turn lead to poor concentration or absenteeism. On the other hand, neurotic conditions are characterised by internal emotional states such as anxiety, which can directly have a negative effect on work behaviour. As far as personality problems are concerned, it is important to note that some experts believe that general personality disorders need not affect the work personality (the work personality is the personality of a person in the work or production situation). Some people, for instance, have a negative perception of work and of their roles as employees — possibly because they were brought up in an environment where work was overemphasised to the extent that it could be equated to something akin to slavery. For some, work may arouse feelings of fear, discomfort or tenseness — for instance if they doubt their abilities or are handicapped.

Psychosomatic disorders refer to cases where physical symptoms and psychological states are closely interlinked. So, for instance, negative emotions like anger, worry and anxiety can contribute to the formation of stomach ulcers. As soon as the physical symptoms are identified, the person begins to worry all over again. Bergh (1992: 233) asserts that "*Psychosomatic problems are among the major work-related problems* encountered among managers. In severe cases these conditions can result in death, early retirement, disability, hospitalization or poor health which leads to losses for both the individual and the organisation."

Organic conditions refer to the negative emotional, intellectual and behavioural implications that brain damage can cause. When there is mental retardation due to underdeveloped intellectual functioning, behavioural problems may also arise in the workplace.

All these types of disorders may have effects that lead to problems like absenteeism, accidents, underachievement, poor productivity and staff turnover. There are also other psychological work adjustment problems such as workaholism, burnout and work alienation.

Work alienation occurs when an employee has a feeling of being detached from his/her work, which seems to have lost its meaning and value. *Workaholism*, on the other hand, is a kind of addiction to work. The person's workload does not decrease at all and there is a compulsion to work continuously. Some may suffer from these symptoms because they have an intense need to be successful, while others may do so to withdraw from unpleasant domestic situations such as an unhappy marriage relationship. *Burnout* refers to the situation where a person eventually becomes listless, ineffective, inefficient and unproductive due to a prolonged period of work overload which has negatively impacted on the physical and mental health of the employee. Such an incapacity at work can in turn lead to stress and behaviour such as an increased use of alcohol and increasing conflict with co-employees.

The potential spectrum of causes is wide, varied, complex and often interlinked. Some factors are unique to the *individual* (such as personality type, intellectual ability, needs, values, attitudes, self-image, occupational concepts and psychiatric problems such as psychotic or neurotic conditions). Sometimes the causes may form part of the *work environment* itself, for example certain managerial processes and practices (such as retrenchments or job design along the lines of Fordism and Taylorism) and physical factors (such as workload, toxic substances, working hours, temperatures, noise and physical dangers in the workplace). (Think, for example, of mines and refer to the quotation earlier in this chapter.) Other factors that may play a role in psychological work adjustment can be categorised as being *external* to the employee or the organisation. These include aspects like family life, traumatic external events such as war or major political change, ecological factors like housing and pollution and economic conditions such as a depression.

Irrespective of the actual problems or their underlying causes, it is essential for organisations to be aware of the importance of OMH. Organisations must strive continually to create a situation where the employees experience, as far as is possible, optimal states of OMH.

19.3.4.2 Stress and work

A topic that has been receiving increasing attention in the area of occupational health over the last three decades is that of work-related stress. As the world around us — and especially the world of work and business — has become increasingly subject to fast-changing forces like increased competition, the pressure for quality, innovation and an increase in the pace of doing business, the demands on employees have grown equally dramatically. This creates stress within employees, which has led some to refer to "the pressure cooker of work" (Joure, Leon, Simpson, Holley & Frye 1989: 92–95). Apart from the stress that arises from the work situation, other sources of stress may relate to personal factors such as relationships with others and the use of free time.

But what is stress?

Stress can be defined as the arousal of mind and body in response to an environmental demand (the stressors).

What is a stressor to one person may not be regarded as such by another, simply because people differ in the amounts of arousal they need to act and the amounts that they can take before the situation becomes personally distressing. Arousal patterns therefore differ from person to person. As human beings we require additional energy as soon as we have to face up to a particularly difficult and stressful situation (the stressor). Thus, as we think of all the things that we have to do (as we worry and plan) energy is released; sometimes, however, it becomes bound within us, building up in areas of the body, for example the neck and shoulders, and then we develop tension headaches and tensed shoulders. This can become even worse, leading to physical problems like ulcers, a lowering of the immune system and even heart problems. It is therefore essential to develop ways of managing stress. Smit and Venter (1996) propose a process approach to the management of stress. The first step is to identify the sources or causes of the stress by tracing whether any symptoms of stress are present. Exhibit F lists various symptoms of stress that one can use as a checklist to determine whether one suffers from stress.

Exhibit F

Symptoms of stress*	
Mental symptoms	*Physical symptoms*
● Feeling wound-up; anxious	● Headaches
● Worry a lot	● Spastic colon
● Irritability	● Indigestion
● Easily frustrated	● Ulcers
● Aggressive outbursts	● High blood pressure
● Poor concentration	● Palpitations
● Forgetfulness	● Hyperventilation
● Depression	● Asthma
● Lack of fun in life	● Stiff, sore muscles
● Poor motivation	● Trouble with sleeping
● Want to be alone always	● Change in appetite
● Poor self-esteem	● Change in sexual drive
● Feel out of control	● Decreased immunity (easily ill)
Other symptoms	
● Increased smoking	
● Increased alcohol intake to try to cope better	
● Increased intake of medication to try to relieve stress-related symptoms	

*Source: Smit & Venter 1996: 11

The next step is to assess whether the stress justifies the end result and whether one's health can sustain the stress. If it justifies the end result and one can sustain it, there is no need to change anything. If the response to either of these two is negative, then one needs to do something about it by working on eliminating the sources, and doing things deliberately to relieve the symptoms. This may include relaxation techniques, hobbies, shrugging off things that you cannot change or cope with, regular exercise, getting sufficient sleep and possibly eliciting help from outside, for example a psychologist, occupational therapist or an addiction clinic (in the case of substance dependence).

One aspect that has been proven to be closely related to stressfulness is the personality type of an individual. *Type A* and *Type B* personalities are relevant in this regard. Type A people have an intense drive to achieve, an eagerness to compete, the need to accelerate the execution of all physical and mental activities, an extraordinary mental and physical alertness, a persistent need for recognition and are constantly involved in many things with deadlines. These people are prone to higher stress levels than Type B people who are basically the opposite.

Although stress management remains, at the end of the day, the responsibility of each individual employee, it is important for organisations to provide the necessary assistance and support. In this regard research undertaken by an American life insurance company (Milkovich & Boudreau 1994: 727–729) led to the ten recommendations listed in exhibit G.

19.3.4.3 Employee assistance

Employee assistance (EA) essentially concerns social services to which organisations can refer troubled employees who seek professional treatment for varying kinds of personal problems with which they cannot cope and which may have a potentially negative impact on their performance and personal lives. Employee assistance (or employee assistance programmes (EAPs)), as a health management intervention, has historical links with alcoholism rehabilitation. The scope of such programmes is, however, much broader nowadays, covering treatment for all sorts of substance dependence, abuse or addiction, as well as therapy and counselling for personal problems such as marital problems, stress and depression, and financial problems (Muller 1988). Alcohol abuse, however, remains one of the major problem areas in South Africa, as can be gathered from exhibit H.

Substance abuse and dependence can have ripple effects that impact negatively on various areas of people's lives. Alcoholism, for instance, causes a person to neglect his/her diet and in this way the nutritional value of food intake deteriorates, which can in turn destroy stress-coping skills, leading to more drinking. This eventually results in more stress and a deterioration of cognitive processes, emotional problems like depression, lack of motivation and aggression, a deterioration in personal affairs (for example family life), poor work performance and absence from work. Finally serious physical health problems and even death can result. It

Exhibit G

Recommendations on handling workplace stress*

1. **Allow employees to talk freely with one another.** "Employees thrive in an atmosphere where they can consult with colleagues about work issues and defuse stress with humour."

2. **Reduce personal conflicts on the job.** Employers should resolve conflicts through "open communications, negotiations, and respect". Two basics: "Treat employees fairly." "Clearly define job expectations."

3. **Give employees adequate control in how they do their jobs.** "Workers take greater pride . . . are more productive and better able to deal with stress if they have some control and flexibility" in how they do their jobs.

4. **Ensure adequate staffing and expense budgets.** "Many organizations are facing the economic reality of smaller budgets", but "a new project may not be worth taking on if staffing and funding are inadequate".

5. **Talk openly with employees.** "Management should keep employees informed about bad news as well as good news" and should "give employees opportunities to air their concerns to management".

6. **Support employees' efforts.** By regularly asking employees how their work is going, listening to them, and addressing issues that are raised, "stress levels are significantly reduced".

7. **Provide competitive personal and vacation benefits.** "Workers who have time to relax and recharge after working hard are less likely to develop stress-related illnesses."

8. **Maintain current levels of employee benefits.** Cuts in pension, health insurance, vacation benefits and sick leave invite employee stress. Employers must weigh potential savings with the high costs of employee burnout.

9. **Reduce the amount of red tape for employees.** "Employers can lower burnout rates if they ensure that employees' time is not wasted on unnecessary paperwork and procedures."

10. **Recognise and reward employees.** "A pat on the back, a public word of praise, a raise or a bonus" for accomplishments and contributions can pay "big dividends in higher employee morale and productivity."

*Source: Milkovich & Boudreau 1994: 728

is generally widely recognised that alcoholism is a disease that needs professional treatment rather than condemnation.

Employee assistance programmes specifically include alcoholism rehabilitation interventions. Aspects like early symptom identification systems should also be included. This will primarily entail the studying of relevant behavioural patterns (such as coming late and absenteeism) and the monitoring of work performance levels. An even more proactive approach to working towards employee wellness would be the inclusion in EA programmes of elements that are aimed at the not-so-troubled employees — those who abuse chemical substances such as alcohol from time to time but not to the extent that it overtly impacts negatively on work behaviour and performance. If such people are not helped in time, the situation may well become more serious. In this regard educational interventions run by

Exhibit H

Alcohol and drugs exact their grim toll*

- There are more than one million alcoholics in South Africa — or 5,8 percent of people older than 15
- The problems of each one affect the lives of up to 15 other people and incur hidden costs such as child neglect and abuse, unemployment and crime.
- Alcoholism costs the South African economy more than R5-billion a year in job accidents, lost productivity, damage to health, crime, and family breakdown and disintegration.
- It is a contributory factor in 11,8 percent of collisions on our roads, 42 percent of drivers and 53 percent of pedestrians involved in accidents at night are over the legal limit.
- Half of all adult drownings and 30 percent of general injuries have been found to be alcohol related. Alcohol abuse by a pregnant woman seriously damages the unborn child.
- Eighty percent of cases dealt with by the SA National Council on Alcohol and Drug Dependence (Sanca) clinics are for alcohol problems. The other 20 percent are for other drugs, although this figure is higher in more affluent areas."

Sunday Times, 24 March 1994: 10

experts from inside or outside the organisation can be very helpful. In general, health awareness campaigns should also include substance abuse warnings.

Although EA programmes may require substantial amounts of money, this should be viewed as an investment with longer-term returns. However, from a management point of view it is important regularly to evaluate the quality of such programmes and to undertake cost–benefit analyses.

One aspect that requires consideration is whether to opt for the *internal* or *external* models of EA programmes. The internal model involves the employment of EA professional staff in the organisation. This may be more cost-effective, but poses the problem of confidentiality — especially in the eyes of those who need to make use of the service, often causing them to shy away from using it. In the external model use is made of professionals from outside the organisation. This may be more expensive, but aspects like credibility and confidentiality may be viewed more positively. Bews and Bews (1988) also list other factors which must be considered when a choice has to be made in this regard, namely: accessibility; availability of expertise; acceptance by employees, unions and management; comprehensiveness of the services; and ease of monitoring the programmes.

Regardless of which model is chosen, it is important — if one wants to create a caring environment — to provide one or another form of employee assistance. Management should make a policy decision in this regard and when the policy is formulated it is important to acknowledge that, at the end of the day, employees must also be willing to help themselves.

19.3.4.4 Occupational diseases, hazards, accidents and injuries

In practice it is often very difficult to distinguish between so-called occupational diseases and non-occupational diseases. This is because the causal relationships between any person's ill health and hazards in his/her work or private life are very complex and interconnected. The World Health Organisation, however, provides a clear definition of an occupational disease (Mets 1992: 91):

"Occupational diseases are defined as diseases which are solely or principally caused by factors which are peculiar to the working environment and are therefore 'arising out and during work', with the qualification that the actual manifestation, ie the disease, may well arise 'after work'."

In the Compensation for Occupational Injuries and Diseases Act 130 of 1993 (COIDA) it is stated that "an occupational disease is any disease mentioned in the first column of Schedule 3 of the Act, arising out of and contracted in the course of an employee's employment" (Mischke & Garbers 1994: 88). Schedule 3 of the Act lists the relevant diseases in the first column and the work which gives rise to those diseases in the second column. It is specifically stated that, if a worker has performed any work involving the handling of or exposure to any of the listed substances in use in the workplace, and he/she contracts the corresponding occupational disease, it is presumed that the disease arose out of and in the course of that workers' employment — unless the contrary is proved.

Various occupational diseases can be identified, such as anthrax, occupational dermatitis, occupational asthma, tuberculosis of the lung, and hearing impairment. What is thus more important is to focus on the *occupational hazards* that may lead to occupational diseases.

Occupational hazards can cause harmful effects to employees in various ways, such as when certain hazardous substances are inhaled, swallowed or even absorbed through the skin. One can distinguish between various categories of occupational hazards, including chemical, mechanical, biological, physical and psychological hazards.

Chemical hazards include gases, vapours, fumes and dust. Mechanical hazards relate mainly to the overexposure of an employee to machine-related vibrations (for example turbines and pressure drills). Employees who work with animals and other people can be exposed to biological hazards such as viral, bacterial or fungal infections. Physical hazards include exposure to radiation, sound and noise, lighting, extreme temperatures and abnormal atmospheric pressures. Psychological hazards relate directly to OMH, and may include aspects like the risks and dangers involved in a particular job and the way in which work is designed (meaningfulness versus alienation, work overload and other factors that can cause work stress).

Accidents and injuries

Workplace safety revolves around creating a work environment in which the chances for and effects of accidents and injuries are minimised and personal security maximised. Hattingh (1992: 33) defines an accident as follows:

An accident may be defined as a sudden, uncontrollable, unplanned, undesirable happening which disrupts the normal functions of persons and causes or has the potential to produce or cause unintended injury, death or property damage and/or business interruption.

There are different types of accidents and injuries. Injuries that result from accidents occurring during the course of work can be minor (requiring only some first-aid treatment) or more serious (causing temporary total disablement). In extreme cases permanent disablement that may be partial, total or fatal may occur. Accidents can be officially classified as follows (Hattingh 1992: 34–35):

- being struck by falling objects;
- caught in, on or between objects;
- stepping on, striking against or being struck by objects;
- falls from a different level (for example from a ladder);
- falls on the same level (for example slipping on a wet floor);
- electrical exposure or contact;
- strain, over-exertion or strenuous movements (pushing, pulling, picking up);
- exposure to or contact with harmful substances through inhalation, ingestion or absorption.

Accidents may be caused by various factors that revolve around *unsafe conditions* and/or *unsafe behaviour* or acts. Unsafe conditions can be caused by equipment deficiencies or inadequacies or by unsafe working environments. Unsafe behaviour and acts result from the human error factor. Factors that can play a role include employee fatigue and boredom, employees' levels of experience, as well as certain social, psychological and physiological factors. Poor eyesight or hearing may lead to accidents and so can certain attitudinal and emotional conditions. On the social side, alcohol usage is often linked to accidents and injuries. Measures to prevent unsafe acts, behaviour and conditions include:

- creating a safety infrastructure with control mechanisms and processes;
- establishing safety standards;
- planning and designing the work and workplace with safety in mind;
- installing safety committees and representatives;
- carrying out regular inspections to ensure that safety standards are adhered to;
- establishing who is accountable and responsible;
- training all employees to be safety conscious;
- ensuring that employees are aware of and alert to safety issues; and
- developing and running accident prevention programmes.

To ensure the success of accident prevention programmes management must lead by example, creating safe, healthy working environments and conditions and inculcating a culture of safe working habits and practices. This calls for management commitment (particularly in terms of resources) right from the top down to the lowest supervisory levels. It also requires the maintenance of day-to-day discipline, as well as a system of rewards and recognition for those who live by the policy of safety first.

19.3.4.5 AIDS in the workplace

People in the Western world first became aware of AIDS in the early 1980s. Although the medical profession soon realised the potential for the disease to develop into a worldwide pandemic, governments were slow to act. This inertia is generally ascribed to the fact that AIDS was seen as a problem affecting already Americanised groups such as homosexuals and drug users. However, as the disease presented itself increasingly in the heterosexual population, and the social, medical and economic implications became clear, the search for a cure gathered momentum. Slowly people came to realise that we are all, or will be, affected by the disease, whether we are infected or not and irrespective of our choice of lifestyle. Employers in particular will be confronted with difficult moral, legal and financial choices, such as:

- Should prospective employees be subjected to pre-employment testing for AIDS/HIV?
- Should AIDS/HIV employees be excluded from the organisation's medical aid fund?
- When may an infected individual be dismissed?
- What is an employer's duty towards his/her other employees?
- What is the extent of an employer's duty of confidentiality regarding the AIDS/HIV status of one of his/her employees?

These and many other difficult issues will have to be dealt with. The purpose of this discussion is not to deal with these questions in any detail, but rather to foster a greater awareness of the problems presented by this emergent pandemic. Research has shown that South African organisations are woefully ill prepared to confront the issue of AIDS/HIV in the workplace head on.

Few South African organisations have developed formal policies to deal with AIDS and are thus faced with issues such as:

- whether to develop an AIDS or General Life-Threatening disease policy, or to continue with existing corporate policies if these in practice cover the rights of employees in respect of life-threatening diseases;
- how to deal with the responses of co-employees;
- how to resolve the conflict between the right of an employee to confidentiality with the right of co-employees to be informed of a potentially dangerous situation in the workplace;

- the question whether the employer has any right to information if the employee has been informed that he/she has been infected with HIV/AIDS;
- the question whether HIV antibody testing should be a condition of employment;
- the question whether the organisation should test current employees;
- the question whether employees who test HIV positive should be allowed to continue to work or whether they should be dismissed or suspended (Bracks & Van Wyk 1994).

Acquired Immune Deficiency Syndrome (AIDS)

The general population's perception of AIDS/HIV is informed by prejudice, stigmatisation and ignorance rather than scientific fact and sober reflection. If there is any doubt about this, reflect on the following questions:

- If someone were to tell you that he/she is HIV positive, would your immediate reaction be concern about the person's wellbeing or would you immediately wonder how the person got infected and/or begin to have doubts about the person's lifestyle?
- Would you be as comfortable disclosing to someone that a near relative of yours is dying of AIDS as you would be disclosing that the relative is suffering from another terminal disease?
- Would you feel uncomfortable in the presence of a known AIDS/HIV carrier?
- Would you invite him/her home or share a meal with him/her?
- Would you be prepared to work with him/her or to share the same ablution facilities?

The social reality presented by the disease is almost as intractable as the disease itself and places a heavy burden on managements first to inform themselves and then to educate their workforces about the disease. AIDS is essentially a disease that destroys the human body's ability to defend itself against the daily onslaught from illnesses of which a healthy individual is largely unaware. Different phases of the disease can be distinguished.

A person can get infected by the virus only through an exchange of body fluids, since the virus does not survive for long in the atmosphere and does not easily transmit from an infected individual to a healthy person. The most common ways of transmission are by sexual intercourse, the indiscriminate use of used needles (as happens when drug users use the same needles to administer drugs intravenously), using infected blood for blood transfusions (rare these days but more common in the early 1980s before proper precautions were taken), or infection of the unborn fetus by the blood of an infected mother. Once the virus is inside the body, the body's immune system recognises it as a threat and this triggers a defence reaction against the virus. However, the immune system's ability to defend the body against any invasive threat is dependent upon its ability to recognise the threat and this is triggered by the so-called T-cells. Without the T-cells mustering the body's natural defence mechanisms, the body becomes defenceless against illnesses, for the simple reason that it does not realise that it has to defend itself. It is at this very core of our bodies' immune system that the AIDS virus directs its attack. The AIDS virus has the ability to penetrate the genetic core of the T-cells and to insert its own genetic material into that of the T-cell. This causes the T-cell to fail to muster the body's defence mechanisms and itself to start producing more AIDS viruses and to release them into the body. Thus ensues a great battle between the remaining healthy T-cells and the virus that can last for many years. It is during this phase that a person is described as being HIV positive and, although free of symptoms, is capable of transmitting the disease to others. It is ironic that it is the human body's ability in the initial stages of infection to fight off the virus to a position of almost stalemate that causes the disease to pose such a threat to humankind. Consider another disease — the Ebola virus — which has gripped our attention in recent years. In the case of Ebola — which is, unlike AIDS, a very contagious disease — the victim rapidly presents with symptoms and becomes debilitated. This rapid onset of debilitating symptoms makes it easy to identify and isolate infected individuals. For this reason, although Ebola is highly contagious, the potential for it to become widespread among the population at large through natural social intercourse is limited. The opposite is true of AIDS: an infected individual may remain undetected for many years during which time he/she may, unbeknown to himself/herself and others, infect others who in turn may remain undetected carriers for many years to come.

At some stage the AIDS virus gets the upper hand in its struggle with the body's T-cells, resulting in a rapid decrease in the number of T-cells present in the body.[1] This destroys the body's ability to defend itself against otherwise non-threatening diseases and the individual becomes increasingly susceptible to opportunistic illnesses such as tuberculosis, skin infections, diarrhoea, ulcerations in the mouth and certain types of rare cancer to which the person finally succumbs. These illnesses which are caused by the body's inability to defend itself against germs and viral infections (called opportunistic because they exploit the AIDS-induced inability of the human body to defend itself) are also referred to as AIDS-related complexes (ARCs).

A carrier of the AIDS virus may look healthy until an illness (which other people can generally fight off) suddenly causes them to fall fatally ill. This is due to the fact that the AIDS virus gradually disables the immune system, resulting in the infected person becoming increasingly vulnerable to almost any infection by another virus, bacterium, fungus or parasite. These opportunistic infections mainly occur in the skin, the lungs, the digestive system, the nervous system and the brain. Medical treatment for pneumonia, for example, may for a time make the symptoms less unpleasant but the AIDS infected person will die within two or three years. Evidence has shown that other infections may accelerate the HIV infection from one stage to the next by stimulating the virus to replicate and infect more cells (Bracks & Van Wyk 1994).

Symptoms at this stage include fatigue, unexplained diarrhoea lasting longer than one month, loss of more than 10 % body weight, fevers and night sweats.[2] Oral thrush or an enlarged spleen may also be present.

The final stage of the disease is what is referred to as full-blown AIDS. At this stage major life-threatening infections invade the body. The sufferers will experience various AIDS-related diseases. The types of disease will vary from patient to patient. Some will experience pneumonia caused by a parasitic *pneumocystis carinii*; others will experience a cancer affecting the skin called *kaposi sarcoma*; whilst some will experience diarrhoea, also referred to as the slim disease[3] which causes the sufferer to waste away and to become extremely thin and grossly fatigued. At this stage the patient would suffer multiple infections such as shingles, thrush, herpes and tuberculosis. Full-blown AIDS is always fatal and sufferers tend to live no longer than three or four years after having been diagnosed.

Magnitude of the problem

The number of full-blown AIDS cases in South Africa is still very low when compared to the rest of Africa. However, there can be very little doubt that HIV infection is already an established epidemic in South Africa. Most experts on the subject agree that, by the end of this decade, AIDS and HIV infection will transcend most other problems in South Africa. This is borne out by the fact that at present an estimated four million South Africans are infected with HIV or have full-blown AIDS. It is also estimated that another 1 000 people are infected with HIV every day and that an expected three million South Africans will die of AIDS over the next twenty years, if behaviour patterns do not change or an effective treatment is not developed.[4] It is clear that the disease will at some time affect many economically active people and have a profound impact on the business sector. In addition to this, most South African employees can expect a reduction in the value of their employee benefits (medical aid cover, retirement funding, etc) because of the increased financial burden that their funds will have to bear due to AIDS.

The AIDS Committee of the Actuarial Society of South Africa has developed a demographic model to project the impact of HIV and AIDS on South Africa.[5] Using this model, the projected deaths due to AIDS and other causes, as well as new HIV infections, are depicted in figure 19.1

Since 1982, when two AIDS cases were reported in South Africa, the incidence of the disease has increased alarmingly. According to some estimates, one in five adults will be infected by the year 2005, with 1 % of GNP lost due to direct health costs. If current trends continue, the prevalence of HIV infection among 20 to 24-year-old blacks will increase from 14,4 % in 1996 to 25,9 % in the year 2000.

What compounds the problem in Africa relative to the rest of the world is the fact that ours seems to be a more resistant strain of the virus than that encountered in, for instance, North America. Furthermore, in Africa there is a greater incidence of transmission of the disease through heterosexual contact and from infected mothers to their unborn children. There also seems to be some resistance to the use of condoms.

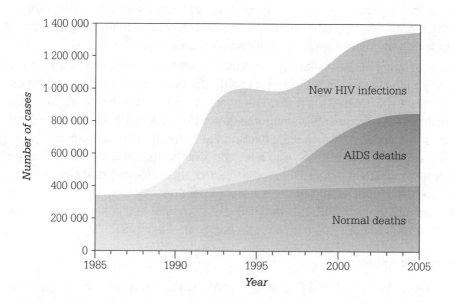

Figure 19.1
Projected new HIV infections and deaths due to AIDS and other causes
Source: Actuarial Society of South Africa AIDS Model *AIDS Analysis Africa* (1997: p 4)

Exhibit I

HIV infection rate 'explodes' among women and children*

Washington — The HIV infection rate exploded this year among women, children, and in previously spared parts of Europe and Asia, says a report by the Joint United Nations Programme on HIV/Aids (UNAids).

During 1996, UNAids says 3,1 million new cases of HIV infection were reported — 8 500 per day — bringing to 22,6 million the number of people with the virus.

Sub-Saharan Africa, which has 14 million people with HIV, 63 % of the world's total, is the hardest hit region, says the report, "HIV/Aids: The Global Epidemic".

Since the start of the epidemic, 30 million people have been infected and 6,4 million have died.

Most of the 2,7 million newly infected adults are younger than 25 years old, and nearly half of the new infections occur in women, the study says.

Some 400 000 children were infected this year, bringing the total number of children with HIV infection to 830 000.

In Nikolayev, in the Ukraine, the number of HIV-infected people who injected drugs rose from 1,7 % in January 1995 to 56,5 % 11 months later.

Meanwhile, in the Russian Federation's Kaliningrad, the number of new cases since January this year has risen from 21 to 387. In these nations, the spread of sexually transmitted disease is leading to fears of an HIV explosion, the study says.

*Sapa-AFP: *The Star*, 29 November 1996, p 10

Countering the threat of AIDS

Presently no cure or vaccination has been developed for AIDS. The most promising treatment regime so far is a cocktail of drugs that attacks the virus on multiple fronts. Experimentation with this approach was first made public in 1996 and holds out the promise that, although it is not a cure, it can arrest the increase of the virus in the body, thereby raising the T-cell count to acceptable levels. This treatment changes the status of the disease from being fatal to being a chronic disease. However, at present this treatment costs something like $50 000 per patient per year, which puts it out of reach of all but the very rich. Given the absence of a cure or a vaccination or affordable medication to arrest the fatal progression of the disease, as well as the nature of the disease and the lack of understanding and knowledge about it among the general population, educating people about the disease is, in the absence of a medical breakthrough, the best way of containing it. Since the major cause of transmission of the disease is through voluntary conduct, behaviour modification on a large scale, if this could be achieved, would be very efficient in reducing the threat of AIDS. For example, abstaining from casual sex or taking precautions when engaging in sexual encounters (by insisting on the use of a condom) or by distributing free needles to drug users or assisting drug users to rehabilitate, could go a long way in countering the spread of the disease. In this employers can play an important role by sponsoring AIDS awareness programmes, by training employees how to avoid being infected and by emphasising the low risk of contracting the disease from a co-worker. Resources expended in this manner would be justified not only by altruistic motives, but, given the speed with which the disease spreads, enlightened employers could also save themselves huge amounts in increased medical aid contributions and the costs associated with replacing experienced employees. It should be remembered that the people most at risk are those who are in the most productive phase of their lives.

South African organisations' reaction to the problem

A survey (Bracks & Van Wyk 1994) conducted in 1994 among South African organisations regarding their AIDS policies and practices found that the majority of organisations have not prepared themselves adequately to deal with the issues raised by the spread of AIDS (see exhibit J). The researchers concluded their report with the following two interesting observations. Firstly, although AIDS will probably affect most organisations and although most of the larger organisations have taken steps to protect their employees against discrimination by the implementation of appropriate policies, research has shown that the majority of the organisations have generally tended not to implement such policies. Secondly, despite the vigour and tenacity with which the unions criticised racial discrimination, they do not seem to make any effort to voice their opposition to discrimination based on AIDS. The reason for this can be assumed to be the prejudices of their own members against infected people, or the fact that AIDS has not yet taken on proportions significant enough to justify union attention.

Exhibit J

South African organisations and AIDS/HIV*

Summary of research results

- Despite the fact that HIV/AIDS is becoming an established epidemic in South Africa, of 166 organisations surveyed, the results indicate that at present the majority of employers do not have AIDS policies protecting the rights of employees. This is despite the emphasis of the significance of the disease in the media, namely newspapers and television, and by various support centres concerned with addressing the problem.

- The results also indicate that a significant majority of the employers would take discriminating or illegal actions against the HIV-infected employee, which is not justified by the nature of the syndrome. A total of 38,4 % of the organisations would inform persons other than those within the management of the organisation and by disseminating such information to them, believe that they are making the work-place safer.

- A total of 66,5 % of the respondents have a policy for assessing applicants to determine whether they are disabled or not, whereas only 36,5 % have policies relating to HIV/AIDS-infected employees. Some 40,6 % of the respondents would employ someone with a life-threatening disease other than AIDS, whereas only 16 % of the organisations would employ someone who has AIDS with no special conditions.

- A very small percentage of the organisations, 16 %, have developed a policy for testing current employees. Of those who carry out tests, the majority, 70 %, assume that testing coincides with pre- and post-counsel testing, and require the informed consent of the employee being tested. The minority of respondents who test for AIDS use the results as a discriminatory practice. Only 1,3 % would fire a person who tested HIV-positive. The majority, 48,4 %, would allow the employee time off for treatment and counselling and 31,2 % would attempt to be accommodating in the employee's work, including holding the position open for an agreed period or until the employee is able to resume work.

- Because many organisations have compulsory benefit schemes in which membership is contingent on negative HIV test results, a very high degree of discrimination would be expected. However, 63,7 % of the respondents' benefit schemes do not restrict or exclude cover for HIV/AIDS-infected employees, and only 30,6 % do have policies which exclude HIV/AIDS-infected employees.

- The results also indicate that 55 % of employers would provide for their employees if they were not adequately covered by corporate benefits. Most employers are more inclined to accommodate present employees who become infected than in the case of job applicants.

- There is some support for the notion that unions have not addressed the issue of AIDS discrimination in the same manner as they have done racial discrimination. This is further supported by the fact that to date only one agreement relating to AIDS has been signed — between the South African Chamber of Mines and the National Union of Mineworkers.

- An analysis of the written policies of organisations has indicated that while there is no uniformity in their format, the majority address issues such as testing, discrimination by co-workers, confidentiality and a safer working place. All attempted to eliminate any form of discrimination against HIV/AIDS-infected employees.

*Source: Bracks & Van Wyk 1994

As the disease spreads, the probability is increasing that employers will sooner or later be confronted with HIV infected and AIDS sufferers in employment. The economic impact of the disease in organisations will be manifested in a loss of productivity as a result of employees absenting themselves from work for treatment, and later dying. This would also result in an increase in the cost of medical aid and pension schemes. Employees could also be discriminated against in the group life policies of organisations because they suffer from HIV/AIDS.

Employers seem to avoid the responsibility of educating employees about the disease, despite the fact that this disease will infiltrate the work situation sooner or later. The impression gained is that many of the larger South African organisations have not adopted an AIDS policy because they feel that if they do create a policy it may raise the concern that there could be an AIDS problem within the organisation.

AIDS, unlike other general life-threatening diseases, raises a number of ethical problems for managers. Issues which have to be considered by employers relate to mandatory testing for prospective employees at recruitment and the responses of fellow employees. The latter issue could raise serious concerns when having to work with employees infected with AIDS.

Discrimination against AIDS/HIV sufferers

Despite the steps being taken to protect HIV/AIDS infected employees, research literature has shown that, in the face of pressure from co-workers, a third of the organisations will discriminate against the infected employee. The problem is exacerbated by the fact that no distinction is drawn between those employees who have tested HIV positive and those who have AIDS (full-blown). The difference is based on the fact that the former could still be alive and well for the next five to fifteen years. Discrimination against infected employees, whether it be HIV or AIDS, places them at a disadvantage; the significance of this has been highlighted in various articles written on the subject, both in South Africa and America.

Discrimination against employees who are HIV/AIDS infected can take on various forms, for example (Bracks & Van Wyk 1994):

- compulsory medical screening at pre-employment level and of employees at any stage of employment;
- denial of employment to potential employees who admit to being HIV positive;
- disciplining of employees who inform their employers that they have AIDS;
- demotion or transfer of employees who test HIV positive or who admit to having AIDS;
- workers forcing the employer to have an employee tested because he/she is suspected of suffering from AIDS;
- the testing of foreigners who enter the country to seek employment;
- suspension with salary of HIV infected employees;
- variation of the conditions of employment (for example, changing the area of work);
- Dismissal

Except in a few situations in which discrimination may be justified (eg an HIV positive health care worker), there can be no justification for discrimination in the workplace. Many eminent writers on the subject have condemned the practice of discrimination in the workplace because, at present, medical consensus is that HIV (the human immunodeficiency virus) is transmissible essentially through body fluids — that is, blood or semen. The prime risk is for the virus to be transmitted from an HIV-positive person to another person during either homosexual or heterosexual intercourse, or when an abrasion or excoriation occurs with resultant exposure of capillaries or cells, involving also the factor of mucosal spread. Blood transfusions pose a threat if the blood or equipment used for the transfusion is contaminated. Based on the above, none of the ways in which infection takes place is directly connected with most work situations as such, or with the social and occupational contact which employees ordinarily have with each other in the workplace. In exceptional cases there may be a relatively minor risk of infection in the work situation. One such situation is in the operating theatre if a doctor fails to take the necessary precautions by wearing surgical gloves, and accidentally cuts himself with a scalpel while operating on an HIV-infected individual. Consequently, the spread of HIV at the workplace is very unlikely. This, however, will not guarantee an AIDS-free workplace, since, judging from the statistics, one or more employees will be infected sooner or later, forcing management to face the question of how to deal with HIV-positive employees.

Despite the increased awareness of and publicity about the disease through the media, many employers have continued to adopt hostile and discriminatory attitudes to HIV-positive employees in a variety of ways, either by insisting that they undergo testing, dismissing them or, in reaction to pressure from co-workers, requesting them to resign. Employers still do not distinguish between employees who have full-blown AIDS and those who are HIV positive. Discrimination against the latter is always prejudicial, since these employees could live long, productive lives and continue to perform their duties as effectively as any other employees suffering from other viral infections such as hepatitis B. Discrimination against those who test HIV positive could have a tremendous effect on the economy and society, both directly and indirectly, and could lead to the loss of skilled labour, which is scarce in our country.

Dismissal of employees who have AIDS/are HIV positive*

Although dismissal will be dealt with elaborately in the last chapter, a brief explanation of those aspects relevant to AIDS/HIV is essential here. All employees have the right not to be unfairly dismissed (s 185 of the Labour Relations Act of 1995). This principle does not allow for any exceptions and is equally applicable to the individual who has AIDS or who is HIV positive. As will be seen in chapter 24, one may only terminate the services of an employee if it can be justified on the basis of

*It is recommended that this section be read in conjunction with chapter 24.

A case at hand . . .

Discrimination at Dan Air*

In an English case, an organisation named Dan Air had as its policy the exclusion of males from cabin staff posts. Dan Air defended this policy by arguing that:

- AIDS mainly affects homosexuals;
- a large number of males (approximately 30 %) were attracted to cabin staff work and were homosexual;
- cabin staff are sexually promiscuous;
- HIV is principally transmitted through sexual intercourse;
- HIV could be transmitted by blood and saliva and could be transmitted to and from passengers when staff cut themselves at work or if passengers required artificial resuscitation.

Members of the Equal Opportunities Commission commented on the issue raised in Dan Air's policy by stating that basic rules of hygiene and common sense were sufficient to prevent any contamination of food and that there had not been any reports proving that the disease was spread by food or those who were responsible for the handling of food. Furthermore, there was no evidence that mouth to mouth resuscitation could result in a person being infected. The Commission therefore ruled that the claims made by Dan Air in defence of their policy were unacceptable, immoral and groundless, and that the airline was in contravention of the Sex Discrimination Act.

*Bracks & Van Wyk 1994

the employee's *conduct*, *capacity* or for reasons relating to the *operational requirements* of the organisation. Failure on the part of the employer to justify the dismissal in terms of one of these grounds will render it unfair. Furthermore, should the dismissal be regarded as discriminatory, it will amount to an "automatically unfair dismissal" in terms of section 187 of the Labour Relations Act. The same principles apply in the case of the employee who suffers from AIDS or who is HIV positive. In dismissal cases it is especially important for employers to distinguish between the case of the employee who is in the latter stages of the disease (that is, who is suffering from full-blown AIDS) and the employee who is HIV positive (that is, who is a carrier of the disease but who does not present any symptoms). In the former case dismissal may be justifiable on the basis of the person's inability to perform his/her duties (as is the case with any employee suffering from a debilitating disease rendering him/her incapable of doing his/her job). In the latter case it may be more difficult to justify the dismissal and to evade the charge of unfair discrimination, since the employee would normally then still be perfectly capable of performing his/her duties. In the following paragraphs the dismissal of infected employees on the basis of one of the three grounds that may be offered as justification is examined in greater detail.[6]

1. (Mis)conduct

This justification would in most instances not be available to the employer. The mere fact of having contracted the disease would obviously not constitute misconduct. Conceivably, an infected employee who knowingly and wilfully exposes a co-worker or customer of the employer to infection could fall under this category.

2. (In)capacity

An investigation into the employee's alleged incapacity is required: this should be done by conducting a fair hearing. During this investigation, certain factors may be taken into account, such as the experience of an employee or the type of work concerned. However, when it is evident that an employee has become incapable of doing the work properly, his/her long service record as such will be to no avail. It should also be established whether the employee's particular disability, such as poor eyesight, could create a dangerous situation for co-workers (or, for that matter, for anybody else) (Brassey, Cameron, Cheadle & Olivier 1987: 445). The fact that AIDS is communicable is irrelevant, because, according to the current knowledge of the aetiology of the disease, there is virtually no risk of communication of the disease in the work situation. What would clearly be decisive would be the degree to which the disease itself, or a secondary condition caused by it, makes the employee unfit to do the required job (which may be manifested by factors such as absenteeism, debility, lack of concentration, confusion, general unproductiveness). When the employee's incapability has indeed been proved (or admitted), alternative employment (and not dismissal) should be considered; the employer should consult with the employee in this regard (Brassey et al 1987: 446). Because the condition of a person with AIDS may deteriorate rapidly (in the last stage the body's defences collapse and bacterial and viral infections which are normally harmless become life-threatening), it would seem that the possibility of alternative employment may often not be feasible.

3. Operational reasons

Under this heading the so-called commercial rationale for dismissal may be put forward. What this justification amounts to is that the employee's continued presence in the employer's workforce frustrates the employer's legitimate objective of being in business to make a profit. A dismissal for being HIV positive may be fair, provided that it can be shown that the news of an employee's HIV-positive status is the direct and only cause of an appreciable decline in business, and all alternatives to the dismissal of the employee have been exhausted (Cameron 1992: 3). It should be cautioned, however, that the commercial rationale as a justification for dismissal is a very tenuous one and may well be found to be unfair, unless the employer has done whatever could reasonably be expected to remedy the situation, short of resorting to the dismissal of the employee. The same applies where co-workers of an infected individual refuse to work with him/her. To dismiss the infected person would most definitely be unfair, unless it is resorted to as a measure of absolute last resort.

Pre-employment testing

As justification for testing, organisations have argued that an organisation requires a healthy workforce which will be productive and not result in a high labour turnover. HIV-infected people have been seen as a high risk. This argument is irrelevant, since organisations do not test for any other life-threatening diseases in particular. Furthermore, available statistics clearly show that more and more people could become infected with the disease while being employed, making an HIV/AIDS-free work environment virtually impossible.

Another reason why pre-employment testing is unjustifiable is that the way in which the disease is identified does not clearly indicate whether a person is HIV-positive or HIV-negative when he/she is tested, first because the disease can be dormant for a long time in the person's system, and secondly because, as a result of human error, a person who is HIV negative could be diagnosed as HIV positive, thereby disqualifying the person unfairly from possible employment opportunities.

Pre-employment testing could result in serious social problems. Tests carried out on a wide scale are expensive, and thousands of people will be unemployed while they are capable of being employed. This means that all these skills (if they are skilled employees) would be lost to the economy.

Managers need to be aware of the impact of tests on employees, and should carry the responsibility of their testing policy by providing necessary support and counselling to those tested. The rejection of an employee solely because he/she tested HIV positive is unwarranted, since statistics have shown that in South Africa the period between testing positive and developing full-blown AIDS is from five to ten years. During this period those who tested HIV positive could fulfil most of their responsibilities in a position. To reject employees with HIV/AIDS has an impact not only in the workplace but also on society, since while an employee with HIV/AIDS continues to work, that person is a productive member of society and does not have to rely on the state for support. Realistically, the employee contributes to the economy and saves the state money because it will not have to make special provision for the employee.

The Labour Relations Act extends the right to fair treatment and the protection against unfair discrimination to prospective employees. This means that the rejection of a job applicant because he or she was shown to be HIV positive by the pre-employment test will amount to unfair discrimination unless the employer can show that the job in question requires a person not to be a carrier of the infection and that no reasonable precautionary measures could be taken to adjust the work content or process to accommodate the person. For instance, a medical doctor who is HIV positive may still be gainfully employed provided that he/she wears protective clothing and is prohibited from doing certain duties. It should be noted that employers may find themselves in a difficult position because by law they are required to provide employees with a safe working environment and they could furthermore be held vicariously liable should a member of the public be infected by an employee during the course of his or her duties. However, these risks should be rare in the case of HIV and should it not be reasonably possible to safeguard co-workers or members of the public due to the nature of the job, an employer will not be guilty of unfair discrimination in refusing to employ an infected job applicant.

19.4 ROLE-PLAYERS IN OCCUPATIONAL HEALTH AND SAFETY

As we have stressed throughout this chapter, the promotion and maintenance of health and safety is important for the wellbeing of the individual, for the success of organisations and for the general success of the country. Individual employees and their representatives like trade unions thus form one stakeholder group, and employers (and managers as their representatives in the workplace) form another group with a vested interest in employee health and safety. The state or government is, however, also an important stakeholder in the sense that healthy and safe working environments and employees who enjoy a general state of wellbeing make up crucial building blocks of any society striving for stability and prosperity. Each of these stakeholder groups thus has a certain role to play.

The government's principal role lies in the realm of promulgating and enforcing legislation such as those Acts which were briefly discussed early on in this chapter. The general duty imposed on employers by the OHSA (section 8(1)) is to provide and maintain, as far as is reasonably practicable, a working environment that is safe and without risk to the health of employees. Furthermore, the OHSA (section 14) imposes the general duty on every employee at work to take reasonable care for the health and safety of him/herself and of other employees who stand to be affected by his/her behaviour. In general the OHSA encourages the parties (employers/ employees) to regulate and promote health and safety in the workplace themselves and to cooperate in this regard. To this end the roles and duties of safety representatives and committees are spelled out in detail in the OHSA (sections 18 and 20). The OHSA furthermore facilitates the policing of the enforcement of the Act's provisions by means of the creation of an **inspectorate**, which is part of the Department of Labour. The inspectorate is headed by a chief inspector (appointed by the Minister of Labour) who is in charge of other inspectors — all of whom are charged with the administration of the OHSA's provisions and regulations. The inspectorate has to monitor continuously compliance with the OHSA's provisions and regulations. The Department of Labour also has a chief directorate of Occupational Health and Safety. This directorate has, in addition, a number of different directors, each charged with the administration of certain delimited areas/aspects of health and safety. Each of the Department of Labour's regional and satellite offices in the country also has a deputy director responsible for matters of occupational health and safety, who is in charge of controlling inspectors who in turn have authority over the ordinary inspectors. The Act also contains provisions for investigations and inquiries that have to be conducted when accidents occur at work.

Another important role-player is NOSA (the National Occupational Safety Association), a not-for-gain incorporated association that is partially funded by the

State Accident Fund. The National Occupational Safety Association was established in 1951 as a joint venture of the then workmen's compensation commissioner and employers through their employer organisations. Its role was basically to carry out preventative occupational accident and disease work, as can be seen from its mission statement in exhibit K (Hattingh 1992: 59).

Exhibit K

NOSA's mission

Mission statement
To provide dynamic, proactive and cost effective consultative services in the fields of Loss Prevention, Occupational Safety and Health in the work environment to all industry and commerce.

Credo
Our profile
- To provide dynamic, proactive and cost effective consultative services in the fields of Occupational Safety and Health.
- To strive for excellence in customer service by motivated employees.
- To uplift our employees and ensure the continued growth of our business.

Our values
We are committed to providing:
- Quality products and services
- Outstanding customer service
- Quality in everything we do.

We believe in recognition and reward for our employees who contribute towards the organisation's stated objective of providing quality in everything we do.

Our goals
- To be the accepted authoritative consultancy in the field of Loss Prevention and Occupational Safety and Health.
- To guide, educate and train all people in the techniques of Occupational Accident and Disease Prevention.
- To continually strive for service excellence.
- To create a work environment which is conducive to encouraging employees to participate in decisions that directly affect their daily work lives.

Although the state and NOSA are important role-players, the bulk of the responsibility for promoting and maintaining health and safety at work lies with the primary role-playing parties: employers and employees.

As explained already, the OHSA spells out a number of duties and prohibitions imposed on employers. These stipulate how the employer must treat employees in order to promote health and safety at work. The *chief executive officer* of an organisation is made responsible for ensuring, as far as is reasonably practicable, that there is compliance with the employer's duties imposed by the Act. An officer who delegates responsibility, as he/she is well entitled to do, is not absolved (either that chief executive officer him/herself or the employer) from the ultimate responsibility of ensuring compliance with the duties of employers in terms of the OHSA.

Thus, although the chief executive officer may make it part of the job of lower-level line management to manage aspects of health and safety, in the eyes of the law he/she will remain responsible at the end of the day.

It is thus clearly evident how important health and safety matters in the workplace are for the government and for employers in general. Each and every manager responsible for other employees under his/her authority should thus have a key performance area dealing with aspects of health and safety promotion and maintenance. Because of the importance of this aspect, however, senior or top management will most likely also want to employ specialists to help ensure that health and safety matters are attended to in a very professional way.

Because health and safety have to do with the human dimension of organisations, it is largely the responsibility of the human resource department to initiate and finally draft and oversee, in collaboration with line management, the implementation of the organisation's health and safety policy, procedures, programmes, etc. Obviously, as stated before, this process ought ideally to be an inclusive one, involving all other role-players and stakeholders — especially all other employees (management and nonmanagement) and their representatives like trade unions.

The horizons of occupational health and safety have broadened to such an extent today, however, that in most cases it is no longer possible or feasible for one individual to be responsible for the whole spectrum of employee wellness promotion and maintenance. The need for various specialist skills has thus developed gradually over time. The overall role of the HR specialist in this regard is summarised by Sounders (1992: 63) in exhibit L.

Exhibit L

General role of HR specialists in health and safety*	
Task	*Specific activity*
• Accident investigator	To carry out investigations into all accidents and dangerous occurrences in order to establish contributory factors.
• Advocate	Establish health and safety as a priority within the organisation and secure its recognition at board level. Secure sufficient resources.
• Auditor	Carry out regular examinations of current health and safety policy, procedures, practice and programmes to ensure satisfaction.
• Leader	Know and understand the workforce and lead by example. Motivate workers and develop schemes and plans to change attitudes and behaviour.
• Planner	Plan, implement, monitor and evaluate remedial measures designed to reduce or prevent accidents from happening.
• Provider	Issue protective clothing and/or equipment. A knowledge of the legal requirements is necessary. Expert help is sought where necessary.
• Trainer	Provide on-the-job training, safe systems of working, indoctrination, workplace rules and regulations, and employee responsibilities.

*Source: Saunders (1992: 63)

As mentioned previously, various other specialist role-players may be involved in the promotion and maintenance of employee wellness in the organisation. These may include medical doctors, occupational nurses, dentists, physiotherapists, psychologists, social workers, ergonomists and safety officers.

19.5 CONCLUSION

In this chapter we have shown how comprehensive and important the field of employee wellness promotion and maintenance is. It was argued that a reactive approach to employee health and safety is no longer applicable or sufficient. What is needed is a holistic and proactive approach to promoting and maintaining the complete wellbeing of an organisation's personnel — all areas that have to be attended to professionally in order to ensure an environment where employees feel and know that they are being cared for — because they are such valuable resources.

SELF-EVALUATION QUESTIONS

1. *"Employee wellness* is something more complex and important than is realised by many South African mangers."
   Critically evaluate and discuss the above statement.
2. Write concise notes on the nature and managerial implications of the following:
   The Mine Health and Safety Act;
   The Occupational Health and Safety Act.
3. Describe the role of health and safety representatives in terms of the OHSA.
4. "Ergonomics and work design hold no implications for employee wellness."
   Do you agree? Why/why not?
5. Describe the general nature and importance of health screening and safety auditing. Explain the problems related to HIV/AIDS in this regard.
6. "Smoking is a personal issue and holds no organisational or managerial implications."
   Critically discuss the above statement.
7. Write brief notes on the nature and importance of being prepared for emergencies in organisations.
8. What does "occupational mental health" entail?
9. Discuss the complexities, interrelatedness between and challenges posed to management by the following:
   O work-related stress;
   O work alienation;
   O work and family life;
   O substance dependency such as smoking and alcohol abuse;
   O personal problems of employees.

10. Differentiate between and cite examples of occupational diseases and hazards.
11. Write brief notes on: "Workplace safety and accidents and injuries at work: meaning, nature and managerial implications."
12. How do South African organisations generally deal with the problems related to HIV/AIDS? What advice would you give to these organisations' managers in this regard? (Refer specifically to discrimination against AIDS/HIV sufferers, pre-employment testing and the dismissal of employees who have AIDS or who are HIV positive.)

ENDNOTES

1. It is this phenomenon that is used to monitor the progression of the disease and the effectiveness of drug therapy. AIDS/HIV infected individuals are regularly tested for the number of T-cells present in their blood; a marked drop in T-cells indicates that the virus is gaining the upper hand.
2. Diarrhoea and weight loss are common in AIDS sufferers due to the inability of the gastrointestinal tract to resist the disease.
3. Due to the rapid weight loss and emaciated appearance of the AIDS sufferer in the latter stages of the disease.
4. Editorial. *AIDS Analysis Africa* 1997: 2.
5. The model is available free of charge by electronic mail from awhitelo@oldmutual.com. The Actuarial Society reserves copyright on the model, but it may be distributed freely (*AIDS Analysis Africa* 1997: 4).
6. Readers who are not familiar with the South African law of dismissal are advised to read chapter 24 which deals with this topic.

BIBLIOGRAPHY

Acutt, J. 1992. Emergencies and disaster planning. In *Occupational Health*, ed AJ Kotzé, 168–169. Cape Town: Juta

Aranjo, JP. 1996. The introduction of a no-smoking policy. *People Dynamics*, 13(12), 39

Bergh, ZC. 1992. Psychological adjustment of the worker in the work environment. In *Occupational Health*, ed AJ Kotzé, 194. Cape Town: Juta

Bews, N & Bews, C. 1988. Employee assistance programes — Internal or external model? The options considered. *IPM Journal*, 7(2), 22

Bracks, R & Van Wyk, MW. 1994. *The Position of HIV/AIDS Employees in South African Companies: A Legal and Empirical Survey* (unpublished MBL research report, Graduate School of Business Leadership, UNISA)

Brase, N. 1995. How safe is safe? *People Dynamics*, 13(1), 24

Brassey, M, Cameron, E, Cheadle, H & Olivier, M. 1987. *The New Labour Law*. Kenwyn: Juta & Co, Ltd

Bryant, W. 1990. Child care options for employers. *IPM Journal*, 9(1), 17–21

Cameron, E. 1992. Comments: AIDS and HIV in employment. *Andrew Levy News*, 1(7)

Covin, TJ & Brush, CC. 1993. Attitudes toward work-family issues: The human resources professional perspective. *Review of Business*, 15(2), 25–29

Editorial: *AIDS Analysis Africa* (Southern African Edition), Dec 1996/Jan 1997, 7(4)

Erwee, C. 1993. Koors, hoofpyne en spierpyne dalk 'siek' gebou se skuld. *Beeld*, 29 Januarie, 13

Gleason, D. 1996. Fighting for survival in a shrinking market. *Financial Mail*, 4 October, 22

Hattingh, S. 1992. Occupational safety. In *Occupational Health*, ed AJ Kotzé, 55. Cape Town: Juta

Hermanus, M. 1991. Occupational health and safety: A NUM perspective. *IPM Journal*, 9(9), 17

Human Resource Management. 1993. Healthcare needs total company involvement. *Human Resource Management*, May, 27

Humphrey, J & Smith, P. 1991. *Looking after Corporate Health*. London: Pitman

Jaire, SA, Leon, JS, Simpson, DB, Holley, CH & Frye, RL. 1989. Stress: The pressure cooker of work. *Personnel Administrator*, March, 92–95

Jensen, DW. 1987. *Worksite Wellness: A New and Practical Approach to Reducing Health Care Costs*. Englewood Cliffs, NJ: Prentice-Hall Information Services

Jones, B. 1996. Poor pay keeps mine safety inspectors away. *Sunday Times*, 14 April, 6

Jones, TH & Kleiner, BH. 1990. Smoking and the work environment. *Employee Relations*, 12(6), 29

Lewis, Peter & Jeebhay, Mohamed. 1996. The Mines Health and Safety Bill 1996 — A new era for health and safety in the mining industry. *Industrial Law Journal*, 17, 429–447

Martinez, M. 1993. Family support makes business sense. *HR Magazine*, January, 38–43

Metz, JT. 1992. Occupational medicine and occupational diseases. In *Occupational Health*, ed AJ Kotzé, 91. Cape Town: Juta

Milkovich, GT & Boudreau, JW. 1994. *Human Resource Management*, Fed. Bar Ridge, Illinois: Irwin

Mischke, C & Garbers, C. 1994. *Safety at Work*. Kenwyn: Juta

Muller, J. 1988. Employee assistance programmes — A new approach to workplace productivity? *IPM Journal*, 6(12), 21

Santhey, C. 1993. Medical costs: Optimise your diagnosis. *People Dynamics*, 11(7), 14–15

Saunders, R. 1992. *Taking Care of Safety*. London: Pitman

Smit, A & Venter, E. 1996. Life in a pressure cooker. *Productivity SA*, 22(1), 10–12

Spearing, S. 1996. Mining safety: Put your fingers away. *Productivity SA* 22(3), 21

Sunday Times Supplement: Primary Health. 1994. Alcohol and drugs exact their grim toll, 1994. 24 March, 10

Taylor, G. 1992. The cost of absenteeism. *People Dynamics* 10(12), 31

Wheeler, BJ. 1984. Nutrition programs. In *Health Promotion in the Workplace*, ed PO O'Donnell & TH Ainsworth, 294. New York: John Wiley & Sons

part six

Managing Labour and Employee Relations

STUDY OBJECTIVES

After studying this chapter, you should be able to:

- write an essay that outlines the essentials of labour relations;
- differentiate between different theoretical approaches to, and perspectives of, labour and industrial relations;
- describe the nature, functioning and role of trade unions in South Africa;
- discuss the meaning and fundamental role that freedom of association and protection against victimisation play in our system of industrial relations;
- explain the different meanings and contexts in which the notion of trade union representativeness is used in the Labour Relations Act (LRA);
- list and explain the organisational rights granted to trade unions in terms of the LRA;
- explain the values and objectives that underpin the LRA;
- describe the role of NEDLAC in our system of industrial relations;
- discuss the statutory regulation of collective bargaining;
- discuss the different bodies created to facilitate dispute resolution in terms of the LRA;
- explain and compare arbitration and mediation as dispute resolution processes; and
- write an essay that outlines the most important principles of industrial action.

20.1 INTRODUCTION

From chapter 2 it ought to be quite clear how important a role the collective aspects of employment relations have played in the historical development of human resource management in South Africa. Especially during the eighties and early nineties trade unions had a tremendous impact on the way management dealt with issues related to their workforces. It is therefore essential that any person interested or involved in human resource management in South Africa be afforded the opportunity to make a study of issues related more particularly (although not exclusively) to the collective dimension of employment relations.

20.2 UNDERSTANDING THE ESSENTIALS OF LABOUR RELATIONS

Before discussing those particular aspects related to the South African system of industrial relations, it is important to clarify some of the general theoretical fundamentals underlying labour relations and collective bargaining.

20.2.1 Clarifying key concepts

Various authors use different terms and concepts when they discuss the more collective aspects of the employment relationship. Terms that are sometimes used interchangeably vary from *labour relations* and *industrial relations* to *employee relations* and even *collective bargaining*. The view taken varies, not only because of differences in the international context but also because of the fact that this topic can be analysed and discussed from many different angles. These range from the legal, economic or sociological to the organisational (managerial) or psychological.

This topic can be viewed as a separate discipline or field of study (usually referred to as *industrial relations*), and it can be studied from the point of view of various fields of study. It is essentially interdisciplinary in nature and as such borrows elements from many disciplines such as sociology, economics, law and psychology. An interdisciplinary approach allows for a coherent study of a very distinct set of phenomena in society — phenomena revolving around certain types of relationships between employer(s) (and/or their representative(s)), employee(s) (and/or their representatives) and government(s) within the context(s) of different countries, organisations and industries. As a distinct field of study it is referred to mostly as *industrial relations* and as such it has its origins in the Industrial Revolution which brought about drastic changes in the world of work and the nature of employment relationships. Nowadays there is an international trend to refer to the field of study as "employment relations", partly because in this post-industrial phase the same phenomena exist and these can also be studied in "non-industrialised" settings.

On the other hand, from a multidisciplinary perspective, it can be said that many aspects related to the field of study of industrial or employment relations can be analysed from the point of view of various academic disciplines. With specific reference to the collective dimension, the student of labour economics can, for instance, study collective bargaining between trade union and management representatives from the angle of its economic and labour market implications. Similarly, the student of psychology (most notably industrial psychology) can, for example, study the human behavioural aspects related to negotiations or conflict dynamics between representatives of labour and the employer. At the same time the sociology student (in particular the student of industrial sociology) can make a study of trade unionism and the labour movement as phenomena in society. The same applies to the student of law (focusing on justice in society) who specialises in labour law and the student of business management who studies union–

management interactions in order to better understand the best ways of dealing with trade unions to enhance the chances of organisational success.

From a multidisciplinary perspective — and specifically from the point of view of business management as a science and academic discipline — we prefer to use the concept "labour relations" when aspects (particularly those having a collective dimension) of *industrial relations* are studied with relation to the successful management of organisations.

Labour relations as a topic in management science is therefore viewed as being concerned with the relations (primarily collective but also to a lesser extent individual) between employer(s) (and/or manager(s) as the representatives of the employer) and workers (and/or their representatives such as trade unions) which develop from employment relationships and which are essentially concerned with balancing the various interests of, and regulating the levels of cooperation and conflict between, the parties involved. In all of this, the government and its relevant representatives, institutions, structures, systems and laws obviously play an important, though secondary role.

From the above it ought to be clear that it is difficult to demarcate precisely the list of issues to be studied under this heading. The reason for this is partly that there is an extremely close interrelationship between labour relations dynamics on the one hand and human resource management on the other. Reference to the definition of human resource management as a field of study, theory and practice as outlined in chapter 2 should help to clarify this intrinsic interrelationship further. In fact, it is desirable, from a management perspective, to approach these topics in a fully integrated manner. Because human resource management as well as labour relations have the employment relationship as foundation, they should be viewed as two sides of the same coin.

In this book, labour relations, as part of management, revolve more around the collective aspects of employment relations. It is, however, not exclusively concerned with issues related to labour unions or other forms of employee collectivities. The notion of 'employee relations' is specifically intended to add the dimension of one-on-one, individual relationships at work — the daily human relationships especially between superiors and subordinates which form such an important element of our working lives.

Employee relations as a topic is thus taken to refer predominantly to those aspects related to the conflict, cooperation, involvement and communication in the relationships between managers and nonmanagement employees, irrespective of the type of work or industry concerned and irrespective of the presence or absence of trade unions.

In this sense, the notion of *labour and employee relations* can be used.

Thus, although the emphasis in chapters 20 and 21 falls on aspects such as South Africa's system that regulates workers' organisational rights, dealing with trade unions, bargaining with labour representatives, handling labour-related disputes and industrial conflict, it is also concerned with issues such as handling grievances (of individuals and/or groups of employees), disciplining employees (as individuals and/or as groups of employees), involving and communicating with employees, and with other aspects that are fundamental to the enhancement of sound human relations in the workplace.

Collective bargaining forms an essential part of labour relations. Drawing on the work of Bendix (1996: 249–250), collective bargaining can quite comprehensively be described as

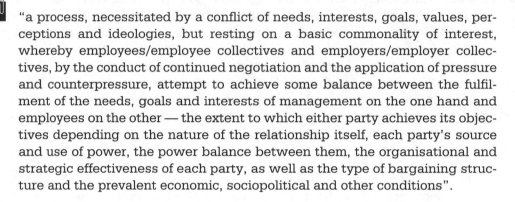

"a process, necessitated by a conflict of needs, interests, goals, values, perceptions and ideologies, but resting on a basic commonality of interest, whereby employees/employee collectives and employers/employer collectives, by the conduct of continued negotiation and the application of pressure and counterpressure, attempt to achieve some balance between the fulfilment of the needs, goals and interests of management on the one hand and employees on the other — the extent to which either party achieves its objectives depending on the nature of the relationship itself, each party's source and use of power, the power balance between them, the organisational and strategic effectiveness of each party, as well as the type of bargaining structure and the prevalent economic, sociopolitical and other conditions".

20.2.2 The employment relationship as the basis of all labour and employee relations dynamics

In chapter 1 it was stated that an employment relationship is essentially one of exchange which comes into being when a person is employed by someone else to be available to work in exchange for some form of remuneration.

Without this employment relationship, then, there can be, by definition, no labour, employee or industrial relations. It is an inherently complex relationship exhibiting a simultaneous need for cooperation between nonmanagement and management employees (due to mutual interests) and a natural state of conflicting interests, perceptions and needs.

This employment relationship is complex partly because of its multidimensional nature.

The *economic dimension* of this relationship derives from the fact that the primary parties are engaged in a relationship of exchange. The employees give their energy, knowledge, skills, abilities and productive time in return for some sort of reward which includes an economic or financial aspect. Money as the exchange medium is thus central to the employment relationship.

The *legal dimension* derives from the fact that the parties enter into a legally binding agreement and that there are specific laws and formal rules which have an official bearing on the relationship between employer and employee. Some legalities pertain to the *individual dimension* of the employment relationship — in other words, to the relationship between an individual employee and his/her employing organisation as a single legal entity. In this regard one can think of the common law (law of contract) which forms the basis of the contract of employment between an employee and employer.

On the other hand, collective labour law ensures that there can be some sort of formality in the relationship on the *collective dimension* — in other words, between labour as a group (including trade unions) with their representatives on one hand and the employer(s) (and/or their representative organisations) on the other. This would include legislation relating to collective bargaining (including dispute settlement and industrial action). The legal dimension can therefore also be referred to as the *formal dimension* of the employment relationship because it forms the basis of the formal rights and duties of the parties.

The *social dimension* gives the employment relationship its informal character; it revolves around the interaction and behaviour between people associated with the human activity of employment or work. The social or *informal dimension* thus refers essentially to human behaviour in organisations within the context of the collective dimension (in a group context which may include labour unions), and/or the individual dimension (in an individual and interpersonal context). Human beings as individuals and as group members all have certain feelings, needs, attitudes, perceptions, etc (see chapter 3), and therefore bring with them to the employment relationship the dynamics which flow from these social and psychological phenomena. This dimension can also be referred to as the soft dimension of the employment relationship.

20.2.3 The parties involved in labour relations and their roles, rights and duties

The industrial relations system in any country is made up of three parties: the two primary parties are employers (and management as their representatives) and labour (and their representatives such as trade unions); the third (secondary) party is the government in its regulatory role (as opposed to its role as an employer).

Sound industrial relations is a prerequisite for the socioeconomic stability and prosperity of any country and the government's primary concern is therefore to provide a suitable statutory framework within which the primary parties can conduct their relationship in an orderly fashion.

The *role of the government* as third party is thus to create and enforce the legal framework which can regulate the rights and duties of the two primary parties. In this sense it plays the role of master and referee in that it also has to enforce all those laws pertaining to the different dimensions of industrial relations in the country. It does, however, also play the role of servant in that it can proffer the necessary assistance to enable the primary parties to conduct their relations in a sound and mutually acceptable manner. The government can, for example, provide the parties with relevant information and guidance regarding industrial relations procedures, structures, institutions, systems, developments and the like. The government, therefore, as protector of the public interest, has a natural interest in overseeing and guiding the conduct of all the parties in order to ensure that the nature and quality of industrial relations does not have a negative impact on the country's inhabitants. The government is also an employer; in labour relations in the public sector the government therefore also becomes a primary party.

Employers (or the owners of organisations) and *management* (as their representatives) form one of the primary parties in the tripartite industrial relations system of a country. Employers or owners of organisations want their organisations to be successful; management must therefore see to it that the right things are done in the right way to ensure the achievement of the organisation's objectives (which may include the financial objective of creating surplus funds or returns on owners' investments). Management's role is traditionally to make the necessary decisions regarding the optimal utilisation of all the organisational resources.

Management's interests in labour and employee relations (and thus in collective bargaining) are therefore quite obvious. Managers have to engage in collective bargaining and related labour relations dynamics in such a way that it ultimately serves the interests of the employer or owner(s) of the organisation. Once nonmanagement employees (workers) are at work, the concerns of management employees revolve around getting the workers (as individuals or as group members) to respond in a positive way to the work situation. They seek ways to control the work process and work-related behaviour and performance so that the objectives of the owners of the organisations can be achieved. The responsibilities of management thus include:

- protecting and serving the interests of employers;
- determining objectives;
- arranging for the optimal utilisation of the organisation's resources (including the human resources);
- ensuring customer satisfaction;
- ensuring that the necessary standards of product and/or service quality are maintained; and
- ensuring that all operations of the organisation are conducted in a cost-effective and efficient manner, which will include the control of labour costs.

It is the particular duty of management to see to it that the quality of labour relations ultimately contributes to the success of the organisation. This will obviously include management's duty to respect and uphold the basic rights of workers.

With regard to the latter, the duties of management include:

- keeping workers in the service of the organisation and not dismissing them arbitrarily;
- paying workers for their work and for services rendered;
- allowing workers to join trade unions;
- negotiating with the workers and/or their representatives;
- providing safe and healthy working conditions; and
- ensuring that all aspects related to the human activity of employment are dealt with within the bounds of the law.

The other primary party in any industrial relations system consists of *the workers and their representative bodies (such as trade unions).* It is the duty of workers to hire out their labour potential (energy, skills, knowledge, abilities, etc) to perform certain work on behalf of the employer (organisation), under the control of management, and ultimately to further the interests of the employer or owners of the organisation. Workers therefore have a particular role to play, which includes duties such as:

● behaving in the required manner at work;
● performing their work as required;
● remaining obedient and loyal to the employer (and management);
● complying with reasonable rules and instructions; and
● exercising the right to associate, bargain and strike in a responsible manner.

The *rights of workers* in South Africa include the right to work, the right to strike, the right to fair remuneration and service conditions, the right to training, the right to associate and form and belong to trade unions, and the right to protection in the workplace (which includes the right to protection against health and safety hazards and to protection against unfair employment practices). The primary role of trade unions and/or other bodies which represent workers (such as staff associations) is to protect and further the rights and interests of the workers and to represent them in collective bargaining.

20.2.4 Some fundamental dynamics underlying labour relations

The way in which labour or industrial relations evolve in any particular organisation or country is dependent on a variety of factors. These include the economic situation in the country, the financial situation of organisations, the politics and power relations both in society and in organisations, the country's legal system and demographics, the characteristics of the labour force, labour market conditions, the nature of the labour movement(s), ideologies of the parties, and many more.

However, a number of aspects are pivotal in any given industrial or labour relations situation. These aspects can be said to be fundamental to the dynamics of labour and industrial relations.

As noted earlier, the natural *conflict* between the employer and employee as parties to the employment relationship forms the basic reason for labour and industrial relations dynamics. The parties have — to some extent at least — conflicting goals, needs, interests and values. The most basic conflict revolves around the economics of the exchange relationship — the economics related to the distribution and sharing of the profits and the value added by the labour process. Owners or shareholders in the private sector want to maximise profits for maximum return on their investments. To this end they have to maximise revenues and minimise costs — most notably, they have to curb labour costs and ensure maximum employee productivity. Conflict therefore develops around issues such as working conditions, remuneration and even matters relating to the organisation of work, the decision-making process and control structures. Conflict in labour relations is natural and the different solutions which are devised to deal with this and to optimise the levels of conflict thus form an essential building block of labour relations.

Another dynamic aspect underlying labour relations (referred to above) is that of *control*. Due to the conflict, both parties seek to control the situation so as to ensure that they derive maximum benefit from it for themselves. Management seeks to control the process of getting the work done in a way that will best serve the interests of the employer or owners of the organisation. Managers try to control the behaviour and performance of workers in such a way that it adds maximum value to the products and/or services rendered by the organisation. From such a perspective organisations can be viewed as structures of control. The parties try to control not only the way in which the work processes are to be performed in order to provide the necessary services and/or products, but also especially the way in which the wealth created in the process of delivering the goods/services is distributed among the various stakeholders (such as the shareholders, management and the workers).

Workers have traditionally been under the control of management as representatives of their employers. However, workers and trade unions have for some time challenged this traditional management prerogative to control and to make decisions. Through collective bargaining processes the primary parties try to conclude agreements about how to institutionalise and jointly control and regulate the conflict inherent in the employment relationship.

Along with these dynamics of conflict and control comes the issue of *power*. Employees join trade unions particularly because as individuals they lack the power to influence the employer or to control the work process or the rewards related to the work they perform. The more dependent one party is on the other, the more power the latter will possess. If an individual employee is totally dependent on one employer to earn a living (in other words, if there are no other job opportunities), the employer will wield most of the power. On the other hand, if the employer is heavily dependent on a particular group of workers because they cannot easily and speedily be replaced, the power balance will be more even. This principle is expressed in the trade union credo of united we stand, divided we fall. There is power in standing together and therefore employees form collectives such as trade unions in order to have more power to influence and control issues related to the employment relationship.

However, conflict, control and power form only one side of the labour relations equation. The other side of the equation relates to the fact that there is interdependency and an inherent *mutual interest* and *need to cooperate* between the two primary parties. Both conflict and cooperation are created simultaneously in the organisation of people and work. Management (and employers) and workers are interdependent: the latter need the former to provide the work opportunities (to be able to earn a living) and to guide and assist them in doing their work; the former needs the latter to perform the work so that the organisation can deliver the needed products/services and so that the owners can earn a satisfactory return on their investments. Workers thus want to earn money by hiring out their labour potential and management is prepared to pay and reward them for their effort, on behalf of the employer.

Both the primary parties, as well as the government as third party, thus have a basic commonality of interest in the continued successful existence of the organisation.

The need to cooperate arises from this mutuality of interests: without the need for cooperation, industrial relations as a field of study, and collective bargaining as a process in practice would never have existed. Unfortunately, the literature dealing with industrial and labour relations often underplays the importance of this natural dynamic which underlies all employment relationships.

Due to the simultaneous existence of elements of mutual and conflicting interests in all employment relationships, there are usually some signs of resistance and some signs of consent on a continuous basis.

20.3 THEORETICAL APPROACHES TO AND PERSPECTIVES OF INDUSTRIAL AND LABOUR RELATIONS

As has been indicated, it is difficult to provide definitive definitions of industrial and labour relations. Different perspectives are taken by different people, partly because they have different frames of reference — due to the fact that the topic can be studied from many different angles.

This also holds true within the context of employing entities or organisations. The particular frame of reference adopted will largely determine the way in which specific labour relations issues and situations are analysed, the way in which the parties are expected to behave, and the means adopted to influence or control their behaviour.

A few of the various theoretical approaches to industrial and labour relations are outlined below.

20.3.1 The unitarist perspective

This approach stresses a so-called natural common goal in all employment organisations and the fact that there is actually no need for divisions in the organisation because all are part of one team. Proponents of this perspective emphasise the fact that generally all members of an organisation have similar needs and values and that conflict is therefore basically unnecessary, unnatural and irrational. Those who challenge or who are in conflict with management are viewed as transgressors or aberrants. Trade unions are therefore seen largely as unnecessary, opposition groupings which actually intrude and try to compete for the loyalty of workers. Collective bargaining is basically seen as an unnecessary waste of time.

20.3.2 The pluralist perspective

Those who adhere to this ideological framework believe that any organisation is basically a coalition of people with a variety of different beliefs, interests, goals and aspirations. Not all employees will share the same goals and conflict is thus seen as a normal occurrence which must simply be managed in such a way that the different interests and goals are kept in some kind of equilibrium. Conflicting views and objectives are thus acknowledged and would be reconciled in such a way that they ultimately contribute positively to organisational success and the wellbeing of all the parties. Some limited common purpose (in the form of the continued successful existence of the organisation) is also acknowledged and the parties who will naturally come into conflict are thus willing to work out ways of ensuring a balance between conflict and cooperation. Trade unions are viewed as the natural consequence of certain individuals who form coalitions because they share certain interests and objectives which differ from those of other individuals or groups. Trade unions are not viewed as a threat or as intruders or troublemakers, but rather as legitimate bodies which can help to restore the power imbalances inherent in all employment relationships and to ensure some form of equilibrium between the natural conflict and common interest between the parties, through a process of collective bargaining.

20.3.3 The radical perspective

This approach is founded on the ideology that no balance of conflict or power can be achieved in any capitalist system and that an alternative, more radical approach has to be taken. This perspective is based on the Marxist thesis that the roots of the conflict and division between the workers who sell their labour and the owners of capital who exploit labour as a commodity are not to be found in the employment relationship as such, but rather in the wider society and in the capitalist way in which the production process is organised. The essence of this perspective is the basic power imbalance which results from the fact that the owners of the means of production in a capitalist system occupy the superior position. Proponents of this perspective therefore take the view that there can be no point of common interest and that the whole capitalist system has to be overthrown and replaced by a system of communal control and the abolition of the social constructs of private property and ownership. It is believed that in a capitalist system of production workers will always be exploited, as they are the only ones who can really add value and increase the profits of the owners of the means of production. Industrial conflict is therefore seen as an extension of the broader conflict in society between the working class and the owners of capital. Trade unions and collective bargaining are viewed to be only instrumental in the process of radical change in society.

20.3.4 The societal-corporatist perspective

Although this ideological framework also acknowledges the natural presence of conflict inherent in employment relationships, it places greater emphasis on the need for more cooperation and coordination between the parties involved in labour relations. In this sense it can thus be viewed to incorporate elements of both the unitarist and pluralist perspectives.

While conflict is regarded as natural, it is also believed that it can be best managed if the parties (state, labour and capital) can focus more on their interdependencies and commonalities of interest. In terms of processes the emphasis therefore shifts away from adversarialism and competitive interactions, towards processes of consensus-building and greater collaboration and coordination. Because the focus is more on common goals, the approach is to take more of a holistic perspective and to create structures through which the role-players can negotiate agreements that are ultimately more beneficial to all the stakeholders over the long term. The needs of broader society are thus incorporated in such an approach, rather than focusing only on short-term, "their loss and our gain" types of negotiation outcomes.

20.4 TRADE UNIONS

As has been pointed out throughout this book (and in particular in chapter 2), trade unions are key stakeholders and role-players in the management of employment relationships in South Africa. Not only have South African trade unions played an important role in transforming the country from an apartheid society to a democracy, but they also remain major stakeholders and role-players in the governance of the country today. In this part of the book the spotlight falls on the nature of trade unions as organisations in their own right.

20.4.1 The anatomy of trade unions: A brief overview

In chapter 1 a definition of "organisation" is provided. From that definition it can be deduced that a trade union is just as much an organisation as any business enterprise. It is a social entity with identifiable boundaries, functioning on a continuous basis to achieve specific objectives.

20.4.1.1 Definition of trade unions

Salamon (1992: 78) defines a trade union as:

". . . any organisation, whose membership consists of employees, which seeks to organise and represent their interests both in the workplace and society and, in particular, seeks to regulate their employment relationship through the direct process of collective bargaining with management".

According to the Labour Relations Act 66 of 1995, a trade union is viewed as:

> . . . an association of employees whose principal purpose is to regulate rela-tions between employees and employers, including employers' organisations.

Although collective bargaining as a process can thus be highlighted as a particular means through which trade unions get involved in representing the interests of their members, there are also other processes that may be used for this purpose. In this regard more cooperative processes such as joint problem solving, indirect par-ticipation in decision making through consultation and even processes of codetermination may form part of how trade unions serve the interests of their members within organisations and society at large. Although the primary interest of trade unions relate directly to the employment relationship, they often also seek to serve the interests of their members more indirectly by serving a macrolevel role in society. In South Africa trade unions (mostly through their federations) take part in political processes such as policy formulation in NEDLAC (National Economic Development and Labour Council).

There are many different *types* of trade unions. Some unions organise their membership and operations without any emphasis on the specific industry, but with a particular focus on certain occupational groups such as related crafts. Examples of such occupational unions in South Africa include the SA Boiler-makers, Iron and Steelworkers, Shipbuilders & Welders Society and the SA Nurses Union. Other unions strive to represent the interests of diverse types of workers, as long as they all work in a particular industry. Examples of such industrial unions in South Africa include the National Union of Mineworkers and the Chemical Workers Industrial Union. Some other unions may, however, prefer to be more gen-eral and open, striving to attain the utopian situation where the whole working class is organised into one association. In this case the emphasis is to a large extent on so-called class consciousness. Examples in South Africa include the Black and Allied Workers Union and the United Peoples Union of SA.

20.4.1.2 Why trade unions exist

From what has already been said it should be quite clear why trade unions exist: they are formed to serve the interests of their members — the workers. The ques-tion arising from this is why certain employees want to belong to a trade union. In essence it can be stated that trade unions exist simply because certain groups of employees do not feel satisfied with their employment relationships. With the advent of the Industrial Revolution, the nature of employment relationships changed considerably due to the rise of mass production, factories and capitalism. The focus was on outputs only and the needs of workers were often grossly neglected. Some groups of employees thus experienced (and many still do today) certain discrepancies between what they felt they were actually getting out of their employment relationships relative to others and what they felt they ought to get (relating to aspects such as job satisfaction, freedom to make decisions for them-selves in the workplace, working conditions, remuneration and/or fringe benefits).

Broadly speaking it is thus the primary purpose of trade unions to restore and maintain some sort of balance or equity in employment relations, as well as in society as a whole, This is especially so when one considers the imbalances in power and inequalities between certain classes of people in society — most notably between the so-called working class and those who own the productive organisations such as business enterprises and government institutions. In practice these imbalances and inequalities largely involve two groups, namely *managers* (employees who are appointed to represent the interests of the owners or real employers in the workplace) in relation to the so-called *nonmanagerial employees* — the workers or labour.

From this one can derive many different generalised objectives of trade unions:

- they try to improve the working conditions of their members as well as their terms of employment;
- they want to ensure that workers are treated fairly at work;
- they strive towards ensuring that workers get a fair share of the wealth generated by organisations;
- they aim at improving social security;
- they want to achieve greater democracy in the governance of individual organisations, industries and society at large by taking part in decision-making processes;
- they aim in particular at getting greater control over the management of employment relationships within organisations; and
- they strive to do away with class structures in societies where some have a great deal while others have very little and many may even not be employed at all.

In order to achieve their objectives, trade unions have to operate efficiently and effectively.

20.4.1.3 How trade unions operate: Their structures and methods

Just as business organisations have to be managed in order to achieve their objectives, trade unions as organisations in their own right also have to be managed. They have to plan and set objectives, they have to be structured (or organised), leadership is essential and control has to be exercised. The topic of how to manage a trade union falls beyond the scope of this book. It is, however, necessary to develop a general understanding of how trade unions operate; we thus focus on the overall structuring and methods employed by these organisations.

Although details regarding the structuring of unions may differ in accordance with variables such as type, size, policy and affiliation to a federation, a general structural pattern can be sketched.

The structure of trade unions

In contrast with most business organisations, the power of a trade union is vested in its membership and not so much in its top hierarchy. Trade unions are democratic organisations and workers usually join them voluntarily. Although top-level leadership, experience and power are important, the real strength of a union lies in its members who form the foundation of any trade union.

The members elect shop stewards to act as the link between the union, the members and the management of organisations. Often the elected shop stewards form shop steward committees within the organisations in which they act as representatives of the workers. These shop steward committees thus make up the next structural layer (on top of the membership base) of the trade union. Typically the next structural level is formed by the trade union's branch offices, which usually include full-time union officials (full-time employees of the trade union) and members of the shop steward committees (or other shop stewards duly elected by the committees).

Should a trade union's membership be significant, it may be necessary to create regional structures in the form of regional union offices. Full-time union officials and branch level members may also be involved at this level.

At the next level there is the national committee and national executive. This structural level usually consists of a president of the trade union or a chairperson, a vice chairperson, a general secretary and a treasurer. These officials are appointed or elected and their roles are determined in accordance with the constitution of each individual trade union. The roles of president and vice president are normally filled by union members who are shop stewards. Full-time union officials usually take on the roles of treasurer and secretary. Sometimes the members of the national committee and national executive come from the ranks of the local or regional committees; in other cases they may be elected by the general congress. The task of the national committee — and in particular the national executive — is to implement the policies of the trade union and also to act and speak on its behalf. Overall responsibility for the smooth functioning of the trade union rests with these structures.

Unions are democratic organisations. All union policy decisions are made at the level of the **national congress.** The national congress represents grassroots membership and elects the executive. The overall management of trade unions thus rests with the executives at the different structural levels. These structures consist of elected union members (office bearers) or officials appointed or elected by the union members who are the employees of business or public enterprises. It can thus truly be said that the members manage the union, in line with the credo of government by the people.

Trade unions may thus not accord organisers or officials appointed from outside (such as the general secretary) a vote in committee or executive decisions. As such union officials become employees of the union. The general management principles spelled out in this book also apply to these employees.

Methods used by trade unions to achieve their goals

Trade unions can make use of various methods in order to achieve their objectives or goals.

In line with the philosophy of trade unionism that unity is power, one of the principal methodologies that they employ is to unite their forces and stand together. This they do by, *inter alia,* affiliating with trade union federations at a national level. Uniting like this at even an international level is not uncommon.

Successful trade unions are founded on two important factors: on their organisation from grassroots level upwards, and on their ability to negotiate and otherwise interact collectively. They also take part in the decision-making processes of various structures, bodies or institutions at a national level. These include, in South Africa, NEDLAC, the Consumer Board, the National Training Board and the Unemployment Board. Sometimes (and in South Africa this has often happened over the past decade and a half), they use power strategies such as organising industrial action in the form of stayaways (protest action), strikes, consumer boycotts, picketing, etc. Trade unions also devote attention to the education and training of shop stewards and officials, especially at the level of the union federation. They also conduct research and publish reports and opinions and many unionists make presentations at conferences to market the role and views of trade unions. It is also well known that, should circumstances warrant it, trade unions will engage in costly litigation to further the interests of their members.

20.4.2 Rights relating to trade unionism in South Africa

In South Africa trade unionism has been entrenched in the country's Constitution and the rights that stem from this have been defined by the Labour Relations Act (hereafter also referred to as the Act). These rights are founded on the right to freedom of association which every South African enjoys. Because of this right, trade unions can legitimately be formed and their rights have accordingly also been spelled out in the Act. It should be noted that, although the focus in this section is on trade union rights and duties, most of these also apply to employers' organisations.

20.4.2.1 Freedom of association

Section 4 of the Act grants employees the right to participate in the formation of a trade union or a federation of trade unions and, subject to the union's constitution, to join that trade union. Union members have the following rights:

- to participate in the lawful activities of their union;
- to participate in the election of any of its office bearers, officials or trade union representatives;
- to stand for election and be eligible for appointment as office bearer or official and, if elected or appointed, to hold office; and

- to stand for election and be eligible for appointment as a trade union represent-ative and, if elected or appointed, to carry out the functions of a trade union representative in terms of the Act or in terms of any collective agreement.

Union members have the same rights in respect of a trade union federation of which their union is a member.

Section 5 of the Act further protects freedom of association by prohibiting dis-crimination, victimisation and so-called yellow-dog contracts of employment. No person may compel or threaten to compel an employee or job applicant to become/ to be or not to become a member of a trade union or a workplace forum or to give up membership of a trade union or workplace forum. Furthermore, no person may discriminate against any person on these grounds or prevent a person from exer-cising any right conferred by the Act or from participating in any proceedings in terms of the Act. No person may prejudice or threaten to prejudice an employee or job applicant because of past, present or anticipated membership of a trade union or a federation of trade unions or workplace forum, or for his/her participation in forming a trade union or federation of trade unions or in establishing a workplace forum, for his/her participation in the lawful activities of a trade union, federation of trade unions or workplace forum, or for his/her failure or refusal to do something that an employer may not lawfully permit or require an employee to do, or for his/ her disclosure of information that the employee is lawfully entitled or required to give to another person, or for his/her exercise of any right conferred by the Act, or for his/her participation in any proceedings in terms of the Act. Furthermore, no person may advantage, or promise to advantage, an employee or a job applicant in exchange for that person not exercising any right conferred by the Act or not par-ticipating in any proceedings in terms of the Act. A provision in any contract that directly or indirectly contradicts or limits freedom of association is automatically invalid, unless the contractual provision is permitted by the Act. (For example, sec-tion 26 of the Labour Relations Act provides for closed shop agreements, which could, but for this provision, be found to be void since it could be argued that the closed shop practice contravenes the principle of freedom of association.)

It should be noted that sections 6 and 7 of the Act extend the right to freedom of association and the protection against victimisation to employers.

According to section 8 of the Act, a trade union (or employers' organisation) has the right:

- to determine its own constitution and rules;
- to hold elections for its office bearers, officials and representatives;
- to plan and organise its administration and lawful activities;
- to participate in the formation of a federation of trade unions or a federation of employers' organisations;
- to join a federation of trade unions or a federation of employers' organisations, subject to its constitution, and to participate in its lawful activities; and

● to affiliate with, and participate in the affairs of, any international workers' organisation or international employers' organisation or the International Labour Organisation, and contribute to, or receive financial assistance form, those organisations.

Disputes arising from any alleged interference with freedom of association or from victimisation may be referred for conciliation to a bargaining council or the Commission for Conciliation, Mediation and Arbitration (CCMA). (Note that, whenever the phrase "bargaining council or the CCMA" is used in this chapter, it is used in the following context and as shorthand to describe the following process: The Act encourages labour and capital to establish their own structures and procedures; thus, if there is a functional bargaining council which has jurisdiction, that council will deal with the dispute. Only in the absence of such a council will the CCMA be required, as the default option, to deal with a matter.) Should the dispute remain unresolved, it may be referred to the Labour Court for adjudication. The process is depicted in figure 20.1.

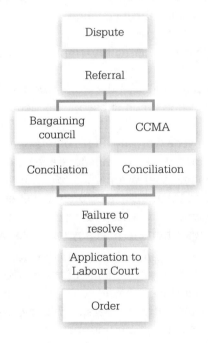

Figure 20.1
Freedom of association disputes

A complainant simply has to prove that he/she has been compelled, threatened, prohibited or detrimentally affected in almost any manner, after which the burden shifts to the defendant to prove that the conduct complained of did not constitute prohibited conduct in terms of this chapter of the Act.

20.4.2.2 *Organisational rights of trade unions*

The freedom to associate would have had little meaning in practice had the rights of the organisations with whom one may associate not also been catered for in the legislation.

Linkage between level of representativeness and entitlement to organisational rights

Depending on how many workers a union represents — its so-called level of representativeness — it will enjoy certain statutory organisational rights. At this point it may be instructive to note the four different types of trade union representativeness encountered in the Labour Relations Act 66 of 1995 as a whole and their attendant rights.

1. Sufficiently representative

   Only a registered trade union (two or more unions may act jointly in order to establish sufficient representation) which is sufficiently representative of employees at a particular workplace will be afforded certain organisational rights. These rights include the following:
   - the right of access to the workplace;
   - the right to hold meetings at the employer's premises (outside working hours);
   - the right to conduct a ballot at the workplace;
   - the right to have trade union subscriptions deducted from members' salaries;
   - the right of employees who are office bearers of the trade union to take reasonable leave during working hours for trade union business; and
   - for registered unions that are parties to a bargaining council, automatic right of access and the right to stop order facilities at all workplaces falling within the jurisdiction of the bargaining council, regardless of the trade union's level of representativeness at any particular workplace.

   In the domestic sector, the right of access to the premises of the employer does not include the right to enter the home of the employer, unless the employer agrees (that is without the employer's consent, a union office bearer may not enter the former's home, although he/she will have to be allowed entry to the premises for the purpose of recruiting members, communicating with members, etc).

   The Act does not attempt to define "sufficiently representative", but one can accept that it does mean a significant membership, albeit falling short of an outright majority.

   Some clues as to what may affect the evaluation of whether the "sufficient representativeness" criterion has been met in any specific case, are to be found in section 21 of the Act, which instructs the adjudicator of a dispute about whether or not a registered trade union is a representative trade union, to seek to minimise the proliferation of trade union representation in a single workplace and to minimise the financial and administrative burden of requiring an employer to grant organisational rights to more than one registered trade union. In addition, consideration must be given to: (i) the nature of the workplace; (ii) the nature of the organisational rights that the registered trade union seeks to exercise; (iii) the nature of the sector in which the workplace is situated; and (iv) the organisational history at the workplace. From these statutory guidelines it is clear that no numerical value can be set as a threshold for sufficient representativeness — it will have to be determined case by case.

2. Majority representation

   Only registered trade unions with a majority support (50 % + 1 support) in a particular workplace will be afforded the following organisational rights (as is the case with "sufficiently representative", two or more unions may act jointly to establish majority representation in a workplace):
   O the right to appoint shop stewards;
   O the right to demand (subject to certain limitations and conditions) that the employer disclose information to the union should such information be necessary to enable the union or its representatives to fulfil their functions;
   O the right to reasonable time off with pay during working hours for shop stewards to perform their functions and to be trained as shop stewards;
   O the right to negotiate specific thresholds for certain rights (see the next paragraph).
   O Only majority trade unions may enter into an agency shop agreement or a closed shop agreement.

3. Collective agreement thresholds

   An employer and a majority trade union (or the employer and employee parties to a bargaining council) may conclude a collective agreement establishing a threshold of representativeness required in respect of the rights associated with the "sufficient representativeness" criterion (that is, access to the workplace, stop order facilities and leave for trade union activities for trade union office bearers). These thresholds may not discriminate between trade unions.

4. Thirty per cent representativeness

   The fourth type of representativeness encountered in the Act is that pertaining to statutory councils. A registered trade union that wishes to establish a statutory council requires a membership of at least 30 % in the sector in question. Two or more trade unions may join together for the purpose of meeting the threshold level of representativeness.

Disclosure of information

One of the most controversial provisions of the Act is the right afforded majority unions to require of an employer to disclose to a shop steward all relevant information that will allow the shop steward to perform his/her functions effectively, and the duty it places on an employer, whenever he/she consults or bargains with a majority trade union, to disclose to that trade union all relevant information that will allow the trade union to engage effectively in consultation or collective bargaining. This is, however, not such a radical innovation to our system as some employers would like us to believe, since there is jurisprudential support for the notion that good faith collective bargaining requires disclosure of information as envisaged by the Act. Neither is the trade union's right to information, and the employer's concomitant duty to disclose the information, without boundaries that should adequately protect the interests of all stakeholders. First, employers may inform the shop steward or the trade union in writing if any information disclosed is confidential. Should a trade union act in breach of its fiduciary duty not to disclose confidential information, a CCMA commissioner may order that the right to disclosure of information in that workplace be withdrawn for a period specified in his/her arbitration award. Secondly, an employer is not required to disclose information that is legally privileged; that the employer cannot disclose without contravening a prohibition imposed on the employer by any law or order of any court; that is confidential and, if disclosed, may cause substantial harm to an employee or to the employer; or that is private, personal information relating to an employee, unless that employee consents to the disclosure of that information. Any dispute about the disclosure of information must be referred to the CCMA who must attempt to resolve it through mediation, failing which the dispute may be arbitrated. The right to the disclosure of information is excluded in the domestic sector (for example, a shop steward may not demand information relating to the financial affairs of the employer of a domestic worker).

Exercising organisational rights

Any registered trade union may notify an employer in writing that it seeks to exercise one or more of the said rights in a workplace. The notice must be accompanied by a certified copy of the trade union's certificate of registration and must specify:

- the workplace in respect of which the trade union seeks to exercise the rights;
- the representativeness of the trade union in that workplace, and the facts relied upon to demonstrate that it is a representative trade union; and
- the rights that the trade union seeks to exercise and the manner in which it seeks to exercise those rights.

Within thirty days of receiving the notice, the employer must meet with the registered trade union and endeavour to conclude a collective agreement regarding the manner in which the trade union will exercise the rights in respect of that workplace. If a collective agreement is not concluded, either the registered trade union or the employer may refer the dispute in writing to the CCMA for resolution. Any dispute concerning the granting or exercise of organisational rights may be referred to the CCMA who must try to resolve it, first through mediation and, if that fails, one of the parties may request that the CCMA-appointed commissioner must arbitrate the dispute.

20.4.2.3 *Trade union registration and relevant statutory requirements*

A simplified registration procedure is provided for in the new Act. Of great importance is the fact that, although the process for registration has been made very simple, all rights in terms of the Act are now granted only to *registered* trade unions. The Act makes no provision for a dual system such as prevailed under the old Act. (It should be noted that all the provisions referred to in the text that relate to the rights and duties of trade unions, except those relating to shop stewards, also apply in essence to employers' organisations.) Unregistered bodies would not be recognised under the new Act although in keeping with the principle of voluntarism, there is no direct compulsion to register in terms of the Labour Relations Act. Any trade union may apply for registration provided that it has adopted a suitable name, its constitution meets the statutory requirements (see below), it has an address in South Africa, and it is independent. The last requirement is an expression of the legislator's disapproval of the practice of some employers to set up trade unions as their puppets in opposition to "difficult" or "radical" trade unions in order to divide the loyalty of the workforce and thus to undermine the undesirable trade union(s). In terms of the Act, a trade union is independent if it is not under the direct or indirect control of any employer or employers' organisation and it is free of any interference or influence of any kind from any employer or employers' organisation. With the exception of the independence requirement, the same provisions apply to employers' organisations that wish to register.

Statutory requirements relating to the constitutions of trade unions *

The constitution of a trade union that intends to register must:

- state that the trade union or employers' organisation is an association not for gain;
- prescribe qualifications for, and admission to, membership;
- establish the circumstances in which a member will no longer be entitled to the benefits of membership;
- provide for the termination of membership;
- provide for appeals against loss of the benefits of membership or against termination of membership, prescribe a procedure for those appeals and determine the body to which those appeals may be made;
- provide for membership fees and the method for determining membership fees and other payments by members;
- prescribe rules for the convening and conducting of meetings of members and meetings of representatives of members, including the quorum required for, and the minutes to be kept of, those meetings;
- establish the manner in which decisions are to be made;
- establish the office of secretary and define its functions;

*Note that these requirements apply (with the necessary changes) also in respect of the constitutions of employers' organisations.

- provide for other office bearers, officials and trade union representatives, and define their respective functions;
- prescribe a procedure for nominating or electing office bearers and trade union representatives;
- prescribe a procedure for appointing, or nominating and electing, officials;
- establish the circumstances and manner in which office bearers, officials and trade union representatives, may be removed from office;
- provide for appeals against removal from office of office bearers, officials and trade union representatives, prescribe a procedure for those appeals and determine the body to which those appeals may be made;
- establish the circumstances and manner in which a ballot must be conducted;
- provide that the trade union, before calling a strike, must conduct a ballot of those of its members in respect of whom it intends to call the strike;
- provide that members of the trade union or employers' organisation may not be disciplined or have their membership terminated for failure or refusal to participate in a strike or lockout if no ballot was held about the strike or lockout, or, a ballot was held but a majority of the members who voted did not vote in favour of the strike or lockout;
- provide for banking and investing its money;
- establish the purposes for which its money may be used;
- provide for acquiring and controlling property;
- determine a date for the end of its financial year;
- prescribe a procedure for changing its constitution; and
- prescribe a procedure by which it may resolve to wind up.

In addition, it is specifically provided that the constitution of any trade union which intends to register may not include any provision that discriminates directly or indirectly against any person on the grounds of race or gender.

In terms of the Act, the Registrar of Labour Relations has a very limited discretion in the matter of registration. If the Registrar is satisfied that the applicant meets the requirements of the Act, he/she **must** register the applicant by entering the applicant's name in the relevant register (register of trade unions or the register of employers' organisations). After registering the applicant, the Registrar must issue a certificate of registration in the applicant's name and send the certificate and a certified copy of the registered constitution to the applicant. If the Registrar is not satisfied that the applicant meets the requirements for registration, the Registrar must send the applicant a written notice of the decision and the reasons for that decision and, in that notice, inform the applicant that it has thirty days from the date of the notice to meet those requirements. Failure on the part of the applicant to meet the requirements within the thirty-day period will result in a notification informing the applicant in writing of the Registrar's refusal to register the applicant.

Any person who is aggrieved by a decision of the Registrar may appeal to the Labour Court against that decision, within sixty days of either the date of the Registrar's decision or, if written reasons for the decision are demanded, the date of those reasons. The Labour Court, on good cause shown, may extend the period within which a person may note an appeal against a decision of the Registrar.

Effect of registration of a trade union *

A certificate of registration is sufficient proof that a registered trade union is a body corporate with limited liability. This means that the fact that a person is a member of a registered trade union does not make that person liable for any of the obligations or liabilities of that organisation. A member, office bearer or official of a registered trade union or a shop steward is not personally liable for any loss suffered by any person as a result of an act performed or omitted in good faith by the member, office bearer, official or shop steward while performing their functions for or on behalf of the trade union.

Duties of registered trade unions and their federations

Every registered trade union (take note again that similar principles apply to employers' organisations) is obliged to do the following:

- keep proper books of account, records of its income, expenditure, assets and liabilities;
- within six months after the end of each financial year, prepare financial statements, including at least a statement of income and expenditure for the previous financial year, and a balance sheet showing its assets, liabilities and financial position as at the end of the previous financial year;
- arrange for an auditor to undertake an annual audit of its books, records of account and financial statements and make the financial statements and the auditor's report available to its members for inspection, and submit those statements and the auditor's report to a meeting or meetings of its members or their representatives as provided for in its constitution;
- preserve each of its books of account, supporting vouchers, records of subscriptions or levies paid by its members, income and expenditure statements, balance sheets, and auditor's reports, for a period of three years from the end of the financial year to which they relate;
- keep a register of its members;
- keep the minutes of its meetings for a period of three years;
- keep ballot papers for a period of three years;
- by 31 March each year, supply the Registrar with a certified membership list as at 31 December of the previous year;
- supply the Registrar, within thirty days of receipt of its auditor's report, with a certified copy of that report and of the financial statements;

*Note that these provisions apply (with the necessary changes) also in respect of employers' organisations

- supply the Registrar, within thirty days of receipt of a written request by him/her, with an explanation of anything relating to the membership list, the auditor's report or the financial statements;
- supply the Registrar, within thirty days of any appointment or election of its national office bearers, with the names and work addresses of those office bearers;
- thirty days before a new address for service of documents will take effect, supply the Registrar with notice of that change of address;
- should a trade union wish to change its constitution or name, it must send the Registrar a certified copy of the resolution;
- should a registered trade union wish to amalgamate with another trade union, the amalgamating trade unions may apply to the registrar for registration of the amalgamated trade union.

Any *federation of trade unions* (or any federation of employers' organisations) is obliged to provide the Registrar with the following:

- within three months of its formation, and after that by 31 March each year, the names and addresses of its members and the number of persons each member in the federation represents;
- within three months of its formation, and after that within thirty days of any appointment or election of its national office bearers, the names and work addresses of those office bearers, even if their appointment or election did not result in any changes to its office bearers;
- within three months of its formation, a certified copy of its constitution and an address in the Republic at which it will accept service of any document that is directed to it;
- within thirty days of any change to its constitution, or of the address provided to the Registrar as required, notice of that change; and
- within fourteen days after it has resolved to wind up, a copy of that resolution.

20.4.2.4 Some prominent South African trade unions

The focus in this section is on the various trade union federations, with some reference also to statistics and trends in the South African trade union movement.

In chapter 2 you learnt how the development of trade unions has over the years influenced South African society in general. Especially during the late seventies and throughout the eighties trade union membership figures grew rapidly. This was largely contrary to international trends. According to some experts, the South African trade union movement was the fastest growing of its kind in the world during the eighties. Whereas the total union membership figure stood at less than three-quarters of a million in 1979, it more than doubled to over one and a half million by 1985. This figure kept on growing to pass the two million mark more than a year before 1990, peaking out at a figure of close to three and a half million employees by 1993 (Levy & Associates 1996: 12). Growth in union membership figures then plateaued out and, according to Department of Labour records, membership figures of registered trade unions went into a decline phase in the period 1993 to 1994.

By the last quarter of 1994, close to two and a half million employees belonged to trade unions registered by the Department of Labour, with just more than half a million more workers belonging to unregistered trade unions. The total union membership figure by the end of 1994 thus stood at a little less (approximately 20 000) than three million. According to the statistics used by Levy & Associates (1997) total union membership figures were just below three million by the end of 1996.

There has thus been a slight downward trend in union membership figures over the period 1993 to 1995. Although this is the first real downward trend since 1979/ 80, one must guard against being misled and should be careful not to read into this trend signs of a decline in collectivism among the South African workforce. It is more likely that this trend is related to economic developments. With the globalisation of markets and fierce international competition, the managements of South African organisations have been forced into situations where aspects like reorganisation, restructuring, downsizing and rightsizing have become the watchwords. All of this has meant large-scale layoffs and retrenchments, severely affecting trade union membership figures. Although economic growth in South Africa has picked up over the period 1994–1996, growth in employment has lagged behind considerably. Union membership figures went up slightly again in the 1995/96 period.

The most prominent trade union federation in South Africa is COSATU (the Congress of South African Trade Unions) with twenty affiliated trade unions, representing approximately one and three quarter million workers by the end of 1996. The National Council of Trade Unions (NACTU) has seventeen affiliated unions, representing an estimated 220 000 workers, by the end of the same year. By mid 1997 the second largest federation was FEDUSA (The Federation of Unions of South Africa). Its total membership stood at approximately 515 000.

Some of the important principles driving COSATU include non-racialism, one union per industry, cooperation between affiliates and a national level, working-class upliftment and worker control. This federation has been instrumental in the turnaround of South African society and is continuing to play a significant role in the country. Although there is still an official alliance between COSATU and the ANC, in 1995 pressure has already started mounting from certain circles within COSATU regarding the wisdom of this alliance. Whether or not this alliance continues in future, COSATU will in all likelihood remain the single most prominent labour federation in the country for some time to come. The Congress of South African Trade Unions has been managed very well strategically and, as circumstances in South Africa change, COSATU not only carries on with intensive research to position itself strategically but also acts as a catalyst for change in the country. This role is also fulfilled primarily within the structure of NEDLAC.

The National Council of Trade Unions stands for worker control and working-class leadership. Traditionally, although it stands for non-affiliation to political parties, NACTU has been sympathetic to the black consciousness/Africanist philosophy (Finnemore & Van der Merwe 1996: 98), and apparently it is still PAC aligned. FEDUSA (Federation of Unions of South Africa) was formed during 1997 by the amalgamation of FEDSAL and others.. The Federation of South African Labour Unions (FEDSAL) used to subscribe to principles such as non-racialism, non-affiliation to political parties, a market-orientated economy, equal opportunities and the rules of union democracy. From a historical perspective, FEDSAL has developed mainly as a federation for white-collar workers. Although it used to propagate a moderate approach to trade unionism, FEDSAL was very active in especially economic politics, made its voice heard very clearly in NEDLAC and supported the reconstruction and development of South Africa.

Some of the prominent trade unions affiliated to COSATU are the National Union of Mineworkers (NUM) with more than 300 00 members, the National Union of Metal Workers of South Africa (NUMSA) with almost 170 000 members and the South African Clothing & Textile Workers' Union (SACTWU) with approximately 160 000 members. Other COSATU unions include SAMWU (South African Municipal Workers' Union), FAWU (Food & Allied Workers' Union), SACCAWU (SA Commercial, Catering & Allied Workers' Union) and NEHAWU (National Health & Allied Workers' Union).

The National Council of Trade Unions' largest affiliates include SACWU (SA Chemical Workers' Union), NUFAW (National Union of Furniture & Allied Workers of SA), MWASA (Media Workers' Association of SA) and BCAWU (Building, Construction and Allied Workers' Union). Some of the more prominent trade unions affiliated to FEDUSA include HOSPERSA (Hospital Personnel Trade Union of SA), IMATU (Independent Municipal and Allied Trade Union) and PSA (Public Servants Association of South Africa).

20.5 STATUTORY PROVISIONS REGARDING STRUCTURES AND PROCESSES FOR COLLECTIVE BARGAINING AND DISPUTE RESOLUTION

20.5.1 General

As mentioned previously, the primary legal source of the rules governing collective bargaining in South Africa is the Labour Relations Act 66 of 1995. At the outset it must be noted that the new Labour Relations Act (hereinafter also referred to as "the Act" or "the new Act") does not make collective bargaining compulsory (with the notable exception of certain issues that are the subject of joint decision making if a workplace forum exists). However, having said this, it is equally important to understand that the Act vigorously encourages collective bargaining. This understandable bias in favour of collective bargaining is evident from the features listed in exhibit A.

Exhibit A

Inducements to collective bargaining in the LRA of 1995

- Granting of strong organisational rights
- Agreements are enforced through arbitration
- A refusal to bargain may be referred to advisory arbitration
- Emphasis placed on central bargaining
- Strong right to strike underpins the need to bargain
- Uncertainties of the Act (better to regulate by agreement)
- Pre-eminence of agreements over provisions of the Act
- Collective agreements are binding irrespective of whether they were concluded at central or plant level
- All agreements must contain a conciliation and arbitration procedure

The objects of the Act, as stated in its long title, are summarised in exhibit B.

Exhibit B

Objects of the Labour Relations Act 66 of 1995

- to give effect to the constitutional right to fair labour practices;
- to regulate the organisational rights of trade unions;
- to promote and facilitate collective bargaining at the workplace and at sectoral level;
- to regulate the right to strike and the recourse to lock out in conformity with the Constitution;
- to promote employee participation in decision making through the establishment of workplace forums;
- to provide simple procedures for the resolution of labour disputes through statutory conciliation, mediation and arbitration, and through independent alternative dispute resolution services accredited for that purpose;
- to establish the Labour Court and Labour Appeal Court as superior courts;
- to provide for a simplified procedure for the registration of trade unions and employers' organisations, and to provide for their regulation to ensure democratic practices and proper financial control; and
- to give effect to the public international law obligations of the Republic relating to labour relations.

In furtherance of these objectives the Act provides for forums to be established by the parties (bargaining councils, statutory councils and workplace forums) on which employers' representatives and employees' representatives can negotiate and consult on matters of mutual interest and prevent or resolve disputes which may arise between them. In addition, the Act grants recognition and strong rights to shop stewards (called "trade union representatives" in the Act). The Act also provides for the establishment of specialist industrial courts (the Labour Court and the Labour Appeal Court) to adjudicate certain labour matters. In addition to the Labour Relations Act, regard must also be taken of the National Economic, Development and Labour Council Act 35 of 1994 which provides for the establishment of a national economic, development and labour council (NEDLAC — see section 20.5.2).

In table 20.1 a brief summary is provided of the primary modes of interaction between the parties, the categories of issues, as well as the statutory structures and processes created to deal with them.

Table 20.1
Union–management interaction: Structures, issues and processes

Structures	Issues	Processes
NEDLAC	National labour market policy (eg labour market flexibility and drafting of labour legislation)	Politics
Bargaining councils	Sectoral and substantive issues (eg wages bargaining and macro-level issues such as industry restructuring)	Politics, conciliation, mediation, advisory arbitration, industrial action
Workplace forums	Workplace issues related to equity and wealth creation	Consultation, joint decision making, conciliation, mediation, arbitration, industrial action
Shop stewards and their Committees	Organisational rights at workplace level and all issues related to agreement administration and the policing of workers' rights	Interpersonal (informal) dynamics, representational facilitation, conciliation & mediation
Commission for Conciliation, Mediation and Arbitration (CCMA)	Certain disputes must be referred to the CCMA; also acts as default option in the absence of a (functioning) bargaining council	Conciliation, fact finding, mediation, arbitration, training, advice-giving
Labour Court & Labour Appeal Court	Disputes of right	Adjudication

20.5.2 The National Economic, Development and Labour Council (NEDLAC)

The National Economic, Development and Labour Council is governed by an executive council and consists of four chambers, namely:

- a public finance and monetary policy chamber;
- a trade and industry chamber;
- a labour market chamber; and
- a development chamber.

The membership of NEDLAC comprises representatives of organised business, representatives of organised labour, parties who represent organisations of community and development interests, and representatives of the state. The functions of NEDLAC are summarised in exhibit C.

Exhibit C

The objectives of NEDLAC

- to strive to promote the goals of economic growth, participation in economic decision making and social equity;
- to seek to reach consensus and conclude agreements on matters pertaining to social and economic policy;
- to consider all proposed labour legislation relating to labour market policy before it is introduced in Parliament;
- to consider all significant changes to social and economic policy before it is implemented or introduced in Parliament;
- to encourage and promote the formulation of coordinated policy on social and economic matters.

In pursuance of these objectives the Act confers on NEDLAC the authority to:

- make such investigations as it may consider necessary;
- continually survey and analyse social and economic affairs;
- continually evaluate the effectiveness of legislation and policy affecting social and economic policy; and
- conduct research into social and economic policy.

It can be expected that NEDLAC will have (and indeed has already had in its short history) a telling influence on the development of economic policy, labour laws and our system of industrial relations. Through the Labour Relations Act 66 of 1995, NEDLAC also has a direct role to play in that it is, *inter alia*, responsible for the issues listed in exhibit D.

Exhibit D

Responsibilities conferred on NEDLAC by LRA of 1995

- Demarcation of the sector and area in respect of which a bargaining council is to be registered
- Nominating members to the governing body of the CCMA
- Preparing Codes of Good Practice relating to industrial relations at the workplace for publication in the *Government Gazette*
- Advising the President on the appointment of judges to the labour courts
- Facilitating consultation between the Minister of Labour and the Minister of Public Service and Administration and NEDLAC on matters concerning the LRA
- Monitoring of socioeconomic issues giving rise to protest action

20.5.3 Bargaining councils

Industrial councils are now called bargaining councils and essentially retain all the powers they formerly enjoyed as industrial councils (plus some additional powers conferred on them by the new Act). As was mentioned previously, the name change was necessitated by the extension of the central bargaining system to the public sector. As before, bargaining councils are to be registered in respect of a specific area and sector. Bargaining councils are established when employers' organisations and employees' organisations come together and decide to create a permanent forum on which to regulate matters jointly in their industry and area. The parties apply for registration of a bargaining council for a specific industry and area to the Registrar who will register the council once he has satisfied himself that the applicants are **registered** employer and employee organisations, that there is no existing bargaining council which has jurisdiction, and that the parties are suf-ficiently representative in the area and industry. In assessing the representativeness of a council, the Registrar may regard the parties as represent-ative of the whole area, even if the trade union or employer parties to the council have no members in part of the area. Representativeness must be reviewed annu-ally. The registration of the council will be in respect of a specific industry and area only (this means that more than one bargaining council can be registered for the same industry, but each will cover different areas or that more than one council will have jurisdiction in the same area, but for different industries). Bargaining councils are permanent bodies and consist of an equal number of representatives from labour and employers respectively. These are, on the employer side, an employer, group of employers, *registered* employers' organisations, group of *registered* employers' organisations, or any mixture of these groups, and a *registered* trade union or group of *registered* trade unions on the labour side.

Any registered trade union or registered employers' organisation may apply in writing to a council for admission as a party to that council. An applicant must be advised of the council's decision within ninety days of that council having received the application for admission, failing which the council is deemed to have refused the applicant admission. If the council refuses to admit an applicant, it must within thirty days of the date of the refusal advise the applicant in writing of its decision and the reasons therefor. The applicant may apply to the Labour Court for an order admitting it as a party to the council. The Labour Court may admit the applicant as a party to the council, adapt the constitution of the council and make any other appropriate order.

A bargaining council can be likened to a mini-parliament which has jurisdic-tion over a particular geographical area and industry (for example, the chemical industry in KwaZulu-Natal). All employers and all employees (and their represent-ative bodies) within that area and industry will thus fall under the jurisdiction of the particular bargaining council registered for that area and industry, irrespective of whether the individual employer or employee organisation is actually repre-sented on the council (membership of a bargaining council is voluntary). This implies that, if a dispute were to arise between an individual employer and a trade union, neither of whom are members of a bargaining council, they would still have to refer their dispute to the council, should both or either of them wish to embark on industrial action. A bargaining council regulates matters of mutual interest in its industry and area by way of collective agreements (these are the "laws" issued by the "mini-parliament"). This lawmaking process proceeds as follows: a decision voted for by the majority (as prescribed in the constitution of the bargaining council) of the council's members will be regarded as a decision by the council.

In the early .1970s a dual system of collective bargaining developed in South Africa: established trade unions bargained at centralised level through the industrial council system while the so-called emergent trade unions rejected the official system in favour of plant-level bargaining and the conclusion of recognition agreements. Unfortunately, the legal status of recognition agreements has always proved problematic and such a dual system inevitably generated its own friction and conflict. The new Act solves this problem by making all collective agreements, whether concluded at centralised or decentralised (individual plant) level, enforceable in terms of the Act. In terms of the transitional arrangements provided for in the Act, existing recognition agreements are regarded as enforceable collective agreements under the new Act.

The Act stipulates that a collective agreement binds the parties and their members to the agreement, as well as those employees who are not members of the trade union which is party to the agreement, if those employees fall within the bargaining unit, the agreement is expressly intended to cover them, and the trade union enjoys majority representation in a particular workplace. Collective agreements continue to bind members of the trade union and employers' association to a collective agreement, irrespective of whether those employees/employers remain members of the trade union/employers' association. Individual employment contracts are automatically amended by the provisions of collective agreements. Unless otherwise specified, any party to a collective agreement may terminate the agreement by giving reasonable notice to the other parties to the agreement.

Procedures for the settlement of disputes regarding the interpretation or application of a collective agreement must be provided for in the agreement. The procedure must first provide for mediation and thereafter for arbitration. Disputes may also be referred to the CCMA for mediation followed by arbitration if the collective agreement does not contain the required dispute settlement procedure, the procedure is not operative, or, a party to the agreement has frustrated the resolution of the dispute in terms of the agreed-upon procedure. In the case of disputes over the interpretation or application of agency shop or closed shop agreements, these *must* be referred to the CCMA for mediation/arbitration.

The parties to a council must attempt to resolve any dispute between themselves in accordance with the constitution of the council. Any party to a dispute who is not a party to a bargaining council, but who falls within the registered scope of the council, may refer the dispute to the council in writing. The party who refers the dispute to the council must satisfy it that a copy of the referral has been served on all the other parties to the dispute. If a dispute is referred to a council in terms of the Act and any party to that dispute is not a party to that council, the council must attempt to resolve the dispute through conciliation. If the dispute remains unresolved after conciliation, the council must arbitrate the dispute if the Act requires arbitration and if any party to the dispute has requested that it be resolved through arbitration, or if all the parties to the dispute consent to arbitration under the auspices of the council. If one (or more) of the parties to a dispute that has been referred to the council do not fall within the registered scope of that council, it must refer the dispute to the CCMA. Every council must apply to the CCMA for accreditation to perform the conciliation and arbitration functions referred to previously, or appoint an agency accredited by the CCMA to perform those functions on its behalf.

Subject to the constitution of the bargaining council, a collective agreement concluded in a bargaining council binds only the parties to the bargaining council who are parties to the collective agreement. However, a bargaining council may ask the Minister in writing to extend a collective agreement concluded in the bargaining council to any non-parties to the collective agreement that are within its registered scope and are identified in the request. This may happen if the employee and employer parties who represent the majority of employees and employers respectively voted in favour of such an extension. A collective agreement may not be extended by notice in the *Government Gazette* unless the Minister is satisfied about the matters listed in exhibit E.

Exhibit E

Extension of collective agreements

A collective agreement may not be extended by notice in the *Government Gazette* unless the Minister is satisfied that:

- the majority of employees employed within the registered scope of the bargaining council are members of the trade unions that are party to the bargaining council;
- the members of the employers' organisations that are party to the bargaining council employ the majority of the employees employed within the registered scope of the bargaining council;
- the non-parties specified in the request fall within the bargaining council's registered scope;
- the terms of the collective agreement do not discriminate against non-parties;
- the collective agreement establishes or appoints an independent body to grant exemptions to non-parties and to determine the terms of those exemptions from the provisions of the collective agreement as soon as possible; and
- the collective agreement contains criteria that must be applied by the independent body when it considers applications for exemptions, and that those criteria are fair and promote the primary objects of this Act.

Especially noteworthy are the last two requirements relating to exemptions. These provisions are supposed to safeguard the interests of small and medium-sized enterprises against the predations and monopolistic tendencies of large corporations. Whether these will prove to be an effective shield remains to be seen. Under the previous dispensation the right to apply for exemption from industrial council agreements was frequently made nugatory by the delays encountered in getting a response to an exemption application.

20.5.3.1 Powers and functions of bargaining councils

The most important functions and powers of bargaining councils are listed in exhibit F.

Exhibit F

Powers and functions of bargaining councils

Bargaining councils are conferred with the following powers and functions:
- to conclude collective agreements;
- to enforce those collective agreements;
- to prevent and resolve labour disputes (mainly through mediation/arbitration);
- to establish and administer a fund to be used for resolving disputes;
- to promote and establish training and education schemes;
- to establish and administer pension, provident, medical aid, sick pay, holiday, unemployment and training schemes or funds or any similar schemes or funds for the benefit of one or more of the parties to the bargaining council or their members;
- to develop proposals for submission to NEDLAC or any other appropriate forum on policy and legislation that may affect the sector and area;
- to determine by collective agreement the matters which may not be an issue in dispute for the purposes of a strike or a lockout at the workplace; and
- to confer on workplace forums additional matters for consultation.

20.5.3.2 Constitutions of bargaining councils

The constitution of every bargaining council must provide for those matters listed in exhibit G on page 642.

Only if the constitution of the bargaining council complies with the requirements spelled out in exhibit G, may the Registrar register the bargaining council. Of particular importance is the requirement pertaining to small and medium enterprises (SMEs). It is often charged that the erstwhile industrial councils (the predecessors of the bargaining councils) did not cater for SMEs and indeed inhibited the growth and performance of these very important sources of business innovation and job creation.

20.5.4 Public service bargaining councils

Prior to the new Act the Public Service Labour Relations Act and the Education Labour Relations Act established the Public Service Bargaining Council and the Education Labour Relations Council respectively as the bargaining forums for these two public service sectors. These two councils, operating under different laws, covered only certain sectors of the public service. The new Act provides for the creation of a single overarching structure, the Public Service Coordinating Bargaining Council which should regulate and coordinate collective bargaining across the public service as a whole, as well as for (subordinate) bargaining councils in sectors in the public service. The old Public Service Bargaining Council and the Education Labour Relations Council became bargaining councils for their respective public service sectors in terms of the new Act.

It should be noted that the state may also be an employer party to a bargaining council in the private sector, if it is an employer in a sector and area covered by a private sector bargaining council.

Exhibit G

Constitutions of bargaining councils

The constitution of every bargaining council must provide for:
- the appointment of representatives of the parties to the bargaining council, of whom half must be appointed by the trade unions that are partly to the bargaining council and the other half by the employers' organisations that are party to the bargaining council, and the appointment of alternates to the representatives;
- the representation of small and medium enterprises;
- the circumstances and manner in which representatives must vacate their seats and the procedure for replacing them;
- rules for the convening and conducting of meetings of representatives, including the quorum required for, and the minutes to be kept of, those meetings;
- the manner in which decision are to be made;
- the appointment or election of office bearers and officials, their functions, and the circumstances and manner in which they may be removed from office;
- the establishment and functioning of committees;
- the determination through arbitration of any dispute arising between the parties to the bargaining council about the interpretation or application of the bargaining council's constitution;
- the procedure to be followed if a dispute arises between the parties to the bargaining council;
- the procedure to be followed if a dispute arises between a registered trade union that is a party to the bargaining council, or its members, or both, on the one hand, and employers who belong to a registered employers' organisation that is a party to the bargaining council, on the other hand;
- the procedure for exemption from collective agreements;
- the banking and investment of its funds;
- the purposes for which its funds may be used;
- the delegation of its powers and functions;
- the admission of additional registered trade unions and registered employers' organisations as parties to the bargaining council;
- a procedure for changing its constitution; and
- a procedure by which it may resolve to wind up.

20.5.5 Statutory councils

During the deliberations at NEDLAC leading up to the new Act a major bone of contention was the demand by COSATU-affiliated trade unions for the inclusion in the Act of a provision making centralised bargaining compulsory in all sectors of the economy. The employer parties to NEDLAC strongly opposed this demand and the outcome was a compromise, namely a proto bargaining council designated a statutory council. In terms of the Act any trade union or employers' organisation which represents at least 30 % of employees or employers in a sector and area in respect of which no bargaining council is registered, may apply to the Registrar for the establishment of a statutory council. Having satisfied himself that the applicant meets the prerequisites of the Act, the Registrar must then invite all registered trade unions and registered employers' organisations in that sector and area to attend a meeting for the purpose of concluding an agreement regarding the parties to the statutory council and a constitution for that council. This meeting is to be chaired by a CCMA commissioner. If an agreement is reached at that meeting, the Minister must still approve of the registration of the statutory council before it can be registered by the Registrar. Should no agreement be reached at the meeting, the CCMA commissioner must facilitate the conclusion of an agreement. However, if this also fails, the Minister must admit any applicant and any other registered trade union or employers' organisation to become a party to the statutory council. In the absence of a registered trade union or a registered employers' organisation to complete the bipartite structure of the council, the Minister must appoint appropriate persons as representatives of employees or employers, as the case may be.

The powers and functions of a statutory council are to prevent and settle labour disputes, to promote and establish training and education schemes and to establish and administer pension, provident, medical aid, sick pay, holiday, unemployment schemes or funds or any similar schemes or funds for the benefit of one or more of the parties to the statutory council or their members. Therefore, statutory councils cannot negotiate wages or conditions of employment (that is, substantive issues), except if the parties to the council agreed to negotiate substantive issues; the purpose of a statutory council is centralised regulations of certain labour matters as a precursor to becoming a fully fledged bargaining council. Statutory councils are mechanisms created in the name of self-regulation but which are essentially undemocratic and counter to the principle of voluntarism in that a basically unrepresentative body can gain power over an area and industry subject only to the approval of the Minister.

20.5.6 Dispute resolution and the Commission for Conciliation, Mediation and Arbitration (CCMA)

20.5.6.1 Establishment and functions of the CCMA

Thus far we have referred several times to the CCMA. The Act provides for the establishment of the CCMA, which is to be independent of the state, any political party, trade union, employer, employers' organisation, federation of trade unions or federation of employers' organisations. The CCMA is governed by a governing body, consisting of a chairperson and nine other members (labour, employers and the state, represented by three persons each), each nominated by NEDLAC and appointed by the Minister to hold office for a period of three years, and the director of the Commission. The Commission has jurisdiction in all the provinces of the Republic. The CCMA can easily be described as the centrepiece of the new industrial relations system introduced by the Act. The CCMA has no one predecessor: in certain respects it fulfils the conciliation functions that the former conciliation boards were supposed to perform (but unfortunately failed to fulfil); in other respects it takes over many of the functions of the old Industrial Court. In addition to this, the CCMA is assigned a host of other tasks not previously given to any specific body. Since most disputes must be processed through the conciliation-arbitration route via either a bargaining council or, as the default option, the CCMA, these bodies have their work cut out for them.

The functions of the CCMA can be broadly grouped into three categories.

- The CCMA must:
  - ○ attempt to resolve, through conciliation, any dispute referred to it in terms of the Act;
  - ○ if after conciliation a dispute still remains unresolved, arbitrate the dispute if the Act requires arbitration and any party to the dispute has requested that it be resolved through arbitration, or all the parties to a dispute in respect of which the Labour Court has jurisdiction consent to arbitration by the Commission;
  - ○ assist in the establishment of workplace forums; and
  - ○ compile and publish information and statistics about its activities.

- The CCMA must further:
  - ○ if asked, advise a party to a dispute about the procedure to follow in terms of the Act;
  - ○ assist a party to a dispute to obtain legal advice, assistance or representation;
  - ○ offer to resolve a dispute that has not been referred to it;
  - ○ accredit councils or private agencies (see below);
  - ○ subsidise accredited councils or accredited agencies;
  - ○ conduct, oversee or scrutinise any election or ballot of a registered trade union or registered employers' organisation if asked to do so by that trade union or employers' organisation;
  - ○ publish guidelines in relation to any matter dealt with in this Act; and
  - ○ conduct and publish research into matters relevant to its functions.

- The CCMA may provide, on request, employees, employers, registered trade unions, registered employers' organisations, federations of trade unions, federations of employers' organisations or councils with advice or training relating to the main objectives of the Act, such as:

○ the establishment of collective bargaining structures:
○ the design, establishment and election of workplace forums and the creation of deadlock-breaking mechanisms;
○ the functioning of workplace forums;
○ the prevention and resolution of disputes and employees' grievances;
○ disciplinary procedures;
○ procedures in relation to dismissals;
○ the process of restructuring the workplace;
○ affirmative action and equal opportunity programmes; and
○ sexual harassment in the workplace.

In addition, the CCMA must perform any other duties assigned to it by or in terms of the Act and may perform any other function entrusted to it by any other law. The CCMA may appoint commissioners in either a full-time or part-time capacity to perform the functions of commissioners.

The CCMA may accredit and subsidise bargaining councils and private agencies to perform conciliation, mediation and arbitration functions. In essence provision is made for the privatisation of dispute resolution. Once the CCMA is satisfied that an applicant agency or bargaining council meets the set standards, the CCMA may accredit such body to perform all or some of the aforementioned functions (on application the terms of an accreditation may be amended). An accredited council or accredited agency may charge a fee for performing any of the functions for which it is accredited, provided that the fee is in accordance with the tariff of fees determined by the CCMA.

20.5.6.2 Resolution of disputes under the auspices of the CCMA

Detailed provision is made in the new Act for the settlement of different types of disputes through conciliation, mediation and arbitration. In an effort to settle a dispute, a commissioner may try many techniques, such as mediation, conducting a fact-finding exercise or making a recommendation to the parties, which may be in the form of an advisory arbitration award. Any party to a dispute about a matter of mutual interest may refer the dispute in writing to the CCMA. The party who refers the dispute to the CCMA must also send a copy of the referral to all the other parties to the dispute. As should be clear by now, the general route any dispute would follow is first conciliation, failing which, arbitration (or, in a few cases, adjudication).

Before looking at these statutory provisions in greater detail, it is first necessary to clarify some concepts and processes from a more general point of view.

● **Conciliation**. This is a collective term for various types of third party intervention to assist parties in settling their disputes themselves. These could include the provision of a neutral venue for the parties to continue their deliberations, the provision of facilities such as secretarial services, fact-finding exercises, and even mediation.

- **Mediation**. Sometimes the parties cannot reach an agreement on their own. When such a stalemate is reached, the parties could, of course, decide to strike (trade union) or to lock workers out (employer). However, it may happen that neither of the parties is willing to take the risk of such drastic forms of industrial action because the potential losses or costs are too high. In such a case the parties can agree to use an objective outsider (the so-called third party) to mediate their negotiations. The negotiating parties may decide to use a mediator when:
  - O both parties have much to lose should their inability to reach an agreement result in direct conflict, but they are nonetheless unable to settle the dispute;
  - O negotiations reach a deadlock and neither of the parties is prepared to concede;
  - O the positions initially taken by the two parties are so far removed from each other than the difference first has to be reduced before an agreement can be reached (here the mediator can assist the parties in making their demands more realistic); and
  - O it is necessary to help one or both of the parties to change its point of view without losing face in the eyes of its interest group.

The basic notion of voluntary mediation is that the parties who find themselves in a polarised position *appoint* a neutral third person, respected and trusted by both parties, to act as go-between and to try to achieve a settlement by affecting a change in the position of one or both parties, so that agreement can become possible. Some features of mediation include the following.

- O Mediation is a voluntary process of settling disputes where the parties use a neutral third party to reach an agreement: the parties must agree to make use of mediation and they must agree on who should act as mediator.
- O The mediator has no decision-making powers: mediation is a nonbinding process of facilitation and persuasion and the parties are, notwithstanding the mediator's involvement in the matter, completely free to reach an agreement in whatever way they think fit.
- O The conflict, communication and people-handling skills of the mediator are of paramount importance (rather than legal or technical expertise): the mediator has to be completely impartial, show understanding for the parties' points of view (be empathetic) and treat confidential information as such. The mediator's primary task is to promote constructive communication and to moderate any aggression and personal acrimony between the parties; the mediator should never take credit for an agreement — the credit must go to the parties. At joint meetings, the mediator should avoid making suggestions and these should rather come from one of the parties. In order to maintain the credibility of the mediation process, the mediator should also be

honest with himself/herself and the parties, and withdraw if he/she sees that he/she cannot help the parties to reach an agreement.

○ The mediation process begins when the parties agree to use mediation. After the mediator has been appointed and a date fixed for the first meeting, the parties compile written submissions about the dispute which are sent to the mediator so that he/she can determine the nature and extent of the dispute. It is better for the parties to meet on neutral territory, such as a hotel, rather than at the employer's factory of the union's offices. The meeting place should preferably have separate rooms where the parties can each caucus in private and can meet with each other (thus at least three rooms). The mediator should first meet with each of the parties separately to determine their (conflicting) views of the dispute and to clarify any obscure points in the written submissions. At this stage the mediator does not make any suggestions — he/she merely encourages the parties to review the matters in dispute calmly, in order to create the right atmosphere for such a review of their respective points of view.

● **Arbitration**. Arbitration involves the appointment of an impartial third party, acceptable to all the disputing parties, to act as final judge in a dispute. The arbitrator gives a final and binding decision regarding the provisions of the settlement. What happens in effect is that the parties renounce their right to further negotiation, request the arbitrator to settle the dispute on their behalf and undertake to be bound by the arbitrator's decision (the arbitration award). The parties usually resort to arbitration when they feel that they cannot possibly settle the dispute themselves but they both have too much to lose by capitulating or by taking the most drastic form of industrial action, namely strikes and/or lockouts. The new Act prescribes arbitration of certain types of disputes, such as dismissal disputes and other rights disputes.

● **Advisory arbitration**. An advisory arbitration award is a nonbinding award and as such can be accepted or rejected by both or one of the parties. The purpose of such an award is to persuade the parties to accept or at least entertain the considered opinion of an outside expert. The new Act requires that an advisory arbitration award be made prior to industrial action over a refusal to bargain.

Keeping these general concepts and processes in mind, we now turn to the specific statutory provisions regarding the settlement of disputes under the auspices of the CCMA.

Resolution of disputes through conciliation

When a dispute has been referred to the CCMA it must appoint a commissioner to attempt to resolve it through conciliation (no provision is made, as is the case in arbitration, for the parties to request a specific commissioner to be appointed to perform the conciliation function). The appointed commissioner must attempt to resolve the dispute through conciliation within thirty days of the date the CCMA received the referral; the parties may, however, agree to extend the thirty-day period. In the conciliation proceedings a party to the dispute may appear in person or be represented only by a co-employee or by a member, an office bearer or official of that party's trade union or employers' organisation and, if the party is a juristic person, by a director or an employee. At the end of the thirty-day period, or any further period agreed between the parties, the commissioner must issue a certificate stating whether or not the dispute has been resolved.

Resolution of disputes through arbitration

Disputes may be resolved through arbitration if:

- it is a dispute about a matter of mutual interest;
- the Act requires settlement through arbitration;
- a commissioner has issued a certificate stating that the dispute remains unresolved; and
- any party to the dispute has requested that the dispute be resolved through arbitration.

The commissioner tasked with arbitrating the dispute may be the same commissioner who attempted to resolve the dispute through conciliation.

However, any party to the dispute may object to the arbitration being conducted by the same commissioner who conciliated the dispute, in which event the CCMA must appoint another commissioner to resolve the dispute by arbitration. Although parties to a dispute may request a specific commissioner to deal with their dispute, the CCMA is under no obligation to accede to their request if it is impracticable to do so. Should the parties have a stated preference, this must be put in writing (listing no more than five commissioners) and must state that the request is made with the agreement of all the parties to the dispute; it must be submitted within forty-eight hours of the date of the certificate stating that the dispute remains unresolved. Provision is also made for the appointment of a senior commissioner to arbitrate in a matter at the request of any party to the dispute. When considering whether the dispute should be referred to a senior commissioner, the director of the commission must hear the party making the application, any other party to the dispute and the commissioner who conciliated the dispute. The director may appoint a senior commissioner to act as arbitrator, after having considered the nature of the questions of law raised by the dispute, the complexity of the dispute, whether there are conflicting arbitration awards that are relevant to the dispute, and the public interest. The director must notify the parties to the dispute of the decision and the director's decision is final and binding and may only be taken on review after the dispute has been arbitrated. The Act expressly provides that commissioners must " . . . *determine the dispute fairly and quickly, but must deal with the substantial merits of the dispute with the* **minimum of legal formalities**" (emphasis added). In addition the Act specifies that, within fourteen days of the conclusion of the arbitration proceedings, the commissioner must issue an arbitration award with brief reasons, signed by that commissioner (the director may extend the period within which the arbitration award and the reasons are to be served and filed).

Fairness, speed and procedural simplicity are the objectives stressed in these proceedings. A commissioner is also granted considerable leeway in the manner in which the arbitration proceedings are conducted; for example, if all the parties consent, the arbitration proceedings may be suspended and an attempt to resolve the dispute through conciliation may be made. During the proceedings a party to the dispute may give evidence, call witnesses, question the witnesses of any other party, and address concluding arguments to the commissioner. In any arbitration proceedings, a party to the dispute may appear in person or be represented by a legal practitioner, a co-employee or by a member, office bearer or official of that party's trade union or employers' organisation and, if the party is a juristic person, by a director or an employee. It should be noted that the only outsiders allowed to represent a party at arbitration proceedings are legal practitioners and even they are excluded in proceedings dealing with misconduct and capacity disputes. A commissioner may make any appropriate arbitration award (including, but not limited to, an award that gives effect to any collective agreement, that gives effect to the provisions and primary objects of the Act, that includes, or is in the form of, a declaratory order). However, a commissioner may not include an order for costs in the arbitration award unless a party, or the person who represented that party in the arbitration proceedings, acted in a frivolous or vexatious manner by proceeding with or defending the dispute in the arbitration proceedings, and/or in its conduct during the arbitration proceedings.

Special provisions for arbitrating certain disputes:

The Act makes special provisions for disputes in essential services, disputes about dismissals for misconduct or incompetency and disputes in respect of which the parties have agreed to waive their right to adjudication by the Labour Court in favour of arbitration by the CCMA.

- **Arbitrating disputes in essential services:** If a dispute about a matter of mutual interest proceeds to arbitration and any party is engaged in an essential service, then the commissioner has **thirty days** (or such longer period as the parties may have agreed upon) from the date of the certificate stating that conciliation has failed to settle the dispute, to complete the arbitration and to issue a signed arbitration award providing brief reasons for the award.

- **Arbitrating disputes about dismissals for reasons relating to conduct or capacity:** If the dispute being arbitrated is about the fairness of a dismissal and a party has alleged that the reason for the dismissal relates to the employee's conduct or capacity, the parties are not entitled to be represented by a legal practitioner in the arbitration proceedings unless: the commissioner and all the other parties consent, or the commissioner concludes that it is unreasonable to expect a party to deal with the dispute without legal representation. In coming to this conclusion, consideration should be given to the nature of the questions of law raised by the dispute, the complexity of the dispute, the public interest, and the comparative ability of the opposing parties or their representatives to deal with the arbitration of the dispute.

Provision is also made for the commissioner, if he finds that the dismissal is procedurally unfair, to charge the employer an arbitration fee.

- **Consent to arbitration under the auspices of the CCMA:** In section 141 provision is made for all the parties to agree to arbitration under the auspices of the CCMA of disputes that, but for that agreement a party would have been entitled to refer to the Labour Court for adjudication. Any party to such arbitration agreement may apply to the Labour Court at any time to vary or set aside that agreement. If any party acts in breach of such an agreement by commencing proceedings in the Labour Court, any party to those proceedings may ask the Court to stay those proceedings and refer the dispute to arbitration, or, to continue with the proceedings with the Court acting as arbitrator.

Arbitration awards

An arbitration award is final and binding and may be made an order of the Labour Court unless it is an advisory arbitration award. An arbitration award may only be amended or rescinded if it was erroneously sought or erroneously made in the absence of any party affected by that award, or, if the award contains an ambiguity, obvious error or omission, or, if the award was granted as a result of a mistake common to the parties to the proceedings.

Any party to a dispute may take an arbitration award on review to the Labour Court asking for an order setting aside the award, based on an alleged defect in the arbitration proceedings, such as improper conduct on the part of the commissioner, or, a gross irregularity in the conduct of the arbitration proceedings, or, the alleged exceeding by the commissioner of his powers, or, that an award has been improperly obtained. Review applications must be made to the Labour Court within six weeks of the date that the award was served on the applicant, unless the alleged defect involves corruption, in which event, within six weeks of the date that the applicant discovers the corruption.

20.5.7 Dispute resolution through adjudication: the Labour Court and Labour Appeal Court

In the place of the Industrial Court, the new Act provides for the establishment of the Labour Court as a open court of law with jurisdiction in all the provinces of South Africa. The Labour Court is a court of record and has the same powers and status as a provincial division of the Supreme Court. The Court is presided over by a Judge President, a Deputy Judge President and as many judges as the President may consider necessary, acting on the advice of NEDLAC and in consultation with the Minister of Justice and the Judge President of the Labour Court. In order to qualify for appointment as a judge on the Labour Court, a person must have knowledge, experience and expertise in labour law, and either be a judge of the Supreme

Court or have been a legal practitioner for a cumulative period of at least 10 years before his appointment. The Labour Court has exclusive jurisdiction in respect of all matters that in terms of the Act are to be determined by the Labour Court but does not have jurisdiction to adjudicate an unresolved dispute if the Act requires the dispute to be resolved through arbitration. Interestingly, the Court may refuse to hear a matter, other than an appeal or review, if the Court is not satisfied that an attempt has been made to resolve the dispute through conciliation. The Labour Court may make any appropriate order or fulfil certain functions, including those listed in exhibit H.

Exhibit H

Powers Of Labour Court

The Labour Court has the power to:
- grant urgent interim relief;
- grant an interdict;
- order the performance of any particular act which order, when implemented, will remedy a wrong and give effect to the primary objects of this Act;
- grant a declaratory order;
- award compensation;
- award damages;
- order costs;
- order compliance with any provision of this Act;
- make any arbitration award or any settlement agreement, other than a collective agreement, an order of the Court;
- request the Commission to conduct an investigation to assist the Court and to submit a report to the Court;
- determine a dispute between a registered trade union, a registered employers' organisation, and one of its members about any alleged noncompliance with the constitution of that trade union or employers' organisation;
- condone the late filing of any document with, or the late referral of any dispute to, the Court;
- review the conduct of any person who performed (or failed to perform) a function provided for in the Act;
- review any decision taken or any act performed by the State in its capacity as employer;
- hear any appeals brought under the Occupational Health and Safety Act; and

deal with all matters necessary or incidental to performing its functions in terms of the Act or any other law

In any proceedings before the Labour Court, a party to the proceedings may appear in person or be represented by a legal practitioner, a co-employee or by a member, an office-bearer or official of that party's trade union or employers' organisation and, if the party is a juristic person, by a director or an employee. The Labour Court may make an order for the payment of costs, according to the requirements of the law and fairness. When deciding whether or not to order the payment of costs, the Labour Court may take into account whether the matter referred to the Court ought to have been referred to arbitration in terms of this Act and, if so, the extra costs incurred in referring the matter to the Court as well as the conduct of the parties in proceeding with or defending the matter before the Court and during the proceedings before the Court. The Labour Court may order costs against a party to the dispute or against any person who represented that party in those proceedings before the Court.

A new court of appeal in labour matters is instituted by the Act. The Labour Appeal Court is a court of law and equity. The Labour Appeal Court is the final court of appeal in respect of all judgments and orders made by the Labour Court in respect of the matters within its exclusive jurisdiction. In relation to matters under its jurisdiction the Labour Appeal Court has the same power and status as the Appellate Division. There is no further appeal from the Labour Appeal Court to the Appellate Division. The Labour Appeal Court consists of the Judge President of the Labour Court, the Deputy Judge President and three other judges of the Supreme Court. The Labour Appeal Court is constituted before any three judges whom the Judge President designates from the ranks of the aforementioned judges, provided that no judge of the Labour Appeal Court may sit in the hearing of an appeal against a judgment or an order given in a case that was heard before that judge. The Labour Appeal Court has exclusive jurisdiction to hear and determine all appeals against the final judgments and the final orders of the Labour Court and to decide any reserved question of law referred to it by the Labour Court.

20.5.8 Industrial action as part of collective bargaining in South Africa

20.5.8.1 General

Industrial action is an intrinsic part of collective bargaining and can be characterised as collective bargaining by other means. Industrial action is serious industrial conflict whereby one party tries to exert the highest degree of pressure on the other. It can take on various forms, such as go-slows, work-to-rule, sympathy strikes, overtime bans, and, on the part of the employer, lockouts.

20.5.8.2 Defining "strike" and "lockout" in South Africa

The Act provides a strong right to strike in that workers engaged in a strike protected by the Act may not be dismissed for striking (although strikers may be dismissed for misconduct or for operational reasons during a strike). The Act defines a strike as follows:

"... the partial or complete concerted refusal to work, or the retardation or obstruction of work, by persons who are or have been employed by the same employer or by different employers, for the purpose of remedying a grievance or resolving a dispute in respect of any matter of mutual interest between employer and employee, and every reference to 'work' in this definition includes overtime work, whether it is voluntary or compulsory".

From this definition the following constituent elements of a strike can be distilled:

- **Concerted action:** This implies first, that one worker cannot go on a strike (two or more workers are needed), and secondly, that the refusal to work, etc must be the result of some form of collusion or understanding between the workers (two or more workers who refuse independently to work, do not constitute a strike as defined).
- **Type of action:** The action constituting a strike may be a refusal to work or the retardation or obstruction of work (thus go-slows and sit-ins could qualify as strikes as defined).
- **Purpose:** This is the crucial and ultimately defining constituent element of a strike. Only strikes in support of a demand in respect of a matter of mutual interest between employer and employee will qualify as strikes in the legal sense.

Only if all three of the above elements of a strike are present can one talk of a strike in the defined sense. Other interesting aspects of the strike definition are the following:

- **Status of workers:** Employees as well as ex-employees employed by the same or different employers may be the participants in a strike.
- **Overtime work:** The positive law position (as developed by the Appellate Division) prior to the new Act was far from satisfactory: a concerted refusal to work compulsory overtime in support of a demand was regarded as a strike whereas the same refusal in respect of voluntary overtime could not be regarded as a strike but could constitute an unfair labour practice. The new definition brings much needed common sense and consistency regarding the refusal to work overtime (see the last part of the strike definition).

The Act defines a lockout as:

"... the exclusion by an employer of employees from the employer's workplace, for the purpose of compelling the employees to accept a demand in respect of any matter of mutual interest between employer and employee, whether or not the employer breaches those employees' contracts of employment in the course of or for the purpose of that exclusion".

It is important to note that a lockout will only be recognised as such, if the conduct and intent satisfy the definition. Two elements need to be present simultaneously, for it to be a lockout in terms of the Labour Relations Act: (i) a particular course of action on the part of the employer; (ii) accompanied by a certain intent. It should further be noted that in order to qualify as a lockout (like in the case of a strike), the demand has to be of a certain type: it must be an economic demand (thus, a demand that the employees should refrain from endorsing the policies of a particular political party, will be regarded as political demands, and, as such, will, per definition disqualify the conduct as a lockout).

Lockouts can be classified as either offensive or defensive. In the case of the defensive lockout the employer locks-out his workforce in reaction to industrial action by his workforce. This could, for instance, be appropriate where the employees are on a go-slow, work-to-rule, partial strike or a sit-in. In these situations the employer is prevented from employing temporary employees to do the work of the strikers (due to the physical presence of the strikers on the premises). By locking them out, he can overcome this obstacle. In other situations it may make strategic sense for the employer to take the initiative during negotiations by embarking on ·an offensive or pre-emptive lockout. This will be the case, for instance, where the employer wishes to avoid a strike at a time when he will be at his most vulnerable (for example, during periods of peak demand and production). By locking out the employees management tries to exert pressure on the employees to accept their offer, thereby hoping to bring the negotiations to a conclusion.

20.5.8.3 Status of strikes/lockouts in terms of the Act

Statutorily speaking strikes and lockouts can be categorised as prohibited, protected or unprotected.

Prohibited strikes/lockouts

These are strikes or lockouts that are absolutely prohibited. These usually occur under the following circumstances:

- if a collective agreement is in force that prohibits industrial action in respect of the issue in dispute;
- if the issue in dispute is subject to compulsory arbitration;
- if the issue in dispute is one that a party has the right to refer to arbitration or to the Labour Court in terms of the Act;
- if the employee is employed in an essential service (see below);
- if the employee is designated as a maintenance worker (see below);
- no strike or lockout may occur during the first year of a wage determination made in terms of the Wage Act that regulates the issue in dispute; and
- no strike or lockout may occur when a binding arbitration award or a ministerial determination that regulates the issue in dispute has been made.

Employees participating in a prohibited strike are guilty of misconduct and may be dismissed provided that a fair procedure is followed.

Protected strikes/lockouts

These are strikes or lockouts that conform with the procedural requirements stipulated in the Act. The most important legal consequence of a protected strike is that the strikers may not be dismissed for partaking in it.

Procedure for protected industrial action:

Every employee has the right to strike and every employer the right to lockout provided that certain procedural requirements are met. In essence these procedures require a dispute to be referred to a council (or, if there is no council with jurisdiction, to the CCMA) which has thirty days to resolve the dispute through conciliation, failing which, the trade union or the employer may give 48 hours written notice of its intention to strike or lockout; after the expiry of the notice period the strike or lockout will be protected (provided of course that the prohibited circumstances are not applicable). The procedure is depicted in figure 20.2.

Figure 20.2
Procedure for protected industrial action

Deviations from the above general procedure are applicable under the following circumstances:

● **Strike/lockout procedure in a collective agreement:** If there is a collective agreement containing a procedure for strikes and/or lockouts then a strike or lockout that conforms with that procedure will be protected industrial action. This is another example of how the new Act promotes collective bargaining. Under the previous Act compliance with the procedure prescribed by a collective agreement would have been irrelevant so far as the legality of the strike or lockout would have been concerned; the only way to have achieved legitimacy was to comply with the provisions of the Act. In stark contrast to this legalistic approach the new Act in effect allows the parties to contract out of the provisions of the statutory strike law in favour of their own (self)-regulated agreed procedure.

- **Defensive strike/lockout in reaction to unprocedural industrial action by the other party:** If the strike or lockout is in response (a so-called defensive strike or lockout) to an unprocedural strike or lockout, then the defensive strike or lockout will be protected under the Act.

- **Constitution of a council:** If the parties to the dispute are members of a bargaining council or a statutory council that has dealt with the dispute in terms of its constitution then the industrial action will be a protected strike or lockout under the Act.

- **Unilateral alterations of employment conditions by the employer:** If the employer unilaterally altered a term or condition of employment or he intends to do so and if the trade union or employee who has referred the dispute to a bargaining council or statutory council or the CCMA at the same time sent a copy of the referral, giving forty eight hours notice to the employer not to proceed or to reverse the unilateral alteration, and the forty eight hour period has ended without the employer having retracted the change (whether implemented or intended), then the strike in reaction to this unilateral action will be protected even though it does not comply with the general procedural requirements set out in figure 20.2.

- **Refusal to bargain:** If the issue in dispute concerns a refusal to bargain, an advisory award must have been made by the CCMA before the forty eight hours notice of the start of the proposed strike/lockout can be given. A refusal to bargain includes a refusal to recognise a trade union as a collective bargaining agent, or to agree to establish a bargaining council; or a withdrawal of recognition of a collective bargaining agent; or a resignation of a party from a bargaining council; or a dispute about appropriate bargaining units, or levels or bargaining subjects.

- **Essential services and maintenance services:** In terms of section 65 no person may take part in a strike or a lockout if that person is engaged in an essential service or a maintenance service. Disputes in these services must first be resolved through conciliation, and, should that have fail to settle the dispute, then through arbitration. The only exception to the no-strike rule in essential services is where the parties to a dispute have previously provided for the maintenance of minimum services in a designated essential service by way of a collective agreement which agreement has been ratified by the Essential Services Committee. For example, a trade union and a hospital may have concluded an agreement in which the trade union undertook to keep certain essential services staffed during a strike. If such an agreement is ratified by the ESC it would mean that workers may strike in the essential service but that they undertake to continue providing certain agreed upon minimum services for the duration of the strike. Considering the right to strike is a constitutionally protected right as well as the fact that there is no real equivalent surrogate for the strike weapon (arbitration remains a very poor second best option), the introduction of minimum services provisions in our strike law is to be welcomed.

The Act defines an 'essential service' as:

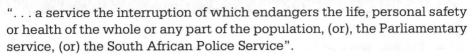

". . . a service the interruption of which endangers the life, personal safety or health of the whole or any part of the population, (or), the Parliamentary service, (or) the South African Police Service".

A special committee, the Essential Services Committee (ESC) is entrusted with the task of determining whether or not the whole or a part of any service is an essential service, and then to decide whether or not to designate the whole or a part of that service as an essential service; to determine disputes as to whether or not the whole or a part of any service is an essential service; and to determine whether or not the whole or a part of any service is a maintenance service. A service is defined (in section 75(1)) as a maintenance service ". . . *if the interruption of that service has the effect of material physical destruction to any working area, plant or machinery.*" An example of a maintenance service could be the operation of water pumps in a mine shaft. Should the continuous pumping of underground water be interrupted because of a strike it may well happen that the whole workplace is destroyed by flooding (thereby causing the permanent loss of jobs, something strikers would typically not intend to cause by their strike). If there is no collective agreement relating to the provision of a maintenance service, an employer may apply in writing to the essential services committee for a determination that the whole or a part of the employer's business is a maintenance service.

● **Scab labour:** An employer may not make use of replacement labour under the following two circumstances: first, to continue or maintain production during a protected strike if the whole or a part of the employer's service has been designated a maintenance service, or secondly, for the purpose of performing the work of any employee who is locked out, unless the lockout is in response to a strike. Replacement labour includes persons engaged through the services of a temporary employment service or an independent contractor.

Unprotected strikes/lockouts

These are strikes or lockouts that fall outside the procedures of the Act. The most important legal consequences are that the Labour Court may interdict such strikes or lockouts and order any just compensation for losses attributable to such strikes or lockouts. In addition strikers participating in an unprotected strike may be dismissed for striking, provided that their dismissal is procedurally and substantively fair.

As a summary, exhibit I contains some comparative perspectives regarding the consequences of these three different categories of industrial action.

20.5.8.4 Specific types of statutory industrial action

Thus far the focus has been on strikes as a form of industrial action in South Africa. The Act however caters for various types of industrial action, including lockouts already referred to.

Exhibit I

Consequences of industrial action

Protected strike/lockout
- Workers cannot be dismissed for striking (but may be dismissed for misconduct during the strike or for operational reasons).
- Involvement in a protected strike/lockout cannot constitute a delict.
- Employer is not obliged to remunerate strikers except in respect of payment in kind.
- Civil legal proceedings may not be instituted against a person for his/her involvement in a protected strike or lockout (except if the conduct constitutes an offence).
- Conduct in contravention of the Basic Conditions of Employment Act or the Wage Act does not constitute an offence.
- Some limitations apply in respect of the employer's ability to employ replacement workers during a protected strike if a part of his operations had been designated as maintenance services.

Unprotected/prohibited strike/lockout
- The Labour Court may interdict the strike or lockout
- The Labour Court may award just and equitable compensation for any loss attributable to the strike or lockout, having regard to a number of considerations [s 68(1)(b)]:
    - whether attempts were made to comply with the provisions of the chapter on strike law and the extent of those attempts;
    - whether the strike or lockout was premeditated;
    - whether the strike or lockout was in response to unjustified conduct by another party to the dispute;
    - whether there was compliance with a Labour Court order or interdict restraining any person from participating in industrial action;
    - the interests of orderly collective bargaining;
    - the duration of the strike or lockout; and
    - the financial position of the employer, trade union or employees.
    - involvement in an unprotected/prohibited strike may constitute a fair reason for dismissal (it is regarded as misconduct), provided that a fair procedure is followed.

Secondary strikes

In line with the trade union credo of united we stand, divided we fall, employees sometimes wish to support workers of another employer in a dispute those workers are having with their employer. The latter workers and their employer are referred to as the primary strikers and the primary employer to distinguish them from the secondary strikers (i.e. those who are not in dispute with their own employer but who wish to embark on industrial action in support of the demands of the primary strikers). Statutory regulation of secondary or sympathy strikes is introduced by the new Act which provides for this type of industrial action, provided certain conditions are met. The Labour Relations Act 66 of 1995 defines a secondary strike as ". . . a *strike,* or conduct in contemplation or furtherance of a *strike,* that is in support of a *strike* by other *employees* against their employer but does not include a *strike* in pursuit of a demand and referred to a *council* if the striking *employees,*

Exhibit J

Protected secondary strikes

A secondary strike will qualify as a protected strike, provided that:
- the primary strike is a protected strike;
- the secondary strikers gave their own employer at least seven days written notice prior to the start of the secondary strike; and
- the harm caused to the secondary employer is reasonable in relation to the possible effect that the secondary strike will have on the business of the primary employer.

Proportionality test

The nature and extent of the secondary industrial action should not be more harmful to the secondary employer than that which is reasonably required to make an effective impact on the primary employer's business. So, for instance, to embark on a crippling secondary strike in circumstances where neither the secondary employer nor his business relationship with the primary employer is such that the secondary strikers' aim of bringing pressure to bear on the primary employer is likely to materialise, would likely render such a secondary strike unprotected.

Three further points regarding the proportionality test and secondary strikes are worth noting:
- The principle of proportionality may often have the consequence that secondary industrial action will have to be paired down to something less than a full-blown strike, for example picketing may be effective as a pressure tactic but entail less harm to the secondary employer.
- For a secondary strike to be a protected strike it is not a requirement that there should be some form of formal relationship between the primary and the secondary employer (such as, for example, that both employers belong to the same group of companies).
- Proportionality requires effectiveness of the secondary action (in the sense that it impacts on the primary employer).

---

employed within the *registered scope* of that *council*, have a material interest in that demand." A secondary strike must therefore qualify as a strike as defined and in order to qualify as a protected industrial action the primary strike must itself be a protected strike (i.e. both the secondary and the primary strikes must be in conformity with the Act). The requirements for a secondary strike to qualify as a protected strike is summarised in exhibit J.

Picketing .

Picketing may be described ". . . as a public expression by workers of their grievances in order to make it known to and elicit support from the general public and other relevant constituencies for their cause. It typically involves some form of public protest directed at the employer and in the near vicinity of the employer's place of business as well as efforts to dissuade the general public and suppliers from normal business dealings with the targeted employer and to persuade other workers to stop working and to join the picket.

The old Act did not make provision for picketing resulting in much uncertainty with the most important source of law relating to picketing being municipal bylaws regulating traffic flow and public disturbance. Under the new Act picketing is recognised as a legitimate form of industrial action worthy of protection subject to certain conditions (see exhibit K). This is not surprising since the right to picket is a constitutionally protected right.

Exhibit K

Protected picketing
Employees who picket enjoy the same protection as workers involved in a protected strike, provided that:

- they are members of a registered trade union;
- that trade union has authorised the picket;
- the picket amounts to a peaceful demonstration;
- the picket is in support of a protected strike or in opposition to any lockout;
- the picket takes place in a public place outside the employer's premises (or, with the employer's permission — which permission may not be refused unreasonably — inside the employer's premises); and
- the agreed upon picketing rules (or in the absence of such agreement, the picketing rules prescribed by the CCMA) are followed.

Protest action

'Protest action' is defined in the Act as ". . . **the partial or complete concerted refusal to work, or the retardation or obstruction of work, for the purpose of promoting or defending the socioeconomic interests of workers, but not for a purpose referred to in the definition of strike.**"

The more common name for protest action is "stayaway", the phenomenon not unknown to most South Africans. Under the old Act (which was silent on the issue of stayaways) the Courts had great difficulty in dealing with stay-aways. Some presiding officers perceived it (correctly it is submitted) as a legitimate form of collective action whereas in other cases the essentially collective nature of the stayaway was simple ignored and employers were allowed to treat workers who participated in stayaways on an individual basis as being guilty of misconduct (the form of misconduct in question being unauthorised absence from work). The purpose element of the definition of a strike (". . .*for the purpose of remedying a grievance or resolving a dispute in respect of any matter of mutual interest between employer and employee . . .*") and more particularly the *mutual interest* component thereof, exclude industrial action aimed at broader socioeconomic issues. The ILOs FFCC stringently criticised our dispensation under the old Act for not recognising workers' rights to protest against things that directly affect them as workers but do not fall within the narrow confines of *mutual interest between employer and employee*". It has of course to be admitted that what constitutes *socioeconomic interests of workers* is not amendable to precise definition. For instance, whereas protest action against proposed new legislation on labour matters or taxation or against the government's intended privatisation of state assets (insofar as job security may be affected) would clearly fall within the ambit of socioeconomic interest of workers, a stayaway for or against the reinstitution of the death penalty or a political party should not be regarded as permissible protest action.

In exhibit L the requirements for protected protest action are summarised. The Labour Court can interdict protest action that does not comply with the laid down prerequisites or grant a declaratory order in respect of such action.

Exhibit L

Protected protest action

Employees participating in action to promote or defend the socioeconomic interests of workers will enjoy the same protection as workers involved in a protected strike, if the following requirements have been met:

- employees must not be engaged in an essential service or maintenance service;
- the protest action has been called/authorised by a registered trade union;
- NEDLAC has been given 14 days' notice of the protest action;
- the matter giving rise to the protest action has been considered by NEDLAC or some other appropriate (tripartite?) forum; and
- the employees do not act in breach or contempt of an order of the Labour Court relating to the protest action

Lockouts

Section 27 of the Interim Constitution of the Republic of South Africa (Act 200 of 1993) guaranteed the fundamental right of employers to take recourse to the lockout. Under pressure from COSATU, the government forced the Constituent Assembly to drop the lockout clause from the draft Final Constitution. It must be understood that apart from the possible negative consequences this may have had in overseas investors' confidence in South Africa as a possible country to invest in, the effect of this omission is zero as long as the right to lockout is provided for in the Labour Relations Act. The constitutional void will only emerge as of crucial importance should a future government wish to outlaw employers' right to lockout (such an amendment to the Labour Relations Act would not have been possible had the lockout provision been retained in the final Constitution). The lockout is the employer's economic weapon during the collective bargaining process to compel workers to accept his offer or proposal. The definition of the lockout contained in the Labour Relations Act 66 of 1995 (see above) read together with other provision of the Act introduces some important changes from the previous regime. These are discussed below.

As was the case under the Labour Relations Act 28 of 1956, the definition of "lockout" contains two elements, namely, first, certain action on the employer's part, and, secondly, this action must be in pursuit of a specific objective. From existing case law it can be accepted that both elements must be present simulta-neously for the employer's conduct to qualify as a lockout as defined. Apart from this similarity between the old and the new definition of "lockout" the following important differences should be noted:

1. The definition of a lockout is substantially narrower than that which obtained under the Labour Relations Act 28 of 1956 in that only the exclusion of employees from the employer's premises is now recognised as action falling within the definition. For instance, the so-called dismissal lockout would no longer be recognised as a form of lockout. Also see the next point .

2. Lockout dismissals are, in terms of s 187, regarded as automatically unfair dis-missals ("a *dismissal* is automatically unfair if . . . the reason for the *dismissal* is . . . to compel the *employee* to accept a demand in respect of any matter of mutual interest between the employer and *employee* . . ."). Thus, not only are lockout dismissals not regarded as lockouts any more, it is in fact stringently censured as constituting an "automatically unfair dismissal (see chapter 19).

3. Employees who go on strike in response to a unilateral change in their condi-tions of employment, will be protected even if they had not complied with the prescribed procedures relating to protected strikes.

4. The total or partial discontinuance by the employer of his business is no longer regarded as a form of lockout.

Once it has been established that the action taken by the employer constitutes a lockout, as defined, it remains to be determined whether the lockout conforms with the requirements of the Act. The requirements are, with the necessary changes, the same as those applicable to strike action. Likewise, the consequences of a pro-tected lockout and an unprotected lockout respectively, are similar to the consequences that follow upon a protected and unprotected strike respectively. Review the discussion under the headings 'Defining "strike" and "lockout" in South Africa' on page 652 and 'Status of strikes/lockouts in terms of the Act' on page 654 above.

20.6 CONCLUSION

In this chapter you were introduced to certain theoretical perspectives underpin-ning industrial and labour relations, and aspects of the South African industrial relations system were discussed in broad terms. This now forms the foundation for the next chapter in which we examine certain organisation-level aspects of labour relations.

SELF-EVALUATION QUESTIONS

1. Explain the concepts "labour relations", "employee relations" and "industrial relations". Are there any differences? If so, what do they entail?

2. Who are the parties involved in labour and industrial relations? What are their respective roles, rights and duties?
3. Describe four theoretical perspectives of industrial and labour relations.
4. Explain why and how trade unions exist and operate.
5. Discuss the organisational rights of South African trade unions.
6. Write an essay explaining the structures and processes for collective bargaining and dispute resolution in South Africa in terms of relevant statutory provisions.
7. "Only some striking workers may be dismissed in terms of the Labour Relations Act 66 of 1995." Explain.

ENDNOTE

1. Section 56 provides for a procedure for the admission of parties to a council

BIBLIOGRAPHY

Bendix, S. 1996. *Industrial Relations in the New South Africa*, 3 ed. Cape Town: Juta

Du Plessis, JV, Fouché, MA, Jordaan, B and Van Wyk, MW. 1996. *A Practical Guide to Labour Law*, 2 ed. Durban: Butterworths

Finnemore, M & Van der Merwe, P. 1996. *Introduction to Labour Relations in South Africa*, 4 ed.Durban: Butterworths

Levy, A and Associates. 1995. *Annual Report on Labour Relations in South Africa: 1995–1996*. Johannesburg: Andrew Levy and Associates

Levy, A and Associates. 1996. *Annual Report on Labour Relations in South Africa: 1996–1997*. Johannesburg: Andrew Levy and Associates

Salamon, M. 1992. *Industrial Relations: Theory and Practice*, 2 ed. New York: Prentice-Hall

chapter (21) Managing Labour Relations at Organisational Level

STUDY OBJECTIVES

After studying this chapter, you should be able to:

- describe the nature and importance of communication in labour relations;
- explain the nature of employee grievances and the value of handling such grievances properly;
- discuss the importance of eliciting greater employee involvement and participation;
- explain how discipline can be successfully maintained in the workplace;
- write concise notes on union-management interactions;
- differentiate between different types of collective agreements;
- explain various broad types or kinds of collective negotiation;
- discuss statutory workplace forums as structures for promoting union-management cooperation;
- write an essay on the management of strikes.

21.1 INTRODUCTION

In chapter 20 you were introduced to the general theoretical basis of labour relations and the nature of South Africa's industrial relations system. The focus now shifts to those aspects which are more directly related to the management of labour and employee relations at the level of the organisation.

In this chapter the emphasis is therefore on how managers can deal with certain aspects in the workplace which relate to labour and employee relations. With regard to the collective dimension, the focus is on actually dealing with trade union–management interaction at the level of the organisation. As far as the individual dimension is concerned, the primary emphasis is on handling different aspects of employee relations, irrespective of whether the employees belong to a union or not. These include communication, discipline and grievances. Due to the fact that a breakdown in relations can always occur, some attention is also paid to issues involved in the handling of strikes.

21.2 ESTABLISHING SOUND EMPLOYEE RELATIONS

Regardless of whether or not employees belong to trade unions, managers have to see to it that the relations between themselves and their subordinates, between the subordinates themselves, and between the employees and their work are maintained at a standard conducive to sound labour relations and to a generally more successful organisation. Activities and practices of managing employee relations can therefore be viewed as those aimed at improving cooperation and optimising conflict levels among various categories of employees, irrespective of the presence or absence of trade unions.

21.2.1 Communicating with employees

21.2.1.1 *The nature and importance of communication in employee relations*

One of the most important things all managers have to do is to communicate with their subordinates. Some experts estimate that up to 80 % of the working time of managers is spent on some form of communication-related activity. Without communication people will not know what work to do, how to do it, how well they are doing it, etc. Just as no marriage relationship can exist without some form of communication, the quality of labour and employee relations depends to a considerable extent upon the nature and quality of the communication between all the parties involved. However, it would be an overstatement to say that good communication is the panacea for all the labour relations problems in the workplace. Although the quality of communication can have an important effect on the quality of labour and employee relations, the causes of labour-related problems lie (as mentioned in the previous chapter) in the more deeply rooted differences between the different role-players in the employment relationship. Communication is, however, a very necessary medium or means through which the parties can identify and address these differences. Effective communication is a necessary but not sufficient precondition for sound labour relations.

Communication can generally be viewed as the process of conveying and sharing information between interacting people. It is a process of information exchange between receivers and senders. In the context of labour and employee relations communication can be viewed as the exchange of information related to anything that flows from or can have an impact on the employment relationship. Through the medium of communication people can relate to one another in the workplace and through communication meaning is given to relationships.

Communication can occur on a one-on-one basis, such as when an individual subordinate informs his/her individual superior that a particular job has been completed. It can also occur on a one-on-group basis, such as when the head of the salary administration section informs all of his/her subordinates at a joint meeting of the newly acquired computerised payroll system.

Representatives of groups of employees also often communicate. During the process of negotiation there is, for example, a constant flow and exchange of information between the members of the negotiating teams, with the aim of influencing and persuading each other to move closer towards an agreement.

Communication can be nonverbal or verbal, in oral or written form. During negotiations a hard slam on the table by one party can convey to the other party how the former feels about something which came to the fore during the course of the negotiations — that would be an example of a nonverbal form of communication. Worker representatives can request a meeting with a manager by means of a written letter or memorandum or by means of a telephonic conversation. An employee who was not given an expected promotion and who gives the boss a note of complaint and later cries in the superior's office as a result of his/her disappointment is communicating in the verbal, written and oral, as well as in the nonverbal form.

Whatever the form of communication, the aim remains the transmission of messages to receivers so that they can understand the intended meanings of the senders' messages. There may, however, be many different obstacles or barriers to successful communication. Before we examine these, it is important to focus briefly on some of the methods used for communication with employees in the workplace.

21.2.1.2 Methods of communicating with employees

It must be remembered that proper communication is two-way process. Because there are two parties (receiver and sender), there is normally some need for a flow of information between the two parties. This is not to say that one-way communication does not sometimes occur. However, when management devises methods to convey information to employees, it is advisable to incorporate checks whether the information has been received correctly and whether the particular communication methods work efficiently and effectively.

Different methods can be used to communicate with employees.

Formal letters or memoranda

Some letters are of a personal nature, such as when an individual is informed that a request for a transfer has been approved. At other times it is necessary for management to inform all or a particular group of employees of something very specific which applies to all concerned. A general letter or memorandum can, for example, be distributed by the personnel department to all the members of the organisation's medical aid scheme when some of the conditions of membership change.

Notice boards

The conventional notice board is still commonly used. Frequently management wants to make information of a general nature available to those who may be interested, while not bothering those who may not be interested. Notice boards can, for example, be used to put up notices of vacancies elsewhere in an organisation — for those who may be interested in a career or job change. Notice boards are also often available to trade union representatives (shop stewards) for putting up union notices. It is a low-cost method, easy to use and often has widespread acceptability due to its convenience. It is, however, suitable mainly for brief messages rather than lengthy, complicated information documents.

In-house newspapers/journals

As a general rule such publications are produced and distributed to all employees free of charge. Such a publication is usually published quite regularly (on a monthly or two-weekly basis) and normally contains interesting and important general information about the organisation and its employees. It can, for example, be used to recognise employees' achievements (both in and out of work), to inform the staff of important new appointments or staff movements, to advertise internal vacancies, to inform the readers of business developments, and so forth. Important and interesting, newsworthy information can thus be made available to all employees and even to outsiders who may be interested.

Special publications or reports

Sometimes it is wise to publicise something very important in a special way. So, for example, when an organisation undergoes a major change in corporate image or business direction, it may be necessary to publish and distribute a high quality booklet which spells out the necessary details about the change in direction or new image.

A case at hand . . .

Communication in Eskom

When Eskom (South Africa's giant electricity utility), for example, realised that a change of culture was needed in its dealing with employees, their representatives and trade unions, the organisation embarked on a new process of union–management interaction. Whereas in the past the approach had often been quite autocratic and paternalistic, Eskom decided to cooperate with organised labour to develop and institute processes to facilitate meaningful input by recognised trade unions over decisions that affected them as key stakeholders. To explain the rationale behind this move and the complexities and benefits involved, a glossy 52-page document entitled *A Vision Unfolding: The Path to Power* was published in 1993.

Sometimes organisations also publish glossy employee reports on an annual basis. These written documents (akin to those for the shareholders) are normally specifically aimed at the employees and provide information relating to the performance and level of success of the organisation for a particular financial year (see also chapter 23).

In-house videos and television technology

A method which can be quite expensive, but often well worth the cost, is the production of video briefings. An organisation sometimes wish to convey complex information where different issues have to be explained in a simple, user-friendly and uniform way to great numbers of employees. When an organisation, for example, introduces a new employee share ownership plan, or when a major reorganisation exercise is embarked upon and it has to be explained to employees why and how it may affect them, a video can be produced with members of the top management team discussing the relevant issues. Big corporations with many establishments can produce such videos in-house and then distribute them to the various business units or establishments for the employees' information. Other forms of television technology can also be used. Different TV watchpoints can be utilised at the various establishments or plants of an organisation by means of an open line rented from a TV broadcasting organisation, one day per week, for a specific time slot.

Electronic mail

In the current era of information technology, there are hosts of opportunities to make use of computer technology to transmit information to employees. Important and urgent messages can, for example, be sent to certain managers via an electronic mail system; they can then pass the necessary information on to their subordinates if not all the employees have access to the system. If, for example, there is a strike and labour unrest in particular areas of a multiplant organisation, managers in other areas can constantly be kept informed of developments in order to monitor the chances of the unrest spreading.

Briefing groups

This is a structured system which can be used on a regular basis by management to cascade down, throughout the organisation or relevant parts thereof, news of particular developments or issues which may be of importance. As a rule a written document containing the relevant information is distributed from a particular level of management downwards, with each manager or supervisor reading the information to the group of subordinates reporting to him or her. Each level of manager does the same right down to the level where the lowest first-line supervisor reads out the same document to his/her small group of workers. The relevant issues are then normally also discussed in question-and-answer sessions (see figure 21.1)

Committees

Although the establishment of formal committees, where representatives of management and nonmanagement employees (including, but not limited to, union representatives) get together to deal with certain issues in a formalised manner, can be viewed as a method of securing more employee involvement, participation and thus (hopefully) identification with and commitment to the organisation's objec-

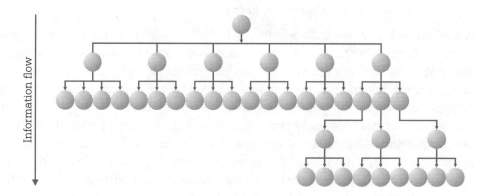

Figure 21.1
Briefing groups

tives, such committees can also be viewed as forums where information is exchanged. At such committees (for example, health and safety committees, workplace forums or other consultative committees), employees can communicate formally about important issues connected to the employment relationship. One of the objectives of a workplace forum is for example, to facilitate better communication on issues such as transport, accommodation, physical working conditions, rest and meal breaks, general worker problems or complaints, or even possible changes in organisation policy. At safety committee meetings safety representatives, exchange information particularly related to the safety of persons in the workplace, often with the objective of making recommendations to management. Similarly, via safety representatives and committees management can disseminate important safety-related information to the workforce.

Diverse face-to-face methods

"Open management" is a concept which is used to refer to a style of management which focuses on promoting the upward flow of information. It is often said that a particular manager or organisation policy statement supports an open door policy. This simply means that as much as possible is being done to enhance opportunities for upward communication from subordinates to superiors.

It is therefore quite an informal method of communication. A particular technique in this regard is sometimes referred to as MBWA (management by walking around). This occurs when a manager is seen walking, talking, listening and observing the job situation. In this way information which may relate to or influence the employment relationship can be exchanged in an informal way.

Another approach may be to hold get-together sessions. This is not the same as the formal meetings scheduled from time to time so that managers and workers in particular departments, sections, or committees can discuss specific issues according to an agenda. *Get-together-sessions* may be more informal and less frequent and enable the parties to talk out or speak up about things that they may like or dislike in the work situation. Sometimes they can even take the form of after-hours social sessions.

Various informal or formal face-to-face interaction opportunities can thus enhance the quality of communication. An example of a very special form of face-to-face communication practised in a prominent South African organisation is cited below.

A case at hand . . .

Honest workplace conversations at SA Breweries*

Brian Fenton, then training manager at SAB, explained in an article in *People Dynamics* that not only the quantity of communication between parties in the workplace is important but also the nature in which communication is opened up. In the case of SAB, a programme to introduce "honest, on-the-level" communication skills to all SAB staff was introduced in the early nineties. The following notion was said to be fundamental to the process: "If I have a view and you have a view and we conduct a conversation in which these views are expressed in a nondefensive way, there may be a good chance that a new, better way will be synergised." SAB therefore ran two-day training programmes designed to give delegates skills and practice at expressing what they are thinking. The programme started off by introducing delegates to the concept of perception in communication and then proceeded to cover the skills and principles of communication. The programme also included case studies and role-plays designed to enable delegates to determine real relevant issues and then to be able to express them. Delegates were also, in the final module, helped to prepare relevant issues for on-the-level discussions back in the workplace.

Said Fenton: "It is our view that as we move into an age where participation becomes the order of the day, organisational teams are going to have to become more efficient at reaching consensus on controversial issues. The skill of being able to quickly identify the issues and express them nondefensively will become increasingly critical."

*Source: Adapted from Fenton 1993: 15–17

Diverse written communication methods

There are many other ways of exchanging information in the workplace. Sometimes it is necessary simply to **inform** employees or their representatives without requiring any feedback or two-way communication.

Often this is the case with the written word. Management may want to remind workers of something or inform them about something, and then use may be made of *notes in pay packets* or *flash notices.*

At other times it may be really necessary to get the attention of employees and use may be made of huge, colourful *placards* or *posters* to convey a certain message. Management may also make use of other forms of written communication such as *brochures* or *pocket cards* which may, for example, contain the mission and value statement of the organisation. Other methods include *information bulletins* and *newsletters.*

Policy handbooks and manuals represent another form of written communication — albeit a more comprehensive form. There are therefore many different written communication methods which can be used.

Special surveys

Sometimes it is necessary to get very specific information from employees. Attitude surveys are, for example, conducted in many organisations on a one-off or regular basis. Use can be made of questionnaires (and/or interviews, for example) to try to discover the views, opinions, feelings — the attitudes — of employees regarding a variety of aspects which relate to the employment relationship.

Management can, for instance, arrange for an audit to check the quality and nature of communication in the organisation. Similarly, labour relations audits and so-called climate surveys can be undertaken.

The idea is to collect the information, interpret it, to draw conclusions and to make recommendations regarding the specific area which has been surveyed. It is also very important to ensure that the relevant employees receive the necessary feedback regarding such survey results.

The scientific nature of these methods may make them more expensive and time-consuming, but if professionally qualified people are employed to conduct a survey properly, it is generally worth the cost.

Mass media communication

Some large corporations have their own phone-in slots on radio stations. Employees are encouraged to raise issues and comments on air, which a management representative responds to. In this way it is hoped to reach a large employee audience (as well as society at large).

Sometimes organisations also use full-page newspaper advertisements to communicate management's point of view (on a critical issue of dispute with a trade union, for example) to its employees (and society at large).

Typically, the mass media are resorted to if the issue is deemed to extend beyond the workplace and employees.

21.2.1.3 Communication barriers

Despite the fact that the importance of communication is widely recognised in organisations, some experts maintain that labour-related problems in the workplace can often be attributed to a failure to communicate properly. Miscellaneous obstacles or barriers are often advanced as the underlying causes of this failure. The objective of this section is simply to draw the reader's attention to this problem, given the limited scope of the book.

Barriers can relate to such things as *differences in frames of reference* (see chapter 3); *language or semantic problems* (not understanding the meaning of a term, phrase or symbol); *selective perception* (paying attention only to that which one believes is necessary); *lack of attention* (due to concentration problems, resulting from noise — physical or psychological, or due to information overload); *contextual problems* (such as timing problems, the size of the unit where communication takes place, or the emotional state of any of the parties); the *deliberate creation of obstacles* (such as refusal to listen or to pay attention, switching off, or deliberately providing misleading information); *incompetent communicators* (people often simply lack the necessary communication skills — they do not understand the dynamics of communication, they are not aware of the possible obstacles and/or they do not know how to overcome them).

A conscious effort has to be made to overcome communication obstacles such as those cited above, and thereby to improve information exchange in the workplace.

21.2.1.4 Communication: concluding remarks

The importance of effective communication in the workplace cannot be overemphasised. To many management experts communication is the lifeblood of the management process. It is omnipresent in all organisations and in life in general. As you read this section, communication is taking place; hopefully the authors' message will be understood as it was originally intended.

There are many other possible forms of communication; these will be highlighted in following sections dealing with establishing sounder employee and labour relations.

21.2.2 Handling employee grievances

As has already been mentioned, sound employee and labour relations are dependent on constant efforts to obtain the best fit in the employment relationship. Both the formal (for example stipulations of the employment contract) and informal (for example expectations in terms of the psychological contract) aspects of the employment relationship can be the root cause of employee dissatisfaction. When an employee is unhappy or dissatisfied with something in the workplace, he/she may ultimately decide to terminate the relationship by resigning if the matter is not resolved. However, before such a drastic, final step is taken, there should be an opportunity to address the relevant issue(s) in a formalised manner.

Grievance handling refers to the process whereby management formally deals with the officially presented complaint(s) of workers relating to the employment relationship (excluding disciplinary matters). A grievance must, however, be distinguished from a worker complaint or problem. A worker may experience a problem that is not work-related, but which may eventually have an influence on the employment relationship — such as personal financial difficulties, family problems or drug addiction problems. These are not grievances because they are not directly related to the employment relationship. On the other hand, a worker may be dissatisfied with something directly related to the employment relationship, but the dissatisfaction may simply be expressed in an informal way — for example by complaining to somebody else. Such a case does not involve a grievance as such because the issue has not been formalised or fed into the official grievance procedure.

Employees' work-related complaints can be formalised as official grievances by means of a *grievance procedure.* By formally presenting such a complaint to management, the worker communicates to management the fact that there is either a real or a perceived breach of the psychological or employment contract. The grievance procedure can therefore be viewed as a method of (mostly) upward communication in the workplace. The formality of the grievance procedure does not preclude management from proactively dealing with worker dissatisfaction or problems even before these become grievances. Such a procedure does, however, help to prevent managers from dodging difficult-to-deal-with worker complaints and to ensure greater consistency in the process of attending to official work-related complaints.

21.2.2.1 *Principles underlying grievance handling*

A number of important principles (some of which have already been referred to in the preceding paragraphs) form the basis of grievance handling and related procedures.

- Management must acknowledge the fact that workers may from time to time be dissatisfied with aspects related to the employment relationship.
- Management must accept the responsibility for addressing and settling all legitimate employee grievances in a fair manner.
- It is best to solve grievances as promptly and as close as practically possible to the point of origin.
- All employees who air grievances must enjoy guaranteed protection against any form of discrimination, victimisation or prejudice whatsoever.
- Management must accept the fundamental right of workers to make use of the help of representatives (either union or otherwise) in the process of airing and handling grievances.
- Management is responsible for the smooth operation of the organisation; although grievance handling is extremely important, the utilisation of the grievance procedure should not unnecessarily disrupt (but rather facilitate) the operation of the organisation.
- A number of time-specified and progressive procedural steps should be spelled out and followed, from the lowest to the highest level of management, in order to arrive at the point where a grievance is solved to the optimum satisfaction of all parties concerned.
- The right of employees to pursue channels of dispute resolution beyond the organisation in cases where grievances cannot be solved through the grievance procedure must be recognised.

21.2.2.2 The grievance procedure

The grievance procedure normally manifests itself in a document which spells out the stages or steps to be followed when employees (as individuals as well as in a group context) have grievances. The exact nature and sequence of steps will vary from organisation to organisation, depending on variables such as their complexity, size and structure. Nonetheless, certain steps can be outlined by way of example.

Step one occurs when the aggrieved person verbally informs the immediate supervisor about the complaint. In this way the grievance is made official and it can therefore be recommended that the event (if solved) be recorded in some way. At this stage it may not yet be necessary for any third party involvement (for example in the form of a worker representative). However, if the issue involves or relates to the immediate supervisor, the grievance procedure normally stipulates the first step to be the referral of the issue to the next higher level of management. If the issue is not solved within a reasonable time (say twenty-four hours), step 2 will follow.

Step 2 generally entails putting the grievance in writing (usually in triplicate), involving a third party like a shop steward (if so wished), and presenting it to a higher level of management (that is, to the superior of the immediate supervisor). One copy is kept by the employee and the other is normally handed to the industrial relations or HR officer. If the grievance is not solved within a reasonable time (say another twenty-four hours), step 3 will follow.

Step 3, the last stage, will (depending on the organisational characteristics) involve consideration of the issue by an even higher level of manager or a formal grievance investigation led by a grievance committee. As a rule such an impartial committee consists of a labour relations/human resources expert, employee representatives, a senior manager and any other experts who may be of particular value with regard to the specific issue at hand. More time is usually allowed at this stage (approximately another two to six days) because at this point it is realised that the issue at hand is quite serious and difficult to solve. The outcome of the grievance committee's investigation has to be announced in writing to all relevant parties. If the issue is not solved, the process of external dispute resolution may be put in motion.

21.2.2.3 Grievance handling: A final comment

It is of utmost importance for sound labour and employee relations, as well as for organisational success in general, to establish and maintain a formally recognised procedure, acceptable to all parties, that can serve as the channel for upward communication when employees are dissatisfied with aspects relating to the employment relationship. In this way unnecessary tension can be relieved and an open climate conducive to a relationship of trust and security can be created. However, it should be noted that, in South Africa, in contrast to the USA for example, the grievance procedure is not used for addressing employee dissatisfaction regarding disciplinary matters. For this purpose appeal procedures are normally necessary. section 21.2.4 focuses on these aspects.

21.2.3 Eliciting employee involvement and participation

In chapter 12 various leadership styles were highlighted. The way management leads subordinates can exert a profound influence on the quality of labour and employee relations within the organisation. As indicated in section 21.2 above, the aim of management with regard to employee relations is to facilitate employee cooperation and to optimise conflict levels. As pointed out in chapter 12, democratic or participative leadership styles often offer the best potential to do just this. According to Kemp (1992: 13), the power struggles and conflict between trade unions and the management of organisations revolve largely around different perceptions of the extent to which employee participation (and thus forms of industrial democracy), as opposed to autocratic management practices, is actually practised.

The concepts *employee involvement* (EI) and *employee participation* (EP) are sometimes used interchangeably and are even viewed by some as having the same meaning as industrial democracy. Without getting you involved in the complex semantic debate which surrounds this issue, the approach taken in this book is that EI and EP basically refer to management initiatives to give employees the opportunity to become involved or to take part in the decision-making processes related to their daily work and the operations of the organisation in general. They refer to any form of altering the power relations within the organisation, either directly or indirectly (through representatives), beyond the traditional form of power sharing embedded in the collective bargaining process. Some methods of facilitating better communication within the organisation can thus also be viewed as forms of EI and EP. Relevant examples cited in the previous section include team briefing, meetings and committees.

In Line with Nel, Erasmus and Swanepoel's (1993: 50–52) view, EI/EP essentially involve those processes whereby non-management employees are given the opportunity to take part in (and to feel part of) and to influence areas of decision making that have traditionally been labelled "management prerogatives". This means, to a certain extent, that management employees will have to yield control and seek more cooperative people management styles and methods.

Employee involvement and participation can take on various *forms* at various *levels* within the organisation and can be introduced in varying *degrees*. Also, the focus of EI/EP can differ from situation to situation. The focus may, for example, be purely financial — such as when all employees can join directly in profit-sharing schemes (see also chapter 17), or involve high-level decision making — such as when indirect participation is facilitated by having trade union representatives on the organisation's board. An example of the latter is found in the case of Eskom, South Africa's giant electricity utility. The form can thus be either formal or informal and direct or indirect. The degree of EI/EP is related to the extent to which employees can exert an influence on the relevant processes, decisions or outcomes. In this regard various techniques of EI/EP can be identified, ranging from simply informing employees, to two-way communication, consultation (where employees' views are sought without any commitment to necessarily incorporate their ideas), negotiation and even co-determination.

In some techniques, like team briefing, employees are primarily informed, although there can sometimes be two-way communication. With other techniques, such as quality circles, the employees' degree of involvement and participation is greater. The most extreme degree of EI/EP is found in organisations which are fully controlled by the workers or employees. Although not very widespread in South Africa, worker cooperatives fall into the latter category. Jaffee (1990: 193) defines this type of organisation as "an enterprise which is collectively and democratically controlled by those who work in it". One such cooperative that has received widespread publicity in the early nineties is the registered company Zenzeleni Clothing Pty Ltd, in which the South African Clothing and Textile Workers Union has played a decisive role.

Many other ways of eliciting EI/EP can be cited. In the case of suggestion schemes, for example, employees are given the opportunity to put forward ideas for improvements in the organisation's operations; these are normally rewarded if greater success actually results. Sometimes work is redesigned to provide for autonomous work teams or other forms of teamwork (see also chapter 6) in which work tasks are assigned to whole groups rather than to particular individual employees. In the case of quality circles all the workers who form part of a particular section or department are trained to become competent participants in a continuous process of problem identification and problem-solving in order to improve the quality of work processes in their section/department/area. As can be gathered from the foregoing paragraphs, EI/EP is aimed largely at eliciting greater employee identification with and commitment to the organisation and the work itself by creating opportunities to improve the quality of their working life. The collective dimension of trade unions should, however, never be neglected in a country like South Africa where they play such an important role. Even when direct forms of participation are considered, it is advisable to involve the trade unions right from the start, especially when the relevant trade unions have high representativity and thus a strong power base. The example of PG Bison (see page 668) serves to illustrate this point.

21.2.4 Disciplining employees

The origin of the term *discipline* lies in the term *disciple*, which can be defined as a learner. This means that the ultimate aim of disciplining employees must be to teach them how to behave and how not to behave within the context of getting the work done in an organisation. Unfortunately too many people view discipline negatively, as being synonymous with punishment and enforcement.

The aim of discipline is therefore, according to Salamon (1992: 592), to ensure that all employees conform to the performance and behavioural standards and cri-

A case at hand . . .

The case of PG Bison*

Implementing emloyee involvement and participation in practice

PG Bison has annual sales of R357 million, and manufactures and distributes timber and industrial products. It has factories and branches throughout the country. The company employs around 5 000 people. PG Bison was not under a significant external threat when a scheme for EI/EP was first conceptualised, although profits had gradually declined. In 1987 Leon Cohen, the CEO of PG Bison Ltd, was concerned by the growing polarisation in the country at the time, and recognised that, if the company was to survive in a posta-partheid SA, it had to change its structure and culture fundamentally. He instituted a number of value-sharing workshops with the intention of building trust between various groups. At the same time existing management styles which maintained traditional, hierarchical structures were challenged by the introduction of participative structures at shop-floor level. These In-a-Groups encouraged employees to participation in decision making. Further, shop stewards indicated that they wanted to participate in decision making as equal stakeholders. A national shop stewards committee was established in October 1989.

In June 1990, one of the three unions represented at PG Bison sent a fax to shop stewards stating that the recently introduced productivity and quality enhancement scheme (TPQ) "is there to co-opt workers and undermine the militancy of the union. Workers need to meet and plan a strategy to stop this."

Two months later management met with shop stewards and union officials to discuss the TPQ process. Union officials said they wanted more than consultation; they sought genuine negotiation and claimed that the process had been unilaterally imposed. Their call for a suspension of the programme until it had been negotiated was agreed to.

After months of discussion, at the request of two shop stewards, negotiations on the TPQ programme were renewed in March 1991. In June, the first national forum attended by elected shop stewards along with union officials and managers met, with sixty people being present. To quote Cohen, "We negotiated an agreed set of company values, full-time shop stewards and other issues. We created joint task forces on matters including company housing policy, human resource development and community involvement." Some of the significant components of the agreement are:

- a medium-term objective of worker involvement in the appointment of managers, peers and team members;
- an undertaking not to use retrenchment to cope with short-term cycles in the economy;
- disclosure of company performance information;
- appointment of full-time shop stewards;
- worker influence in the policy, principles and values that drive the business and other decisions which affect their work life, such as training programmes (Cargill 1991).

A literacy programme is now in place, and there is a strong emphasis on skills training and internal promotion. The agreement falls short of full worker participation in that there is no worker representation on the board of directors, and no profit-sharing or employee ownership. Strategic and policy decisions are made by management. However, Cohen has indicated that management has not taken an uncompromising stand on these issues.

*Source: Adapted from Horwitz & Townsend 1993: 927–928.

teria necessary for the successful operation of the organisation. From a positive point of view, discipline is therefore a constructive element of management designed to facilitate learning and opportunities for personal growth, as well as the achievement of organisational objectives.

The process of disciplining employees entails both informal and formal aspects. The informal part of discipline forms an integral part of managing the performance and behaviour of employees on a continuous basis. Just as the creation of opportunities for employee involvement is aimed at eliciting better performance, the ideal of continuously teaching subordinates what is right and what is wrong, acceptable and unacceptable, lies at the very heart of people management. On an informal basis employees are supposed to be taught not simply to conform to minimum requirements related to performance and behaviour, but actually to display superior behaviour and work performance. The first stage of disciplining employees is therefore informal by nature.

At times, however, some employees fail to adhere to the basic minimum standards and requirements. This is normally where the formal dimension of discipline comes into play. It is therefore advisable for organisations to have a system for formally disciplining those employees who fail to comply with the organisation's requirements. Apart from an organisation's formal policy statement regarding discipline, this formal disciplinary system usually consists of a written disciplinary code and procedure which has to be applied by management.

21.2.4.1 The disciplinary code

As a general rule a disciplinary code is drafted to assist management in the identification of offences warranting formal disciplinary measures and to help ensure consistency in disciplinary matters. Such a code therefore usually contains a list of possible offences and the concomitant sanctions to be considered by management. It is mostly used as a guideline rather than a set of hard and fast rules. In this way employees can be made aware of the rules and requirements related to behaviour and performance (and of the potential consequences of not adhering thereto). It is good practice to educate all new employees on the disciplinary code and procedure during the course of induction programmes.

Due to the fact that the nature of various offences may differ in terms of seriousness (ranging, for instance, from minor, to moderate, to very serious), some form of progressive discipline is usually built into the disciplinary code's section dealing with the penalty guidelines connected to the various types of offences. The first step in a formal disciplinary process is normally a written warning and this progresses to a final warning and ultimately even to dismissal. The dismissal of employees for misconduct should, however, always be viewed as the last option and not as a penalty in the true sense of the word. Termination should never be imposed overhastily or in an improper manner. Under normal circumstances, terminating the service of employees in essence means ending the employment relationship. However, if this is not done fairly, it may very well happen that an order is eventually made (by the Labour Court or in terms of an arbitrator's decision) for the employment relationship to continue. The last chapter of this book focuses specifically on the termination of employees' services.

It is important to note that, in respect of first-, second- and third-time offences, where the penalties will have to become progressively more severe in order to rectify (or eliminate) undesirable behaviour, time limits will normally have to be applied. Depending on the type of offence, warnings can be taken to cease to apply after a "clean period" of, for instance, three to twelve months. In order to incorporate the principle of progressive discipline, other types of penalties which may be warranted (depending on the relevant circumstances) can include suspension without pay (only if the parties agreed to this), or demotion (it may similarly not be imposed unilaterally), before dismissal as a last option may be decided upon.

An example of a disciplinary code of a South African organisation is provided at the end of this chapter (see the appendix to this chapter, starting on page 719).

21.2.4.2 Aspects of the disciplinary process and procedure

The disciplinary process should start off in an informal way; once a superior has determined that a violation of rules or of required behavioural standards has occurred, some form of counselling should take place. If this does not help and rehabilitation does not take place, the transgressor has to be informed of the possible consequences should his/her behaviour not change.

Should an employee be charged with misconduct that could possibly lead to dismissal, management must act in line with the fundamental rights of employees regarding procedural fairness in discipline. As a general rule, these rights may include the following:

- the right to be told the nature of the offence or misconduct with relevant particulars of the charge;
- the right to a timeous hearing;
- the right to be given adequate notice prior to the enquiry;
- the right to some form of representation (the representative can be anyone from the workplace — either a shop steward, workplace forum representative, a colleague or even a supervisor — who can assist the employee and ensure that the disciplinary procedure is fair and equitable);
- the right to call witnesses;
- the right to an interpreter;
- the right to a finding (if found guilty, the employee has the right to be told the full reasons why);
- the right to have previous service considered;
- the right to be advised of the penalty imposed (eg verbal warnings, written warnings, termination of employment); and
- the right of appeal, for example to a higher level of management (which is usually the case).

The process of disciplining an employee should therefore be based on principles of professional and reasonable management. As can be seen from the guidelines spelled out above, it is advisable that a disciplinary hearing normally forms an integral part of this process.

First of all it is essential to ascertain whether sufficient grounds exist for the holding of a hearing. A form of preliminary investigation is therefore normally necessary before one proceeds with the actual disciplinary hearing.

The *disciplinary procedure* concerns the detailed steps to be followed in the case of alleged employee misconduct. An example of a disciplinary procedure is provided in figure 21.2.

As can be seen from the above example, a formal disciplinary hearing may form an essential part of the disciplinary procedure and process. Although, in terms of the Act, a formal hearing is not always required, it became the custom during the previous dispensation for such formal hearings to be viewed as prerequisites for any decision to dismiss an employee.

A disciplinary enquiry can be divided into two basic stages. The first stage is an investigation to resolve the question of whether the employee did in fact commit the act of which he/she is accused (this involves the valid reason requirement and the employee's personal circumstances may not be discussed or considered here). Should the employee be found guilty of the misconduct as charged, the second stage is entered where a decision has to be taken as to the appropriate disciplinary action. Here the employee's personal circumstances (such as his/her service record, disciplinary record and period of service with the enterprise) are considered. For example, assume that employees X and Y are both found guilty of being under the influence of alcohol at work. Assume that employee X has received two warnings during the past year for the same offence, while employee Y has a clean record and has been working for the enterprise twice as long as employee X. Under these circumstances the employer could possibly be justified in dismissing employee X and not employee Y.

21.2.5 Sound employee relations: Concluding remarks

In the previous paragraphs you were introduced to the complex management task of working towards sound employee relations on primarily the individual dimension. These efforts will, however, all be in vain if insufficient attention is paid to the collective dimension as represented primarily by union–management relations.

21.3 TOWARDS SOUND UNION–MANAGEMENT RELATIONS

Because trade unions play such an important role in South African organisations today, it is essential for management to be professional in its dealings and interactions with such employee representative bodies. No matter how much attention is paid to the individual dimension of employee relations — in other words, to ordi-

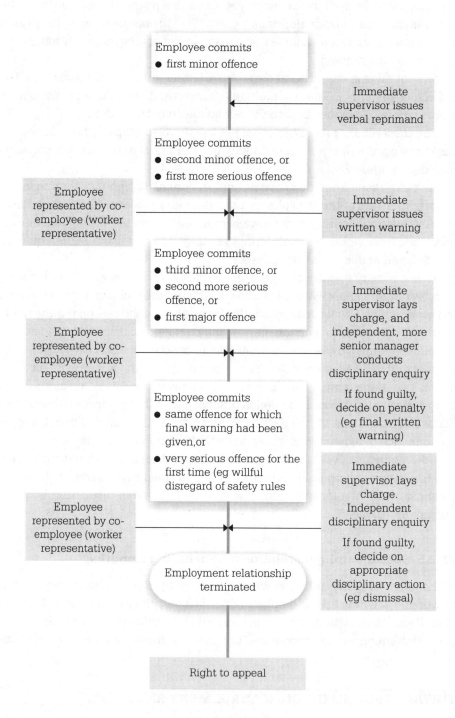

Figure 21.2

Flow diagram of a disciplinary procedure: an example

nary human resource management practices and to one-on-one employee relations — negligence in respect of the collective dimensions (particularly as far as trade unions are concerned) can have serious negative consequence for an organisation's quest for success.

From a strategic perspective (see chapter 6), one of the most fundamental management decisions in this regard relates to the organisation's general approach to dealing and interacting with trade unions.

21.3.1 Deciding on a comprehensive general approach

As explained in chapter 6, the frames of reference or mind-sets of managers (and of unionists) may have a significant influence on how management/union relationships develop over time. As explained, an organisation's strategies and policies regarding dealings with trade unions are often strongly influenced by the decision makers' mind-sets or ideologies. Different mind-sets are based on managers' differing beliefs about, perceptions of and reactions to trade unions and their leaders. Obviously these mind-sets are formed over time and are therefore often influenced by the attitudes and methods of trade unions in their interactions with management. A country's labour history, trends in collective bargaining, and factors such as the economy and political situation also obviously play a role in shaping the mind-sets of managers.

In general it can be said that decision makers will be either relatively positive or predominantly negative towards trade unions. In reality, a continuum ranging from extremely negative to extremely positive can be drawn.

The more negative the mind-set, the more of a unitarist the person concerned is (see chapter 7). People who fall towards the other end of the continuum are more pluralist in their thinking. The more unitarist a person is, the more adversarial his/her approach towards trade unions will be. If circumstances allow, a top management team whose members share a very strong unitarist frame of reference will in all likelihood prefer to oppose trade unions with every available means because they do not really believe that unions should exist or that they should interfere in any way with the management of employee affairs. This resistance towards (or even fear of) union involvement may then result in strategies to avoid unions and to keep them out as far as possible.

Towards the middle of the continuum, but still towards the negative, lie those who favour a broad approach of *union containment*. This is still basically an adversarial type of approach towards union–management relations. Management may perhaps realise that the trade unions cannot really be kept out, perhaps because of legislation. Attempts may therefore be made to devise ways and means of restricting trade union involvement. In such cases interaction with trade unions will be limited to issues such as conditions of employment, remuneration and working conditions (and these aspects will often be rigidly codified into agreements). Slightly more to the right of the neutral point, where pluralism becomes the shared frame of reference, management may realise that a more professional and peaceful relationship with the trade unions must be sought. Unions are thus accepted as part of organisational life and are respected as the legitimate representatives of the workers. Although generally more positive towards trade unions and their role, management may still be critical of certain aspects of trade union involvement, and initially may still generally oppose trade union demands. In general, however, a spirit of *accommodation* may start to develop: management is prepared to accommodate the union by establishing an ongoing pragmatic working relationship with it. In such a relationship there will thus be scope for real compromise and flexibility in a process dominated by more win–win bargaining.

Managers who fall towards the extreme positive side of the continuum will prefer to establish *cooperative* relationships with trade unions. Although the accommodation type of approach allows a certain degree of joint or cooperative interactions, it is only where a very strong pluralist stance is taken that trade unions are in essence welcomed as important stakeholders in the organisation. The emphasis in this approach shifts to mutual concerns, common ground, real joint problem-solving and integrative, win–win interactions and negotiation. Fundamental to this approach is the belief that, although the parties are distinct groups with different values and objectives, they are dependent upon each other and will be able to achieve their objectives better if they support each other overall. The way in which management deals with trade unions will thus vary, depending on the decision taken at top management level.

21.3.2 Handling initial trade union contact

Even though an organisation's management may not be involved with a trade union at a particular point in time, it may still be wise to decide beforehand upon a particular broad approach (as spelled out in section 21.3.1) regarding dealings with trade unions. At some point a trade union may approach or contact management for the first time. This initial contact may be in the form of a letter or by means of a telephone call. In some instances it may be a direct person-to-person contact between a union official or a person who says that he/she has been elected as shop steward, and a management representative. The issue at hand may be a request for recognition as the ongoing representative of a group of workers or it may entail a once-off representation of an employee regarding an issue such as a grievance, the alleged unfair dismissal of another employee, or the need to negotiate improved wages and/or working conditions for employees.

Whatever the form of the initial contact and irrespective of the reason put forward for the contact, it is important for management not to lose the initiative or to panic, or to engage overhastily in interaction with the trade union. The approach should be handled correctly and it is therefore essential to gather the necessary information first. As much as possible should be found out about the trade union and, if the first contact is by telephone, it is advisable to obtain the name of the trade union, its address and telephone numbers, the name of the official and details regarding the issues/requests/demands at hand.

It is also advisable to request the person to fax through a letter confirming the discussion details. At that stage it is normally not wise to make any overhasty commitments other than that the union will be contacted again as soon as possible. If the initial approach is in writing, or when the fax has been received, a prompt written response is professional. Receipt of the letter should be acknowledged and the contents of the letter should be studied carefully. The next step should be to set up, as far as its practically possible, a face-to-face meeting with the appropriate official at the earliest possible opportunity.

The purpose of the first meeting should involve getting to know each other better. It is therefore imperative to make it clear that, in order to have a fruitful first meeting, the parties should be willing to exchange certain information.

In this regard it is sound practice for management to request a copy of the union's constitution, as well as its registration certificate in advance. A first meeting could then be arranged at a date, time and venue convenient to both parties. A reasonable time should be set aside for such a meeting and the time and duration thereof ought to be specified.

The first meeting is normally important for setting the tone or climate for future interactions. The maxim "first impressions last" is especially true in this regard. If an approach of union–management cooperation is preferred, the first meeting should preferably end off on a positive note. However, because of our history of very adversarial union–management relations — especially during the 1980s and early 1990s — it should be borne in mind that a trade union will often not be prepared for a cooperative type of meeting initially. At the first (and later meetings) it is thus largely up to management to keep the initiative in setting up an appropriate climate for the future, long-term collective relationship.

21.3.3 Formalising the union–management relationship

21.3.3.1 General

Formalising the relationship with a trade union usually involves some kind of an agreement between the parties. The process of formalisation will often depend to a large extent on the level of the union's representativeness in the organisation. This means that generally, before such a relationship is formalised, the trade union will be required to present proof of its membership. This normally includes the submission of signed and correctly completed union membership forms that have to be verified.

The next step is then to make known to the trade union management's approach regarding the type of representativeness required before a trade union will be recognised as an official representative body of the organisation's workers, or of some of them. In terms of the old dispensation, management could choose between an *all-comers* approach, the *majoritarian* approach or the *sufficiently representative* approach. Furthermore, *bargaining units* (particular employee interest groups — for instance, per geographic area and occupational interests and job grades) played an important role in this decision during the 1980s to mid 1990s. In the *all-comers approach* management was basically prepared to recognise any trade union having membership of some employees in a particular bargaining unit. In the *majoritarian approach* management usually only recognised a trade union on a quantitative basis — that is, once the union could prove that it had a membership figure of 50 % + 1 of the employees in a particular bargaining unit. The *sufficiently representative approach* was often based on a qualitative evaluation of the wisdom of recognising a trade union even if it had less than 50 % + 1 membership. In the latter case factors such as the unique skills of certain employees (who are union members) and the ease with which they could be replaced would play a role.

In terms of the new dispensation, management will have to be guided by the principles laid down in the new Act (see chapter 20). The new Act has subordinated the importance of bargaining units to the notion of majoritarianism in the workplace. This means that a trade union has now only to provide proof of sufficient or majority representation in order to be able to exercise certain organisational rights, depending on its level of representativeness in the workplace (see chapter 20). Management's discretion in this matter has thus to a large extent been curtailed by the new labour relations legislation.

As soon as a decision has been made in principle to recognise a trade union and thus to formalise the relationship by means of a collective agreement, the parties start to negotiate the nature of the agreement itself. In the previous dispensation recognition agreements were non-statutory agreements — the Labour Relations Act 28 of 1956 did not cater for them in the sense that collective agreements as such were not defined and the consequences of recognition agreements were only minimally regulated.

In Act 66 of 1995 a *collective agreement* is defined as any written agreement regarding conditions and terms of employment or any other matter of mutual interest concluded by one or more registered trade unions on the one hand, and — among others — one or more employers on the other (it could also include one or more registered employers' organisations).

It should be noted that, in terms of the new Act 66 of 1995, most recognition agreements which came into existence under the previous dispensation are deemed to be collective agreements under the new dispensation. Recognition agreements are procedural agreements. Procedural agreements should be distinguished from substantive agreements; while the former spell out the "how to" of the collective relationship, the latter contain the detail regarding the "what of" the relationship (for example, conditions of service, wage levels, etc).

Formalising the recognition relationship thus essentially entails recognition of the fact that a particular union (or unions) will act as the collective bargaining and representative agent of a specified group of employees. According to Bendix (1996: 289–290), a recognition agreement will confirm that management accepts the union as a bargaining agent and it will also stipulate the parameters of the future relationship and the way in which it will be conducted. The issues and procedures that will be subject to bargaining will be spelled out in the recognition agreement. In this regard it can be said that a recognition agreement is the plant-level equivalent of the constitution of a bargaining council. Bendix (1996: 289–290) also distinguishes between different **types of recognition agreements.** A written recognition agreement may take on the form of a *skeletal agreement* or a *full agreement*. While the former simply states the broad principles involved, the latter is a comprehensive agreement containing detailed procedures and providing for most eventualities. A full procedural agreement can be advantageous in that it may serve to eliminate some of the uncertainties encountered by the lower-level managers and shop stewards who have to implement and live by the agreement on a day-to-day basis. In such agreements the rights and obligations of all role-players are usually also clearly stipulated, facilitating contract administration and any litigation that may be necessary should there be a breach of the agreement at any stage. Full procedural recognition agreements can, however, often be extremely complicated and too legalistic. On the other hand, a skeletal agreement, while allowing for more flexibility, could lead to greater uncertainties. Skeletal agreements naturally presuppose a more mature relationship and greater trust between the parties. The majority of recognition agreements which have been signed in South Africa to date have, however, been full procedural agreements; this is understandable considering the lack of trust which has characterised our labour relations history.

A general pattern has developed over time with regard to the contents of such full procedural recognition agreements. Typically such an agreement will start off with a preamble that sets the tone of the collective relationship. This is usually followed by a section containing definitions and the clarification of terminology used further on in the agreement. The so-called recogition clause, whereby the organisation's management officially commits itself to recognising the trade union(s) as the representative and bargaining agent of a group of employees who are union members, usually follows the definition section.

Other aspects usually covered by the recognition agreement include the regulation of access by trade union officials to the organisation's premises and arrangements regarding stop-order facilities. As a rule a separate section deals with the election, rights, role and functions of the recognised trade union's shop stewards in the workplace.

Although the number of shop stewards to be appointed is guided by the Act 66 of 1995, the number of shop stewards may still be arranged in accordance with the nature of the workplace. It has become customary to divide eligible employees into constituencies and to allocate specific numbers of shop stewards per constituency. Management may also agree to appoint full-time shop stewards. Typically these people will have special privileges and a special role to play in the workplace.

The rights and duties of different categories of shop stewards are normally stipulated in the recognition agreement, for instance that shop stewards may not leave their places of work without permission from their supervisors. Shop stewards are, however, usually granted reasonable time off and access to their members. The recognition agreement usually also regulates the holding of shop steward meetings within normal working hours, as well as aspects such as time off for the training of shop stewards to enable them to fulfil their functions properly. The Act spells out these functions clearly.

In terms of the Act, shop stewards (designated "trade union representatives" in the Act) essentially have the following functions in the workplace:

- assisting and representing workers in grievance and disciplinary proceedings;
- monitoring the employer's compliance with the relevant provisions of the Act;
- reporting any contraventions of workplace-related provisions of the Act to the employer, to the union, or to the responsible authorities (usually the Department of Labour); and
- performing any other functions agreed to between the union and the employer.

The Act also provides that an employee who is a trade union representative or office bearer of a registered majority trade union has the right to take reasonable leave during working hours for the purpose of union activities. The parties may put into the agreement the number of (paid or unpaid) days' leave and the conditions of leave to which the shop stewards or office bearers will be entitled.

Other aspects normally covered by a recognition agreement include a procedure and parameters for further negotiations in the future (for example on substantive issues like wages/working conditions on an annual basis), procedures for dealing with disputes, stipulations regarding the duration and amendment of the recognition agreement, as well as a section containing the physical addresses of both parties.

21.3.3.2 Two specific types of collective agreements

In terms of the new Act, management and a trade union may opt to enter into so-called closed and/or agency shop agreements. Management and a majority trade union may conclude an agreement in terms of which all employees covered by the agreement are compelled to become members of that trade union. This is known as a *closed shop agreement* and is very controversial because of its compulsory nature and, as some allege, the curtailment of the freedom of association as a basic human right, which makes it somewhat uncertain whether the closed shop provision would survive a constitutional challenge. It is therefore not surprising that the drafters of Act 66 of 1995 found it necessary to build in various checks and balances (for example a mandatory ballot must be held in which at least two-thirds of employees must vote in favour of the closed shop agreement) in an effort to protect the closed shop from possible constitutional challenge. The Act explicitly provides that it would not be unfair to dismiss an employee who is refused membership or who is expelled from a trade union party to a closed shop agreement (if the refusal/expulsion is in accordance with the trade union's constitution and the reason for the refusal or expulsion is fair, including, but not limited to, conduct that undermines the trade union's collective exercise of its rights), or for refusing to join a trade union party to a closed shop. Only two exceptions to this rule are allowed: the existing employees at the time a closed shop agreement takes effect may not be dismissed for refusing to join a trade union party to the agreement, and, employees may not be dismissed for refusing to join a trade union party to the agreement on grounds of conscientious objection (in both these instances employees may be required by the closed shop agreement to pay an agreed agency fee).

An *agency shop agreement* is an agreement between an employer and a trade union in terms of which the employer is compelled to deduct from the wages of employees within the bargaining unit who are not trade union members an amount equal to or less than (and in lieu of) the membership fees paid by the trade union members. The agency shop was introduced to counter the free rider complaint of trade unions. This refers to the situation where non-union member employees within the bargaining unit enjoy the benefits of the trade union's efforts and its members' contributions without incurring any of the costs borne by the trade union members. On the other hand, it may be regarded as morally questionable to require of someone to belong to a trade union against his/her wishes (as is the case where a closed shop agreement prevails). In terms of the Act, an amount equal to or less than the subscription dues may be deducted from non-union members and paid into an account administered by the trade union, to be used to advance the socioeconomic interests of employees in general. Note that in both the closed shop and the agency shop agreement, the union party to the agreement must enjoy majority support in the workplace

Although a collective agreement, such as the recognition agreement, need not be put in writing to make it a legally binding contract, when a recognition agreement is duly signed by the parties for the first time it can be said that the relationship has been truly formalised. This, however, is only the beginning of the formal union–management relationship. Although it may be true that a good start can help the parties halfway towards the winning line, much work still needs to be done to maintain sound union–management relations over the longer term. Much of the challenge lies in the way in which the parties interact during the course of ensuing collective negotiation encounters.

21.3.4 Broad types of collective negotiation

Negotiation can be described as a process of interaction between two or more parties in a situation in which the parties believe they have to be jointly involved so that the resultant agreement can be balanced and acceptable to all parties concerned.

In this process the parties, although they may have certain different needs or objectives, realise that there are common interests and that a mutually acceptable outcome can be arrived at through processes involving information exchange, communication, reasoning and persuasion.

Although some may hold the view that negotiation and bargaining as concepts have different meanings, Pienaar and Spoelstra (1991: 5) argue that these terms can be used in much the same way, implying that they have much the same purpose and meaning and follow the same methods. This does not mean, however, that *collective bargaining* and *negotiation* are synonymous concepts.

Collective bargaining and collective negotiation are, however, used interchangeably in this book. The qualification "collective" indicates that the negotiations are conducted by representatives on behalf of their constituencies comprising a particular group of people — the group of employees who are union members and the group called management who represents the interests of the employer at the bargaining table.

21.3.4.1 Distributive negotiation

Many people think that this is all that management–trade union bargaining is about. The parties' behaviour during the processes of negotiation is driven primarily by their conflictive and opposing needs, interests, objectives and positions. The parties view the negotiation process as a zero-sum game where the only real outcome of the situation can be one party winning and the other losing. What the one party wins, the other party will have to lose. The size of the pie over which the parties negotiate is viewed as a given and the purpose of the interaction between the parties is seen as being to fight for a fair share for their constituencies. The parties often display hostile behaviour towards each other, viewing each other as the enemy. In this type of bargaining the parties are generally antagonistic and display little reasonableness in the process. Focusing on positions and using power are seen as central elements of this type of negotiation. Trade unions usually view management as equating the owners of capital who want to exploit all workers and to control fully the labour or work process. Likewise management often negotiates from the assumption that the trade union is an unnecessary intruder making management's life difficult and serving no real economic purpose as they simply cause labour costs to rise. This type of negotiation is associated with the collective side of employment relations, with the result that the collective bargaining process is traditionally viewed as being of an adversarial, win-lose nature.

The process of distributive negotiation

In distributive collective negotiation management and trade unions make demands, counterdemands and offers so that agreements can be reached. Each negotiation situation is unique. For this reason (and in line with the scope of this book) only broad guidelines regarding distributive collective negotiations can be provided. Three phases or stages of the process of distributive negotiation can be identified, namely the prenegotiation phase, the interactive phase and the postnegotiation phase.

PHASE 1: THE PRENEGOTIATION PHASE

Thorough planning, preparation and organising are vital for successful negotiation. Preparation and planning for initial negotiations start with the first contact between the parties. When an agreement is concluded, the preparation phase for the next round of negotiations has already started. The more comprehensive and complex the topics for negotiation, the more time and energy will have to be spent on the prenegotiation phase. The topics can vary from procedural aspects such as grievance, disciplinary, staff-reduction or dispute-settling procedures to substantive aspects such as working hours, wages, leave, job evaluations, bonuses, equal opportunities, health and safety, and so on.

Even before the first negotiations commence, decisions have to be made about prenegotiation aspects such as the levels at which to negotiate and the appropriate scope of issues about which to negotiate. Obviously, the broad negotiations approach must also fit in with the overall strategic posture (see chapter 6).

Furthermore, during this phase of negotiation, the wide range of environmental influences which could have an impact on the negotiations must also be taken into consideration. For instance, the other party's envisaged positions, objectives and tactics must be considered and the negotiation mandate of the management negotiation team itself must also be clearly established. Intra-organisational negotiations thus typically form an important element of the prenegotiation phase — that is negotiation among managers themselves regarding their own priorities, objectives and positions. Furthermore, it is also important to appoint competent negotiation teams during this phase, to train them and to synchronise their efforts.

The prenegotiation phase thus involves a great deal of time and effort. At this stage the collection of all sorts of information is extremely important. The underlying organisation of the negotiations will also have to take place, with aspects such as dates, times, venues with appropriate facilities for caucusing, teabreaks, meals, secretarial and record-keeping facilities, and media coverage arrangements being attended to.

The methodology used and the quality of these preparations and planning efforts are of cardinal importance in ensuring successful negotiations. An important part of this phase relates to setting objectives and structuring negotiation priorities.

It is very important, before the bargaining team actually enters into the physical or interactive phase of negotiating with the trade union representatives, to analyse and identify exactly what issues are at stake. As far as possible one should divide and subdivide the issues into subissues by carefully analysing the range of issues and considering which may be dealt with as stand-alone topics and which need to be combined. As this process progresses, it also becomes necessary to prioritise the negotiation issues. When this is done it is also wise to consider the likely priorities of the other party.

A so-called bargaining range is also established for each issue. The bargaining range determines just how much the parties to the negotiation process can shift their positions. If, for example, the issue at hand is the monthly wage levels of workers and the current level is R1 900,00 per month, management's bargaining range may be between R1 995,00 and R2 280,00. This will mean that the most optimistic outcome for management would be an increase of 5 %. On the other hand, the highest increase that management will be prepared to settle for (if trade-offs with other issues can be made) is 20 %. This means that the bargaining range of management is between 5 and 20 %. Within this range there will be some point of realism — in other words, what management could actually expect the realistic outcome to be. This point or subrange will, however, only be determined once the likely bargaining range of the other party is also considered and the area of overlap is identified. This overlapping range would give the most likely range of settlement. If, for instance, the bargaining range of the trade union is between 32 % and 14 %, the realistic settlement range would in all likelihood amount to anything between 14 and 20 %.

In this way the negotiating team prepares all the issues by prioritising them in terms of relative importance, establishing opening positions and working out bargaining ranges with ideal and fall-back positions. Planning fall-back positions is extremely important. Anstey's (1991: 134–135) views in this regard speak for themselves.

"It is important for an employer to plan fall-backs from the onset of the bargaining process. Usually projections have to be made for labour costs into the future to allow for accurate business planning and budgeting, and competitiveness. Where an employer must tender for business in a highly competitive industry this becomes particularly important. However, many employers do not think through their fall-backs, often carelessly identifying an inflationary increase as the point of no further offers. This is often naive, being based on what they desire rather than what is practicable.

In one negotiation, the union reduced its demand from 25 to 22 %, to which the company made a 'final offer' of 12 %. A mediator spent considerable time with the management team discussing the implications of this. If a final offer was made too early and too bluntly it would not allow the union side time and room to reconsider its position for purposes of further movement. It would be left with a 'take it or leave it' situation, in this instance, with a large gap to close. If the company stated that this was a final offer, but then moved at the first sign of a strike, it would be saying to the union that its 'finals' could not be trusted and inviting the union to strike every year to test the seriousness of a position. The factory manager stated that 12 % was the limit of the mandate, beyond that they had been directed from board level to 'dig the trenches and do whatever fighting was necessary'. The union rejected the offer and indicated to the company that it would be taking a strike ballot. When the factory manager returned to head office that afternoon he advised the directors that deadlock had been reached and that a strike was probable. Looking again at the order book and stock levels, the directors realised that a strike would be very damaging to the business — and immediately raised their offer to 21 %! This reflects some wise last minute shifts, but very bad planning and poor use of the bargaining process — in effect the union called a bluff which the company did not consciously consider making!

Companies might need to plan several fall-back scenarios, based on various business conditions, for example, stock levels, orders, competition, peak periods, etc. A series of 'what-ifs?' need to be considered. A distinction between what would be desirable and what is possible under various conditions is necessary. An employer may actively resist movement from a given point, but whether it would accept a strike for two months at that point, or stand the risk of severing relations with workers is another issue. Points of resistance signal to the other party that a final position may be close, but it is incorrect to state that it is 'final' if it is not! It locks parties into battles of trust and entraps them in principles that might be expensive to live out."

By doing this sort of planning for all the negotiation issues or items, one can start to develop an overall plan regarding aspects such as opening moves, pressure tactics and when and how concessions may be made on what issues. Obviously, in mapping out this negotiation plan it is essential to take into consideration the power dynamics in the relationship. In this regard aspects like the general state of the economy, the strength of the trade union in terms of membership figures and leadership, the organisation's market, financial and logistical/stock situation, the overall climate in the country/region in terms of industrial action, all have to be considered. Only if such variables have been carefully considered within the context of the bigger picture relating to the total bargaining situation and employment relations in general, can one really start to work out the different tactics that may be used during the course of the actual interactive phase of negotiation.

PHASE 2: THE INTERACTIVE PHASE OF NEGOTIATION

In this phase the two parties face each other and systematically try to persuade each other to change points of view regarding the positions of the parties.

During this stage particular negotiating tactics are applied within the context of the broad negotiation approach or strategy. Remember that "strategy" refers to the overall approach, plan and policy in respect of the negotiation process, while "tactics" refers to the particular conduct of the parties during the actual negotiations.

Knowledge and particular skills play a major role during this stage. Exhibit A lists some potentially useful hints to help during this phase of negotiations.

During the course of the interactive phase the core aspects revolve around communication, persuasion and debate. Getting down to the nitty gritty of the actual conduct of negotiations basically boils down to the various parties discussing and debating the merits of each other's arguments. One must always remember that collective negotiations take place in order to reach agreements and that negotiating for the sake of negotiating can only be to the detriment of all.

The final stage of this interactive phase — that is, agreeing on solutions, recording the agreements and summarising the bargains that have been struck should be sought on a continuous basis. Finally, all parties should explicitly accept responsibility for communicating and implementing the agreed-upon issues. Make sure, before you depart, that you understand everything and do not rush the final stages of the interactive phase. Remember, how you greet and depart sets the climate for future negotiations and for the spirit in which the parties will go out and implement the agreements.

Exhibit A

Guidelines for the interactive phase of negotiation

- Keep to the agenda as far as possible.
- Maintain order at all times.
- Stick to the facts and do not discuss people as such (separate problems from people).
- Take note of and use body language and gestures effectively.
- Listen more and talk less (two ears, one mouth)–ask a lot of appropriate questions, in the right way to get the right information.
- Remain alert all the time.
- Regularly confirm when you have understood and get confirmation that others understand.
- When in doubt or uncertain about anything, call for a caucus.
- Take your time and never talk, act or make decisions overhastily.
- Be pleasant, true and decent all the time.
- Treat everyone else with due respect.
- Be sensitive to cultural and language differences.
- Make careful notes and keep looking for alternatives and inaccuracies in information and arguments.
- Offer various possible choices of options to the other party and make sure that everything is understood within the context of the real interests at hand.
- Be emotionally stable — do not become unnerved by militant action or provocation. Let a colleague talk when you are angry.
- Regularly check progress and summarise where the process stands — seek confirmation of common understanding on this.
- Always keep some flexibility in your negotiation positions or stances and always remind others of the interests at hand.
- The negotiator should not only be concerned with what the other party says and does, but must constantly find out the real interests and the reasons underlying these positions or stated problems.
- If something is not well understood, ask for thorough explanations.
- Respect the importance of face-saving for the other party and be graceful. Give other parties the necessary dignity.
- Be constantly alert to the real intents of the other party, not only with respect to objectives and positions but also to priorities and real interests.
- Build a reputation for being fair but firm.
- Make each negotiation decision in relationship to the other decisions — that is, link all interests into a whole.
- Pay close attention to communication, do not interrupt and listen with interest to what is being said and what not. Never hesitate to make sure that you understand things as they are meant to be understood.
- Remember that collective negotiations in the labour area should essentially be a process of compromise. There is no such thing as winning or getting your own way in everything.
- Try to understand the people on the other side of the table, their personalities, fears, interests, perceptions, needs, concern, and so forth — it could bear fruit during negotiations.
- Always consider the impact of the current negotiations on future negotiations — remember that collective bargaining revolves around long-term relationships.
- Remain positive and assertive.
- Sanctions may be used but not misused.
- Pay close attention to the wording of each clause of agreements negotiated. Words and phrases (or expressions) are often the source of valuable information.
- Read agreements carefully before signing and do not ignore the fine print.
- Close the negotiations by summarising key, agreed points and by breaking the eye contact — then get up and shake hands in a pleasant, decent manner.

PHASE 3: THE POSTNEGOTIATION PHASE

The importance of implementing agreements correctly cannot be overemphasised. The interactive phase usually concludes with some sort of agreement (or contract) which is usually put in writing. This means that differences have been settled or that agreements have been reached on particular issues. Negotiations can also, of course, be less successful at times. Further dates must then be set for future negotiations, or the parties must follow the relevant dispute-settling procedures in the event of deadlocks.

Both parties must, however, respect all agreements — even in difficult circumstances — because this builds trust and mutually beneficial long-term relationships. Contract administration is the key concept.

The postnegotiation phase usually refers to the total validity period stated in agreements. During this period the parties make sure that all role-players abide by the agreed-upon procedures and substantive issues (such as wages and other conditions of service). The role of the grievance and disciplinary procedures applied during this phase is, of course, extremely important.

During this phase the role of the lower-level supervisors and shop stewards is of equally crucial importance. Good communication and day-to-day contact between all the other relevant role-players are some of the other key elements of this phase. The supervisors and shop stewards have to ensure that all clauses in the agreements are adequately maintained. Where negotiations are conducted at sectoral level, the inspectors of bargaining councils also have an important part to play.

The whole concept of good-faith bargaining becomes quite watered down if the postnegotiation phase is neglected by any of the parties. All agreements have to be implemented and adhered to in a decent, honest, truthful and sincere manner. This is the phase where the quality of the long-term collective employment relationship can really be developed or undermined.

The interactive phase may very well be the dramatic highlight of collective bargaining, but the actual proof of the pudding lies in contract administration and adherence by both parties. Trade unions are often more interested in the postnegotiation phase — this is why shop stewards and supervisors play such an important role during this phase. These key role-players have to ensure that agreements operate smoothly on a day-to-day basis, otherwise the agreements are not worth the paper on which they are written. Any problems which arise in this regard have to be brought to the attention of the trade union and/or management, so that the necessary follow-up meetings and discussions can be arranged.

Competencies and characteristics of successful negotiators

Exhibit B lists some essential characteristics of successful negotiators, based on the works of Salamon (1990); Kniveron (1974); Bendix (1996); and Alfred (1984).

Exhibit B

Essential characteristics of successful negotiators

- They have to be well trained and knowledgeable in the intricacies of negotiations.
- They have to possess good social interpersonal skills.
- They have to like dealing with people, especially in difficult circumstances.
- They have to be good planners and thus need good information-processing skills.
- Their nature should be positive towards mutual gains and not filled with greed and egocentrism.
- They have to be good communicators, being able to listen sincerely and express themselves clearly.
- They need a lot of persuasive abilities.
- They should be very alert and perceptive to what is happening around them (and what is not).
- They need high quality discretionary judgement and analytical skills.
- They have to be patient and should possess good stress tolerance.
- They have to be able to control their emotions (keeping cool under heated circumstances).
- They need good conceptual abilities in order to relate aspects and continually to see the bigger picture.
- They have to be long-term orientated.
- Although they have to be goal orientated and persistent, they also have to be flexible, open-minded thinkers.
- They have to be creative in order to come up with counterproposals and alternative arguments.
- They have to be intellectually well developed with a quickness of mind, coupled with the ability not to act overhastily.
- They have to have a good sense of humour.
- They have to be reasonable and prepared to compromise when necessary.
- They have to have the ability sometimes to take a backseat and they should not be overconcerned with defending the self (being modest).
- They have to possess diplomatic abilities and must be sincere, honest people.
- They have to be hard on facts and soft on people.
- High levels of perceived integrity are essential for long-term success in negotiations.

21.3.4.2 Integrative negotiation

The parties to negotiation sometimes wisely recognise and emphasise the fact that there is indeed common ground between trade unions and management. According to this approach to bargaining, the parties explore the possibilities of creating win-win situations. The parties, although they acknowledge the basic conflict in perceptions, goals and interests, deliberately channel their energies towards enlarging the areas of common concern. They thus concentrate on interacting in such a way that the outcomes of the negotiation process eventually lead to overall mutual gains. The parties are not as adversarial in their behaviour and relationships and they are prepared to grant concessions in order to move to situations where both parties gain something. More emphasis is placed on trust, openness, information sharing, constant meaningful two-way communication and joint problem-solving. The parties emphasise the fact that they have to solve problems jointly in order to reach optimum solutions. Examples include negotiating on measures to reduce absenteeism and labour turnover in order to improve the work processes and the quality of the organisation's products/services, thus saving (and creating) jobs, increasing turnover and revenue, and increasing the size of the pie. Negotiation is thus not viewed as a fixed-sum game.

Another example could be where the parties deal with the health, education and housing problems of workers, which in turn enhance the workers' ability to perform better on the job (because they feel better physically, are not as unhealthy and do not suffer from fatique as a result of travelling problems). This could in turn help the organisation to be more successful — thus increasing the size of the pie. The parties could then also look at the fair redistribution of the bigger pie — eventually all can win! The parties would thus be more positive towards each other and prepared to underplay their differences in order to channel their energies towards common goals. Openness, trust, concessions and mutual support are emphasised rather than opposition, competition, power and adversarial behaviour.

An analysis of the literature (Fisher & Ury (1981); Fisher & Brown (1988); Hock (1991/92) and Power (1991)) reveals that there are certain approaches or styles which can be used to bring about or facilitate more integrative types of collective negotiation. Two such styles are *interest bargaining* and *target specific bargaining*.

Interest bargaining: Some principles

One of the key ideas of this approach is that parties who engage in collective bargaining should focus on the *interest* which motivate the parties and their claims rather than on the claims themselves. For example, if a trade union's claim is a 20 % across the board wage increase, the question ought to be asked: why? Similarly, if an organisation's position is an offer of 2 %, the question ought to be asked: why? As the parties explore these underlying questions, they will most likely discover that the reasoning behind the claims or bargaining positions represents the interest range of the parties, and that for every interest range there is normally more than one possible settlement position which could satisfy the interest underlying the initial position. In this way they are more likely to identify common ground or interests which are compatible. These interests are explored during prebargaining meetings, even before letters of demand are tabled by the union.

The parties thus acknowledge that the real conflict lies not so much in their respective bargaining positions, but that these should rather be viewed as the *symptoms* of conflicting desires, needs, concerns and interests. In focusing on their respective interests, the parties have to be open and frank, and have to discuss their interests honestly and sincerely. Parties should be flexible and should be prepared to recognise each other's interests, fears and needs; they should look to the future rather than dig up the past; and they should be prepared to list consisely the specific problems and their causes.

In this way the focus of attention is drawn away from the opposing parties' respective positions so that progress is no longer measured in terms of successively relinquishing and adopting a sequence of positions. During the collective bargaining process the parties do not try to defend their positions by saying "we have given in here, there and on these and those aspects", but instead they defend the underlying real needs, concerns and interests of their constituents. The elements of egoism and face-saving thus become less important.

Another important element of interest bargaining is to *separate the people from the problems*. Thus, although a party may be hard on defending their interests (not their positions as such), they will be soft on the people — that is, the other party's negotiators. To this end it is important, when following the interest bargaining approach, to accept the legitimacy of the other party's negotiators as the representatives of certain real interests which are important to them and to those whom they represent. Parties should thus be prepared to try to understand each other's needs and concerns, the fact that people are people (all with different personalities, emotions, feelings, fears, needs, etc) and that, at the end of the day, the failure to reach workable agreements could be to the detriment of all. Furthermore, the parties must be committed to exchanging the necessary information and to opening up communication in order to understand each other's interest better. Fisher and Brown (1988: 85) suggest that good quality communication does not necessarily equate with being best friends and that it is almost even more important (and certainly more difficult) to communicate successfully with those whom one has conflict than with those with whom one has no conflict and whom one likes.

Yet another extremely important principle of interest bargaining that also relates to the human side of the collective bargaining process is that of *trust*. Flanders (1973: 371) states that "If one had to select one particular factor . . . as having the greatest influence on the system of collective bargaining it would probably be the level of trust between the parties." Furthermore, Walton and Mckersie (1965: 358) assert that: "Trust plays a more central role in integrative bargaining. It does more than circumscribe conflict behaviour of the participants; it enables them to increase their joint gain. The integrative process requires open communication which in turn depends on trust. Moreover, the more trust and other positive attitudes exist in the relationship, the more sincerely motivated each party is to work on the problems of the other, irrespective of anticipated substantive or attitudinal pay-offs." This quotation underscores the importance of this element when it comes to switching from a distributive approach to an integrative one, when it comes to the restructuring of attitudes and to the adoption of an approach of interest bargaining.

Within this context the importance of integrity, of being honest and sincere, of being reliable and of sticking to agreements and avoiding unlawful or unprocedural actions, cannot be overemphasised. The *manner* in which negotiations take place is also of fundamental importance. Fisher & Brown (1988: 132) put it as follows: "Just as my ability to negotiate with someone is affected by the quality of our relationship, so the quality of the relationship is affected by the way I negotiate. How we try to influence each other has a significant impact on the ability to deal with future differences." It is thus obvious that less adversarial, hostile types of behaviour will have to be demonstrated. Less reliance will have to be placed on power *positions* and coercive tactics such as verbally attacking people during the course of negotiations, or threatening to withdraw if a certain demand (or position) is not adhered to. Emphasis will instead have to be placed more on persuasive tactics. Bostrom (1983: 11) describes persuasion as ". . . communicative behaviour that has as its purpose the changing, modification, or shaping of the responses (attitudes or behaviour) of the receivers".

Persuasive tactics, as a primary means of bringing about attitudinal restructuring, also form an important component in the move from distributive to more integrative types of bargaining. This is the case because the actual collective bargaining process is viewed as only one part of the collective employment relationship. The quality of this relationship can, in terms of this perspective, only be built on principles such as respect, trust, integrity and fairness. In all of this the softer aspects of mutually beneficial relationship building through, *inter alia*, interest bargaining are viewed as being more important than the harder aspects of legalism and the actual eventual formal written agreements flowing from the negotiation encounters.

The process of target specific bargaining

Power (1991: 15–20) provides quite an elaborate discussion of this relatively new approach to collective bargaining. According to him, the results of this approach in the USA have ". . . been extremely encouraging for parties seeking an alternative to pure adversarial bargaining", and he proposes that it ". . . may represent a creative alternative for South African employers and unions interested in developing sounder relations, based on shared information, and for parties locked into the crises induced by interaction of rising expectations and problems of economic survival and growth" (Power 1991: 20).

This approach is based on the idea of changing the bargaining process to one which is actually productive for both parties, through the use of valid information and with the aim of generating less confrontation. It thus contains similar characteristics and principles as interest bargaining, but it also has, as is illustrated below, certain distinct features — especially as far as the process is concerned. As an approach it is claimed to fall somewhere between win-win and win-lose types of bargaining and extensive use is made of a mediator. Again, one of the fundamental elements is that of trust. Power (1991: 15) states, for example, that ". . . trust and information, has been characterised in the historic past of adversarial bargaining . . . Target Specific Bargaining requires the joint identification and organisation of information to solve problems brought forward by labour and management. This gives validity to the information brought forward through a joint process."

Power (1991: 16–20) then proceeds to describe a seven-step process which structures the target-specific bargaining approach.

Step one is a problem-seeking process during which both management and the union go back to their members (constituents), where they meet in small groups to record, in a uniform format, all problems and issues, their symptoms and causes or sources. In this way the factor of trust is reaffirmed because the members identify **their problems** as well as the real reasons why they exist — thus focusing on the true interests.

Step two is a procedural step where each party lists their problems (including the symptoms, reasons, etc) and lodges the list with a central source. This information is kept confidential at this stage.

Step three has two stages. Each party goes separately to the mediator with whom they review their list of problems. The mediator asks questions, probes into reasons, points out potential inconsistencies or duplications and helps each party to finalise their list. Up to now the parties have done everything separately. Stage two of this step commences when the management and trade union teams come together to exchange lists and clarify uncertainties. The parties get the information from each other in order to understand the interests better — they are not allowed to criticise each other or to question the legitimacy of any item on the list. The exchange of information is aimed purely at clarifying what each item entails.

Step four commences with each party clearly understanding the nature of each problem and its perceived causes. The parties now move to a situation of joint ownership of the problems where they decide jointly what information will be needed to address each specific problem listed by the two sides. The extremely important prerequisite of target-specific bargaining — that is, to disclose fully all **information** relevant to solving the problems — now comes into play. There is, by now, a joint list of problems, symptoms, possible causes and information needed to address each aspect, all structured in an agreed-upon problem classification system. Use is made of brainstorming techniques to get all the information for this joint bargaining manual. The parties will furthermore decide on how and when joint teams will gather all the necessary data.

Step five is the final prebargaining meeting where the parties jointly, with the aid of the mediator, set the "bargaining agenda by sequencing the order of discussion by groupings of classifications" (Power 1991: 16).

Step six sees the beginning of the actual negotiation process; the joint problem-solving processes are now constructively facilitated by the mediator. As the processes develop, the problem-solving becomes more and more complex, in turn requiring various techniques ranging from brainstorming, discussions, constructive debate, analyses and consensus-seeking processes. The mediator focuses especially on dovetailing the interests of the parties and on using consensus processes to arrive at solutions from which all parties will benefit in the interest of those whom they represent. The target-specific bargaining approach requires that agreement be reached on a solution for each listed item (problem or issue).

Step seven revolves around the ratification and follow-up processes. The parties go back to their members and present them with the agreed-upon solutions. All the parties are jointly trained with regard to the changed situations (contracts) and the parties implement the agreements. Agreement administration is thus also conducted jointly with all parties understanding the new situation. Attitudes are thus more positive and perceptions are streamlined. In this way the possibilities of improved relationships are enhanced and a move from distributive types of collective bargaining to more integrative styles is thus facilitated.

21.4 COOPERATING THROUGH STATUTORY WORKPLACE FORUMS

21.4.1 General

Under the old Labour Relations Act (28 of 1956) an employer and his/her employees, or some of his/her employees, could set up in-house structures, called works councils, to fulfil such functions as they might jointly determine. The only constraint placed upon the works council was that at least half of its members had to be elected by the employees. The functions of the works council could be agreed upon by the employer and the employees concerned. A works council under the old Act was therefore a representative body through which the employees met with management on a regular basis through elected representatives to discuss matters of common interests. In South Africa works councils were generally not used for the purposes of collective bargaining, but served mainly as a forum for communication and consultation between managers and workers, and also as advisory bodies. Works councils therefore served mainly to promote sound labour and employee relations. In practice, aspects normally dealt with at the works council level were internal matters such as grievance handling, disciplinary matters and issues such as promotion and transfers, transport services, accommodation facilities, hygiene, sports and recreation facilities, cafeteria facilities, payment procedures and safety standards.

Works councils must not be confused with workplace forums introduced by the LRA 66 of 1995. This Act introduced workplace forums as in-house institutions for employee participation and representation at the workplace. The idea is that, whereas collective bargaining can be used for distributive issues in the time-honoured adversarial fashion, workplace forums should be used to foster cooperative relations through dialogue, information-sharing, consultations and joint decision making. The nearest thing the old Act had to workplace forums were works councils. For various reasons, most notably political and historical, these works councils were deeply distrusted by black trade unions (since many employers and politicians abused works councils by trying to use them to undermine black trade unionism).

Given the historical baggage relating to works councils, the workplace forum is perhaps the most controversial innovation introduced into our system of industrial relations by Act 66 of 1995. Despite opposition and scepticism from representatives of labour as well as business at the NEDLAC negotiations over the new labour relations Bill, the government persisted in its resolve to have provision made in the new dispensation for some form of in-house institution which could be used for more cooperative and participatory endeavours between management and labour.

21.4.2 Rationale for and establishment of a workplace forum

For the purpose of workplace forums, the term "employee" excludes senior managerial employees.

A *senior managerial employee* is defined as a person whose contract of employment or status confers the authority to represent the employer in dealings with workplace forums; or to determine policy and take decisions on behalf of the employer that may be in conflict with the "representation of employees in the workplace".

In terms of the Act, the functions of a workplace forum are to strive for the promotion of the interests of all employees in the workplace, whether they are trade union members or not, and to improve efficiency in the workplace. In order to promote these objectives, it has the right to obtain certain information from the employer, to be consulted on certain matters, as well as to participate in joint decision making on other matters (see below).

The general process for the establishment of a workplace forum is depicted in figure .

A workplace forum may be established in any workplace in which an employer employs more than 100 employees. Any representative trade union may apply to the CCMA for the establishment of a workplace forum.* The applicant must satisfy the CCMA that a copy of the application has been served on the employer. Once the CCMA receives the application, it has to ascertain whether there are 100 or more employees employed at that workplace, whether the applicant is a representative trade union, and whether there is no functioning workplace forum already established in terms of the Act. Thereafter the CCMA must appoint a commissioner to assist the parties to establish a workplace forum by collective agreement or, failing that, to establish a workplace forum in terms of the Act. The commissioner must convene a meeting with the applicant, the employer and any registered trade union that has members employed in the workplace, in order to

---

*For the purposes of this section of the Act, "representative trade union" means a registered trade union, or two or more registered trade unions acting jointly, that have as members the majority of the employees employed by an employer in a workplace.

facilitate the conclusion of a collective agreement between those parties, or at least between the applicant and the employer. If a collective agreement is concluded, the role of the commissioner regarding the establishment of a workplace forum is completed. If a collective agreement is not concluded, the commissioner must once again try to convene a meeting between the relevant stakeholders (or at least between the applicant and the employer), with a view to reaching agreement on a constitution for the workplace forum in accordance with the Act. If agreement is not reached on a constitution, the commissioner must establish a workplace forum and determine the provisions of the constitution in accordance with the Act. After the workplace forum has been established, the commissioner must set a date for the election of the first members of the forum and appoint an election officer to conduct the election.

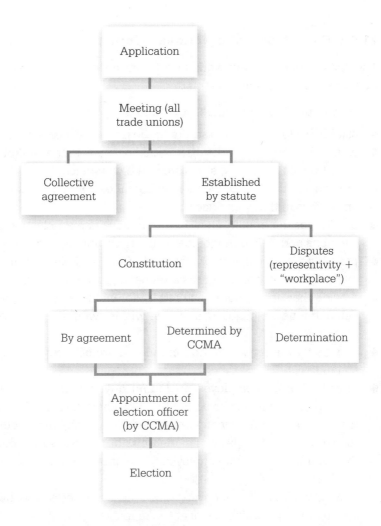

Figure 21.3

General process for the establishment of a workplace forum

If a majority trade union enjoys sole bargaining rights in respect of all employees in a particular workplace, that trade union may apply for the establishment of a trade union based workplace forum. In this case the applicant trade union may choose the members of the workplace forum from among its elected representatives in the workplace. The constitution of the applicant trade union governs the nomination, election and removal from office of elected representatives in the workplace. A trade union based workplace forum will be dissolved if the collective agreement granting sole bargaining rights to the trade union is terminated or whenever the trade union loses its status as the majority trade union. It should be noted that trade union based workplace forums will be rare, since, in terms of the Act, the majority trade union must represent all employees at a workplace and it is not common in South Africa to have one trade union representing workers as well as supervisors and middle management.

21.4.3 Constitution of a workplace forum

The constitution of every workplace forum **must** provide for certain matters and **may** provide for certain other matters.

The constitution of a workplace forum **must**:

- establish a formula for determining the number of seats in the workplace forum;
- establish a formula for the distribution of seats, in the workplace forum so as to reflect the occupational structure of the workplace;
- provide for the direct election of members of the workplace forum by the employees in the workplace;
- provide for the appointment of an employee as an election officer to conduct elections and define that officer's functions and powers;
- provide than an election of members of the workplace forum must be held not later than twenty-four months after each preceding election;
- provide that, if another registered trade union becomes representative, it may demand a new election at any time within twenty-one months after each preceding election;
- provide for the procedure and manner in which elections and ballots must be conducted;
- provide that any employee, including any former or current member of the workplace forum, may be nominated as a candidate for election as a member of the workplace forum by any registered trade union with members employed in the workplace, or a petition signed by not less than 20 % of the employees in the workplace or 100 employees, whichever number of employees is the smaller;
- provide that in any ballot every employee is entitled to vote by secret ballot and to vote during working hours at the employer's premises;
- provide that in an election for members of the workplace forum every employee is entitled (unless the constitution provides otherwise) to cast a number of votes

equal to the number of members to be elected and to cast one or more of those votes in favour of any candidate;

- establish the terms of office of members of the workplace forum and the circumstances in which a member must vacate that office;
- establish the circumstances and manner in which members of the workplace forum may be removed from office, including the right of any representative trade union that nominated a member for election to remove that member at any time;
- establish the manner in which vacancies in the workplace forum may be filled, including the rules for holding by-elections;
- establish the circumstances and manner in which meetings must be held;
- provide that the employer must allow the election officer reasonable time off with pay during working hours to prepare for and conduct elections;
- provide that the employer must allow each member of the workplace forum reasonable time off with pay during working hours to perform the functions of a member of the workplace forum and to receive training relevant to the performance of those functions;
- require the employer to take any steps that are reasonably necessary to assist the election officer in conducting elections;
- require the employer to provide facilities to enable the workplace forum to perform its functions;
- provide for full-time members of the workplace forum where there are more than 1 000 employees in a workplace;
- provide that the forum may invite any expert to attend meetings of the workplace forum, including meetings with the employer or the employees, and that an expert is entitled to any information to which the workplace forum is entitled and to inspect and copy any document that members of the workplace forum are entitled to inspect and copy;
- provide that office bearers or officials of the representative trade union may attend meetings of the workplace forum, including meetings with the employer or the employees; and
- provide that the representative trade union and the employer, by agreement, may change the constitution of the workplace forum.

In addition, the constitution of a workplace forum **may** provide for the following:

- establishing a procedure that provides for the conciliation and arbitration of proposals in respect of which the employer and the workplace forum do not reach consensus;
- establishing a coordinating workplace forum to perform any of the general functions of a workplace forum and one or more subsidiary workplace forums to perform any of the specific functions of a workplace forum; and
- including provisions that depart from those set out in the Act.

21.4.4 Meetings of workplace forums

The Act specifies that there must be regular meetings of the workplace forum. It then proceeds to specify three different types of regular meetings, namely: (i) meetings between the employer and the workplace forum; (ii) meetings between the workplace forum and employees; and (iii) meetings between the employer and employees at a workplace.

1. **Meetings between the employer and the workplace forum:** At these meetings the employer must present a report on its financial and employment situation, its performance since the last report and its anticipated performance in the short term and in the long term; and consult the workplace forum on any matter arising from the report that may affect employees in the workplace.

2. **Meetings between the workplace forum and employees:** At these meetings the workplace forum must report on its activities generally, on matters in respect of which it has been consulted by the employer, and on matters in respect of which it has participated in joint decision making with the employer.

3. **Meetings between the employer and employees at a workplace:** Each calendar year, at one of the meetings with the employees, the employer must present an annual report of its financial and employment situation, its performance generally and its future prospects and plans.

Meetings with employees — (2) and (3) above — must be held during working hours, at a time and place agreed upon by the workplace forum and the employer, without loss of pay on the part of the employees.

21.4.5 Using workplace forums for the purposes of consultation

Consultative decision making may be described as a process in which one party retains the right unilaterally to make and implement a decision, subject to the qualification that he/she must, as part of the decision-making process, allow other stakeholders to make representations; these representations must be seriously considered by the decision maker before making the decision. It should be noted that good faith consultation requires of the decision maker to suspend the final decision until he/she has elicited and seriously considered the proposals of the other stakeholders. To reach a decision *before* considering the other parties' proposals would constitute consultation in bad faith, and would therefore not constitute consultation at all. What distinguishes consultative decision making from joint decision making is the fact that the former remains a *unilateral* process, whereas the latter is a *bilateral* process (in the sense that the authority to make a decision is shared between two or more parties, which in turn implies that each party has a veto over each of the other parties). As a unilateral process, consultative decision making does not impose a duty on the decision maker to reach any agreement with the non-decision-making parties to the procedure (accordingly, the Act provides that, after having complied with the statutory duty to consult, the employer may implement the proposal, even in the absence of agreement).

According to the Act, the purpose of consultation is to reach agreement. Before an employer may implement a proposal in relation to any of the listed matters, the employer must first consult the workplace forum and attempt to reach consensus with it. The employer must allow the workplace forum an opportunity during the consultation to make representations and to advance alternative proposals. The employer must consider and respond to the representations or alternative proposals made by the workplace forum and, if the employer does not agree with them, he/she must state his/her reasons for disagreeing. If the employer and the workplace forum do not reach consensus, the employer must invoke any agreed procedure to resolve any differences before implementing his/her proposal.

Except where a collective agreement determines otherwise, a workplace forum is entitled to be consulted by the employer about proposals relating to any of the matters listed in exhibit C.

Exhibit C

Matters for consultation

The employer must consult the workplace forum about any proposals relating to:
- restructuring the workplace, including the introduction of new technology and new work methods;
- changes in the organisation of work;
- partial or total plant closures;
- mergers and transfers of ownership, in so far as they have an impact on the employees;
- the dismissal of employees for reasons based on operational requirements;
- exemptions from any collective agreement or any law;
- job grading;
- criteria for merit increases or the payment of discretionary bonuses;
- education and training;
- product development plans;
- export promotion; and
- other matters specifically provided for (see discussion below).

The list in exhibit C could be expanded in the following manner.

- A bargaining council may confer on a workplace forum the right to be consulted about additional matters in workplaces that fall within the registered scope of the bargaining council.
- A representative trade union and an employer may conclude a collective agreement conferring on the workplace forum the right to be consulted about any additional matters in that workplace.
- Any other law may confer on a workplace forum the right to be consulted about additional matters.
- Subject to any applicable occupational health and safety legislation, a representative trade union and an employer may agree:

    O that the employer must consult with the workplace forum with a view to initiating, developing, promoting, monitoring and reviewing measures to ensure health and safety at work;

    O that a meeting between the workplace forum and employer constitutes a meeting of a health and safety committee required to be established in the workplace by that legislation; and

    O that one or more members of the workplace forum are health and safety representatives for the purposes of that legislation.

● A newly established workplace forum may request the employer for a review of existing merit systems, disciplinary codes and procedures and work-related conduct (see below).

In the case of workplace forums in the public service, matters may be removed from the list of consultative issues, but none may be added.

21.4.6 Joint decision making with workplace forums

Except if a collective agreement determines otherwise, an employer *must* reach consensus with a workplace forum before implementing any proposal concerning those matters listed in exhibit D. This list of issues may be amended by either a collective agreement between the employer and the majority trade union, or by any other statute that may confer on a workplace forum the right to participate in joint decision making about additional matters.

Exhibit D

Matters for joint decision making
Except if a collective agreement determines otherwise, an employer must reach consensus with a workplace forum before implementing any proposal concerning: ● disciplinary codes and procedures; ● rules relating to the proper regulation of the workplace, in so far as they apply to conduct not related to the work performance of employees; ● measures designed to protect and advance persons disadvantaged by unfair discrimination; and ● changes by the employer or by employer-appointed representatives on trusts or boards of employer-controlled schemes, to the rules regulating social benefit schemes.

Should the employer not reach consensus with the workplace forum, the employer may either refer the dispute to arbitration in terms of any agreed procedure, or, if there is no agreed procedure, refer the dispute to the CCMA. The employer must satisfy the Commission that a copy of the referral has been served on the chairperson of the workplace forum. The Commission must attempt to resolve the dispute through conciliation. If the dispute remains unresolved, the employer may request that the dispute be resolved through arbitration (see figure 21.4).

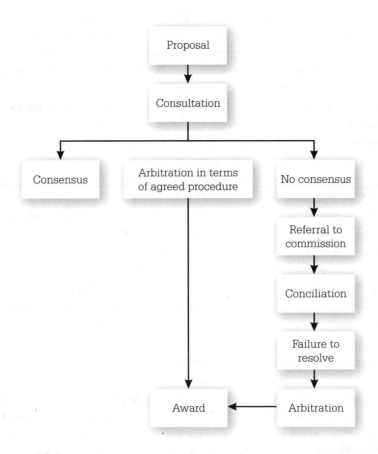

Figure 21.4
Procedure to resolve failure to reach consensus with workplace forum

21.4.7 Matters for review

Once it has been established, the workplace forum may request a meeting with the employer to review the criteria for merit increases or the payment of discretionary bonuses, disciplinary codes and procedures, and rules relating to the proper regulation of the workplace, in so far as they apply to conduct not related to work performance of employees in the workplace. The employer must submit the necessary criteria, disciplinary codes and procedures, and rules, if any, in writing to the workplace forum for its consideration. A review of the merit increases criteria must be conducted in terms of the prescribed consultative process, whereas a review of the disciplinary codes and procedures, and rules, must be done by way of a collective agreement or conducted in accordance with the procedure depicted in figure 21.4.

21.4.8 Disclosure of information

One of the aspects of the new Act with which employers are least comfortable concerns those provisions relating to disclosure of information to both shop stewards (see the discussion of organisational rights above) and/or workplace forums. In terms of the Act, an employer must disclose to the workplace forum all relevant information that will allow the forum to engage effectively in consultation and joint decision making. An employer is not required to disclose information that is legally privileged, that the employer cannot disclose without contravening a prohibition imposed on the employer by any law or order of any court, that is confidential and, if disclosed, may cause substantial harm to an employee or to the employer, or that is private, personal information relating to an employee, unless that employee consents to the disclosure of that information.

If there is a dispute about the disclosure of information, any party to the dispute may refer the dispute in writing to the Commission. The party referring the dispute to the CCMA must satisfy the Commission that a copy of the referral has been served on all the other parties to the dispute. The CCMA must attempt to resolve the dispute through conciliation. If the dispute remains unresolved, any party to the dispute may request that the dispute be resolved through arbitration.

In any dispute about the disclosure of information the commissioner must first decide whether or not the information is relevant. If the commissioner decides that the information is relevant, and if it is confidential or private personal information, the commissioner must balance the harm that the disclosure is likely to cause an employee or employer against the harm that the failure to disclose the information is likely to cause the workplace forum in its effective participation in consultation and joint decision making. If the commissioner decides that the balance of harm favours the disclosure of the information, the commissioner may order the disclosure of the information on terms designed to limit the harm likely to be caused to the employee or employer. When making such an order, the commissioner must take into account any past breach of confidentiality at that workplace and may refuse to order the disclosure of the information or any other confidential information that might otherwise be disclosed for a period specified in the arbitration award.

Lastly, the Act provides for the appointment of full-time members of a workplace forum and for the dissolution of workplace forums.

21.4.9 Appointment of full-time members

In a workplace in which 1 000 or more employees are employed, the members of the workplace forum may designate from their number one full-time member. The employer must pay a full-time member of the workplace forum the same remuneration that the member would have earned in the position the member held immediately before being designated as a full-time member. When a person ceases to be a full-time member of a workplace forum, the employer must reinstate that person to the position that person held immediately before election or appoint that person to any higher position to which, but for the election, that person would have advanced.

21.4.10 Dissolution of workplace forums

A representative trade union in a workplace may request a ballot to dissolve a workplace forum. If a ballot to dissolve a workplace forum has been requested, an election officer must be appointed in terms of the constitution of the workplace forum. Within thirty days of the request for a ballot to dissolve the workplace forum, the election officer must prepare and conduct the ballot. If more than 50 % of the employees who have voted in the ballot support the dissolution of the workplace forum, the workplace forum must be dissolved.

21.5 ASPECTS OF STRIKE MANAGEMENT

No matter how much is done by management to improve the quality of employee and labour relations in an organisation, conflict always forms an inherent part of the employment relationship. From time to time this conflict may increase or decrease. The aim of management will, however, always have to manage conflict levels to facilitate better chances of the overall success of the organisation. Sometimes this does not happen and it may then even lead to the manifestation of serious forms of organised, collective labour–management conflict such as strikes. Should this occur, it is necessary to manage such situations professionally.

21.5.1 General

As mentioned in chapter 20, strikes are to be regarded as a natural and integral part of the collective bargaining process. It is the ultimate form of power used by labour. The intention of strikers is to suspend the relationship temporarily, not to terminate the relationship. This should always be borne in mind when dealing with strikes.

When dealing with strikes and other forms of work stoppages, it is important to realise that workers may have legitimate grievances related to the employment relationship and that the strike may be a last resort effort to demonstrate their dissatisfaction and to pressurise management to concede to their demands. Management should deal appropriately with the strike and the striking workers, irrespective of the legality or the exact form of the industrial action as manifestation of conflict.

As is the case with all employment-related issues, managers should always consider how their actions could affect the operations of the organisation, as well as the ongoing relationship with the employees.

21.5.2 Strike management phases

Strike management entails more than strike handling. Strike handling actually refers to the active phase of strike management — the phase when all the plans and preparations are activated and implemented.

The different phases of strike management thus include:

- strike preparation (planning and organising prior to any actual strike action);
- strike handling (the active phase of strike management);
- poststrike action (evaluation of actions and decisions after the strike has ended).

21.5.2.1 The prestrike or preparatory phase

Because conflict is naturally inherent in the employment relationship — conflict which, if not dealt with professionally, may eventually grow into serious industrial conflict such as a strike — management has to manage all aspects of the employment relationship in such a way as to minimise the possibilities of disruptive labour actions. It can thus be said that the best way to manage a strike is to engage in management practices that prevent strikes.

However, no management team can be 100 % assured that they will never have to deal with any form of industrial action. It is therefore necessary to take relevant precautionary measures and to be prepared, just in case.

One of the first questions to be answered is: "In the case of industrial action like a strike, what would the objectives of management be?" The basic step of the management process, *objective setting*, thus comes into play.

The **primary objective** of management must be to handle the situation in such a way that workers become productive again as soon as possible. The idea is to minimise the disruption of operations and to restore order and the normal business processes in the shortest possible time so that financial losses are limited. Obviously this will include the objective of resolving the underlying causes of the conflict. If this is not achieved, labour productivity levels will not be acceptable, even though workers may have returned to work.

It is thus necessary for management to take the required planning and organising steps in order to reach the said objectives. Through preparatory action such as drawing up a strike handling and contingency plan, management should be more able, when a strike does take place, to identify and address quickly the real causes of the conflict, to relieve unproductive conflict levels, to prevent any form of damage to property or injuries to people, to arrive at mutually acceptable settlements in the shortest possible time, and thus to minimise the disruptions to the normal business processes. The idea is thus to be prepared so that there is little need for impulsive action. By being prepared management can create a better sense of certainty regarding how such situations should be dealt with. In this way panic can be minimised and uniformity in management thought can be enhanced.

During the preparatory phase the management of an organisation must thus reassess their objectives and see to it that their strike handling and contingency plans are geared towards the achievement of these objectives.

Even before a strike occurs it is therefore necessary to compile a contingency plan and organise all of those who will have to play an additional role in the event of a strike. Management must appoint a strike handling team and ensure that all team members are fully informed and sufficiently competent to fulfil their tasks. It is also advisable to ensure continuously that all parties are satisfied with the relevant prestrike dispute handling procedures and, in addition, plan how to deal with customers in the event of a strike. This will involve, for example, ensuring that contracts with customers contain clauses that will prevent them from having claims against the organisation for damages which may result from strike action.

With regard to the contingency plan and the organising of a strike handling team, it is always necessary to appoint a strike-handling leader. This person should ideally hold a very senior position in the organisation and must have the responsibility and mandate to make all final decisions regarding the strike situation. He/she should be available at all times during strike action and usually acts as the link between parties like the negotiating team, the operational team, the consultants, the media and the top management team.

The members of the *negotiating team* will as a rule be responsible for negotiating with the representatives of the strikers. Such a team will obviously have to include some of the most competent and experienced negotiators in the organisation. On the other hand, the business *operations team* will consist of senior persons who have the best knowledge of the core business operations, activities and processes of the organisation (such as the production manager in a manufacturing business), as well as the most important support personnel (such as a plant maintenance engineer who has to ensure the smooth functioning of all technical equipment and production machinery). A group of *special consultants* (internal and/or external) may also form part of the strike management team. The particular members of this subteam will vary in accordance with the nature of the strike and the strikers' demands. Normally it will include experts in the legal field, language experts, media experts, security specialists and also key personnel who are experts on the administrative and financial implications of any decisions and actions which may be considered during the course of the strike handling phase. The HR procurement specialist should also be a team member to give the necessary inputs on the procurement of human resources to help ensure continued business operations.

Apart from organising a strike management team, it is also necessary as part of the preparations to train the role-players and even to arrange strike handling exercises. Furthermore, it is necessary to organise the physical infrastructure. This includes aspects such as a strike monitor and control room with the necessary equipment (for example telephones, fax machines, photocopy facilities, radio communication devices, megaphones, etc). Evacuation procedures must also be available should the situation get out of control. Lists with contact details of important parties (for example the police, customers, suppliers, Department of Labour, CCMA, relevant bargaining council) must also be available. Other facilities may include normal stationary, flip charts (for brainstorming and discussion sessions) and tape recording and video equipment. It is also advisable for management to negotiate (as part of the recognition and procedural agreement) a code of conduct to be applicable in strike situations. This code can spell out the rules of behaviour during strikes.

As can be gathered from the above, the strike preparatory phase involves a multitude of complex planning and organising decisions and actions.

21.5.2.2 The active phase of strike management

As soon as any rumours or suspicions develop that industrial action may be looming, the appropriate member of the strike management team must be informed. This person may then analyse the information and, if necessary, assemble the strike management team.

The strike management team will collect and analyse all the information, discuss possible courses of action, and commence with their functions as stipulated in the strike handling plan. The negotiating subteam will, for example, get together to analyse relevant information and to prepare their negotiating strategies and tactics.

One of the most important things to be done throughout any strike episode is to record accurately all relevant events which take place during the strike. Use is often made of a so-called strike diary. With the objectives of strike handling in mind, it is obviously extremely important to open up communication with the representatives of those on strike in order to identify the grievances and the real causes of the industrial action. Although a policy of "no work, no pay" is advisable, management must always try to get the workers productive again as soon as possible, and a deviation from the "no work, no pay" rule can be used as a trade-off in return for those who resume normal work promptly.

As communication and even negotiations progress, more information will be gathered which has to be analysed in order to identify the relevant facts necessary for appropriate decisions. Whatever the strike handling team decides to do, however, the need to encourage dialogue and to reach the set objectives must always be facilitated. The sting of a strike is often eased by the spirit in which management deals with the demands, the anger (sometimes the violence) and the people with whom management negotiate. Although strictness and discipline are always important, it is also necessary to show an understanding of the emotions of those involved in the strike. Strikes are usually very traumatic for the strikers themselves, emotions often run high, there is a great deal of uncertainty and aspects like intimidation and violence can also form part of severe forms of industrial action. It is therefore normally advisable not to address mass meetings of striking workers, but rather to work through their representatives. The most important issue is to settle the relevant issues to the satisfaction of all parties as soon as possible.

Deciding on the dismissal of strikers

It should be borne in mind that strikers in South Africa enjoy constitutional protection (see section 23 of the Constitution). However, this right, like any other fundamental right, cannot be absolute and must therefore be subject to some ascertainable limitations. The Constitution contains a general limitation clause in section 36 detailing the principles to be applied in determining whether a limitation of any constitutional right is constitutional. The question of the limitation of fundamental constitutional rights is one of the most complex issues in constitutional law and certainly falls beyond the scope of this book. Leaving constitutional issues aside, the question still remains whether strikers may be dismissed in terms of the Labour Relations Act.

In the case of *protected* strikes, strikers may not be dismissed for striking: to do so would amount to an automatically unfair dismissal. However, this does not mean that strikers involved in a protected strike enjoy immunity from dismissal; it only means that they cannot be dismissed because they are legitimately exercising their right to strike. They may still be dismissed for misconduct during the strike (for example because they assaulted non-strikers or damaged company property) or for operational reasons such as plant closure (which may itself be caused by the strike).

In the case of *unprotected* strikes, different principles apply. In this case workers may be dismissed for striking. This, however, does not mean that an employer may dismiss unprotected strikers with impunity: he/she must still act in accordance with the precepts of fairness as enunciated in the Act. A fair dismissal in the context of an unprotected strike will involve an enquiry into a number of issues, including those summarised in exhibit E.*

Exhibit E

Questions regarding the fair dismissal of unprotected strikers

- Was a proper ultimatum given?
  - Did it reach all the strikers?
  - Did it clearly indicate the consequences for the workers if they persist in their strike (ie that they will be dismissed)?
  - Did it contain a specific deadline to return to work?
- Were the workers given enough time to consider the ultimatum?
- Did the employer try to contact the trade union?
- What attempts were made to follow the procedures?
- Did the employer provoke the strike?

21.5.2.3 The poststrike phase

After an episode of serious industrial conflict, it is important to take certain steps immediately in order to rebuild the relationship between the parties. These include the following:

- It is essential to ensure that all undertakings (agreements and promises) relating to the negotiations during the strike episode are fulfilled.

*This should be read in conjunction with chapter 24.

- It is necessary to work at restoring relations. During strikes emotions often run high and trust, respect and communication often suffer. Steps have to be taken to normalise all of these as soon as possible. Without restoring communication between all parties concerned, the quality of the relationships cannot be expected to return to normal.
- It is important to acknowledge that serious conflict and a breakdown in relations has occurred. More important, however, is to acknowledge the real causes and to start focusing on the prevention of a recurrence.
- It is important to ensure that all the normal procedures and processes (such as disciplinary and grievance procedures) are confirmed as operative and applied.
- It is important to adhere to all relevant legal requirements.
- The so-called industrial action *post mortem* must be attended to. Here the whole incident is reviewed and special attention is paid to the process of strike handling, the effectiveness of the strike handling and contingency plans, mistakes that were made, the competency of the strike management team members and the lessons to be learned from the strategies and tactics followed by the parties.
- Appropriate media liaison must take place. Normalising the relations with customers, suppliers and the general public can be facilitated by a proper media release on the incident.

21.6 CONCLUSION

In this chapter the focus was on the management of various aspects of labour and employee relations at the organisational level.

Establishing sound labour and employee relations at the level of the workplace is certainly one of the most important challenges facing South African organisations. This is the case largely due to the historical development of this country, with the resultant huge trust gaps existing between labour and management in many organisations. Even though legislation may go a long way to facilitating more sound and constructive industrial relations in the country, it is ultimately up to the primary parties to work hard at building relationships of trust and cooperation at organisational level.

In this regard we have focused on the important role of communication, grievance handling and especially worker participation and involvement. We have also highlighted how the representatives of labour — most notably trade unions — and those of the employer (ie management) can interact with each other. In this regard the focus was on collective bargaining and negotiation dynamics. Workplace forums as structures for cooperation and worker participation were also examined. Lastly we also briefly explained the nature and role of strikes in labour relations, and we specifically pointed out some guidelines regarding the management of strikes.

SELF-EVALUATION QUESTIONS

1. Explain at least ten methods of communicating with employees.
2. Briefly describe barriers to good communication.
3. List the principles underlying the handling of employee grievances and related procedures.
4. What is meant by "employee involvement and participation"? How can this be achieved?
5. Differentiate between a *disciplinary code* and a *disciplinary procedure*.
6. Explain how one should handle initial contact with a trade union.
7. Describe the issues involved in formalising a relationship with a trade union.
8. Distinguish between a *closed shop agreement* and an *agency shop agreement*. Comment on the merits and demerits of each.
9. Discuss in detail the process of distributive negotiation.
10. List twenty competencies and characteristics required of distributive negotiators.
11. Explain the principles underlying interest bargaining.
12. Describe the seven steps of the process of target-specific bargaining.
13. How can a workplace forum be established?
14. Write concise notes on the constitutions of statutory workplace forums.
15. List the issues earmarked by the Labour Relations Act for consultation and for joint decision making.
16. What has to be done during the planning and preparation phase for strikes?

 BIBLIOGRAPHY

Alfred, N (Ed). 1984. *Bargain, Don't Fight!* Johannesburg: Thompson

Anstey, M (Ed). 1990. *Worker Participation*. Cape Town: Juta

Anstey, M. 1990. Worker participation: Concepts and issues. In *Worker Participation*, ed M Anstey. Kenwyn: Juta

Anstey, M. 1991. *Negotiating Conflict: Insights and Skills for Negotiators and Peacemakers*. Kenwyn: Juta

Bendix, S. 1992. *Industrial Relations in South Africa*, 2 ed. Cape Town: Juta

Bendix, S. 1996. *Industrial Relations in the New South Africa*, 3 ed. Cape Town: Juta

Bostrom, R N. 1983. *Persuasion*. Englewood Cliffs, New Jersey: Prentice-Hall

Fenton, B. 1993. Honest workplace conversations at South African Breweries. *People Dynamics*, 11(7), 15–17

Finnemore, M & Van der Merwe, R. 1992. *Introduction to Industrial Relations in South Africa*, 3 ed. Johannesburg: Lexicon

Finnemore, M & Van der Merwe, R. 1996. *Introduction to Labour Relations in South Africa*, 4 ed. Durban: Butterworths

Fisher, R & Brown, S. 1988. *Getting Together: Building a Relationship that Gets to Yes.* Boston: Houghton Mifflin

Fisher, R & Ury, W. 1981. *Getting to Yes.* London: Hutchinson

Flanders, A. 1965. *Industrial Relations: What is Wrong with the System?* London: Institute of Personnel Management

Höck, C. 1991/92. Interest bargaining: The way ahead? *IPM Journal,* 10(4), 15–18

Horwitz, F M & Townsend, M. 1993. Elements in participation, teamwork and flexibility in South Africa. *International Journal of Human Resource Management,* 4(4), 917–932

Jaffee, G. 1990. Worker co-operatives: Their emergence, problems and potential. In *Worker Participation,* ed M Anstey. Kenwyn: Juta

Kemp, N. 1992. *Labour Relations Strategies: An Interactional Approach.* Kenwyn, Cape Town: Juta

Kniveron, B H. 1974. Industrial negotiating: Some training implications. *Industrial Relations Journal,* 5(3), 27–37

Nel, P S, Erasmus, B J & Swanepoel, B J. 1993. *Successful Labour Relations: Guidelines for Practice.* Pretoria: Van Schaik

Nieuwmeijer, L. 1988. *Negotiation: Methodology and Training.* Pretoria: Owen Burgess

Pienaar, WE & Spoelstra, HJ. 1991. *Negotiation, Theory Strategy and Skills.* Cape Town: Juta

Pondy, L R. 1969. Organisation conflict, concepts and models. *Administrative Science Quarterly,* 12, 27–36

Power, D F. 1991. Target specific bargaining. *IPM Journal,* 9(8), 15–20

Salamon, M. 1992. *Industrial Relations: Theory and Practice,* 2 ed. New York: Prentice-Hall

Walton, R E & McKersie, R B. 1965. *A Behavioral Theory of Labour Negotiation.* New York: McGraw-Hill

APPENDIX: DISCIPLINARY CODE OF A SOUTH AFRICAN ORGANISATION

Examples of mandatory offences

Consider Dismissal (by Formal Disciplinary Enquiry)

- Repeated similar misconduct after Final Written Warning within a period of six months.
- Absent from work without a valid reason within a period of six months after a Final Written Warning for a similar offence.
- Late for work without a valid reason within a period of three months after a Final Written Warning for a similar offence.
- Absent from work without a valid reason or notifying the supervisor of the reason for absence for a period of three or more consecutive days. Confirmation of dismissal will be taken on, at the latest, the sixth working day.
- Gambling or unofficial money lending on company premises.
- Causing injury to person(s) or damage to company property by driving any vehicle without a driving permit.
- Assault.
- Serious disrespect, insubordination, impudence or insolence.
- Wilfully clocking another employee's clock card or allowing another employee to clock his/her clock card.
- Possession and/or consuming intoxicating liquor on company premises without permission.
- Fighting on company premises.
- Unauthorised possession of weapons on company premises at any time.
- The making or publishing of false, vicious or malicious statements concerning an Employee, Supervisor, the company, or its products, the Employee Council and the Union.
- Misuse or removal from the premises of employee data and company records without proper authorisation or the conveying of confidential information of any nature.
- Falsification of personnel or other documents.
- Theft or misappropriation of company property or the property of employees in any manner.
- Disposing of or concealing defective work either directly or as a party to any deception in this regard.
- Wilfully restricting output or attempting to influence other Employees to restrict output or stop work except if all existing grievance channels have been used to no avail.
- Refusal to carry out work related instructions or orders from supervisor.
- Permitting a person who is not an Employee of the company to use your identity card to gain entry to premises.
- Entering or leaving the company premises other than through recognised gates.
- Threatening, intimidating, coercing Employees or supervision at any time.
- Tampering with his/her or another Employee's clock card in any manner.
- Distribution of written or printed matter of any description or soliciting of any kind without the company's permission.
- Serious immoral conduct or indecency.
- Carelessness or negligence, or committing any act which may result in injury to person or damage to company property, depending on seriousness.
- Posting or removal of notices, signs or writing of any form on notice boards or company property at any time without specific authority of management.
- Tampering with sick certificate.

- Wilful disregard of safety rules and common safety practices.
- Using another Employee's identity card or permitting another Employee to use his/her identity card to gain entry to company premises.
- Unauthorised driving of any company vehicle.

Examples of non-mandatory offences

Formal verbal warnings (by Foremen/Immediate Supervisor)

- Late for work without a valid reason.
- Leaving own work place or department during working hours without permission from the supervisor.
- Stopping work or making preparation to leave work (such as washing or changing clothes) before the signal sounds for lunch/tea breaks or before the specified knock off-time.
- Loitering in work area or other departments 15 minutes after having clocked out at end of shift.
- Running in the company premises.
- Failure to use refuse drums — strewing litter on company premises.
- Wearing canvas shoes or sandals on company premises.
- Failure to perform assigned tasks timeously and according to set quantity and quality.
- Overstaying lunch or tea breaks or reporting late at work stations or commencement of shift.
- Wilfully obstructing movement of stock or vehicle in company premises in any manner.

First written warnings (by Foreman/Immediate Supervisors countersigned by General Foremen)

- Similar misconduct repeated after Formal Verbal Warning within a period of six months.
- Late for work without a valid reason within a period of two months after having received a Formal Verbal Warning for a similar offence.
- Spitting on the floor or walls in any areas within the company premises.
- Horseplay, i.e. playing in a manner that distracts others from their jobs or causing confusion that may lead to accidents, injuries or personal friction.
- Absent from work without a valid reason.
- Unauthorised operation of machinery, tools or equipment.
- Consuming any food stuff in other than prescribed eating places or unauthorised sitting in vehicles at any stage of production, or unauthorised switching on of car radios of such vehicles.
- Failure to report for overtime without a valid reason if required to do so.
- Absent from work for a period of up to two consecutive days without notifying supervisor.
- Obstructing movement of stock or vehicles by wrong parking or stacking which may cause injury to person(s) or damage to company property.
- Sleeping while on duty.
- Unauthorised removal of safety guards.

Final written warnings (by Departmental Superintendent/Manager)

- Repeated similar misconduct, after a Formal Written Warning within a period of three months.
- Absent from work without a valid reason within a period of six months after a Formal Written Warning for a similar offence.
- Late for work without a valid reason within a period of two months after a Formal Written Warning for a similar offence.

- Absent from work for a period of up to two consecutive days without a valid reason.
- Smoking in an area which is prohibited due to high fire hazard and/or smoking in vehicles at any stage of production and other nonsmoking areas.
- Poor performance as reflected by a Performance Appraisal.

part seven

Special Topics in Human Resource Management

After studying this chapter you should be able to:

- explain the nature of change;
- describe the internal and external forces driving change;
- explain individual and organisational resistance to change;
- identify strategies for reducing resistance to change;
- describe the change process, and different change options and interventions;
- discuss some contemporary issues in change management;
- explain the importance of change and transformation in South Africa.

22.1 INTRODUCTION

As indicated throughout this book, South Africa is experiencing extraordinary change and transformation in all sectors of life and business. In all likelihood, however, when reflecting on the late 1990s and early twenty-first century, future management historians will conclude that the turbulence of these times was nothing compared with that which was to come.

For South African organisations, therefore, change and transformation are management issues that have and will become a way of life. There can be no hiding or escaping from the intensity and frequency of events that will confront South African organisations. As indicated in chapter 4, factors such as globalisation, reduced technological cycles, shifting demographics, changing customer demands and worker expectations, international economic trends and international competition are some of the forces driving change in South African organisations.

Different types of changes, however, demand different ways of managing it. How these organisational changes are managed will play a crucial role in the extent to which organisations remain competitive and successful — in fact, in their very survival. Yet, the question remains whether South African organisations and their managers and workers in all sectors of the economy are able to cope with the turbulence with which they are faced. Can South African organisations compete globally and succeed, much less survive, in the "New Age"? The material already covered in this book has focused on ways in which to manage employment relationships in order to be able to succeed in this era of turbulence. However, organisational change and transformation must itself be professionally managed. This topic forms the focus of this chapter.

A study by Human and Horwitz (1992) conducted half a decade ago concluded that South African business is inward looking and "closed". At that stage they found that South African managers did not rate issues such as globalisation, strategic alliances and relationships with the state and community as very important. Indeed, they found that South African managers had shut themselves off from their organisations and had adopted a siege mentality. Vermaak (1996: 14) supports this view and points out that the isolation of the past and the lack of competition have made South African organisations quite "lethargic and myopic", and he suggests that they must "wake up and change".

In recent years South African organisations have been exposed to so many unprecedented major changes in their external as well as internal environments, that managers do not have a choice any longer — it is rather a case of transform or cease to exist.

Understanding and successfully managing this challenge has become one of the most important issues for nineties' managers in general, and especially for those managing the people who have to accept, implement and live with the dramatic changes taking place in South African organisations.

While some of the conclusions drawn from earlier research may reflect a rather depressing prognosis for the status of change management in South African organisations, a growing body of evidence from management literature all over the globe offers some clues for South African managers about how to manage their organisations in the face of an uncertain future. Some of these ideas are highlighted in this chapter.

22.2 THE NATURE OF ORGANISATIONAL TRANSFORMATION AND CHANGE MANAGEMENT

The term *transformation* can be defined as follows:

Transformation is the move which an organisation makes to start everything from scratch.

It involves an enquiry into the underlying paradigm of the organisation and a systematic attack on the strategy and operations of existing organisational elements (Nadler & Tushman 1988). Transformation occurs when the majority of individuals in an organisation change their behaviour (Goss, Pascale & Athos 1993).

For example, when a vaccine for the disease of polio was discovered, the American organisation whose sole purpose had been to eradicate polio by raising funds for research into this disease (that is, March of Dimes); had to transform its mission and operations in order to survive. It therefore transformed its mission to focus on a broader purpose — that is, to cure "birth defects". Its organisational structures, systems, management styles, core competencies and the types of behaviours required from all employees for this new venture radically changed in line with the all new reality.

On the other hand, *change* is about tweaking the organisation's strategy and operations. It is about going back to basics or searching for new tools and techniques that will propel the organisation forward.

Change, according to Jick (1993a: 1), is ". . . in its broadest sense, a planned or unplanned response to pressures and forces". Organisational change is defined by Bennis (in Vermaak 1996: 14) as ". . . a response to change, a complex educational strategy intended to change beliefs, attitudes, values and structures of organisations so that they can better adapt to new technologies, markets and challenges, and the dizzying rate of change itself".

An important factor is that the changes facing organisations today are very different from those of the past in that they are not continuous (that is — more of the same thing). In fact, what's complicating things in today's world is the fact that these changes are not part of a past pattern of events — they are often characterised by radical new factors that are driven by, *inter alia*, technology and global issues in which new tools and techniques are required (Jick 1993). Let us take a closer look at the forces that are driving the trends of change and transformation.

22.2.1 The driving forces for change

A number of forces, either individually or in combination, can compel organisations to change. One broad set of forces consists of external or environmental forces that are pressures or opportunities that arise from outside the organisation. Most of these have been discussed in chapter 4. Another set of forces is composed of internal organisational forces, some of which relate to those discussed in chapter 3.

22.2.1.1 External forces

Organisations often have to transform and change as a result of external forces, rather than from an internal desire or need to change (Goodstein 1991). As mentioned already, in South Africa extra-organisational factors include the major political, economic and social changes that have forced organisations to adjust their businesses so that they are aligned with new realities. The challenges posed by the simultaneous need to expand the economy and to establish a just and equitable society have been clearly spelled out in earlier chapters. Other external forces that South African organisations face have been emphasised throughout this book and especially in chapter 4.

It is a well-known fact that globalised economies are creating increased threats and opportunities, forcing organisations to make dramatic improvements not only to gain a competitive advantage but simply to survive. Kotter (1996: 18) states in this regard that "globalisation, in turn, is being driven by a broad and powerful set of forces associated with technological change, international economic integration, domestic market maturation within the more developed countries, and the collapse of worldwide communism".

22.2.1.2 Internal forces

Inside South African organisations, changes are occurring as a result of, *inter alia*, organisational life cycle evolution, the redesign of core structures and processes, changing expectations of workers and the role of unions in the workplace. Changes in workforce demographics towards a more culturally diverse population, in part because of affirmative action and equal opportunity programmes, also create an impetus for the way organisations will need to change traditional management practices.

While both external and internal changes are forcing South African organisations to continuously reassess their strategies and operations, it can generally be said that the methods and timing in which employees all over the world respond to change and transformation differ. Indeed, organisations will have to learn to cope with different responses to change. Research shows that for organisational transformation and change management to be successful and to help organisations to survive and eventually to prosper through employee buy-in, certain fundamentals will have to be retained (Nadler & Tushman 1988).

For example, Goodstein (1991) indicates that, in the face of organisational transformation, organisations need to retain some stability in the form of the organisation's ultimate purpose, core technologies and key people. Indeed, embarking on a transformation initiative when an organisation has a cash crunch crisis, a leadership vacuum, or too much of an adversarial management-union relations climate, should be avoided if at all possible. Such factors should be dealt with first before embarking on any full-scale transformation process.

The principle here, drawn from the field of psychotherapy, is that in order to be able to cope with large-scale and complex change and transformation, people need to have something stable to hold on to. Change must thus be brought about by keeping some aspects the same, by building some stability into the process of change (Nadler 1983). The paradox facing managers in organisations undergoing change and transformation is therefore how much turbulence to expose their employees to, while, at the same time, retaining some form of continuity and stability in order to obtain their employees' commitment to the transformation process. Indeed, planned change — that is, change designed and implemented in an orderly and timely fashion, is preferable to reactive change — that is, a piecemeal response to problems as they develop (Griffen 1987). While planned change and reactive change are interesting theoretical concepts, the reality facing most South African organisations today is that they no longer have the luxury of always controlling which option to select.

Whichever option is chosen, managers need to understand the dynamics of change if they want to manage it successfully. Much of this relates to the human

side of things. In this context, resistance to change is perhaps the greatest imped-
iment to managing change and transformation processes successfully.

22.2.2 Resistance to change (RTC)

Some of the best-documented findings in studies of organisational change relate
to the existence of individual and organisational sources of resistance to change
(RTC) (Robbins 1997; Carrell, Jennings & Hearin 1997; Strebel 1996; Kotter 1995
and Nadler 1983). Inherent congruence in an organisation will make it resistant
especially to "frame-braking" changes (Nadler & Tushman 1988). According to
Robbins (1997), organisations with a history of lengthy periods of success tend to
be particularly resistant to change. Furthermore, Dalziel and Schoonover (in Jick
1993a) have found that organisations with historical barriers to change are likely
to continue this pattern of resistance. Jick (1993b) argues further that if an organisation has a track record of opposing change, more care should be taken to design
a gradual, non-threatening participative implementation process for future
changes.

In a classic experiment conducted by Coch and French in the mid-1940s (Coch
& French 1948), the researchers noticed that factory workers were resistant to
changes in products and production methods. They asked two questions: why do
people resist change and what can be done to overcome that resistance?

The authors went to an American plant (Harwood Manufacturing) and examined the after-change learning curves of several hundred workers who had been
rated as standard or better prior to the job changes. They learned that 38 % of those
workers achieved the new standard of production shortly after change was introduced, but that "62 % either became chronically substandard operators or quit"
(Coch & French 1948: 514).

These results showed that *relearning* was often slower than initially learning
the job, and so they designed two experiments to illustrate: (1) the forces creating
resistance and (2) the mechanisms for overcoming them. In the study, they
employed two variations of democratic procedures in handling two different
groups (all members of both groups participated in the planning and execution of
the change). In a third group, they used representatives of the workers in designing
job changes. A fourth group, with no participation at all, served as the control
group.

After the job changes were complete, the control group did not improve. Frustration was high, some aggression was seen, and 17 % of the group resigned. The
group with representation improved markedly after the job changes, but the two
groups with complete member participation improved even more.

About three months after the initial experiment, the remaining members from
the control group (thirteen workers) were brought together in a job change intervention that involved total participation. With this approach, their performance
improved rapidly up to the level of the other groups.

Interestingly, Coch and French's (1948) study was repeated at a Norwegian shoe factory but without producing the same results. The authors speculated on the role played by cultural differences in mediating variables in the results.

As indicated in previous chapters, and especially in chapter 4, the contexts within which organisations operate play a significant role in the way in which one has to manage the human side of organisations. This seems to hold true also for the management of organisation transformation and change as such. Within a South African context, for instance, it would be quite unthinkable for a highly unionised organisation to expect to succeed with any change or transformation intervention if trade union representatives are not viewed as full stakeholders in the process. Union representatives have to be involved in order to avoid eventual collective resistance to change by the workforce. Any form of organisation change or transformation will impact on the employees of the organisation. Although the degree and nature of such impact will vary from organisation to organisation, the representatives of the workforce can be instrumental in dealing with it. The impact experienced by employees (management as well as nonmanagement) collectively, is one of the most important factors requiring professional attention during any process of change and transformation.

The general nature of the impact of change and transformation on managers and workers was studied by Richardson (1995), who found the following predictable sequence of responses from employees:

- **Fear:** People become fearful and anxious about the impact of change on themselves (they do not mind change, but resist being changed).
- **New faces:** New faces appear in the organisation, frequently at senior-level positions initially.
- **New questions:** Surveys and studies which are conducted to obtain feedback raise new questions about existing practices and new options.
- **New structures:** Roles and responsibilities, as well as lines of authority, change.
- **New goals and standards:** The organisation creates a new culture, aims and standards in line with the new mission and purpose.

22.2.2.1 Individual resistance to change

Resistance to change may stem from the individual, the organisation, or from both.

Several research studies, as summarised by Robbins (1997), Carrell et al (1997), and Greenberg and Baron (1997: 560–561) have identified the following individual resistance factors to change.

- **Fear of the unknown:** This concerns uncertainty about the causes and effects of change. Employees may resist change because they are worried about how it will affect their work and their lives. Even if they have some appreciable dissatisfaction with their present work, they may still worry that things will be worse when the proposed changes are implemented. When the change is initiated by someone else, they may feel manipulated and wonder about the real intention behind the change.

- **Habit:** To cope with the complexity of work and of life itself, people often rely on habits or programmed responses. Change requires new ways of doing tasks and challenges people to develop new competencies. This tendency to respond in accustomed ways may then become a source of resistance.
- **Self-interest:** This relates to the unwillingness to give up existing benefits. Appropriate change should benefit the organisation as a whole but, for some individuals, the cost of change in terms of lost power, prestige, salary, quality of work, etc will often not be viewed as sufficiently offset by the rewards of change.
- **Economic insecurity:** Changes in the organisation often have the potential to threaten employees' job and economic security, either through loss of jobs or reduced pay, and people may therefore resist change.
- **Failure to recognise the need for change:** Employees need to recognise, fully understand and appreciate the reasons for change, otherwise the vested interests that they may have in keeping things the same may result in resistance to the change.
- **General mistrust:** Even though people may understand the arguments in favour of change, they may not trust the motives of those advocating the change. This is especially true in South African organisations where the history of the country has impacted dramatically on people's mindsets.
- **Social disruptions:** Many organisational changes threaten the integrity of friendship groups that provide valuable social rewards; individuals may therefore fear that change will disrupt existing traditions and working relationships.
- **Selective perceptions:** As explained in chapter 3, people have different perceptions and process information selectively. Changes in the organisation may be perceived by some employees as threatening and by others as challenging.

22.2.2.2 Organisational resistance to change

A number of authors have documented various organisational factors that can hinder the implementation of change management processes (Carrell et al 1997; Greenberg & Baron 1997). The following are a few examples of such factors.

- **Structural inertia:** Traditionally organisations are designed to maintain order and stability. The selection process, induction and organisational socialisation, formalisation of tasks and processes and bureaucracy are all aimed at creating order and stability. When confronted with change, these forces creating stability often resist change and cause structural inertia.
- **Cultural inertia:** Some organisations have cultures that emphasise stability and tradition. In such cultures those who advocate change are often seen as being misguided.
- **Work group inertia:** Because of the development of strong group norms that help to guide member behaviour, potent pressures exist to perform jobs in a

certain way. Change often disrupts these established normative expectations, leading to formidable resistance.

- **Threats to existing power relationships:** Any redistribution of decision-making authority can threaten long-established power relationships within the organisation. Certain individuals may resist change because they fear the loss of their power base. Changes from autocratic to participative management or self-managed teams are often seen as threatening by supervisors and middle managers.
- **Threats to expertise:** Individuals and groups within the organisation develop certain specialised expertise. Changes in organisational patterns or structures may threaten the expertise of these specialists, causing resistance to change.
- **Threats to resource allocation:** Individuals and groups may believe that change will threaten future resource allocation. In particular, those groups or individuals who control sizeable resources often see change as a threat.
- **Previously unsuccessful change efforts:** Organisation members who went through previously unsuccessful change efforts may resist change and may be very cautious about accepting any further attempts at introducing change into their system. Individuals may also resist change because they are aware of potential problems that have apparently been overlooked by the change initiators.

22.2.2.3 Overcoming individual and organisational resistance to change

Resistance to change on the part of employees could signal to managers that there may be two problems. The first of these could be the proposal for change or transformation itself. Secondly, the problem could lie with mistakes made in the presentation of the proposal. Managers encountering employee resistance need to re-evaluate their strategies after determining the actual causes of resistance, and then remain flexible enough to overcome the resistance in an appropriate manner. Two somewhat different approaches to overcome resistance to change are presented by Kotter and Schlesinger (1969) and Beer, Eisenstat and Spector (1990).

Kotter and Schlesinger (1969) proposed the following six methods to overcome resistance to change:

- **Education and communication:** If the need for and the logic behind the change are explained early — whether individually to subordinates, to groups in meetings, or to entire organisations through elaborate audiovisual education campaigns — the road to successful change may be smoother.
- **Participation and involvement:** According to a classic study undertaken by Coch and French (1948), resistance to change can be reduced or eliminated by having those involved participate in the design of the change. Leavitt (1964) came to a similar conclusion, suggesting that in order to avoid resistance, managers should take into account what he called the social effects of change.
- **Facilitation and support:** Easing the change process and providing support for those caught up in it is another way in which managers can deal with resist-

ance. Retraining programmes, allowing time off after a difficult period, and offering emotional support and understanding may help.

● **Negotiation and agreement:** It is sometimes necessary for managers to negotiate with avowed or potential resisters to change, and even to obtain written letters of understanding from the heads of organisational subunits that would be affected by the change. In South Africa this may include the negotiation of such agreements with representative trade unions.

● **Manipulation and co-option:** Sometimes managers covertly steer individuals or groups away from resistance to change, or they may co-opt an individual, perhaps a key person within a group, by giving him or her a desirable role in designing or carrying out the change process.

● **Explicit and implicit coercion:** Managers may force people to go along with a change by explicit or implicit threats involving loss or transfer of jobs, lack of promotion and the like. Such methods, though not uncommon, risk making it more difficult to gain support for future change efforts.

A particular process approach to overcoming resistance to change and transformation is postulated by Beer, Eisenstat and Spector (1990). According to these authors, the following six steps in overcoming resistance to change should be implemented sequentially.

● **Step one:** Mobilise commitment to change through joint diagnosis of business problems. Help all employees to develop a shared diagnosis of what is wrong in an organisation and what can and must be done about it.

● **Step two:** Develop a shared vision of how to organise for competitiveness. Once commitment is obtained to the analysis of a problem, managers lead employees toward a task-aligned vision of the organisation that defines new roles and responsibilities.

● **Step three:** Foster not only consensus for the new vision, but also the necessary competence to enact it and required cohesion to move it along. Since employee commitment to change is uneven (some are enthusiastic, others are lukewarm, etc) everyone needs to develop competencies to make the changes work and support mechanisms need to be in place. Managers who cannot adapt to change and transformation issues during this period must be replaced.

● **Step four:** Spread revitalisation to all departments without pushing it from the top. Use teams to break down resistance by enlisting their feedback about how to organise their department and responsibilities.

● **Step five:** Institutionalise revitalisation through formal policies, systems and structures. Enact changes in structures and systems that are consistent with change and transformation during this step (not earlier).

● **Step six:** Monitor and adjust strategies in response to problems in the revitalisation process. Monitoring the change and transformation process needs to be shared by all employees through use of an oversight team — key manager(s), union leaders, secretary, engineer, someone from finance, etc. Regular attitude surveys to monitor behaviour patterns are also essential.

The literature on change management therefore indicates that when organisational change occurs, the climate must be conducive to the change, employee understanding, participation and support are needed, and some of the changes need to be incremental, step by step and congruent with the existing culture, in order to maintain some form of stability. Furthermore, any such changes must be implemented with the utmost care and sensitivity. Managers need to balance the opposite ends of the continuum concerned with how to rejuvenate an organisation (change) and yet not demoralise its loyal workforce (stability).

22.3 PROCESS ASPECTS OF MANAGING ORGANISATIONAL TRANSFORMATION AND CHANGE

As has already been mentioned, the literature suggests that the different antecedents to change necessitate different change responses. When the antecedents include major shifts or changes in the external environment, such as those factors facing most organisations in 1990s, these antecedents call for a reorientation (revitalisation) that implies discontinuous, multilevel, frame-braking (radical, revolutionary or transformational) or second-order change. This kind of change focuses on reforming the mission and core values of the organisation, altering power and status, modifying structures, systems and procedures, revising interaction patterns and often also even appointing new executives from outside the organisation to implement and drive the transformation (Orlikowski & Hofman 1997: 12; Jick 1993a: 1–5; Beatty & Ulrich 1993: 60–62; Tushman, Newman & Romanelli 1986: 482–485; Nadler & Tushman 1988: 226–229; Greenwood & Hinings 1996: 1024; Robbins 1997: 518–519). However, in the process of changing or transforming an organisation, many other aspects are also important. In this respect cognisance should be taken of aspects like change action roles and different change management models.

22.3.1 Change action roles

Jick (1993a: 192–193) points out that when implementing change there are three broad action roles in the organisation: (i) *change strategists*, who are responsible for identifying the need for change, creating a vision of the desired outcome, deciding what changes are feasible, and choosing who should sponsor and defend the changes (ii) *change recipients*, the largest group, comprising the employees (management included) who must adopt and adapt to the changes (their adoption of and adaptation to the changes determine whether or not the transformation is successful); and (iii) the *change implementers*, who implement the actual day-to-day process of change. They help to shape, enable, orchestrate and facilitate successful progress. They are actually the people in the middle, responding to demands from the change strategists while attempting to win cooperation from the change recipients. This is a challenging role indeed.

Nadler (1983), Kotter (1995) and Jick (1993b) point out that in order for a change agent to bring about effective change, he or she must have the formal authority, position and legitimate power base to put transformation into practice throughout the organisation. Hart and McMillan (1996), Kotter (1995) and Tushman et al (1986) all point out that change can be brought about more effectively by an outside person or group of persons who act as change agents.

Indeed, Hart and McMillan (1996) suggest that ". . . in transition to another phase of the company's life cycle, (the) leadership profile must yield to one more appropriate for the challenges . . .". Kotter (1995) adds that the renewal process typically goes nowhere until enough real leaders are promoted or hired into senior job levels. Beatty and Ulrich (1993) point out that leadership does not only come from bringing in new leaders but also from empowering existing leaders by building competencies. They state further that "mature organisations renew by creating empowered employees who act as leaders at all levels . . ." (Beatty & Ulrich 1993: 66).

22.3.2 Change management models

An important theory which examined the interaction of pressures for change and pressures for stability is the force-field model of Kurt Lewin (Marrow 1969). Two concepts from this theory that illustrate the process of change are especially useful.

First, Lewin (Marrow 1969) concluded that whatever is occurring at any point in time between people in an organisation is the result of opposing forces. Employees on a production line determine their level of production through equilibrium points in a field of forces, with some forces (people) pushing for higher levels of production and other forces (people) pushing for lower levels. For example, a supervisor may believe that he or she can achieve improved production by telling subordinates that time off will not be allowed until productivity increases. But, despite the supervisor's directive, subordinates might respond by becoming distrustful, hostile and resistant, leading to additional declines in productivity.

Indeed, the natural response from individuals who are asked to change (to increase production levels) is to push against it. And the natural tendency of the person who is driving the change is to push back. According to Lewin (Marrow 1969), driving forces activate their own restraining forces. The best way to overcome resistance and to encourage change is to decrease the restraining forces instead of increasing the driving forces. Thus, in the above example the supervisor would be more likely to achieve high rates of production and to overcome resistance by identifying pointless bureaucratic bottlenecks and eliminating them.

Lewin (Marrow 1969) developed a technique called the Force Field Analysis to depict the field of forces and to develop action plans for moving the equilibrium point in one direction or the other. Programmes of planned change are directed towards removing or weakening the restraining forces while creating or strengthening the driving forces that exist in organisations.

Lewin's second contribution to an understanding of change and transformation was his belief that behaviour change frequently lasts for just a short period of time (Marrow 1969). Thus, after a brief period of trying to do things differently, individuals often return to their traditional patterns of behaviour. To overcome these constraints, Lewin (Marrow 1969) proposed a model for analysing what things must occur for permanent change to take place. The model holds good for individuals, groups or organisations. He conceptualised change as a three-stage process: unfreezing the old behaviour, changing to a new level of behaviour, and refreezing the behaviour at a new level. Stoner and Wankel (1986) describe this process as follows:

- *Unfreezing* involves making the need for change so clear and obvious that the individual or group can quickly understand and accept the reality.
- *Changing* requires a trained change agent to foster new values, attitudes and behaviour through the process of identification and internalisation. Organisation members identify with the change agent's values, attitudes and behaviour, internalising them once they perceive their effectiveness in performance.
- *Refreezing* means locking the new behaviour pattern into place by means of supporting or reinforcing mechanism, so that it becomes the new norm.

Further research into Lewin's process undertaken by Schein (1980) indicates that change and transformation efforts may fail for three reasons. *First*, change or transformation strategies will fail if too much energy is needed to move the system to the point where change is desired. *Secondly*, change and transformation strategies will fail if those seeking the change do not put enough energy into attempts to bring it about. *Finally*, if the unfreezing step is too difficult, the change effort will fail.

Lippitt, Watson and Westley (1958) subsequently refined Lewin's three phases into the "planned change model", a seven-phase model of the change process which unfolds as follows:

- **Phase 1:** The development of a need for change. (This phase corresponds to Lewin's unfreezing phase.)
- **Phase 2:** The establishment of a change relationship. This is a crucial phase in which a client system in need of help and a change agent from outside the system establish a working relationship with each other.
- **Phase 3:** Diagnosis of the client system's problem.
- **Phase 4:** The examination of alternative routes and goals; establishing goals and intended action.
- **Phase 5:** The transformation of intentions into actual change efforts. (Phases 3, 4 and 5 correspond to Lewin's change phase.)
- **Phase 6:** The generalisation and stabilisation of change. (This corresponds to Lewin's freezing phase.)
- **Phase 7:** Achieving a terminal relationship.

The following is a simple formula proposed by Gleicher (Beckhard & Harris 1977) to help managers assess the extent to which a transformation or change effort is likely to succeed:

$$C = (A \times B \times D) \, X$$

where:

    C   = change
    A   = level of dissatisfaction with the status quo
    B   = clearly identified desired state
    D   = practical first steps toward the desired state
    X   = cost of the change (in terms of energy, emotions, financial costs, etc).

Stoner and Wankel (1986) elaborate on this formula by indicating that change (or transformation) takes place when the cost of the change is not too high. The cost of change will be too high unless dissatisfaction with the status quo (A) is quite strong; unless the desired state (B) is quite evident; and unless practical steps can be taken towards the desired state (D). The multiplication signs indicate that if any of the factors A, B or D is zero, there will be no change. For example, if employees are satisfied with the status quo (A), they are not likely to change even if they can imagine a more desirable state (B) and they can see practical steps to move towards it.

Gleicher (Beckhard & Harris 1977) indicates that in addition to diagnosing how ready the system is for change, and predicting how likely it is that change will take place, the formula can also suggest ways of making the system more ready for change. For example, if dissatisfaction with the current state of affairs is high on everyone's part but there is no concrete notion of how things could be better, a vision of a future ideal state has to be created and communicated.

A more recent model that reflects today's turbulent, flexible and uncertain organisational conditions is proposed by Orlikowski and Hofman (1997). Their model assumes that change implementation is an ongoing process, rather than an event with an end point. It also assumes that although some changes may be planned, organisational change as an ongoing process can, by definition, not be anticipated ahead of time. This model recognises three different types of change: (i) anticipated or planned change, (ii) emergent changes that arise spontaneously and that are not originally intended or anticipated, and (iii) opportunity-based changes that are not anticipated, but are introduced purposefully and intentionally during the change process in response to an unexpected opportunity, event or breakdown.

22.4 APPROACHES TO ORGANISATIONAL TRANSFORMATION AND CHANGE MANAGEMENT

Up until now we have described the importance of change and transformation to managers in South Africa. In addition, the nature and process of organisation transformation and change management have been highlighted and employee resistance factors, as well as steps to overcome these factors, have been identified.

This section describes the various elements of the organisation to which the transformation and change process can be applied, and answers the question: what aspects of the organisation can be changed?

Leavitt (1964) states that an organisation can be changed by altering three things: its structure, its technology and its people. Robbins (1997: 523–526) expands upon Leavitt's three levels and proposes five levels on which change can take place in the organisation: the structural, cultural, technological, people and physical setting levels. Beatty and Ulrich (1993) refer to possible changes in the organisation's hardware (strategy, structure and systems) and in its software (employee behaviour and mindsets).

22.4.1 Structural approaches

Changing the organisation's structure may involve bringing about change in organisational design, decentralisation and flow of work (Leavitt 1964).

Classic organisational design seeks to improve organisational performance by carefully defining employees' job responsibilities and by identifying divisions of labour and lines of authority. Spans of control, job descriptions, areas of responsibility, reporting relationships, etc are all elements of this design.

Decentralisation creates smaller, self-contained organisational units that increase the motivation and performance of team members. Decentralisation enhances team flexibility and allows each unit to adapt its own structure and technology to the performance of tasks and to the external environment.

Modifying the *flow of work* and careful grouping of specialities may also lead directly to an improvement in productivity and to higher morale and satisfaction (Chapple & Sayles 1961).

22.4.2 Technological approaches

The influence of technology on work and motivation has been well documented (Stoner & Wankel 1986). Essentially, this approach involves designing work — using approaches like job enrichment and job enlargement (see chapter 7) — that is user-friendly to people and technology (for example, designing work that integrates automation and data-processing technologies). In addition, changes that result from introducing new office equipment, information-processing systems, work sequence and work processes and how these changes impact on performance are also addressed. *Technostructural* approaches to change and transformation are a firm's attempt to improve performance by changing both the firm's structure and technology. For example, small teams are formed around tasks that involve operating new equipment or other technologies.

22.4.3 People approaches

Both technological and structural approaches attempt to improve organisational performance by changing the work situation, which should cause employee behaviour to become more productive. On the other hand, people approaches to change and transformation attempt to change the behaviour of employees directly by focusing on their skills, attitudes, perceptions and expectations.

Efforts to change people's behaviour and attitudes can be directed at individuals, groups or at the organisation as a whole. Many (but not all) such efforts are known as organisational development (OD) techniques. Other (non-OD) approaches for changing people include management development, behaviour modification and management by objectives.

22.4.4 Physical setting approaches

Robbins (1997: 525) points out that physical settings per se do not have a substantial impact on organisational or individual performance, but that these issues can make certain employee behaviours easier or harder to perform. The layout of work space and of physical settings should therefore not be a random activity, but a thoughtful consideration of work demand, formal interaction requirements and social needs, so that appropriate decisions can be made regarding space configurations, interior design and equipment placement.

22.4.5 The organisational development approach

Organisational development has been defined by French and Bell (1984: 89) as:

"a top management-supported, long-range effort to improve an organisation's problem-solving and renewal processes, particularly through a more effective and collaborative diagnosis and management of organisation culture — with special emphasis on formal work team, temporary work team, and intergroup culture — with assistance of a consultant-facilitator and the use of the theory and technology of applied behavioural science, including action research"

Organisational development practitioners employ a variety of techniques to change and transform behaviour. These include survey feedback methods that systematically report the results as a basis for change (Carrell et al 1997). Team building is an initiative aimed at improving group effectiveness by improving task performance and relationships between team members. Finally, Grid OD, a six-phase programme based on the concept of the managerial grid (see French & Bell 1984), uses a variety of OD activities to bring about a high level of concern for people and production in the firm.

22.4.6 Organisational culture approaches

A number of authors have highlighted the importance of changing and transforming organisational culture (Sathe 1983; Peters & Waterman 1982). Sathe (1983) defines organisational culture as a set of important understandings (often unstated) that members of a community share in common. These shared understandings consist of the norms, values, attitudes and beliefs of members in the organisation. Furthermore, these understandings may be as wide as a society or industry, or as narrow as a organisation, department or work unit.

Managers wishing to change their organisational culture are advised to proceed cautiously. Changing culture is more difficult than changing behaviour and usually takes longer (Sathe 1983). Indeed, there is evidence to suggest that only the managing director has the power and influence to institute a change in overall organisational culture. This involves not only changing structure and technology but also changing shared symbols, rituals and beliefs (Uttal 1983).

Kotter (1995, 1996) examined the multiple approaches to change and transformation that were adopted by more than 100 organisations going through a transformation process and concluded that (i) the change process goes through a series of phases that, in total, require a considerable length of time, and (ii) critical effects in any of these phases can have a devastating impact, slowing momentum and negating hard-won gains. He identified eight errors common to organisational change and their consequences.

These errors include the following:

- underestimating the importance of having a clear vision;
- failing to communicate such a vision;
- allowing obstacles to block a new vision;
- failing to create a sufficiently powerful guiding coalition;
- allowing too much complacency;
- not anchoring changes in the corporate culture;
- not creating enough short-term gains;
- declaring victory too soon.

As a result of such errors new strategies may fail to be implemented successfully, downsizing may fail to get costs under control, quality programmes may fail to deliver what was hoped for, and re-engineering efforts may not yield anticipated results.

Kotter (1995, 1996) not only identified common errors but also proposed remedies. He pointed out that the methods used in successful transformation are based on the fundamental understanding that major change will not happen easily for the reasons we have already covered in this chapter. He proposed a multi-stage process for designing change strategies (Kotter 1996: 20–173). Each stage in the process is associated with solving one of the fundamental errors that undermine transformation efforts.

- The *first* step in Kotter's (1996) model is to establish a sense of urgency. Nadler and Tushman (1988) argue that energy — which results from this sense of urgency — is necessary to shake up the status quo so that change can be initiated and executed.

- The formation of a powerful guiding coalition is *step two* in Kotter's model. A group with enough power — in terms of aspects like titles, information, expertise and reputation — needs to be developed to lead the change effort.

- Creating a shared vision and strategy is the *third step* in Kotter's model. Before change implementation can begin, the change agent must first craft a vision, formulate corporate strategies, transpose these into human resources strategies, and then communicate the vision, strategy and core values to the employees on a continuous basis (Warren 1992).

  To build stability into the change process, the past can be incorporated into the vision for the future, as Hurst (1991) observes, the ". . . purpose is to reinterpret the past and visualise the future, for it is the weaving for the 'texts' or lessons from the past with the expected scenarios or 'contexts' of the future that constitutes the cognitive pattern that we call a 'vision' of the future".

- According to Kotter (1995: 63), the importance of *step four* — communicating the vision and strategies — cannot be overemphasised. These visionary strategies and their core values must be communicated down to everyone in the organisation, using every possible communication vehicle (see chapter 21) — memos, meetings, workshops, forums or industrial theatre. Warren (1992: 74) points out that it is crucial to accomplish employee understanding and acceptance of the visionary strategies when bringing about change; he also emphasises that frequent and repetitive communication of a simple message is necessary to do this.

  Strebel (1996) has identified a common root cause of change problems in organisations that ties in with this step: managers and workers view change differently. Top management sees change as an opportunity to strengthen the business by aligning operations with strategy, as well as an opportunity to take on new professional challenges and risks. However, for many workers, including middle managers, change is both disruptive and intrusive. It is essential, therefore, not only to communicate the vision and strategy to employees at all levels on a continuous basis but also to communicate what is in it for them and how the changes will impact on job descriptions and specifications, personal relationships with colleagues, and on communication with management.

  Hart and McMillan (1996) support Strebel's conclusions by emphasising that for the mission to be aligned with the organisation, it must be communicated to employees in such a way that they see in it a role for themselves that is aligned with their personal ambition. Lynn (1993) details an elaborate communication process that can help to create a (new) mindset in employees — causing them to accept, associate and adapt to change quickly and positively.

- *Step 5* involves "empowering broad-based action" — involving the process of getting rid of obstacles, encouraging a culture of risk-taking and creativity, and changing structures or systems that undermine the change.

- *Steps 6 and 7* involve the generation of short-term wins (create performance opportunities and reward them) and the consolidation of gains.

- The *last step* entails anchoring the new approaches in the culture of the organisation. In this regard it is very important to articulate the connections between new behaviours and organisational success.

In summary, the value of change and transformation often lies in the process — the journey — and not so much in the actual changes or the end result, because the end result is ever-changing in response to internal and external factors facing the organisation. Indeed, organisations need to instil a culture of continuous change for improvement — which may, or may not, involve minor or even radical changes in operations in order to survive and meet competitive challenges. When change is viewed as an ongoing learning process and as a form of continuous organisation innovation and renewal, organisations will have a process that is woven into the fabric of organisational life (Gebert 1996; Robbins 1997).

22.5 SOME CONTEMPORARY TRENDS IN MANAGING CHANGE AND TRANSFORMATION

Because change and transformation have become such universally important topics, many methods of dealing with them have been proposed. Some are very similar and buzzwords are frequently used to offer new ideas — which very often are not as new as their tags would indicate. In this regard concepts often used include rightsizing, downsizing, restructuring, reorganisation, business process re-engineering, redesign, etc. In this section a brief overview is provided of two of these relatively recently proposed methods of dealing with organisational transformation and change.

22.5.1 Re-engineering

The process of re-engineering is different from conventional organisational change approaches. While conventional organisational change approaches involve some stability through links with the past and step-by-step incremental changes, re-engineering means radically redesigning the organisation's core processes by starting with a blank sheet of paper and ignoring the way things have been done in the past. The question underlying re-engineering is "if we could start from scratch, how would we do this?" Carrell et al (1997: 629) point out that the proponents of re-engineering regard it as neither downsizing nor a programme for bottom-up continuous improvement (although this may be included in the process). Instead, they start from the future and work backward, as if unconstrained by existing methods, people or departments. Indeed, as has already been noted in this chapter, the process of re-engineering is consistent with the notion of organisations undergoing transformation rather than change.

Thus, even though Robbins (1997) concludes that re-engineering is one of the most favoured management tools for implementing radical change, it comes as no surprise to learn that Carrell et al (1997) have found that 50–70 % of re-engineering efforts fail because of factors such as individual and organisational resistance to change.

22.5.2 The learning organisation

The concept *learning organisation* refers to an organisation that is continually improving and developing (Senge 1990). Robbins (1997) concludes that this management concept has become to the mid-1990s what Total Quality Management (TQM) was to the 1980s. Greenberg & Baron (1997: 548) and Robbins (1997: 535) define a learning organisation as follows:

A *learning organisation* is an organisation that has developed the continuous capacity to adapt and change. It is successful at acquiring, cultivating and applying knowledge that can help it to adapt to change.

The importance of change and transformation management in a learning organisation is obvious: in the learning organisation, change is seen as an ongoing process, not as an event. Change is woven into the fabric of organisational life as a way of functioning and continuously developing.

22.6 THE IMPORTANCE OF CHANGE AND TRANSFORMATION IN SOUTH AFRICA: SOME RECENT RESEARCH

Recently documented findings concerning the attitudes of South African managers to a number of human resource management related issues have revealed a number of priority rankings (Hofmeyr, Rall & Templer 1995). Table 22.1 lists these rankings and illustrates two important trends. *First*, managers regard their priority activity as managing organisational change. *Secondly*, managers indicate that they are having to spend more time dealing with traditional industrial relations issues and training activities instead of handling issues relating to change management. Furthermore, table 22.2 reveals that managers believe unanimously that the pace of change in the training of employees and managers, in affirmative action and in the advancement of women is too slow.

This evidence, along with anecdotal and informal feedback from managers and executives attending executive and management courses at the University of South Africa's Graduate School of Business Leadership, indicates that the management issues of change and transformation are both current and important. South African managers will have to understand and accept these realities if they are to help their organisations to compete successfully in the international arena. External factors — such as shifts in government regulations, trade union dynamics, the government's social and economic initiatives such as GEAR, social responsibility pressures, an irregular economy, international competition, deregulation, the increasing importance of informal business, mergers and acquisitions, crime, etc — all combine to create unusual pressures that require radical shifts in management thinking and practice in South African organisations.

Table 22.1

Importance of human resource management activities in South Africa*

Activities	Importance	
1 = most important 18 = least important	*now*	*should be*
Industrial relations	1	7
Training	2	4
Organisation change	3	1
Management development	4	5
Introducing participative management	5	3
Affirmative action/black advancement	6	2
Human resource planning	7	6
Employment equity and the removal of discrimination	8	8
Remuneration	9	14
Recruitment and employment	10	12
Performance appraisal and review	11	11
Job evaluation and design	12	15
Cross-cultural communication	13	10
Human resource records and computer systems	14	17
Cross-cultural management	15	9
Health and safety	16	16
Community upliftment and involvement	17	13

*Source: Hofmeyr, Rall & Templer. 1995. The future challenges facing South African human resource managers. *South African Journal of Business Management*, 26 (3), 108–114.

Table 22.2

Pace of change in South African companies*

	Too fast	Right pace	Too slow	No opinion
Training of employees	0,5	41,8	57,4	0,5
Training of managers	1,0	32,1	65,3	1,5
Affirmative action/black advancement	1,0	16,9	79,0	3,1
Advancement of women	0,5	36,4	55,4	7,7

*Source: Hofmeyr, Rall & Templer. 1995. The future challenges facing South African human resource managers. *South African Journal of Business Management*, 26 (3), 108–114.

Factors such as affirmative action, especially in management and executive positions, and a major shift in the cultural profile of workforce demographics, are also creating profound adjustments in the organisational culture, management style and practice of South African organisations.

One of the major challenges facing South African organisations is therefore how to create structures, policies, systems and practices that are consistent with the cultural profiles of their workers. After years of isolation in a siege economy, new human resource management strategies and practices mean that South African managers will have to grasp the fundamentals of change and transformation management issues.

22.7 CONCLUSION

This chapter introduced you to the nature and importance of successfully managing change and transformation in South African organisations — both now and into the next millennium. While transformation concerns an organisation starting from scratch, change concerns tweaking (or improving) existing operations. Regardless of whether an organisation is having to deal with change or with transformation, there are major implications for all levels of employees and for the way in which the changes have to be managed in the context of the human dimension of competitiveness.

Even though there is ongoing debate regarding the current readiness of South African managers to confront radical changes that will affect the organisation's strategies and operations, a growing body of management literature offers insights into the nature and process of change and transformation management. The need to retain some degree of organisational stability while undergoing change and transformation was emphasised and theories that describe the process of change and transformation were highlighted. Resistance to change was also covered and ways in which this resistance can be dealt with, were explained. Finally, several approaches that organisations can use to institute change and transformation processes were described. The subject of organisational culture and the difficulties involved in changing or transforming an organisation's culture were also briefly covered. Lastly, specific challenges facing change management and transformation issues in South Africa were also described.

SELF-EVALUATION QUESTIONS

1. Why is it important for South African managers to understand the nature of and the problems involved in the management of change and transformation? Explain in detail.
2. Give a brief overview of the forces underlying change and transformation in organisations today.

3. Write an essay in which you explain the nature of and the challenges posed by resistance to change.
4. Explain the different ways in which one can deal with resistance to change (RTC).
5. Discuss in broad terms the process of organisational transformation and change.
6. Describe Lippitt, Watson and Wesley's (1958) seven-phase model of the change process.
7. List and discuss seven different approaches to organisational transformation and change.

BIBLIOGRAPHY

Anstey, M. 1997. New ball game. *Productivity SA*, Jan/Feb, 7–10

Beatty, RW & Ulrich, DO. 1993. Re-energising the mature organisation. In *Managing Change, cases and concepts*, edited by Todd O Jick. Boston Richard D Irwin, Inc

Beckhard, R & Harris, R. 1977. *Organisational Transitions: Managing Complex Change*. Reading. Mass: Addison-Wesley

Beer, S. 1975 *Brain of the Firm*. New York: Herder & Herder

Beer, M, Eisenfat, R, Spector, B. 1990. "Why Change Programs Don't Produce Change". *Harvard Business Review*. November-December, 158–167

Bennis, W & Mische, M. 1995. *The 21st Century Organisation: Reinventing through Re-engineering*. San Diego: Pfeiffer & Company

Carrell, MR, Jennings, DF & Hearin, C. 1997. *Fundamentals of Organisational Behaviour*. New Jersey: Prentice-Hall, Inc

Chapple, E & Sayles, LR. 1961. *The Measure of Management*. New York: MacMillan

Coch, L. & French, JR. 1948. Overcoming resistance to change. *Human Relations*, August, 512–532

Cooper, HJ, Leavitt, (eds) 1964. *New Perspectives in Organisation Research*. New York: Wiley

French, W & Bell, CH. 1984. *Organisation Development: Behavioral Science Interventions for Organisation Improvement*, 3 ed. Englewood Cliffs, NJ: Prentice-Hall

Gebert, D. 1996. Organisation development. In *International Encyclopaedia of Businesss and Management* vol 4, edited by Malcolm Warner. New York and London: Routledge

Goss, G, Pascale, R & Athos, A. 1993. The reinvention roller coaster: Risking the present for a powerful future. *Harvard Business Review*, November-December, 7–108

Greenberg, J & Baron, RA. 1997. *Behaviour in Organisations*, 6 ed. New Jersey: Prentice-Hall, Inc

Greenwood, R & Hinings, CR. 1996. Radical organisational change: Bringing together the old and the new institutionalism. *Academy of Management Review*, 21(4), 1022–1054

Goodstein, L. 1991. Creating successful organisation change. *Organisational Dynamics*, Spring, 5–17

Griffen, R. 1987. *Management*. Boston: Houghton Mifflin Company

Hackman, JR & Lawler, EE. 1971. Employee reactions to job characteristics. *Journal of Applied Psychology*, 55, 259–286.

Hart, E & McMillan, J. 1996. Leadership and organisational transformation. *HRM*, February, 4–12

Hilliard, V. 1996. Transforming the public service — no room for despondency. *HRM*, April, 9–14

Hofmeyr, K, Rall, J & Templer, A. 1995. The future challenges facing South African human resource managers. *South African Journal of Business Management*, 26(3), 108–114

Human, P & Horwitz, F. 1992. *On the Edge: How South African Companies Cope with Change*. Kenwyn: Juta & Co

Hurst, DK. 1991. Cautionary tales from the Kalahari: How hunters become herders (and may have trouble changing back again). *Academy of Management Executive*, 5(3), 74–86

Jick, TD (ed). 1993a. *Managing Change, Cases and Concepts*. Boston: Richard D Irwin, Inc

Jick, TD. 1993b. Implementing change. *Managing Change, Cases and Concepts*, edited by Todd D Jick Boston: Richard D. Irwin, Inc

Kotter, JP. 1995. Leading change: why transformation efforts fail. *Harvard Business Review*, March-April, 59–67.

Kotter, JP. 1996. *Leading Change*. Boston: Harvard Business School Press

Kotter & Schlesinger, 1969. Choosing strategies for change. *Harvard Business Review*. January-February

Leavitt, HJ. Applied organisation change in industry: Structural, technical and human approaches.

Lippitt, R, Watson, J & Westley, B. 1958. *The Dynamics of Planned Change*. New York: Harcourt Brace Jovanovich

Lynn, AI. 1993. Managing the challenges of trigger events: The mindsets governing adaption to change. In Jick, TD (ed). 1993a. *Managing Change, Cases and Concepts*, edited by Todd D Jick. Boston: Richard D Irwin, Inc.

Manning, T. 1996. Transformation or profit checkmate for SA businesses? Part 1. *People Dynamics*, Nov/Dec, 16–20

Manning, T. 1997. Profit through transformation. Part 2. *People Dynamics*, January, 16–19

Marrow, AJ. 1969. *The Practical Theorist: The Life and Work of Kurt Lewin*. New York: Basic Books

McRae, H. 1996. Seismic forces of global change. *Strategy and Leadership*, Nov/Dec, 6–11

Nadler, D. 1983. *Concepts for the Management of Organisation Change. Section V: Organisation Adaptation and Change.* New York: Delta Consulting Group.

Nadler, D & Tushman, M. 1988. Organisational frame bending: Principles for managing reorientation. *Academy of Management Executive*, August, 194–204

Orlikowski, WJ & Hofman, JD. 1997. An improvisational model for change management: The case of groupware technologies. *Sloan Management Review*, Winter, 11–21.

Peters, T & Watermann, B. 1982. *In Search of Excellence.* New York: Harper & Row

Richardson, B. 1994. The political-aware leader. *Leadership and Organisation Development Journal*, 16(2), 27–35

Robbins, PR. 1997. *Managing Today!* New Jersey: Prentice-Hall

Sathe, V.J. 1983. Implications of corporate culture: A manager's guide to action. *Organisational Dynamics*, 12(2), Autumn, 5–23

Senge, PM. 1990. *The Fifth Discipline.* New York: Doubleday

Schein, EH. 1980. *Organisational Psychology*, 3 ed. Englewood Cliffs, NJ: Prentice-Hall

Stoner, J & Wankel, C. 1986. *Management*, 3 ed. New Jersey: Prentice-Hall

Strebel, P. 1996. Why do employees resist change? *Harvard Business Review*, May-June, 86–92

Tushman, M, Newman, W & Romanelli, E. 1986. Convergence and upheaval: Managing the unsteady pace of organisation evolution. Section V: Organisation adaptation and change. Reprinted from the *California Management Review*, 29(1), 477–489

Uttal, B. 1983. The corporate culture vultures. *Fortune*, 17 October, 66–72

Van Schalkwijk, O. 1997. Global competition, demanding clients, limited resources challenges for 1997. *HRM Yearbook*, 4–6

Vermaak, T. 1996. Revitalising South African organisations. *Boardroom*, 1, 14–16

Vinton, DE. 1992. A new look at time, speed and the manager. *Academy of Management Executive*, 6(4), 7–16

Warren W. 1992. Changing corporate culture or corporate behaviour? How to change your company. *Academy of Management Executive*, 6(4), 72–77

chapter (23) Aspects Related to Human Resource Management Information

STUDY OBJECTIVES

After studying this chapter, you should be able to:

- describe the role of research in human resource management;
- critically discuss the role and nature of evaluation of human resource management;
- distinguish between and describe different models for the measurement of HRM;
- write an essay on the role and nature of record keeping and human resource information systems;
- discuss the nature and importance of human resources reporting.

23.1 INTRODUCTION

Throughout this book we have focused on the nature and importance of managing the human resource systems of organisations successfully. It has been pointed out on various occasions that the world around and within our organisations has been undergoing (and still is undergoing) substantial change. As we move into the *information age*, the need for organisations to develop learning cultures becomes more and more pressing. Generating knowledge and learning depends to a large extent on *information*! All decision making in organisations — and thus also all decisions relating to the human resource systems of organisations — must be based on information.

In this chapter we focus on some of the management implications of this information-driven society — particularly as they relate to human resource management. We start off with a brief explanation of the nature and value of *research* to facilitate informed decision making in the human management arena, as opposed to intuition-based decision making. This is followed by a discussion of information related to the *evaluation* of human resource management. The other two sections deal with human resource related *information systems* and the *reporting* of human resource information.

23.2 THE ROLE OF RESEARCH IN HUMAN RESOURCE MANAGEMENT

Managers obviously prefer making informed decisions rather than relying on guesswork. The relevant information and 'knowledge' is therefore necessary in order to manage human resources effectively. Although there are different ways of acquiring knowledge, scientific research is a method that can yield reliable and valid data on which to base human resource management decisions. In research-based decision making an attempt is made to manage the human resource system of an organisation on the basis of objective information. Human resource research is thus a means of acquiring knowledge about aspects of the human dimension of the organisation in the most objective and scientific way.

23.2.1 Research areas

Whereas academically orientated HR research focuses on aspects such as testing, refining or developing theories, many managers in practice also prefer a stronger research focus. For instance, research needs to be conducted on aspects such as:

- the changing environment for which HR strategies have to be formulated;
- the climate and culture in the organisation;
- the training needs of employees;
- staff attitudes and levels of satisfaction;
- the acceptability of and problems relating to certain managerial practices, processes or systems;
- the remuneration system of the organisation (for example establishing pay grades and levels of pay that are market related);
- required staffing levels and, in particular, labour force demographics;
- data regarding labour litigation cases;
- conducting organisational diagnostic interventions to determine scope for improvement;
- the abilities, potential and personality traits of job applicants.

23.2.2 Research approaches

The way in which human resource related research is carried out can vary from purely *quantitative* to purely *qualitative* methodologies. We do not believe that any one approach or methodology is the correct or best one. Rather, a combination of various research methods ought to be used covering both quantitative and qualitative techniques, the mix of which will ultimately depend upon what phenomena one is trying to obtain information about.

Different techniques are employed to gather human resource-related information in a *qualitative* way, such as direct observation, interviewing, group processes, document reviews and other archival measures. Again, one must be careful not to be led to believe that there is one best technique. More often than not more than one technique ought to be used, often in conjunction with other methods which are more quantitative in nature.

One of the more popular techniques used to conduct HR-related research is survey research, which is a quantitative method. Survey research has quite a wide spectrum of applications and is popular with most experienced and professional HR practitioners. Through surveys one can gauge the perceptions, opinions, attitudes, beliefs and intentions of the organisation's employees. In this way one can gather reliable information relatively quickly, covering large numbers of employees. For instance, the survey method can be used to determine training needs and to evaluate the reactions of trainees on the training they have undergone. One popular and frequently used type of survey is the so-called EAS (employee attitude survey), also referred to by some as an audit.

23.2.3 Employee attitude surveys (EAS)

These surveys have also been referred to in chapter 21.

An employee attitude survey (EAS) **can be defined as a systematic, objective investigation into the perceptions, feelings, behaviour, attitudes, opinions, etc of the employees of an organisation.**

The rationale underlying such surveys is that, as managers, we have to have knowledge about how satisfied our employees are, about their needs, desires, attitudes, opinions and fears. In larger organisations in particular it is not possible to know how your staff feel simply by applying MBWA (management by walking about). In this day and age when organisations so often assert that their employees are their most valued assets, it becomes increasingly important to pay serious attention to their views, opinions, feelings, ideas, attitudes, etc.

It is unfortunate that some managers tend to shy away from the EAS, especially when everyday indicators like high absenteeism and staff turnover, generally low morale and motivation levels, and labour productivity problems point to an unhealthy state in organisations. They are generally reluctant to commission this kind of HR research, probably because they fear stirring up more trouble, even though they often instinctively 'know' that they are guilty of neglecting their most valuable assets — the people who work for them. Furthermore, some are reluctant to execute an EAS simply because they really have no idea what such research entails — often thinking that it is some mysterious way of uncovering employees' most secretive thoughts and ideas. Some also resist it because they maintain that one cannot exactly or precisely measure or use statistics to investigate the human side of the organisation. While there may be some truth in this, we reiterate our contention that quantitative analyses are also important. In EAS use is usually made of both hard and soft data (ie, quantitative as well as qualitative).

Although statistical analysis is an important component of employment attitude surveys, information gathered through qualitative processes such as focus groups, unstructured or semistructured interviews, or brain storming, normally makes up a critical part of EAS. In larger organisations with greater numbers of employees it may well be important to have sufficient knowledge of statistics (for example in respect of sampling and measurement scales) in order to execute EAS, but this does not mean that soft data resulting from more unstructured, qualitative research methods must be ignored. On the contrary, in such EAS there is often quite a heavy reliance (in addition to the objective, reliable hard data) on soft data emanating, for example, from interviews and group processes such as the NGT (nominal group technique).

The hard data is usually collected by means of written questionnaires. It is of crucial importance to design the questionnaire in a professional way, simply because the data thus collected normally constitutes the backbone of the EAS. Before the questionnaire design is finalised, however, a number of other aspects have to be attended to.

First of all it is necessary to be clear what the objectives of and underlying reasons for the decision to conduct an EAS actually are. This will determine the scope of the survey research and thus the specific areas or topics to be investigated. As a rule this requires an initial diagnostic phase which is primarily qualitative. Through group processes and interviews the potential problem areas are detected and the survey population demarcated. The essential purpose is thus to determine the scope and nature of the EAS; the information gathered is used to construct or adapt the questionnaire. During this phase it is very important to make all the stakeholders part of the process by involving all of them. This may include top management, other levels of management, the workers themselves, as well as their representatives. In some instances it may even involve discussions with customers, suppliers or consultants and subcontractors who may have relevant knowledge. Ownership and commitment from all stakeholders are thus essential ingredients and, right from the very first moment, the involvement of all the stakeholders' representatives is of crucial importance.

Once the questionnaire has been finalised (this may be after a pilot study), it is distributed to all relevant employees. If possible the questionnaire should be distributed to all employees. This may not always be feasible and sampling may sometimes be necessary. Be that as it may, it is important to follow up and to ensure a high rate of return of completed questionnaires. Often it is wise to let relevant employee groups complete the questionnaire at specific time slots, so that an expert can assist with the completion of the questionnaires. This very often requires the assistance of an interpreter, especially if the workers are illiterate.

Once the questionnaires have been completed, the data is computerised, processed and interpreted. The findings (results and conclusions) are then normally presented in report format. This may include recommendations; alternatively, all the stakeholders could discuss, debate and brainstorm the findings in order to arrive at decisions regarding subsequent action. The emphasis of this kind of human resource research has to be on *action*. The intelligence generated by the research should lead to the necessary action to improve the human dimension of the organisation.

Exhibit A

Employee attitude surveys (EASs) in South Africa over the years*

A Chicago-based organisation, International Survey Research (ISR), has been surveying employee attitudes in 92 countries since 1974. South Africa is one of these countries, and the ISR has been carrying out its research on local organisations since the early 1980s. This has made it possible for South African organisations to compare the attitudes of their employees among one another and with their competitors elsewhere in the world. Here are some of the overall conclusions drawn over the years from ISR's EASs:

- In general, employee attitudes in South Africa became more negative during the years 1994–1996.
- South African employees' perceptions of management rate lower than those of employees in global high-performing organisations, especially on providing leadership.
- Employees feel there is a lack of trust/confidence in their judgement.
- Compared to organisations in other countries, South African organisations score low on employee satisfaction with opportunities to input ideas.
- The management style in South Africa is perceived by employees to be characterised by words and phrases such as:
  - centralised decision making,
  - directive,
  - bureaucratic, and
  - task-orientated.
- Compared to employees in global high-performing organisations, South African employees show less commitment to their employers.

---

*Source: Adapted from Hofmeyr 1997a; 1997b.

23.3 THE EVALUATION OF HUMAN RESOURCE MANAGEMENT

Nowadays there is little debate about the fact that the human resource management system of an organisation should be subject to evaluation. The contribution of this subsystem to the success of the organisation as a whole forms part of such an evaluation. Evaluation of human resource functions dates back to the 1920s; by the late 1970s it had become "common practice" (Phillips & Seers 1989: 54–58).

23.3.1 The need for the evaluation of human resource management

The following are some reasons why the evaluation of human resource management is necessary.

- **The quality of human resource management is improved**: The evaluation of human resource management may lead to increased awareness of this area of management. Evaluation can facilitate a new way of thinking about human resource management and ensure better identification of areas for possible improvement.

- **Goal achievement is facilitated**: An evaluation system for human resource management clarifies expectations and gives direction. As soon as goals with regard to cost, time, quality and quantity have been set, the parties know what is expected of them. Performance standards and acceptable deviations from standards are then known. When goals are set, for example, to decrease employment costs and grievances and to increase on-job training time, employees know what is expected of them. As the old saying goes: What gets measured, gets done.

- **Decision making and information provisioning are facilitated**: Evaluation data contribute towards improved decision making. According to Ameiss and Williams (1981: 113–118), evaluation data facilitate the planning of human resource expenses in both the short and the long term. Individual projects can be assessed on a comparative year-to-year basis and information on human resources can be provided to external stakeholders.

- **Control over the contributions of human resource activities can be maintained**: Evaluating the contribution of human resource management towards organisational goals for the purposes of cost control or profit improvement programmes can help to control input/output ratios. This helps to ensure that the human resource management system of an organisation adds value to the organisation as a whole. After all, the effectiveness of cost control programmes can only be realistically assessed if changes in the value of the contribution made by human resource management are also taken into account.

23.3.2 Some arguments against the evaluation of human resource management

Despite the well-recognised need to evaluate human resource management, it appears that many of the models which have been developed to date are quite theoretical in nature and have not been properly tested.

The following problems have been identified with regard to the evaluation of human resource management.

- **Perceptual problems**: To some extent the perception exists that the evaluation of human resource management will always be subjective. According to McCarthy (1980: 101–105), this subjectivity myth developed from the idea of the intangibility of human resource management and is based on the view that management as such is abstract and difficult to measure. Fitz-enz (1984) has identified the following (not insurmountable) problems which contribute to the subjectivity myth.
  - ○ Specialist human resource staff do not know how to measure their activities.
  - ○ There appears to be a conflict in values; that is, some people regard it as simply impossible to evaluate human resource management objectively.

○ Human resource managers often fear that evaluation might expose their managerial shortcomings and inefficiencies.

○ Top management seems to accept the absence of a human resource management evaluation system; this seems to reflect a general lack of interest in human resource management.

● **Accounting problems**: The evaluation of human resource management requires an interdisciplinary approach. Accountancy concepts play an important role in this approach. Unfortunately, the accounting practice has traditionally neglected the value of human resources. The employee is traditionally regarded largely as an expense or cost factor. The fact that employee-related expenses (like training) often hold substantial long-term advantages for the organisation is traditionally largely ignored. The most important accounting problem related to the measurement of HRM involves categorising the employee as an asset. According to Flamholtz (1985), it is not *humans* that should be regarded as assets, but the *service* expected from them by the organisation; in other words their work performance.

● **The image of HRM**: Traditionally the HR function does not enjoy the same status as other functions in the organisation such as operations or marketing. As a result of the neutral perception of HR by top management, the need for an evaluation system is often underplayed.

● **Lack of time and funds**: The additional work created by the collection of data, compiling the data into the report format, etc, takes time and increases costs.

23.3.3 Models for the evaluation of HRM

A variety of approaches for the evaluation of HRM have been published to date. In spite of this, no universally, acceptable approach has been developed. Possible reasons for this relate to the problems discussed in the previous section.

The emphasis here will be on two major approaches to the evaluation of HRM, and on a brief assessment of their respective merits. The first is human resource accounting (HRA) and the second human resource cost–benefit analysis. Other approaches will be referred to only briefly.

Two important factors must be taken into account with regard to these models. The first is that precise measurements should not be expected because of the various uncontrollable variables which form part of the measures. Secondly, it must be realised that every organisation is unique as regards its size, values, culture, climate, general nature, staff composition, etc; each evaluation system will thus also be unique.

23.3.3.1 *Human resource accounting (HRA)*

The American Accounting Association (1973) defines HRA as the process of identifying and measuring HR data and the communication of this information to interested parties.

The purpose of HRA is to improve the quality of financial decisions which are made both internally and externally regarding the organisation. Human resource accounting thus aims at providing a more quantitative framework for HRM decision making.

Human resource accounting models are divided into two major groups, namely HR *cost models* and HR *value models*.

A *cost* in this sense can be viewed as a sacrifice which is made in order to obtain an anticipated benefit. A cost is normally incurred to obtain tangible benefits. An *expense* is that part of cost consumed during the current accounting period, while *asset* refers to that part of cost expected to bring about benefits during future accounting periods. Human resource costs thus comprise costs incurred to acquire, develop or replace employees and include expense and asset components.

Two major cost models have been developed, namely the *historical cost model* and the *replacement cost model*. These models are outlined in figures 23.1 and 23.2.

With regard to HR value models, two concepts require definition. Flamholtz (1985: 174) defines value as the current value of future services. Human resource value is thus the current value of expected future services to be rendered by employees.

The HR value models can be categorised into the three groups as shown in exhibit B.

Exhibit B

HR value models*

Non-monetary behavioural models	Monetary approach
• social-psychology indicators approach	• unpurchased goodwill model
	• adjusted present value model
	• discounted remuneration model
	• discounted wage flows model
	• current monetary value model
	• group model based on Markov-matrix

Combination of non-monetary behavioural aspects and monetary economic value
• human organisation effectiveness model
• dollarised attitudes model
• behavioural economic outcome model
• behavioural cost model
• stochastic rewards valuation model
• certainty-equivalent net benefits model

*Source: Sackmann, Flamholtz & Bullen 1989

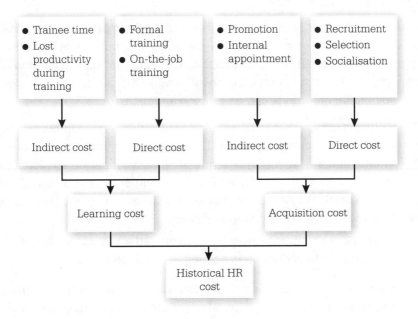

Figure 23.1
Historical cost model
Source: Flamholtz (1985: 63

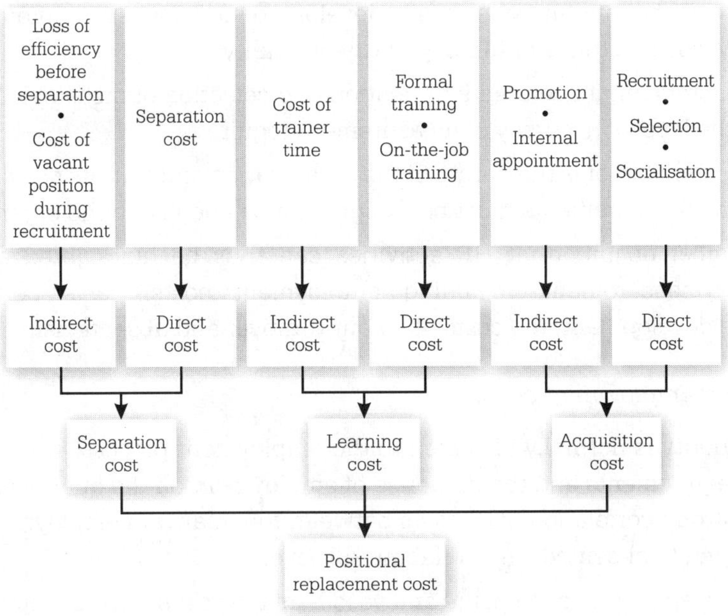

Figure 23.2
Replacement cost model
Source: Flamholtz (1985: 63)

Evaluation of the HRA approach

Human resource accounting formed the basis for the measurement of HRM and proponents of this approach played a major role in putting evaluation on the agenda of HR researchers. It appears, however, that after more than two decades of research, HRA is not operational, theoretically or practically, on a significant level. Two general objections can be levelled against HRA:

- The inclusion of human assets, which are regarded as intangible assets, is not foreseen in the accounting system. To overcome this problem, an extension of the parameters of accounting is required. An investigation by Vorster (1977), some two decades ago into fifty well-known companies found that HRA had no significance in South African organisations. No evidence can be found to suggest that the situation has changed since.

- It seems to be very difficult to establish an operationally acceptable HRA model that conforms to the requirements of validity and reliability.

Human resource accounting thus seems to have failed as an operational evaluation approach. Possibly a more practical approach is human resource cost–benefit analysis.

23.3.3.2 *Human resource cost–benefit analysis*

Before evaluation can take place, objective measures must be established. Human resource cost–benefit analysis entails developing such measures in order to evaluate HRM costs in terms of time, quantity or quality.

Two factors influence the identification and selection of measures. The first of these is the level of accuracy of measurement required.

The second factor is the nature of the organisation and thus its specific requirements. The measurements must be of significance and use to the organisation.

A number of important HR activities can thus be highlighted as possibly requiring measurement, including employment costs, costs pertaining to employee development, the costs of labour turnover and absenteeism.

Measuring employment costs

A high priority is normally allocated to the employment process, often as a result of legal requirements and the influence of employment on the quality of the workforce. A strong correlation also exists between the quality of employment and the costs related to absenteeism and labour turnover.

The first employment measure analysed here is a cost measure, namely cost per hire. The cost elements associated herewith are set out in table 23.1.

No generally accepted method exists for the computation of cost per hire — any of the components included in table 23.1 may be excluded or others added according to the needs of the organisation.

Table 23.1
Cost elements of hiring an employee

Type	Expense
Source cost	Advertising and agency fees paid to generate applicants; hire and/or referral bonuses.
Staff time	Salary, benefits, and standard overhead costs of staff meeting with the manager to discuss sourcing; working with the media and/or agency to commence the search; screening applications, calling applicants in for interviews, interviewing and reference checking; reviewing candidates with the manager and scheduling interviews; making or confirming the offer.
Management time	Salary, benefits, and standard overhead costs of the requesting department relating to plan the sourcing, discuss and interview candidates, and make a hiring decision and offer.
Processing cost	Manual or automatic data system cost of opening a new file; cost of medical exams; cost of employment and record verification (mail or telephone), security checks, etc.
Travel and relocation	Travel and lodging costs for staff and candidates; relocation costs.
Miscellaneous	Materials and other special or unplanned expenses. The cost of new employee orientation may be included or considered as part of the training expenses.

Determining cost per hire (C/H) is not as simple as it may appear. Various decisions must be made. As far as source cost is concerned, for example, the cost of one advertisement for one position can easily be allocated to that position. However, when a combination of advertisements is run for more than one position, allocating cost per hire gets more complex. An advertisement, for example, may be placed for the positions of supervisor of accounting, senior accountants and bookkeepers. A supervisor, senior accountant and three bookkeepers may be appointed. As it is more complicated to appoint a supervisor than a bookkeeper, the advertisement cost could not simply be divided by five to compute advertisement cost per hire. One way to overcome this problem is to weigh the costs by the salary level of each hire. Then it must be determined whether to use actual salary, entry-level salary, or the midpoint of the salary range.

According to Fitz-enz (1984: 56), the way the computation is made is not the critical factor. What is important when cost per hire is being calculated over a long period, is consistency in the methodology used. Consistency ensures comparable results over time. The basic formula for computing source cost per hire (SCH) is illustrated in exhibit C.

Exhibit C

Source cost per hire*

$$\frac{SC}{H} = \frac{AC + AF + RB + NC}{H}$$

where:

AC = advertising costs, total monthly expenditure (eg R28 000)

AF = agency fees, total month (eg R19 000)

RB = referral bonuses, total paid (eg R2 300)

NC = no-cost hires, walk-in, non-profit agencies, etc (ie R0)

H = Total hires (eg 119)

Example:

$$\frac{SC}{H} = \frac{R28\ 000 + R19\ 000 + R2\ 300 + R0}{119}$$

$$= \frac{R49\ 300}{119}$$

$$= R415$$

*Fitz-enz 1984: 61

Exhibit D

Determining the quality of hires*

Response time

RT = RD − RR

where:

RT = response time

RD = date of first qualified candidate referred for interview (eg 22 January)

RR = date the requisition is received (eg 4 January)

Example:

RT = 22 − 4

= 18 days

Time to fill

TF = RR − SD

where:

TF = time to fill the job

RR = date the requisition is received (eg 4 January)

SD = date the new hire starts work (eg 10 March)

Example:

TF = 4 January − 10 March

= 65

Referral factor

$$RF = \frac{R}{O}$$

where:

RF = referral factor, relationship of candidates to openings

R = number of candidates referred for interview (eg 76)

O = number of openings (eg 22)

Example:

$$RF = \frac{76}{22}$$

= 3,5

*Fitz-enz (1984: 70)

Determining the cost of hires for different positions according to the various hiring methods is not sufficient information. What is also important is determining the *quality* of hires. According to Fitz-enz, a trade-off must be established between the quality of the hire and the time to fill the position. Three measures are important: response time, time to fill and referral factor (see exhibit D).

In addition to the measurement of the cost and quality of employment, measuring *efficiency* is also important. A number of efficiency measures are outlined in exhibit E.

Exhibit E

Determining hiring efficiency*	
Internal hire rate	*Example:*
$IH = \dfrac{IA}{H}$	$IH = \dfrac{49}{76}$
	$= 64,5\ \%$
where:	
IH = percentage of jobs filled internally	
IA = jobs filled by internal applicants (eg 49)	
H = total hires (eg 76)	
Interview time	*Example:*
$ALI = \dfrac{h}{HI}$	$ALI = \dfrac{6}{5}$
	$= 1,2\ \text{hours}$
where:	
ALI = average length of interviews	
h = total hours spent interviewing (eg 6)	
HI = total number interviewed (eg 5)	
Hit rate	*Example:*
$HO = \dfrac{OA}{OE}$	$HO = \dfrac{42}{50}$
	$= 84\ \%$
where:	
HO = percentage of offers which result in a hire	
OA = offers accepted (eg 42)	
OE = offers extended (eg 50)	

*Fitz-enz 1984: 75–83

Thus far measures for cost, quality and efficiency of employment have been discussed. It is also important to measure the *effectiveness* of employment. According to Fitz-enz (1984: 86), a measure of effectiveness is the quality of hire (QH).

QUALITY OF HIRE

$$QH = \frac{PR + HP + HS}{N}$$

where:

QH = quality of the people hired

PR = average job performance ratings of new hires (eg 4 on a 5-point scale)

HP = percentage of new hires promoted within one year (eg 45 %)

HS = percentage of new hires retained after 1 year (eg 90 %)

N = number of indicators used (eg 3)

Example

$$QH = \frac{80 + 45 + 90}{3}$$

$$= \frac{215}{3}$$

$$= 71,7\%$$

The percentage of 71,7 is a relative value. It is up to the person constructing the equation to decide if that number represents high, medium or low quality. The decision can be based on historical comparison, present performance standards or objectives, or management mandates.

Measuring training costs

Cascio's (1991) approach is used as an example of the determination of training and development costs. Cascio (1991: 35) identifies three main elements of training costs.

The *first* is cost of information/literature (T1) aimed at formal socialisation and training. This is computed by multiplying the unit cost of information/literature (for example R10) with the number of trainees (for example 300).

$$T_1 = R10 \times 300$$

$$= R3\ 000$$

The *second* cost element is instruction in a formal training programme (T2). This cost is computed as follows:

$$T_2 = (LO \times OV \times AP) + (LV \times CL \times LO)$$

where:

LO = length of the training programme (for example 40 hours)

OV = average remuneration rate of trainer(s) (for example R25 per hour)

AP = number of (similar) programmes presented in a year (for example 10)

LV = average remuneration rate per trainee (for example R12 per hour)

CL = number of trainees who participated in the training programmes (for example 300)

Example

$T_2 = (40 \times R25 \times 10) + (R12 \times 300 \times 40)$

$\quad = R10\,000 + R144\,000$

$\quad = R154\,000$

The *third* element is costs associated with on-the-job training (T3). Suppose that the trainees (for example 300) are subjected to coaching where two trainees per trained employee are subjected to an on-the-job training period of 60 hours. The remuneration rates of the trainers and trainees are R17 and R12 per hour respectively. While the trainer is busy with the on-the-job training, his/her productivity is lowered by 40 %.

$T_3 = 60 \times [(R17 \times 40\,\% \times 150) + (R12 \times 300)]$

$\quad = 60 \times R1\,020 + R3\,600$

$\quad = 60 \times R4\,620$

$\quad = R277\,200$

Total training cost (T4) is the summation of the above three elements.

$T_4 = R3\,000 + R154\,000 + R277\,200$

$\quad = R434\,200$

Two factors must be taken into account in determining training and development costs. The first, according to Cascio (1991: 259), is the differentiation between recurring and non-recurring costs. The development stage of a course prescribed more than once contains cost elements such as equipment (overhead projectors, video machines, etc) and salaries of course developers, which are incurred only once. The way in which differentiation between costs is made, and how the costs are allocated between courses, depends on the person doing the accounting. What is important, however, is consistency in determining and allocating recurring and non-recurring training costs.

A second factor to be considered in determining training costs is the computation of the cost of lost productivity time (cost of disruption) while employees involved in the training are away from their jobs. These costs are categorised as opportunity costs and inclusion thereof in cost models depends on standards of accuracy maintained in cost determination.

Not only the cost but also the benefits of the training and development effort should be measured. Models developed to date for measuring benefits are, however, mostly of a qualitative nature.

As you know, the result or outcome of training can be measured at reaction level, by the change in knowledge, skills, attitudes and work performance (see chapter 16). Information on this may be obtained by means of pre- and post-testing, questionnaires, interviews, observation and performance appraisal.

Measuring labour turnover and absenteeism

Three factors must be taken into account when assessing the importance of measuring labour turnover and absenteeism. The first is the impact of labour turnover and absenteeism on HR activities, for example the cost of training and sick leave. Secondly, it is important to note that labour turnover does not only influence the organisation negatively — new employees may also create new ideas and turnover may thus have a cleansing effect on the organisation. A third aspect is that turnover and absenteeism — whether of a voluntary (resignations) or involuntary (dismissals) nature — should be calculated.

LABOUR TURNOVER:

Fitz-enz (1984: 169) proposes two basic measures for labour turnover, namely the *accession rate* and the *separation rate*.

ACCESSION AND SEPARATION RATES

Accession rate: $AR = \dfrac{H}{E}$ Separation rate: $SR = \dfrac{NT}{E}$

where:

AR = accession rate

SR = separation rate

H = number hired during the period (eg 725)

NT = number terminated during the period (eg 656)

E = average employee population (eg 3 097)

Example:

$AR = \dfrac{725}{3\ 097}$ $SR = \dfrac{656}{3\ 097}$

$\quad = 23{,}4\ \%$ $\quad = 21{,}2\ \%$

The following are other significant measures for calculating labour turnover.

STABILITY AND INSTABILITY FACTORS

Stability factor: $SF = \dfrac{OS}{E}$ Instability factor: $IF = \dfrac{OL}{E}$

where:

SF = stability factor of an existing population

OS = original employees who remain for the period, for example 1 year (eg 832)

IF = instability factor of an existing population

OL = original employees who left during the period (eg 80)

E = employee population at the beginning of the period (eg 912)

Example:

$$SF = \frac{832}{912} \qquad IF = \frac{80}{912}$$
$$= 91{,}2\ \% \qquad\quad = 8{,}8\ \%$$

Obviously, SF and IF are reciprocals. In this case, 91,2 % of the employees with 5+ years of service stayed and 8,8 % left during the past year. This information can be compared with previous experience and a value judgment can be made.

The survival or loss rate of new hires is conceptually identical to the stability factor, only here the base population is new hires and not existing employee groups.

SURVIVOR AND LOSS RATES

$$\text{Survivor rate: } SR = \frac{HS}{H} \qquad \text{Loss rate: } LR = \frac{HL}{H}$$

where:

SR = survival rate of new hires

HS = number of new hires from the period who are still employed, stayers (eg 209)

LR = wastage or loss rate

HL = number of new hires who left, leavers (eg 79)

H = total number of new hires during the period (eg 288)

Example

$$SR = \frac{209}{288} \qquad LR = \frac{79}{288}$$
$$= 72{,}6\ \% \qquad\quad = 27{,}4\ \%$$

Hall (1981) presents a detailed and practical model for the calculation of labour turnover cost. This is depicted in table 23.2.

The costs attached to labour turnover should never be underestimated. In 1997 it was reported, for instance, that it could cost as much as R4 million to replace a top executive (see exhibit F).

It is therefore often necessary to execute certain measurements relating to labour turnover (and absenteeism).

ABSENTEEISM

For the measurement of absenteeism, two measures are of importance: the absence rate and the labour utilisation levels (Fitz-end 1984: 164).

Table 23.2

Labour turnover cost model*

Activity	Cost in rands
1. Recruitment advertising	55 000
2. Agency fees	30 737
3. Internal referrals	14 779
4. Applicant expenses	9 818
5. Relocation expenses	82 132
6. Remuneration of employment personnel	35 200
7. Other employment office expenses	2 300
8. Expenses of recruiters	3 500
9. Direct employment cost (sum of 1–8)	233 466
10. Number of appointments	362
11. Direct cost per appointment (9 ÷ 10)	645
12. Indirect cost per appointment (sum of 18–20)	5 000
13. Total cost per appointment	5 645
14. Number of replacement appointments (labour turnover)	250
15. Total labour turnover costs (13 × 14)	1 411 250
16. Target percentage reducement	25 %
17. Potential saving (15 × 16)	352 813
18. Cost of management time per appointment	390
19. Training cost per appointment	610
20. Productivity loss (or performance difference)	4 000
21. Total indirect employment cost per appointment	5 000

*Source: Hall 1981: 45

Exhibit F

Top brass can break the bank*

It can cost as much as R4 million to recruit or replace a top executive, according to estimates by Renwick Management Services. The bulk of the cost of recruiting or replacing management is in the cost of training the new employee. The second largest contributor to the cost is the loss of work by the outgoing employee. According to Renwick, it will cost more than R980 000 to replace a technical manager, just over R1 million to replace a marketing or sales manager, around R274 000 to replace an engineering manger, and R328 000 for a financial manager.

Cost estimates of recruiting/replacing management in various disciplines

Cost area	Technical	Marketing/Sales	Engineering	Financial	GM/MD
Writing/production/placing of one advertisement in the newspaper	R9 000	R9 000	R9 000	R9 000	R9 000
Interviewing applicants	R4 500	R4 500	R4 500	R4 500	R4 500
Response administration	R10 000	R10 000	R10 000	R10 000	R10 000
Testing and checking references	R1 750	R1 750	R1 750	R1 750	R1 750
Loss of work output by departing employee	R105 000[1]	R88 000[1]	R74 000[1]	R93 000[1]	R270 000[1]
Cost of training new employee	R850 000[1]	R930 000[1]	R175 000[1]	R210 000[1]	R3 700 000[1]
TOTAL COST	R980 250	R1 043 250	R274 250	R328 250	R3 995 250

[1]Replacement costs calculated on 5 % of organisational turnover

**Sunday Times Business Times*, 25 May 1997

ABSENCE RATE

Absence rate: $AR = \dfrac{WDL}{e \times WD}$

where:

AR = absence rate

WDL = worker days lost through absence (eg 400)

e = average employee population (eg 550)

WD = number of work days available per employee (eg 22)

Example

$$AR = \dfrac{400}{550 \times 22}$$
$$= \dfrac{400}{12\ 100}$$
$$= 3,3\ \%$$

As with most other ratios, this one can be computed by department to find locations where absence levels are relatively high. It can also be applied to job groups to search out types of employees who are often absent. There are two prerequisites which will determine whether or not an absence control programme will work: accurate employee time records and a standard acceptable absence rate.

EFFECT OF ABSENTEEISM ON LABOUR UTILISATION

$$U = \dfrac{Nh}{h}$$

where:

U = labour utilisation percentage

Nh = non-productive hours: absence, breaks, downtime, prep time, rework (eg 380 hours)

h = work hours available (eg 10 employees × 40 hours × 4 weeks = 1600 hours)

Example:

$$U = \dfrac{380}{1\ 600}$$
$$= 24\ \% \text{ (utilisation} = 76\ \%)$$

To show the effect of absenteeism, subtract absent hours (eg 80) from Nh and recompute.

JUTA

Example

$$U = \frac{380 - 80}{1\ 600}$$

$$= \frac{300}{1\ 600}$$

$$= 19\ \%\ (\text{utilisation} = 81\ \%)$$

Utilisation would have been 5 % higher if no employees had been absent.

For the calculation of absenteeism cost, a flow diagram devised by Cascio (1991: 61) can also be used. This is presented in figure 23.3.

A number of other areas (for example compensation) can also be subjected to cost–benefit analyses. There are also various other approaches to the evaluation of the organisation's human resource system.

23.3.3.3 *Other ways of evaluating aspects of human resource management*

As has been mentioned, there are various approaches to, or ways of evaluating, aspects of the organisation's HRM subsystem. Thus far we have focused in detail on the HRA and the cost–benefit analysis approaches. In section 23.2 we referred to the attitude survey approach which, to some extent, can also be viewed as a way of measuring/evaluating the net result of managing the organisation's HR system.

Another approach is referred to by some as *HRM auditing*. When one conducts an HRM audit, a systematic evaluation of the quality of various HRM systems, structures, practices, procedures and processes is undertaken. Cost benefit analyses can form part of such an audit, and so may an EAS. The audit, however, normally emphasises qualitative methods like document reviews. For instance, the disciplinary and grievance handling systems can be evaluated by studying the actual procedures, by analysing how the cases have been dealt with, and by interviewing the employees to determine their satisfaction with these systems.

Two other approaches often referred to are the *key indicators model* and the *reputational approach*.

23.4 RECORD-KEEPING AND HUMAN RESOURCE INFORMATION SYSTEMS

Human resource record and information systems are important for various reasons, to facilitate decision making in all areas related to the management of employment relationships and also to facilitate feedback to other stakeholders regarding human resource related matters.

Although in the past, and in some instances still today (such as in very small organisations), human resource records used to be maintained through manual systems, today such record-keeping systems cannot adequately fulfil the important role being played by HR information. This is especially true in the context of the trend towards more strategic human resource management.

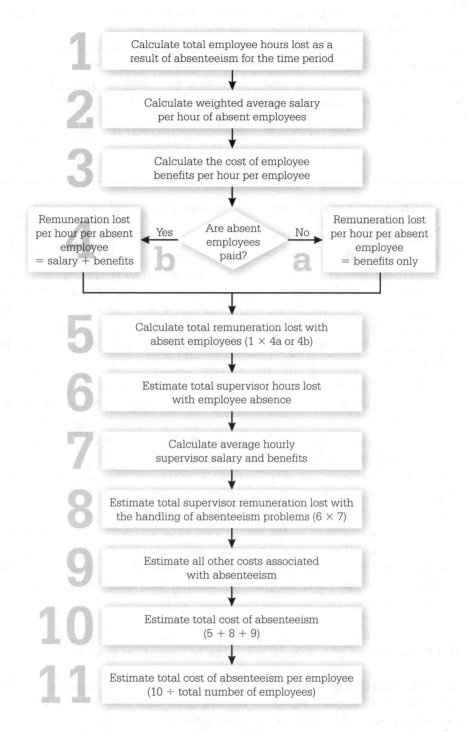

Figure 23.3

Estimated cost of absenteeism

Source: Cascio 1991: 61

With the increasing importance of human resource issues in general strategic and business planning and decision making, the capacity of human resource information systems (HRISs) to organise, store, process and manipulate employee-related data has become very important. To be of value to any organisation, the information must, however, be kept up to date and be complete, correct, flexible and accessible. Well-designed and maintained human resource information systems (HRISs) — especially if they are computerised — can play a major role in aligning human resource related goals and management practices with the business strategies and goals of the organisation as a whole.

23.4.1 The need for HR-related records and information

The overall purpose of any HRIS must surely be to provide the users (that is, all the HR staff as well as top, middle and lower management, and also workers and their representatives), with the relevant information that they need in order to make sound decisions about the management of employment relationships. The point of departure for any organisation is thus to analyse the kinds of HR-related decisions made within the organisation and the types of human resource information that such decisions require. After all, as we mentioned at the start of this chapter, good HRM decisions require good HR information.

All HR-related decisions require information. However, this information need not necessarily be complex and comprehensive. Those instances when more detailed information is actually required include forecasts of personnel needs (supply and demand) which are undertaken in the process of workforce planning and the compilation of data about jobs for job specifications (which must always be kept up to date). Similarly, records about each individual employee (for example biographical data, career history, tax details, absenteeism record, pension and medical information) must be maintained. There is also a general need to keep some form of collective database on the workforce as a whole, covering aspects such as numbers, job grades, occupations, labour turnover and absenteeism rates, total wage/salary bill, training records, overtime statistics and demographic characteristics of the staff (for example age, education, race and gender distributions). All of these aspects require a good HRIS.

23.4.2 Definition of a human resource information system

An HRIS is used to systematically collect, organise, store, maintain, retrieve and validate all human resource related data that may be needed in the process of managing employment relationships.

Such a system need not be computerised. When it is, however, it can be referred to as a CHRIS (**C**omputerised **H**uman **R**esource **I**nformation **S**ystem). In the rest of this section the emphasis will be on CHRISs.

A computerised human resource information system (CHRIS) is usually part of the organisation's larger management information system (MIS), which would then also be computerised.

Any HRIS is characterised by three main activities, namely inputs, transformations and outputs. Control in the system is achieved through feedback. Feedback helps to ensure that the HRIS outputs are those required by the system's users.

The system inputs generally consist of work and employee information, and sometimes also include organisation policies and procedures and other related information. Transformation components have to do with the inner part of the system itself, for example, the computer. A CHRIS usually includes hardware (computer itself — personal or mainframe), software or written instructions that tell the computer what to do, how to do it and when to do it, the procedure manuals, the data and peripheral devices like the printers. The output of the system is the actual utilisation of the processed data by the users, for example, a printed report categorising all employees in terms of age, gender and race distribution.

23.4.3 The potential value of computerised human resource information systems

A number of potential benefits can be derived from the proper utilisation of a well-designed CHRIS within an organisation. These include greater speed, the reduction of errors, increases in efficiency and reductions in costs (paperwork will be reduced, forms may be standardised and information is generated and gathered faster). As mentioned already, a CHRIS can be used as a tool in strategic planning. Information technology is so advanced nowadays that many functions and operations can be performed which were impossible when manual systems were the only systems available. Computerised human resource information systems can link with other information systems and, in this way, provide valuable information to decision makers and alert them to potential complexities and dynamics. Computerised systems are also much more flexible and can be more easily manipulated to suit the needs of the data users. A CHRIS is also much more mobile in the sense that it can allow communication between various organisations or link different parts of an organisation which may be spread across international borders. Generally speaking, the greatest value of a CHRIS lies in the fact that it speeds up decision making and saves on administrative costs.

23.4.4 Basic components of a CHRIS

A computerised human resource information system consists of various components, including hardware, software, procedures, data and users.

23.4.4.1 Hardware

Different types of hardware are available. "Hardware" basically refers to all *physical* equipment used in the computer system. The nature of the required hardware will be dictated largely by the applications for which the CHRIS is to be used — in other words, the types of decisions that will have to be made, the kinds of information that will be needed, the nature of the required databases, the software and programmes required, etc. These factors will determine what amount of memory will be required, as well as the networking, speed and storage requirements. This will in turn determine whether mainframe computers or personal computers (PCs) will be needed.

Each computer system has a central processing unit (CPU). This is basically the brain of the computer. Here the programme instructions are executed so that data can be read, stored, written or otherwise processed. The different types of CPUs are basically mainframe and personal computers (including different versions of these such as minicomputers, microcomputers or desktop computers). Technological developments have made PCs so powerful that the distinction between minicomputers and PCs has become less obvious. Mainframe computers are the largest computers and also the most expensive. There are also other hardware components, such as scanners, keyboards, modems, printers, diskettes, etc.

23.4.4.2 Software

Software is the second basic component of a CHRIS and refers in essence to the set of programs that make a computer work. A wide variety of software packages are available, ranging from simple programs that can track applicants or maintain organisational charts to more complex programs. A number of HR software programs that can be purchased in South Africa are listed in table 23.3

23.4.5 The process of managing a CHRIS

Changing from a manual to a computerised HR information system can be a significant intervention requiring careful management. It is imperative that top management should support such a switchover. The HR department should take overall responsibility for the changeover intervention, although they will depend a lot on the data processing department for technical assistance. In such an intervention a number of important steps must be followed. Kavanagh, Guetal & Tannenbaum (1990) have identified three main phases in this process, namely needs analysis, design and development, and implementation and maintenance.

23.4.5.1 Conducting the needs analysis

This phase is extremely important and involves a number of activities. First of all one must evaluate the HR information needs of the HR department and of the organisation as a whole. It must be ascertained how well HR operations are being performed and whether a CHRIS could bring about improvements. The current state of automation must also be established and it must be ascertained whether similar HR computer applications exist elsewhere in the company. It must always be borne in mind that a new or improved CHRIS should support the company's goals, strategies and business and thus provide better services to the organisa-

Table 23.3
HR software available in South Africa

Package	Description (Minimum hardware requirements shown in brackets)
Accsys Personnel Manager	Universal solution for personnel administration, data base to provide profiles on employees, instant access to data on skills, education, courses, disciplinary/job history, etc. (Single/multi-user DOS & Unix)
Ajax	A breakthrough methodology for a holistic & integrated approach to HR management, based on accepted principles. (PC386, 4 MB RAM, 30 MB HD, Hayes compatible modem)
Huroles	Integrated HR-payroll management system for enterprise solution backed by HR consulting & BPR support. (Mainframe & midrange on application)
Profile	Character-based personnel administration system providing cost-effective method of HR management. (PC386, 13 MB s/w 9k/employee)
SalaryBase 9.00	The personnel system that "pays". unique ability to customise system to suit individual company requirements. (DOS 6.2/Windows/Windows 95)
Unique	Fully integrated personnel administration/payroll management solution for the PC & midrange platforms. Offers incredibly powerful functionality, superb management facilities. (PC386, 30 MB HD, s/w, etc)
Vision	The first locally developed LAN-based human resource information system for windows covering all aspects of human resource management. (PC486, Windows 3.1, 8 MB RAM 50 MB HD)
Paywell Payroll/Wages	Paywell's power & flexibility makes it a unique product catering for both payroll & wages. Paywell is parameter driven. (PC386, 4 MB RAM, 40 MB HD. Also LAN & Unix)
Peodesy Human Resources System	Fully integrated, modular human resource information management system. Extremely flexible windows + network compatible, internationally recognised. (PC386, 4 MB ram, 50 MB HD)
Personnellease	Human resources management system which enables management to acquire up-to-date personnel information with speed & accuracy. (PC386, 4 MB ram, 40 MB HD. Also runs on networks)
Survey Tracker for Windows	Provides the current best approach for survey planning, scheduling, budgeting/survey design/audience design, administration, sampling, data collection, statistical analysis, plus. (486 PC Windows)
Unipayper	Package which solves all & any HR administration scenarios. Operates on mainframe & PC platforms including integrated download facilities. (IBM compatible mainframe 386 DX, 4 MB RAM)
VIP Human Resource Management System	Sophisticated employee database management system including advanced leave management. Fully integrated with the VIP payroll system. (DOS, Unix Windows LAN. PC 386 4 MB RAM)

tion's clients. The next step is to form a project team who will guide the intervention from start to finish. Another important issue is to determine the automation needs. The key here is to identify and prioritise the exact needs. According to the results of the needs analysis, detailed system specifications should be drawn up, specifying the desired outputs, inputs and system processing requirements.

It is also necessary to analyse current and future reporting needs by determining what reports are currently being used, what types of reports are needed, and how these will be changing.

All of this will culminate in a *request for proposal* (RFP) document. This document specifies what the organisation's needs are and invites vendors to submit proposals regarding how they will meet these needs and what the costs will be. In this way computer packages offered by various vendors are evaluated. It is important not to change the vendor at a later stage, as this may give rise to many problems. After this, a proposal will be submitted to management. The proposal will include an indication of costs and other necessary resources in comparison with the potential benefits expected to be derived from the system.

With the completion of the needs analysis phase, the second phase (that is, the design and development of the system) can be initiated.

23.4.5.2 *Designing and developing the system*

The design/development phase can be executed with or without the assistance of external vendors. It is, however, important for the relevant HR staff to be involved throughout. During this phase a detailed project plan is developed, user groups are identified and the hardware is purchased once it has been determined what software will be used to meet the processing and storage requirements of the data. The evaluation of appropriate software packages should be guided by factors such as ease of access, back-up support, guides for users and their general user-friendliness.

One very critical step in the process is the establishment of procedures and guidelines to support the system. These guidelines and procedures must reflect organisational realities and the system's limitations. It is also important to conduct a test run of the system. The necessary data must then be entered into the system. If an organisation, for example, has job codes, each job and its respective code should be entered into a job table on the CHRIS.

A further important step is the establishment of a Human Resource Information Centre and the training of its staff. Spirig (1988) spells out the functions of the HRIC staff as including:

- managing database integrity and data quality, with the goal of enabling more users to add and change data;
- establishing and maintaining hardware and software standards to assure compatibility between systems and optimal communication between users and systems, and to minimise duplicative or redundant procedures;

- safeguarding employee privacy and implementing and administering security policies and procedures;
- marketing CHRIS products and services throughout the company to ensure that all employees understand the available services and use them to the benefit of the organisation; and
- training new employees to use CHRIS products and services.

23.4.5.3 Implementing and maintaining the CHRIS

Once it has been established that the system has been set up successfully (in other words, after having conducted pilot or dummy runs), the system has to be made available for use. Certainly the most important aspect of managing a CHRIS is to ensure that it is used correctly in order to improve human resource management decisions. An important task is thus to provide users with information about the new system and to train them so as to overcome initial resistance. Support to users is important, for example through easy-to-understand manuals, guidelines and procedures and through providing an easily accessible support system such as a telephone hotline.

An extremely important aspect of system maintenance is continuously to evaluate the system's effectiveness. Techniques that can be used include error analysis, user surveys and audit reports. Evaluating the system over time may lead to a decision to update the CHRIS at some stage, and the cycle discussed above may then have to be repeated.

23.4.6 HRM application areas of CHRISs

Computerised human resource information systems can be used in almost all the areas of human resource management, including various personnel administrative matters, workforce planning, employment (recruitment and selection), performance management, training and development, career management, remuneration and labour relations. Only a few areas of application are elaborated upon here.

23.4.6.1 Workforce planning

With the help of a CHRIS, projections and estimates of future labour supply and demand can be undertaken professionally by extrapolating current staffing levels and skill mixes, turnover, promotions and other staff movements. Part of this process involves skills inventories which answer questions such as whether the organisation will have enough people with specific competencies to accomplish production goals over a specified period.

23.4.6.2 Tracking and recruiting job applicants

The CHRIS could maintain information on vacancies and candidates for those jobs. In this way applicants can be tracked and information on their resumés can help match candidates on file to the vacant jobs. Lists of potential candidates can be sent to any manager who has a vacancy. The CHRIS can thus carry certain data on individual employees, such as names, addresses, experience, skills, ages, etc. It may also contain data on results of selection tests, reference checks, interview results and any previous job offers.

23.4.6.3 Training and development

An individual's training and development needs can be compared with the training and development options available within an organisation. On the basis of the PDPs (personal development plans), both the subordinate's and the superior's evaluations of training needs can be put onto the system. The training component of a CHRIS can be quite extensive, carrying complete training course information on relevant internal and external courses, training course evaluation data, instructors, costs, room assignments and employees scheduled to participate. Individual records can also be captured, such as educational achievements, further studies and degree certifications, courses taken in-house and outside, results of courses and areas of multiskilling. This and other information can be used as part of the organisation's career management system, as well as for workforce planning purposes.

23.4.6.4 Compensation administration

One very common area of application is that of wages, salary and fringe benefit administration. Computerised human resource information systems are typically used to administer salary programming (grades and salary ranges), to track and control various incentive, bonus, and commission schemes, and to administer employee share ownership plans (ESOPs).

23.4.7 CHRIS developments in South Africa: Some early research

It is interesting to note the extent to which computerised human resource information systems are used in South African organisations. The results of a survey undertaken in 1987 among 165 companies with a staff complement ranging from less than 100 to more than 10 000 revealed that a large number of these companies were using computers in the HRM area. Areas of usage appear in table 23.4.

Table 23.4

*Areas of CHRIS application: research results**

Application area	% of companies (n = 165)
Basic payroll processing	96,9
Payroll management reports	90,3
Salary increase data/calculations	86,6
Pension fund administration	71,5
Employee records	69,0
Medical aid fund administration	66,6
Other fringe benefit administration	66,0

*Source: Beukes 1987: 30

Exhibit G lists those areas of human resource management which are not currently receiving the attention they deserve. The use of computerised information systems in these areas could lead to a vastly improved utilisation of employees and could provide valuable information in the decision-making process.

Exhibit G

Application areas that have received very little attention*
• Manpower planning
• Succession planning/career pathing
• Skills inventory/requirements planning
• Job descriptions/evaluation
• Training needs analysis
• Training/development administration
• Performance appraisal/assessment
• Applicant tracking and analysis
• Affirmative action
• Psychometric testing and other forms of applicant tracking
Fewer than 30 % of the companies paid attention to these areas.

*Source: Beukes 1987: 30

From the above it is clear that a decade ago South African companies were using CHRISs more for administrative than strategic purposes. Although more recent research results are lacking, there seems to be a slight trend towards the development of more strategic applications.

However, if South African organisations want to become more competitive in international markets, they will have to make better use of CHRISs. There is a definite need for action research and research in this area.

23.4.8 Internet and human resource management

With the advent of Internet, revolutionary application possibilities for human resource management have come to the fore. Heyns (1996) reports as follows:

"Unprecedented software for employers or their human resources departments is being launched with the new Labour Relations Act to provide users with the most revolutionary medium for personnel management, research and communication. By connecting your computer to a phone and loading your software, you could join the millions of people surfing the information highway, swopping opinions and information, networking with other employers and mobilising resources to deal with the challenges industrial relations will offer in the new dispensation.

With the implementation of the new Labour Relations Act, a consortium of organisations has launched a computer software product called Labournet which they say no employer can be without. The product aims to support employers through the Internet as it was felt that a need exists for such support to employers who will be faced with the significant changes introduced by the new Labour Relations Act."

Heyns goes on to illustrate how one can, by the click of a button, have, for instance, the International Labour Organisation, COSATU, NEDLAC, NUM (National Union of Mineworkers) or the Constitutional Assembly on line. In this way aspects like ILO conventions and documents or, for example, COSATU policy documents and newsletters, can be obtained within minutes. Through Labournet one can also gain access to the CCMA and the Labour Court. In addition, E-mail forms part of the Labournet package. Labournet can provide organisations with access to research material and contact with employer organisations so that, within minutes, help can be obtained in the drafting of collective agreements or other labour-related documents.

Heyns (1996: 24) summarises this exciting development as follows:

> "The future for human resources people and the Internet is bright. Those who choose not to board the 'information superhighway' will soon find themselves as technologically disadvantaged as those who work without telephones or fax machines. Information will increasingly become your armoury. Your ability to get it quickly enough may win the battle for you."

23.5 HUMAN RESOURCE REPORTING

Through a human resource report an organisation can provide various stakeholders with information about the organisation's human resources and issues relating to its human resource management system. As a rule such a report will be contained in the organisation's annual report which serves as the main corporate vehicle for providing information to stakeholders such as shareholders, employees, potentially interested investors and the general public.

In a world dominated by financial and bottom-line concerns, the human resource report is often the Cinderella in the corporate reporting stakes; 40 % of the companies registered on the Johannesburg Stock Exchange do not provide any information about their human resources (Visser 1995). One possible reason for this neglect is the absence of statutory requirements compelling organisations to include human resource related information in their annual reports (unlike the situation in some other countries). This situation is, however, likely to change in the future when legislation on employment equity (see chapter 5) is enacted. A further reason for the lack of human resource information is that a standard for a human resource report has not yet been established. Consequently, when human resource information is provided, it is done mostly in an unstructured manner and on an ad hoc basis. While a frame of reference for providing financial information through relevant financial statements (balance sheet, income statement, value added statement, etc) is well established, no such frame of reference exists for human resource information.

In this section a brief overview is provided of initiatives to improve corporate accountability on human resources. Reference is made to the *King Report on Corporate Governance* (1994), which recommended greater transparency and accountability on corporate non-financial affairs. Proposed legislation on employment equity also aims to introduce statutory requirements relating to the reporting of human resource-related information.

23.5.1 Greater accountability in respect of the human resource: Background

23.5.1.1 The King Report on Corporate Governance (1994)

Following the publication of the Cadbury Committee Report on Corporate Governance in England, in December 1992, the Institute of Directors in Southern Africa established a committee to investigate corporate governance in South African organisations. Mervyn E King, Chairman of the Frame Group of companies, served as Chairman of this committee; the committee subsequently became known as the King Committee.

The final version of the King Committee Report was published in November 1994 following widespread consultation and comment. The recommendations of the King Committee were widely reported on and enjoyed much acclaim in the business and financial press. Although the King Report advocates many sweeping changes to the way business is organised and controlled, one of its major recommendations deals specifically with the need for transparency and greater accountability on human resources:

> "Reports and communication must be made in the context that society now demands transparency and greater accountability from corporations in regard to their non-financial affairs, for example, their workers . . . " (1994: 29)

The King Report clearly identifies corporate stakeholders as including "shareholders, employees, bankers, suppliers, customers, environmentalists, the community or country in which it operates and the State". It then suggests that the director's reports (annual report) should be directed at all stakeholders and not only shareholders. In this regard the content of a human resource report is likely to be influenced by the information requirements of its particular stakeholders.

The King Report also gives some indication of the type of issues to be addressed in a report to all stakeholders: ". . . employment, such as staffing levels, skills levels, new jobs created, retrenchments, affirmative action policy, unionisation, training programmes, etc". The report does not specify every facet of human resources to be reported on, thus allowing organisations much scope in the development of a report which will address the information requirements of the relevant stakeholders.

The King Report further recommends that information be supported by figures. It therefore suggests that the tendency to adopt only a narrative approach in reporting on human resource issues be supported by quantified information. The Report also recommends that ". . . a balance between the positive and negative aspects of the activities of the company . . ." be attained. This recommendation supports the notion that organisations develop a human resource *balance sheet* reflecting both the positive (asset) as well as the negative (liability) side of their human resource. An example of a human resource balance sheet is provided in the *World Competitiveness Yearbook* (1996: 270) which reflects on the people dimension when comparing South Africa's competitiveness with that of forty-six other countries (see table 23.5).

Although the King Report does not identify all the issues to be addressed in a human resource report, the need for a comprehensive report dealing with human resource issues is clearly indicated. The King Report thus confirms and sanctions the provision and inclusion of a human resource report as part of the annual reporting process.

23.5.1.2 *The Green Paper on Employment and Occupational Equity*

Further support for comprehensive reporting on human resource issues is being provided by the *Green Paper on Employment and Occupational Equity* (see also chapter 5). A key feature of the *Green Paper* is the suggestion that employers report and provide information on employment and training in terms of race and gender. Information that is likely to be required includes:

- profiles of employees by race, gender and disability;
- employment, pay and benefits in major categories by race, gender and disability;
- programmes and policies on human resource development;
- language competence of the workforce.

Although the *Green Paper* is only the first step towards legislation on employment and occupational equity, it is already clear that statutory directives will be implemented which will require employers to provide comprehensive information on their human resources. The *Green Paper*, however, is also not very clear on what human resource information should be provided, other than that a differentiation should be made on the basis of race, gender and disability.

23.5.1.3 *Quantifying human resource information*

As mentioned already, the current trend is to adopt a narrative approach when reporting on human resource issues. Such information is often vague and inaccurate. For this reason it is recommended that information be supported by figures — that is, by quantified information.

It is suggested that quantifying human resource information makes it less vague. Statements like: "The organisation has spent R3,5 million on training" or "9 900 mandays have been spent on training . . ." are less vague than: "A major contribution, in terms of time and money, is being made towards people development." Quantified information allows for clear interpretation, ease of analysis and comparison.

Accountability with regard to human resources can be improved by quantifying information and expressing it in terms of aspects such as:

Table 23.5
National competitiveness balance sheet: South Africa

Assets	Rank	Liabilities	Rank
Management		*Management*	
Remuneration of HR Director	14	Industrial relations	44
Compensation levels	15	Change in overall productivity	43
Social responsibility	22	International experience and senior managers	41
Productivity in manufacturing	24	Total quality management	40
People		*People*	
Youth unemployment	13	Equal opportunity	46
Female labour force	14	Skilled labour	46
Working hours	14	Economic literacy	46
Population	17	Worker motivation	46
Employment	20	Brain drain	45
		Unemployment	45
		The education system	45
		Values of the society	45
		Employment %	44
		Illiteracy	43
		Human development index	41
		Competent senior managers	40
		In-company training	39

Criteria

✓Remuneration of HR director: annual gross salary

✓Compensation levels: total hourly compensation levels for manufacturing workers

✓Social responsibility: extent to SR issues

✓Productivity in manufacturing: value added per manufacturing worker

✓Youth unemployment: unemployment of population under the age of 24 as a % of total employment

✓Female labour force: average number of working hours per year

✓Population: estimates in millions

✓Employment: total employment

✗Industrial relationship: relations between managers and employees (are fragile)

✗Change in overall productivity: annual compound % change of real GDP per person employed

✗International experience and senior mangers: more than 10 years experience in international management

✗Total quality management: extent to which TQM is comprehensively applied

✗Equal opportunity: race, gender or family background poses a handicap in society

✗Economic literacy: low among the population

✗Worker motivation: don not identify with company objectives

✗Brain drain: many well-educated people emigrate

✗Unemployment: % of labour force

✗The education system: does not meet the needs of a competitive economy

✗Employment %: % of population

✗Values of the society: do not support competitiveness

✗Illiteracy: adult illiteracy — % of population

✗Human development index: combines economic, social, educational indicators

✗Competent senior managers: difficult to find

✗In-company training: neglects training employees

- money, for example: cost of staffing, cost of training, minimum wages;
- numbers, for example: number of employees (various categories), number of people trained;
- mandays, for example: lost through labour unrest, absenteeism, sick leave, spent on training;
- indexes or ratios, for example: safety ratings, qualification levels, literacy levels, productivity ratios, etc.

23.5.1.4 Towards a definition of "accountability in human resource management"

Within the context of the foregoing and the country's drive to devolve democracy to lower levels of society, and in light of the importance of greater overall transparency in this process, we can conceptualise *accountability* in respect of human resource management issues as:

the obligation imposed on the management of an organisation to identify, measure, record, and provide relevant information to stakeholders about the organisation's human resources in terms of its responsibility to attract, employ, develop, utilise and reward this resource effectively, efficiently and fairly.

23.5.2 The human resource report vs the employee report

Because of the current practice to produce an employee report, in addition to an annual report, it is necessary to distinguish between the two.

The **human resource report** is a section within an annual report which contains comprehensive information about an organisation's human resource. When the King Committee recommended greater transparency and accountability from corporations with regard to their non-financial affairs, they were in fact making a case for the inclusion of, *inter alia*, a human resource report, a social responsibility report and an environmental report as part of the annual report.

An **employee report**, on the other hand, is a layman-friendly version of the annual report and is normally produced in addition to the annual report. The content of the employee report usually covers the whole spectrum of an organisation's activities with the intention of creating an awareness on the part of all employees of the financial and economic factors affecting the organisation's performance. The employee report addresses the information needs of the employee as a corporate stakeholder. The focus is on providing information in a format that enhances understanding. While companies are encouraged to produce employee reports, *inter alia* through the CA/Anglo Alpha Employee Report Award, a fair amount of criticism has also been directed at these reports, namely that biased information could be provided and also that the employee report suggests that employees are regarded as a less sophisticated audience.

23.5.3 Research in South Africa: Establishing a frame of reference for human resource reporting

Visser (1995) undertook research to determine how companies portray their human resources in their annual reports. The objective of the research was to establish a frame of reference for human resource reporting based on current practices.

An analysis was made of the 1993 annual reports of 362 companies in South Africa. Most of the companies identified in the *Financial Mail* 1994 Special Survey of Top Companies were included in this analysis. A comparative analysis was also made of the annual reports of forty-four selected companies from seventeen foreign countries. In the process valuable perspectives were gained of the human resource reporting practices within the corporate world. Through this research it was also possible to develop a structure and format for a human resource report which can go a long way towards meeting the requirements of comprehensiveness and relevance. The format suggested in section 23.5.4 is based on Visser's research.

23.5.3.1 Human resource accountability rating

In order to answer the questions "How accountable are organisations with regard to their human resources?" or "How well are organisations doing in reporting on their human resources?", it is necessary to adopt a particular standard and to utilise an appropriate evaluation instrument. One such instrument has been developed (refer to table 23.6). Through this instrument a human resource accountability rating has been determined which is defined as follows:

The Human Resource Accountability Rating (HRAR) is a numerical value, determined through a given standard or 'mark plan', indicating the extent to which relevant human resource information is provided to organisation stakeholders, usually through and included in the annual report, thus reflecting the organisation's accountability regarding their human resources.

By applying this instrument to the 1994 annual reports of 337 companies, most of which are listed on the Johannesburg Stock Exchange, it was possible to gain a picture of the extent to which companies provide information about their human resources. This research indicated that only 7 % of the companies reviewed had an HRAR of more than 20. A rating of 20 — out of a maximum of 90— implies that at least some information had been provided about the organisation's human resources. Only three companies had an HRAR of more than 30: Anglo-alpha (45), Adcock Ingram (33), Sasol (31). Seventy-one per cent of the companies had an HRAR of 8 or less, indicating that very little human resource information had been provided. The conclusion reached was that South African companies are not accountable with regard to their human resources.

It has been suggested that part of the reason for this is the absence of a Generally Accepted Human Resource Practice (GAHRP) which could provide guidelines to the human resource practitioner and general managers on how to compile and

Table 23.6

Human resource accountability: Annual report evaluation mark plan

	A	B
Company: *Year:* **Listing category:** *Number of employees:* HR in chairman's report (1); HR in CE's report (1); Operational report on HR (2); Other location: . . . .(2)(max 4)		
Mission statement (max) HR Objectives stated (2) Attitude toward HR statement (2)	4	
Senior management (max) Information provided, eg name, qualifications, age, years service, portfolio	2	
Value-added statement (max) Included plus definition or elaboration (2); VA per employee (1)	3	
Productivity/quality (max) Priority indicated (2); Indicators: Re people utilisation (4)	6	
Employee numbers (max) Explanation given on (1); Comparative numbers over . . . years (1); Provide per category/division (1); Provided per sex and race	4	
Employee information (max) Retrenchments (1); Employee turnover (1); Service record (1); Qualification distribution (1); Work days lost on industrial action (1); Absenteeism (1); Other . . . . (1)	6	
Employee benefits (max) Remuneration (2); Minimum wages (2); Pension/provident fund (2); Medical aid/health care (2); Housing (2); Education assistance (2); Other . . . . (2)	10	
Safety (max) Issue addressed (2); Relevant information provided (2)	4	
HR development (max) Attitude and commitment to (2); Information on cost, numbers (2); Management development (2); Skills training (2); Technical and apprentice training (2); Education and further studies support (2); Literacy training and ABE (2); Other people development initiatives (2); Training status of industry (2)	12	
Industrial relations (max) Relationship with unions (3); Issues at stake (3); Employee participation strategies (3)	9	
Affirmative action (max) Issue addressed (2); supporting employee information (2); Programmes/strategies (2)	6	
Other HR issues (max) Recruitment issues (1); HR audits/research (1); The disabled employee (1); AIDS (1); Performance management (1); Job creation (1); Ethics (1); Communication with (1); Harassment (1); Policies (1); Equal opportunities (1); Elimination of discrimination (1); Working environment (1); Address HR issues on a national level (1); Other . . . . (1)	12	
Qualitative evaluation (max) Quantitative support for HR issues (2); Comprehensiveness in HR reporting (2); Layout: use of appropriate headings (2); Style (2)	8	
TOTAL . . . . .%	90	

present human resource information effectively. It is also suggested that an effective human resource report will not only reflect people utilisation within an organisation but will also enhance effectiveness in leadership and human resource management in general.

23.5.4 The human resource report: A framework

On the basis of the current practices in human resource reporting in annual reports, determined through research, the following basic structure for providing human resource information could be adopted.

23.5.4.1 Supporting information

The value of the human resource component of an organisation is underscored by the current practice of providing information on human resources outside the proposed human resource report. This practice should be encouraged. Such additional information can be provided in the following sections of the annual report.

Mission statement

It has become common practice to include the mission statement in the annual report. It is assumed that human resources will be clearly reflected in this statement.

Chairman or Chief Executive statement

It is likely that the Chairman's statement will address human resources on a strategic level. Issues to be addressed could then include broad strategies in respect of human resource and labour relations management; job creation strategies; affirmative action strategies and programmes; strategies to eliminate discrimination in the workplace; staff development; people productivity, etc. Reference could also be made to strategic human resource issues on an industry or national level. In this regard the Chairman's statement is likely to reflect a vision or perspective of the future.

Executive management

It is a statutory requirement that the names of directors should be included in the annual report. Additional information on the directors is usually also included, for example age, qualifications, date appointed as director, experience and portfolio within the company. The same information is also provided in respect of senior management.

Value added statement

It is becoming increasingly common for companies to include a value added statement with their year-end financial statements. This statement reflects the relationship between the various stakeholders in the enterprise, giving an indication of their respective contributions. The stakeholders are:

- customers — providing turnover and standards of quality;
- suppliers — providing materials and services;
- employees — providing added value;
- shareholders — providing permanent capital;
- financiers — providing financing and loan capital;
- government — providing a stable, disciplined growth environment;
- entrepreneurs/leadership — providing increased wealth through retained value.

Productivity/quality

Many annual reports feature a commitment to improved productivity, while recognising the contribution made by the human resource component in this regard. Use is made of particular productivity indicators, for example turnover per employee, assets per employee, value added per employee, etc.

23.5.4.2 Specific human resource information

In practice a human resource report usually provides operational information regarding the organisation's human resource system. As a rule, the following operational information is included.

Employee numbers

The number of people working in the organisation is indicated. Changes in employee numbers could be explained. Employee profiles in terms of race, gender and disability will be required. A further breakdown of employee numbers in various categories could also be provided.

Employee information

Further information about employees is often provided, including employee turnover, service record, age profile, absenteeism, qualifications profile, literacy levels and language competence.

Remuneration and employee benefits

Information in this regard could include remuneration levels, profit-sharing schemes, minimum wages, retirement benefits, medical aid, housing, education assistance, employee loans, share incentive schemes, reward systems for suggestions, etc.

Health and safety

Information is often provided on efforts to improve health and safety in the work environment and relevant statistics.

HR development

Information on human resource development includes aspects such as management development, literacy and numeracy training and adult basic education, training and development in support of affirmative action, focus of training courses and programmes, reference to training on an industry or national level, technical training, further training scheme, cross-cultural training, multiskills training, etc. Quantitative information is provided.

Labour relations

Information includes the names of participating unions and their membership figures, the status of relations with unions, issues at stake and being addressed, the extent and types of disciplinary and grievance activity, employee participation strategies, etc.

Affirmative action

Information includes the extent to which this issue is being addressed, relevant programmes and strategies in place, employee profiles (and changes in profiles) in terms of race, gender and disability.

Other HR issues

Other human resource information could include: recruitment issues, HR audits and research being conducted (such as EAS), efforts to accommodate the disabled worker, dealing with AIDS, performance enhancement strategies, job creation strategies, ethics, strategies to enhance communication, dealing with harassment, employment policies, equal opportunity, elimination of discrimination, working environment issues, addressing HR issues on an industry or national level, etc.

23.6 CONCLUSION

It is often said that the world has now moved into the information age. Our organisations are therefore required to become increasingly information driven. Linked to this is the fact that the world is experiencing an era of revolutionary developments in the field of information technology. All of this, coupled with increasing pressure to become more competitive in the global village of business warfare, cause organisations constantly to change and develop through the acquisition of knowledge — the trend towards the so-called learning organisation. Knowledge and information go hand in hand. World-class human resource management decisions and practices have to be based on information of the same standard. In this chapter we have focused on a number of specific areas relating to the management of information within the context of an organisation's human resource system. We looked briefly at human resource related research as an important means of collecting HR-related information, as well as on approaches to the evaluation of various aspects related to an organisation's HRM system. The nature and value of switching to computerised human resource information systems was discussed and the nature and importance of human resource reporting was also highlighted.

23.7 SELF-EVALUATION QUESTIONS

1. List and explain ten areas of human resource related research.
2. What is meant by "employee attitude surveys"? How should such surveys be executed?
3. Discuss arguments for and against the evaluation of human resource management aspects.
4. Critically discuss the human resource accounting model.
5. Explain briefly what human resource cost–benefit analysis entails.
6. Critically comment on the need for and nature of the measurement of labour turnover and absenteeism.
7. What is a CHRIS? Explain the basic components thereof.
8. Discuss the process of managing a CHRIS.
9. Explain the HRM application areas of CHRIS's.
10. Discuss the value and nature of human resource reporting and comment on developments in this regard in South Africa.

23.8 BIBLIOGRAPHY

Ameiss, RP & Williams, DE. 1981. Human resource accounting in industry. *CA Magazine,* August, 113–118

American Accounting Association. 1973. Report of the Committee on Human Resource Accounting. *The Accounting Review,* XLIX (2), 169–185

Anthony, RN. 1990. The bad and the good of experience. *Management Accounting,* 71 (7), 36–37

Anthony, WP, Perrewe, PL & Kacmar, KM. 1993. *Strategic Human Resource Management.* Orlando: The Dryden Press

Beukes, D. 1987. The use of computers in South African human resources management. *IMP/IPB Joernaal,* 6(2), 30

Cascio, WF. 1991. *Costing Human Resources: The Financial Impact of Behavior in Organizations,* 3 ed. Boston: PWS Kent

Fitz-enz, J. 1984. *How to Measure Human Resources Management.* New York: McGraw-Hill

Flamholtz, EG. 1985. *Human Resource Accounting.* San Francisco: Jossey-Bass

Hall, TE. 1981. How to estimate employee turnover costs. *Personnel,* July-August, 43–52

Heyns, A. 1996. Internet as HR's new assistant. *People Dynamics,* 14(7), 21–22

Hofmeyr, K. 1997a. Employee attitudes: a key dimension in organisational success. *People Dynamics,* 15(8), 31–35

Hofmeyr, K. 1997b. *SA Employee Attitudes: A Key Factor in Organisational Change.* Upublished paper delivered at the IPM Convention, Sun City, October.

Kavanagh, MJ, Guetal, HG & Tannenbaum SI. 1990. *Human Resource Information Systems: Development and Application.* Boston: PWS-Kent

King Committee Report on Corporate Governance 1994. Johannesburg: The Institute of Directors in Southern Africa, 29 Nov 1994

McCarthy, JP. 1980. Memo to senior management: Is your personnel department effective? *Best's Review,* July, 101–105

Phillips, JJ & Seers, A. 1989. Twelve ways to evaluate HR management. *Personnel Administrator,* April, 54–58

Republic of South Africa. 1996. *Green Paper: Policy Proposals for a New Employment and Occupational Equity Statute.* Notice 804 of 1996, *Government Gazette* 17303. Pretoria: Government Printers

Sackmann, SA, Flamholtz, EG & Bullen, ML. 1989. Human resource accounting: A state-of-the-art review. *Journal of Accounting Literature*, 8, 235–264

Spirig, JE. 1988. Selling the HRIS. *Personnel,* October, 26–34

Visser, CJ du T. 1995. *Corporate Accountability on Human Resources — A Review of Human Resources Accounting Practices as Reflected in Corporate Annual Reports.* Harrismith: PiERD Resources

Vorster, HJS. 1977. *Die Wenslikheid van die Rekenkundige Verantwoordings van Menslike Hulpbronne in die Gepubliseerde Finansiële Jaarstate van Ondernemings.* D Com-proefskrif, PU vir CHO, Potchefstroom

World Competitiveness Yearbook 1996. Lausanne, Switzerland: International Institute for Management Development

STUDY OBJECTIVES

After studying this chapter, you should be able to:

- explain what counts as *dismissal* in terms of the LRA;
- list dismissals that will be characterised as *automatically unfair dismissals;*
- briefly discuss three grounds of justification for dismissal and explain the fairness standards for dismissal associated with each of these; and
- discuss the statutory remedies for unfair dismissal.

24.1 INTRODUCTION

Despite all human resource management efforts to ensure that employment relationships remain sound and that the match or fit between the parties adds value to the organisation's quest for success, the employment relationship between individual employees and the employing organisation will inevitably break down from time to time. Sometimes employees terminate the relationship by resigning in order to take up a position elsewhere. It may also happen that the initiative to terminate the relationship may come from the employer's (or rather management's) side. This chapter focuses on the latter situation.

Both internationally and in terms of South African law the services of an employee may be terminated for any one of the following reasons: as a result of misconduct on the part of the employee; for operational reasons; or because of the incapacity or incompetency (poor worker performance) of the employee. In order for a termination of employment to be fair, the employer must comply with the necessary standards of substantive and procedural fairness and must be able to justify the termination of the employee's services in terms of any one of the above-mentioned three reasons.

Through its jurisdiction in terms of the "unfair labour practice" definition contained in the Labour Relations Act of 1956, the Industrial Court has, over a period of little more than fifteen years, developed an impressive body of law dealing with issues relating to, *inter alia*, dismissal law (both collective and individual). In Chapter VIII of the Labour Relations Act 66 of 1995 the legislator has endeavoured to codify the dismissal law formulated in terms of the Industrial Court's jurisprudence.

24.2 DEFINITION OF "DISMISSAL"

In the Act the chapter on unfair dismissals starts by stating in the clearest terms possible that *"(e)very employee has the right not to be unfairly dismissed"*. It then proceeds to spell out in some detail what is meant by "dismissal". It should be noted that at this stage the fairness or unfairness of a dismissal is not at issue; the Act simply tells us what conduct will, legally speaking, amount to dismissal. Logically, an enquiry into the fairness of a dismissal should be preceded by asking whether or not there has, in fact been a dismissal in the first place. This is also the sequence followed by the Act. The definition of "dismissal" in terms of the Act is outlined below.

"Dismissal" is defined as any one of the following:

- an employer has terminated a contract of employment with or without notice;
- an employee reasonably expected an employer to renew a fixed-term contract of employment on the same or similar terms, but the employer offered to renew it on less favourable terms, or did not renew it;
- an employer refused to allow an employee to resume work after she took maternity leave in terms of any law, collective agreement or her contract of employment;
- an employer refused to allow an employee to resume work after she was absent from work for up to four weeks before the expected date, and up to eight weeks after the actual date, of the birth of her child;
- an employer who dismissed a number of employees for the same or similar reasons has offered to re-employ one or more of them, but has refused to re-employ another; or
- an employee terminated a contract of employment with or without notice because the employer made continued employment intolerable for the employee.

24.3 THE FAIRNESS OF A DISMISSAL

24.3.1 Automatically unfair dismissals

Obviously, employers should be entitled, given appropriate justification and having followed a fair procedure, to dismiss employees; not all dismissals are unfair. Having ascertained that a dismissal, as defined above, has indeed occurred, the next step is to determine whether the dismissal was fair or unfair. The new Act introduces an innovation into dismissal law by providing that certain types of dismissals constitute automatically unfair dismissals. One could say that the legislator regards the listed instances of automatically unfair dismissals as the worst kind of unfair dismissal. The reason why these instances of dismissal have been given special treatment is not difficult to ascertain: the listed reasons involve instances of undermining collective bargaining, undermining the authority of the Act and dismissals that amount to unfair discrimination. Dismissing an employee for any of the reasons listed in exhibit A will be regarded as automatically unfair.

Exhibit A

Automatically unfair dismissals*
Dismissing a worker for any of the following reasons will be regarded as automatically unfair: • victimisation or interference with the freedom of association; • the employee participated in or supported, or indicated an intention to participate in or to support, a protected strike or protected protest action; • the employee refused, or indicated an intention to refuse, to do any work normally done by an employee who at the time was taking part in a protected strike or was locked out (unless such work is necessary to prevent the actual endangering of the life, personal safety or health of other persons); • the employer wanted to compel the employee to accept a demand in respect of any matter of mutual interest between the employer and employee; • the employee took action, or indicated an intention to take action, against the employer by exercising any right conferred by this Act or by participating in any proceedings in terms of this Act; • the employee's pregnancy, intended pregnancy, or any reason related to her pregnancy; • the employer unfairly discriminated against an employee, directly or indirectly, on any arbitrary ground, including (but not limited to) race, gender, sex, ethnic or social origin, colour, sexual orientation, age, disability, religion, conscience, belief, political opinion, culture, language, marital status or family responsibility (despite the preceding, a dismissal may be fair if the reason for dismissal is based on an inherent requirement of the particular job, or, in the case of a dismissal based on age, if the employee has reached the normal or agreed retirement age for persons employed in that capacity).

*In terms of the Labour Relations Act

In the light of the above, the following observations are worth noting.

• Dismissing an employee for participating in a protected strike is unfair.
• An employer may not compel non-striking employees to do the work of protected strikers or of workers who have been locked out by the employer, except in crisis situations where life or health are endangered.
• The so-called lockout dismissal that enjoyed statutory recognition under the old Act now attracts the extreme censure of being designated as automatically unfair.
• Dismissing an employee for exercising his/her rights as a worker will not be tolerated.
• Women who are pregnant or intend to become pregnant, enjoy job security for the first time. The ambit of the disconcertingly wide "*or any reason related to her pregnancy*" will have to await clearer definition through arbitration awards and court decisions.

● A dismissal amounting to discrimination in terms of any one of the listed protected grounds will be automatically unfair unless it falls within the ambit of the savings clause. A few examples will serve to illustrate how this discrimination clause will work. Assume that a woman has been dismissed for using foul language and she challenges her dismissal on the basis that men using similar language are not even disciplined, let alone dismissed. She, as applicant, will bear the onus of proving the fact of her dismissal, after which the onus will shift to the employer to prove that the dismissal did not amount to discrimination and was therefore not unfair (automatically or otherwise). The employer may discharge himself/herself of this onus either by showing that men who use foul language are similarly disciplined or by showing that the inherent requirements of the job are such that foul-mouthed women cannot be tolerated (it is difficult to think of a justification in this example that would not in itself amount to an impermissible expression of male chauvinism!). Assume that the minister of a protestant church is dismissed after he has undergone a change of faith and has converted to catholicism. The dismissal would have been for religious reasons (one of the listed protected grounds), but the employer would be able to justify it on the basis that the inherent requirements on the particular job (that is, ministering to protestant members of the congregation) justified his dismissal.

This antidiscrimination provision proscribes direct as well as indirect discrimination. Direct discrimination occurs where the discrimination is explicit, for example when an employer unfairly refuses to employ women. On the other hand, indirect discrimination occurs when an employer follows standards which appear to be neutral on the surface, but which have the effect of unfairly disadvantaging a particular group. An example of indirect discrimination would be the use of selection criteria such as height and weight, which could, although neutral, exclude more women than men. In the case of indirect discrimination, the American term, *disparate impact discrimination*, is perhaps more appropriate: the criteria have a disparate impact on one group when compared with the impact on another group. It should be borne in mind that after the complainant has proved that direct discrimination or indirect/disparate impact discrimination has taken place (usually by adducing statistical evidence) and the onus has shifted to the respondent (employer), the latter can still show that either the discrimination was not unfair or that the discriminatory dismissal was "based on the inherent requirements of the particular job" (section 187(2)(a)).

24.3.2 Other unfair dismissals

If a dismissal was not automatically unfair, it must still be determined whether the dismissal was fair or not. Employers will have less trouble in acting fairly when dismissing employees if they take note of the points summarised in exhibit B.

Exhibit B

Fairness standards and the 3 justifications for dismissals

Fair reason for dismissal + Fair procedure

1. There are only THREE justifications (fair reasons) for dismissals:
   (a) (mis)conduct by the employee;
   (b) (in)capacity on the part of the employee; or
   (c) because of the operational requirements of the employer.
   The fairness standards differ depending on which of the above reasons is relied upon to justify the dismissal

2. Regardless of the reason for the dismissal, a fair procedure must always be followed, which procedure can be summed up by the following two principles:
   (d) *Nemo judex in sau causa:*[*] The person hearing the matter must be unbiased and not have an improper interest in the outcome of the case; and
   (e) *Audi alteram partem:*[†] The employee must be given a proper opportunity to state his/her side of the story

[*] No one may be a judge in his own case.
[†] I have heard the other party.

A dismissal must be both *substantively* as well as *procedurally* fair: the one element of fairness cannot substitute for the other. Thus, to dismiss an employee for some extremely gross form of misconduct (for example, a grievous and unprovoked assault on a co-worker) may very well be substantively fair, but it will be procedurally unfair if the dismissed employee is not given an opportunity to state his case; the dismissal as a whole will then be tainted with unfairness.

Exhibit C

Requirements for a fair dismissal

Fair dismissal = Substantive fairness + Procedural fairness

The Act places the onus on the employer to show:

- that the reason for dismissal is a fair reason (related to the employee's conduct or capacity or based on the employer's operational requirements); and
- that the dismissal has been effected in accordance with a fair procedure.

Exhibit D

Shifting onus in dismissal disputes

Proof of dismissal	*Proof of fair dismissal*
On employee ⟶	On employer

In addition, the person considering whether or not the reason for dismissal is a fair reason or whether or not the dismissal has been effected in accordance with a fair procedure must take into account the **Code of Good Practice** contained in

Schedule 8 of the Act. It should be noted that Schedule 8 deals only with dismissals based on misconduct or incapacity; dismissals based on the operational requirements of the employer are dealt with in section 189 of the Act.

We now discuss in more detail each of the three grounds of justification for terminating the services of an employee: namely conduct, capacity and operational reasons.

24.4 DISMISSAL FOR MISCONDUCT

Schedule 8 to the Act contains a Code of Good Practice relating to dismissals based on conduct or capacity. Although it would be technically wrong to state that Schedule 8 represents a codification of our labour law on dismissals, it is in fact largely reflective of the positive law. As the Code itself makes clear, one should, when interpreting and applying the Code, always bear the following key principles in mind.

- The Code is general in nature; therefore, departures from the norms established by this Code may be justified in appropriate circumstances.
- The Code is not intended to replace collective agreements; therefore disciplinary codes and procedures which have been agreed to between the parties (either during collective bargaining or as the outcome of joint decision making with a workplace forum), will take precedence over the guidelines provided in the Code of Good Practice.
- Mutual respect: The Code states that the

  "... key principle in this Code is that employers and employees should treat one another with mutual respect ... [a] premium is placed on both employment justice and the efficient operation of business . . . [w]hile employees should be protected from arbitrary action, employers are entitled to satisfactory conduct and work performance from their employees."

Therefore, formal compliance with the Act and the guidelines set out in the Code may be seen simply as an operationalisation of this basic norm: employers and employees should treat one another (as well as each other's divergent interests) with respect.

Mindful of the fact that the **Code of Good Practice** provides guidelines which may be departed from under appropriate circumstances, the Code suggests that the following principles should be adhered to with regard to dismissals based on conduct. (Note: The following section has largely been taken from Schedule 8.)

24.4.1 Disciplinary procedures prior to dismissal

All employers should adopt disciplinary rules that establish the standard of conduct required of their employees. The form and content of disciplinary rules will obviously vary according to the size and nature of the employer's business. In general, a larger business will require a more formal approach to discipline. An employer's rules must create certainty and consistency in the application of discipline. This requires that the standards of conduct are clear and made available to employees in a manner that is easily understood. Some rules or standards may be so well established and known that it is not necessary to communicate them. The courts have endorsed the concept of corrective or progressive discipline. This approach regards the purpose of discipline as a means for employees to know and understand what standards are required of them. Efforts should be made to correct employees' behaviour through a system of graduated disciplinary measures such as counselling and warnings. Formal procedures do not have to be invoked every time a rule is broken or a standard is not met, informal advice and correction is the best and most effective way for an employer to deal with minor violations of work discipline. Repeated misconduct will warrant warnings, which themselves may be graded according to degrees of severity. More serious infringements or repeated misconduct may call for a final warning, or other action short of dismissal. Dismissal should be reserved for cases of serious misconduct or repeated offences.

24.4.2 Dismissals

Generally, it is not appropriate to dismiss an employee for a first offence, except if the misconduct is serious and of such gravity that it makes a continued employment relationship intolerable. Examples of serious misconduct, subject to the rule that each case should be judged on its merits, are gross dishonesty or wilful damage to the property of the employer, wilful endangering of the safety of others, physical assault on the employer, a fellow employee, client or customer and gross insubordination. Whatever the merits of the case for dismissal might be, a dismissal will not be fair if it is not done in accordance with a fair procedure. When deciding whether or not to impose the penalty of dismissal, the employer should, in addition to the gravity of the misconduct, consider factors such as the employee's circumstances (including length of service, previous disciplinary record and personal circumstances), the nature of the job and the circumstances of the infringement itself. The employer should apply the penalty of dismissal consistently with the way in which it has been applied to the same and other employees in the past, and consistently as between two or more employees who participate in the misconduct under consideration.

24.4.2.1 Fair procedures

Normally, the employer should conduct an investigation to determine whether there are enough grounds for dismissal. This does not need to be a formal enquiry. The employer should notify the employee of the allegations using a form and language that the employee can reasonably understand. The employee should be allowed the opportunity to state a case in response to the allegations. The employee should be entitled to a reasonable time to prepare the response and to the assistance of a trade union representative or fellow employee. After the enquiry, the employer should communicate the decision taken, and preferably furnish the employee with written notification of that decision. Discipline against a trade union representative or an employee who is an office-bearer or official of a trade union should not be instituted without first informing and consulting the trade union. If the employee is dismissed, the employee should be given the reason for dismissal and reminded of any rights to refer the matter to a council with jurisdiction or to the Commission or to any dispute resolution procedures established in terms of a collective agreement. In exceptional circumstances, if the employer cannot reasonably be expected to comply with these guidelines, the employer may dispense with pre-dismissal procedures.

Exhibit E

Guidelines in cases of dismissal for misconduct

Any person who is determining whether a dismissal for misconduct is unfair should consider:
1. whether or not the employee contravened a rule or standard regulating conduct in, or of relevance to, the workplace; and
2. if a rule or standard was contravened, whether or not—
   (a) the rule was a valid or reasonable rule or standard;
   (b) the employee was aware, or could reasonably be expected to have been aware, of the rule or standard;
   (c) the rule or standard has been consistently applied by the employer; and
   (d) dismissal was an appropriate sanction for the contravention of the rule or standard.

24.4.2.2 Disciplinary records

Employers should keep records for each employee specifying the nature of any disciplinary transgressions, the actions taken by the employer and the reasons for the actions.

24.4.3 Dismissals and industrial action

Participation in an unprotected strike is misconduct. However, like any other act of misconduct, it does not always deserve dismissal. The substantive fairness of dismissal in these circumstances must be determined in the light of the facts of the case, including the seriousness of the contravention of the Act, whether attempts were made to comply with the Act, and whether or not the strike was in response to unjustified conduct by the employer.

Prior to dismissal the employer should, at the earliest opportunity, contact a trade union official to discuss the course of action it intends to adopt. The employer should issue an ultimatum in clear and unambiguous terms that should state what is required of the employees and what sanction will be imposed if they do not comply with the ultimatum. The employees should be allowed sufficient time to reflect on the ultimatum and respond to it, either by complying with it or rejecting it. If the employer cannot reasonably be expected to extend these steps to the employees in question, the employer may dispense with them.

24.5 DISMISSALS RELATING TO THE EMPLOYEE'S CAPACITY

24.5.1 Case one incapacity: Poor work performance

A newly hired employee may be placed on probation for a period that is reasonable, given the circumstances of the job. The period should be determined by the nature of the job and the time that it takes to determine the employee's suitability for continued employment. When appropriate, an employer should give an employee whatever evaluation, instruction, training, guidance or counselling the employee requires to render satisfactory service. Dismissal during the probationary period should be preceded by an opportunity for the employee to state a case in response and to be assisted by a trade union representative or fellow employee. After probation, an employee should not be dismissed for unsatisfactory performance unless the employer has: (i) given the employee appropriate evaluation, instruction, training, guidance or counselling; and (ii) after a reasonable period of time for improvement, the employee continues to perform unsatisfactorily: The procedure leading to dismissal should include an investigation to establish the reasons for the unsatisfactory performance and the employer should consider other ways, short of dismissal, to remedy the matter. In the process, the employee should have the right to be heard and to be assisted by a trade union representative or a fellow employee.

Exhibit F

Dismissal for poor work performance — guidelines*

Any person determining whether a dismissal for poor work performance is unfair should consider:
1. whether or not the employee failed to meet a performance standard; and
2. if the employee did not meet a required performance standard, whether or not—
   (a) the employee was aware, or could reasonably be expected to have been aware, of the required performance standards;
   (b) the employee was given a fair opportunity to meet the required performance standard; and
   (c) dismissal was an appropriate sanction for not meeting the required performance standard.

*Source: From item 9 in Schedule 8 (Labour Relations Act 66 of 1995)

24.5.2 Case two incapacity: Ill-health or injury

Incapacity on the grounds of ill-health or injury may be temporary or permanent. If an employee is temporarily unable to work in these circumstances, the employer should investigate the extent of the incapacity or the injury. If the employee is likely to be absent for a time that is unreasonably long in the circumstances, the employer should investigate all the possible alternatives short of dismissal. When alternatives are considered, relevant factors might include the nature of the job, the period of absence, the seriousness of the illness or injury and the possibility of securing a temporary replacement for the ill or injured employee. In cases of permanent incapacity, the employer should ascertain the possibility of securing alternative employment, or adapting the duties or work circumstances of the employee to accommodate the employee's disability. In the process of this investigation the employee should be allowed the opportunity to state a case in response and to be assisted by a trade union representative or fellow employee. The degree of incapacity is relevant to the fairness of any dismissal. The cause of the incapacity may also be relevant. In the case of certain kinds of incapacity, for example alcoholism or drug abuse, counselling and rehabilitation may be appropriate steps for an employer to consider. Particular consideration should be given to employees who are injured at work or who are incapacitated by work-related illness. The courts have indicated that the duty on the employer to accommodate the incapacity of the employee is more onerous in these circumstances.

Exhibit G

Dismissal arising from ill-health or injury — guidelines*

Any person determining whether a dismissal arising from ill-health or injury is unfair should consider:
1. whether or not the employee is capable of performing the work; and
2. if the employee is not capable—
    (a) the extent to which the employee is able to perform the work;
    (b) the extent to which the employee's work circumstances might be adapted to accommodate disability, or, where this is not possible, the extent to which the employee's duties might be adapted; and
    (c) the availability of any suitable alternative work.

*Source: From item 11, Schedule 8 (Labour Relations Act 66 of 1995)

24.6 DISMISSALS BASED ON OPERATIONAL REQUIREMENTS

It has been observed that the sequence in which the three grounds of justification for dismissal (namely because of misconduct or incapacity or for operational reasons) are normally listed represents a descending order of fault or guilt that can be attributed to the employee. Whereas an employee is clearly at fault in cases of misconduct, the employee who loses his job because of events not of his making and beyond his control, such as economic forces impacting on the employer's business (or because of other reasons such as technological innovation), is blameless. The so-called no-fault dismissals are deemed to be deserving of special treatment. It has been said that losing one's job is economic capital punishment. Losing one's job when one has not even committed the "murder" (of committing serious misconduct) is doubly unfortunate and cries out for special compassion on the part of the employer. The requirements of a fair dismissal for operational reasons are summarised in exhibit H.

Exhibit H

Fair dismissals for operational reasons

Substantive fairness
- A valid and fair reason for the retrenchment

Procedural fairness
- Prior consultation
- Prior consensus over certain matters
- Disclosure of certain information
- Allowing employees to make representations
- Genuine consideration of these representations
- Selection of employees to be retrenched
- Payment of retrenchment package

We shall now look at the above requirements in greater detail.

24.6.1 Substantive fairness

The Act does not tell us what will constitute a valid and fair reason, but this has been well-established by the Industrial Court. In brief, the employer's reason for the dismissal must be a genuine reason based on the operational requirements of the business. The factors that caused the to-be-retrenched employees' services no longer being needed can be as diverse as a downswing in the economy, the implementation of new technology, restructuring of the business or the shutting down of a plant or part of the business or even the closing down of the business as a whole.

If an employer tries to rid himself/herself of employees for whatever reason (for example, because they had joined a trade union or because the employer is dissatisfied with their conduct or capacity) under the guise of operational reasons, such scheme will indubitably be found to be grossly unfair. If an employee's conduct or ability to perform his duties is not to his employer's satisfaction, the fairness standards relating to dismissal for misconduct or incapacity must be complied with; to dismiss the "undesirable" employee under the pretence of operational reasons (eg because the employer has insufficient proof or wants to save the costs of holding a hearing or does not want to waste time on the employee, or for whatever reason), will always be unfair.

24.6.2 Procedural fairness

The seven requirements (see exhibit H above) for a procedurally fair retrenchment will now be discussed.

24.6.2.1 Step 1: Consultation

"When an employer contemplates dismissing one or more employees for reasons based on the employer's operational requirements, the employer must consult . . ." (s 189(1)).

"Consultation" means that the decision maker must seek advice or information from someone else. It does not mean that the decision maker must accept the advice or that he/she is constrained to reach consensus with the other party. A duty to consult is not a duty to reach agreement, it is simply a duty to give another party the opportunity to provide inputs into the decision-making process and to consider these inputs seriously before the decision maker makes a final decision (unilaterally). Secondly, the duty to consult arises before the employer reaches the final conclusion that retrenchments will have to take place. This in effect means that, as soon as the employer senses that there may be a possibility of retrenchments, the duty to consult arises. That this must be so is clear from the use of the word "contemplates" in section 189(1), as well as the meaning of "consultation", as explained above: the decision maker cannot seriously consider representations made to him/her (for example trade union suggestions on how to avoid retrenchments), if he/she has already reached a final decision on the course of action to be taken (that is, prior to hearing the representations). The primary purpose of consultation is to inform the employees (and their trade union) of the possibility of retrenchments and to invite their inputs on how the retrenchments may be avoided or on how the impact on the affected employees can be ameliorated as much as possible.

Who must be consulted? In section 189(1) the legislator prescribes a preferential sequence of persons with whom the employer must consult:

- **First**, if the employer is bound by a collective agreement, and that agreement specifies with whom he/she must consult regarding retrenchments, the employer is obliged to consult with that person or party.
- **Secondly**, if there is no such collective agreement, the employer must consult with the workplace forum, if such a forum exists.
- **Thirdly**, if there is no workplace forum, the employer must consult with any registered trade union whose members are likely to be affected by the proposed dismissals.
- **Fourthly**, if there is no such trade union, the employer must consult directly with the employees likely to be affected by the proposed retrenchments, or other representatives nominated for that purpose.

24.6.2.2 Step 2: Attempt to reach consensus on certain matters

The second procedural step is specified in section 189(2) of the Act and entails an effort on the part of the consulting parties to try to reach consensus on certain matters.

"The consulting parties must attempt to reach consensus on—

(a) appropriate measures
  (i) to avoid the dismissals;
  (ii) to minimise the number of dismissals;
  (iii) to change the timing of the dismissals; and
  (iv) to mitigate the adverse effects of the dismissals;

(b) the method for selecting the employees to be dismissed; and

(c) the severance pay for dismissed employees." (section 189(2))

The matters specified in section 189(2) over which consultations take place can be summarised in the following words: avoidance, minimise, timing, mitigation, selection and compensation. The process is summarised in figure 24.1.

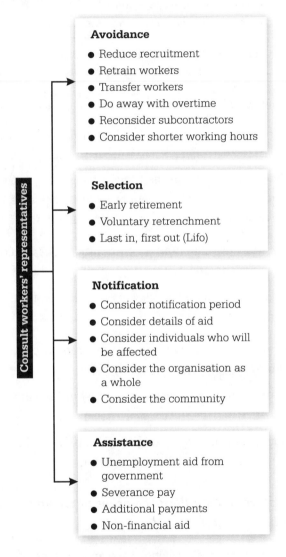

Figure 24.1

Procedural fairness in dismissals for operational reasons

24.6.2.3 *Step 3: Disclosure of information (s 189(3))*

The Act (s 189(3) read together with s 16) places an explicit duty on an employer to provide the other party, in writing, with any information relevant to the possible retrenchment. This information is summarised in exhibit I.

Exhibit I

> ### Retrenchments: written disclosure of information
>
> The employer must disclose all relevant information, including, but not limited to:
> - the reasons for the proposed dismissals;
> - the alternatives that the employer considered before proposing the dismissals, and the reasons for rejecting each of those alternatives;
> - the number of employees likely to be affected and the job categories in which they are employed;
> - the proposed method for selecting which employees to dismiss;
> - the time when, or the period during which, the dismissals are likely to take effect;
> - the severance pay proposed;
> - any assistance that the employer proposes to offer to the employees likely to be dismissed; and
> - the possibility of the future re-employment of the employees who are dismissed.

Furthermore, it should be noted that the provisions relating to the disclosure of information in section 16 of the Act also apply to the disclosure of information during retrenchment consultations. This implies, *inter alia* that:

- "all relevant information" would entail all information that would put the other party in a position to consult effectively;

- the employer would not be obliged to disclose information that:

  o is legally privileged;

  o the employer cannot disclose without contravening a prohibition imposed on the employer by any law or order of any court;

  o is confidential and, if disclosed, may cause substantial harm to an employee or to the employer; or

  o is private personal information relating to an employee, unless that employee consents to the disclosure of that information.

24.6.2.4 Step 4: Employer must afford the other party an opportunity to make representations (s 189(5))

> "The employer must allow the other consulting party an opportunity during consultation to make representations about any matter on which they are consulting."

The employer must, in good faith, consult with the trade union about the intended retrenchments. Should the employer not allow the trade union (or other party) to make representations during consultations, the retrenchments will be unfair. Issues on which the other party may make representations include "any matter" and would presumably include at least those matters mentioned in section 189(2).

24.6.2.5 Step 5: The employer must consider and respond to the representations made by the other party (section 189(6))

> "The employer must consider and respond to the representations made by the other consulting party and, if the employer does not agree with them, the employer must state the reasons for disagreeing."

Having received the representations of the other party, the employer is under a statutory obligation to consider these proposals in good faith, and to give reasons should he/she not agree with them. Although not explicitly required, it would be best to give this response and reasons in writing to the other party. It is important to note that, although an employer is obliged to consider the representations carefully, he/she is under no obligation to reach agreement on these issues. On the other hand, true consideration of representations implies that at the time these are under consideration the employer must not have already firmly decided upon a course of action: considering representations against the background of a *fait accompli* cannot amount to good faith consultations. The employer is, of course, not bound to either accept or reject all the representations made as a package; for instance, the employer could reject (with supporting reasons) the proposals made relating to alternatives to retrenchments (for example to work short time), but still accept representations made in respect of certain deserving individuals who were earmarked for retrenchments and who, but for these representations, would have been dismissed.

24.6.2.6 Step 6: The selection of employees for retrenchments (section 189(7))

> "The employer must select the employees to be dismissed according to selection criteria
> (a) that have been agreed to by the consulting parties; or
> (b) if no criteria have been agreed, criteria that are fair and objective."

It will be recalled that the employer must inform the trade union (or whoever is the other consulting party) in writing regarding "the proposed method for selecting which employees to dismiss" (section 189(3)(d)). If the employer and trade union have agreed on the selection criteria, these must be applied; if no agreement was reached, the employer must apply criteria that are fair and objective. "Fairness" in this context would entail a balancing of the interests of the various stakeholders, including, for example: retrenchees, the employer, the workers not to be retrenched, the trade union, shareholders of the organisation, and the public at large. "Objective" would mean criteria that are susceptible to external or third party verification. Please note that criteria other than the popular last-in-first-out (LIFO) may be used, as long as these criteria are not left to the subjective opinion of any individual. For instance, productivity would be an acceptable criterion if it could be objectively verified by means of production figures, and/or absenteeism figures, and/or accident figures, and/or reject figures. But productivity measurement by asking the subjective opinion of supervisors regarding which of their subordinates they would regard as more or less productive will not do.

24.6.2.7 Step 7: Payment of retrenchment packages (section 196)

Prior to the new Act there was no obligation on an employer to pay a severance package to retrenchees, except under the following circumstances: if the employer had paid packages in the past or if he/she had promised to pay a package or if he/she was contractually bound (either in terms of a collective agreement or in accordance with an employment contract) to pay a package. The payment of retrenchment packages was held to be a substantive issue over which the courts had no jurisdiction (except in the case of any of the three circumstances listed above); it had to be regulated by agreement between the employer and his/her employees. However, although the principle is sound that the courts should not involve themselves in substantive issues, there are some very cogent reasons (if not legal, then at least moral and as a matter of sound industrial relations) why retrenchment packages should be paid. First, remember that a retrenchment is an instance of no-fault dismissal (that is, the worker loses his/her livelihood through no fault of his/her own (as opposed to the case of dismissal for misconduct). Under these circumstances it seems appropriate that the employer should pay the employee something in recognition of his/her loyal service and the hardship of losing his/her job. Secondly, the obligation to pay retrenchment packages may act as a deterrent or brake on employers who may otherwise too easily resort to retrenchments. Thirdly, in terms of the organisation's wider social responsibility, it may be expected of an employer to tide the employee and his/her family over for the period that the employee will be unemployed. Fourthly, keeping in mind the interest that the employer has in a motivated workforce, it may make good business sense to pay retrenchment packages, if only in order to reassure the remaining employees of their employer's good faith and loyalty towards his workforce. After a retrenchment exercise the morale among the survivors is typically low and some show of compassion on the part of their employer may go some way towards addressing the survivors' fears and feelings of job insecurity.

As has been intimated earlier, the new Act contains fairly detailed provisions regarding retrenchment packages. Some of the most important provisions are summarised in exhibit J. Some aspects warrant special mention.

One can define a retrenchment package (or severance pay as it is also called) as monetary and other benefits which are given to an employee in addition to any other benefit to which he/she may be legally entitled.

From this definition it is clear that the payment of accrued leave, pro rata bonuses, contractual notice pay, withdrawal benefits in terms of a pension/provident fund, etc, cannot be regarded as part of the retrenchment package. Secondly, should an employee be offered a reasonably similar position and he/she unreasonably refuses to accept the alternative employment, he/she loses the entitlement to a severance package. Lastly, note that, for the purposes of calculating the monetary value of the package, it is only *completed* years of service (which service must have been *continuous*) that are used to calculate the severance package. For example, an employee who worked for an employer for two years, then resigned and was later re-employed by the same employer, for whom he then worked uninterrupted for ten and a half years prior to retrenchment, will be regarded as having had only ten years' service for the purpose of calculating the severance package (although in reality the person had had twelve and a half years of service with the employer).

Exhibit J

Prescribed severance pay

Severance pay (section 196)
- An employer must pay a retrenchment package equal to at least one week's remuneration for each year of continuous service with the employer.
- Remuneration includes payment in kind.
- Employers may apply for exemption from the duty to pay retrenchment packages.
- The payment of a package is in addition to any other amount the worker may be entitled to in terms of law.
- An employee who unreasonably refuses to accept the employer's offer of alternative employment with that employer or any other employer forfeits the right to a retrenchment package.

Before we consider the next topic in this chapter, you are reminded that there are only **three grounds of justification for dismissal** — each dismissal must be **capable of being classified as either a conduct** or a **capacity** or an **operational reasons** dismissal, and must be justified in terms of the **standards of fairness** pertaining to those particular grounds of justification.

24.7 COMMERCIAL RATIONALE

Another type of termination of services that warrants attention is the case where it would be unreasonable to expect an employer to keep an employee in service, even though misconduct in the traditional sense cannot be proven. An employer should be entitled, in a more or less free-market society, to dismiss an employee whose continued presence negatively affects the economic prospects of the business (that is, to dismiss an employee for a valid commercial or economic reason). The following are examples of such situations.

1. **Where the employee does not comply with a request to do something voluntarily, which is necessary for the successful running of the business.**
   An example of such a situation could be where the employee refuses to work voluntary overtime and the operations of the organisation are of such a nature that the working of overtime is essential for the continued viability of the business. The Industrial Court in such cases seems prepared to accept that, although the employees are not guilty of misconduct since they are within their rights to refuse to work voluntary overtime, the specific circumstances of the employer's business require employees who can do so to work overtime. The

employer may then be entitled to dismiss those employees who could not or would not work overtime. Management must, however, ensure that a dismissal for an economic reason is procedurally fair. This may, for instance, include exploring the possibility of transferring the employee to a job in which overtime is not required or to a location closer to the employee's home. These investigations should take place in consultation with the employee.

2. **Where special circumstances necessitate the employee's dismissal.**
   An example of this situation could be where some employees commit industrial sabotage, but it is not possible for the employer to identify the specific culprits in the group or department. In this situation the employer cannot dismiss the whole group on the grounds of misconduct since it would be unfair to dismiss employees for this reason without proving that each individual employee is in fact guilty as charged. It may, however, be fair if management were to terminate the services of all the employees on the basis of commercial rationale.

3. **Where the employee's presence indirectly impairs the profitability of the business.**
   The presence of an employee may indirectly impair the profitability of the business where his/her presence prejudices or jeopardises other employees' employment opportunities or work security. This could also be the case where an employee's presence disrupts the business of the employer, or creates or promotes labour unrest, or detrimentally affects the relationship between the employer and the rest of the employees. The courts generally seem to regard the dismissal of such an employee as valid for economic reasons.

   The court, however, normally requires that the economic reason should be legitimate, that the dismissal should be procedurally fair (the employee must have been consulted about the problems that his/her conduct and presence have been causing), and that management must have considered alternatives to dismissal.

Exhibit K

Checklist for fair dismissal: some questions to ask

- Was/is there an employment relationship?
- Was there a dismissal? (Onus on employee)
- Was the dismissal automatically unfair or just unfair?
- What are the grounds for justification? (Conduct, capacity or operational reasons?)
- Legality?
- Substantive fairness?
  - Valid reason?
  - Proportionality of sanction?
- Procedural fairness?
  - *Nemo judex in sua causa* (chairperson must be unbiased and must not have any interest in the outcome of the hearing)
  - *Audi alteram partem* (timeousness, reasonable notice, cross-examination, translator, call witnesses, appeal, etc)

24.8 REMEDIES FOR UNFAIR DISMISSAL

The natural remedy for an unfair dismissal is reinstatement or re-employment.

 Reinstatement occurs when an employee is placed back in the same position that he/she held before his/her putative dismissal.

 Re-employment occurs when an employer is required to accept the dismissed employee back into service, but not necessarily in the same position.

In both instances the order may be from any date between the date of the order and the date of the unfair dismissal.

In terms of the new Act the person adjudicating an alleged unfair dismissal must, upon a finding in favour of the employee, order reinstatement or re-employment, unless (section 193(2)):

- the employee does not wish to be reinstated or re-employed;
- the circumstances surrounding the dismissal are such that a continued employment relationship would be intolerable;
- it is not reasonably practicable for the employer to reinstate or re-employ the employee; or
- the dismissal is unfair only because the employer did not follow a fair procedure.

Of great importance to employers is a new provision in the Act which limits the amount of compensation that may be granted to an employee who has been unfairly dismissed. In the past employers suffered great prejudice when disputes, frequently due to no fault on the part of either party, were resolved after lengthy delays between the date the matter was brought to court and the date of the dismissals. Unfairly dismissed employees should not be disadvantaged by these limits since the Act requires disputes regarding allegedly unfair dismissals to be resolved speedily (hence the absence of any status quo remedies, as provided for under the previous Act, in recognition of the fact that the final determination of dismissal disputes frequently could take very long, resulting in the need for some interim relief). The limits on compensation are summarised in exhibit L.

24.8.1 Urgent interim relief

In terms of section 158(1)(*a*)(i) of the act, the Labour Court may grant urgent interim relief. The purpose of granting relief is to come to the speedy assistance of an applicant pending the final resolution of a dispute by the ordinary (and more time-consuming) court procedures. In common law the requirements for the granting of urgent interim relief are as follows:

- the matter must be **urgent**;
- a *prima facie* **right**[2] in respect of which irreparable harm will be suffered if the relief sought is not granted;

- no adequate **alternative remedy**; and
- the damage and inconvenience that the applicant will suffer should the application be refused, will be greater than the damage and inconvenience that the respondent will suffer, should the application for interim relief be granted.[3]

Exhibit L

Limits on compensation awards for unfair dismissals

Limits on compensation (section 194)
Three types of limits are placed on compensation:
- **If a dismissal is substantively fair but procedurally unfair** . . . the compensation must be equal to the remuneration that the employee would have been paid between the date of dismissal and the last day of the hearing of the arbitration or adjudication, as the case may be, calculated at the employee's rate of remuneration on the date of dismissal.[1]
- **If a dismissal is substantively unfair** . . . the compensation must be just and equitable in all the circumstances, but not less than the amount specified in respect of a procedurally unfair dismissal and not more than the equivalent of 12 months' remuneration, calculated at the employee's rate of remuneration on the date of dismissal.
- **If the dismissal is automatically unfair** . . . the compensation must be just and equitable in all the circumstances, but not more than the equivalent of 24 months' remuneration, calculated at the employee's rate of remuneration on the date of dismissal.

It should be noted that under the old Act the mere fact of dismissal was not deemed to be sufficient cause upon which to launch a successful application for urgent interim relief. Added to the dismissal there had to be some other consideration, such as ejection from the organisation's accommodation, in order to constitute urgency for the purposes of an application for urgent relief. Presumably the Labour Court will follow the same approach.

24.9 CONCLUSION

In this final chapter we have focused on the appropriate way to go about terminating employment relationships. Technically speaking, if the services of all an organisation's employees have been terminated, this will mean that the full cycle of the human resource management process has been completed. In practice this is, however, very rare — except in those instances where organisations actually close down or go out of business. In most cases organisations continue to exist, work still needs to be done and employees are still needed to perform that work. The termination of employment relationships in a procedurally correct and equitable manner under such circumstances therefore implies the start of the human resource management process all over again. Already then, generally speaking, one will have to start planning and organising around the work to be done and the replacement employee/s required to do the work. If employment relationships are not terminated fairly and in the correct way, this could have major negative effects on the organisation in the sense that its image in the labour market may be damaged to such an extent that it may become difficult to attract, employ and keep the right numbers and quality of employees. Such an approach clearly does not fit in with a strategic approach to the management of human resources, as advocated throughout this book.

ENDNOTES

1. Compensation may, however, not be awarded in respect of any unreasonable period of delay that was caused by the employee in initiating or prosecuting a claim.
2. *"Prima facie"* means that "on the face of it" or from the documentation before the court it appears as if the applicant's rights are infringed; no oral evidence is led and the final determination of whether the applicant indeed has a right which has been violated is left for the proper court proceedings that are to follow in due course.
3. One could call this a "balance of harm" test. Typically an employee who allegedly has been unfairly dismissed and ejected from the organisation's accommodation would suffer greater prejudice should an order not be granted than his/her employer would, should it be granted.

SELF-EVALUATION QUESTIONS

1. Define "dismissal" in the South African context.
2. When will a dismissal be regarded as automatically unfair? Explain.
3. What are the two basic requirements for ensuring that a dismissal is regarded as fair? Explain.
4. Differentiate between fair and unfair dismissal, and discuss fair dismissal in the context of:

   O misconduct,
   O incapacity, and
   O operational requirements.

5. Write brief explanatory notes on the idea of terminating employment relationships fairly on the basis of commercial rationale.
6. Explain the different potential remedies for unfair dismissal in South Africa.

Index

Note: Page numbers in **bold type** refer to definitions

H

Trade union (*continued*)
  organisational rights   626
  reasons for existence   620
  registration and relevant statutory
    requirements   629
  relations with management   681, 685
  rights   623
  some prominent unions   632
  structure and methods   621
Traditional learning   499
Training   191, 479, 499, 776
  advisers   474
  behavioural-modelling   497
  boards   468
  bodies responsible in SA   449
  can it correct a performance
    deficiency?   484
  centres   471
  computer-based   493
  cycle   482
  department   482
  evaluation
    behaviour   501
    learning   500
    reaction   500
    results   501
  financing of   451
  identifying objectives   486
  industry centres   472
  knowledge of results   489
  levies   473
  macrolevel perspectives   447
  measuring costs   762
  methods for nonmanagerial
    employees   491
  monetary value   503
  needs assessment   481
  of persons who are not apprentices or
    minors   471
  organisational-level perspectives   477
  private centres   472
  SA problems   450
  schemes   471
  sensitivity   496
  strategy, national   451
  systematic, model for   480
  transfer of   489
Trait theories   371
Transactional and transformational
  leaders   384
Transactional leadership   381

Transactional theories   378
Transformation   725, **726**
Transformational leadership   383
Transitory career pattern   438

U

Understudy assignments   496
Unemployment Insurance Act   135
Unfair discrimination   **186**
Unit labour cost   **120**
  changes   120
Unitarist perspective   617
United States, lessons from   168
Units of learning and qualifications   456
Unsafe behaviour   587
Unsafe conditions   587
Urgent interim relief   809

V

Vacation work   301
Validity   314, **314**
Value added statement   785
Values   81, **81**, 517
Variability   96
Variables   104, 391
  of organisation structure   249
Variety   300
Vertical work redesign   240
Visual outlay   300
Vroom-Jetton-Jago leadership-participation
  model   377

W

Weighted application blank   **316**
Weighting   520
White, Isobel
  address to IPM   39
  advent of personnel management in
    SA   33
Wide incentive schemes   545
"Wild wests"   253
Work and family life interactions   573
Work design, ergonomic
  considerations   243
Work domain   59, 61
Work redesign   **239**
Work team   **246**
Worker obsolescence   440
Work–family conflict   441, **441**